The North Carolina

Railroad, 1849–1871,

and the Modernization

of North Carolina

**THE FRED W. MORRISON
SERIES IN SOUTHERN STUDIES**

*The University of
North Carolina Press*

Chapel Hill and London

ALLEN W. TRELEASE

The North Carolina

Railroad, *1849–1871*,

and the Modernization

of North Carolina

The paper in this book meets the guidelines for permanence
and durability of the Committee on Production Guidelines for
Book Longevity of the Council on Library Resources.

95 94 93 92 91   5 4 3 2 1

Library of Congress Cataloging-in-Publication Data

Trelease, Allen W.
    The North Carolina Railroad, 1849–1871, and the
modernization of North Carolina / by Allen W. Trelease.
        p. cm. — (The Fred W. Morrison series in
Southern studies)
    Includes bibliographical references and index.
    ISBN 0-8078-1941-7 (cloth : alk. paper)
    1. North Carolina Railroad Company—History.
    2. Railroads—North Carolina—History—19th century.
I. Title. II. Series.
HE2791.N82398 1991
385'.06'5756—dc20   90-39189
                                                  CIP

CONTENTS

MAPS AND ILLUSTRATIONS

TABLES

PREFACE

IN SOME RESPECTS the North Carolina Railroad was typical of America's early railways: small in size, built and operated on a shoestring, run by inexperienced and often part-time managers, and destined soon to be swallowed by larger roads. Even in the NCRR's own day, physical structures and rolling stock were seldom described and less photographed; most of the pictures we have date from later times.

In other respects the NCRR was not so typical. Largely a state-owned enterprise, it was subject to continuing political influence; the governor appointed a majority of its board of directors as well as a state proxy empowered to cast 30,000 of the 40,000 votes at stockholders' meetings. The NCRR was also the state's largest business corporation, its longest railroad (223 miles), its largest source of revenue, and its chief reliance for economic growth and modernization. Leased (but not sold) to other roads after 1871, it became a vital link in the Southern Railway system forged by J. P. Morgan in the 1890s. Unlike most parts of that network (now the Norfolk Southern), the NCRR remains in the ownership of the corporation that built it in the 1850s, three-quarters of whose stock still belongs to the state of North Carolina.

North Carolina was often characterized in the 1840s as the Rip Van Winkle State—asleep for the past generation, increasingly backward and poverty-stricken, and closed to new ideas, especially if they cost money. The NCRR did much to remove that image, contributing over the years to the economic growth of its own territory and that of the world beyond. The Piedmont Urban Crescent, following the road from Raleigh through Greensboro to Charlotte, is clearly attributable to it, although existing towns helped attract the railroad in the first place. The NCRR's broader impact is not easily measured, given the road's rapid integration into an ever-larger regional, national, and international transportation network. In the following chapters, especially the final one, I will attempt to describe and assess that impact during the latter half of the nineteenth century.

The greatest attention, however, will go to the NCRR's development as an independently operating railroad from the time of its charter in 1849 until its lease to the Richmond and Danville Railroad in 1871. These twenty-two years fall naturally into three parts—before, during, and after the Civil War—each relatively distinct. The prewar years were the time of inception, construction, and early operation, including the first through traffic agreements with connecting roads north, south, and east. During the war the

NCRR played a vital role in supporting (not always adequately) the Confederate military effort in Virginia, and many of the war's last scenes were played out along its tracks in April 1865. After the war the road experienced several kinds of reconstruction. Physical rehabilitation of its property and the recovery of the regional economy on which the road depended took place amid political changes that inescapably affected its management. Finally, the postwar railway consolidation movement, creating a national rail network, soon engulfed the NCRR, putting its operations into the hands of "outsiders and strangers."

The NCRR charter of 1849 was a product of sectional compromise. Western North Carolinians wanted a railroad to connect projected South Carolina and Virginia roads running northward to Charlotte and southward to Danville, Virginia. This north-south axis promised to confirm the existing flow of western North Carolina products to neighboring states. Easterners agreed to charter a road from Charlotte, therefore, only if it headed eastward and connected at Goldsboro with an existing railroad that terminated in Wilmington. Their purpose was to direct western trade as much as possible toward North Carolina ports.

That aim was frustrated from the beginning by several factors. In the first place, Wilmington and the other North Carolina ports were inferior to those of Norfolk and Charleston. Secondly, shipping and insurance rates around Cape Hatteras were higher than those to Norfolk in particular. Finally, the two existing railroads of eastern North Carolina, both of which were to connect with the NCRR, led toward Virginia. If the southern terminus of the Wilmington and Weldon Railroad was Wilmington, its northern terminus was on the Roanoke River, with easy rail access to both Norfolk and Richmond. The second road, the Raleigh and Gaston, would soon also run to Weldon and the same rail connections into Virginia. The NCRR thus became from the outset primarily a north-south railway linking South Carolina and points farther south with Norfolk, Richmond, and points farther north. Later wartime construction of the controversial link from Danville to the NCRR at Greensboro reinforced that role.

The NCRR was built to more than the minimal standards prevailing in the 1850s. But abrupt grades and inadequate ballasting and drainage facilities would create perennial maintenance and operational problems and even take a few lives. The repair shops, built at the road's midpoint in Alamance County, served as the nucleus of a new railroad-owned town, Company Shops, which a generation later would take the name of Burlington.

The road was built, as it was operated, primarily by black labor. Neighboring slaveholders took construction contracts and used their slaves to clear and grade the roadbed. The road itself hired slaves by the year to hew crossties, lay track, and build water tanks, stations, and bridges. Hired slaves subsequently filled the section gangs that maintained the roadway, and they comprised most of the station hands and train crews as well. After the war, with a brief exception, free blacks performed the same roles. Whites held the prestigious jobs as engineers, conductors, foremen, machinists, and other skilled shopworkers, but they also served along with blacks as firemen, brakemen, and relatively unskilled shopworkers.

Train service began in 1854 at opposite ends of the line while construction proceeded in the middle. With the completion of the road in January 1856, agreements were quickly made for through service, both freight and passenger, with connecting roads; almost immediately the NCRR became an important link in a chain of railroads and steamship lines providing service between New York and New Orleans. As on most railroads, there was always tension between through service and local service for travelers and shippers who lived along the NCRR. It extended to both schedules and fares. Local users preferred daytime trains and cheap local rates. But since they had almost no alternative to the NCRR, they lacked bargaining power. The NCRR and its connecting roads were competing for through traffic with rival lines along the coast and on the other side of the mountains. Hence they usually fixed train schedules and charged rates to suit long-distance users. The result was higher rates and middle-of-the-night trains for the road's closest and most dependent customers.

The state, as primary stockholder, responsive to the voters of North Carolina, might have been expected to intervene in behalf of local interests. It did not. With very few exceptions the state adopted a passive role, allowing the private stockholders and ordinary business considerations to dominate the road's policies and management. Succeeding governors appointed directors and proxies who agreed with them politically, but these officials seldom took the initiative. Public and private directors acted in concert, usually following the lead of the president. Until after the war, he was more often a private than a public director, elected to the board by the private stockholders. Even as Reconstruction era governors (of both parties) sought to bring the road more nearly under political control, public and private directors seldom differed. With the advent of Republican party control in 1868, operational jobs were awarded to party faithful for the first time, but that policy hardly outlived the year.

Seven presidents headed the NCRR from its incorporation in 1850 until its lease in 1871. The first and ablest, former Governor John Motley Morehead, was in large measure the road's founding father, but he stepped down in 1855 before the construction was finished. The mercurial Charles F. Fisher led the road as a part-time endeavor from his home in Salisbury until the outbreak of war, when he went off to die a hero's death at Manassas. After less than a year of trying to cope with wartime emergencies Paul C. Cameron (probably the state's wealthiest man) gave way to Thomas Webb, a young Hillsboro lawyer who carried the road through the war and was its first full-time president. Reconstruction brought a succession of three one-year presidencies until the election of Republican William A. Smith in 1868. Smith performed admirably, even winning over the predominantly Democratic stockholders who fully backed his negotiation of the lease.

Most railroads experienced financial problems in their first years. The NCRR was no exception. Originally capitalized at $3 million, two-thirds contributed by the state, it requested and received an additional $1 million from the state before construction was finished. The final cost, including the shops complex, was just under $5 million. The last million came from a $350,000 bond issue and from operating revenues. The first dividend was deferred until 1859, when a suspicious legislature had undertaken to investigate the road's management. Inflated wartime profits were largely illusory and, in any event, could not be used to replace degenerating rails and rolling stock, which were unobtainable. The road's only two years in the red came immediately after the war, when rehabilitation costs were high and revenues from an impoverished countryside were low. Cash dividends reappeared in 1870.

State ownership may possibly have impeded NCRR managers in undertaking new initiatives such as acquiring control of other roads in the postwar consolidation battles; but the NCRR and the state had little capital with which to fight these wars, and the results would probably have been the same anyway. North Carolinians felt they had an interest and a voice in the policies of this road beyond what they felt regarding other, privately owned lines. That feeling helped keep the road in public ownership, despite postwar efforts to sell the state's stock and despite the lease that removed operational management from local control.

The Richmond and Danville Railroad had itself come under northern control by 1871 when it leased the NCRR for thirty years. Had the NCRR persisted in rejecting that offer, it faced the near-certainty of a parallel road, built with seemingly inexhaustible northern capital, between Danville and Charlotte. That road, part of a consolidated line from Washington to New Orleans under the same management, would have reduced the NCRR to a poverty-stricken local carrier subject to the predations of every railroad combination in the region. As it was, the lease proved a blessing to the stockholders, including particularly the state of North Carolina, who collected a dependable annual dividend from the stipulated rental, often during years when the "victorious" roads were unable to pay dividends to their own stockholders. The new Southern Railway renewed the lease in 1895 for ninety-nine years. As that agreement nears expiration, the state as majority stockholder considers its options.

ACKNOWLEDGMENTS

No book is is a single-handed effort. My obligations are legion. The University of North Carolina at Greensboro afforded me time and money to do the necessary research, for the most part in its Jackson Library, the North Carolina Archives in Raleigh (where the NCRR records are housed), Duke University, the University of North Carolina at Chapel Hill, and the Association of American Railroads in Washington, D.C. I am particularly grateful for the generosity and general helpfulness of Dr. James H. Thompson, Kathryn M. Crowe, and Nancy C. Fogarty of the Jackson Library; of Dr. H. G. Jones and Alice R. Cotten of the North Carolina Collection at UNC-Chapel Hill; of Dr. Carolyn A. Wallace and Dr. Richard A. Shrader of the Southern Historical Collection at UNC-Chapel Hill; of the late Dr. Mattie Russell of the Manuscripts Division at the Duke University library; and of Helen M. Rowland, supervisor of library services at the Association of American Railroads.

Further obligations are owing to those individuals who helped supply illustrations of what must be one of the least-photographed railroads in the nation. I am grateful in this respect to R. B. Carneal of Winter Park, Fla. and to several residents of Burlington, N.C. (the former Company Shops) who thus absorbed an interest in the NCRR and its physical remains in the natural order of things: W. T. Lasley, Allen B. Cammack, and Paul E. Morrow, Jr. One of their neighbors, so to speak, Professor Durward T. Stokes of Elon College, the historian of Company Shops, kindly led me to them.

I cannot omit a third category of debt otherwise poorly acknowledged in the bare bibliographic listing that terminates this book: the debt to other scholars whose own work helped make mine possible. Professor Harry L. Watson of UNC-Chapel Hill raised the suggestion in a symposium a decade ago that a history of the NCRR and its impact upon the state would not be amiss. I am the first and perhaps last person to take up that suggestion, but I have derived enormous benefit along the way from the work of others on closely related subjects. Durward Stokes's *Company Shops* certainly falls in that category. Thomas E. Jeffrey's perceptive articles on North Carolina politics in the antebellum era helped to inform my account of the NCRR's origins. John F. Stover's and Maury Klein's railroad histories are models of the genre and Klein's accounts of the consolidation movement were indispensable to me. I am particularly in debt to Professor Charles L. Price of East Carolina University for his many works on North Carolina railroads during and after the Civil War—some published and others not, but all of them thoroughly researched and carefully written. Every historian of railroading in North Carolina must be grateful for Cecil M. Brown's classic work of sixty years ago on the state's railroad beginnings. A final mention should go to John H. White of the Smithsonian Institution, whose books and articles on railroad technology are also classics and indispensable to historians of American railroading.

The North Carolina

Railroad, 1849–1871,

and the Modernization

of North Carolina

Map 1. The NCRR and Its Stations

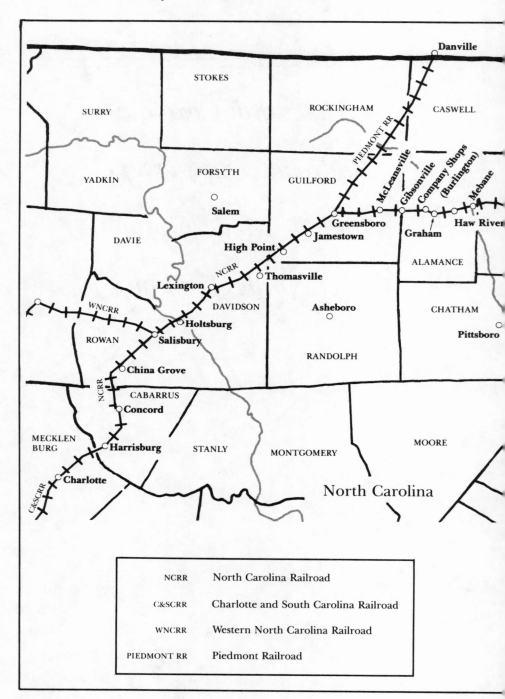

NCRR	North Carolina Railroad
C&SCRR	Charlotte and South Carolina Railroad
WNCRR	Western North Carolina Railroad
PIEDMONT RR	Piedmont Railroad

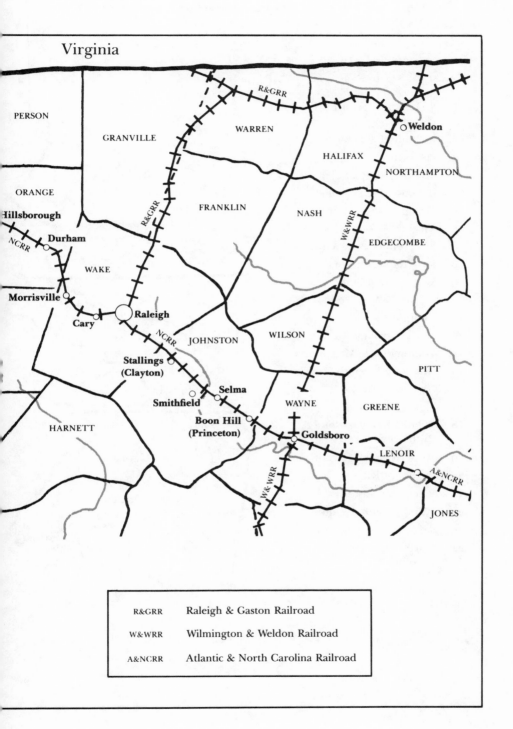

Map 2. The NCRR and Its Connecting and Competing Roads

Numerical Key to Railroads

1. Richmond, Fredericksburg & Potomac
2. Richmond & Petersburg
3. Petersburg RR
4. Seaboard & Roanoke
5. Richmond & Danville
6. Orange & Alexandria
7. Virginia & Tennessee
8. East Tennessee & Virginia
9. East Tennessee & Georgia
10. Western & Atlantic
11. Atlanta & West Point
12. Georgia RR
13. South Carolina RR
14. Wilmington & Manchester
15. Charlotte & South Carolina
16. Northeastern RR
17. North Carolina RR
18. Wilmington, Charlotte & Rutherford
19. Western North Carolina
20. Piedmont RR
21. Raleigh & Gaston
22. Wilmington & Weldon
23. Atlantic & North Carolina
24. Northwestern North Carolina RR

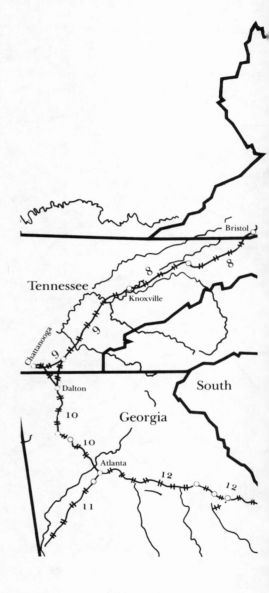

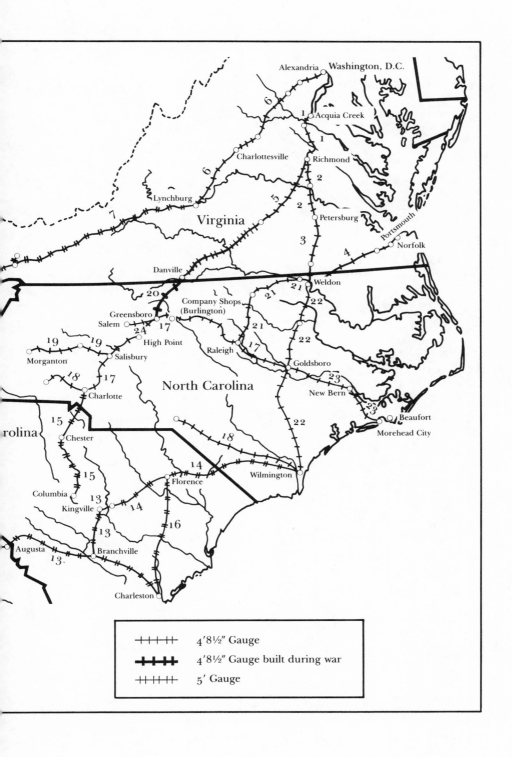

Alexandria Washington, D.C.

1 ○ Acquia Creek

6

Charlottesville

6   Richmond ○

2

5   2   Petersburg ○   Portsmouth

Lynchburg   Virginia   ○ Norfolk

7   3   4

Danville   Weldon

20   21 21   22

Company Shops
(Burlington)

Greensboro ○   21

Salem ○ 24   17   22

19   19   High Point   Raleigh   17

Morganton   Salisbury   Goldsboro

18   17   North Carolina   23

Charlotte   New Bern

15   23

...rolina   ○ Beaufort

Chester   18   Morehead City

14

15   Florence   Wilmington

Columbia   13

Kingville   14

13   16

Augusta   Branchville

13

Charleston ○

┼┼┼┼┼┼	4′8½″ Gauge
╋╋╋╋╋	4′8½″ Gauge built during war
┼┼┼┼┼┼	5′ Gauge

PART 1

Before the War

1

Waking Rip Van Winkle: Organizing the NCRR

MOTHER NATURE distributed her blessings to North Carolina with an uneven hand. The state was endowed with no good seaports and few navigable rivers. Within the Outer Banks the sounds were shallow and treacherous for navigation, as were the perennially shifting inlets that provided access to them. The best port, Wilmington, was handicapped by shallow waters at the mouth of the Cape Fear River, the main interior water route. But that river was navigable for shallow draft steamboats only to Fayetteville, and water levels were frequently undependable that far upstream. The Roanoke, Neuse, and Tar also carried steamboat traffic, but they were smaller and even more subject to the same limitations. The major piedmont rivers, the Yadkin–Pee Dee and Catawba, were too full of rapids and shallows to carry much more than downstream flatboat traffic during favorable seasons. The navigational value of the mountain streams is sufficiently indicated by their current popularity with whitewater rafters and canoeists. Most of the state was therefore dependent on roads for transportation.

It was a perilous dependency. Southern roads in general were bad before the Civil War; those of North Carolina were notorious. Some examples from 1853 will make the point. In January, Frederick Law Olmsted, traveling through the South as a correspondent for the *New York Times*, stopped for dinner at an inn in Weldon. Upon completing his meal he discovered that his stagecoach had left without him. He decided to run after the vehicle, and in half an hour caught up with it. "The road," he reported, "was as bad as anything under the name of a road can be conceived to be. Wherever the adjoining swamps, fallen trees, stumps, and plantation fences would admit of it, the coach was driven, with a great deal of dexterity, out of the road. When the wheels sunk in the mud, below the hubs, we were sometimes requested to get out and walk. An upset seemed every moment inevitable. At length, it came." No one was hurt, the passengers helped right the conveyance, and it proceeded on its way, covering fourteen miles in about four hours.[1]

Several days later, on his way from Raleigh to Fayetteville, Olmsted took another stage that had overturned the previous day, requiring its passengers to camp out overnight. This road passed through "an undulating pine forest, the track tortuous among the trees, which frequently stood so close that it required some care to work between them. Often we made detours from the original road, to avoid a fallen tree, or a mire-hole, and all the time we were bounding over protruding roots and small stumps. . . . Now and then [there was] a deep slough. In one of these we found a waggon, heavily laden, stuck fast, and six mules and five negroes tugging at it." The last ten miles went rapidly and smoothly, he noted with relief, over one of the new plank roads into Fayetteville.[2]

Almost simultaneously, the *Carolina Watchman* of Salisbury noted that, owing to recent heavy rains and muddy roads, "it has been difficult for some weeks, for our citizens to obtain wood enough to keep up their fires—wood haulers finding it almost impossible to get through the mud."[3]

Several months later, in July, the westbound stage from Raleigh overturned while fording the rain-swollen Eno River near Hillsboro. The *Hillsborough Recorder* noted that although the nine passengers were saved, some baggage was lost and the mails "were in a sad condition, being saturated with water."[4] Olmsted noted that in leaving Raleigh by stage for Fayetteville, he was following one of the state's main mail routes. But in averaging two miles per hour one day and four the next, his stage failed to make its mail and passenger connections.[5]

In 1849 President David L. Swain of the University of North Carolina reported only triweekly service from Goldsboro to Charlotte. Barring delays, the 210-mile trip took three and a half days, or eighty-four hours, thus averaging two and a half miles per hour. (Fast coaches on the National Road between Cumberland, Maryland, and Wheeling averaged five and a half miles per hour in the 1840s, with exceptional runs averaging up to ten miles per hour.)[6]

Four years later, in 1853, the Raleigh to Charlotte service had been upgraded in order to expedite traffic between two railroads that now terminated in those towns. An advertisement of Bland & Dunn's "Great Northern & Southern Stage Line" promised daily service from Charlotte via Salisbury, Lexington, Salem, and Greensboro to Raleigh in twenty-three hours. The accommodations, it continued, "have been arranged at great expense, and are unequalled in this country: fine Teams; superb Troy built Coaches; careful and experienced Drivers; in fact it is a Model Line."[7] Olmsted regarded this route to New Orleans (his ultimate destination) as too expensive at eight cents a mile, as well as "hazardous & awfully tiresome," so he headed south to Fayetteville and Charleston.[8] That was six months before one of those coaches overturned in the Eno River.

Mud roads had a comparable effect on freight transportation. Farm produce would occasionally come 200 miles to market by wagon, but only the most valuable crops, like cotton or tobacco, could bear such long hauls.

With other produce, the costs of transport over much shorter distances usually outweighed the proceeds. A farmer below Raleigh told Olmsted that it cost too much to get corn to market by the wagon roads available, so most farmers in the vicinity raised only enough to supply their own needs. At the same time, turpentine farmers around Fayetteville were unable to raise the food their workers needed and purchased corn and bacon from Ohio. These products came by northern railroads, the sea, and the Cape Fear River.[9] Olmsted saw 3,000 barrels of rosin, worth $1.50 per barrel in New York, thrown away because the cost of transportation was greater than the product was worth.[10]

Where railroads existed, they offered a dramatic improvement. Using the Raleigh and Gaston Railroad (R&G), a farmer near Raleigh sold a quantity of wheat in Petersburg, Virginia, for $1.20 per bushel. At the same time, forty miles away and off the railroad line, wheat sold for only 60 cents per bushel. It was common for the profits of half a farmer's crop to be consumed in getting the other half to market. Only the shortest hauls of less than twenty miles found wagon transportation competitive with railroads.[11]

An intermediate improvement was the plank road, which saw a brief period of popularity in the 1850s. These roads were built on a graded roadway, using heavy pine planks laid across parallel stringers. The whole was covered with sand or shavings, and graded shoulders were provided to make room for passing vehicles. As Olmsted found, plank roads were speedier and more comfortable by far than the common dirt roads. But they were also expensive to build and maintain and were unable to compete with railroads when the latter were constructed parallel to them.[12] Had more plank roads been built sooner, they might have delayed or deflected the construction of railroads. (Fayetteville, at the head of navigation on the Cape Fear and the center of plank road construction, was the last major town in the state to be well served by railroads.) But coinciding with the advent of the railroad era, plank roads served primarily as feeders, and temporary ones at that, to the new iron horse.

North Carolina in the 1840s was overwhelmingly rural and agricultural. Commercial agriculture, based on cotton, tobacco, and other salable produce, was restricted primarily to the coastal plain and other limited areas within reach of a market. The more dubious that access, the more farmers were relegated to an unwilling self-sufficiency. The southeastern quadrant of the state found its chief markets in Fayetteville, Wilmington, and New Bern. (Fayetteville received the largest wagon trade, hence its interest in plank roads in the 1850s.) The northeast was largely tributary to Norfolk. The west divided according to the direction of its rivers. The upper piedmont counties traded with Danville, Petersburg, and other Virginia towns while the produce of the southern piedmont gravitated by flatboat or wagon to Cheraw and Camden, South Carolina, and thence to Charleston.

Such produce as the mountains could send to market either followed the preceding courses or went westward to Tennessee.[13]

Most North Carolina towns were too small and remote to serve as markets to any but nearby farmers. Inhabitants of Wilmington, the largest city in the state, numbered only 7,264 in 1850. The next three towns, New Bern, Fayetteville, and Raleigh, each had a little over 4,500 souls. In general, those places that were not sea or river ports owed their existence primarily to service as seats of county or state government and as marketing centers for the immediate environs. Industry was small and geared to nearby markets. The few textile and other mills tended to locate at waterpower sites on the rivers, where they created their own villages.

Farming, industry, and trade produced so little profit for the bulk of the state's population that large numbers, often the most productive persons, sought relief through flight. The Westward movement drew people from every eastern state, of course, but North Carolina contributed her full measure. So did her central counties. Twice in the fall of 1851 the editor of the *Hillsborough Recorder* noted the exodus from Alamance and other neighboring counties and pleaded with people to stay until the North Carolina Railroad (NCRR) and other projected internal improvements should be built and rejuvenate the state.[14]

The suggested internal improvements took several forms. Included were river navigation projects ranging from the elimination of snags and dredging of sandbars to the construction of dams, locks, and sluices to overcome rapids and shoals. Canals were suggested where the terrain appeared to permit them, and plank roads were widely projected. Above all, railroads were called for as the most practical invention of the age to lessen distances, end isolation, stimulate the economy, and in general usher in a new era of progress and prosperity.

The first serious proposal for railroad development in North Carolina had come in 1827–28 with the appearance of a series of articles in the *Raleigh Register*, later reprinted in pamphlet form as *The Numbers of Carlton*. The author, President Joseph Caldwell of the state university, was aware of work already underway in Maryland on the Baltimore and Ohio Railroad (B&O) and in South Carolina on the Charleston and Hamburg Railroad designed to connect those cities with existing river transportation routes into the interior. (Both roads opened in 1829.) Caldwell proposed a more ambitious railroad, to cross North Carolina from the port of Beaufort through New Bern, Raleigh, and Lexington to the Tennessee border. In August 1828 the state's first public railroad meeting, consisting of over 200 persons from several neighboring counties, assembled in Chatham County. Participants called for a similar railroad.[15]

This project was not to bear fruit for another twenty years and more, but growing railroad agitation in the 1830s produced concrete results. North Carolina's first two railroads, both chartered in that decade, were completed in 1840. The Raleigh and Gaston connected the capital with the navigable Roanoke River to the northeast, and the Wilmington and Weldon (W&W) linked the state's largest port with the Roanoke at Weldon, a few miles downstream from Gaston.[16] (The Wilmington and Weldon was originally named the Wilmington and Raleigh, but it never went to Raleigh. Its name was changed to reflect its actual termini in 1852.) In time, Weldon would become something of a railroad hub, with a short link to the R&G at Gaston and additional lines running north to Petersburg and northeast to the Norfolk area. (That is how Olmsted happened to be there in 1853; the link to Gaston was not yet built and he had to take his memorable stage-coach ride there to catch the Raleigh train.)

Like many other early railroads, both of these lines were built with strap iron rails fastened to wooden stringers. In time, the strap iron was apt to come loose at the ends and project upward as trains passed over, sometimes penetrating the wooden coach floors. (These lethal objects were commonly referred to as snakeheads.) The R&G in particular was poorly maintained, and it became increasingly rickety, hazardous, and uncertain. The editor of the *Petersburg Intelligencer* wrote sarcastically of a ride in July 1851:

> There is scarcely a piece of iron on [the road] of six feet continuous length. But what of that? The cars jump from the iron to the wood rail, then skip a while on mother earth, and then jump fiercely on a snake-head, mash it down, and go on their way rejoicing in a speed of some eight miles an hour. As to a 'run off' [derailment], the Engineer does not care the smack of his finger for that. He is used to it, and can, with his assistants, replace a train before the snoozing passenger knows that it has encountered any thing more formidable than an ordinary bump with a snake-head. . . . There never was such travelling, over such a road.[17]

Soon after this account the road was reorganized and rebuilt. Thereafter it was regarded as one of the best-run railroads in the region, and Olmsted noted its benefit to farmers who were within reach of it.[18]

By far the greatest benefit received by the Raleigh and Gaston was the construction in the 1850s of a connecting line, the North Carolina Railroad. Extending from Goldsboro through Raleigh, Greensboro, and Salisbury to Charlotte, this central road embodied an important segment of Joseph Caldwell's early plan for a mountains-to-sea railroad across the state. Eastern and western connections were soon added, linking the NCRR with the coast at New Bern and Beaufort and (prospectively) with the Tennessee border near Asheville. More importantly, the NCRR's connection with the Charlotte and South Carolina Railroad (C&SCRR) running southward to Columbia would make both the NCRR and the R&G vital links in a developing north-south trunk railway system extending from New York to New Orleans.

That outcome was diametrically opposed to what many of the founders of the North Carolina Railroad and its eastern and western connections had wanted. They sought to implement something very like the Caldwell plan, diverting western North Carolina's commerce away from Virginia and South Carolina and toward the state's own seaports. They hoped that Beaufort, New Bern, and Wilmington would thereby rival if not surpass Norfolk and Charleston. East and west would be united as never before by ties of common interest; this would be, in substance as well as in name, the North Carolina Railroad.

However desirable that program might be in the abstract, it was delayed for nearly a generation by its great cost. Private capital was inadequate, and the legislature long refused to tax the public for state aid. That reluctance was overcome only when a greater danger materialized in the late 1840s: the prospect of a north-south trunk railway from Danville to Charlotte. Such a road, with connections upward through Virginia and downward through South Carolina, would seemingly confirm for all time the west's existing commercial reliance on those two states. Except possibly for Wilmington, served by her own railroad, North Carolina's ports would continue to languish while her neighbors waxed rich and powerful at her expense. She would remain what many of her citizens ruefully admitted her to be, a backwater, the Rip Van Winkle State.

The imminent cause of this alarm was the construction of two railroads, the Charlotte and South Carolina coming up from Columbia and the Richmond and Danville (R&D) linking those two Virginia cities. Each road would have further connections to the south and north, respectively. All that was lacking to achieve a through trunk line was to fill the 150-mile gap between Danville and Charlotte. Western North Carolinians demanded with increasing fervor that this be done, ending their long dependence upon muddy roads and whitewater rivers for contact with the outside world. Their request for a legislative charter was particularly hard for easterners to deny as it involved no state aid. The proposed road would be of such widespread economic value that it was expected to generate ample outside investment.

The legislature that convened in November 1848 faced two pressing transportation issues, apart from the general backwardness inherited from preceding decades. The first was this Charlotte-to-Danville link, embodied in a railroad charter bill introduced by Representative John W. Ellis of Rowan. The other was the dilapidated Raleigh and Gaston Railroad. That line had suffered from a lack of population centers to generate local traffic and an absence of railroad connections south of Raleigh to provide through traffic. The state had bought the road at a foreclosure sale in 1845 and needed somehow to make it profitable.

In his opening message, Governor William A. Graham lamented the state's abominable transportation facilities and addressed the two imminent questions with a single proposal: charter a central railroad to connect with a refurbished R&G at Raleigh, to proceed by way of Salisbury to Charlotte, and to connect there with the Charlotte and South Carolina Railroad, now under construction. Graham doubtless hoped that this proposal would appease the western demand for a through railroad while routing it eastward to provide the Raleigh and Gaston with badly needed through traffic. On the other hand, his suggestion offered nothing to the North Carolina seaports; it would feed traffic to South Carolina and eastern Virginia. For this reason easterners found it little more palatable than the Danville Connection, as it was called, contained in the Ellis bill.[19]

For a time it looked as if the Danville Connection might prevail, given its seeming justice to the west and the fact that no state money was requested. Western Whigs, moreover, were threatening to disrupt their party if their eastern colleagues did not support the measure. At this point a compromise was worked out by representatives of both sections, including Rufus Barringer, a Whig from Cabarrus County, and William S. Ashe, a New Hanover County Democrat and later president of the Wilmington and Weldon Railroad. This compromise embodied much of the Graham plan but with a saving benefit for Wilmington and its railroad. The new bill would charter a North Carolina Railroad running from Charlotte through Salisbury to Raleigh, as Governor Graham had proposed, but then proceeding onward to Goldsboro where it would connect with the Wilmington and Weldon. One might expect, therefore, that through traffic on the new railroad would choose one of three eastern connecting routes: the R&G from Raleigh toward Virginia, the W&W from Goldsboro toward Virginia, or the W&W from Goldsboro to Wilmington. The proposal was thus calculated to defeat the Danville Connection by attracting eastern support for what was still largely a western railroad, but now with eastern connections. The only region to lose obviously by this arrangement would be the region around Danville. The NCRR itself was estimated to cost $3 million; of this, the state would pay two-thirds, once a million dollars in stock had been pledged privately.

In order to attract further legislative support, the measure's backers agreed to provide state aid for several other internal improvements: a turnpike from Salisbury to the Georgia border, a plank road from Salisbury to Fayetteville, and navigational improvements on the Neuse and Tar rivers.

These efforts were successful, and the North Carolina Railroad charter passed both houses of the legislature by small margins in January 1849. The House vote on 18 January was 60 to 52; that in the Senate a week later was 23 to 22, Senate President Calvin Graves of Caswell casting a tiebreaking vote before a hushed chamber. Although Graves received a deafening ovation after his vote, he would later be denied renomination by the Democrats of his home county, located adjacent to Danville. Historians differ as to whether the bill was primarily a Whig measure or a western measure. It was largely both, but entirely neither. Party membership was almost evenly divided in both houses. About three-quarters of the Whig members in each chamber voted for the bill, while nearly the same proportion of Democrats opposed it. At the same time, the west favored the measure more strongly than the east; there were exceptions in both regions, however, including opposition around Danville and support in Wilmington. In truth, some Democratic and eastern support was required to furnish the necessary majorities.[20]

Included in the NCRR charter and other bills enacted before the session ended were appropriations for the turnpike, the plank road, and the river improvements as well as provisions to aid the two existing railroads.[21] It was a package designed to appeal to supporters of internal improvements in every section of the state.

Some of those persons had been urging the modernization of North Carolina for a generation and longer and had about lost hope. They were particularly happy with the new central railroad. "If this beneficent measure had been defeated," the *Raleigh Register* editorialized, "North Carolina would have lost almost every claim to the respect of enlightened communities, and many of her intelligent and enterprising citizens would have abandoned her in a body." And again, "A great system of Internal Improvements has been adopted, which will redeem and disinthrall the State and the people. A movement has been made which will shake off the incubus of lethargy and sloth for which we as a people have become proverbial; and which . . . has palsied every effort at improvement."[22] The *Register* was a Whig paper. Hardly less enthusiastic was the Democratic *North Carolina Standard* of Raleigh, whose editor, William W. Holden, noted that eight of the eleven Democratic papers in the state favored the new program. But he acknowledged ruefully that the issue was a divisive one among Democrats, many of whom bitterly opposed this expenditure of the taxpayers' money. In fact, Holden himself had only recently dared to avow publicly his advocacy of state-supported internal improvements. In March 1850 he admitted having lost about 200 subscribers because of his position.[23]

In the next legislative session, 1850–51, two efforts were made to repeal the charter. The House voted them down, 105 to 10 and 80 to 36. In the latter case, actually a "request" that the NCRR surrender its charter, 90 percent of the Whigs and 52 percent of the Democrats joined to kill the measure, as did the vast majority of western members. Some Democrats, regardless of their original views of the charter, were also unwilling to impair the state's credibility by reneging on its legal commitment.[24]

FEW PEOPLE were opposed to railroads on principle. Many were opposed, however, to government support, involving taxpayers without their individual consent. Yet public aid to internal improvements, including railroads, was popular in nineteenth-century America. It came from every level of government—local, state, and eventually federal. It was most apt to occur in areas, like the underdeveloped West and South, where private capital was least able to finance such projects by itself. It is estimated that 55 percent of the cost of antebellum southern railroad construction came from the public sector. Seldom was government money employed alone; mixed enterprise involving both public and private investment was more common, as with the North Carolina Railroad. The sources of public aid varied from state to state, counties and municipalities playing a larger role in some places than others. In North Carolina fully 89 percent of all public aid for railroads before the war came from the state itself.[25]

Raising the million dollars of private investment in the NCRR proved a monumental effort. The charter required that the million dollars be subscribed and half of it actually paid in before any state aid was forthcoming. It seems to have been assumed from the beginning that substantial out-of-state stock purchases were unlikely, despite the road's interstate implications. Thus the ensuing fund-raising campaign was aimed largely within the state, and virtually all of the money raised came from North Carolina. The procedure followed was in line with precedents established around the country during the first two decades or so of railroad promotion.[26] (Although virtually all of the stock was sold in North Carolina, the state bonds that financed the state's subscription were sold to American and foreign investors in New York.)

The charter named fifteen commissioners, including former Governors Edward B. Dudley, John Motley Morehead, and William A. Graham (whose term had just expired), to conduct the fund-raising campaign. Most of the fifteen lived in counties that the road was expected to traverse—Morehead from Guilford and Graham from Orange, for example—while Dudley resided in Wilmington, where substantial backing was hoped for. Subscription books were authorized to be opened at twenty-three towns around the state, both near and far from the expected route. In each case the books were placed in charge of several of the locality's leading citizens, specified by name, who were to be responsible to the general commissioners. The books were to be open for at least thirty days. Stock subscriptions would be for shares costing $100 each, of which $5 had to be paid immediately. As soon as the full million dollars (10,000 shares) was subscribed and the $5 per share paid in, the company was authorized to organize formally. Its board of directors was then entitled to determine a schedule of subsequent subscription payments.[27]

The ensuing effort was the work primarily of a small group of men drawn from the political and financial leadership of a rural state where few persons saw $100 in the course of a year.[28] Besides Morehead and Graham, these figures included former Governor David L. Swain, then president of the state university; Calvin Graves; and Romulus M. Saunders, recently minister to Spain and once Morehead's opponent for the governorship. Morehead, Graham, and Swain were Whigs; Graves and Saunders, Democrats. The campaign was bipartisan. In fact, most of the promoters were seasoned political campaigners who conducted this effort in accustomed fashion, courting dollars rather than votes. They wrote letters to the newspapers, the overwhelming majority of which supported the campaign, and they addressed public meetings of various sizes that were assembled around the state and, in a few cases, in Virginia.

The arguments advanced to support the subscription campaign were impressive in their diversity and ingenuity. One of the best statements appeared as a broadside by legislators John A. Lillington, Hamilton C. Jones, Rufus Barringer, and Joseph W. Scott, representing Rowan, Cabarrus, and Davie counties. It was reprinted in a number of newspapers. They argued that the railroad would redeem the declining fortunes of western North Carolina by generating passenger and freight traffic and stimulating economic activity along its route. The products of the region's farms, factories, and mines would be put in reach of markets and would sell for at least double their present prices. The telegraph that inevitably accompanied railroads would provide market news for producers, enabling them to find the best markets and prices. All railroads multiplied land values along their routes. They also stimulated activity on feeder routes; the NCRR would bring steamboats to the Yadkin River, which with slight improvement could be made navigable for 150 miles above the Narrows. (The Narrows were inundated by the construction of Badin Lake dam during World War I.)[29] Construction of the road would provide work for underemployed slaves, doubling the income of such owners as took out construction contracts. "A few miles of Rail Road would keep a whole neighborhood in employment for a year or so." And the road would be a source of continuing employment thereafter.[30]

These arguments were elaborated upon in countless speeches and newspaper articles. North Carolina was compared with other parts of the country having supposedly fewer natural advantages—like "cold, barren Massachusetts"—but made to "blossom as the rose" with the advent of railroads. The greater access to markets would increase productivity and stop the westward emigration that had been debilitating North Carolina for years. The state could then hold up her head and become independent of her proud and patronizing neighbors north and south.[31] Similarly, the road would end the ruinous sectional antagonism that had pitted east against west in North Carolina. That objective would be enhanced still further by the construction of connecting railroads to the coast and the mountains.[32] Papers in New Bern and Fayetteville reported Wisconsin wheat and Mississippi Valley bacon being sold in those towns for lack of means to get such commodities from interior North Carolina.[33]

Arguments of immediate economic interest to residents of the state received the greatest attention, especially the prospective increase in land values and decrease in freight costs. "The rich lands of Davie, Iredell and Rowan as a body are unsurpassed, and but give their proprietors . . . a market for their productions and their fortunes are immediately secured without the necessity of a trip to California," wrote a supporter in March 1849 as the gold rush was getting underway. "Sedge will no longer be permitted to wave over deserted fields, fences will be rebuilt, gullies filled up, delapidated [*sic*] buildings repaired, and the acre which [presently] yields twenty or twenty-five bushels of corn will tripple [*sic*] its production." The value of real estate would increase by at least 50 percent, he added. The *Raleigh Register* predicted an advance of at least 50 percent in both property values and population locally if the NCRR were built.[34] Former Governor Swain argued that the strip of land four miles wide on each side of the railroad would increase in value by 33 percent to 100 percent, based on the experience of landowners in this and other states. He added that land tax revenues increased by 32 percent between 1837 and 1847 in those counties traversed by the Wilmington and Weldon, compared with a rise of only 20 percent statewide. State Treasurer Charles L. Hinton claimed similar benefits for those living along the Raleigh and Gaston.[35] (Some promoters threw caution to the winds. A correspondent of the Raleigh *Star* predicted that "the bare completion of the Road, will add to the value of real estate in each town through which it passes from two to three hundred per cent. and within five years thereafter tribble [*sic*] the population and five hundred per cent. on the value of real estate.") In May 1850 Hamilton C. Jones of Salisbury, trying to raise the last few dollars needed to end the campaign, claimed that real estate values there had already risen at least 50 percent, in mere anticipation of the railroad, since the legislature passed the charter.[36]

The railroad would give farmers a far wider choice of markets than most of them now had. They could choose between Wilmington, New Bern, Raleigh, Charleston, Petersburg, and Norfolk, wrote a correspondent of the *Raleigh Register*. It would also diminish greatly the cost of shipping their crops to market. It used to cost at least $20 to wagon a hogshead of tobacco 100 miles, he said, besides the discomfort of bad weather and having to camp out overnight; nowadays, on the rickety Raleigh and Gaston, the cost is $6 per hogshead, warranted to be delivered in good order. In addition, that road had roughly halved transportation costs of cotton, salt, lime, and other commodities, according to State Treasurer Hinton.[37] Cadwallader Jones of Hillsboro wrote that it cost $1.50 to haul a barrel of flour from that place to Wilmington or Petersburg, where it brought $4.50. One third of its value was consumed in transportation. The railroad, he estimated, would cut that cost by at least a dollar. In the case of many farm commodities, it was often argued, the cost of transportation simply precluded their being raised commercially in many places. Existing transportation conditions amounted in effect to a tax on the merchant, farmer, and consumer. A correspondent of the Salisbury *Carolina Watchman* wrote that the United States grain crop in 1848 was 900 million bushels, of which 120 million were exported abroad. Not one bushel of that export came from central or western North Carolina. We lose annually $400,000 from our inability to export grain, he concluded.[38]

The railroad was expected to promote manufactures as well. Fledgling cotton mills in piedmont North Carolina could use the railroad to expand their markets and to obtain greater cotton supplies than local growers provided. In fact, said Cadwallader Jones of Hillsboro, North Carolina's future as a textile manufacturing state depended on readier access to the cotton-growing regions farther south that only railroads, and this railroad in particular, could provide.[39]

In July 1849 former Governor Swain wrote a letter, which was widely reprinted, calling attention to the comparative costs of passenger travel by stagecoach and railroad. He had recently completed a trip from Goldsboro via Charlotte to Dalton, Georgia, taking stagecoaches 210 miles along the proposed route of the NCRR, and railroads for 831 miles (a very circuitous trip) in South Carolina and Georgia. The stagecoach travel cost him 11 cents per mile at a speed of less than two and a half miles per hour. The railroad travel cost 2½ cents per mile at an average speed of 12 miles per hour, nearly reversing the two figures. He too referred to the discrepancy as a tax imposed on the people of North Carolina.[40]

Another consideration of NCRR promoters was the fate of the Raleigh and Gaston Railroad. Some people regarded the new road as essentially a lifesaving extension of the older one. As the *Raleigh Register* pointed out, it was generally understood that if the NCRR failed, the R&G would also go down. This was a major argument in Raleigh and points northward into Virginia, but it also had relevance for North Carolina taxpayers who were aware of the state's ownership of the Raleigh and Gaston.[41]

The NCRR itself was expected to be highly profitable, its backers assured prospective subscribers. As evidence they cited the experience of earlier railroads in South Carolina and Georgia, which paid regular dividends and helped support the state governments that had financed them.[42]

The greatest enthusiasm for the enterprise, first and last, lay in the piedmont areas that expected to be its immediate beneficiaries. Within a month of the charter's passage, promotional meetings, addressed by John W. Ellis, Hamilton C. Jones, Rufus Barringer, John A. Gilmer, Robert P. Dick, David F. Caldwell, and other dignitaries, were held in Salisbury and Greensboro. A meeting was held in Raleigh on 3 March with State Treasurer Charles L. Hinton as featured speaker and editor William W. Holden as secretary.[43] Raleigh and Salisbury were specified in the charter as intermediate points along the road. But the route between them was left open, and supporters in Greensboro, Hillsboro, and elsewhere hoped to influence the decision by heavy stock subscriptions in their localities. Accordingly, many of the subscriptions were made contingent upon an acceptable route. A sort of regional alliance seems to have formed early for this purpose. In March a meeting at Hillsboro offered financial support only if a route through Orange and Guilford counties was adopted.[44] In June a Jamestown meeting made its support dependent on a route through Hillsboro, Graham, Greensboro, Jamestown, Fair Grove, and Lexington. The *Greensboro Patriot* argued that a route through Greensboro was only ten miles longer than one through Asheboro and would pass through a richer and more level region, but the *Patriot* promised to support the NCRR whichever path it took.[45]

The region east of Raleigh, being served already by the two older roads, felt it had less to gain from the new railroad. The subscription books in Raleigh were originally scheduled to open in April, but the date was twice postponed.[46] In fact, subscriptions were lagging everywhere, and a general convention was called for Salisbury on 14 June to rejuvenate the campaign.

The prospect of such a meeting had an effect. Local conventions around the state elected delegates to Salisbury and passed resolutions supporting the railroad. Such meetings were even held in Norfolk and Portsmouth, Virginia, where civic leaders saw the NCRR and its connections as a potential bonanza for their adjoining seaports. Similarly, persons in Warren, Halifax, Granville, and other counties dependent upon the Raleigh and Gaston Railroad saw its future as tied up with that of the NCRR.[47] The Salisbury convention attracted 225 delegates from twenty-two counties and Virginia, plus a number of unofficial visitors. The *Raleigh Register* enthusiastically called it "one of the most numerously attended, the most enthusiastic, and one of the most able and enlightened Conventions ever assembled in North Carolina."[48] The members did in fact constitute a who's who of North Carolina business and politics, including General Alexander McRae, president of the Wilmington and Weldon Railroad; former Governors Swain, Morehead, and Graham; George W. Mordecai, William Boylan, and Charles L. Hinton of Raleigh; James W. Osborne of Charlotte; John W. Ellis, Archibald Henderson, and Hamilton C. Jones of Salisbury; John A. Gilmer of Greensboro; Calvin H. Wiley of Franklin County; and Edward R. Stanly of New Bern. John Motley Morehead was unanimously chosen president.

The three former governors urged that the survey and selection of the route be delayed until after the stock subscriptions were complete and the company was organized. There seems to have been a general understanding that the road would pass through Orange, Alamance, and Guilford counties, and the finer delineations had better wait.

The convention passed up a suggestion made earlier by Dr. Josiah Watson of Johnston County and renewed in the convention by former Governor Swain to form a body of 100 men, each pledging $10,000 to supply the $1 million stock subscription.[49] Quite possibly, 100 such men could not be found. Instead the convention provided for a renewed subscription campaign throughout the state and in Virginia, welcoming even the smallest amounts.

Another resolution recommended that stockholders be given a preference in the awarding of construction contracts. By this means subscriptions might be expected from men with limited funds who could pay a part of the cost of their stock by work—or more accurately in most cases, by working their slaves. This arrangement had recently been employed successfully in Georgia and South Carolina.[50] Although the Salisbury convention had no power to authorize such a policy, there seems to have been a general understanding that it would be adopted, and much of the promotion campaign assumed it.

So the campaign was renewed. County committees were appointed in over forty counties, and even more localized committees in some of them. Thirteen were chosen in Guilford.[51] More meetings were held and speeches delivered. The services and talents of leading men were called upon as never before. Morehead, Graham, Swain, Saunders, Graves, Gilmer, John W. Thomas of Davidson County, Rufus Barringer of Cabarrus, and others crisscrossed the piedmont and occasionally the coastal plain addressing crowds in places large and small.

But progress was slow. Although the Wilmington and Weldon Railroad subscribed $50,000, it was payable in transportation once the new road was in need of construction materials. The *Carolina Watchman* of Salisbury lamented in August that while Rowan County ought to raise $200,000, so far it had subscribed only $32,500. The figure in Guilford at that time was about $47,000, in Raleigh $25,000.[52] Efforts were made in Raleigh to secure a municipal appropriation of $25,000, but this required legislative authorization as well as a popular vote, and neither was achieved. A similar effort was made, with no greater result, in Salisbury. The *Greensboro Patriot* lamented, "Is there nothing that will arouse our old Rip Van Winkle State? Is she too lazy to put forth her hand for dear life? . . . What somniferous influence is it . . . that depresses our energy? . . . The Railroad," it added, "*must be built.*"[53] By early September there was a growing consensus for another general convention to redirect the campaign once more. That meeting, originally scheduled for 18 October in Greensboro, was postponed to 29 November.

Meanwhile, subscriptions began to pick up, especially when six men stepped forward at a Raleigh meeting to pledge $10,000 apiece: Governors Morehead and Swain, Dr. Josiah O. Watson of Smithfield, and William Boylan, Charles L. Hinton, and John D. Hawkins of Raleigh. News came soon afterward that Davidson County subscriptions had topped $100,000, more than doubling any other county. In Salisbury Nathaniel Boyden and several other men agreed to form a company of twenty to raise $100,000 among them. Similar efforts in Guilford—spurred by Morehead, Gilmer, and David F. Caldwell—reportedly raised that county's total to $150,000 by the time of the November meeting.[54]

Delegates from twenty-four counties plus representatives of the city of Petersburg, Virginia, the Petersburg Railroad, and the Greenville and Roanoke Railroad assembled in the Presbyterian Church at Greensboro on 29 November. Many of them had been at Salisbury in June. Calvin Graves was elected chairman after Morehead recounted once again the thrilling scene in the Senate when Graves cast his deciding vote for the charter.[55] Members made extraordinary efforts to complete the subscription process at this meeting, fifty-one of them agreeing each to take on $^1/_{100}$ of the as yet unsubscribed shares—about $8,000 apiece. But on the afternoon of 30 November only $610,000 had been subscribed—well short of the needed $1 million. The convention ended with yet another appeal to the people, yet another round of county meetings along the route.

The meetings were held during December 1849 and January 1850 at intervals of several days, in two groups, east and west of Greensboro. Romulus M. Saunders, only recently returned from his diplomatic assignment in Spain, was the featured speaker at most of the eastern meetings, performing prodigious labors. Morehead, Gilmer, Graves, and others spoke at the western meetings.[56] The effort now was to enlist the remaining 49 members of the 100 begun at Greensboro. Progress was gradually made: 4 in Wake County, 4 in Davidson, 4 in Rowan, 1 in Randolph, 5 in Cabarrus—but not a nibble in Charlotte, where Morehead and company received cheers but no dollars. That city, like Goldsboro and Raleigh, already had her railroad—the Charlotte and South Carolina—then under construction. Residents pleaded in extenuation the heavy subscriptions they had made to that road. By 17 January, Morehead could report 73 shares of the 100 taken; by early February it was said to be 88.[57]

Accordingly, a third general convention was called for late February in expectation that the subscriptions would then be complete.[58] But when the delegates assembled at Hillsboro on 26 February, they found themselves still about $150,000 short. They resolved to make up that deficiency before the meeting adjourned. Seven additional shares of the 100 were subscribed, leaving some $100,000 to go. Heroic measures were called for, and at length Morehead proposed that a list of ten men be drawn up, each promising to be responsible for $10,000 of additional subscriptions. This was agreed to, and under the compulsion of the circumstances the list began to form: first John W. Thomas of Davidson; then Morehead; a company of New Bern men including Alonzo T. Jerkins and Edward Stanly; Dr. Edmund Strudwick of Hillsboro; William Boylan of Raleigh; George W. Mordecai of Raleigh; Paul C. Cameron of Orange County; and Dr. A. J. de Rosset, Jr., of Wilmington. At this point the list reached eight and no one else stepped forward. It had been agreed that if the list could not be completed before adjournment it would not be binding on those who had signed. Mordecai moved to adjourn, but no one seconded. Thomas made a speech. Mordecai again moved to adjourn, but still no second. Morehead, looking "the picture of despair," made a desperate appeal, aimed particularly at the local Orange County men, and finally moved adjournment himself. This spurred Giles Mebane of Alamance (just separated from Orange) to step forward as number nine, amidst loud cheering. Then a company of Hillsboro men agreed to take the remainder, completing the ten. The meeting adjourned, confident that the campaign was finally over the top. When the news reached Raleigh, a *feu de joie* of 100 guns was fired, followed by a parade and speechmaking by Saunders, Boylan, Hinton, Governor Charles Manly, and others. Most of the Hillsboro Ten had already made subscriptions, and some were now committed to the extent of $18,000, a very large figure for the time and place. Subsequently others made subscriptions in order to ease the burden on these men.[59]

The general commissioners of the railroad, named in the charter, met in Greensboro on 30 March to complete the formalities and collect the 5 percent initial installments. Once there, they found that payment had been made on only 8,680 shares of the whole 10,000. (For one thing, the stockholders of the Petersburg Railroad in Virginia had objected to a $40,000 subscription made in their name.) So the books were reopened until 1 May. On that date there was still a deficit, and the books were ordered to remain open for another month.[60] Local meetings resumed, with still more exhortations by the dignitaries who had done so much in the past. Subscriptions gradually edged upward.

Finally, at a meeting in Chapel Hill on 5–6 June, timed to coincide with the university's commencement exercises, the commissioners announced that all 10,000 shares had been subscribed and the necessary 5 percent, or $50,000, was paid in. They formally declared the North Carolina Railroad Company to be in existence and called the first stockholders' meeting for Salisbury on 11 July.[61] Measured from the legislative charter enactment in January 1849, the subscription campaign had required nearly a year and a half of tireless effort by a relatively small number of men.

Although more than 1,100 individuals subscribed to stock, the great bulk of it similarly was held by a relative few. As the president and directors pointed out later, "This great work . . . has been commenced, not by the mass of the people of the whole State, nor even of the counties through which the road passes, but by an exceedingly small portion of our people." Unlike many railroads around the country, the NCRR received no aid from local governments, county or city, despite efforts to obtain it in Raleigh, Salisbury, and perhaps elsewhere.[62] Geographical distribution was also uneven, as shown in table 1. Eighty-five percent of the stock subscribed by March 1850 was held in the counties along the expected route from Goldsboro through Raleigh, Hillsboro, Greensboro, and Salisbury to Charlotte. And, as between these counties, interest lagged perceptibly among residents of Wayne and Johnston at the eastern end of the line and Mecklenburg at the western terminus. Wayne (Goldsboro) and Mecklenburg (Charlotte) were already served by railroads. The only shares subscribed out of state were 173 in Petersburg, Virginia, which already had railroad connections to Raleigh and Goldsboro and wished to see them extended.[63]

The charter had specified Salisbury as the first meeting place. It empowered the stockholders to adopt bylaws and to elect twelve directors annually.[64] Late in June, Morehead (as chairman of the commissioners) asked George W. Mordecai to draw up a set of bylaws and bring them to Salisbury for the stockholders to consider. When the meeting assembled on 11 July a committee including both men presented a set of bylaws that the stockholders adopted.[65]

Another committee, under William A. Graham, was chosen to recommend a system of apportioning and nominating the twelve directors. Its report seems to have called for a division of the stockholders into regional caucuses, each to nominate one or more directors. This was adopted, and the stockholders elected a panel drawn from ten counties, seven of them along the expected route. The three laggard counties of Wayne, Johnston, and Mecklenburg were unrepresented, while Rowan and Guilford each received two directors. This formula was retained until 1853, when the seating of eight state directors forced a modification.[66]

Most if not all of the directors chosen in 1850 were men who had been identified with the subscription campaign. All had to be stockholders; most were substantial ones, including John M. Morehead with 180 shares, A. J. de Rosset of Wilmington with 150, John I. Shaver and John B. Lord of Salisbury with 106 each, and Alonzo T. Jerkins of New Bern with 100. Other directors included Francis Fries, the Salem textile manufacturer; John W. Thomas of Davidson; John A. Gilmer of Greensboro; former Governor Graham; and Romulus M. Saunders. Half of these men were reelected in 1851 and again in 1852. With one exception, replacements were chosen from the same counties. They included John W. Ellis of Salisbury, sponsor of the Danville Connection bill and a strong supporter of the NCRR substitute, and textile manufacturer Edwin M. Holt of Alamance.[67]

The bylaws required the board of directors to elect from their number a president, who was to receive a salary of $2,500 plus any expenses incurred in out-of-state travel. A secretary-treasurer was provided for, at a salary of $1,250. The president and directors were authorized to employ all other officers at their discretion. The directors were to meet quarterly, or oftener on call of the president. Their only compensation was 10 cents per mile in traveling to and from meetings.[68]

As soon as the stockholders adjourned, the board of directors met and elected John M. Morehead president. He was the obvious choice, having been chairman of the preceding board of commissioners and the acknowledged leader of the subscription campaign. The board's first choice as secretary-treasurer, John U. Kirkland of Hillsboro, declined, and the position went to Jeduthun H. Lindsay of Greensboro. Next to the presidency, the most important office to be filled was that of chief engineer, which went to Colonel Walter Gwynn of Virginia. He would be in charge of construction—a task far different from launching the company but quite as demanding.[69]

2

Building the Road

HARDLY A BETTER MAN could have been selected as chief engineer. Colonel Walter Gwynn was a West Point graduate—as were most civil engineers in the United States before the Civil War—class of 1822. Until 1850 or so West Point was almost the only institution in the United States offering systematic training in engineering. At first the army lent its engineers to the Baltimore and Ohio and other pioneer railroads to conduct their surveys and supervise construction. When Congress forbade this practice in 1838, officers increasingly resigned their commissions to go into the lucrative civilian practice.[1]

Lieutenant Walter Gwynn was one of the young officers who received their practical training on the B&O, beginning in 1827. After ten years he resigned from the service and began a notable career as a canal and railroad builder. From 1833 to 1836 he was chief engineer in charge of constructing the Portsmouth and Roanoke (later Seaboard and Roanoke) Railroad, between Portsmouth, Virginia, and Weldon, North Carolina; in 1842 he returned for four years as president of that road. During the interval he supervised construction of the Wilmington and Raleigh (renamed the Wilmington and Weldon) Railroad and conducted surveys for several other railroad and canal projects in Virginia, North Carolina, and Florida. Beginning in 1846 Gwynn served first as president, then as chief engineer of the James River and Kanawha Canal Company. This ambitious enterprise was designed to connect and make navigable those two rivers flowing in opposite directions on either side of the Virginia mountains. He was so employed in 1850 when he accepted appointment as chief engineer of the North Carolina Railroad.[2]

In fact, Gwynn engendered a fair amount of controversy in North Carolina by his stated intention to hold both positions simultaneously. He apparently gave most of his attention to the Virginia post until the fall of 1853, when he resigned it and moved from Richmond to Raleigh. By that time the NCRR survey was complete, and construction was well underway. Gwynn superintended the construction until its completion early in 1856. But between 1853 and 1855 he also conducted the surveys for the Atlantic and North Carolina (A&NCRR) and the Western North Carolina (WNCRR) railroads, the eastern and western extensions of the NCRR. And from 1848 to

1855 he was listed as chief engineer of the Wilmington and Manchester Railroad (W&M). Although some North Carolina newspaper editors (and doubtless some of their readers) thought the state was being slighted and was paying too much for this Virginian's absentee services before he moved to the state in 1853, the NCRR seems not to have suffered much by his other activities. (Gwynn's part-time salary with the NCRR before 1853 was $3,000 at a time when the governor earned $2,000.)[3] Gwynn's professional qualifications were as highly regarded during and after his association with the NCRR as before, and of course most of the field work was done by subordinates.

Little time was wasted in beginning the survey. Gwynn organized four parties, each under a principal assistant engineer, to survey four approximately equal sections of the road. The first section, running from the eastern terminus near Goldsboro to about six miles west of Raleigh, was in charge of Lewis M. Prevost, Jr. The second, from that point to the eastern Guilford County line, was under John C. McRae. J. L. Gregg led the third party, from eastern Guilford to Lexington. The fourth section, from Lexington to Charlotte, was under a second John McRae. Each party included two assistant engineers plus draftsmen, rodmen, chainmen, and axemen. The first party began work near Goldsboro on 21 August, the others by 18 September. The survey took approximately eight months, Gwynn submitting his report on 5 May 1851. In that time his men ran 1,494 miles of lines, including experimental ones; the final route measured 223 miles.[4]

The charter required that the road run from near Goldsboro to Raleigh, Salisbury, and Charlotte. A great deal of the stock had been subscribed in Orange, Alamance, Guilford, and Davidson counties by persons expecting the route to run through Hillsboro, Greensboro, and Lexington. They did not remain silent when the stockholders met at Salisbury. A resolution was passed instructing the directors "to ascertain by actual surveys whether said route, all things considered, is not the most practicable."[5] The directors complied, and that was the route ultimately chosen.

Gwynn denied taking the resolution as a mandate and explored every alternate route between Raleigh and Salisbury. But he soon learned what residents of the state already knew, that a straight line west from Raleigh to Salisbury via Pittsboro and Asheboro involved difficult terrain. Anyone who had traveled that way by the existing road, Gwynn said, must be impressed by the many ups and downs. To maintain a practicable grade the railroad would be forced either to construct an endless succession of cuts and fills across the hills and valleys or to take a serpentine course around them, or some of both. A route farther south would encounter the same problems. The most practical route from an engineering standpoint, he concluded, was along the ridge line farther north, nearer the headwaters of the south-flowing tributaries of the Haw, Deep, and Yadkin rivers, where the streams were not so wide nor their valleys so deep as they became farther south.[6]

Gwynn could have made a further argument, just about as cogent. So far as possible, railroads are supposed to serve people where they live and do business. The existing towns of Hillsboro, Greensboro, Lexington, and the smaller villages and farming regions between them had a substantially greater capacity to generate traffic (and subscribe railroad stock) than the poorer and less populated regions of Chatham and Randolph counties farther south. The NCRR is credited with creating the prosperous urban Piedmont Crescent between Raleigh and Charlotte. Over time it did have that effect, but an earlier "incipient crescent" probably helped to locate the railroad in the first place.[7] A shorter line bypassing these existing towns would have injured them needlessly, apart from whatever consideration they were entitled to as a result of their stock subscriptions.[8] It would also have injured the railroad. As it was, the chosen route was only about twenty miles longer than the shortest possible route farther south. The people of Chatham and Randolph seem to have recognized their disadvantages from the beginning. They subscribed very little of the stock and made next to no effort to secure the railroad themselves. In fact, it seems to have been generally conceded all along that the road would take approximately the route that Gwynn recommended.[9]

This is not to say that the survey engendered no controversy. There was intense interest as to the precise location of the road in a number of localities. State Senator John W. Thomas of Davidson County, one of the road's foremost champions in the legislature and in the later subscription campaign, was eager to have the road pass through his Fair Grove plantation in eastern Davidson. He personally accompanied the surveyors much of the time as they ran their experimental lines in the vicinity during March 1851; he showed great solicitude about their findings, and he had them to dinner at his house. But Gwynn decided upon a more direct line between Greensboro and Salisbury, passing several miles north of Fair Grove. Thomas swallowed his disappointment, bought a sizable tract of land on both sides of the chosen route, and began building the village of Thomasville. A little farther south, a straight line would have taken the road several miles east of Lexington.[10] But the county seat was a more valuable destination than Thomas's estate, and the road bent westward to pass closer to town.

Other towns were not so fortunate, probably because the costs of deflecting the line outweighed the expected benefits of passing through them. Most of these problems arose on the eastern half of the road. Alamance County had been created by the same legislature that chartered the NCRR in 1849; its county seat of Graham was subsequently planned in the expectation that the railroad would pass through it—or so a public meeting of its citizens declared in February 1851. But they were disappointed to find the survey passing a short distance north of town and were unable to get it changed.[11]

A few miles farther east, the railroad had to cross the Haw River. The main stage road between Hillsboro and Greensboro crossed over Trollin-

ger's bridge at the mill village of Haw River, where General Benjamin Trollinger had built the Granite cotton mill in 1844. Although Gwynn favored
an alternate crossing to the north as being a mile shorter and $5,000
cheaper, the board of directors chose to cross at Trollinger's bridge. General Trollinger was a member of the board and expected to be a major
construction contractor. These considerations surely helped influence the
decision, but his mill's traffic-generating capacity may also have played a
part.[12]

Still farther east, residents of Hillsboro were disappointed to find the
engineers recommending a route south of town, on the far side of the Eno
River. Former Governor Swain remarked that no one in the history of
Hillsboro had ever gone to that site except on his way to the gallows. At
least one public meeting was held, but residents failed to relocate the road
through town.[13] Nonetheless, Hillsboro was close to a depot, however inconvenient it might have been.

That advantage might well have been at the expense of Chapel Hill.
Swain (now president of the university) and others lobbied in vain for a
route through or at least near the college town. Gwynn reconnoitered such
a route, bypassing Hillsboro, but found it so hilly that considerations of
grade, curvature, distance, and cost ruled it out.[14] In 1855–56 a nine-mile
wagon and coach road was laid out from Chapel Hill to what was called
Strayhorn's Turnout, the closest point on the railroad. A depot was later
built there, called University Station. Building lots were even advertised in
contemplation of a town, but the plans never materialized. When President
James Buchanan attended the university commencement exercises in 1859,
he took a special train from Raleigh to Durham, then a horse-drawn coach
to Chapel Hill.[15]

Nearby Durham owes its very existence to the railroad. The original survey called for a station to be built at a hamlet called Prattsburg, southeast of
Hillsboro. But William Pratt, the local landowner, asked such an exorbitant
price for land on which to build the depot that the road relocated two miles
west onto the land of Dr. Bartlett Durham, who donated the needed property. Durham's Station became the nucleus of the later city.[16]

One of the greatest controversies involved the route to be taken through
Raleigh and the connection to be made with the Raleigh and Gaston Railroad. Both engineering and economic concerns were at stake. Gwynn's
preference was a route through the southern and western part of the city.
However, the gradient was such as to make difficult the installation of a
depot or a connection with the R&G within the city limits. He recognized
the practical objections to having either of these points located outside the
city and believed that modifications were possible to accommodate local
opinion.[17]

A greater problem by far, surprisingly, turned out to be whether or not to
make a connection with the R&G at all. One of the arguments in the subscription campaign had been the necessity of making such a connection, in

the interest of the R&G and the state as well as the NCRR. It had been assumed all along that a connection would be made, and it was specifically provided for in the recent charters of both roads. The R&G of course eagerly sought it. But eastern North Carolinians, especially those associated with the Wilmington and Weldon Railroad, saw an opportunity to defeat the connection. Their argument—and a clear-sighted one—was that it would divert most of the state's produce into the lap of Virginia at the expense of Wilmington and other North Carolina ports. To this was added the voice of the Raleigh hotel and drayage trades, which stood to benefit from an absence of close railroad connections. Debate and no little hard feeling persisted over this question for more than two years.[18] Opponents of the connection prevailed temporarily, but it was finally effected in 1854. A temporary depot was constructed in the southwestern part of the city, and the R&G built a connecting link to that point from its own station a mile north.[19]

In Johnston, the next county southeast of Raleigh, the railroad chose to bypass the county seat of Smithfield in favor of a straighter line across the Neuse River four miles upstream. The saving in distance was a little over a mile, in cost about $11,000. Townspeople were predictably unhappy, but the decision stood. A depot, called Mitchener's Station, was built near the closest place to Smithfield; some years later its location was shifted slightly and it was renamed Selma.[20]

Easily the greatest controversy was generated over the location of the eastern terminus near Goldsboro. The charter required the road to connect with the Wilmington and Raleigh (soon to be renamed Wilmington and Weldon) Railroad "where the same passes over Neuse River, in the County of Wayne."[21] The idea was to effect a junction at this point not only with the other railroad but also with the river, where a dock or boat landing was to be provided. Literal compliance with the charter proved impossible owing to swampy terrain subject to frequent flooding. The Wilmington and Raleigh approached the Neuse on trestle work above the low ground. The nearest place for a boat landing was at the old town of Waynesboro, a half-mile upstream from the W&R bridge. After exploring three alternate routes, Gwynn recommended a line passing through Waynesboro from the west, then proceeding a short distance to the W&R and intersecting with it a mile south of Goldsboro. He recommended that the depot be established in Goldsboro, where the W&R already had a station and warehouses that could be shared by the two roads. Goldsboro itself was a relatively new byproduct of the Wilmington and Raleigh Railroad, located halfway between its termini of Wilmington and Weldon; it was incorporated in 1847. Waynesboro, incorporated in 1787, was the first seat of Wayne County. It grew to perhaps 500 people before the county seat was moved to Goldsboro in 1850, and then it began to decline.[22]

Gwynn's proposal was not entirely satisfactory either to Goldsboro, which disliked the idea of a junction a mile south of town and perhaps bypassing its businesses, or to construction contractors, who still thought the route covered too much low ground. Accordingly, Gwynn recommended moving the road to higher ground near Waynesboro and shifting the proposed W&R connection into Goldsboro. But this in turn excited the fears of New Bern and other points down the Neuse, who suspected an effort to divert traffic away from the river. These fears were only partly laid to rest by assurances that the railroad would still pass through Waynesboro and touch the river by means of a short spur before reaching Goldsboro.[23]

NCRR stockholders in the New Bern area met in February 1852 and denounced any effort to steal traffic from the Neuse. Some of them threatened to seek relief in the courts for what they regarded as a violation of the charter. The president and directors therefore sought legal counsel themselves in April and agreed to a literal compliance with that document if the route so far chosen was found not to be in conformity. In November 1852 the matter was referred for settlement to Gwynn and another engineer, William Beverhout Thompson, apparently representing the New Bern interest. As late as September 1853, some New Bern stockholders continued to protest by refusing to pay their stock installments.[24] The road was actually built in 1854 according to the revised survey, with a short branch line to Waynesboro, where a warehouse was built along the river.[25] The matter was rendered largely moot by the decision next year to construct the Atlantic and North Carolina Railroad from Goldsboro to New Bern and Beaufort. Steamboat traffic on the Neuse almost disappeared thereafter. When the NCRR's warehouse at Waynesboro burned in 1862, it was being used as a barn by a neighboring farmer.[26]

As finally surveyed by May 1851, the North Carolina Railroad extended 223 miles. The terrain to be crossed was not very difficult, for the most part. Perhaps the roughest was around Hillsboro in some hills euphemistically known as the Occoneechee Mountains. The lowest elevation at any station, 104 feet above sea level, was at Goldsboro. The highest, 943 feet, was at the future site of High Point, so named for that reason. The western terminus at Charlotte was 743 feet.[27] There were few swamps to equal those near Waynesboro, and only three rivers of any size: the Neuse above Smithfield, the Haw at Haw River, and the Yadkin near Salisbury. Gwynn reported only modest grades and curves, but both would be criticized in later years as unnecessarily difficult. (See Chapter 3.)

President Morehead was at work acquiring rights of way as early as February 1851, several months before the survey was complete. The right of way embraced 100 feet on each side of the contemplated track. The greater part of the route, passing through open countryside, was donated by willing landowners eager to have the railroad come. In Orange County only four or five landowners refused to do so.[28] And most of the demands for compensation were reasonable. The total expenditures for right of way amounted to just over $20,000.[29]

Where consent was not forthcoming or the demanded price was judged too high, the railroad had the power of eminent domain. In such cases a court was empowered to appoint five commissioners to assess the landowner's damages and benefits by having the railroad pass through the property. After a public hearing the court could condemn the strip of land and award monetary damages. In the case of Barnabas Johnson of Wake County, for instance, on petition by the NCRR the Court of Pleas and Quarter Sessions appointed commissioners on 3 November 1852 to examine his property; on 1 December they reported his estimated damages at $95 and his benefits nothing. Accordingly, in May 1853 the court condemned the 200-foot-wide strip of Johnson's land and awarded him $95.[30]

As early as April 1849 an anonymous South Carolinian offered to grade the entire road within three years, using 1,000 to 3,000 slave laborers. He volunteered to subscribe $100,000 in stock, paying for it in work.[31] The offer was not accepted. It was understood from the beginning that the grading (they called it graduation) and much of the additional construction would be done by neighboring landowners using slave labor. This policy had recently been adopted in the building of railroads in Georgia and South Carolina. From the railroad's point of view, slave labor was apt to be the cheapest available. Moreover, the prospect of work contracts utilizing underemployed slaves was a major inducement to secure stock subscriptions from farmers and planters along the route. Commonly they were permitted to receive part of their payment in cash, the rest in railroad stock.[32]

John W. Thomas and his neighbors in northern Davidson and southern Guilford were not alone in trying to influence the course of the road by offering subscriptions with work contracts in return for a specified route. Thomas offered to take a contract for one mile, others for as little as a quarter-mile each.[33] Throughout the successive promotional meetings of 1849–50, resolutions were passed asking that stockholders be favored in the awarding of construction contracts. Many subscriptions were solicited and given with that understanding, and the stockholders repeated the request at their initial meeting in July 1850.[34]

The directors had the power to decide. They confirmed the policy in May 1851 upon accepting Gwynn's survey report: contractors would receive half of their pay in cash, the other half in stock, nominally valued at $100 per share. (Most of the railroad's promoters—at least those reported in the newspapers—had led prospective contractors to believe that they would receive as much as two-thirds in cash and one-third in stock.)[35] The president and chief engineer were directed to let contracts as soon as possible for grading, masonry, bridging, and timber supplies. That process began in June. Although contractors were not required to start until January 1852, the target completion date was optimistically set at 1 January 1854.[36] In actuality, the road was not completed until January 1856.

In letting contracts the road's four main divisions were subdivided into sections of a half-mile to two or three miles' length. For the most part, the process of awarding contracts went quickly. Most if not all of the contractors were stockholders, and nearly all were inexperienced at this kind of work.[37] Some were middling to large farmers along the route. Others were among the chief backers of the road, members of the state's political and business elite. In Orange County—claiming a disproportionate share of that elite— the number included former Governor Graham, Colonel Cadwallader Jones, Josiah Turner, Sr., and Paul C. Cameron.[38] In the Guilford-Davidson division, as elsewhere, some of the contractors organized in companies. Cyrus P. Mendenhall and Company contracted for six miles of road; Joel McLean and Company had about twice that distance, extending from President Morehead's house in Greensboro to the Alamance County line. In Rowan County, 114 bids were received for the 22 sections available. Most of these sections went to a single contractor each, although some bidders had desired more.[39]

The one exception to the rule of relatively small contractors lay in section 1, from Goldsboro to about six miles west of Raleigh. Support for the railroad had always been weakest in this region, and too few local contractors could be found to perform the necessary work. Yet construction of the road, apart from grading, almost had to begin in this section, with its existing rail connections to convey equipment and supplies. In May and again in June 1851 the directors suggested that the stockholders in Wilmington and New Bern unite and take a contract for the entire section. After considerable negotiation John C. McRae of Wilmington, an assistant engineer under Gwynn, agreed in October to organize a company for that purpose. He subsequently recruited his brother Alexander McRae (president of the Wilmington and Raleigh Railroad), Colonel John McRae (another assistant engineer on the NCRR), and two other men. With their backing he assumed the contract and began work in January 1852.[40]

Contracts for bridge and masonry work lagged behind those for grading, but in that same month Gwynn was finally able to report that the entire road was under contract.[41]

Meanwhile a formal groundbreaking ceremony took place at Greensboro on 11 July 1851, following the second annual stockholders' meeting. Probably the largest crowd in the town's history was in attendance, according to the *Greensboro Patriot*'s account. A procession formed, headed by the clergy and followed in order by stockholders, Odd Fellows and Free Masons, and the general public. Reaching a point on the railroad right of way, the crowd arranged itself ten or twenty deep around a 100-foot square and awaited the ceremonies. The stockholders had chosen Calvin Graves to lift the first spadeful of earth. After a long introductory speech by Morehead, recalling again Graves's moment of glory in the Senate, Graves himself spoke, then dug some earth and deposited it in a copper box that had been prepared for the occasion. Enclosed with the dirt was a copy of the charter, the names of the original subscribers to the stock, some newspapers of that day or month, coins, and a scroll to be read on the one-hundredth anniversary. The box was not to be opened until that occasion. The ceremonies closed with a barbecue.[42]

The grading, masonry, and bridge building, unlike the later tracklaying, required little outside material, and each contractor proceeded more or less independently. Actual work seems to have begun in July 1851 soon after the groundbreaking, but many contractors, occupied with farming, did not get started until the following January.

None of the contractors were destined to be paid until a year (more or less) had elapsed and their work was essentially done. The charter authorized the state to begin stock payments only after the private stockholders had paid half of their subscriptions, or $50 per share. Until that occurred, the road was dependent for funds upon periodic installment payments by the stockholders. As Morehead pointed out to the legislature, the contractors were in an anomalous position: they were being asked to "do the work first and raise the means to do it with afterwards." The directors called for periodic installments following the initial 5 percent paid at the time of subscription. The crucial 50 percent was requested by November, but payments lagged enough that a further 10 percent had to be called for that month in order to secure the state's subscription. That much-hoped-for event came in December. By the time of the annual stockholders' meeting in July 1853, the state treasurer had remitted $500,000.[43] To raise this money the state issued $500,000 in state bonds. They sold in New York on 31 March 1853 at a premium of 5 percent, or $25,100 above the face value, reflecting the state's high credit rating.[44]

The plans called for a single track, with double-width cuts through hills in contemplation of a later second track and in order to provide enough dirt fill for the low places. The roadbed was to be of gravel a foot deep, supporting the then-standard wrought iron T-rail weighing sixty pounds per yard. Drains and culverts were to be made of stone or brick. Wooden bridges, also standard at the time, were to rest upon masonry piers and abutments. Gwynn pronounced the soil throughout the line to be well adapted as a base for the roadbed. There was ample timber adjacent to the road for crossties (usually called sills at the time) although some of the bridge timber and building stone would have to be brought from a distance.[45]

Railroad building in the 1850s was heavy, arduous work. Animal power was used where possible, but there was very little mechanical help. Gunpowder was used for blasting rock. Earth, gravel, timber, building stone, and other materials were hauled in carts and wagons. Much of the grading was done by plows and scrapers drawn by mules, horses, or oxen. But rocky or hilly terrain, embankments, cuts, and drainage ditches often required men with picks and shovels. Axemen felled trees more or less adjacent to the site, cut them to the proper length, then hewed them into crossties. The iron rails were fastened down by hand-driven spikes.[46]

The great majority of railroad construction laborers in the South before the Civil War were slaves. On the NCRR as generally, contractors usually owned their laborers or hired them from other owners. Slave laborers were economical and efficient: they received almost no compensation beyond their upkeep, they did not strike, and they were often underemployed otherwise during much of the year.[47] In 1851 and 1852 NCRR contractors hired unskilled slaves for $100 to $125 per year—or less often, $6 to $8 per month. But all the railroad construction created a labor shortage. The Charlotte and South Carolina Railroad, nearing Charlotte, advertised there in March 1852 for "50 Negro Fellows" at an annual rate of $140 plus clothing. In January 1856 farm hands (equivalent to unskilled construction workers) were hired for $125 to $150 in Charlotte.[48]

NCRR contractors also hired free wage laborers. Some of these were Irishmen, who were found on railroad construction gangs almost everywhere in the United States. Dozens of Irish reportedly came to Hillsboro by early 1852, seeking work on the railroad. William A. Graham's foreman paid two of them $9 and $10, presumably per week. This was in line with wages for comparable labor in Louisiana and on the Illinois Central Railroad, which was built at the same time. Such workers commonly put in a twelve-hour day six days a week. Masonry and other skilled labor was sometimes subcontracted to workers from out of state. In July 1852 the *Standard* in Raleigh reported that some hands were being hired for as little as 50 cents per day.[49]

One blanket rule imposed by the NCRR directors was a ban on the use of ardent spirits among construction workers.[50]

As construction started, contractors began advertising for slaveowners to hire out their "hands" by the month or year. Some were interested in buying. During the early weeks especially, newspapers along the route eagerly reported on the activity. The following came from Greensboro in November 1851: "The array of carts and horses and wheelbarrows, and hands with their mattocks and shovels, digging and throwing up the earth, and passing and repassing like ants on an ant hill, presents a most animating spectacle."[51] In January 1852 the railroad began advertising for crossties from landowners along the route. The president was authorized to purchase the first rails as well as two locomotives and a number of freight cars to assist in construction work at either end of the line.[52] (Tracklaying at the western end would be facilitated by the completion of the Charlotte and South Carolina Railroad to Charlotte in October 1852.) President Morehead reported that in November 1852, 1,493 men, 425 boys, 581 carts, 49 wagons, 758 horses and mules, and 54 oxen were employed on the road. Half of the grading was completed at that time, and bridges were under construction. By July 1853 most of the grading was done and the force had diminished somewhat. But sixteen tracklayers had been added.[53]

The first shipments of rails arrived at Wilmington and were delivered to Goldsboro on the Wilmington and Weldon Railroad in May 1853. They were of Welsh manufacture, like most of the rails used on the early American railroads. Tracklaying began at the eastern terminus, just south of Goldsboro, on 23 June accompanied by the firing of a cannon and the drinking of champagne. Initial progress was exceedingly slow, only twelve miles having been laid by December.[54] Although rails began reaching Charlotte via the C&SCRR in October, tracklaying there did not begin until February. The major cause of delay was inability to procure crossties locally at an acceptable price. When the road finally sent to South Carolina for them, local farmers lowered their prices and the supply improved.[55] The NCRR's first locomotive (manufactured by Norris in Philadelphia) was in service in Charlotte by April 1854, pulling flatcars in construction work. Early in May the Raleigh and Gaston finished its connection to the NCRR in Raleigh, and tracklaying immediately commenced westward from the capital.[56]

On the eastern section John C. McRae's contract called for him to complete the road, including tracklaying. Elsewhere the company decided to lay the track itself. Henceforth two corps of tracklayers consisting of eighty-five black laborers and two overseers were at work on the line. One group worked west from Raleigh, the other north from Charlotte.[57]

Progress continued to be slow, however. The Salisbury *Banner* reported in May that the company had fifty-five hands laying track above Charlotte, the largest number that could be used efficiently. But they were laying only 1¼ to 1½ miles per week and had completed only eleven miles. By November it was 1¾ miles per week. Near Raleigh the speed was only 1,000 feet per week in July, though the force employed there was expected to increase.[58]

Everywhere, in the construction of roadbed, track, and buildings, progress seems to have been slowed by the shortage of labor engendered by this massive enterprise. In addition there were vexatious delays in receiving rails, partly because the railroad was running out of money.[59] Sometimes there were difficult terrain to cross and difficult bridges to build. Heavy rains also impeded activity and caused considerable damage to fresh earthen embankments.

Regular train service began on the western end of the line in September 1854. The short daily train ran between Charlotte and Concord, extending its run as track was laid northward. In the same fashion a train began running from Goldsboro to Stalling's Station (now Clayton) at the other end of the road in October; it reached Raleigh in December and Hillsboro in April 1855. In July these trains reached Lexington and Haw River, respectively. Both were delayed some weeks by tardy completion of the Yadkin, Eno, and Haw River bridges.[60]

North of Charlotte and west of Raleigh no railroad had ever been known before, and towns began holding celebrations upon the arrival of the first trains. Salisbury did so on 4 January 1855. Rufus Barringer, the grand marshal, led a procession from the court house to the depot (not yet finished), accompanied by the Salisbury and Concord brass bands. At 11 A.M., amidst the music and booming cannon, a locomotive whistle signaled the arrival of the first passenger train, decorated with banners. The crowd cheered. Judge John W. Ellis delivered a speech during which two more trains arrived crowded with passengers. John Motley Morehead then spoke, describing the progress of the road to date. When he repeated the familiar story of Calvin Graves's vote, there were renewed cheers and locomotive whistles. All of the road was graded, he said, and 118 of the 223 miles of track were laid. He informed his audience that the road was going to need another million dollars to complete and equip itself but doubted not that the legislature would make this sum available. At this point Nathaniel Boyden of Salisbury proposed three times three cheers for the legislature. The ensuing cheers were echoed by steam whistles. After Morehead's speech there was a barbecue featuring 24 hogs, 16 sheep, 6 beeves, 10 opossums, and 1,400 pounds of bread. Later a Professor Elliott staged a balloon ascension, drifted five miles, and descended in time for a ball that evening at Murphy's Hall. It was followed by a lavish midnight supper. Altogether, 10,000 to 15,000 persons were present during the day, exceeding the town's public and private sleeping accommodations as well as the supply of barbecue.[61]

Some 5,000 persons attended a smaller ceremony in Lexington on 4 July, their arrival delayed by torrential rains that washed out a new culvert. At Thomasville on 9 November, barbecue, speeches, and short train rides were offered to about 6,000 persons. Master of ceremonies and supplier of the food (at least) was a radiant John W. Thomas.[62]

The westbound trains reached Greensboro on 13 December. The *Greensboro Patriot* greeted the event as the beginning of a new era. So did everyone else. "The arrival of the train was hailed by an almost *unanimous* concourse of the inhabitants of the town, old and young, great and small, male and female, white, black, including all the rest of mankind who sojourn here, besides not a few from the surrounding country." There were train rides and other pleasantries, but no elaborate ceremony. As it became apparent that the two construction parties would soon meet near neighboring Jamestown, the Greensboro city fathers decided to schedule their major celebration for that event: the completion of the road, only a few miles from where the groundbreaking had taken place four and a half years earlier.[63]

On Christmas Eve 1855 the two tracklaying crews were only four miles apart. Observing the holiday season, work was suspended until after New Year's Day. When it recommenced, work was impeded by bitter cold and heavy snows. But finally, on 29 January 1856, the two parties met and the track was united about midway between Greensboro and Jamestown. The last spike was driven by David F. Caldwell of Greensboro, a longtime backer of the road. The two labor crews then ran their trains into Greensboro, where "such hallooing, singing and cheering by the negroes—commingled with the bellowing of two engines, perhaps was never heard before by our citizens." Next day, 30 January, through trains ran along the whole line from Charlotte to Goldsboro.[64]

In anticipation of this event, his major work completed, Walter Gwynn submitted his final report as chief engineer on 8 January. He resigned two days later.[65]

For various reasons, including inclement weather (the coldest temperatures and heaviest snowfall in years), the Greensboro celebration was postponed, at the request of NCRR officials, until the road should be in good working order. In February a date in May was anticipated; in March it was postponed until July. Then in June the cryptic announcement was made that, "for various reasons unnecessary to mention here, but well understood in this community," the celebration was canceled altogether.[66] No satisfactory explanation was ever made. The Charlotte *Western Democrat* blamed the cancellation on Whig party machinations and specifically Greensboro's John A. Gilmer, that party's candidate for governor in 1856. In another view it arose from NCRR officials' refusal to grant free passage to persons attending the ceremony.[67]

Although trains ran the length of the road after January 1856, many construction chores remained. Many stations, water towers, warehouses, and other buildings were not yet completed. Bridges needed to be covered. Ten culverts on the eastern division had to be rebuilt. Above all, the road's repair shops had to be finished. Much of this was done in the next year.[68]

Nearly all railroads of any size possessed repair shops for the maintenance and even the construction of rolling stock and other equipment. The NCRR clearly needed such a facility. The major questions to be answered related to location, size, and cost. Locomotives in the 1850s needed inspection and maintenance every hundred miles or so. On a road of 223 miles, that pointed to a location for the major shops as near the center of the line as possible. Auxiliary repair facilities should exist at each end. Such was the advice of leading authorities who were consulted by Colonel Gwynn.[69]

Predictably, several communities were eager to secure the shops; they were expected to attract substantial business and population. Goldsboro and Raleigh were interested, but the most ardent contenders (particularly when it became known that the shops should be near the middle of the road) were Greensboro and Hillsboro. The exact center of the road lay in western Alamance County near the community of Glen Raven. When the board of directors met to decide the issue in August 1853, they took their advisors literally and voted for a site within five miles of the center. Greensboro in particular took this decision as a calculated affront, the local press persisting for years about the folly of building shops "in the woods" instead of in an established town.[70]

In the light of this rivalry to secure the shops, there was some surprise when the owners of the selected tract near Glen Raven refused to sell their land. Reportedly the directors then chose a site five miles east, on the edge of the new town of Graham. But that village also objected to having the shops so close, citing the attendant noise, sparks, and general commotion.[71] At this point General Benjamin Trollinger came to the rescue, offering to sell lands between the first two sites and only three or four miles east of the road's center. These tracts belonged to Trollinger and several friends and relatives, who sweetened the offer by promising to raise money around the county to reimburse the road for at least part of the purchase price. The company accepted this offer, acquiring about 632 acres at a cost of just under $7,000. In a subscription campaign many local residents joined to reimburse about half of that amount.[72] Construction began in the summer of 1855 and continued into 1859. During those four years the NCRR created not only a shops complex but a company town, including a hotel, stores, and employee houses.

In September 1850, as the railroad survey was getting underway, Walter Gwynn estimated that the $3 million capitalization provided in the charter would "be amply sufficient to put the Road into thorough operation." In May 1851, as the survey ended, his estimate for construction and necessary operating equipment rose to $3,405,132. In July 1856, with the road in operation but the shops and some other structures not yet complete, the figure climbed to $4,350,000. In January 1859, with the shops virtually finished, President Charles F. Fisher gave the total as $4,912,652.93 in one place and $4,907,982.44 in another.[73] In 1867 two successive presidents placed it at $4,950,755.68 and $4,922,982.93, respectively.[74] As bills continued to come in for payment years after construction was finished, the 1867 figures are probably nearest to the mark.

All of the estimates from 1859 and later calculate at close to $22,000 per mile. In 1850 the average figure nationally was $34,521 per mile; in the South Atlantic states it was $21,491.[75] The NCRR was thus in line with the regional average.

Only about a third of the nearly $5 million total was raised in North Carolina. Against the $1 million in stock sold locally, the state's $3 million (it later increased its original $2 million) came from state bonds that were sold in New York. Of the remaining $925,000 or so, $350,000 came from NCRR bonds subsequently issued and sold within the state; the rest came from operating revenues paid by passengers and shippers both inside and outside the state.

Except for the hotel near the shops, a road master's house, two water tanks, and perhaps some rolling stock, the final cost included items that had been planned from the beginning. Primarily responsible for the cost overrun was an unrealistically low original estimate—an error that was endemic in railroad planning in that period. The lower the estimate, the more attractive and salable it was. Also responsible was a sharp rise in the cost of labor and materials within a year after construction began. The total cost of iron alone rose about $400,000 above the original estimates based on 1851 prices.[76] The inflation in wages and locally produced supplies reflected the increased demand caused by the NCRR itself within a very limited market; the increase in iron and other commodities bought from afar was the result of massive railroad building throughout the United States and abroad in the 1850s.

Inevitably charges of extravagance were made at the time and later. Some of the criticisms were inconsistent, accusing the road's management of profligacy in one breath and unwise parsimony in another. In general they had little merit.[77] Ideally the road should have been built to higher standards, with consequent savings in the years ahead. But in common with most railroads of its time, it lacked sufficient funds for that. The road was as well built as the company could afford, and that was reasonably well.

William W. Holden's *North Carolina Standard* and others accused Morehead of mismanagement for failing to foresee the rise in the price of iron and not ordering it early, borrowing the funds if necessary against expected state contributions. Not only was the critics' hindsight clearer than Morehead's foresight, but they overestimated the road's ability to borrow money. Morehead explained that he and the directors lacked authority to borrow so much money or means to repay it, even if they had foreseen the necessity. He confessed to William A. Graham in March 1855 that the company treasury was bare. Neither Greensboro nor Raleigh banks would lend any money against forthcoming state payments, and he lacked means to pay a $2,000 debt falling due in a few days.[78]

Morehead was more alert to the possibility of a higher tariff on iron than to prospective fluctuations in its market price. In 1850, as the survey was still in progress, he asked Graham, then secretary of the navy, to warn him of any impending tariff increase so that he could order the NCRR's rails from Britain before it was imposed. The tariff was not raised at that time, and he decided to defer ordering until the rails were needed. But soon the price began to rise, by 60 percent to 75 percent between September and December 1852 alone.[79] In October 1853 Morehead ordered another 5,000 tons at $50 per ton. By that time the duty on foreign iron was 30 percent, increasing the cost of American railroad construction by an estimated $1,500 per mile.[80] The arrival of these rails the following spring and the necessity of paying for them on arrival occasioned great financial distress for the NCRR.[81]

During the railway construction boom of the early 1850s, Britain supplied over three-quarters of the rails consumed in America. British rails were cheaper and were regarded by many as of better quality.[82] The price rise of 1852–54 in Britain came in response to growing demand from both the United States and Russia. Perhaps encouraged by the United States tariff, American iron production grew steadily. That, plus increased British production, occasioned a price drop in 1854. American production exceeded British imports in 1856 and every year thereafter.[83] But by 1856 construction was complete on the NCRR.

Another charge against the Morehead management was the overpayment of construction contractors. Both Gwynn and President Charles F. Fisher denied this in later years, Fisher arguing that many contractors had in fact been saved from loss only by an appreciation in the value of their lands as a result of the railroad.[84]

Critics also claimed that the shops had been built too lavishly, or at least that the company had not needed to build so much of the town surrounding them. The shops proper appear to have cost about $130,000; the other buildings in town, $65,000. Fisher (who continued Morehead's plans in this respect) stoutly defended all the expenditures as vital to the railroad's operations and worth more than their original cost.[85]

Again, it is often difficult or impossible to determine the exact costs of NCRR operations. Figures that purport to cover the same items sometimes vary. Those critics who accused the company of sloppy bookkeeping were right on target. It was a common complaint concerning railroads of this era. As the nation's first big businesses, they learned by trial and error.

For the NCRR, the transcendent fact was that the road was in full operation. Even before its completion North Carolinians were thrilled by the sight of its trains and the premonitions it brought of a new era. In June 1855 the *Hillsborough Recorder* noted the completion of the road to that place, bringing daily trains to and from Goldsboro: "On the Central road may be daily seen trains of new and elegant cars propelled by splendid and powerful engines, speeding their way through the heart of the Old North [State]. What North Carolinian can survey this great State work without emotions of pride that Old 'Rip' has waked up and in her strength presumes to compete with sister States in the great improvements of the age."[86]

3

The Road and Its Equipment

NINETEENTH-CENTURY American railroads tended to be underfinanced and underbuilt. Lacking the capital to start in first-class condition, they made do with what they had in hopes of repairing the deficiencies from operating revenues later on. The results were often steep grades and sharp curvatures through hilly terrain, flimsy rails spanning infrequent crossties that lay upon the bare ground, inadequate drainage, narrow and danger- ous embankments, and cuts barely wide enough to admit the passage of trains. Trees "drooped their branches over the track, and [adjacent] under- growth . . . beat like an Aeolian harp against the . . . sides of the passing cars." Bridges were apt to be wooden trestles subject to rapid decay, and culverts were too small to handle the water flowing through them. Sidings were too few and too short to handle the business of the road. Depots and warehouses were similarly inadequate and sometimes nonexistent.[1]

These conditions, though common, fell far short of the highest construc- tion standards of the 1850s. Engineers were already writing treatises on railway construction, setting forth higher goals to be aimed at if not always achieved. John B. Jervis, a celebrated civil engineer, published the best of these early works, *Railway Property*, in 1861. His book provides a useful basis of comparison for the engineering of the NCRR, finished five years earlier. Although Jervis set high standards, he recognized that some had a higher priority than others. Few railroads could afford to go first class in all re- spects. Engineers like Walter Gwynn and even Jervis knew that their liveli- hoods depended on building roads within their employers' means.

The NCRR was built to better standards than those described above, but not always much better. In the first place, there is a question concerning her maximum gradient. Colonel Gwynn reported it as 50 feet per mile (1-foot rise in 106, or just under 1 percent). But two postwar superintendents re- ported the maximum grade at 70 feet per mile—1 foot in 75, or 1⅓ per- cent. More troublesome from an operational standpoint was the frequent alternation of ascents and descents, the result of too little grading. This was a common feature of economically built American railroads; had such com- promises not been made, some of the roads could not have been built. These flaws on the NCRR, according to an informed observer in 1862, required the use of heavier and more expensive locomotives than would otherwise have been needed. Many of the engines, he said, could pull twice as many cars at either end of the road as in the middle.[2]

Gwynn reported the road's tightest curves at five degrees and said that these occurred in very few cases. But the critic of 1862 called many of them too sharp; they had the effect of slowing the trains passing over them, wasting energy and wearing out the equipment. NCRR President Thomas Webb conceded in 1867 that the road's trains were limited in size by both heavy grades and curves.[3]

The United States before the Civil War presented an array of conflicting railroad gauges. The broadest was the Erie Railroad's six feet, measured from the inside of one rail to the inside of the other. Most southern roads had a five-foot gauge. But the majority in North Carolina and Virginia adhered to a width of four feet, eight and a half inches. Inherited from England, where it had originally been the standard spacing between wagon wheels, that gauge was gradually becoming standard in the North and would eventually become so nationwide.[4] The NCRR was thus built to the standard gauge. This put it in harmony with most neighboring roads, present or prospective, but not with the Charlotte and South Carolina or with the Richmond and Danville, which it would one day meet in Greensboro. This discrepancy would cause increasing problems as through service developed in the years ahead.

Meanwhile the new road received favorable comment from several newspaper editors who traveled over it during the first two or three years. After a ride to Charlotte and back in 1857, the editor of the Salisbury *Carolina Watchman* found it to be in tiptop order. "The cars glide along almost as easy as a boat on a river," and under the "direction of careful and gentlemanly officers, everything is well-ordered and pleasant to the traveller." Newspaper editors sometimes received (or at least hoped for) free passes in return for such bouquets. As a result, firm reliance cannot be placed on generalized flattery concerning comfort of ride and attentiveness of personnel.[5]

In forested terrain (such as the greater part of North Carolina) John B. Jervis called for clearing all trees that by falling would reach the track. The best method, he said, was to clear all the timber within 100 feet of the rails. According to the specifications in a standard NCRR construction contract, the roadway was to be cleared at least 80 feet wide; it does not specify on each side.[6]

In company with every authority on the subject, Jervis emphasized the importance of good drainage. At best, a muddy roadbed caused the track to subside in places, warping the rails and causing derailments. At worst, rampaging waters swept away tracks and the embankments on which they lay. Jervis emphasized both ballasting and ditching. They were complementary: the less a railroad provided of one, the more it needed of the other.

Ballast, consisting of permeable material like gravel or crushed rock, raised the track above the soil level, permitting water to drain away. It also provided the track with necessary elasticity when the base was solid rock or frozen earth. Jervis prescribed ballast at least a foot deep and extending to at least a foot on each end of the crossties. It should be deepest in cuts where the land sloped downward toward the track.[7]

The NCRR specified the use of whatever acceptable ballast was available locally. The result was a marked lack of uniformity along the line. Gwynn called for a roadbed "of gravel or other suitable material to the depth of a foot." The construction contract cited above repeated that objective and specified the cleanest gravel available on that section.[8] But if none were available close by, presumably none was laid down; it soon became clear that the road was not thoroughly ballasted. As early as January 1856, before the road was finished, the mail train derailed just west of Raleigh, owing to wet weather and a roadbed that had "sunk considerably in several places."[9] President Fisher admitted in 1857 that ballasting was needed at many points, and a great deal was done by 1861, especially in cuts and other wet spots. A stockholders' inspection committee in 1860 recommended that the entire road be faced with gravel, which the inspectors said was abundant at many points along the line. This would not only preserve the roadway, they said, but protect passengers from clouds of dust.[10] Most if not all of the connecting and neighboring roads were similarly deficient and spent years ballasting the most sensitive places.[11]

Drainage ditches, like ballasting, were particularly necessary in cuts and wherever water did not naturally flow away from the track. The wetter the soil, the deeper the ditches should be. Jervis recommended making them at least two and a half feet deeper than track level and eight feet wide on either side of the track. As a single track ideally measured at least ten feet wide, including proper ballasting to contain the crossties, that meant cuts at least twenty-six feet wide. When economic considerations produced narrower excavations, as they often did, the result was apt to be perennial drainage problems and high maintenance costs.[12]

Colonel Gwynn and the 1851 construction contract called for a single track road except that cuts should be excavated in contemplation of a double track. The contract also called in a general way for ditching on either side of cuts but did not mention other places.[13] The excavations seem not to have been wide enough for two tracks, and they were not faced with rock. For several years, therefore, landslides were a problem during rainy weather. Owing to this as well as to poor ditching and ballasting, the roadbed was so damaged during the winter of 1858–59 that train speeds had to be curtailed.[14] Despite improvements, the problems persisted, especially in the east, sometimes delaying trains. The stockholders' inspection committees of 1860 and 1861 reported that ditching was badly needed along the entire line. After torrential rains in January 1861 President Fisher was so concerned about the condition of the roadway that he personally supervised repairs.[15]

Embankments or fills, said Jervis, should extend at least three feet beyond the crossties on each side to give firm support to the track. With nine-foot ties, that meant a roadway fifteen feet wide. When embankments were so high as to cause great damage to a derailed train, they should extend seven or even ten feet beyond the ties. The NCRR was distinctly lacking in this respect. The roadbed barely extended to the ends of the sills in many places, if not generally. The 1862 observer recommended, like Jervis, that the roadbed be widened by at least thirty inches at each side to provide adequate support.[16]

Commonly embankments run across the courses of streams, and culverts are required to let the water pass through. Too often these openings were made too small to carry all the water after heavy rains. Turbulent rising waters were then apt to erode the embankments, perhaps washing them away altogether. Jervis prescribed arched stone or brick culverts for all but the smallest streams, where rectangular structures were permissible. Wing buttresses, he said, were frequently necessary to protect both culvert and bank against flood damage.[17]

Gwynn called for all drains and culverts to be built of stone or brick, although the surviving construction contract permitted wooden drains. Embankments along waterways, it said, were to be faced with rock. The contract was specific concerning the structure of the masonry culverts, rectangular if small and otherwise arched. Abutment walls had to be at least two and a half feet thick to repel flood waters.[18] Gwynn left to his assistants along the road the choice of brick or stone, based on local cost.[19] In 1871, when the road was leased, there were 148 culverts along the line.[20]

Some culverts proved to be too small. In June 1854 a heavy rainstorm washed away part of the embankment over Sugar Creek, near Charlotte, soon after it was constructed. The break was quickly repaired by means of temporary trestlework and later a bridge.[21] This problem was greatest on the eastern end of the road, built by John C. McRae. Near Boon Hill (now Princeton) in Johnston County an embankment gave way under a freight train in September 1856, killing the conductor and a free Negro train hand. Responsibility was assigned to heavy rains and too small a culvert. Within a year ten culverts on this end of the line were reconstructed or replaced with temporary trestling. As these construction flaws were corrected, roadbed problems diminished, giving way to more routine maintenance. But culverts at the eastern end of the road remained a source of trouble. A locomotive plunged into a washed-out culvert near Selma in 1862, killing two train crewmen.[22]

The earliest railroads sometimes used stone blocks as crossties. But apart from their original cost, they proved too rigid and damaging to both rails and rolling stock. Wooden sills or sleepers, as they were usually called, soon came into general use. Their great disadvantage was that they were subject to decay and had to be replaced periodically, especially in the absence of proper ballasting. But suitable timber (and the labor to cut it) was cheap and plentiful along most early railroads, especially in the South.

Hard woods were required, to prevent the rails from sinking into the sills, and woods that were relatively resistant to decay. Railroads generally made do with the best kinds locally available. In the South these were white oak, first and foremost, unless cedar or cypress were available. Long leaf and southern yellow pine were also used widely, especially the inner heartwood, which was regarded as more rot-resistant. Unlike Europe and the northeastern United States, where timber soon came to be scarce and expensive, the South was heavily wooded, and preservatives were not cost effective for some time to come. The average life of sills in the eastern states was about seven years, between four and five in the South.[23]

Ties were hand-hewn, and the most common practice was to hew two sides parallel, leaving the other two in their natural state; the flattened sides served as top and bottom. On standard gauge railroads, like the NCRR, sills were usually cut seven to nine feet long. Jervis recommended that each be at least seven inches wide and six and a half inches thick to provide good support. They should be placed at two-and-a-quarter-foot intervals, adding up to 2,347 per mile.[24]

The NCRR set a reasonably high standard in its original specifications and apparently thereafter. Its first advertisements for bids, early in 1852, called for sills eight feet long, hewn on two sides parallel, eight inches thick, and the other two sides to be either barked or hewn. They were to be made of good white or post oak and were to be delivered in quantities of twenty at fifty-foot intervals, indicating a spacing of two and a half feet. These specifications were modified from time to time as to length, width, and thickness. By November the road was permitting a wider latitude in the kinds of wood, depending partly on what trees were available on different sections of the road. Red or black oak ties were permitted on the western section, but they had to be thicker and wider. All had to be eight feet long, and the same implied spacing was observed.[25] By 1860 it had become obvious that red and black oak were not satisfactory; they rotted faster. Henceforth, only white or post oak and yellow heart-pine were accepted. The oaks predominated on the central and western portions of the road, pine at the eastern end.[26]

There were about 490,000 sills in the road, including sidetrack, spaced two and a half feet apart.[27] The first extensive replacement appears to have come in 1858–59. Thereafter 70,000 to 98,000 (on average, about 90,000) of them were replaced annually. These figures indicate a life expectancy of 5.4 years. The sills were laid on top of the dirt roadbed, which was the usual practice in the absence of proper ballasting. The critic of 1862 approved their length and spacing but recommended burying them with dirt (for lack of ballast) to deter weathering. He believed that faster rotting would not equal the current damage from weathering.[28] This recommendation, like most of his others, was not followed.

By the 1850s the standard rail in use on American roads was wrought iron, T-shaped in cross section, commonly coming in eighteen-foot lengths. Size or weight varied, but the usual range was from 56 to 65 pounds per yard. (Modern steel rail weighs 110 to 150 pounds per yard.) Such rails generally measured three and a half inches in height. Although heavier rails might carry heavier loads, lighter rails were apt to be better wrought and sometimes more durable. Jervis found a 60-pound rail quite acceptable for major railroads as long as it rested on a proper foundation. Rail ends were usually joined by an iron device called a chair, which was fastened to the tie. Sometimes they were joined by fishplates bolted to the sides of each rail. Whatever method was used, rails tended to wear out first at the ends. The average life of such rails was ten years, or less under heavy traffic. When rails wore out they could be re-rolled and used again.[29] At the outbreak of the Civil War a number of southern roads, including the Richmond and Danville and the Charlotte and South Carolina, still had at least a few miles of older strap, U, or flanged iron rail laid on wooden stringers. (U-rail looked in cross section like an inverted U.) For the most part these were replaced as they wore out, but as late as 1870 the Charlotte, Columbia and Augusta (CC&A) (successor to the C&SC) laid ten miles of new stringer track on its Charlotte division.[30]

The NCRR from the beginning used sixty-pound T-rail, purchased from Britain, on the seventeen miles of sidetrack as well as on the 223-mile main line. By July 1859 less than two miles of iron had had to be replaced. Wear occurred first on curves, from the lateral pressure of the trains, and near stations where trains applied their brakes to stop. It also tended to occur unevenly from one section to another, reflecting uneven quality in the rails themselves. But in 1861 the rails were in better condition than the roadbed beneath them.[31]

Stone arch bridges—like the culverts but on a much larger scale—were apt to last indefinitely, like the B&O's Carrollton Viaduct at Baltimore, constructed in 1829 and still in use today. But they were almost prohibitively expensive.[32] Wooden bridges were all but universal in the United States until after the Civil War, when iron structures began to appear, mostly in the North. Wooden bridges were inexpensive, but they were subject to water, fire, and even wind damage. They weakened invisibly from stress and decay. The normal life of an ordinary wooden road bridge roofed over and protected from the weather was generally thirty to forty years, while those without covering would last only about a third as long. On the other hand, a roofed railway bridge was more susceptible to fire from locomotive sparks. Railroads could choose their hazards.[33]

The timber bridge was a product of evolutionary development. A number of designs were used almost interchangeably by common roads and railways. All could be and were frequently roofed over and covered at the sides. Many designs were later adapted to iron construction. In 1806 Theodore Burr patented a truss bridge with a supplemental supporting arch. By the 1880s thousands of Burr bridges were built around the country.[34]

Also important in early railroad history was the Town lattice bridge. This was developed by the Connecticut Yankee Ithiel Town, who built his first one across the Yadkin River near Salisbury, North Carolina, in 1818. A year later he built another across the Cape Fear at Fayetteville, which continued to serve until burnt by General Sherman. Its name came from the fact that it was constructed from intersecting diagonal boards in a lattice pattern arranged between vertical end posts and horizontal top and bottom chords. Like other bridges, it was often built in multiple spans resting on masonry piers or pillars. The great advantage of the lattice bridge was that it could be constructed inexpensively by ordinary carpenters out of common planks. Its disadvantages were its flexibility and tendency to warp or twist, especially in long spans and under heavy loads. To remedy this deficiency it was sometimes built with supplementary arches.[35]

William Howe, an uncle of Elias Howe, the inventor of the sewing machine, created a more satisfactory truss bridge after 1840. The Howe truss was stronger and more capable of bearing the heavy moving weight of locomotives and cars. As a result it became the standard American railroad bridge after 1850. The structure, which Howe continued to develop, combined horizontal chords and diagonal braces of wood with vertical rods of wrought iron. Sometimes supplementary arches were added. Railroad spans on this pattern were built either as conventional through bridges with the trusswork on either side of the track and above track level or as deck bridges with the track passing over the truss. In either case the bridge could be covered, the through type with a roof and side walls, the deck type with siding and a top surface immediately below the track. Sometimes this surface was covered with sheet iron as a protection against sparks.[36]

Today covered bridges evoke nostalgia for bygone days and are preserved as historical landmarks. They are regarded as picturesque. It was not always so. Contemporaries feared their aptitude for catching fire, resented their constant need for maintenance, and tended to see them as eyesores when they were allowed to deteriorate. In the words of a *New York Post* correspondent in 1864: "They are all built of wood, and must be constantly patched and mended, and will rot away in a very few years. They are enormous blots on the landscape stretching as they do like long unpainted boxes across the stream." He also resented the way they blocked the view from trains: "You are riding along in a railroad car enjoying the scenery. A river gleams ahead. You approach its banks and prepare to catch expected glimpses of beauty up or down the stream. But suddenly a roaring sound is heard. You plunge into a great wooden tunnel; wooden walls on either side hide the view; a wooden roof blocks out the light of day. After a minute of deafening noise you emerge, but . . . the stream is passed, and the delicious bit of scenery is lost to you."[37] Travelers on the NCRR were treated to the same experience, though none recorded their reactions.

Colonel Gwynn's plan in 1851 was for wooden bridges with substantial arch bracing, resting on stone abutments. All the work was to be as permanent as anything found in the country.[38] Twenty-four bridges were constructed altogether, ranging in length from 40 feet to 658 feet. (See table 7.) Only four were long enough to require more than one span: those over the Yadkin, the Neuse, the Haw, and Abbott's Creek near Lexington. All were of timber construction and rested on masonry abutments and piers, where the length justified piers. Brickwork was common at the eastern end of the line; cut stone prevailed elsewhere.

Over the years bridges were occasionally rebuilt or replaced as a result of flood, fire, military destruction during the Civil War, or old age. At least seven were replaced in 1866–69. Wooden trestlework was sometimes resorted to on these occasions to keep service going. Unlike many railroads of the section and time, the NCRR regarded trestles as temporary, but they occasionally saw protracted duty. One at Cates Creek near Hillsboro, erected to replace a burned bridge in 1856, was apparently still in service until 1869.[39]

In 1871 eleven of the bridges were listed as Howe truss types, including those built after the war. The Little River bridge near Goldsboro was first constructed as a Burr truss in 1853.[40] It was destroyed by retreating Confederates in 1865, replaced by pursuing Federals with a temporary trestle, and then supplanted with a Howe truss in 1867. The remaining thirteen were lattice bridges dating from the road's construction. About ten of the total (both Howe and lattice) were through bridges, at least three of them having shingle roofs. The remainder (both Howe and lattice) were deck bridges covered with planks and often with sheet iron strips between the rails.[41]

There was no correspondence between the length of structures and whether they were through or deck bridges, or lattice or Howe truss. Rather, these categories tend to appear in series when the bridges are viewed in geographical order, as if a given builder constructed two or more in a row and chose a particular construction style.

Owing to a desire to cover the bridges with seasoned lumber, their covers or roofs were not finished for some months after being put in use. At his departure in 1856, Gwynn recommended that the bridges be painted. Eighteen were covered and perhaps painted in 1856 and 1857. In more heavily populated areas pedestrians used the structures as foot bridges, taking advantage of the sheet iron strips between the rails. This reportedly hastened their deterioration.[42]

The first serious mishap to a bridge occurred in March 1856, when the small span over Cates Creek near Hillsboro was destroyed by fire. Owing to the presence of mind of Thomas Webb, who lived nearby—surely the same Thomas Webb who became president of the road in 1862—an approaching train was prevented from plunging into the creek. In three days a trestle was built and service restored. Soon afterward a blaze was extinguished on a nearby bridge across the Eno River. The first fire was initially attributed to sparks from a passing train, but the second appeared to be arson. Watchmen were then posted at both bridges.[43] By 1860 resident guards were maintained at the most important bridges on the road.[44]

Two timber bridges served as street crossings over the railroad in Salisbury and Charlotte.[45] Charlotte newspapers were indignant at the NCRR's delay in building the bridge there while the railroad was under construction in 1854. It made the neighboring streets impassable, they said, and effectively blocked access to town from the east. Similar problems troubled Salisbury, but they all subsided that fall as the local construction ended.[46]

The NCRR was obligated by its charter to maintain all public road crossings, including bridges. It seems to have done so with reasonable satisfaction in most places. In Rowan County in 1871, however, a horse pulling a wagon fell through a bridge over the railroad and was killed. Its owner sued the railroad for negligence in failing to maintain the bridge and carried the case to the state supreme court. But that body, speaking through Justice Nathaniel Boyden (a former president of the NCRR), agreed with the railroad that the bridge was not on a public road and therefore not its responsibility.[47]

The vast majority of road or street crossings were at grade. They seem not to have occasioned much trouble, or at least much comment in the press, once construction was finished. (Muddy streets in the vicinity of stations were another matter.) Trains ran relatively infrequently and at comparatively slow speeds. Most accidents along the railroad occurred away from road crossings. But an exception took place in November 1854, just weeks after the railroad's opening. The stage road between Concord and Salisbury crossed the NCRR at least ten times as they made their not-quite-parallel ways between those two towns. After a fatal accident at one of these crossings local newspapers called for a rerouting of the dirt road.[48]

Every railroad required a variety of buildings and other structures, from freight and passenger stations to water tanks and housing for section gangs. Along the NCRR these waited until the track construction was underway. Some, in fact, could hardly be more than temporary until actual operations determined the nature, extent, and distribution of the road's business.[49] Deferral of permanent structures also helped to hold down the road's initial construction costs, a troublesome matter. But a number of the temporary buildings had to be replaced within five years.

Early in 1852, arrangements were made with the Charlotte and South

Carolina Railroad for a joint depot, well before either railroad was built to Charlotte.[50] As the roads were to be of different gauges, continuous running was impossible and their tracks would not meet. But as through traffic would have to move from one to the other, they were to terminate side by side. Joint freight and passenger stations were built in 1856–57. Whether from poor temporary construction or not, an open car shed blew down in a heavy windstorm in June 1860.[51]

Similar arrangements were made at other connection points. At Goldsboro the NCRR was chartered to run only to its junction with the Wilmington and Weldon, which it established just south of town. But that road already had a station in the middle of Goldsboro that seemed a more logical place to terminate. So the NCRR extended its own parallel track to that point. The two roads seem to have shared the W&W passenger station, and they erected a joint freight warehouse nearby in 1856–57.[52] Soon the new Atlantic and North Carolina Railroad, from Goldsboro to Morehead City, would also share the passenger station. The W&W track (now joined by the NCRR) ran up the middle of Center Street, the main north-south artery, and the passenger station was located at the corner of Walnut. In effect, Goldsboro had been created by the W&W after 1840. The town grew up around the W&W facilities, especially after the NCRR and the A&NCRR joined it there. But it had a population in 1860 of only 985.[53]

At Raleigh, the Raleigh and Gaston extended its line to the new NCRR depot in the southwest part of town. Here several buildings were erected, including an engine house and a joint freight warehouse. They seem to have been badly planned and constructed. Although the warehouse was described in the *Standard* as a large brick building when it was under construction in 1854, it was regarded two years later as too small to accommodate the growing business of the two roads. They could not afford to replace it, however, nor did they build a needed joint passenger station. In 1860 the engine house, described as a badly built "old eyesore," was partially dismantled and the remainder renovated.[54]

With the construction of the Western North Carolina Railroad westward from Salisbury, beginning in 1857, that town also became a junction. The two roads agreed that year to build joint freight and passenger stations. This action was taken despite the fact that only two years earlier the NCRR had completed its own depot on the same spot, with a "mighty, gigantic and ponderous roof" big enough to replace the Yadkin River bridge if need be, according to a local editor. Indeed the earlier building, now found inadequate, was to be demolished and its materials used in construction of the new.[55] Three joint buildings were erected, one for local freight, another for through freight, and a passenger station that also housed the WNCRR offices. These buildings were completed in 1859. Unfortunately, the passenger shed was blown down in a windstorm the next summer, a month after the shed at Charlotte was similarly destroyed.[56]

Even at little High Point, newly called into being by the railroad, the freight warehouse was too small for the volume of business transacted there and was enlarged in 1860. "No station on the road presented more the appearance of an active trade," remarked the inspection committee that year.[57] Much of this trade originated in or was destined for Salem and Forsyth County; High Point was their closest rail depot, accessible by plank road.

By January 1859 twenty-five stations had been established on the road, eleven on the eastern division, thirteen on the western, and one at Company Shops, the midpoint. Each had a building called a warehouse and, except for the places with joint passenger stations, many of these buildings must have accommodated passengers as well as freight. Water tanks and woodsheds were also provided at each station to serve the wood-burning steam locomotives. Engine and car sheds were built at Goldsboro, Charlotte, and Company Shops to protect the rolling stock that frequently had to stop over at those places. There were three large and three small turntables at the shops, Raleigh, Goldsboro, and Charlotte, among other places.[58]

As early as 1860 the engine and car sheds at Goldsboro, the car shed at Charlotte, the Salisbury and High Point depots, and the buildings mentioned at Raleigh were all found wanting. Most were too small and some were badly built.[59]

For maintenance purposes the road was divided into nineteen sections, nine in the eastern division (east of Company Shops) and ten in the western. They averaged about twelve miles in length. On each section a house was provided for the section master and another for section hands. Similarly, every station had a house nearby for station hands. Most if not all of these dwellings were in place by July 1857.[60]

Company officials regarded the sylvan location of the repair shops as a great advantage. The shops were expected to occupy a number of buildings and to employ many men. Company headquarters would also be placed here. Since employees and their families would need to live within walking distance, a town would necessarily develop. As President Fisher later put it, the locality was beautiful, "elevated, healthful, and in the midst of a fruitful region where the large mechanical working force . . . can have pleasant homes, pure water, and abundant supplies at a cheap rate, remote from all the disturbing influences of even a village residence." He added that the company had designedly acquired a large enough acreage to ensure its own police control of the jurisdiction. In short, the directors planned to build a company town. These were a common feature of the nineteenth-century American industrial scene, and the NCRR was by no means the only railroad to sequester its shops in one.[61] In this case the town was even called Company Shops and (with a brief respite) so it remained until 1887, when the name was changed to Burlington.[62] The exception came in 1863–64, when it was called Vance as part of an ill-timed town development scheme. (See Chapter 10.)

Colonel Gwynn advised, in the interests of efficiency and long-run economy, building the shops entirely and at once rather than making do with temporarily cheaper but inferior facilities. This advice was followed—as it was not with some of the depots and other buildings along the road—but the company still had to use small smith shops at Charlotte and Goldsboro for over two years until the main shops were ready.[63]

Construction began in the summer of 1855 and continued to 1859. Seven major buildings were erected: a carpentry shop (195 by 60 feet), two engine or machine shops (237 by 66 feet and 180 by 100 feet), a blacksmith shop (128 by 40 feet), a foundry, engine shed, and car shed. A number of small homes were built nearby for workers and three larger houses for railroad officials; one of the latter doubled as company headquarters. Still another structure served as passenger and freight station, general store, post office, telegraph office, and (upstairs) public meeting hall. One of the grander buildings was a two-story hotel with thirty-odd rooms, providing eating facilities and overnight accommodations for passengers, other visitors, and local residents. It was lined on three sides by a large colonnaded porch and on the fourth by a row of outhouses. Most of these structures (probably not the outhouses) were made of brick manufactured at the site from local clay; the bigger ones were said to be the largest brick buildings in the state at the time. In addition, private individuals erected homes, stores, and other structures for their own use. In 1857 the village boasted twenty-seven buildings; in 1859, fifty-seven.[64] A railroad passenger in 1859 called it one of the prettiest places she had ever seen.[65]

Inevitably this production evoked cries of extravagance from editors, legislators, and stockholders. The latter voted in 1858 to ban any further buildings at the village without their specific consent.[66] State Senator Ralph Gorrell of Greensboro, still smarting from the shops' placement "in the wild woods," referred to them in 1859 as "an instance of the most reckless extravagance ever beheld in America. . . . How came that extraordinary, unnecessary pile of machine shops—those brick houses—that store house—that hotel?" A legislative committee reached a similar conclusion the same year.[67] But President Fisher and others stoutly defended the enterprise. In his estimation the shops were the heart of the railroad, ensuring its safety, efficiency, and profits. By 1858 he was defending both the quality and cost of the work performed there compared with that obtained from the temporary facilities previously depended upon in Charlotte and Goldsboro. In 1860 the stockholders' inspection committee saw the shops as a "fruitful nursery for the mechanical genius" of North Carolinians and, in 1861, as an indispensable southern resource in the war just begun.[68]

The South would have great need of such resources. Virtually all locomotives in service on southern roads were of northern manufacture. Southern railroads, moreover, having less traffic on average than those in the North, owned less rolling stock. The South Carolina Railroad (SCRR), oldest in the region and 242 miles long, had more locomotives than any other southern road, sixty-two at the outbreak of the war. By contrast, the NCRR, with 223 miles, possessed only about twenty-five engines at that time.[69] (See table 8.)

The great majority of locomotives on the NCRR as elsewhere in the country were of the so-called American 4-4-0 type: a movable forward truck of four small wheels followed by four large drive wheels. This conformation became identified with the United States because it was well adapted to the uneven track and sharp curves so often encountered on American railroads. Nearly all of these engines on the NCRR before the war weighed twenty-four tons. They were used in both passenger and freight service and were the mainstay of the road. In addition, two of the NCRR's early locomotives, the Traho and Pello, were of the 4-2-0 type, having only two drive wheels. These engines, weighing only fourteen tons, had predominated on American railroads in the early 1840s but lacked traction and were generally replaced by the 4-4-0s and even heavier engines. The NCRR used these two locomotives to pull "gravel trains" in construction and maintenance work. In 1856 the road bought two 4-6-0s. These twenty-eight-ton locomotives with six drive wheels were used in freight service, where longer and heavier trains required greater tractive power.[70]

In 1860, three-quarters of all American locomotives were manufactured in Philadelphia and in Paterson, New Jersey. The largest firms were Norris, Baldwin, and Rogers. Although Virginia promised to be a production center for a time, with the Tredegar Iron Works in Richmond turning out over 100 locomotives in the 1850s, the NCRR was a relatively faithful customer of the Norris Locomotive Works in Philadelphia.[71] Of the twenty-four locomotives that the road appears to have bought before the war, twenty-two were Norris products. (The other two were made by Rogers of Paterson and by Breese and Kneeland of Jersey City.) Colonel Gwynn recommended in 1856 that the road continue to patronize Norris, not only because he found their engines satisfactory but also to ensure standardization of parts and thereby lessen repair costs. Nationally, the price of a standard 4-4-0 locomotive averaged about $8,000.[72] The NCRR paid for its first locomotives in 1854: $9,250 each for passenger engines, $9,000 for freight engines, and $6,250 for the gravel-train locomotives.[73]

Relatively few railroads built locomotives in their own shops, but much of the repair work they did was tantamount to new construction. Such was the case with the NCRR. In 1859 its shops transformed one of the road's first locomotives, the 4-2-0 Traho, into a 4-4-0 called the Carolina.[74] More of this work was done during and after the war as the 1850s locomotives wore out. (See table 8.)

Most American locomotives in the 1850s and all those on the NCRR were wood burners. They were massive consumers of the nation's forests—equivalent to 100,000 acres per year.[75] Conversion to coal came first in the urbanized Northeast, where wood was becoming scarce. Locomotive cordwood, like the timber for crossties, was cut by hand, in the South by slave labor for the most part. The NCRR purchased it by contract from landowners adjacent to the road, who delivered it to the road's woodsheds along the line.

In the early 1850s a locomotive could expect to get at least twenty-five miles per cord of wood, and it used about 1,000 gallons of water in the same distance. A tender commonly could carry these amounts of wood and water, so trains had to stop and restock every twenty-five miles. As a result stations, including woodsheds and water tanks, were distributed along the line at that or lesser intervals. Later in the decade larger tenders came into use with doubled capacity, permitting comparably longer runs. Freight locomotives, often heavier in themselves and pulling heavier loads, consumed more fuel than passenger engines.[76]

NCRR locomotives used 6,000 to over 8,000 cords of wood annually. During the two intervals for which data are available, 1857–62 and 1867–70, the average consumption by each engine was 67.8 and 41.4 cords, respectively.[77]

Seasoned hardwoods and pitch pines were favored, and generally North Carolina had these in abundance. By 1870, however, NCRR officials noted that timber was becoming scarce along the road, and they intervened to prevent other roads from buying crossties along their line. After the war, if not before, the NCRR specified for fuel wood of original forest growth, two feet long. It paid from $1.75 to $2 per cord.[78]

The common practice in the 1850s and earlier was to name locomotives, as opposed to the impersonal numbering that later came into vogue. The NCRR derived its earliest names from classical mythology. The first sixteen locomotives included the Pactolus, Cybele, Ajax, Sisyphus, Midas, and Apollo. In 1856 most of the new engines began receiving geographical names like Guilford, Yadkin, Watauga, and Rowan. During and after the war prominent men, including NCRR directors and presidents, came to be honored, among them General Washington, Governor John Motley Morehead, Paul C. Cameron, Giles Mebane, and Governor William W. Holden.

The earliest American locomotives of the 1830s and 1840s were relatively unadorned. The 1850s and 1860s, by contrast, were an era of gaudy decoration featuring bright colors, polished brass, and gilt lettering. Few railroads kept records of the precise color combinations they favored, and we must depend largely on illustrated brochures released by the locomotive manufacturers. Green and red seem to have been favored especially. Almost all the illustrations show red wheels and flat black smokestacks and smokeboxes. Elaborate striping and lettering were common, often with scrollwork. Decorative panels sometimes carried vignettes of factories, eagles, landscapes, or portraits of the persons for whom the engines were named. Natural wood finishes were popular on engine cabs. Frequently in this period, locomotives were assigned on a regular basis to the same train crews, who took pride in their engines and kept them clean and polished.

When this policy disappeared in the 1860s and later, and elaborate decoration and constant cleaning came to be regarded as unnecessary luxuries, colors became more subdued and utilitarian.[79]

Unfortunately the NCRR kept no record of the decoration on its engines and other rolling stock. More surprising is the virtual absence of description by the general public. Of the many references I have seen to NCRR locomotives, passenger cars, and other equipment, none specified colors or decoration except the mention in 1869 of elaborate gilt lettering, flags, and a portrait of its namesake on the locomotive Governor William W. Holden.[80] One may learn that bright colors were in use from the periodic inventories of the paint shop, in which red and yellow ocher, vermilion, Venetian red, chrome yellow and green, and other paints were listed as on hand in considerable quantities. But there is no indication of what colors were used where. All of these inventories date from the postwar period, but decoration was likely similar before the war.[81]

In the 1850s nearly all American railroad cars, passenger or freight, were made of wood and rode on two movable trucks of four wheels each. The typical freight car was only twenty-six to thirty-four feet long with a capacity of eight to ten tons. There were three main types: boxcars, platform or flatcars, and gravel cars or gondolas, which resembled flatcars but had low sides to contain dirt, gravel, or coal. Freight cars often cost less than $500, especially those built by railroads in their own shops.[82]

Passenger cars of the 1850s were forty to fifty feet long, nine to ten feet wide, and sat fifty to sixty persons. They had plain arched roofs until the 1860s, when the windowed clerestory roof made its appearance. Platforms at each end sheltered boarding and exiting passengers. Many cars had cushioned seats, some of which reclined; others afforded only wood slat seats. Candles (often limited to one or two at each end) provided most of the lighting; oil lamps, used in home illumination, were regarded widely as a fire hazard by railroad managers. Many cars had tanks of drinking water and a toilet at one end; many did not. Heat was provided by wood- or coal-burning stoves, often one at each end. In basic design these cars were "as unimposing as a shoe box." Nonetheless, they were much more expensive than freight cars, ranging from $2,000 to $5,000 apiece.

Much of this cost was spent in decoration. Like the locomotives, they were often highly ornamented inside and out, with bright colors, illustrated panels, striping, scrollwork, and rich carpeting. "All surfaces were varnished and rubbed to a mirror-like finish." The basic body color before 1870 was yellow, in different shades. But light blue, pea green, gray green, and Indian red were also used. The favorite, pale yellow, served as background for accent decorations in vermilion, ultramarine, lake, and gold and silver leaf. "Yellow was also basic camouflage for the clay dust churned up by the train." After the Civil War more subdued design and darker colors came into vogue, in cars as well as locomotives.[83]

In 1860 the NCRR had only 27 passenger and 286 freight cars. (See table 9.) The South Carolina Railroad, a generation older but only nineteen miles longer than the NCRR, possessed 59 and 720, respectively, that year.[84]

Until the NCRR shops were sufficiently completed to begin manufacturing cars, the road purchased its first cars from individual craftsmen, some of them local. John R. Harrison of Raleigh made passenger coaches for both the NCRR and the Raleigh and Gaston. Silas Burns of Raleigh got a contract in 1854 to build fifty boxcars for the NCRR. The road's first baggage cars were made by Harrison and a builder in Richmond.[85] (Both Harrison and Burns were NCRR construction contractors as well as members of the board of directors after the war.) The first flatcars were made by three different builders. Lacking uniformity in height, they caused problems in loading and especially in operation. Eventually many of them had to be rebuilt.[86] According to President Morehead's account in 1854, the first coaches cost $2,450, baggage cars $1,600, boxcars about $700, flatcars about $525, and gravel cars $235 or less.[87]

The NCRR shops began car construction in 1858–59, turning out three passenger coaches and nine boxcars that year in addition to repair work. The stockholders' inspection committee of 1860, in oblique reference to the ornate and expensive passenger cars then in vogue, expressed the wish "that hereafter every thing that rolls on the track of this road shall issue from the shops of the Company, substantially fashioned to suit the condition of the Company and the taste of a plain people."[88]

The passenger car roster in 1855, when the road was not yet complete, consisted of seven coaches and four baggage or express cars; the number grew almost every year thereafter. The 1860 total included thirteen first-class coaches, four second-class and baggage cars, four "Mail, Smoking and Servants" cars, and six "Baggage and Express" cars.[89] (See table 9 for other years.) These classifications, apart from first-class coaches, varied in successive annual lists and are impossible to chart accurately. The second and perhaps third categories probably embraced the familiar combination car, with a small baggage or mail compartment and most of the space devoted to passenger seats. These cars were combined with freight cars to form mixed or accommodation trains, providing service for small numbers of passengers traveling short distances. Sometimes they were also provided, as the third category suggests, for smokers and for blacks, slave and free. The baggage and express car carried both passengers' baggage and any less-than-carload freight that required expedited handling.[90]

The freight- and work-car roster in 1855 included 39 boxcars, 100 flatcars, 20 gravel cars, 11 polecars, and 4 crank cars. The last two categories comprised small hand-operated cars for road workers. The gravel cars were used primarily in road maintenance. The typical gravel train consisted of a locomotive, tender, and several of these cars. Flatcars were sometimes used in the same service as well as for general hauling. By 1860, with construction complete, there were still 20 gravel cars, but the flat cars had declined from 100 to 83. At the same time the boxcar roster grew from 39 to 142 as freight traffic increased. At this time many if not most of the cars were being made in the road's own shops. In 1861 at least one conductor's car or caboose was in use carrying a freight train conductor and crew. It might have been a converted boxcar.[91]

Trains rarely exceeded twenty cars. The NCRR's master machinist in 1869 estimated the average number that each engine then in service could pull at what he called fast and slow speeds. The most powerful locomotive, the Guilford, a 4-6-0, was listed at seventeen and twenty cars, respectively; the averages were about thirteen and fifteen.[92]

This, then, was the physical plant—the roadbed, track, and rolling stock —of the NCRR during its first years of operation. We turn now to those operations and the men who made the wheels roll.

4

The Men and Their Work

THE EARLY RAILROAD president was something of a political figure within the railroad and often in the larger community as well. Often he was an experienced businessman with little practical knowledge of railroads except for what he picked up in the job. Certainly that was the case with the NCRR's first two presidents: John Motley Morehead, a former governor with widespread business interests but no previous railroad experience, and Charles F. Fisher, a politician and businessman with even narrower experience. The president dealt with the stockholders, the board of directors, and sometimes even with the general public in a public relations sense. He and the board determined general policy, but they usually had little to do with operational detail.[1]

It was customary on all but the smallest roads to place operations in the hands of a general superintendent responsible to the president. He was in charge of freight and passenger transportation, road maintenance, and the purchasing of equipment and supplies. It was the superintendent's business to know the traffic of his and other roads and to schedule trains and fix rates in such fashion as to maximize profits without at the same time inciting shippers and travelers to insurrection.[2]

Despite the centrality of this position, and provision for it in the NCRR's early regulations, the road operated without a superintendent during most of its first five years of full operations. Theodore S. Garnett, one of Walter Gwynn's principal assistants, succeeded him as engineer and superintendent for a short time while the road was in the last stages of construction. But when Garnett left in September 1856 to take charge of another railroad, the position was left vacant until 1861. During those years President Fisher performed most of the superintendent's duties himself—even while serving also as a principal construction contractor on the Western North Carolina Railroad.[3]

As the shops had been placed at the middle of the line to facilitate inspection and repair, it was decided in 1856 to work the road in two divisions, east and west of the shops. Each division was slightly over 100 miles long and was subdivided for maintenance purposes into sections of about twelve miles. At first, engines, passenger cars, and train crews were largely confined to one division; only loaded freight cars passed the length of the road. By 1867, conductors at least were making the entire run too.[4]

The road master was in charge of maintenance. Thomas J. Sumner, an assistant engineer under Gwynn, became the first road master as the construction process neared completion in January 1856. He soon left to become superintendent of the Charlotte and South Carolina Railroad and was succeeded by Captain James E. Allen, who had been in charge of tracklaying on the eastern half of the road. Allen held the position until 1860, when his duties were divided between two division masters.[5]

The initial regulations of 1854 required the road master to traverse the entire road in a hand car at least once a week; this grueling requirement was relaxed to once a month in 1857. On these trips he saw to all necessary repairs as well as to obtaining and inspecting wood supplies for the locomotives. Subject to him were nineteen section masters, who were obliged to inspect their respective sections every three days (daily in the 1854 regulations). These inspections were especially important after heavy winds and rains. The section masters and their work gangs were responsible for the actual maintenance work and for seeing that the water tanks were full.[6]

Larger railroads were apt to have general ticket and general freight agents. They were responsible for compiling and publishing information about passenger and freight rates and service and coordinating these with other railroads.[7] On the NCRR these offices were combined into a general transportation agent during the first year or two of operation. Then the position remained vacant until 1860, when Edmund Wilkes, a veteran of several years' experience on other roads, took it up. Under him were clerks in charge of passenger freight service. Wilkes rapidly became a kind of man Friday to President Fisher, performing some of the duties of a superintendent. By 1862 he would be superintendent in name as well as in fact.[8] (See table 5.)

Well below the officers of the road, but vitally important to its welfare, were the agents in charge of each station. They were responsible on the NCRR for the placement, loading, and unloading of cars; the receiving and sending of both freight and passengers; the proper setting of switches; and the filling and maintenance of water tanks.[9] They were also the business managers and record keepers of their respective stations. Agents were often recruited from the local mercantile community. By 1860 every station had an agent, though he might not always work full time. There were twenty-six stations before the war. Agents at the larger ones not only worked full time but supervised a clerk and a number of station hands. In 1860 Raleigh was the only station with two agents, one for freight and the other for passenger traffic. Business was heavy enough to require clerks at Salisbury, High Point, Greensboro, Raleigh, and Goldsboro. Charlotte's station agent had no clerk listed, but he got the largest salary and perhaps hired a clerk himself.[10]

Early agents were known to use railroad facilities to engage in business on their own. In 1858 "A Farmer" wrote from New Garden, near Greensboro, charging NCRR station agents with buying and selling produce such as molasses, sugar, coffee, flour, and fish at the ticket windows and shipping these commodities over the road. In this fashion, he said, one unnamed agent—it had to be J. P. Balsley at Greensboro—claimed to have earned more than double his $600 railroad salary. The stockholders forbade this practice in 1859.[11]

On the NCRR as generally, the operating personnel of the road were organized into three departments: train, road, and machinery. The train department was concerned with the movement of both passenger and freight trains. Included within it were engineers, firemen, woodpassers, conductors, brakemen, and baggage masters. The road department (under the road master) included the section masters and their hands, the station agents and hands, bridge carpenters, switchmen, and the crews of gravel trains and switch engines. The machinery department embraced the shop employees: machinists, boilermakers, smiths, patternmakers, moulders, tinners, carpenters, painters, car cleaners and greasers, and others.[12] (See table 6.)

Railroad record keeping was a primitive art before the Civil War. Many statistics were not reported, and others were given inconsistently in successive years, making comparison difficult or impossible. In this respect too the NCRR was a child of its time. Employment records were published for the first two full years of operation—1856–57 and 1857–58—but for no others until the end of the war. They survive in only fragmentary form before 1864 in the manuscript NCRR Records. Perhaps record keeping seemed an unnecessary extravagance to managers beset with cries for dividends out of slender profits. Employment, below the managerial level, totaled 442 and 414, respectively, in these two years. This averaged two men per mile of road, less than half the numbers who manned the nation's busiest railroads.[13]

The train department amounted to about eighty men, a little under one-fifth of the total force. A typical train crew in the 1850s consisted of an engineer, a conductor, a fireman to stoke the boiler, a woodpasser to feed him wood from the tender, a brakeman, a baggage master if it were a passenger train, and sometimes a mail guard.[14] The NCRR in 1856–58 had about twenty engineers, nine conductors, thirty firemen, and fifty train hands including brakemen. (Some of these worked on gravel trains and were part of the road department.) With so few conductors, compared with engineers, it is unlikely that every freight train carried a conductor.

Within the road department were the twenty-six station agents, several clerks, and about fifty-five station hands to load and unload cars and do other physical chores. Most of these laborers were employed at the largest stations, especially the junctions of Charlotte, Salisbury, Raleigh, and Goldsboro. Nearly thirty gravel-train hands performed maintenance work along the road, particularly ditching and ballasting. A dozen or so bridge and station watchmen rounded out the department.

The machinery department in 1856–58 was restricted to 39 men working in temporary shops. In July 1859, about the time the permanent shops were fully opened, the number was 58. After the war, when total employment on the road was only a little greater than in these early years, there would be from 70 to 140 shopmen of different descriptions.

Two-thirds of the NCRR personnel in 1856–58 were blacks, the great majority of them slaves. They served in all three departments, primarily as unskilled laborers. Over half were section hands; many others worked as train, station, and shop hands. But some of the slaves employed in the shops were apparently mechanics. Twenty-seven of the thirty firemen in 1857–58 were blacks, twenty-one of them slaves. Although brakemen were not itemized in the employee lists, there is evidence that most of them were blacks and probably slaves. A correspondent of the *Greensboro Patriot* wrote indignantly in 1857 that the NCRR was discriminating in favor of blacks on the ground that they were more dependable than whites. No wonder young men emigrated to the West by the thousands, he exclaimed.[15]

Slave labor was the rule on antebellum southern railroads. Some roads owned substantial numbers outright; the South Carolina Railroad possessed 103 slaves in 1860.[16] But most were like the NCRR in hiring the bulk of these laborers from their owners. The general rule was to contract with slaveowners by the calendar year. Early in the 1850s unskilled slaves brought $75 to $100 per year plus their upkeep. Skilled workers brought up to $250 per year.[17] Some were hired out year after year to the same employers.

Owning or hiring was a matter of economics, and the path of true economy was not always clear. Growing demand for slave labor in the 1850s, especially among farmers in a decade of rising crop prices, so increased the price of slaves that some railway managers thought purchases to be a bad investment. But the same factors raised the cost of slave hire as well. A slave normally rented for 10 to 15 percent of his total value. The NCRR in 1859 was paying at least $160 per year for firemen and other train hands and $200 for mechanics. At Salisbury in January 1860, "Negro fellows, for rail road work," were being hired for $175 to $200; the demand was very strong, said the *Carolina Watchman*, with bidders coming from far and near.[18] Around Atlanta the average cost of slave hire and subsistence doubled during the 1850s. As a result, railroads in that area began to replace slave laborers with whites, who were hired by the month or even the day and could be laid off during slow times.[19]

Some railroad managers, including President Fisher of the NCRR, saw the rising cost of slave hire as a signal to buy slaves instead.[20] In 1856 the NCRR had 276 hired slaves working on the road at an average annual wage of $150. Every year, said Fisher, a large proportion of these laborers were new and inexperienced. It was time-consuming and expensive not only to train them, but also to negotiate all the contracts every year. Many of those contracts, moreover, specified that the slaves could not be employed at certain tasks or outside certain areas. He added optimistically that directly owned slaves would take greater interest in their work and maintain better discipline. All things considered, Fisher believed that ownership was more economical by twenty percent. He recommended buying at least 100 slaves at $1,000 each, borrowing the necessary money. But the stockholders, citing the road's financial condition, turned him down.[21] Fisher repeated his proposal in 1859, with little more success. The road's expenses for Negro hire in 1859–60 were $37,787.98.[22]

The NCRR did buy two slaves before the war, however. Master Machinist Thomas E. Roberts bought a man in 1857 for $1,150, presumably for the shops, and another was purchased for only $414.58 the next year.[23]

Life on the railroad was probably not much better or worse than the farm life that most slaves experienced otherwise. Plantation slaves were traditionally allowed a week's vacation at Christmas; the NCRR did likewise. The road's work regulations of 1854 and 1857 permitted the superintendent and road master to let slaves visit their homes when occasion required it.[24] The road contracted with their owners to furnish slaves with food, clothing, and shelter during the year. These provisions were hardly lavish: the usual clothing consisted of a hat, shoes, and a blanket. Occasionally, hired hands —probably including slaves—were permitted to earn extra money by cutting wood. One man, Dave, cut at least twenty-five cords in 1857, for which he received the princely going rate of 25 cents per cord, or $4.75.[25]

Railroad section gangs worked under overseers outdoors in all weather, much as did plantation fieldhands. Train, station, and shop hands worked in smaller numbers and sometimes at less onerous tasks. A few had skilled jobs involving some responsibility and satisfaction. After the war and probably before, blacks worked in the shops as painters, carpenters, smiths, and tinners as well as laborers and helpers.

On many southern roads, including the NCRR, slaves often worked as brakemen.[26] This was the most hazardous and disagreeable position on the road, especially in freight service. It entailed scrambling over the roofs of moving cars in all weather in order to set the wheel-operated brakes at the car's end. It also required moving between supposedly stationary cars in order to couple or uncouple them. The link and pin coupler was in general use in this period, requiring someone (usually the brakeman) to place a metal pin from one car into a loop device on the other car. If the cars moved during this process, the man could be crushed between them or lose his footing and fall under the wheels. Automatic couplers and air brakes were not introduced until the 1870s or generally required until the 1890s. Until then, brakemen appear to have suffered 35 to 50 percent of all railroad worker injuries and fatalities while constituting only 10 percent of the work force.[27]

Free Negroes were also hired by railroads across the South, but in relatively smaller numbers. Slaves were often preferred to free blacks and whites because they were subject to greater control. But some employers favored free laborers, black or white, for work that was considered too hazardous to risk valuable slave property.[28]

The NCRR employed only 20 free blacks in 1856–57, compared with 276 slaves; next year it was 12 and 263.[29] Free blacks performed the same jobs that slaves performed, mostly of lower status.

White men, constituting only one-third of the NCRR labor force in 1856–58, held almost every low-status job that blacks held, but in lesser numbers and perhaps for lesser periods of time. They were more likely than blacks to be promoted but more apt than slaves to be laid off. (Free blacks were on the losing side of both equations.) Whites were absent from only two job categories: section hands and lumber-train hands. Of course they monopolized the higher status positions such as engineers, conductors, station agents, section masters, and even watchmen.

Nationally, one of the most striking aspects of nineteenth-century railway labor policy was the lack of job security. "Work gangs were assembled, enlarged, reduced, and abolished with astonishing frequency. If there was some ditching to be done, a gang was hastily assembled and put to work, and whenever the job was finished the men were instantly dismissed. Even regular section crews were enlarged or reduced almost on the spur of the moment."[30] If this description of conditions on the Illinois Central Railroad had less application in the South, it was owing to the widespread use of slaves on southern roads.

Unskilled workers tended to be young, especially if the work required great exertion or agility. Some (if white) looked forward to promotion in time, but it seldom came rapidly and often never. Nearly all blacks, and Irish too in some degree, were locked permanently into low-status and low-paying jobs. In the South these unskilled workers—black or white—were almost all natives of the areas where they worked.[31]

Skilled shopworkers fell into two categories, those with machine skills and those practicing more traditional hand crafts. The former included machinists, boilermakers, patternmakers, and coppersmiths; the latter were primarily carpenters and painters. In Georgia and probably elsewhere in the South, carpenters and painters, practicing skills obtainable in the local building trades and elsewhere, could generally be recruited in the surrounding area. Machine workers were scarcer because of the South's predominantly agricultural economy. Many of them originally had to be recruited in the North, whence they were lured by higher wages.[32]

The aristocracy of the operating personnel were the engineers and conductors. (They were not in full agreement among themselves as to where the precedence lay.) Engineers (with their firemen) customarily were assigned their own locomotives and took a proprietary interest in them. They saw to it that their iron chargers were well tuned, oiled, greased, and polished and sometimes even presided over their decoration. Engineers carried heavy responsibilities and required considerable mechanical skill. Their work was also dangerous; they were on the front line in case of boiler explosions and derailments. Locomotive drivers (as they were sometimes called) initially were scarce in the antebellum South, as were their usual sources—locomotive works and large machine shops. As a result, many of them (like mechanics generally) were imported from the North in the early days.[33]

The conductor was captain of the train, the supervisor of its crew. He needed a degree of intelligence, practical judgment, literacy, record-keeping ability, and (in the case of passenger conductors) courteous manners. Despite the conductor's greater authority, his job required less training and was easier to fill than that of the engineer, who almost always commanded a higher salary. (NCRR engineers in 1856 made $85 per month, conductors about $50.) Thus southern conductors were much more apt to be native sons. Sometimes they were promoted through the ranks, but where so many of the lower ranks were filled with slaves, appointments often came from the outside. According to a study of Georgia railroaders, family connections and personal friendships often influenced appointments. This was quite likely the case in North Carolina and on the NCRR. In Georgia, moreover, a distinction had developed by 1860 between freight- and passenger-train conductors. The latter were ticket takers and sellers with a degree of public exposure that freight conductors did not have. As a result they acquired more prestige and pay.[34]

On the NCRR no apparent distinction in either rank or pay was made between passenger and freight conductors. But the number of conductors, which averaged eight between 1856 and 1858 and rose to twelve in 1866, fell to only four between 1868 and 1870. As there were obviously more than four trains being run, it is likely that freight conductors were dispensed with altogether after the war, their work being delegated to the engineers and other members of the train crew. Gravel-train conductors also disappear from the list after 1866. (See table 6.)

Conductors were in a unique position to defraud their employers, and (around the country) many improved that opportunity. Without posting spies, which some railroads did, there was no way of telling whether a conductor allowed passengers to ride free or pocketed their passage money if they bought tickets from him on the train. This problem was not unknown to the NCRR. A suggested solution called for preventing anyone from boarding a train without a ticket in hand or, alternatively, for charging more for tickets bought on the train. The NCRR introduced the higher rate in 1857. But trains sometimes picked up passengers at depots where there was no ticket agent. The question then was whether the suspected conductors stole enough to repay the cost of additional ticket agents.[35]

Railroads customarily adopted codes of regulations for employee behavior, which were distributed to the workers in pamphlet form. The NCRR issued such regulations in 1854 and again in 1857. The first paragraph set the tone: "Employees of the Company, disapproving of these or other Regulations of the Road, or not disposed to aid in carrying them out, are requested not to remain in the employ of the Company." The next rule advised that "each person in the employ of the Company is to devote himself *exclusively to its service* attending during the prescribed hours of the day or night, and residing wherever he may be required." Employees were to render prompt obedience to instructions on pain of "immediate dismissal."

The rules also enjoined courtesy and safety. "Rudeness or incivility to passengers, will, in all cases, meet with immediate punishment, if a slave, and dismissal if white." All employees were required "to exercise the greatest care and watchfulness, to prevent injury or damage to persons or property." Each person was held legally liable for injuries caused by his own negligence, and his pay might be docked to defray the losses. These regulations, like those of virtually every other railroad, forbade the use of both liquor and tobacco. The ban on alcohol applied even to off-duty hours, and "any individual who shall become intoxicated, will be immediately dismissed."

In the absence of a standard uniform—they were not in general use in this period—every NCRR conductor, engineer, baggage master, and brakeman on passenger trains was to "wear upon his hat or cap a badge" indicating his office and the NCRR initials. The great body of the regulations then went on to define the duties of specific officers and groups of employees.[36]

Railway wages were determined by supply and demand. That in turn depended upon the number of persons seeking a job, the level of skill required, and the danger involved. It was to the railroad's interest to minimize danger and simplify skills as means of lowering labor costs. That interest was not always immediate or clearly recognized, however. Railroads generally fought legislative efforts to mandate the use of safety devices; so did many workers whose jobs were thereby threatened.[37]

Nationally, railway wages compared favorably with those for other work. They kept pace with inflation, except during the war. Skilled workers in the South earned substantially more than those elsewhere in the country, owing to their scarcity. In the mid-1850s, when locomotive engineers in the North got $55 to $60 per month, southern engineers received up to $100. After the war this southern advantage narrowed but still remained. The reverse was true for unskilled positions, although comparisons are difficult because of the use of slaves. After the war, when unskilled black labor was still plentiful and cheap in the South, station and track hands there were paid 80 cents to $1 per day, compared with $1.50 to $1.75 in the North.[38]

Pay varied greatly within ranks as well, depending on the character of work done, length of service, and of course race. Agents assigned to larger and busier depots got more money than those at small ones. Passenger-train workers often received more than those in freight service. Shopmen were paid according to their personal skills and responsibilities. On some roads there was a seniority system of sorts, rewarding long service with higher pay.[39]

Some kinds of workers were paid at a monthly rate, others by the day. Track crews and shopmen were usually paid at a daily rate for only the days actually worked. Agents, foremen, clerks, station hands, conductors, and brakemen were variously paid by the day, month, or even year on different roads. Before the war, engineers and firemen were commonly paid by the day or month. But owing to these workers' unusual and uncertain hours, a kind of piecework formula evolved for determining a day's or a month's work: 100 miles per day and 2,500 miles per month. Usually there was no overtime pay for extra mileage or for longer hours caused by breakdowns or other delays. In the 1860s and 1870s, railroads began to introduce the piecework system more formally, and engineers and firemen were paid by the number of miles run. Fixed rates were assigned to specific runs. Under this system, employees worked and were paid only when called.[40]

To encourage higher productivity, some roads began experimenting in the 1850s with bonuses for good performance such as accident avoidance, low fuel consumption, or least broken equipment.[41] There is no evidence of such a policy on the NCRR—or much evidence of innovative management generally.

Prewar employment information for the NCRR is fragmentary. Workers probably put in a ten-hour day when there was enough to keep them busy that long. In 1856 section masters received $25 per month plus an allowance for board; in 1859, $33 with no mention of board. Conductors earned $600 per year, less than the national average of $764. On the other hand, locomotive engineers, being in shorter supply, received $85 per month or $1,020 annually, which compares very favorably with the national average of $721. NCRR brakemen in 1859 were making $20–$25, firemen $25. Shopworkers were usually paid by the day, foundrymen making $2.50 and carpenters up to $2.25, but mostly $1 to $1.50. Most of the shopworkers were paid for twenty to twenty-five days per month in June and July 1859, indicating a usual six-day workweek. A very few were paid for more than thirty-one days—a form of overtime.

NCRR station agents' pay in 1860 ranged from $150 per year at China Grove to $1,000 at Charlotte. The average was $442, compared with a national average of $624 per year; agents, like conductors, were easily recruited locally. Their compensation bore a relationship to the volume of business at their stations. The highest salaries were at Charlotte, Salisbury, High Point, Raleigh, and Goldsboro. All except High Point (the depot on the plank road to Salem and Forsyth County) were junctions with other railroads.[42]

One may deduce something of NCRR management attitudes from a comment of the 1860 stockholders' inspection committee. Noting that they had hardly met an employee who did not complain of his wages, the committee doubted if anyone had come into the company's employ without improving himself financially. And from careful inquiry, they added, they were convinced "that the most importunate are those who are the most indolent and disposed to shirk duty." The chairman of the committee was Paul C. Cameron, one of the largest landowners and slaveholders in the state and destined to be president of the road in another year. Despite its hard-nosed attitude, management was accused of laxity by a sharp-eyed stockholder in 1859 who discovered the road paying a substitute worker as well as the regular employee who was out sick. However admirable this was from a humanitarian standpoint, warned the critic, it was unfair to the stockholders.[43]

There is even less information as to the hours of labor on the NCRR. Very likely it approximated the national norm of ten to twelve hours, six days per week. An hour was often allowed for dinner. Shopmen nationally worked ten- or eleven-hour days, office workers twelve hours. The hours of trainmen varied most, owing to seasonal factors, breakdowns, and other delays. In general, they worked a seventy-hour week: twelve hours on weekdays, ten on Saturday. But fifteen- to seventeen-hour days were common.[44] In the mid-nineteenth century, and in North Carolina, there was virtually no effort on the part of government to regulate wages, hours, or other conditions of labor.

Nor did employers of that era have a legal obligation to compensate sick workers or those who were injured or killed on the job, unless it could be proven that management itself was negligent. Courts generally ruled that workers accepted the risks of hazardous occupations when they took the jobs. Slaveholders actually fared better in the courts than free workers when they sought compensation for injuries to their hired property. Such relief as there was for disabled workers or the families of those killed in the line of duty came as a matter of Christian charity or perhaps public relations. Few roads made compensation a matter of policy, and each case was decided on its own merits.[45]

The NCRR followed usual custom, therefore, in stipulating that "the regular compensation will cover all risks incurred, or liability to accident, from any cause, while in the service of the Company. And when disabled from sickness or any other cause, the right to claim compensation will not be recognized." By the same token, wages were to be docked in case of absence from work by reason of sickness or any other cause.[46]

As it was in sickness, so it was in old age. Some roads developed an informal seniority system, providing older workers with less demanding jobs, sometimes without reduction in pay. But again, this was a matter of choice. Formal pension plans did not begin until the 1880s. As a matter of fact, the problem seems not to have been a major one before the Civil War.

Early railroaders tended to leave the industry before reaching retirement age.[47] There is little evidence of a problem or of a settled policy on the NCRR.

Needless to say, this was not a climate favorable to labor unions, locally or nationally. Except for a brief and unsuccessful organizational effort by locomotive engineers in the 1850s, railway unions did not get started until the 1860s, and then it was primarily in the North.[48] The NCRR knew neither unions nor strikes.

The highest-ranking northerner in the NCRR seems to have been Master Machinist Thomas E. Roberts of Massachusetts.[49] As superintendent of the shops, he busily recruited men while the machinery was being installed. By July 1857, fifty-two men were employed at the shops. A majority of them hailed from nine other states, the District of Columbia, Ireland, and Scotland.[50] Roberts made an effort to hire local men, however, telling a Cane Creek man that if he did not accept the position as head of the blacksmith shop the road would have to send to Virginia for someone.[51] There is little information as to the origins of the NCRR's early locomotive drivers. The senior one on the road in 1860, E. H. Marsh, was identified as a southern native. When Roberts retired that year, Marsh was promoted to succeed him. Another engineer, a northerner, was permitted to return North after the outbreak of the war.[52]

As the conflict impended, southern roads looked uneasily at some of their northern employees and even more uneasily at any continuing dependence upon the North for additional workers. But that dependence rapidly diminished as southern railroads trained local men in the requisite skills, fostering regional independence.[53] This was very much on the mind of Paul C. Cameron, speaking for the inspection committee of 1860, when he praised the new Company Shops as "a fruitful nursery for the mechanical genius" of North Carolinians. So far as practicable, he urged the NCRR to give preference to "native labor and talent, [so that] this great work built by home labor shall be worked by home men."[54]

Unlike some other southern railroads, the NCRR was almost exclusively southern, even North Carolinian, in its ownership, directorship, and management.[55] Master Machinist Roberts early incurred the ire of at least one North Carolinian who noted his Massachusetts origin and accused him of having no more "interest in common with the people of N.C. than an Arab!" Although President Fisher was generous in his praise of Roberts upon the latter's retirement in 1860, he made it a point to note that his successor was a native southerner.[56]

5

Trains and Their Operation

WHEN THE NCRR commenced operations in 1854, it had a considerable body of experience and precedent from other railroads to draw upon. President Charles F. Fisher claimed in 1860 that "the System of the Road . . . has been adopted after careful examination of the manner of working the best Roads in the Country—we have introduced whatever was deemed to be of value, wherever found, and have made such changes as were applicable to the latitude and people."[1] In general, the NCRR, running through lightly populated regions generating only a modest traffic compared with some of the northeastern roads, was not in the vanguard in railroad organization or management, nor did it need to be.

The business of railroads is to run trains. Freight engines of the 1850s could seldom pull more than twenty loaded cars—even thirty-foot cars—without damage to themselves, the bridges, or the roadbed. Ten to fifteen cars was nearer the average.[2] The Greensboro *Times* noted in February 1856 that the first regular eastbound freight train on the NCRR had just passed through town with seventeen cars so heavily loaded with upcountry produce that at least three carloads of freight had to be left behind in Greensboro alone. The use of double-headers—two locomotives—was apparently rare on the NCRR; at least they were rarely mentioned. One such train was used in August 1856 to bring eighty tons of guano—agricultural fertilizer—into the interior.[3]

In 1856, after the road's completion and the initiation of through service, three passenger engines were assigned to each half of the road, east and west of Company Shops. Each of them ran the 110 miles or so from the shops to either Goldsboro or Charlotte and back again, then laid over for two days of inspection overseen by the locomotive engineer. (Before completion of the shops in 1858 this service was performed at nearby Haw River.) Presumably freight engines received the same attention. A locomotive in good condition commonly ran 25,000 miles or more per year.[4] Freight cars necessarily ran the length of the road, and passenger cars did so too in time. But as late as December 1856 through passengers were required to change trains at the shops.[5]

Mixed trains, combining passenger and freight cars, were a regular fixture of nineteenth-century railroading. They generally involved the attaching of one passenger car (or a combination passenger/baggage car) to the end of a freight train for the accommodation of local travelers. In fact, this was often referred to as an accommodation train. Passenger service, needless to say, was slower than on the through express or mail trains. The NCRR used mixed trains at both ends of the line during the construction process. Soon after the ends met in early 1856, the practice was abandoned, but only temporarily.[6] Mixed trains became a common feature of service on the NCRR.

When freight and passenger cars were combined in this fashion, the passenger car was placed at the rear of the train as far as possible from the engine's smoke and sparks. It was also farther removed from two of the sources of greatest danger to moving trains—boiler explosions and derailments owing to collisions and broken track. This rule was of such importance that NCRR regulations called for the dismissal of any employee who violated it. By the same token, baggage, express, and mail cars were placed at the front of passenger trains. Apparently carrying this logic a step farther, second-class coaches carrying slaves were placed ahead of the first-class cars.[7]

Passenger trains, whether local or express, were commonly much shorter than freight trains. On some busy roads in the North they might run to ten cars, but three to five coaches were more common, combined usually with an express, baggage, or mail car, or some combination thereof. NCRR passenger trains consisted typically of only two cars before the war.[8] Through passenger trains, not always stopping at every station, were often called mail or express trains; they carried mail or express shipments or both as well as passengers.

Train speeds were governed more by the limitations of the roadway and the braking apparatus than by the capacity of the engines. An NCRR engineer in 1855, eager to impress the dignitaries aboard an excursion train on the new western section, took them from Charlotte to Lexington at speeds frequently reaching fifty miles per hour.[9] There are many examples of speeds faster than that, but almost never under regular operating conditions. John B. Jervis, the famous railway authority of that era, estimated that a train operating at thirty miles per hour cost twice as much as one running twenty miles per hour, considering wear, tear, and fuel consumption. "No intelligent railway manager will run at a higher speed for express trains, than 25 miles per hour, including stops, unless compelled by some competitor for the passenger traffic." A study was made in 1852 of the schedules of the fastest trains on 113 different railroads around the country that year. Based on total elapsed time, including stops, the average speed was about twenty-two miles per hour; actual running speed was of course somewhat higher. Northern roads had faster runs than those in the South and West. Passengers demanded faster speeds, and these were gradually achieved by means of heavier rail, stronger bridges, and straighter track. By

1864, American express trains were averaging up to thirty-two miles per hour.

For freight trains, speed was less important than tractive power, permitting locomotives to pull longer and heavier loads. Average freight-train speeds rarely exceeded fifteen miles per hour before 1900, and the figure was often closer to ten. Jervis recommended a maximum of twelve. Even with frequent stops, this bettered the time of canal boats and Conestoga wagons, as historian John F. Stover remarked. Daniel C. McCallum, another noted railwayman and superintendent of the Erie, agreed with Jervis that the best way to improve running time was to have fewer and shorter stops, not to run at faster speeds.[10]

In his valedictory report of January 1856 Walter Gwynn also agreed with all the authorities in urging the NCRR to adopt low rates of speed. He recommended actual running speeds of sixteen miles per hour for passenger trains and twelve for freight trains. Under that regimen the mail train would take sixteen and a half hours (including stops) getting from Goldsboro to Charlotte. In fact, the local trains had been averaging a faster sixteen miles per hour including stops at each end of the line during 1855. Many people thought Gwynn's caution was carried to excess when, after the road's completion, the crack passenger and mail train ran at a scheduled *fourteen* miles per hour, including stops, between Charlotte and Goldsboro. The *Greensboro Patriot* reported widespread complaints, even ridicule, at the slow pace. Even in the light of Gwynn's arguments, which the paper quoted, it asked pointedly how much business the NCRR expected to get at this rate.[11]

No doubt the greatest pressure for higher speeds arose from connecting roads and the necessities of competitive through traffic. The Raleigh and Gaston and the Charlotte and South Carolina both asked in 1857 for an NCRR express-train speed of twenty-two miles per hour in order to expedite connections at Raleigh and Charlotte. President Fisher complied, entailing a running speed of twenty-six miles per hour between stops, but the slower mail train continued to operate at seventeen miles per hour, including stops. (See table 10 for examples of running times and average speeds.) A hypercritical legislative committee then attacked Fisher for failing to heed Gwynn's sage advice.[12]

In 1860, in the words of historian Robert C. Black,

> the North Carolina Railroad could boast of no faster schedule than that of the westbound mail. Following a noisy departure from Goldsboro every morning at half-past six, the little train coasted into Raleigh, some forty-eight miles away, at approximately nine-thirty. Forty-four miles farther its engine stood hissing in the noonday sun at Hillsboro. At three-thirteen it was solemnly inspected by the loungers of Greensboro. It lurched into Salisbury in deepening twilight and, if all went

well, its headlight would sweep the houses of Charlotte at a quarter past nine. From Goldsboro it would have come 223 miles in a little less than fifteen hours. Such was a typical day's run upon one of the larger railroads of the South in 1860. Including twenty-three intermediate stops, the mail rolled across the Tarheel State at an average speed of about fifteen miles per hour.[13]

The freight trains received less publicity; presumably they maintained an even more sedate and (for them) satisfactory ten or twelve miles per hour.

Punctuality and precision in timekeeping are essential to railroad operations; trains have to arrive and depart at stated times. On a single-track road with trains constantly approaching each other, keeping to a predetermined schedule was a matter of life and death. Conductors' watches had to be both accurate and synchronized. By March 1856 the NCRR had an official timekeeper, a Mr. Root of Raleigh. His clock, by which the road regulated its trains, was said to be corrected every day through the Washington Observatory.[14] Raleigh was at that time the only place on the road with telegraphic communication. By 1857 the NCRR maintained an official clock (perhaps governed by the one in Raleigh) at Company Shops, and all conductors and engineers were required to regulate their watches by it.[15] The system worked so well that the Greensboro *Times* reported in April 1856 that most businessmen there were setting their watches by the passing trains. It recommended the same to other communities. The clock was still functioning at Company Shops in 1863, perhaps regulated more directly by telegraph, which had come there the previous year.[16]

Railroads of this period generally followed the "time interval system" of train dispatching. Trains were classified as superior or inferior according to their class and the direction in which they moved. Inferior trains had to give way to superior ones, often waiting an hour or more for the higher priority train to pass. Thus freight trains had to give way to passenger trains, and gravel or work trains gave way to both. On single-track roads, including the NCRR and most other American railways, where traffic moved in both directions on the same track, it was imperative that rules be established for the proper movement of each kind of train and that everyone know what the rules were. Sidings or turnouts were placed along the road at frequent intervals to permit lower priority trains to get out of the way. On the NCRR these turnouts were usually five to ten miles apart and usually (but not always) located at stations; in fact, the operating necessity of a turnout might occasion the establishment of a rural depot there.

Elaborate rules were established to govern the movement of each class of train under varying circumstances. On the NCRR, for instance, no train was permitted to leave a station unless the timetable showed that it had enough time, traveling at its normal rate of speed, to reach the next station at least fifteen minutes before an approaching higher priority train was scheduled to leave that station. Extra trains, whether a second section of a regularly scheduled train with its own locomotive or a special excursion train, were sources of particular anxiety. Their existence and schedules had to be made known to operating personnel throughout the distance they were to travel.[17]

Ultimately there were no more regular, important, or devoted users of the new magnetic telegraph than the railroads. That relationship developed only gradually in the 1850s. Despite the seemingly obvious advantages that the telegraph brought to train dispatching and other railroad operations, the earliest roads either forbade telegraph wires along their rights of way or barely tolerated them. The Erie led the way to telegraphic operation after 1851 by creating a central dispatcher who knew the location of every train on the road at any given time and then directed their movements, all by telegraph. That instrument practically doubled the capacity of a single-tracked road, and Erie Superintendent Daniel McCallum remarked in 1855 that such a road with the telegraph was safer than a double-tracked road without it. By 1870 the use of the telegraph had become almost universal.[18]

At the time the NCRR was chartered and for several years afterward, the only telegraph line in North Carolina belonged to the Washington and New Orleans Telegraph Company, connecting those two cities via Petersburg, Raleigh, Fayetteville, and Cheraw.[19] In 1854 a line was built from Columbia to Charlotte along the Charlotte and South Carolina Railroad, and there were hopes to extend it northward along the NCRR.[20] For some reason apparently beyond the power of the NCRR management, the matter was perennially delayed. President Fisher signed a contract with the Magnetic Telegraph Company in 1858 to put up a line along the road from Goldsboro to Raleigh.[21] That too miscarried, and a year later Fisher urged that the road build its own telegraph line. "No road of the length of this should ever be without one," he said. The stockholders authorized the project, but two years later, in 1861, it had only been constructed from Goldsboro to Raleigh.[22] The completion from Raleigh to Charlotte came in 1862.

The chief value of the telegraph was to help avoid accidents, particularly collisions between trains. There were surprisingly few accidents in the first years of American railroading, probably because of slow speeds and generally light traffic. But the year 1853 for some reason ushered in a new era. The first major accident of that year occurred in January when President-elect Franklin Pierce and his wife were injured in a New England train wreck that killed their twelve-year-old son. Total deaths that year were well over 100, and for the next half-century, railroad disasters were commonplace.[23] The *American Railroad Journal* in 1865 listed the following as the primary categories or causes of railroad accidents:

1. Persons getting caught between cars, either employees involved in coupling them or passengers jumping from one car to another and falling between them

2. Collisions when trains meet or when cars of the same train telescope

3. Broken rails, and switches thrown in the wrong direction

4. Derailments, involving locomotives more than cars, owing to vertical or horizontal movement of the track; this in turn arose from rotten ties or subsiding roadbed and faulty ballasting

5. Broken axles, wheels, or trucks, chiefly owing to defective iron or bad workmanship.[24]

In respect to accidents as otherwise, the NCRR belonged to its era. It had at least fifty accidents before the war, falling into each of the categories above. Five were collisions, three of them in 1854 and 1855, before the road was completed and while train crews were still inexperienced. In the first case, a locomotive stalled on the track for lack of water. A slave was sent on ahead to warn the oncoming passenger train, but he reportedly sat down and fell asleep; several people were injured in the ensuing wreck. A year later two passenger trains collided, one of them having been left on the track overnight by its crew while they slept; some cars were smashed but no lives were lost. The first collision fatality occurred in January 1861 when two passenger trains collided head-on near Charlotte. One of the engineers was killed, and several train hands were injured; the two engines and several coaches were demolished. Among the passengers slightly injured was Rufus Barringer, a founder and stockholder of the NCRR, long active in its affairs.[25] The first two cases obviously were products of negligence, and some of the others were so characterized at the time.

NCRR regulations automatically placed the blame for collisions on the conductors and engineers of the trains involved, until the facts proved otherwise. A number of trainmen were dismissed following accidents, including the engineer and others held responsible for the 1861 collision.[26]

The first noncollision fatalities long preceded that event. In November 1854 a man was crushed between two cars. In March 1856 a young brakeman was run over as he attempted to uncouple a car. In September of that year a conductor and a free Negro hand were killed as a new embankment collapsed under their freight train.[27] A month later a gravel train ran over and killed a man as it was backing up. In May 1859 a fireman at Company Shops was run over as he attempted to uncouple his locomotive. And in January 1861 a freight-train conductor was killed as the car in which he was riding suffered a broken axle, derailed, tipped over on top of him, and burned.[28]

These fatalities were suffered by employees of the road. In the United States generally, crew members were injured or killed more often than passengers. Until the 1861 collision President Fisher boasted regularly in his annual reports that no disaster had yet happened on a passenger train; he even stretched the truth to say that no passenger had ever been injured on the trains.[29] At least two men broke their legs jumping from trains, and another lost part of a leg trying to retrieve his hat from under the train.[30] It would remain true in 1861 that no passenger had ever lost his life.

One of the most common accidents—on the NCRR as elsewhere—involved persons (chiefly drunks) lying or walking on the tracks and failing to respond to the locomotive's whistle. There were at least eight such cases on the NCRR by 1861. North Carolina courts ruled that engineers were not negligent in failing to stop as soon as they saw persons on the tracks— assuming that it was even possible to stop in time. Trains could not be stopping all the time and still perform their public service; engineers had a right to suppose that people would get out of the way when the whistle blew. The state supreme court confirmed this ruling in the case of a deaf mute slave run over by an NCRR gravel train in 1857.[31]

About a dozen accidents or near-accidents arose from sabotage, in which persons deliberately placed logs, rocks, and other objects on the track to cause derailments. Most of these obstructions were discovered in time to avert an accident or were pushed aside by the locomotive cowcatcher. Several others led to derailments without causing serious personal injury. In one case, two slaves confessed to placing rocks on the tracks near the Rock Creek culvert in eastern Guilford County where the road passed over a high embankment (see fig. 12). The train narrowly avoided plunging down the embankment. The sentence passed upon the slaves—thirty-nine lashes and sale outside the state—created widespread indignation at its lenience; one paper suggested lynching.[32]

There were four cases of arson. Two of these involved the bridges near Hillsboro mentioned in Chapter 3. The other two cases, both near Selma in Johnston County, involved the more novel offense of burning the track itself. In the first instance, fire was set to cordwood stacked along the road for the locomotives, causing adjacent crossties to catch fire as well. About a thousand cords of wood were consumed in that effort, and 300 yards of track were damaged in each incident. The first case detained trains for several hours, the second not at all.[33]

Virtually every American railroad faced the problem of livestock straying onto the tracks. It was especially troublesome in the South, where the open range prevailed widely until well after the Civil War. Here it was up to farmers to fence in their cultivated fields (or railroads their tracks) against straying livestock, not stockmen to enclose their animals.[34] The North Carolina Senate in 1857 defeated by a vote of 40 to 1 a measure that would have required railroads to fence in their rights of way. One North Carolina road, the Wilmington and Manchester, did authorize this action wherever it could be done at the joint expense of the road and adjoining landowners.[35] Otherwise the open range continued to prevail.

The result was a continuing series of confrontations between locomotives and livestock, especially cows. Cowcatchers, those distinctive devices on the front of locomotives, came into general use during the 1850s. If substantially enough constructed, they were often effective in lifting or pushing aside animals or other obstructions.[36] This commonly averted derailments, but it was hardly gentle with the cow.

A North Carolina law that *was* enacted in 1857 declared that when any livestock were killed or injured by a railway train, it was prima facie evidence of negligence by the railroad. If a road could show that its engineer had slowed down and blown his whistle to warn the animal, this could sometimes satisfy the court.[37] But to avoid endless lawsuits in which they bore the burden of proof, railroads developed formulas for settling such claims out of court. The NCRR paid half the value of the animal as determined by the owner and a nearby railroad officer such as a station agent or section master.[38] When the matter did get to court, judges sometimes appointed two freeholders of the region to assess the damages.[39] Before the war the NCRR paid an average of $900 per year settling livestock claims, usually out of court.

Most cases of animal injury were accidental and were regretted by all parties involved. But it was a widely held belief around the country that some farmers derived secondary incomes from such incidents. The *American Railway Times* remarked in 1864, with more than a trace of bitterness, that for such farmers the best way to sell an otherwise unsalable animal was to lead him onto a railway track, then sue the railroad and depend upon anticorporation jurors to award substantial damages. It is suggested that some stockowners in Alabama (at least) deliberately salted the tracks in order to entice animals to them.[40]

Railroads were always coping with emergencies, and these took many forms. On 17 January 1857 a blizzard swept over much of the state, exceeding, some said, anything seen in the past fifty years. The storm covered most of the NCRR line and immobilized the road for nearly a week. The snowfall at Greensboro was about two feet on level ground. Drifts in some of the railroad cuts approached fifteen feet, higher than the tops of the locomotive smokestacks. Passengers were stranded for several days at Jamestown and Haw River, the railroad paying their expenses, as road crews worked to clear the track. Three attached locomotives, the first with a massive plow fastened to its cowcatcher, gradually rammed their way through the drifts. "At a speed of about 60 miles an hour," reported an observer, "they would pitch into a snow bank, and if not too deep, would clear it the first dash, throwing the snow right and left, sometimes clear out of the cut, and high into the air." But it was slow going; on the nineteenth they progressed only 200 yards. Miraculously, no one was reported injured in the operation; apparently not even a derailment occurred. The first trains got through after five days, and the road earned much praise for its handling of the crisis.[41]

By contrast, the road received little but censure in the nettlesome matter of Sunday operations. Railroads all over the country faced great public pressure to observe the Sabbath by operating six-day weeks. On the other hand, many through travelers, connecting railroads, and others resented the interruption of daily service, including daily mail delivery. Faced with such conflicting pressures, railroads reacted in different ways. A common compromise was to run Sunday trains only on exceptional occasions, but the exceptions tended to multiply. Economic considerations usually encouraged Sunday operation although some railroad leaders, like Henry Varnum Poor, editor of the *American Railroad Journal,* joined those opposing it on moral grounds. One of the main arguments for Sunday trains was the need to carry the mails expeditiously. Shielded by this excuse, Poor objected, some railroads would go on to attach a train of passenger cars. The concerns of opponents included disturbing church congregations, attracting idlers to the depots on the Lord's Day, and denying railroad employees their right to observe the Sabbath. Poor charged that railroads operating on Sunday were "schools of vice" that deprived their workers of self-respect. By 1856 there appeared to be a national trend away from Sunday trains, but it was short-lived. After the Civil War, Sunday operations became more and more commonplace.[42]

The question arose with the NCRR even before it began operations. As early as May 1854 the *Hillsborough Recorder* urged the stockholders to ban Sunday trains at the outset, before bad habits became established. The subject seems not to have come up at the 1854 annual meeting, and the stockholders rejected the *Recorder's* advice in 1855.[43] At that point the Charlotte and South Carolina appeared to be the only connecting railroad that forbade Sunday trains. When the NCRR began full operations early in 1856 it ran Sunday trains and incurred criticism thereby.[44] One man—an NCRR stockholder—attributed a recent disaster on the Seaboard and Roanoke Railroad (S&R) to that road's policy of operating on Sunday. He congratulated the S&R management for later rescinding the policy and urged his fellow stockholders to take heed at their own forthcoming meeting.[45]

The stockholders did comply, to a degree, with what seemed to be a growing trend. On motion of former Governor David L. Swain, they approved a resolution that condemned Sunday trains but stopped short of forbidding them altogether. In effect they encouraged the board of directors to abandon Sunday service if such a prohibition seemed expedient. Despite continuing editorial pressure, nothing happened. The *Greensboro Patriot* remarked in October that if the directors had given a moment's thought to the resolution, there was no evidence of it; they "regularly desecrate the Sabbath . . . with impunity."[46]

The directors may have been seeking collective action by all connecting roads, or they may all have been dragging their feet collectively. In May 1857 Fisher and other southern railroad presidents and superintendents, meeting at Augusta, Georgia, passed a very cautious resolution to discontinue one Sunday train on each road, provided the Post Office Department concurred.[47] In September, after the postmaster general agreed and several South Carolina roads took the plunge, the NCRR, Wilmington and Weldon, and Raleigh and Gaston followed suit. Henceforth the NCRR Sunday mail train was discontinued although the Sunday accommodation train continued to run. In August 1859 Sunday mail service on the NCRR was halted altogether.[48] While some newspapers had sought this action for years and applauded it, others now objected to the newless Sundays. Charlotte's *Western Democrat* lamented in March 1861 that the only mail reaching that town from Saturday evening to Monday evening was the horse-drawn mail from Davidson College.[49]

The relationship between the Post Office Department and the railroads was not always a happy one. The department wanted to expedite service and urged the roads to accelerate their speeds and coordinate their schedules to that end. The roads, on the other hand, resisted the call for higher speeds—harmful to their equipment and roadbeds—until competition or public demand required it of them. Coordinated schedules often called for nighttime running, which the roads and many passengers (especially local passengers) disliked. Nor were roads always content with the compensation they received for carrying the mails. In 1859 the mails on 137 of the 318 railway routes in the United States were being carried on a day-to-day basis by railroads that refused to sign contracts at the going rates. By the 1870s the roads and the department compromised through a revised compensation system and better technology, permitting faster trains and more rapid handling of the mail en route.[50]

Until the 1860s, when the railway mail car was introduced, mail was usually sorted at local post offices; most railroads simply carried the bags or pouches of mail from one station to another. Their compensation depended on a classification system that varied according to the size and importance of the mails they carried and the speed at which they did it. Roads of the first class received up to $300 per mile per year, second class up to $100, and third class $50.[51]

The NCRR began carrying the mails early in 1855, soon after train service started and while the road was still under construction. Through mails, like through passengers, were obliged to transfer to stagecoaches for passage across the narrowing distance between the two tracklaying crews.[52] Initially the road was paid an annual rate of $100 per mile from Goldsboro to Raleigh, $50 per mile west from Raleigh, and $75 per mile on the western end. (Bland and Dunn's stagecoach line received $85 per mile across the middle.) Conflict arose almost immediately over the rate that was to apply for the four years beginning in July 1855. The road asked $100 per mile; the Post Office Department offered $75. In his final annual report President Morehead (a member of the normally protariff Whig party) lashed out sarcastically at a federal government policy that taxed railroads oppressively for the rails they had to buy abroad, then refused them a just compensation for carrying the mails. The NCRR appears to have won this dispute; after July 1855 it was compensated at the rate of $100 per mile.[53] (See table 11.)

The mail it carried was more or less local, destined for points along the line of the NCRR and tributary stage routes. By contrast, the "Great Southern Mail" from New York to New Orleans traveled the coastal route of the Wilmington and Weldon and its connections. One of those roads, the Wilmington and Manchester, repeatedly delayed the service by missing train connections with its neighbors. This encouraged the NCRR, the Charlotte and South Carolina, and the Raleigh and Gaston to tighten their own connections early in 1857 so as to provide faster service and, they hoped, capture a larger share of both the through mail and through passengers. The three presidents went to Washington to press their case with the postmaster general. But such changes required unanimity among all roads party to the existing contracts, including in this case the Wilmington and Manchester. Its refusal to agree foiled the plan so far as the mails were concerned. Subsequently the Great Southern Mail was awarded to the newer and shorter transmountain route through western Virginia, eastern Tennessee, and northern Georgia.[54]

In July 1859, when the existing mail contracts expired, the NCRR and its connections joined the great number of roads that refused to sign new contracts at the same rates. The NCRR, the R&G, and the C&SC asked $150 per mile annually in return for twice daily service. Pending action by Congress to increase the rate of compensation, they continued to carry the mails as before, but without contract. Congress did not act, and on 1 May 1860 the three roads discontinued mail service altogether. The ensuing public outcry caused the roads to resume service after about a week at the existing rates—they hoped temporarily. But the policy of the government generally was to revise rates downward rather than upward. Postmaster General Joseph Holt cited that fact as well as the relatively low volume of mail along their routes as reason for denying their request.[55] This time the government had its way; until the war the NCRR continued to receive $100 per mile as a second-class mail carrier. This represented between 5 and 7 percent of the road's total receipts. (See table 11.)

Even less important were express revenues. The early express companies, like American, Adams, and Wells Fargo, specialized in the fast shipment of high-ticket and perishable items, generally of small bulk, using railway passenger trains where these were available. These shipments included money and even slaves on occasion. The express companies either rented space in the railroads' baggage or mail cars or supplied their own express cars. The latter were more apt to run through from one railroad to another, a practice that became increasingly common in freight service generally. The Adams Express Company, founded in 1840 with headquarters in Philadelphia, absorbed several smaller firms in the South in 1854 and moved on to become the major express company in the Southeast. (Its major rival, the American Express Company, dominated a more northerly territory.) Adams's business expanded with the growth of the southern railway network.[56]

The NCRR seems to have made its first express agreement with a local firm, Keith & Flanner of Wilmington, in June 1856. According to President Fisher's offer, apparently accepted and treated as a contract, the NCRR agreed to haul twice weekly from Goldsboro to Salisbury and back a marked car furnished by Keith & Flanner. They were to be charged twenty-four dollars per trip plus first-class freight rates for the commodities shipped. Fisher stipulated that the car was to be of such good appearance that the road could admit it as a part of its regular passenger train. The express company was permitted to send an agent with the car.[57]

It is not clear how long this arrangement lasted, but an agreement was made with the Adams Express Company early in 1859. In this case the NCRR promised to make room for express shipments in "the baggage apartment of the Mail Train" between Raleigh and Charlotte. In return it was to receive $4,000 per year from the express company and more if the volume of business justified it. This agreement was part of a larger through express arrangement including the Raleigh and Gaston; hence the stipulation of Raleigh rather than Goldsboro. (The NCRR affirmed its freedom to continue carrying fish and oysters from Goldsboro outside of this agreement.) The contract took effect in March 1859 and continued until the war. The volume of business in that period never exceeded the minimum compensation rate. (See table 11.)[58]

6

Passenger Service

THE NCRR'S FIRST passenger service was inaugurated in September 1854 between Charlotte and Concord. The twenty-one-mile trip took one hour and cost a dollar. In October service was instituted westward from Goldsboro. It reached Raleigh in December, covering the forty-nine miles in three hours.[1] By January 1855 this daily service was extended to Salisbury and Durham, respectively. For the next year, as the two tracklaying crews moved toward each other, train service followed them, station by station. In between, passengers and mail were carried as before, by stagecoach. This service was contracted by the NCRR with "Messrs. Bland & Dunn's mail line of four horse post coaches," running daily between the two rail heads. The coaches were to average at least four miles per hour and to charge no more than $5 per sixty miles. In general they adhered fairly closely to the railroad's projected route, following the old stage road. But that included a westward divergence from the railway route, required by the postal service, to include Salem in Forsyth County. The route then went southward to Lexington, Salisbury, and Charlotte.[2]

The contrast in service was striking to people who were treated to both. Editor Dennis Heartt of the *Hillsborough Recorder* reported a jolting thirteen-mile stage ride to Durham at a speed of a little over three miles per hour followed by a delightful twenty-six-mile glide to Raleigh in a splendid new railway car, taking hardly more than an hour. By December 1855 the stagecoach gap amounted to only ten miles in a nearly twelve-hour trip from Raleigh to Salisbury. (Salem had now been omitted.) A little over a year earlier, reported a traveler, the same trip had taken three and a half days.[3]

For years to come travelers remarked on the smoothness of the ride on the NCRR, compared with other roads, as well as the comparative freedom from dust. These were the products of well-laid track on a new and reasonably well-constructed roadbed. A passenger in 1857 also complimented the road on its absence of cinders and sparks, although these emanated from the locomotive and it is hard to see how they could have been averted, given the wood-burning engines in use. Wartime and later flatcar loads of cotton were highly susceptible to NCRR locomotive sparks.[4]

Cinders and sparks were to be avoided only by keeping the windows closed, for which a different price was paid. "Those who have never experienced it can hardly realize the sensations of thirst, half suffocation and blindness, which are occasioned by a long day's travel in unventilated cars. If you close your window, you parch; if you open it for air, your eyes are filled with heated cinders and smoke, while your clothes are covered, and your nose and throat are choked with the dust you respirate."[5] Inventors were constantly at work devising means of ventilation that would simultaneously prevent admission of smoke, dust, and cinders. None was particularly effective until the introduction in the 1860s of the clerestory roof, with small windows along the ceiling. Although this did not fully solve the problem, it helped and remained in general use until the 1930s.[6]

Then there was the problem of heating the cars in winter. A writer in the *American Railway Times* in 1865 declared the method of warming cars to be barbarous. The stoves were packed with fuel until they became red hot. It was impossible to sit near them, while remoter parts of the car remained cold. By the same token, the air near the roof became too warm while that around the passengers' feet was too cold. The stoves were also a fire hazard, especially in case of accident. This danger soon came home to the NCRR when a stove fire ignited and consumed a passenger car at Haw River in October 1856.[7]

Racial segregation seems to have been universal on southern roads before, during, and immediately after the war, as it was on many northern roads. Nearly all southern railways, and some northern ones too, possessed both first- and second-class coaches. The precise meaning of this distinction was so well understood at the time as not to require writing down. As a result we must guess at it today. Very likely the second-class coach was equivalent to the better-known postwar Jim Crow car: open to whites (perhaps as a smoking car) and mandatory for all blacks except those who might be attending their employers in a servile capacity farther back in the train. If that is so, it is a little baffling to see in the NCRR car roster of 1860 separate categories of first-class, second-class, and "Mail, Smoking and Servants" cars. But the smoking and servants designation appeared in no other year, while second-class coaches were listed throughout the period. Commonly the servants' or second-class coach was a combination car, partly given over to baggage, mail, and express. But if traffic were heavy enough a full (often older) passenger car might be assigned to this service. An NCRR passenger conductor referred in 1858 to a group of slaves riding "in the negro car."[8]

Some railroads of the 1850s, and especially those in the South, carried separate ladies' cars to which men were admitted only by invitation. The NCRR had such accommodations in 1865 and probably before.[9] White men and women, ladies and gentlemen or otherwise, generally traveled in the first-class coaches. Some may have smoked there too—the rules on this subject have not survived.[10]

Washing and toilet facilities were another subject of general reticence. Commonly water for washing was obtainable by means of a hand pump from tanks suspended beneath the car. (The NCRR Regulations and Instructions of 1857 merely mention water cans.) Toilet facilities often consisted simply of an enclosed traveling privy emptying to the roadbed below.[11]

Sleeping cars were coming into use in the North by 1860 but were almost unknown in the South until after the war. Many railroads were still so short and running cars through from one road to another was so rare—sometimes impossible due to gauge differences—that even through travelers often spent no more than a few hours in a single car. Under these conditions sleeping cars were impractical.[12]

Certainly the NCRR, with its ten- to fifteen-hour runs (often overnight) between Charlotte and Raleigh or Goldsboro, could have used sleeping cars from the beginning of through service. It did not use them until 1866. This is a little surprising, given the intense effort that the road and its connections made from the beginning to secure through passenger traffic. But train schedules were so impermanent that overnight runs could not be counted upon unless they were made a matter of policy, and these cars were costly to buy and maintain. Local travelers, for their part, resented overnight trains, and they carried a good deal of weight as long as the road operated only one passenger train per day.

Through travelers who did not choose to ride overnight in the day coach had to stay in hotels along the way, if train schedules permitted. These establishments sprang up adjacent to all but the smallest stations. The largest and most popular were apt to be in the larger towns, especially the junctions of Charlotte, Raleigh, Goldsboro, and later Salisbury and Greensboro, where through passengers sometimes had to lie over for considerable times between trains.

These railroad hotels often did a bigger business in feeding travelers than in putting them up overnight. Dining cars were not generally introduced on American railroads until after the Civil War and not until about 1880 in the South. Travelers could often buy food from vendors on the platform during station stops, or even on the train.[13]

Food vendors were not unknown to travelers on the NCRR although little evidence of them survives. The road's operating regulations of 1857 forbade the sale of books, papers, or refreshments on trains without written permission; how easily that permission was obtained does not appear. But conductors were enjoined to "keep news boys and other annoyances out of the cars."[14] Most through travelers seem to have depended on hotel restaurants adjacent to the stations along the way. Trains made scheduled meal stops, often for no more than twenty minutes, and commonly there was no choice among places to go. Train schedules in effect dictated which eating places travelers could patronize. Perhaps that is why the NCRR in 1857 dropped an original regulation forbidding employees to influence passengers for or against any particular hostelries. The regulation would have been particularly awkward after 1856, when the NCRR itself sponsored such an establishment.[15]

Given the mechanical requirement that locomotives be changed after a hundred miles' run, trains were required to stop at the middle of the road, and it was convenient to schedule a meal stop at the same time. Construction of the repair shops and allied buildings began in 1855, but they were not ready for use until 1858. In the meantime trains stopped, engines were changed, and passengers ate at Haw River, four miles east.

Late in 1855, several months before the road's completion and the beginning of through service, an agreement seems to have been made with General Benjamin Trollinger, the dominant figure thereabouts, to build and operate a hotel and eating place for NCRR passengers, train crews, and other personnel working at Haw River. The railroad gave him a tract of land on the east side of the river, adjacent to Trollinger's Granite cotton mill, the NCRR depot, and the railroad bridge that he had recently built. The Haw River House, as he called it, was serving meals to passengers and employees even before its completion in July or August 1856. It also provided overnight accommodations, but these were limited to ten rooms; presumably few passengers spent the night there.[16]

In early September Trollinger hosted a massive open house featuring a barbecue and a ball. It reportedly attracted 3,000 people, including three militia companies from Raleigh and Hillsboro. Unfortunately Trollinger's hospitality did not equal the anticipations of his guests. They were charged a dollar each for the barbecue, which many thought extravagant. At a late hour (after the ball) the three militia companies marched off to Graham, where they were hospitably received, fed, and lodged free of charge. Meanwhile, those who paid for the barbecue were fed expansively—women in the hotel dining room, men in the engine sheds. The ball was held in the station house.[17]

Trollinger soon gave up personal management of the hotel, leasing it to others in 1857 and 1858. It was in the latter year that the NCRR shops (and the new railroad hotel) began operations four miles away.[18] Thither went the eating and sleeping business on which the Haw River House had been founded. As the permanent shops had been located (with Trollinger's vital assistance) and were under construction when he built the Haw River House, his investment of $8,000 in that enterprise, for two years' worth of business, might seem ill advised. At any rate the hotel failed and with it his other enterprises as well. Trollinger went into bankruptcy, and his entire property was disposed of at a sheriff's sale. Pioneer textile manufacturer Edwin M. Holt bought the mill and placed his son, Thomas M. Holt, in charge. (Thomas would one day be president of the NCRR, after its period of independent operation.)[19] The hotel was bought by a partnership headed by George W. Swepson, soon-to-be NCRR station agent at Haw

River, later cotton manufacturer several miles downstream at Swepsonville, and still later railroad speculator.[20]

The new brick NCRR hotel, with its two-story balustraded veranda, was larger (about thirty rooms) and doubtless more ornate. It fed shop employees and train crews as well as passengers, who commonly got twenty minutes or so to bolt down their meals before the new engine was attached and the train was ready to resume its run. Apart from the mealtime trade, the hotel seems to have been well patronized by overnight visitors. For years the road either rented out the establishment or hired a manager, sometimes a husband and wife, to operate the place. The first manager was Nancy Hilliard, an experienced hotel keeper from Chapel Hill. Her cuisine and service seemed genuinely popular at a time when newspaper editors praised any place that gave them a free meal.[21] Railroad-owned and -operated hotels were not especially common around the United States at that time, nor were they generally very profitable.[22] With the mechanical necessities and arrangements as they were at Company Shops, however, it is hard to see how the place could have done without such a hotel. If the railroad had not built it, someone else would have, and Company Shops was a company town.

A privately owned Railroad Hotel was built in Charlotte in 1856, the proprietors making a point of their location in full view of the NCRR and C&SCRR depots. Advertised as "entirely new, commodious and tasty in appearance," the establishment was up for sale by the end of the year.[23] A traveler through Salisbury in 1857 told of being taken in a cart-like concern to eat at a hotel presumably some distance from the station. By 1860 Salisbury too boasted a Railroad Hotel, but Raleigh editor William W. Holden rang a familiar note in complaining of the short time allowed for supper there.[24] In his own city as early as 1855 the three principal hotels sent omnibuses to meet the trains, the Raleigh station being about a half-mile from the main business district.[25]

Accommodations in Raleigh appeared to be satisfactory to most visitors, but such was not the case everywhere. Holden's associate editor reported being "thrown into Greensboro" about 2 A.M. in December 1855, at a time when ten miles of stagecoach travel was still required in that neighborhood. He and forty other passengers were put up at Hopkins' Hotel "where the sleeping accommodations were bad, the fare indifferent, the attentions none, and the charges tuned to the highest note."[26] When the road was completed a month later, trains ran through, and Hopkins' Hotel must have lost a great part of its patronage.

Trains have never been able to arrive and depart from every station at convenient times of the day. Local travelers in particular resented having to ride or catch trains in the middle of the night, and railroad managements avoided night running when they could, if only for safety's sake. But through traffic, necessitating connections with other roads, usually required it. The NCRR started with one daily passenger train in each direction. It necessarily served both local and through travelers, with attendant and predictable conflicts.

Train scheduling was a matter of the utmost sensitivity, requiring decisions at the highest level. No railroad, as business historian Thomas C. Cochran pointed out, could be an island to itself.[27] Almost every road aspired to have as large a volume of through traffic as possible, even if its survival did not require it. Through traffic was by definition traffic from one railroad to another. To secure, maintain, and expand it required continuing consultation and cooperation between roads, often between many of them. Possessing a common interest, these roads retained other interests that were not in common. Nor did they always agree on how the burdens and benefits of the through traffic should be apportioned among all the participants. One of the hallmarks of early railroading—after the initial stage of small, isolated roads had given way to the dream and reality of through traffic—was a pattern of informal alliances, sometimes constant but more often shifting according to the perceived interests of the independently operated roads and their successive managers. Interrailroad relations, in short, were much like international relations.[28]

Neither its founders nor its neighbors ever regarded the NCRR as an island unto itself. The original impetus for its charter was the desire to build a railroad between Charlotte and Danville, to which other railroads were already under construction. President Edward G. Palmer of the C&SCRR, regretting that he could not manage the stagecoach ride from Charlotte to Greensboro to attend the groundbreaking ceremonies in 1851, noted that the two roads shared a strong common interest. They "are destined at no distant day to become one of the great lines of travel between the North and the South."[29] He and others envisioned an inland trunk line between New York and New Orleans, including the Danville Connection if possible but doing without it if necessary. Still others preferred to think of the NCRR as a link between the Atlantic ports of North Carolina and the Great West. Their favorite connections were an eastward one to the coast and a westward one to the Tennessee mountains.[30] In either case, the NCRR's future lay in conjunction with other roads.

This attitude shaped the policies of the Morehead and Fisher administrations from the beginning. Fisher reminded the board of directors in 1857 that they had always approved the closest connections possible with other roads, "even when the doing so involved a sacrifice . . . of comfortable hours for our way [local] travel—upon the ground that the interest of the whole Road—to the State particularly—was of more consequence than the convenience of any communities on the Line."[31] That put the case very clearly. It was not that local passengers (or shippers) were to be disregarded. But through traffic was competitive with other routes and could be won or lost, while patrons along the road had little alternative but to accept the service provided them.[32]

From the very beginning, the through traffic adhered primarily to the pattern envisioned by President Palmer in 1851. Even before its completion the NCRR became one of the links in a chain of railroad and steamboat (and Bland & Dunn's stagecoach) lines connecting New York with New Orleans. Only those links in Virginia and the Carolinas directly affected the NCRR very much, but the interests and necessities of a host of carriers always had to be considered. Passengers traveling south from Baltimore had a choice between railroad travel on a succession of lines through Washington, Richmond, and Petersburg or steamship travel on Chesapeake Bay to Norfolk. From Norfolk, or rather its neighbor Portsmouth, one took the Seaboard and Roanoke Railroad to Weldon, North Carolina, as Frederick Law Olmsted did in 1853. From Petersburg one took the short Petersburg Railroad to Weldon. At that little railway hub there were two southward routes to choose from. The first was via the Raleigh and Gaston to Raleigh (again like Olmsted) and thence westward and southward on the NCRR to Charlotte. The second choice was to proceed southward on the Wilmington and Weldon through Goldsboro. There one could catch the NCRR westward or continue on to Wilmington. From that city the Wilmington and Manchester Railroad proceeded into South Carolina, where it connected with the South Carolina Railroad at Kingsville, near Columbia. The SCRR (originally known as the Charleston and Hamburg, one of the nation's pioneer railroads) then took one to Augusta, Georgia. Meanwhile, a passenger taking the NCRR at either Goldsboro or Raleigh would be deposited at the Charlotte depot shared with the Charlotte and South Carolina Railroad. That line would take the traveler to Columbia for a junction with the South Carolina Railroad and conveyance thence (indirectly) to Augusta. From that point there was a succession of railroads across Georgia, Alabama, and Mississippi to New Orleans—unless one chose to take an Alabama River steamboat to Mobile and a Gulf Coast steamer to the Crescent City.

In all of this travel it was necessary to change trains when passing from one railroad to another. In this respect freight was usually treated with greater deference than passengers. But continuous service from one road to another was often physically impossible: the rails did not connect, either because of gauge differences or the preference of some cities (outside North Carolina) that passengers cross town in hacks and patronize local businesses on the way. The NCRR shared a common gauge (the later-standard four feet, eight and a half inches) with both the R&G and the W&W and with their connections onward into Virginia. From the beginning its track physically joined both of those roads, so cars could pass from one road to the other. Freight cars increasingly did so, passenger cars almost never in this period. To the south, however, the C&SC had a five-foot gauge that was standard in South Carolina and throughout most of the South until the 1880s. The Richmond and Danville also had a five-foot gauge, which would become significant for the NCRR when the Danville Connection was finally effected during the war.

Prior to the NCRR, through north-south rail traffic in North Carolina necessarily followed the W&W to Wilmington and thence (as soon as the W&M was completed) into South Carolina. The NCRR opened an alternate route from Goldsboro to Augusta—or if the R&G were included, from Weldon to Augusta. The new route was twenty-eight miles longer if it included the R&G, but passengers might be induced to overlook that if the scenery, the service, the rolling stock, the roadbed, or the fares were appealing enough. This situation made the NCRR an obvious and natural ally of the C&SC at Charlotte, but it created an anomalous relationship with the W&W. That road was always the NCRR's chief competitor but also its ally if the NCRR chose to route its through traffic via Goldsboro rather than via the R&G at Raleigh. It was advantageous for the NCRR, of course, to have two rivals at its eastern door vying for its patronage. (The Atlantic and North Carolina between Goldsboro and Morehead City would presently become a weak third.) From the beginning it frequently had to choose between them in making its alliances.

The alliance it chose in 1854, at the beginning of operations, was with the W&W, despite the fact that the R&G had the advantage of a shorter route by twenty-nine miles—a more or less direct run from Raleigh to Weldon versus the roundabout trip via Goldsboro. All other things equal, travelers (and freight shippers) would favor the former. But Walter Gwynn and other early policymakers on the NCRR favored the longer route as entailing an additional fifty miles' use of their road, with correspondingly greater revenues.

This was a matter of more than marginal interest to the R&G; its hopes for through traffic and perhaps its very survival hung in the balance. It was to achieve a through traffic that R&G stockholders had advocated the NCRR charter and participated in its subscription campaign. In May 1854 the R&G constructed at its own expense a track connection between the two roads in Raleigh. As soon as the NCRR agreement with the Wilmington road became known to him, therefore, President Lawrence O'Bryan Branch of the R&G attempted to get Gwynn to change it. When that failed he asked Governor David S. Reid to intercede, arguing that the state had a financial interest in both roads.[33] For the time being, Branch's efforts were unavailing. During 1855 and 1856 NCRR trains made most of their close connections with the W&W, and the two roads developed a joint ticket arrangement with reduced fares. As a result, most through travelers went via Goldsboro.[34] There was no such arrangement with the R&G.

President William Johnston of the Charlotte and South Carolina argued that the additional distance and higher fares entailed in going through Goldsboro were driving more passengers to the coastal route than the policy was worth to the NCRR.[35] His argument was persuasive. In September 1856, the NCRR made a through ticket arrangement with both railroads, equalizing fares between the two routes.[36]

The demands of through travel went far to determine the nature of train schedules. Early in 1855, westbound trains left Goldsboro at the awkward hour of 3 A.M., shortly after the arrival of the southbound mail trains on the W&W. Raleigh, forty-nine miles away, was almost as badly served from the standpoint of local travelers.[37] Connections at the other end of the line, in Charlotte, were not originally as close, and critics charged the NCRR with forcing the mails and through travelers to spend the night there unnecessarily. So schedules were tightened to provide closer connections—this at a time when the trip from Goldsboro to Charlotte consumed twenty-four hours, most of it still by stagecoach.[38] For that reason most long-distance travelers found the coastal route vastly preferable.

With the NCRR's completion in January 1856, its competitive position improved. The total run was shortened from twenty-four to fourteen hours. This improvement in turn called for another round of schedule changes by the C&SC if close connections were to be maintained at Charlotte. For one reason or another—probably an unwillingness to alienate local passengers by running night trains—that road failed to revise its schedule, forcing through passengers again to spend the night in Charlotte. President Fisher responded by running the NCRR trains in the daytime too, at the price of longer stays at *both* ends of the line for through passengers.[39] The result of all this was to give the coastal route an advantage of ten hours' time in a trip from Columbia to Richmond.

President Johnston of the C&SC—one of the most capable railroad leaders of the time and region—offered as a solution two daily passenger trains on both roads instead of the single train hitherto in service. This would accommodate through travelers with a night train to make close connections north and south as well as provide a day train for local passengers. Fisher at first refused, saying that he lacked the rolling stock and thought it would not pay.[40] But after several months of vacillation the NCRR instituted double daily trains in March 1857 in conjunction with both the C&SC and the R&G. This attracted enough through passengers to the R&G that the NCRR briefly discontinued its express train between Raleigh and Goldsboro altogether.[41]

Although through traffic increased, it failed to meet expectations. E. J. Hale, editor of the *Fayetteville Observer*, wrote in August 1857 that despite its superior service and facilities (except in distance and time) the NCRR seldom ran more than one passenger car half filled with passengers; by contrast the W&W ran four to seven cars with 100 to 200 passengers. He criticized the new route for not advertising itself to an unfamiliar public.[42] But that criticism was not entirely accurate. Conscious of their newcomer status, the allied roads had already begun to advertise, hiring both local and traveling agents to boost the advantages of their route. "Our time . . . will surely come," Fisher confidently predicted in July. "A Road, whose first Train ran through the line little more than twelve months ago, and which has only, at this very day, completed its actual construction, can hardly . . . expect to enter at once upon the business of Transportation that all other Roads have required years to reach gradually."[43]

In April 1858 a desired twelve-hour cut in running time was achieved between Kingsville, South Carolina, and Weldon. As part of the arrangement Fisher increased the speed of his express train to twenty-six miles per hour, not including stops. The time between Goldsboro and Charlotte was shortened from about fourteen hours to ten. This arrangement persisted, with some further schedule tightening, until January 1859, when Fisher felt that it endangered life and equipment beyond its financial return. He claimed nevertheless that the fast express did much to protect the road against the effects of the financial panic of 1857–58; the NCRR, he said, was one of the few roads to increase its receipts that year.[44] The twice-daily trains continued operating until the war. An advertisement in the spring of 1861 pointed out that in addition to the through express, daily passenger trains were available, giving travelers the opportunity to stop at night and travel only in the daytime.[45]

In April 1859 the through ticket agreement was expanded to include for the first time all of the eastern lines from New York to New Orleans, the coastal route as well as the NCRR's.[46] This arrangement broadened the understanding already reached between the NCRR, the R&G, and the W&W in the fall of 1856. The new agreement, like the former one, by no means ended competition between the two routes; rather, it was intended to mitigate the severity of their competition in the face of a new and dangerous common enemy across the mountains. It was followed by a further agreement between the NCRR and W&W to dismiss their respective sales agents and discontinue negative advertising.[47]

Early in 1858 the Virginia and Tennessee line opened for traffic through Lynchburg, Knoxville, and Chattanooga. It provided the shortest route between Washington and New Orleans and thereby captured the Great Southern Mail. The two eastern routes were left to compete primarily for the traffic of points east and south of Atlanta. The effect was greatest on the formerly thriving coastal route. As early as May its trains were reportedly running nearly empty. Both the Wilmington and Weldon and the Wilmington and Manchester reported sharp declines in through passenger receipts for the fiscal year ending in September 1858 compared with the previous year; most of this was attributed to the decrease in through travel.[48]

The impact was by no means as great on the NCRR and its nearer relations of the inland route. Although the *Greensboro Patriot* reported that NCRR cars too were often empty, the road's passenger records actually show a modest increase in through traffic until the secession crisis broke in December 1860.[49] The same was true in general of the R&G and the C&SC.[50]

A small part of the NCRR's increase in through traffic was attributable to two new connecting roads, the Atlantic and North Carolina and the Western North Carolina. Both were designed, with the NCRR, to provide the mountains-to-sea railway line envisioned by Joseph Caldwell in the 1820s and by John Motley Morehead and others in the 1840s. Together they would link the ports of North Carolina with the great continental interior and place the Old North State in the forefront of national commerce. They were not created as one road in 1849 when the NCRR was chartered because the state lacked the money and self-assurance to take on such a large project all at once. The highest priority had attached to a road linking South Carolina with the existing roads in eastern North Carolina, thereby defusing the Danville Connection issue. But the seeming success of the NCRR encouraged supporters of the original plan to press on with the connecting roads east and west. Both roads were chartered in 1854, the state providing two-thirds of the capital as it had originally done with the NCRR.

As completed in 1858, the Atlantic and North Carolina Railroad ran ninety-six miles from Goldsboro through New Bern to Beaufort. Actually, it ended on Beaufort Harbor across from that old but isolated seaport, and a new town was developed as its terminal. As John Motley Morehead was the leading spirit in creating this railroad, like the NCRR, and was also the prime developer of this new seaport and railhead, it fittingly was named Morehead City. At Goldsboro the new road built a depot adjacent to the NCRR and W&W stations. They shared common facilities and the hope of enlarged through traffic.[51]

The Western North Carolina Railroad was intended to run from Salisbury to the Tennessee line, either at Paint Rock on the French Broad River beyond Asheville or, alternatively, near Murphy in the extreme southwest corner of the state. It reached Statesville in 1858 and Morganton at the foot of the mountains by 1861, when the war began and new priorities supervened. From that point, the road faced formidable topographic obstacles, and many years were to elapse before the first locomotive surmounted Swannanoa Gap and found its way onto the streets of Asheville. In the meantime, the NCRR looked for the western road to be a valuable feeder line; Fisher hoped in 1858 that it might contribute $100,000 to the road's business in the next year.[52]

In fact, both roads were destined to be disappointments to their managers and stockholders, to the state, and to the NCRR. Neither was capable of providing much more than local traffic from its own territory to the larger central road. The WNC was for many years a dead-end road, linked to the NCRR at Salisbury but having no other connection west of Statesville. It helped make Salisbury the NCRR's second-busiest passenger station. But its limited usefulness to the NCRR was further diminished on the eve of the war by the construction of the Atlantic, Tennessee, and Ohio Railroad. That grandiosely named line from Charlotte to Statesville created a shortcut between western North Carolina and Charlotte, bypassing Salisbury and the NCRR for southbound traffic.

The A&NC was dependent, as more than a local carrier, upon the ports of New Bern and Beaufort/Morehead City. Neither was a considerable seaport at the time, nor did they become so despite many years of promotional effort by local residents and patriotic North Carolinians farther inland. The only access to New Bern was through the Outer Banks at Ocracoke Inlet and thence through Pamlico Sound. The entrance to Beaufort Harbor was across a sandbar, sometimes deep enough to accommodate large sailing vessels and steamships, sometimes not. Both ports were the victims of shallow water and shifting sands. The approaches to both, moreover, were disconcertingly close to the treacherous winds and seas off Cape Hatteras, the graveyard of the Atlantic. Maritime insurance rates were therefore higher to those ports than to more favored ones farther north and south, especially Norfolk. In 1862 Morehead City consisted of little more than "a railroad depot at the end of a long wharf."[53]

Efforts were made, nonetheless, to open regular steamship service between one or both places and the major northeastern seaports. Such connections would presumably foster the development of the A&NC as a through carrier comparable with the railroads farther inland; that in turn would further encourage traffic on the NCRR. In the fall of 1860 the A&NC was instrumental in establishing a new steamship line between New York and Morehead City, with trimonthly service.[54] Whatever prospects this effort might have had in normal times, the war quickly disposed of them.

Through ticket arrangements, in which one railway sold passage on other roads as well as its own, required regular payments between all parties to the agreement. Each road received a pro rata share of the proceeds of the through ticket, based on its share of the mileage traveled by each passenger. (The NCRR, with a relatively long 223-mile road, received a larger share than most of its partners.) Each road thus kept a separate account of the through tickets it sold and the proceeds it received from those sold by the others. From 1857 onward the great bulk of NCRR through ticket revenues came from other roads; this approached three-quarters after 1858. The NCRR also kept track of eastbound and westbound revenues. They were about equal, but the NCRR itself sold a much larger share of eastbound through tickets than it did westbound. More North Carolinians, in other words, traveled north than south out of the state. Tickets sold by other roads were predominantly westbound, indicating that the allied railroads situated east and north of the NCRR generated more traffic than did those to the south. A large share of the through passengers seem to have been northerners.

Despite the overwhelming emphasis on through travel, and owing in large part to the failure to attract a great deal of it, there was not a year between 1856 and 1861 in which local passenger traffic on the NCRR did not far exceed through traffic, both in number of passengers and in revenue generated. Local passenger receipts varied from $93,000 in the first year of full operation to $117,000 in the last prewar year. Except for a slight dip in the depression year of 1858–59, the trend was gradually upward.[55] Through passenger receipts never exceeded the $50,000 of 1859–60; the figure was usually $40,000 to $45,000 after the adoption of the double-train policy in 1857. Through passengers of course generated more receipts per capita, but collectively they never brought in half as much revenue as local travelers. The highest prewar passenger revenues were earned in 1860–61, when local passengers produced $117,000 compared with $43,000 from through travelers. (See table 14.)[56] Local traffic resembled through traffic in that eastbound and westbound passengers were nearly equal in number.

Passenger traffic was somewhat seasonal, summer and fall being the heaviest seasons, spring the lightest. August and September were the favorite months for through travelers, October and December (but not November) most preferred by local passengers. As already deduced, a substantial proportion of the through travelers were northerners. May 1861—anything but a normal month—was at once the least traveled month of that fiscal year (June to May) by through passengers and the most heavily traveled by local passengers. Many of the latter were in uniform.[57]

The annual reports for 1860 and 1861 list the number of passengers leaving each station, the latter giving their destinations as well. In both years the five stations contributing the largest numbers of passengers were Raleigh, Salisbury, Greensboro, Goldsboro, and Charlotte, in that order. Raleigh was well ahead of the others, with about 10,000 departures each year; Salisbury had 7,000. About one-third of Raleigh's passengers went to Goldsboro and a like proportion of Salisbury's to Charlotte. Many of these were no doubt through passengers planning to travel on other roads. The leading stations were large receivers as well as contributors. But a substantial proportion of all the travel, from large stations as well as small, was to nearby locations. Eighteen percent of all passengers went only to the next station in either direction. Over half of those leaving Greensboro, for instance, were headed for destinations less than twenty-five miles away; almost a third went to Jamestown and High Point.[58]

Antebellum railroad rates were largely determined by what the traffic would bear. There were almost no government regulations beyond maximum rates stipulated in a few railway charters. The NCRR charter contained no such restrictions. According to a study made in 1850 of passenger rates on over 125 American railways, fares ranged from a low of 1.33 cents per mile to a high of 6.25 cents; the average was near 3 cents per mile. (The few roads approximating 5 cents per mile were chiefly found in the South.) Rates declined somewhat by the mid-1850s. On the eve of the Civil War, the average fare in Virginia was 4 cents per mile first-class and 3 cents second-class.[59]

The first NCRR rate tariff was prepared by Walter Gwynn and adopted at the beginning of operations in September 1854. It provided for a passenger rate of 5 cents per mile, close to the national and sectional high.[60] (This was presumably for first-class accommodations; second-class is not mentioned.) That relative standing did not go unnoticed, and a year later the rate was lowered to 3½ cents per mile.[61] Even then the *Greensboro Patriot*, the road's most persistent critic, found the rates too high. It particularly objected to the practice, on the NCRR as generally, of charging through passengers somewhat less per mile than local travelers.[62] In this matter as in that of train scheduling, competitive through traffic usually retained an advantage over noncompetitive local traffic. The 3½-cent rate seems to have been regarded generally as a moderate one and persisted until the war.[63] It bears notice, however, that even at that rate it would have required $7.80, over a week's wages, for most NCRR employees (or unskilled laborers generally) to ride the 223 miles from Charlotte to Goldsboro.[64]

Special rates, even free passes, were available to certain kinds of passengers, besides through travelers. Following widespread custom, the road granted half-fare, or a free return, to roundtrip passengers attending events that the road, or society generally, sought to encourage. This consideration was extended to persons attending a State Medical Society convention in 1855 and, more unusual, a "great sale of lots" at the new town of Morehead City in 1858. The latter was in the nature of a special excursion trip to the coast, something that would become more common after the war.[65] The NCRR joined other railroads in according half-fares to persons visiting the annual state fair, with free transportation of animals, implements, and other items to be exhibited there.[66]

Far more controversial was the matter of free passes. The holders of these privileged tickets were commonly referred to as dead heads by members of the community not so honored. Every free pass obviously diminished a road's revenue, but the impulse or pressure to issue them was difficult to resist. In the first place, the board of directors and officers of the road seemed deserving and could hardly be denied. Lower-ranking employees who had legitimate reason to travel on the road were also reasonable, even necessary recipients. There were people of great political or other importance, the governor for instance, who had to be remembered, as well as some reasonable charity cases. Some roads included members of the clergy. In the interest of comity with other roads, particularly connecting lines and those regarded as allies, their presidents, superintendents, and directors were likely recipients, especially if they had already extended a like favor. A group particularly clamorous for attention were newspaper editors, who were ready to praise to the skies a railroad and all its attributes and employees in return for a free pass. (Free meals or beds could evoke similar encomia for the enterprises that furnished them.) In fact, once started, the practice was hard to stop without offending or even outraging important interests.

Most railroad officials tended to deplore the custom even as they perpetuated it. Part of the problem was one of reciprocity between roads, and railroad conventions often tried to cope with the problem cooperatively. Resolutions were passed, but they were unenforceable and were quickly abandoned. Henry Varnum Poor of the *American Railroad Journal* regarded free passes as an unavoidable product of human nature with some real benefits. He believed that travel on other roads was broadening for railway officials; it spread knowledge and fostered improvement. Off-duty travel by employees and their families at the road's expense cost little while it boosted morale and imparted better attitudes toward the road. And subsidizing newspaper editors was a cheap way to secure valuable publicity. The public, he said, eagerly read travel accounts describing the route, the experiences encountered along the way, and the potentialities of the region being traversed.[67]

Most editors appreciated sentiments like these, though not all were as eloquent in expressing them. The *Charlotte Whig* opined in 1854 that "All Editors and Publishers living at the termini and along the lines of Rail Roads, should have free passage tickets to ride and reride at their free will and pleasure. This is so at the North, and why not so at the South?" On the other hand, William W. Holden of the *Standard* in Raleigh welcomed the expressed desire of railroads to withhold free passes; editors could then ride along without feeling they had to extol the locomotive, the conductor, and the president and directors of the road.[68] (Holden himself did a good deal of this, with or without subsidy.)

The NCRR addressed the matter in its Regulations and Instructions of 1854. Free passes were to be extended to officers and directors of the road, their families when accompanying them, ex-presidents, conductors, engineers, wood agents, and other employees with a job-based need to travel on the road as well as the presidents and superintendents of eight connecting or neighboring railroads. These categories were substantially repeated in the regulations of 1857. All free passes were good for a year or less.[69]

President Fisher by no means adhered to these restrictions religiously. In 1856 he issued a pass to director Paul C. Cameron with the following addendum for other railroads: "The courtesy of pass is extended by this Road to all gentlemen connected with Southern Roads." In 1857 the presidents and superintendents of southern railroads, meeting in Augusta, adopted a resolution to restrict free passes.[70] Fisher attended this meeting but seems to have felt no pressure to restrict his own policies. In 1858 Thomas Ruffin, acknowledging a free pass in his capacity as a member of the NCRR's Sinking Fund Commission, promptly secured like rewards for his two colleagues on that board. One of them, President David L. Swain of the state university, remarked that he would use it a good deal, partly on university business. "I anticipate no other dividend upon rather an inconvenient amount of stock in the road."[71]

When Fisher denied in 1859 that editors were riding free on the NCRR, the proprietor of the *Greensboro Patriot* replied that he himself had been so honored by Fisher, but only rarely. The stockholders that year tabled a motion giving themselves and families one free ride a year; at the same time they substituted a five-dollar-per-day expense allowance to members of the board of directors in lieu of the free mileage they had hitherto received. Then, refusing to condemn free passes altogether, the stockholders called for yet another southern railroad convention to address the matter.[72] The free pass issue remained a hardy perennial for years to come.

7

The Beginnings of Through Freight

WHEREAS PASSENGER TRAINS ran on fixed schedules—at least theoretically—freight service was more flexible. The frequency of trains was apt to vary according to the volume of business to be done.[1]

With the NCRR's completion in January 1856, it instituted a triweekly freight train in each direction, running west on Tuesday, Thursday, and Saturday and east on Monday, Wednesday, and Friday. This schedule was always subject to change. During the ensuing wheat season the road ran daily trains.[2] And when business failed to repay even triweekly service, it reserved the right to omit a train and lay off its crew on those days.[3] In 1857, at a time when daily freight trains were running, it cut back service between Charlotte and Salisbury to every other day, presumably for lack of business.[4] Only occasionally was the road accused of letting produce and other shipments pile up at stations.[5]

The earliest American railroads derived far more revenue from passengers than from freight. But freight traffic rose to the point by the 1850s that the two branches of business were roughly equal on most roads. After the Civil War, freight prevailed heavily. Of course, there was variation among roads. The Wilmington and Weldon and the Wilmington and Manchester, the NCRR's two eastern rivals for through traffic, were both primarily passenger roads. But most of Virginia's prewar railways had greater freight than passenger income. So did the South Carolina Railroad.[6] The Charlotte and South Carolina and the Raleigh and Gaston got two to three times more revenue from freight during the mid- and late 1850s.[7]

Similarly, NCRR freight receipts predominated throughout the prewar years; the margin would increase after the war. From 1855 to 1861, on average, freight revenues accounted for 51 percent of all receipts, compared with 42 percent from passengers. The remainder came from the mails, express, and other miscellaneous sources. (See table 11.)

Economic conditions were not particularly auspicious during the NCRR's first years. Serving a predominantly agricultural constituency, the road encountered some indifferent crop years and sagging crop prices. The national business panic in 1857 slowed economic activity. And hopes of introducing steamboat traffic on the Yadkin River, making it a valuable feeder, never materialized. (More useful in that respect was the Western North Carolina Railroad, which reached the Catawba Valley in 1858.) Nevertheless freight receipts increased steadily, from $120,000 in 1855–56 when full operations began, to $214,000 in 1860–61.[8]

In freight even more than in passenger service, rate making was a complex and delicate operation. If the general rule was to charge as much as the traffic would bear, there was a host of modifications. Competition from other roads or water routes almost always brought lower rates. Long hauls cost a railroad less per ton mile than the same items hauled shorter distances; they were often charged lower rates, therefore, especially if there was competition from other routes. Bulky items of low unit value won lower rates per pound than high-priced items of smaller size. Big shippers commanded lower rates than small shippers because they brought in greater revenue, even at lower rates. Shippers often regarded rates as too high, particularly when they saw themselves as victims of discrimination. In such cases public outcry occasionally forced rate reductions, though railway managers were seldom much moved by these appeals. The argument that lower rates would foster a larger volume of traffic, hence greater revenues, usually fell on deaf ears. Only competitive routes or a very flexible local economy offered much hope of winning additional revenue through cutting rates.

These considerations recurred on a larger scale when joint rates were worked out by cooperating railroads in a through line. Then there was an additional problem of deciding the pro rata share of each participating road.[9]

Nationally, there was a good deal of variation in rates. Northern roads, with greater traffic volume, usually charged less than southern roads. The general tendency everywhere was downward as volume increased and technology and business methods improved. The national average in the early 1850s was between 3 and 4 cents per ton mile. By the end of the decade the larger northeastern roads were charging 2 cents or a little less.[10] These of course are broad averages. By 1860 most roads were classifying freight by type and charging different rates for different classes.

On the NCRR the first freight tariff was set in 1854, substantially the work of Walter Gwynn. It was revised from time to time as changing conditions warranted. In 1857 President Fisher said that rates averaged less than three cents per ton mile, which was close to the national average. Two years later he said they were as low on average as those of any southern road.[11]

However that may be, NCRR freight rates during the first three years of operation were an object of protest, even outrage, among many persons along the road. Particularly odious to small farmers was the rule that low-volume shippers had to pay higher rates per unit—per barrel of flour, for instance—than larger shippers. The complaint regarding flour was quickly rectified in 1855, but discrimination persisted with other products. The protests were particularly vehement at the western end of the line, between Salisbury and Charlotte. Repeated comparisons showed that rates on wheat in particular were lower via the South Carolina roads to Charleston than they were to Wilmington. (Both were regarded as too high.) Not only was the grain trade being diverted unnecessarily to South Carolina, it was claimed, but farmers who could do so were wagoning their harvests to Charlotte to avoid even a short haul on the NCRR.[12] The Concord *Weekly Gazette* bitterly attacked the road as "an immense swindling machine. . . . All our business men here have been bled by this vampyre, to a greater or less degree, and many have determined hereafter to hire wagons."[13]

Some of the protesters were stockholders; one of them, Caleb Phifer of Concord, had recently been a director. In 1856, after a formal request by the stockholders as a whole, the board of directors lowered the freight tariff.[14] Particularly large were the reductions on the local staples of wheat, flour, corn, and tobacco, as well as salt. At the same time, the W&W and the connecting roads in South Carolina cut their rates. Very likely these actions were taken in concert in response to a national downward trend. They placed pressure, in turn, on the Raleigh and Gaston and its northern connections.[15]

The reductions of 1856 were substantial enough to alarm President Fisher, who blamed them in part for the road's lackluster improvement in freight receipts in 1856–57. The increase from $120,000 in the previous year to $146,000 was undeniably modest considering that this was the first full year of through traffic. But the other reason he assigned, a "deplorable and general failure of crops everywhere," was surely at least as important. In lecturing the stockholders on their poor judgment, Fisher did not address the question of general downward freight revisions, which the NCRR could hardly have resisted alone. But the NCRR and the South Carolina roads all felt that they had gone too far with their 1856 reductions and raised them again slightly in 1857.[16]

The most vocal objection to these new rates focused less on their overall level than on a long haul/short haul differential that was now built into them for the first time. Shippers of the major agricultural staples to Goldsboro paid the same rates from the intermediate station of Greensboro as they did from all of the stations farther west. This was a common feature of nineteenth-century railroad rates, universally execrated by those living in the areas discriminated against. The most common reason for the differential was that favored areas had alternative transportation choices, and attractive rates were offered to draw their business. In this case the region southwest of Greensboro could (and frequently did) ship its produce southward to Charleston instead of eastward to Goldsboro. Residents of that southwestern area were the chief complainants against the earlier rates.

The differential was introduced to attract their business eastward over a longer stretch of the NCRR.[17] In 1859–60 the stations west of Salisbury continued to ship most of their grain through Charlotte. Stations from High Point eastward shipped primarily to the east. Those from Salisbury to Thomasville divided their trade about equally.[18]

The territory served by the NCRR was not blessed with major industries able to command preferential rates because of large-volume shipping. Although the directors authorized the president to make such rates, he had little occasion to do so. Only one case has come to light before the war, an agreement with Francis Fries, the Salem textile manufacturer, who was building a new mill adjacent to the railroad at Haw River in 1857. Not only did the road promise Fries a most-favored-customer rate, but it used his warehouse for its own freight and agreed that the station agent should be an employee of his Haw River Company.[19] The agent after 1859 was George W. Swepson.

The NCRR was an indifferent record keeper. Its published records were neither full nor very consistent in their coverage. This was a common criticism at the time, applied to most railroads. After 1857 the annual reports contain breakdowns of freight receipts by month as well as direction, whether eastbound or westbound. In the two years 1858–59 and 1859–60 the principal items of freight were variously listed by month, station, direction, and quantity. Even these data are not entirely comparable, but between them one can gain a fair idea of the road's business.[20]

Railroads serving agricultural regions necessarily did a seasonal business. The heaviest eastbound freight traffic on the NCRR occurred in August, September, and October, near the harvest time of the leading crops. Westbound freight, more diversified in character, peaked in March, April, and October. In both cases, traffic in the busiest month was apt to be twice as heavy as in the lightest month.[21] Yet the NCRR was not as season-bound as some Deep South roads, most of whose annual profit was made just after the cotton harvest.

Unlike the passenger traffic, which split about evenly between eastbound and westbound, freight traffic was predominantly westbound, both in terms of tonnage and value. In 1860–61 the disparity in revenue was two to one. (See table 15.)[22] The most important items of westbound shipment (in 1858–59 at least) appear to have been iron and machinery, castings, boxes of tobacco, bacon, and general merchandise.[23] Many of these were manufactured items of relatively high value compared with the predominantly eastbound agricultural staples. The NCRR freight pattern, in short, reflects an unfavorable balance of trade between economically underdeveloped North Carolina and the industrial North.

From the beginning, six stations accounted for over two-thirds of the freight revenues. The proportion exceeded three-quarters in 1859–60; during and after the war it would exceed 80 percent.[24] Salisbury and Golds-

boro each ranked first or second during the prewar years, followed by
Charlotte, High Point, Raleigh, and (well behind) Greensboro. In tonnage
(as opposed to receipts) the four leading stations were Goldsboro, Raleigh,
Salisbury, and Lexington.[25]

Surprisingly, Charlotte, the western terminus, accounted for less than
fifteen percent of the freight revenues before the war. Its tonnage in 1858–
59 scarcely exceeded that of nearby Concord. Not only was eastbound
freight less heavy or valuable than westbound, but nearly all of it originated
along the line; very little came from the Charlotte and South Carolina Railroad and points south. The C&SC itself had so little through freight that it
simply attached one or more freight cars to its daily express train.[26]

Of course, interchange with the C&SC required transfer of goods at the
joint depot because the roads had different gauges. (At Raleigh and Goldsboro, where gauges were the same, through freight cars were soon instituted.) But the gauge difference did not prevent a considerable southbound traffic through Charlotte, consisting chiefly of agricultural staples
from western North Carolina. Charlotte's own trade had previously been
toward Charleston, and it largely remained so.

At the other end of the road, Goldsboro surpassed Charlotte in both
freight revenue and tonnage before the war. In 1858–59 Goldsboro sent
off more than twice as much by weight as Raleigh, the next-highest station
and also a junction. Their combined tonnage amounted to 36 percent of
the total. In the following year they contributed 30 percent of the road's
freight revenue, twice the amount at Charlotte. The great bulk of this
westbound freight, at Goldsboro particularly, was received from connecting
roads. The W&W contributed most of it, primarily from Wilmington, but
some came from Petersburg and Norfolk. A little came from the A&NC.
Much of Raleigh's contribution came from the R&G. A substantial proportion of it all seems to have originated in the North.

Wheat and flour were among the NCRR's largest and most valuable
freight items. Nearly all of the 135,880 bushels of wheat shipped in 1859–
60 originated between Greensboro and Harrisburg Depot, near Charlotte.
Salisbury and Lexington alone were responsible for over three-quarters of
the total. They lay in the midst of a fertile wheat-growing region which the
NCRR made vastly more productive for a time—until midwestern wheat
came to dominate the eastern market after the war. Flour originated in a
wider spectrum from Charlotte to Morrisville, near Raleigh; Salisbury and
High Point were the largest shippers.

Some of these commodities were headed for the North via Norfolk and
Wilmington. The Wilmington and Weldon Railroad showed a dramatic increase in wheat shipments in 1856, when the NCRR began sending wheat
from western North Carolina. (Most of it went via Wilmington rather than
directly north via Weldon.) But the greater part of this trade disappeared
by 1860, lost to the Raleigh and Gaston and the port of Norfolk.[27]

Some of western North Carolina's wheat went to the Deep South as well, primarily through Charlotte on its way to Charleston and Savannah. Those two cities had long depended on Virginia and North Carolina for grain, receiving it chiefly by sea.[28] The NCRR now offered a cheaper and more plentiful supply from a region hitherto isolated by transportation barriers.

The direction in which these commodities moved fluctuated from year to year, depending on changing prices and freight rates as well as proximity to market. In 1858–59 the bulk of the wheat and flour went eastward. In the next year, more than two-thirds of the flour continued to move east while wheat divided slightly in favor of Charlotte. The most productive region from Greensboro to Salisbury was almost equally accessible to the eastern and southern markets and was apt to send its crops in the direction that seemed most beneficial at the time.[29]

Corn, the ubiquitous crop, was raised primarily for home consumption. It was not a major freight item on the NCRR. Salisbury was the only place shipping any considerable quantity of it in 1859–60, nearly all toward Charlotte.

Some 33,000 pounds of vegetables were shipped that year, nearly all eastward from Graham and High Point. Commercial truck farming was in its infancy during the 1850s. In the absence of refrigeration, fruits and vegetables could not be carried far unless in dried form. (Truck farming began around Norfolk in this decade, initiating what would become a major economic activity along the coast.)[30] The NCRR contributed importantly to the growth in piedmont North Carolina of a dried fruit trade as well as a nursery trade specializing in fruit trees.

Joshua Lindley established a nursery at Greensboro in 1842. After the arrival of the NCRR, that town became something of a nursery center, with several firms eventually carrying on an extensive mail-order business. One such company belonged to Cyrus P. Mendenhall, secretary of the NCRR during the 1850s. Most of this development occurred after the war, but as early as 1859–60 the NCRR shipped from Greensboro 561 bundles of fruit trees and 3,580 pounds of peach seeds.[31]

The NCRR shipped small quantities of dried fruit in 1855 and 1856;[32] by 1860 the annual volume reached 1,683,778 pounds. Just over half of that amount was loaded at High Point, most of it originating in Forsyth County. But Salisbury, Lexington, and Greensboro also shipped over 100,000 pounds each. All of the shipping points were between Salisbury and Durham, and nearly all of the fruit was headed eastward toward the northern urban market. Leading the list were blackberries, which grew wild in the fields throughout the region and were used in wine making. Orchard crops, particularly apples and peaches, soon found their way into the trade as well. The fruit was dried on boards in the sun or—after the war, anyway—in "dry houses" or kilns not unlike the later tobacco-curing barns.[33]

Before the advent of the railroad there was no market for these products at home, and growers had no means of reaching distant markets. Now they became a new source of income for farm families. Blackberries in particular, which were free for the taking, were gathered and processed primarily by rural women and children. The novelty of the crop was reflected when the Raleigh *Standard* noted in 1859 that 4,000 pounds of dried blackberries had just passed over the NCRR from Lexington toward New York City and asked, What next?[34] In 1858 alone the growers' cash return from these fruits was estimated at $300,000 or more. Around Guilford County these proceeds reportedly equaled the annual return for all farm produce ten years earlier.[35]

Bacon was the only meat itemized among the shipments in 1859–60, except for a few head of livestock. Salisbury and Durham, each with about 6,500 pounds, were the largest shipping points, although Greensboro and Jamestown sent off large amounts too. Except for Durham, it was all shipped from Greensboro and points south, most of it headed toward Charlotte.

Virginia was the chief tobacco-growing and manufacturing state in the Union during the 1850s. Production centered in the southern part of the state and spilled over into the northern tier of counties in North Carolina. Tobacco prices were high in these years and this, with railroad construction, caused its production to expand. The major marketing and manufacturing centers were at Richmond, Petersburg, and Lynchburg, with smaller ones at Danville and several other places in Virginia and North Carolina. Most of the North Carolina leaf was sold at Petersburg, though some found its way to Danville and other markets above or below the Virginia line. Outside Richmond and Petersburg, tobacco factories were typically small. The 1860 census counted ninety-four of them in North Carolina, nearly all in the northern piedmont. Durham's first factory was established in 1858. By far the greatest part of the manufactured product took the forms of plug and twist chewing tobacco.

The major consumer market for tobacco was in the North, although peddlers and other retailers sold it throughout the South, sometimes from the backs of their wagons. Because of its high value per pound, tobacco could be wagoned greater distances than grain or other farm products. But it went by river, canal, or railroad whenever possible. Leaf tobacco on its way from farm to market and factory was commonly shipped in 1,500-pound hogsheads; manufactured tobacco went in 125-pound boxes.[36]

From the beginning, tobacco was an important freight item on the NCRR, shipped in both boxes and hogsheads. Virtually all of it was put on the railroad at points between Durham and Salisbury. The leading sources of manufactured tobacco in 1859–60 were Greensboro, High Point, Hillsboro, Gibsonville, and Lexington, each with over 2,000 boxes; about three-quarters of them were sent westward and southward. Durham, Haw River, and Lexington were the main shippers of leaf, with over thirty hogsheads each, most of them heading east. (This was before the rise of Durham as a manufacturing center.) Nearly all of the tobacco shipped from Greensboro and High Point (at least) had been wagoned for distances of up to 125 miles from Virginia and the northern tier counties of North Carolina. (Before the road was completed, in 1855, about 14,000 boxes were shipped southward from Lexington, which was the railhead at that point.)[37] The 11,662 boxes shipped from Greensboro in 1859–60 represented a third of all the tobacco shipped in that form that year. Virtually all of it went toward Charlotte, seeking a market farther south. High Point sent over 8,000 boxes in the same direction.[38]

More than 2,000 barrels of liquor were shipped in 1859–60, more than half of them from Salisbury. Gibsonville (east of Greensboro), High Point, and Graham also sent off large quantities. Well over half went east.

Turpentine and rosin, products of the pine forests of eastern North Carolina, were shipped in large quantities from Selma and Boon Hill (later Princeton), most of it heading the short distance eastward to Goldsboro and thence on the Wilmington and Weldon.

Rags, used in paper manufacture, were a large freight item, at least in weight. Salisbury and High Point as well as Charlotte each shipped more than 100,000 pounds of rags in 1859–60, and eight other stations sent off at least 10,000 pounds each. All of these shipments were headed for Raleigh, presumably to a paper mill at the falls of the Neuse River nearby.

Southeastern cotton found its way to market in Europe or the northern ports almost entirely by sea before the Civil War. The quantity moving northward by rail was rising, from almost nothing in 1857–58 to 143,424 bales in 1860–61, but it would not be a significant portion of the crop until after the war.[39] (Mississippi Valley cotton, to a much greater degree, found its way north and then eastward by rail during the 1850s.)[40] Only 6,870 bales were shipped on the NCRR in 1859–60, two-thirds of them originating between Charlotte and Concord. Virtually all of them were destined for textile mills along the road.[41]

Most of North Carolina's antebellum textile mills were located in the rural piedmont, adjacent to waterpower sites. The mills bought raw cotton from farmers of the region and spun it into yarn for sale primarily to general stores, also in the region. If they could get their products to a more distant market, they jumped at the opportunity, but originally they were dependent upon wagon transportation over miserable roads. It is no wonder that John Motley Morehead, Edwin M. Holt, Francis Fries, Benjamin Trollinger, and other early textile manufacturers were ardent railroad promoters, particularly of the NCRR.[42]

The NCRR broadened the range and encouraged the growth of these mills, bringing them closer to their markets as well as their sources of supply. In 1859–60, the road shipped 1,879 bales of "domestics," approximately equal quantities in each direction. The major shipping points were High Point, Gibsonville, and Hillsboro. (High Point, again, was the depot for Salem and vicinity, and Francis Fries, the Salem cotton and woolen manufacturer, maintained a warehouse at the High Point depot.)[43] In the same year, 338 bales of cotton yarn were shipped, the vast majority eastward from the mill town of Haw River. The mills were small, however, and they contributed a very small part of the road's business.

Some 22,000 pounds of leather were shipped in 1859–60, two-thirds of it eastward and two-thirds from High Point. The next-largest shipping points were Mebanesville, on the Orange-Alamance line, and Gibsonville.

Lumber in the amount of 391,000 board feet was sent on the NCRR in 1859–60. Nearly all of it came from Thomasville and Morrisville, which shipped the commodity toward the center of the road.

Gold, silver, copper, and lead ores were shipped in large quantity from several stations between Harrisburg and Jamestown. But Jamestown, with nearly 1,500 tons of copper and gold ore, contributed the vast majority. The nearby Gardner and Guilford mines shipped 666 tons of copper ore to Baltimore in the first three months of 1860.[44] Thomasville and High Point, also close by, were remote second- and third-place shippers of these two ores. Surprisingly, Concord, adjacent to the recently active Gold Hill mining region, shipped no ores in 1859–60, although Salisbury and Harrisburg sent off small quantities. All of these ores were shipped eastward.

One of the predominantly westbound commodities was guano—dried bird manure—the most widely used agricultural fertilizer of the period. Guano was imported largely from South America and the Pacific. Baltimore was the largest southern port of entry although some was shipped to Wilmington as well. The NCRR and other railroads carried guano and other fertilizers at cost or even at a loss on the theory that the more farmers used it, the larger their crop yields and shipments would be. It was carried throughout the year, but, in 1858–59 at least, August and September were the heaviest months. That likely resulted from the greater availability of empty cars to haul it inland while the wheat harvest was being taken eastward to market.[45]

In summary, the NCRR shipped North Carolina products, chiefly agricultural commodities, to other railways—southward through Charlotte and eastward or northward through Raleigh and Goldsboro. (Virginia tobacco was the only important outgoing commodity that originated elsewhere.) Similarly, incoming freight was distributed within the state rather than passed through. Heavy rail shipment between the North and the Deep South would develop after the war; until then it went by sea. A great part of the through traffic that the NCRR did enjoy in the 1850s was headed for (or arriving from) neighboring seaports—Charleston, Wilmington, Morehead City, New Bern, and Norfolk or Portsmouth—where it was loaded on (or unloaded from) ships sailing back and forth from northern ports. Although southeastern railroad freight traffic was overcoming state and local barriers in the 1850s, it was still more regional than national.

Interchanges from one railroad to another constituted a greater problem for freight than for passengers. Travelers could change trains under their own power. Freight had to be unloaded from one train and reloaded onto another. In the late 1850s and early 1860s, a single transshipment was estimated to cost from 7 to 25 cents per ton and required at least a day's delay. Where gauge differences like that in Charlotte did not exist, there was a great incentive to provide continuous running of cars from one road to another.

Such operations required a high order of cooperation and record keeping. When this effort developed, it represented a new phenomenon in American business, historian Alfred D. Chandler explains. Participating roads had to set uniform freight classifications and rates as well as make through ticketing and scheduling arrangements. Each road had to get its pro rata share of the proceeds from each shipment. The first of these agreements was begun in the mid-1850s. Meanwhile, a freight shipment over three railroads was handled as three separate transactions. Where alternative ocean transportation was available, it was usually cheaper.[46] The NCRR faced this problem from the start and might have been in the vanguard (with its connecting roads) in addressing it.

Before the NCRR began operations, Orange County farmers wagoned their flour to Raleigh and sent it off toward Norfolk on the Raleigh and Gaston Railroad. In February 1855, with the NCRR open to Orange County from Goldsboro, the Wilmington and Weldon tried to divert trade to Wilmington by negotiating a favorable through freight agreement with the NCRR.[47] This was during the period when the NCRR management favored the W&W in order to encourage traffic to go on to Goldsboro rather than stop at Raleigh. But in May 1856 the NCRR gave up this alliance. It now agreed with the R&G and the Petersburg Railroad to run freight cars through from Charlotte to Petersburg on all three roads without the necessity of breaking bulk, or transshipment. This major agreement was quickly followed by similar ones with the Seaboard and Roanoke (running from Weldon to Portsmouth, Virginia, near Norfolk) and with the W&W. Together these accords enormously facilitated through freight traffic between Charlotte at the one end and Petersburg, Norfolk, or Wilmington at the other.[48]

A unique feature of the W&W agreement was the two roads' joint ownership of twenty boxcars to carry through freight between Wilmington and Salisbury. (Beyond Salisbury, shippers were apt to deal with Charleston.) Trains using these cars were to provide weekly service. But merchants in Salisbury soon complained about delayed shipments.[49] The experiment did not work well and was apparently abandoned by 1859. The freight agreement continued, however, using through cars of each road.

It is difficult to measure the results of the 1856 accords independent of other phenomena. West- or southbound freight entering the road at Goldsboro and Raleigh increased very little during the first year of the agreements (1856–57), but the volume more than doubled from 1857 to 1860. Goldsboro and Raleigh accounted for 53 percent of the increase in freight receipts during those three years. (Northbound shipments from Charlotte contributed only 16 percent of the increase.) Furthermore, Goldsboro (with the W&W) maintained almost a three-to-one lead in westbound freight traffic over Raleigh (with the R&G). It is unlikely that a great deal of the Goldsboro traffic came from Weldon; it was a more roundabout trip than by the R&G, and only a little of the Goldsboro traffic came from the A&NC. So far as incoming freight is concerned, therefore, Wilmington retained its primacy compared with Norfolk and Petersburg. (See table 16.)

The new state-controlled A&NC and Western North Carolina roads were not party to these agreements. When upcountry merchants did send for goods by way of New Bern or Morehead City, they complained of delays by the NCRR in forwarding the shipments at Goldsboro.[50]

The state board of internal improvements grew restive at the failure of its three railroads to promote through traffic more seriously among themselves—especially when much of the traffic was being diverted through Virginia. The state had both a financial and a sentimental investment in these roads as well as the North Carolina seaports. In April 1859 Governor John Ellis, at the board's behest, called upon the presidents of all the roads in which the state held stock—and that included the R&G and W&W—to meet and form a through freight agreement among themselves, free of any transshipments.[51]

The meeting was held at Raleigh on 17 May. It produced the kind of agreement asked for, focusing on the three roads converging at Goldsboro. The NCRR, W&W, and A&NC agreed to send and receive through freight cars among themselves without delay. There was even provision for entire trains to pass from one road to another if the volume of shipments warranted it. The WNC (which seems to have had some such arrangement already) promised to support the agreement. And the NCRR promised to apply it to the R&G, whose president could not attend.[52]

This treaty did little to change the established routes of trade. But it may have encouraged the W&W to new efforts to increase its own share of the interior North Carolina trade with the Northeast. Noting that Norfolk, Charleston, and Savannah all had bi- or triweekly steamship service to New York and Philadelphia while Wilmington lacked regular service, the W&W instituted it with New York on at least a bimonthly basis (depending on demand) early in 1860. It advertised through billing and forwarding from inland North Carolina to New York, free of intermediate charges along the way. It also made a serious play for traffic as far away as Charlotte for the first time.[53]

The Atlantic and North Carolina responded to this challenge by initiating its own steamship service to New York. It took some time to decide where the ships would land, because New Bern and Morehead City/Beaufort were in a sometimes precarious balance in the councils of that road. The nod went to Morehead City, and regular service began in October 1860. In February 1861 the A&NC initiated a special freight train to connect with the steamer.[54]

The Wilmington and Morehead City efforts were matched by counteractivity in behalf of Charleston. Attempting to direct more upcountry traffic that way, the C&SC and the South Carolina Railroad in October 1860 instituted daily freight service between that city and Charlotte, advertising that no transshipment was necessary between them at Columbia.[55] None of the three efforts had time to achieve very much before the war cast all such plans into discard.

8

Management and Finance: Morehead

RAILROADS WERE America's first big business. Operating on a larger scale than previous enterprises, they necessarily were innovators in devising methods of organization and procedure.[1] The pioneer in this respect was the Western Railroad of Massachusetts, in the 1840s.[2] It was followed on a larger scale in the 1850s and 1860s by the Baltimore and Ohio, the Erie, and the Pennsylvania. Building on each other's precedents, they developed managerial and operational systems that served almost concurrently as models for the industry as a whole.[3]

Virtually every railroad company was a corporation, chartered by its home state and owned by a body of stockholders. They chose boards of directors who in turn appointed presidents and other company officers. Very few directors or presidents in the 1850s were professional railroad men or had much experience with the industry at all; it was too new and expanding too rapidly for that to be possible. The first large investors in railroads, some of whom became directors, presidents, and other officers, were typically merchants, manufacturers, and farmers of the vicinity whose primary concern was to develop the local or regional economy. Later, as the process of expansion and consolidation took place, railroads had to look farther afield for financing. Presidents and boards came increasingly to represent entrepreneurs in the major financial centers, especially in the Northeast. By contrast, the operating managers subordinate to the president were (wherever possible) professional railroad men. As salaried employees, they usually owned little or no stock in the company. Another type of railroad leader, the professional speculator, emerged during the 1850s. Represented by Daniel Drew, Jim Fisk, and (a bit later in North Carolina) George W. Swepson, these men were not primarily engaged in transportation and had no long-term interest in the roads they headed. Their profits usually came from manipulating the roads' securities.[4]

As a writer in the *American Railroad Journal* put it, railroad directors of the 1850s accepted their positions on the board partly as an honor, partly through interest as substantial stockholders, and generally under the impression that little work was required. Receiving only token compensation, they had no idea of rummaging through the account books to determine how well or badly the road was being run. They depended on the officers they had chosen. Everything hinged, therefore, on the caliber of those officers.[5]

According to Henry Varnum Poor, editor of the *American Railroad Journal*, the best-run railways were those whose presidents were least trammeled by their boards of directors. Good management, said Poor, required strong direction by a single executive who knew the business thoroughly. Generally ignorant stockholders and directors fostered good management by letting presidents have their own way, but the ignorance should stop with the stockholders and boards. Too many presidents, Poor said, were financiers who scarcely knew one end of a locomotive from the other. As a result they exercised too little control over those below. Presidents as well as superintendents, Poor believed, should be promoted from the ranks and should enjoy a large measure of job security.[6]

John Motley Morehead epitomized the typical antebellum American railroad president. Aside from having served as governor (1841–45), he was a successful textile manufacturer and businessman with varied economic interests.[7] He was easily one of the wealthiest and most influential men in the state. What he lacked in practical railroad experience—he had none at all when he became president in 1850—he more than made up in financial and political skills. In Morehead's case, practical railroad experience was almost irrelevant; he retired less than a year after limited train service began and six months before the road's completion. His central tasks as president were to hire a competent engineer, preside over the business end of construction, and obtain additional support from the legislature. These things he did, with ability and style.

The NCRR differed from most railroads in that two-thirds (soon three-quarters) of its stock belonged to the state. According to the charter, however, the state was not to make any payments on its stock until half of the $1 million of private stock subscriptions was paid in. That occurred late in 1852, whereupon the state made an initial payment of $100,000.[8] The remainder came in periodic installments over the next two years.[9] The state raised its $2 million through the issuance of bonds that were marketed periodically in New York beginning in January 1853. By that means, two-thirds of the NCRR's initial capital was indirectly supplied by northern (and probably European) capital.[10] North Carolina had borrowed little in previous years, and the state's credit was so good that most of the bonds sold at a premium of 3 to 5 percent.[11]

In 1854 it became clear that another $1 million, at least, would be needed to finish building and equipping the road. Morehead and the directors, still struggling to collect the last payments on the original $1 million private subscription, knew that they could not sell that much in additional stock.

Theoretically they could borrow the money by issuing company bonds; struggling railroads all over the country were doing this. But they were reluctant to saddle the NCRR with such a large debt, if indeed they could sell the bonds at all in a "market already glutted with stocks of every hue and dye and uncouth name," as Morehead put it. The remaining alternative was to ask the state for another $1 million. This he did in an able petition to the legislature in December. By that month the estimated construction costs had climbed to $4,235,300, and bills continued to come in.[12] The final cost was to exceed $4,900,000. (See Chapter 2.)

The legislature, in an expansive mood, responded favorably to Morehead's appeal, as it did in further appropriations to the Atlantic and North Carolina and the Western North Carolina railroads, similarly circumstanced. The response in the case of the NCRR came as a subscription to an additional $1 million of stock with the stipulation that it should be preferred stock—entitled to an annual dividend of 6 percent before any dividends were paid on the remaining stock.[13] The author of the Senate bill making the desired appropriation was Charles F. Fisher of Rowan County, chairman of the committee on internal improvements, an NCRR stockholder and director, and soon to be Morehead's successor as president. Conflict of interest was not a well-refined concept in the mid-nineteenth century.[14]

Morehead also asked for an exemption of NCRR property from state and local taxation. He noted facetiously that every county and town along the route not only clamored for a fine station to adorn its community but "manifests a becoming vigilance to see that [such edifices are] duly taxed." The company, he added, "are desirous to make the road useful to every portion of our citizens, yet they are not ambitious of distinction in this line of usefulness." The legislature replied with a tax exemption on all NCRR property as long as the road's annual dividends did not exceed 6 percent— practically an invitation not to issue larger ones.[15]

These provisions—and others to be mentioned presently—came in the form of amendments to the NCRR charter and had to be approved by the stockholders. A special stockholders' meeting approved them unanimously in March 1855.[16]

The state financed its new subscription as it had its last, with a bond issue. This time the NCRR, at its own request, took most of the $1 million of bonds directly and sold or paid bills with them as needed. The Norris Locomotive Works even agreed to accept them at a 2 percent premium.[17]

Even before the 1855 charter amendments, state ownership entailed a measure of state control. The form and extent of this control seem to have occasioned little consideration or controversy at first. The practice of other states varied widely. (So, in time, did that of North Carolina with other railroads.) The general preference around the country in cases of mixed enterprise, where governments subsidized private corporations in various ways, was for government to adopt a passive role. When public stock ownership entitled states and localities to representation on boards of directors and to vote in stockholders' meetings, such governments generally deferred to private leadership. Virginia, for instance, limited its stock-voting rights to two-fifths, even after the commonwealth increased its stock ownership to three-fifths.[18]

North Carolina policy was more ambiguous. The NCRR charter of 1849 simply gave the state two-thirds of the 30,000 shares of stock, corresponding to its share of the original capitalization. No mention was made of the state's voting rights or of how or by whom they would be exercised. The governor was empowered, however, to appoint eight of the twelve members of the board of directors (proportionate to the state's stock ownership) once its financial subscription was made.[19] In the interim, the private stockholders elected all twelve directors at their annual meetings in July 1850, 1851, and 1852.

When the time for the state subscription arrived in December 1852, Governor David S. Reid called attention to the charter's silence concerning state representation in the stockholders' meetings.[20] The legislature responded on Christmas Day with a set of proposed charter amendments that required private stockholder acceptance (as a unit) to take effect.[21] One amendment would have limited the state to 1,000 votes, probably allowing the private stockholders to outvote it under an accompanying voting scale. The state votes would be cast by an agent or proxy appointed by the governor. After what the Salisbury *Whig* characterized as "excited and spicy debate," the stockholders decisively rejected the amendments at their July 1853 meeting. The center of controversy seems to have been less the state's role in company management than the proposed voting scale among private stockholders, which threatened to diminish the power of the larger owners.[22] A year later the stockholders rejected the amendments again.[23]

Shortly before the 1853 meeting, Governor Reid appointed as state proxy Judge John W. Ellis of Salisbury, a director of the NCRR, one of its early promoters, and later governor of the state. If the amendment authorizing the governor to appoint a proxy were accepted by the stockholders, Reid directed Ellis to serve accordingly. If the amendment were rejected, Reid believed that he still possessed an implied right to appoint a state proxy. But the stockholders, after rejecting the amendments, denied this claim and refused to seat Ellis.[24] The eight state directors appointed by Governor Reid in 1853 were seated, however, in accordance with the charter. Henceforth the private stockholders elected only four members of the board.

In 1855 new charter amendments, including another million dollars of state aid, proved much more acceptable to the stockholders. That consideration overrode the fact that these amendments were more protective of the state's interest in the road. These were the amendments adopted unanimously at a special stockholders' meeting in March. Henceforth the state, with 30,000 of the total 40,000 shares of stock, would be represented by a state proxy appointed by the governor and entitled to cast 30,000 votes on all questions except the election of the private directors. All board members, moreover, were required to own at least five shares of stock—a standard not always met by the previous state directors.[25]

The state's power was exercised very lightly. Robert P. Dick of Greensboro, the first state proxy to serve, in 1855 and 1856, did not use his vote, announcing that he would reserve it for major contingencies that he did not foresee. This precedent was followed by his immediate successors, and neither the state proxies nor the governors who appointed them played a significant role in determining company policy before 1865.[26] In 1857 Governor Thomas Bragg deliberately left his proxy, Judge Thomas Ruffin, without instructions, first, because he was not sufficiently informed about company affairs and, second, because of his confidence in Ruffin's judgment.[27] Apparently on his own volition, Ruffin tried twice, in 1857 and 1858, to have the board of directors declare a dividend on the state's $1 million of preferred stock. He was turned down both times.[28] Even in the month-to-month operations of the road, involving the directors more than the stockholders, the state's hand was not heavy. President Charles F. Fisher reported in 1859 that "as between the State and stockholders interest, no conflict whatever has at any time occurred." Both he and his predecessor Morehead had been chosen from the private directors, he pointed out, and in effect the road remained in private hands.[29] In 1867 a legislative investigating committee, after inquiries among persons in a position to know, reported the same harmony between the presidents and state and private directors until the end of the war.[30]

Nearly all of the 10,000 shares of private stock were held by individuals or business partnerships in North Carolina. (Two of the stockholders were other railroads, the South Carolina and the Charlotte and South Carolina, each of which seems to have accepted about fifty shares in payment for transporting NCRR iron during construction. Aside from these, the only shares known to be held out of state by 1870 were 173 owned in Petersburg, Virginia.) In 1854 as in the original subscription of 1850, over 80 percent of the private shares were held by persons in counties along the route.[31]

The largest early transfers of stock occurred as men like John Motley Morehead, George W. Mordecai, Francis Fries, John W. Thomas, and William Boylan unloaded some of the shares that they had subscribed at a sacrifice to get the railroad started. Nearly 900 of these shares were transferred to John C. McRae and Company, the construction contractor for the eastern end of the road, as partial payment on its contract.[32]

In 1859 there were 923 stockholders, apart from the state, with an average of 10.8 shares each.[33] Their holdings ranged from single shares to the 885 of John C. McRae and Company. That partnership consisted of John C. McRae of Wilmington, his relatives John McRae and Alexander McRae (president of the Wilmington and Weldon Railroad and an NCRR director),

Zebulon Latimer, and Jere Nixon. Slightly over half of the private shares were held in blocks of 40 or more, owned by sixty-two persons or companies. The other ten owners of 100 or more shares were Shaver and Simonton (a construction firm based in Salisbury) with 314 shares; Cyrus P. Mendenhall of Greensboro (secretary-treasurer of the NCRR), 157; President Charles F. Fisher of Salisbury, 143; William Murdoch of Salisbury, 140; Michael Brown of Salisbury, 133; Francis Fries of Salem, 114; Richard J. Ashe of Chapel Hill, 110; John B. Lord of Salisbury, 106; John H. Caldwell of Charlotte, 105; and Richard Smith of Raleigh, 100. (See table 2.)

Most of these owners derived the bulk of their stock as contractors. In fact, a substantial proportion of the private stock was originally issued to contractors (both individuals and partnerships) in partial compensation for their construction work. This was true of former Governor and Navy Secretary William A. Graham, 40 shares; later NCRR President Paul C. Cameron, 38; and Thomasville's John W. Thomas, 75. Other well-known stockholders of 1859 (large and small, some of them former contractors) were lawyers Daniel, Victor, and Rufus Barringer of Concord and Charlotte; John Motley Morehead (88 shares), David F. and William A. Caldwell, Robert P. Dick, John A. Gilmer, and Ralph Gorrell, all of Greensboro; Alamance textile manufacturer Edwin M. Holt and his brother William R. Holt of Davidson County; Giles Mebane and Benjamin Trollinger of Alamance; Archibald Henderson of Salisbury; editors Dennis Heartt (*Hillsborough Recorder*) and William W. Holden (Raleigh *North Carolina Standard*); Romulus M. Saunders and George W. and Jacob Mordecai of Raleigh; and former Governor David L. Swain of Chapel Hill. Both political parties were represented, but according to common repute the great majority were Whigs.[34]

As time passed, stock ownership became more concentrated. The number of private stockholders shrank from 923 in 1859 to 832 in 1865 and to 765 in 1870.[35] By the same token, the average holding increased from 10.8 to 12.0 to 13.1 shares. The number of shares held in blocks of 100 or more grew from 2,307 to 3,023 to 3,595. By 1870 a majority were held in blocks of at least 50.

At the same time there was substantial continuity in stock ownership. Nearly half (47.5 percent) of the shares held in 1870 were in the hands of the same persons who had owned them in 1859, and that figure understates the case. Most of the early construction partnerships had dissolved by 1870, but a large proportion of their shares were now held by the former partners as individuals—men such as the McRaes and John I. Shaver. Many shares were owned by widows, children, and other heirs of 1859 holders. The number of shares represented in the annual meetings from 1853 to 1870 varied from 9,197 to 5,094; the average was 7,210. There was no consistent trend upward or downward.

Although the state's holdings dwarfed those of the private stockholders once it made its subscription in 1853, the larger private shareholders attained considerable influence in company affairs, both in the stockholders' meetings and through election to the board of directors. That influence was only slightly diminished by public control, given the state's passive role.

Directors served one-year terms and met at least quarterly. Originally these gatherings, like the annual stockholders' meetings, rotated among the major towns along the road. But in 1859 and later, board meetings were usually held in the new offices at Company Shops.[36] Five members, including the president, constituted a quorum until 1858, when the number was raised to seven, a majority. They received no pay except traveling expenses of ten cents per mile to attend meetings.[37] The four private directors were elected by ballot during the July stockholders' meeting; the eight state directors were appointed by the governor in advance of that meeting.

The elections were sometimes hotly contested after 1853, when the number of private directors dropped from twelve. Coalition tickets seem to have formed in some years.[38] These contests were only scantily reported in the press. Even less appeared in the road's *Annual Reports*, which seldom gave more than the vote totals and not always those. As a result, understanding of the issues involved (if any) did not often survive the place and time.

With the advent of state directors in 1853, both they and the private directors continued to be selected with a partial eye to geographical distribution. New Bern soon transferred its affections to the A&NC and was dropped from the NCRR board. But Wilmington and vicinity held both a private and a state directorship almost every year into the war. General Alexander McRae, a partner in John C. McRae and Company and recently president of the Wilmington and Weldon Railroad, was a private director for seven of the years from 1855 to 1863; John D. Bellamy of Wilmington was a state director during all eight years. That region was seldom represented after 1863, however. Forsyth County also had a private director during the road's first eight years; for seven of them it was Francis Fries. Philemon D. Hawkins of Franklin County served eight years as a state director during the 1850s and early 1860s.

The remaining board members were distributed more or less evenly along the NCRR's route. Private directors were apt to own substantial amounts of stock, but not always. Dolphin A. Davis of Salisbury compiled the longest tenure on the board before 1871: nine years as a private director (1851–54 and 1865–71) and two years during the war as a state director. He never owned more than 34 shares in these years and usually about 20. His fellow townsman John I. Shaver, who alternated with him (usually as a state director), was by contrast one of the largest stockholders, with 503 shares in 1870. So were Alexander McRae, John Motley Morehead (at first), and his son John L. Morehead. (See table 4.)

State directors, appointed by the governor, were less likely than private directors to own large amounts of stock, although several did. In fact, ten of the seventy-eight board members between 1850 and 1871 served at different times in both capacities. A number of state directors owned only the legal minimum of five shares, and in a few cases less than that requirement before it was instituted in 1855. Four of five state directors replaced by Governor Thomas Bragg that year owned less than the new minimum.[39] Governor William W. Holden seems to have suspended the requirement temporarily in 1865; there is no record of his appointee William A. Smith owning any stock at all during his first two years on the board. Later, as president of the road, Smith acquired seventy-three shares by 1872.

Many directors, public and private, were chosen because they had evidenced an interest in the road as stockholders, legislators, or as promoters during the subscription campaign. Men with proven business talents were sought and were kept on by stockholders or governors for years at a time. The tendency of public and private members to form a common front reflects the absence of any clear distinction between them. State directors were seldom chosen entirely for political reasons. Paul C. Cameron, a state director during eight of his ten years on the board, was perhaps the wealthiest man and largest slaveholder in the state. He was known more as a shrewd planter and businessman than as a political figure. At the same time, among the private directors elected by their fellow stockholders, John Motley Morehead and Romulus M. Saunders had been rival gubernatorial candidates in 1840 and remained politically active for many years after.

The board of directors chose the officers of the road. Only a president, secretary, and treasurer were stipulated in the charter and bylaws; others were added as needed. Directors elected the president annually from their own membership. Former Governor Morehead, chairman of the commissioners who conducted the stock-subscription campaign, was the logical choice as president in 1850. After five years he retired, to be replaced by Charles F. Fisher of Salisbury, who served until 1861.

On most roads the secretary was, in effect, clerk to the board of directors and keeper of the records. The treasurer, of course, collected and disbursed company funds.[40] The NCRR combined the two positions until 1856. Jeduthun H. Lindsay of Greensboro was the first secretary-treasurer in 1850, soon being succeeded by Cyrus P. Mendenhall, also of Greensboro, who continued as treasurer until 1859. Peter Brown Ruffin (a son of Judge Thomas Ruffin) took his place, serving throughout the war. When the two offices were separated, the treasurer was the official in charge of the accounts; the secretary was little more than a bookkeeper.[41] Julius D. Ramsey and R. W. Mills each served briefly as secretary before the war.[42]

Company headquarters were maintained in Greensboro as long as Morehead was president. Fisher ordinarily conducted the road's business in Salisbury, his home, although he seems to have traveled frequently to the new offices at Company Shops after 1857. Soon all officers except the president were required to live there.[43] In 1859 Fisher noted the difficulty of hiring a satisfactory treasurer to succeed Mendenhall, given the small salary ($1,500 or less) and the difficulty of a family man finding a suitable place to live in Company Shops.[44]

Neither Morehead nor Fisher was much interested in organizational structure or in pioneering in the field of business management. The subjects get very little attention in their annual reports. In 1854–55, when train service began amidst continuing construction work, no clear line was drawn between officers in the two lines of activity. Chief Engineer Walter Gwynn doubled as superintendent in charge of operations. Subject to the board of directors, he developed the first rate schedules, for instance, with their implications for relations with other roads and the general public. After 1856 President Fisher performed most of the superintendent's duties, despite a willingness by the directors to fill the position.[45]

By 1855, with train service underway, a master mechanic (or master of machinery) was appointed to take charge of the rolling stock. This position went to the New Englander Thomas E. Roberts, who held it until 1860. With the road's completion early in 1856, a road master was chosen to be in charge of track and roadbed maintenance. Thomas J. Sumner, the first road master, soon left and was replaced by James E. Allen. A general transportation agent, in charge of the clerical aspects of passenger and freight operations, also appeared in 1854 or 1855.[46]

President Fisher presided over a substantial administrative reorganization between 1858 and 1860. A clearer managerial hierarchy emerged with the creation by 1859 of separate road, machinery, and transportation departments—roughly in line with developments a few years earlier on the Erie, the Baltimore and Ohio, and other railroads. (Some of the more sophisticated reforms on other roads were dependent on telegraphic communication between regional and central officers, an impossibility on the NCRR before 1862.)[47] There was also a significant turnover in managerial personnel.

In 1860 James Allen resigned, to be replaced as head of the road department by two division masters, each responsible for half of the road, east and west of the shops. The machinery department remained under the master mechanic, but Thomas E. Roberts gave way in 1860 to E. H. Marsh, a locomotive engineer promoted from the ranks.[48] In 1859 Edmund Wilkes became head of the transportation department, as general transportation agent. Presumably subordinate to him were newly instituted freight and ticket (passenger) clerks. These seem to have been watered-down versions of the general freight and general ticket agents instituted by Daniel C. McCallum on the Erie by 1856.[49] Wilkes was both capable and experienced, and Fisher gradually delegated to him many of the operational responsibilities he had carried since Superintendent Theodore Garnett's departure in 1856.[50] In 1861 Wilkes formally became superintendent.

Fisher reported in 1860 that "the System of the Road ... has been adopted after careful examination of the manner of working the best Roads in the Country—we have introduced whatever was deemed to be of value, wherever found, and have made such changes as were applicable to the latitude and people."[51] His actions were likely triggered by the severe criticism he received from a legislative investigating committee under Jonathan Worth in 1859. That investigation clearly produced a conflict between Fisher and Treasurer Mendenhall, causing the latter's resignation. It probably also induced payment of the first dividend that year. In general, the reorganization improved record keeping and seems to have increased managerial efficiency as a whole.

NCRR salaries were below the national average. Railway presidents of the 1850s typically received $3,000 to $6,000 per year, while superintendents were often paid almost as much.[52] Until the war, the NCRR president received $2,500 a year plus traveling expenses—exactly half the salary of Chief Engineer Walter Gwynn before his resignation early in 1856. At $2,500, the salary of Gwynn's successor, Garnett, equaled that of the president during Garnett's short tenure as superintendent. So did the master mechanic's. Road Master Allen earned $1,500 in 1856, and Treasurer Mendenhall received $1,250.[53] Although NCRR salaries lay near the bottom of the national range, many stockholders thought they were exorbitant. In 1855 they voted a reduction "to the lowest figure that will enable [the road] to retain or secure . . . efficient and competent men, especially in the engineering department."[54] The board probably believed that it had already reached that point, and there was no general reduction.

State control, however lightly exercised, carried undeniable political ramifications. Governor David S. Reid, a Democrat first elected in 1850, had opposed the NCRR charter the previous year. As governor, however, he supported the road and the state's interest in it.[55] That support did not preclude a measure of Democratic partisanship in his railroad appointments, which began in 1853. John W. Ellis, his would-be state proxy, was a Democrat, as were six of his eight appointees as state directors; next year he eliminated the two Whigs. Opposition newspapers criticized the appointees in both years, partly for being young and inexperienced and partly for the political basis of their selection. Democrats replied that the stockholders had also acted politically by electing four Whigs and no Democrats as private directors.[56]

In 1855 Reid's Democratic successor, Thomas Bragg, appointed a largely new slate of seven Democrats and one Whig. Most of these men were reappointed throughout Bragg's four years in office and were continued by the ensuing Democratic Governors John W. Ellis and Henry T. Clark until 1863. Reportedly, only one state director was turned out involuntarily during these years: Robert P. Dick, allegedly for his indiscretion in supporting Stephen A. Douglas over John C. Breckinridge for the presidency in 1860.[57]

The effect of the Bragg, Ellis, and Clark policy was to enhance the degree of experience and continuity on the board. In fact, the state directors

served almost twice as long on average as did the private members during
the eight years from 1855 to 1863—5.8 years as against 3.2 years.

Less effort was made to provide continuity in the office of state proxy,
which usually required service only during the annual stockholders' meeting and which was deliberately kept inactive in these years. Political affiliation was so unimportant in this position that two of the four proxies appointed by Governors Ellis and Clark were Whigs.[58]

Ordinarily, partisan affiliation played little part in stockholders' balloting
for directors, in the directors' voting for president, or in the everyday
management of the road. There was some talk that the proposed charter
amendments voted on in 1853 and 1854, including a scale of voting in
stockholder meetings, would diminish not only the power of the state and
the larger private stockholders but that of Democratic shareholders as well.
However that might have been, the preponderantly Whig stockholders defeated the measures in both years.[59]

In 1853, with the advent of state directors, there was a concerted effort to
replace Morehead, a Whig, with his old gubernatorial rival Judge Romulus
Saunders, a Democrat. This action was politically motivated in part, but it
also arose from personal and management differences. Some stockholders
charged Morehead with arbitrariness and a failure to report his activities
and expenditures adequately. William W. Holden's Raleigh *Standard*, among
others, accused him of extravagance in the failure to buy rails more cheaply
and in construction cost overruns generally. Some contractors, on the other
hand, especially John C. McRae and Company at the eastern end of the
line, blamed him for not paying them more for their work. Wilmington
interests charged him with partiality toward Virginia (he was a constant
advocate of the Danville Connection) and toward Beaufort (whither he was
preparing to help build the Atlantic and North Carolina Railroad and its
terminus of Morehead City).[60]

When the stockholders voted for the four private directors, Morehead
came in fourth and was the only winning candidate requiring a second
ballot. And when the new board (now equally divided politically with the
seating of the state directors) met to choose a president, Morehead was
reelected only after several ballots.[61] Among those voting against him was
the McRae company with its 885 votes.[62] The scene was repeated in 1854,
when Francis Fries was the chosen rival. Morehead barely secured the
fourth directorship by a margin of 10 votes out of 8,202 votes cast. The
board that elected him to a fifth term that year consisted of nine Democrats
and three Whigs. Newspapers on both sides were at a loss to explain his
survival; obviously party politics was not the controlling influence.[63]

Not surprisingly, Morehead chose to step down in 1855. Apart from the
criticisms and his other business interests, he was burdened by the strain of
building the road with inadequate funds. He wrote William A. Graham in
March, before the additional state aid had become available, that the road's

funds were entirely spent. Bills were unpaid and banks refused to extend short-term credit. "I have resorted to every expedient in my power to keep going this long. I am now out of expedients, and my financial tact is exhausted." Six weeks later, despite the renewal of state aid, he added, "I am worried out of my life, almost, with the Rail Road, and am determined to quit the Presidency." He did not mention partisan politics as he referred to "malcontents" who had combined against him, and his second choice as a successor (after Graham) was the Democrat Calvin Graves.[64] In addition, Morehead had new interests to pursue. A month after leaving the presidency, he took a construction contract for twenty-six miles of the new Atlantic and North Carolina Railroad just as that road decided to locate its eastern terminus at his well-placed real estate development, the future Morehead City.[65]

As it turned out, Morehead's friends and enemies all united behind a different Democrat to succeed him. Charles F. Fisher was a proven friend of the road as a state director during the previous two years and more recently as a state senator. Born in 1826, he was the only son of Charles Fisher, a tireless supporter (with Morehead) of internal improvements in legislatures gone by, despite their party differences. When the elder Fisher died in 1849, his son managed his extensive properties and edited the Democratic Salisbury *Western Carolinian* before winning election to the state senate, his first office, in 1854. Despite his lack of seniority, Fisher served as chairman of the committee on internal improvements and piloted the charter amendments of 1855 to passage. It was probably to enhance his eligibility as president that Fisher agreed to seek election as a private director in 1855 rather than accept reappointment as a state director. When the balloting took place, a large majority of the stockholders, including Morehead, voted for Fisher. The board then elected him president unanimously.[66]

9

Management and Finance:
Fisher

DESPITE THE EVIDENCE of internal unity manifested in Fisher's election, his administration was to suffer even greater criticism than had Morehead's, most of it partisan. The road provided a larger target once it commenced full operations early in 1856. Hardly had that year's political campaign opened when the Whig/Americans, led by their gubernatorial candidate John A. Gilmer, began accusing Governor Bragg of using the road as a patronage machine. (They referred primarily to his appointment of directors; almost no one before the war suggested that railroad employees were hired or fired for political reasons.)[1]

No aspect of the road's operation or management seems to have escaped criticism. The mounting construction costs continued to alarm some people, as did the means employed to finance them. Actually, Fisher's management was competent, although he was guilty of spreading himself too thin. Office and management personnel were held at Spartan levels both in numbers and pay in the interest of economy. As a result, details were overlooked, and the operation was neither as efficient nor probably as economical as it might have been. Had he appointed a superintendent, he might have escaped the charge that he let thousands of dollars' worth of unused iron rails and crossties lie scattered along the road, exposed to the elements.[2] (Whatever the facts in this case, the accuser, the *Greensboro Patriot*, was capable of politically misrepresenting what might have been a foresighted policy of stockpiling and strategic distribution as one of utter waste and abandon.) Fisher was accused of arbitrary behavior, of intimidating the board of directors and stockholders, of incompetence, and, less often, of fraud.[3]

Unquestionably, Fisher invited conflict-of-interest charges by becoming a major construction contractor on the Western North Carolina Railroad. State Senator Jonathan Worth accused him of getting the NCRR to ship WNCRR construction materials at below cost in order to enrich himself as a contractor and of getting the NCRR shops to do work for the WNCRR without accounting for it properly.[4] Fisher replied that the NCRR carried construction materials for the WNCRR at cost, just as other roads had previously done for the NCRR. The shops, he said, did only emergency work for the WNCRR and charged top prices.[5] He defended his role as a contractor on the WNCRR by saying that no one else would take up the contract, thereby threatening to prevent the construction of that road, which was considered vitally important to Salisbury, western North Carolina, and the NCRR.[6]

For several years, controversy swirled around the Company Shops complex, which was not completed until early in 1859. Here, too, the *Greensboro Patriot* led the hue and cry against Fisher. In the first place, it resented the site chosen for the shops, having strongly favored Greensboro. Secondly, it believed the costs were "shameful and ruinous," not only in the construction but in subsequent operation.[7] The project of course originated with the Morehead administration. But as Morehead was a fellow Whig and Greensboro's most distinguished citizen, the *Patriot* restrained its criticism of the road's management until after 1855.

Fisher had supported the project as a director, and he continued to do so as president, even expanding the original plans to include the hotel and an additional officer's house. He consistently defended the shops and the village around them, insisting that they were vital to the road's prosperity if not its very existence.[8] On this issue as most others, Fisher enjoyed the support of a majority of the directors and stockholders, which led in turn to the false charge that he intimidated them. From Fisher's own perspective, as he told his confidant Paul C. Cameron in 1857, some directors (specifically Alexander McRae) were caving in to the clamor against the shops.[9] There was some talk in the piedmont that a malign "McRae-Wilmington policy" was at work to orient NCRR policy toward that port and the east generally.[10] The charges were notably lacking in corroboration, especially after the NCRR's abandonment of its exclusive traffic alliance with the W&W in 1856. McRae declined reelection in 1857 and was replaced on the board by Ralph Gorrell of Greensboro.[11]

To friends and critics alike, the basic issue was profit and loss. Accounting practices in the 1850s did not recognize depreciation. Seldom was money set aside before the calculation of profit to pay for normal wear and tear. As a result, profits were exaggerated and dividends (when declared) were paid partly from the original capital. To have done otherwise would have required lessening reported profits when they were already too low in the stockholders' eyes. Railroad officials were eager to maximize rather than minimize their profit statements. They hoped and, to some extent, believed that repair and replacement could be paid for out of earnings when necessary. This was a particularly appealing idea in the first years of operation, when revenues were unsteady and little repair or replacement was necessary. A few railroad authorities like Henry V. Poor advocated the routine setting aside of a depreciation fund, and a few railroads did so. But most did not, and the NCRR was with the majority.[12]

Within that context the NCRR's performance bore favorable comparison with other roads of similar age. Both passenger and freight receipts rose in each year of Fisher's administration. In fact, annual earnings as well as profits almost doubled during the years 1855 to 1861: earnings rose from $230,301 to $434,957, and profits (earnings less operating expenses) increased from $122,092 to $234,167. The operating ratio (expenses as a percentage of receipts) was between 45 and 47. (See table 11.) The Pennsylvania Railroad, with profits ten times greater, had a less favorable ratio of about 50 percent, which was average for a well-run railway of that period. The figures for contemporaneous Virginia railroads ranged from 30 to 76 percent, with the average about 48.[13] The NCRR's rate of return on its capital investment in 1859–60 (the last prewar year for which the necessary data were reported) was 4.8 percent.[14]

These favorable statistics did not automatically translate into stockholders' dividends. They seldom did on any new railroad, as John B. Jervis pointed out at the time.[15] It was a rare road that could be built out of its stock subscriptions alone. Most roads had a bonded debt that equaled or exceeded the amount of stock. The holders of that debt ordinarily had a prior claim on the road's operating surplus, hence the right to receive payment before stockholders received any dividends.[16]

In the case of the NCRR, the bonded debt in 1855 ($3 million) amounted to three-quarters of the amount of stock, but it was an obligation of the state rather than the railroad directly, issued by the state to finance its stock subscription. The road had other debts, however. Like most railroads, it cost more to build and equip than had been predicted. The capitalization, as increased in 1855, was $4 million; the total cost of construction as reported in 1859 came to slightly over $4,900,000. Operating revenues were not large enough to cover all of these bills as they came due.

Fisher's first expedient (like Morehead's) was to make short-term loans from local banks. They charged up to 12 percent interest, however, which he (and his critics) regarded as extortionate. To escape the banks, spread the payments over a longer period, and also to finance about $80,000 worth of new rolling stock, the stockholders decided in 1856 to borrow money elsewhere, this time in the form of a $350,000 bond issue maturing in ten years.[17]

As originally issued, the NCRR bonds bore 6 percent interest, but the company found no buyers at that figure. So the board once more approached the legislature, this time asking permission either to raise the interest rate or to have the state endorse the bonds and, in either event, to exempt them from taxation.[18] The enabling bill almost failed to pass the House as members condemned the road's management for requiring a third bailout. But a thin majority acceded after NCRR lobbyists virtually promised that the bond income would enable the road to pay the state a 6 percent dividend on its $1 million of preferred stock in 1857. (That promise was not kept.)[19] As passed in February 1857, the act exempted the bonds from taxation and permitted an interest rate of up to 8 percent.[20]

The NCRR promptly sold the bonds at 8 percent, several of them at a premium over face value. The new bondholders, seventy-one in all, were mostly if not entirely North Carolinians. A number were stockholders, even directors and officers of the road—not Fisher, however. The three largest individual holders were bankers George W. Mordecai, Charles Dewey, and Cyrus P. Mendenhall (the NCRR treasurer).[21] The legislature required that the road create a sinking fund to provide for the debt's retirement at maturity in 1867. It did so, mandating the appropriation of $25,000 annually.[22]

The bond issue still left something over $550,000 in debts, which fell due over several years' time and were paid out of earnings. That process was nearly finished by July 1859, although unanticipated bills continued to appear for years.[23] This fact suggested another well-founded criticism: the NCRR accounting system and the reports based on it were chronically deficient.

Railroads, as the nation's first big business, pioneered in the accumulation of data and the development of new accounting methods to measure financial performance. The Erie and the Pennsylvania railroads in particular, under Daniel McCallum and J. Edgar Thomson, were in the vanguard. They required the monthly (in some cases daily) tabulation of operational and financial data that in turn served as the basis of annual reports. Managers were guided by this information on a continuing basis. By the mid-1850s the Pennsylvania's annual reports showed for each month the number of passengers departing from each station, the tonnage of local and through freight shipped from each station, and statistics relative to more than 200 major kinds of freight. To process and analyze this data, the Pennsylvania and other leading railroads developed large accounting departments; by 1860, according to Alfred D. Chandler, they probably employed more accountants and auditors than the federal or any state government.[24]

Most railroads failed to match these standards of both collecting and reporting. As Henry V. Poor put it in 1858, the great majority were so new and their managers so inexperienced that railway reports were lamentably incomplete or inaccurate; they tended to contain what the managers believed to be interesting and important and, at the same time, what reflected favorably on themselves. James M. Whiton in his 1856 treatise on railroad management concluded that most reports were of little or no practical value. In consequence, "a great part of the experience of the last twenty years may now be regarded as irretrievably lost."[25] The *American Railway Times* also pointed to a general lack of systematic and digested information in railroad reports. Of forty railroads the *Times* observed in 1863, no more than a dozen kept track of the ton miles of freight they carried. Less than half knew their maximum track gradient.[26]

Writers on railway matters repeatedly urged reform. This was particularly true of Henry V. Poor: "A short table of figures, exhibiting a company's affairs in a clear and intelligible light, is better than the longest and most eloquent exposition of the peculiar merits of its road, or the wonderful amount of business which it is destined to do next year, but which unavoidable circumstances prevented it from accomplishing last year."[27] Expense records were especially open to abuse, intentional or otherwise. The annual report, said Poor, should specify for each year the quantity and cost of rails installed, the total number of ties on the road and the number replaced, and provide equally explicit statements regarding machinery, bridges, and every perishable structure so as to show the value of the property and its management. Inadequate reports, he observed, either reflected bad management or caused it.[28] John B. Jervis argued that the most important statistics were those showing the working expenses in each department and the net cost of each kind of traffic. Too many roads failed to determine what kinds of business were profitable or unprofitable, perhaps in a well-intended effort to save clerk hire. As a result they had only general impressions to guide them in deciding what kinds of traffic to carry and what rates to charge. A zeal for business is commendable, Jervis observed, but it should never be pursued at a loss. Any money devoted to clerk hire for this purpose was money well spent.[29]

Again, the NCRR was a child of its age. Its records got better—or fuller, at least—during the 1850s and 1860s, but there was a lack of consistency throughout the period. In keeping with Jervis's observation, NCRR receipts were reported much more fully than expenses. Receipts were reported for each branch of service (passenger and freight) by month and by station. They were often broken down further into through and local traffic, eastbound and westbound. Passenger departures and receipts as well as freight receipts were reported by station nearly every year. But expenses were given only by year and by broad category (locomotives, bridges, rails, etc.) without distinguishing between branches of service. The annual mileage and maintenance costs of each locomotive were given. But little effort was made (or at least reported) to calculate operating receipts or costs per mile overall, much less separately for passenger and freight trains. Fisher usually pointed to overall receipts and their ratio to overall costs. Only occasionally was information reported as to the kinds and quantities of freight shipped, its points of origin, and the directions in which it was sent.[30]

As early as 1852 the stockholders' finance committee pointed out Treasurer Cyrus P. Mendenhall's occasional practice of making large payments without the president's warrant and apparently in his absence. Mendenhall lived and worked in Greensboro while Fisher spent most of his time in Salisbury. Given that eccentric arrangement, Mendenhall may have had little choice if the bills were to be paid on time. At any rate, no one objected very much, the funds were properly directed, and the practice continued.[31]

The most persistent and embarrassing problems were the construction bills that kept popping up for payment, without warning, for years after the materials or services had been rendered. This lasted throughout the road's history of independent operation. Apparently fraud was not involved; record keeping was so loose that liabilities were not always recorded at the time contracts were made. As a result, the road never knew about all of its outstanding debts—a subject of perennial surprise and criticism.[32]

The stockholders' finance committee for some reason suppressed its discontent at these conditions until 1858. Only then did it publicly note "the entire want of system in keeping the Books of the Company. . . . Bookkeeping [the committee said] has been long ago reduced to a perfect system, simple and easy to be understood, and there is nothing in the principle of keeping the books of this corporation, which varies from that of . . . any well regulated mercantile establishment." But as a result of inadequate books, the committee had never been able to determine the company's exact debt. "This state of things ought no longer to exist," it concluded, recommending an increase in the office force.[33]

The responsibility for inadequate records was shared in some measure by all the officials in charge. President Fisher, it may be repeated, was not obsessed with managerial efficiency, else he would have required (among other things) that all company offices be located in one place. He seems to have kept the position of secretary (or bookkeeper) unfilled for a couple of years after 1856 in the interest of economy. Treasurer Mendenhall was apparently in charge of the books in that period, until the castigation by the finance committee. At that point R. W. Mills was hired as secretary to clean up the mess. He painstakingly recast the books back to 1850 in what Fisher claimed was proper form.[34]

The relationship between Fisher and Mendenhall, once cordial enough, came to an abrupt end in February 1859. In seeking to defend himself against a barrage of accusations by the Worth committee, Fisher wrote a public letter that incidentally imputed a measure of disloyalty to Mendenhall and described Mills's assignment in terms that reflected on the treasurer's competence. Mendenhall replied with a public statement questioning Fisher's veracity.[35] As the *Winston Sentinel* remarked concerning Fisher, "self-possession and mildness of temper, under exciting circumstances, are certainly not the chief charms in his excellent character."[36] Under fire by a legislative committee for incompetence if not dishonesty, Fisher lashed out angrily at all his attackers, not the least of them this subordinate officer whom he now regarded as deserting to the enemy for political favor. Blaming Mendenhall for the bookkeeping errors that had "caused so much abuse and trouble, and censure to all of us," he promised satisfaction on the field of honor should the treasurer seek it. Of course the Quaker-bred

Mendenhall did not seek it, instead terminating the correspondence as well as his employment.[37]

In July 1859 both the board of directors and the finance committee (composed of the same persons as a year earlier) noted a great improvement in the books, presumably extending back beyond Mendenhall's resignation. Moreover, the committee risked Fisher's anger by paying tribute to "the honesty, integrity, and correctness" with which Mendenhall had kept his accounts.[38] Perhaps these remarks sprang from considerations of policy or gentility; it is hard to reconcile them with all the complaints of slovenly bookkeeping and reporting that would persist for years.

It was inevitable that some of the stock subscribers of 1849–50 would fail to make the scheduled payments. Even before the final installment fell due on 1 May 1854, the road began selling the stock of delinquent subscribers in order to raise the money necessary to secure the state's continuing subscription. The shares were sold at a series of public auctions from Goldsboro to Salisbury during February 1854. Several of the delinquents had subscribed up to eighty shares apiece, but most were owners of less than five.[39] The prices received were well below the $100-per-share par value, ranging from an average of $32.50 at Raleigh to $51 at Salisbury.[40] In January 1856, when another block of forfeited stock went on sale, it brought an average of $48.[41]

These prices reflected, at least in part, pessimism regarding the likelihood and amount of any dividend return on the investment. Criticism of management on this score mounted after the road's completion in 1856, when the price continued to fall. NCRR shares were never publicly traded outside the state or quoted on any stock exchange. Except for the blocks already referred to, they were usually sold in small amounts, privately and (before the war) without published prices. Critics of the Fisher administration charged that the price had fallen to as low as $12 by the end of 1858. In July 1860 there was still an unpaid balance of $27,561.35 on the original stock issue.[42] Given the low price at which it could sell these shares, the NCRR eventually decided to retain them in its own name. In 1863, the first year in which the road appeared as one of its own stockholders, it owned 213 shares.

Fisher was never allowed to forget that the NCRR was a public enterprise, subject to the same political pressures that governed the state, its largest stockholder. Whig criticism persisted. The *Greensboro Patriot* in particular attacked the road and its management throughout his administration—all in terms reminiscent of the Democratic attacks on Morehead. By the same token, Democratic papers regularly came to Fisher's defense. The *Patriot* claimed in November 1857 that no one knew the extent of the NCRR debt, that the twelve directors were as ignorant of its financial condition as they were of the railroads of New York, and that they all yielded quietly to Fisher, who was incompetent. Some of these attacks were petty and obviously partisan; others, particularly on the road's accounting system, were close to the mark. Whigs soon focused on the road's failure to pay dividends before 1859 as well as on the fall in the price of its stock.[43]

At the annual meetings in 1857 and 1858, State Proxy Thomas Ruffin, apparently on his own volition, formally requested that the state be paid a 6 percent dividend on its $1 million of preferred stock. In both years the directors (including state directors) refused, arguing that outstanding debts had to be paid first.[44]

Reports circulated before the 1857 annual meeting that Fisher intended to step down as president.[45] Next year he himself indicated that desire but declined to do so for fear that he would appear to be surrendering to his critics.[46] Although the turnout was low that year, some stockholders reportedly made an effort to replace him with Francis Fries.[47] As it turned out, Fisher was reelected to the board by a much smaller margin than previously, and Fries was narrowly defeated for reelection, thereby ending his presidential hopes. In the previous three years the two men had run a strong first and second, respectively, among the four private directors. Fisher seems to have had no trouble in getting reelected president by the board in either year.

When the legislature assembled in November 1858, two measures were introduced that bore directly and importantly on the NCRR: a bill to permit the private stockholders to elect seven of the twelve directors, and a resolution to investigate the road and its management. Proponents of the bill blamed state control for the road's failure to pay a dividend. Management, said Senators Jonathan Worth, Josiah Turner, and Ralph Gorrell (Whigs all), should be left to those who were personally interested. Turner, in one of those flights of rhetorical excess for which he would become famous after the war, "denied that politicians were the right sort of men to manage public works—they did not get up early enough in the morning." The bill's opponents, mostly Democrats, defended the Fisher administration and argued that it would be unfair to the state and its investment in the road to diminish its share of control. The measure was killed by the Senate on 4 January 1859 by a margin of one vote.[48] Fisher claimed to take no public position on the bill, but he made it a point to tell senators that there had never been any conflict between state and private directors, that Morehead and he had both been chosen from the private sector, and that the road, in effect, had remained in private hands.[49]

While this bill was pending, Ephraim Mauney, a pioneer miner at Gold Hill, near Salisbury, and now a leading figure in that industry and community in their heyday, asked the legislature for permission to lease the NCRR for five years at $120,000 per year. A disgruntled shipper as well as a stockholder, Mauney promised to operate the road more efficiently, to lower freight rates, and to pay a small dividend. Nothing came of his request, but it reinforced the attacks being made on Fisher's management and seemingly justified the legislative investigation then underway.[50]

That inquiry was spearheaded by Whig Senator Jonathan Worth of Randolph County, who (in striking contrast with modern practice) became chairman of the joint Senate and House committee despite a heavy Democratic majority in both houses. His one Whig and three Democratic colleagues played a subordinate part in the investigation and in preparing the final report. Worth's chairmanship no doubt resulted from his authorship of the enabling resolution. That initiative ostensibly arose from his concern as a member of the finance committee that the state was receiving no income from the NCRR three years after its completion.[51] (Although the resolution ultimately included all railroads in which the state owned an interest, in practice the inquiry was limited almost entirely to the NCRR.) In his proceedings Worth echoed the partisan attacks on the Fisher administration that had filled the pages of the *Greensboro Patriot* and other Whig papers since 1856. Whigs welcomed the investigation while Democrats tended to decry it.[52] The investigation took place in January 1859, with the report appearing early in February.

The right of a legislature to investigate a business corporation, even one in which the state owned stock, was by no means universally conceded at this time. The *Tarboro Mercury* in 1860 published a learned argument denying any such right. If a railway were thought to be violating the law, the remedy was for the attorney general to bring suit against it in the courts. The only two North Carolina laws binding upon the NCRR stockholders, wrote the correspondent, were the charter of 1849 and the amendments of 1855; neither authorized a legislative investigation. Thus the stockholders' charter or property rights prevailed over any generalized notion of a public interest. In fact, the writer concluded, it was the governor who was charged with the state's interest in the NCRR, and his appointed directors and proxy were the proper officials to safeguard the state's interest, short of a lawsuit.[53]

Worth conceded at the outset that there was no authorization in the charter for a legislative investigation, but the state's majority ownership made it a legitimate undertaking. Fisher agreed with this as a matter of policy and publicly welcomed the enquiry while lashing out against it privately.[54] His cooperation was unenthusiastic, to say the least.[55]

Along with Treasurer Mendenhall and Secretary Mills, Fisher appeared before the committee in Raleigh but was promptly excused to attend his duties as president. These turned out to include the preparation of a lengthy special report to Governor Bragg (not requested by him) justifying Fisher's policies and especially the failure so far to declare a dividend.[56] Fisher required that Mills attend him in Salisbury with some of the company books as he prepared this report, keeping that officer and the books away from the committee for a week. Mendenhall remained, however, with other records and a much greater knowledge of the company's affairs. His testimony and cooperation with the committee were to cause his breach with the president. Personal relations between Fisher and Worth deteriorated even sooner, the president privately characterizing the chairman as a "miserable rascal."[57] The two men were singularly alike in their readiness to criticize others and in their inability to accept criticism gracefully themselves. In Worth's case particularly, there was a formidable strain of self-righteousness as well.[58]

Even with full and cordial cooperation, the committee would have lacked time for a thorough investigation before the legislature's scheduled adjournment. As it was, the inquiry was hasty, superficial, and partisan. It found nothing at all to praise in Fisher's management. Worth probably never intended an objective examination; he found no subject too trivial to take up if it promised to embarrass Fisher and the Democrats. He conspicuously avoided criticism of Fisher's Whig predecessor even when the logic of his position seemed to demand it, as in his attack on the Company Shops complex and the settlement of the McRae construction contract. His report, accusing the Fisher administration of extravagance and general mismanagement, was largely an elaboration of charges ventilated by the *Greensboro Patriot* and other Whig journals in the past three or four years. Worth even told the *Patriot*'s proprietors that they were "entitled to the thanks of the State" for their longstanding opposition to "the little president." The report was so satisfactory in a political sense, he boasted after its release, "that a purse has been made up to print a large number of extra copies."[59]

The biggest surprise is the acquiescence to the report by two of the three Democratic committee members. The one dissenter did not address its substance but objected that there had been too little time to permit a thorough or fair investigation.[60]

Fisher took the report as a politically inspired personal attack. Hypersensitive to a fault, he seems not to have challenged Worth to a duel only because of the certainty of a refusal. Instead he penned a blistering reply combining factual refutation with biting ad hominem attacks on Worth. Some of the committee's "objections, complaints, and observations," he concluded at one point, "are so manifestly in a spirit of captious faultfinding, that I let them pass for what they are—worth."[61] Fisher addressed his reply to Senate Speaker Henry T. Clark. When Clark started to read it aloud in the Senate chamber, Whigs protested vociferously, causing pandemonium in the chamber and forcing a suspension of the reading.[62] Fisher now leveled his guns at the Senate itself—including some "Democratic knaves"— for its refusal to give him a hearing. His reply evoked a rejoinder from Worth, and an acrimonious newspaper exchange followed for more than a year featuring further charges and countercharges.[63]

Taken as a whole, the more important accusations and responses may be reduced to several categories:[64]

1. The committee accused Fisher and other directors in 1855 (during the Morehead administration) of overpaying John C. McRae and Company $6,643 (about 1 percent of its contract) for the construction work on the

eastern end of the road. Fisher's purpose (Worth later added) was to enlist that company's 885 stock votes in an effort to replace Morehead as president. Fisher and McRae both denied this, the latter pointing out that he had already voted against Morehead in 1852, 1853, and 1854 without any such inducement. As Fisher recalled, he was chosen president in 1855 with no opposition and did not need the McRae votes. Later, when he could have used them, they were cast against him because of his criticism of the quality of the McRaes' construction work. No substantiation was ever provided for Worth's corruption charge, and he eventually receded from it.[65]

2. The Fisher administration was charged with recklessly squandering money on the shops complex, and more especially on the residences and other buildings nearby that were not directly involved in railway maintenance. This echoed the charges from Greensboro, where there was continuing resentment at being passed by in favor of building a brand new town in the "wild woods." Although the committee acknowledged the necessity of the shops themselves, Fisher championed the company town surrounding them as well. He pointed out that both the idea and the locale had been chosen by the preceding administration.[66]

3. The committee found fault with the NCRR board's fixing an 8 percent interest rate on its 1857 bond issue without first consulting the stockholders, who had previously stipulated a 6 percent limit. As explained above, when the board found that bonds could not be sold at 6 percent, it went to the legislature for a tax exemption on the bonds and either a state endorsement of them or an 8 percent interest limit. The endorsement and the tax exemption lay exclusively in the power of the legislature; the offense in not going back to the stockholders for the 8 percent authorization was relatively venial.[67]

4. Management was charged with accumulating too much wood fuel along the road, thereby wasting money and risking losses from fire and decay. Fisher attributed the surplus to the preceding Morehead administration, but the committee produced evidence that his own regime had contracted for about 40,000 cords since 1855. About $50,000 was involved, and nearly all of the remaining wood was still usable, according to Fisher.[68]

5. Fisher was accused of paying for an unnecessary water tank and other work at Haw River at a cost of $2,000. Fisher replied that this tank was the locomotives' chief water supply for twenty miles of road during dry weather.[69] Still more water facilities had to be built in that vicinity during the war.

6. The committee criticized Fisher's introduction of a fast express train in March 1857, arguing that its benefits failed to equal its cost, including the damage it did to the track and roadbed. Fisher replied that running two daily trains, including the express train, was the only way to accommodate through passengers without long layovers and also to carry local passengers at reasonable hours of the day.[70]

7. Finally, the committee charged great irregularity in the road's book-keeping operations. In this respect the committee stood on firm ground. As already explained, the NCRR was clearly guilty of careless accounting practices, in company with most other railroads of its time. Fisher never conceded this publicly, but he did so privately, blaming it on Mendenhall. The committee report relentlessly attached all blame to Fisher.[71]

Although the *Greensboro Patriot* in particular continued to attack Fisher, he received a stunning vindication from the stockholders at their annual meeting in July. Of 8,140 votes cast for directors, Fisher came in first with 6,648. (Each stockholder was entitled to vote for four candidates; Giles Mebane, the runner-up, received 6,322.) The board then reelected him president.[72] Among the predominantly Whig stockholders voting for Fisher was John Motley Morehead. That fact as much as Fisher's reelection was a source of mortification to Jonathan Worth.[73] Morehead in fact had played no visible part in the recent inquisition, although he was a member of the House of Commons during that session.

The declaration of the road's first dividend in March 1859 surely contributed to Fisher's enhanced popularity. In refusing to pay a dividend until the debts were either paid or (in the case of the bonds) provided for by a sinking fund, Fisher and the directors followed the sound financial policy preached by the leading railroadmen of the day.[74] Nor was the NCRR far out of step with other roads in its first years. Less than half of the nation's railroads paid regular dividends in the 1850s. In 1859 less than a quarter of them did so; outside the Northeast the proportion was one in seven.[75] Viewed from this perspective, the NCRR was on solid footing.

The picture was not so clear to the NCRR stockholders. (In fact, few American stockholders of that day knew anything of investments outside real estate.)[76] Their inexperience, together with the extravagant promises of the subscription campaign, encouraged unreasonable expectations of profit. Even if three-quarters of the stock had not belonged to that sovereign entity, the state, Fisher and his colleagues would have had to listen to the stockholders' demand for a return on their investment. Many managers around the country succumbed to the pressure sooner and with less justification.[77]

One may suspect that the Worth committee investigation hastened the dividend, but Fisher justified it wholly on financial grounds. Back in 1857, after NCRR lobbyists virtually promised a 6 percent dividend on the state's $1 million of preferred stock in return for legislative support of the new bond issue, State Proxy Thomas Ruffin formally requested such a distribution. He repeated the demand in 1858. Both times the board refused, citing the large remaining debt. But in his special report of January 1859 Fisher announced that the floating debt (i.e., all debts except the bonds) had finally been liquidated. That fact and continually rising receipts, he said, offered the prospect of an early dividend.[78]

This time the promise was fulfilled: a dividend of 6 percent on the preferred stock and 2 percent on the remaining $3 million of common stock. The state's share of this distribution was $100,000.[79] Fisher seems originally to have contemplated paying the state in NCRR bonds, which it refused.[80] The same dividend was paid in 1860, with an increase on the common stock to 3 percent.[81] None was paid in 1861 and no explanation was given; although receipts were up slightly over 1860, expenses appear to have been heavy. The 1861 annual report was even less meticulous than usual—hastily assembled as Fisher prepared to take his newly raised regiment to Virginia.[82]

Fisher expressed a desire to retire in 1860. In what he probably intended as his valedictory, he announced that the NCRR "is now on firm and safe ground. Its success [is] fully established—its future beyond doubt."[83] But he had voiced the same wish in previous years, perhaps not as strongly, and his friends had learned that the feeling could be overcome. Now he again permitted himself to be reelected to the board (by a much-diminished majority) and agreed to another year as president.[84] At the same time, he ran for the state senate in Rowan and Davie counties in order (as he said) to better defend himself against the attacks to which he had been subjected in the last legislature. In this contest he was narrowly defeated.[85]

In the summer of 1861, with the nation at war and Fisher himself busily recruiting and training a regiment, few questioned the authenticity of his retirement. The stockholders passed a resolution of appreciation for his past services and tendered "their best wishes in the dangerous and arduous duties, which he has now assumed in the defence of our liberties and homes and families."[86] Fisher had already left Raleigh with his regiment, bound for northern Virginia. Only nine days later he died a hero's death, leading his men on the field of First Manassas or Bull Run.[87]

PART 2

Wartime

10

Management and Finance: Cameron and Webb

CHARLES F. FISHER's departure for military service in July 1861 brought a new president and superintendent, but it did not change the road's ownership or the relations between private stockholders and the state. Among state directors, the prewar pattern of continuity persisted until 1863. Only Robert P. Dick of Greensboro was removed involuntarily in that time, reputedly for supporting Stephen A. Douglas for president in 1860.[1] Dick was one of the original state directors, having served continuously since 1853. He was also the first state proxy, in 1855 and 1856. (Fittingly, one of his daughters married a son of Stephen A. Douglas after the war.)

In 1863, by contrast, every head rolled. The absence of formal political parties during the war obscures the fact that they did exist in substance. Zebulon Vance's election in August 1862 represented the first political turnover in the governorship since David S. Reid's election in 1850. It was the first, therefore, since the state took majority ownership of the NCRR. It was a victory in large measure of reluctant secessionists and Whigs over more ardent secessionist Democrats. Both groups were, for the moment, supporters of the Confederate war effort, but some of the "Conservatives" who had supported Vance broke away after 1863 to advocate a negotiated peace. In 1864 they rallied behind editor William W. Holden in an unsuccessful effort to defeat Vance for reelection.[2] The political divisions of both 1862 and 1864 were reflected in subsequent changes on the NCRR board.

Most of the eight men named by Vance in 1863 were well qualified by almost any standard. Cyrus P. Mendenhall had been treasurer of the road; Dolphin A. Davis, William C. Means, and John Berry (the Hillsboro architect and builder) had served on the board a decade earlier; Albert Johnson, for many years master mechanic of the Raleigh and Gaston Railroad, was the first workingman to serve on the board. Johnson was a Holden supporter, however, and in 1864 he alone was replaced, even losing his job with the R&G. (After the war Johnson would return to the board by Governor Holden's appointment; in 1868 he became NCRR superintendent.) Johnson's successor in 1864, C. W. D. Hutchings, was also identified as a mechanic.[3]

There had never been much continuity among the state proxies. John W. Thomas of Davidson County compiled the seniority record, up to 1871 at least, by serving three years, 1859–61. A Whig, he received all three appointments from Democratic Governor John W. Ellis, an old personal friend from the stock subscription days. His successor in 1862 was William A. Graham, and in 1863 and 1864 it was Ralph Gorrell of Greensboro.

Vance's appointments to the NCRR board were a matter of patronage rather than policy. Despite the political controversy they generated in the press, there was little if any impact on the road's policies or operations. The state's voice in NCRR control was still passive; private and state directors continued to act in harmony, with no visible difference between them. Paul C. Cameron in 1861 would be the first president elected from the state directors, but his choice was unanimous.[4] His subsequent resignation under fire had no political bearing. He remained a state director until 1863, and when Vance dropped him that year, the stockholders elected him for two more years.

Occasionally during the war, Governors Clark and Vance asked the NCRR, as other railroads, to do certain things—to allow "foreign" trains on the road, for instance, to relieve freight congestion—but these wishes were never issued as commands. The road's leaders were not quite free to ignore the governor, but they sometimes argued with him, conceding less than he asked. Only once did the state proxy officially request stockholder action at the governor's behest—when Ralph Gorrell offered a resolution in 1863 to stop further rate increases—but he refrained from casting the state's controlling vote for the motion, and it died.[5] The principle of laissez-faire was well ingrained.

Fisher's departure in July 1861 left the presidency open. Paul C. Cameron, the board's unanimous choice, was an original stockholder and construction contractor and a state director since 1855. With over 12,000 acres and 470 slaves in Orange County in addition to plantations in Alabama and Mississippi, Cameron was probably the wealthiest man in the state.[6] His election was widely hailed on account of his business acumen and his long-time association with the road. Yet within six months there was a rising shout for his official head amidst charges of inefficiency, incompetence, and even senility. (He was fifty-three at the time of his election and would devote another thirty years to his interests as planter, businessman, and philanthropist.) Most of the accusations arose from conditions beyond his control, and Cameron was clearly wounded by them. (In 1856, while reluctantly accepting a state senate nomination in Orange County, he had expressed "a positive repugnance for any sort of strife, especially of a political character.")[7] Without public comment, he resigned the presidency on 7 February 1862 after only seven months in office.

Morehead and Fisher had both been part-time presidents, although the road must have occupied most of their time. Cameron seems to have given it less of his attention, as he continued to look after his plantations and other business affairs. Probably for that reason Edmund Wilkes was named superintendent, the first time this office had been filled since Theodore Garnett's resignation in 1856. Reportedly an experienced railroader, Wilkes had joined the road in 1859 and won Fisher's praise as general transportation agent and, later, as master of transportation. He may already have been superintendent in fact, with or without the title, as Fisher raised his regiment and prepared to leave.[8]

When the war came, it brought problems for the road that were unprecedented in their character, volume, and complexity. The road did not, could not adjust to them as quickly as an uninformed and equally inexperienced public would have liked. Public anger of course focused on management. Cameron and Wilkes, but especially Cameron, were exposed to merciless criticism during the winter of 1861–62. "If there ever was a man in public station who richly merited the abundant execration[s] for neglect of duty that are daily heaped upon him, that man is Paul C. Cameron," intoned a letter to the *Concord Flag* in January 1862. It cataloged his shortcomings as a railroad manager: During his brief administration to date, there were more collisions and derailments than in all of Fisher's tenure, and these were of almost daily occurrence; at Concord the engineer frequently overshot the station, forcing ladies to walk in the mud while boarding the train; Negro section hands ran off with much greater frequency than under Fisher, because of bad treatment; the Charlotte depot was overflowing with freight awaiting shipment, unlike the adjacent Charlotte and South Carolina depot, and so was the Concord station; and Cameron was guilty of nepotism in filling offices on the road. People were suggesting an indignation meeting at the county courthouse, the letter concluded, but that seemed useless since everyone was indignant at the road's management already.

The Salisbury *Carolina Watchman*, a much more influential paper, reprinted this diatribe with approval. "Mr. Cameron is almost universally denounced here as totally unfit for the office of President. There is scarcely a day that we do not hear somebody complaining of the bad management of the Road, or denouncing the President and Mr. Wilkes . . . for incompetency, neglect, inattention, &c." The Salisbury depot too had been packed for months with rotting produce and other goods. The *Watchman* facetiously reported great joy at recent news that Cameron had resigned; the rejoicing subsided when it was learned that the news related to Lincoln's Secretary of War Simon Cameron.[9] A week later, editor J. J. Bruner detailed again the failures of the NCRR to carry accumulating stores of freight despite offers of the Western North Carolina Railroad to help with its rolling stock, now idled because of this dereliction. "There is no one here capable of rendering an excuse for him [Cameron], or if capable, willing to do it. He therefore stands before this community as the author of many losses and any amount of vexation and trouble sustained by its citizens, and will be held responsible for them until he shall have rendered a satisfactory account for the wretchedly inefficient use made of the public property entrusted to his management for the public good."[10]

Not all editors were so quick to arraign Cameron and Wilkes. The Charlotte *Western Democrat* defended them, calling attention to the doubled volume of business, especially priority government freight, and bad weather. Holden of the Raleigh *Standard* was also supportive while calling for an investigation of the facts.[11] But after he learned of Cameron's resignation under this barrage, Holden joined the pack: What the NCRR requires, he said, is "a strong, young, sober, sensible, energetic, business man—a man, if possible, of experience in Railroad matters. A man *who has his fortune to make*,—not a superannuated, broken down man of wealth and ease, who is as hard to stir as a loggerhead in winter time. Nor is this a time for consulting the wishes of kinsfolks [*sic*] and class politicians. The State demands the services of . . . a man who would remove his family to the Shops, and devote his whole time to the Road."[12]

The situation was worst at the western end of the line between Salisbury and Charlotte. This was owing largely to the gauge difference and necessity of transshipment at Charlotte and the shortage of NCRR cars to carry the predominantly northbound freight. Wilkes complained that the Confederate government was constantly commandeering NCRR cars and it was all he could do to keep them on the road. As it was, they were run constantly, without opportunity for proper maintenance.[13]

Although these conditions improved by 1863, it was partly due to greater experience and even more to government aid that was withheld in the first two years of the war. After 1863, moreover, the public had become resigned to erratic service and was better educated to its causes. It was always tempting to scapegoat but not so easily as in the naivete of 1861 and 1862.

Both Cameron's successor Thomas Webb and President William Johnston of the Charlotte and South Carolina spoke well of his work as president. Johnston, one of the most respected railroad leaders in the region, heard of Cameron's desire to resign and asked him to reconsider. When Cameron had agreed to accept the office, said Johnston, there was general gratification "that a gentleman of high reputation, sound judgment and practical business character had assumed control of this great state work. . . . The groundless effusions of a newspaper here and there can avail nothing." Editors wrote in ignorance of what the railroads were facing. None of the roads were equipped for the volume of freight with which they were deluged. Johnston asked Cameron to stay on until July, when the NCRR's swollen business would be reflected in its earnings statements; he predicted that this would be the best year by far in its history. Johnston closed with a second word of advice: Cameron needed an experienced railroader like Wilkes to help run the road; watching the finances and seeing that everyone did his duty was all the president could do on a road the length of the NCRR and carrying the volume of traffic that it had to carry.[14]

Cameron resigned less than a week after this letter was written. The resignation was "accepted under the regret and remonstrance of every member of the Board," as Thomas Webb put it a few months later when required to deliver the annual report for 1861–62. During at least part of the time that Cameron was at the helm, Webb stated, he labored under the great disadvantage of having no secretary to write up the books, hence no source of information as to the company's financial affairs. Yet "by his industry and ability he has systematized the whole operations of [the] road, and marked out a broad way, which it will be well for those to pursue who succeed him."[15] It is unclear how much substance there was in this tribute; Webb did not elaborate upon Cameron's system or broad way or why he did without the services of a bookkeeper.

In choosing Hillsboro lawyer Thomas Webb as president, the directors picked both the youngest man on their board (he was thirty-four) and its junior member (he was in his first year). Webb was no stranger to the road, however. While disclaiming railroad experience, he had been an interested if small stockholder from the beginning and had served several times as secretary of the annual meeting. He was probably the same Thomas Webb who in 1856 flagged down an approaching train on discovering that the bridge near his home had burned.[16]

Webb in fact stood in striking contrast to his three predecessors. Morehead and Fisher had been prominent politicians, the former one of the leading statesmen of his time and region. All three were businessmen of wealth and standing. Webb was a young lawyer of relatively modest estate and family whose highest offices had been Orange County clerk and Hillsboro town councilman.[17] He was the road's first full-time president, having little to divert him from this remarkable career opportunity. Lacking the political influence or powers of articulation belonging to Morehead and Fisher, he was, as the Raleigh *Standard* described him in June, a "sensible, energetic young man," doing his utmost.[18] He would remain on the board until 1869 as a private director, almost always securing first or second place in the balloting. He continued as president until July 1865 and served a fifth year in 1866–67. Webb was a successful if unspectacular administrator during very difficult times.

In July 1862, five months after Webb's accession, a group of stockholders quietly tried to replace him with Thomas J. Sumner, superintendent of the Charlotte and South Carolina Railroad, and elected Sumner to the board for that purpose. Sumner had an obvious qualification that Webb lacked: he was a practical railroader associated with a connecting road that had a regional reputation for good management. He would also have been remembered as one of Walter Gwynn's assistant engineers during the NCRR's construction and then as its first road master for a short time. It does not appear which stockholders were behind the Sumner boom, but they seem to have been a distinct minority. In the balloting for directors, Webb came in first with 3,822 votes. Sumner was in fourth place with 2,510 votes, less than a majority of those cast; he was elected on a second ballot. When the directors met to choose a president, they were unable to do so. They adjourned for a week, returned, and reelected Webb. The delay was owing more to absenteeism among the directors than to any strength for Sumner, who never received more than one vote.[19]

Sumner's supporters shifted to the office of superintendent, causing Edmund Wilkes to decline a second term. Sumner was elected on the first ballot, perhaps as part of a deal growing out of the presidential contest.[20]

Wilkes had been subjected to almost as much criticism as Cameron. But Webb praised him (before Wilkes's resignation) as "a thorough Railroad man . . . who has made it the business of his life. . . . He is faithful, energetic, competent, and of untiring industry; . . . to him in a great measure is due the credit of [the] past year's success."[21] Before the year was out, Wilkes and his brother contracted to build the Piedmont Railroad between Greensboro and Danville. That may have been the inducement to leave the NCRR.[22] Wilkes would return in 1865 as NCRR superintendent, replacing Sumner. Meanwhile, Sumner's simultaneous service as director (for one year) and superintendent was an anomaly little noted nor long remembered. In 1863 the stockholders replaced him on the board with Paul C. Cameron, who had just been dumped as a state director by Governor Vance.

There may also have been an effort to derail Webb in 1863. The *Raleigh Register* implied this as an objective of the Vance administration. But if so, it is unclear who his opponent was. Webb was the only man that year to win election to the board on the first ballot; he then was reelected president with the support of eight directors.[23]

Even before Wilkes's resignation as superintendent, editor William Holden criticized the road for changing its subordinate officers too often, thereby depriving itself of experienced management. The charge had merit. Most personnel changes were not as well documented or publicized as the Fisher-Mendenhall feud, and the reasons for them are hard to determine. But Fisher and others in authority before the war were on record as favoring the hiring of people at the least possible wages. This was false economy, said Holden: "It is the old way of 'saving at the spigot and letting out at the bung.'" Good management required good personnel, well paid. A case in point was James E. Allen, one of the best road masters in the land, according to Holden; why was he not kept in 1860? The road would be in better shape if he had been. Holden held up the Raleigh and Gaston as a worthy example, hiring only the best people it could find and then keeping them.[24] (His good opinion of the R&G would suffer a blow when Albert Johnson, one of his prime examples of a longtime, skilled employee, was forced to resign under political pressure for having supported Holden's own gubernatorial race in 1864.)[25]

The office of secretary was also in need of stability. R. W. Mills, who had been hired in 1858 to clean up the books, did so in a fashion apparently satisfactory to Fisher.[26] But after reelection in July 1861, he was discharged in August. Mills's work had not brought universal satisfaction, as Webb later made clear in uncharacteristically caustic terms: "Owing to the gross negligence or the total inability of your former Secretary, the books . . . were filled with errors and misstatements, and I may safely say that this company has lost thousands of dollars by not having a competent officer in charge of them during the last two or three years." Two other men were elected to the job in quick succession before a third, John H. Bryan, Jr., was hired in October. He and an assistant were subsequently credited with correcting many past errors. In June 1862 Webb announced the inauguration of a new bookkeeping system under Bryan's charge.[27] Quite possibly the books were put in better order, but poor accounting methods continued to merit criticism for years to come. In 1864 Bryan gave way to Francis A. Stagg, who had served since 1861 as general ticket agent.

The treasurer throughout this period, and one of the few elements of continuity in the higher ranks, was Peter Brown Ruffin of Hillsboro. A son of Judge Thomas Ruffin, Sr., he was also the brother-in-law of Paul C. Cameron. One of the charges against Cameron was that he practiced nepotism, particularly in the case of Ruffin.[28] But Ruffin had become treasurer under Fisher in 1859 and continued until the end of the war under Webb. When Webb returned to the presidency for a year in 1866, Ruffin returned as treasurer for the same period.

The master of machinery at the beginning of the war was E. H. Marsh, who had been promoted in 1860 from a locomotive engineer. By 1863 Marsh had given way to James Anderson, who left in September 1864 to become superintendent of the Charlotte and South Carolina. His successor for the next several years was Rufus D. Wade.

Maintenance of the road was still under two division masters, provided for when James Allen left as road master in 1860. The men occupying these positions also changed several times during the war.

Officers' salaries rose during the war, in response to wartime inflation. Morehead, Fisher, and Cameron had received $2,500 per year. So did Webb until 1863, when the stockholders granted him a $500 increase, retroactive to a year earlier. In 1864 his salary was raised to $6,000, also effective a year earlier. In the same fashion, the treasurer's salary was raised to $2,500, then $5,000; the secretary's to $2,000, then $4,000.[29] These increases fell far short of the inflation rate by 1864.

Corporate headquarters were firmly established at Company Shops, which remained a rustic village lacking churches, schools, and some other amenities of urban life. It did not appeal as a residence for many company officers or mechanics, save as their jobs required it. To make more housing available for additional needed employees and also to enhance the quality of the place, Webb asked in 1862 that the prewar ban on further building be rescinded and that lots be made available for sale to private individuals. The ban on building was partially lifted that year, and in 1863 the stockholders approved the laying off of streets and of lots for private sale.[30]

To foster the new town-building campaign, it was decided to drop the descriptive but dowdy name Company Shops and give the village a title of more dignity. The one chosen was "Vance." (Eight of the twelve directors had just been appointed by that official.) The new name appeared in a newspaper notice of October 1863 advertising a forthcoming sale of town lots. (The lots were 200 feet square, the streets 100 feet wide.)[31] Not surprisingly, the sale of lots was slow until after the war, although company housing construction helped the village grow. It numbered 300 persons by July 1864, but there was still no church or school.[32] The name Vance persisted in NCRR communications until July 1864, when the stockholders voted to return to "Company Shops."[33]

President Cameron seems to have spent no more of his time at Company Shops than Fisher had done. Webb's surviving correspondence is dated predominantly at Company Shops, however, and it seems likely that he moved his family there. He was, again, the first full-time president. A resolution was offered at the 1863 annual meeting to require all the road's officers except the president to live at the Shops—something the directors had already mandated in 1858. The order may have been inspired by the town-building effort that year, but in any case the motion was tabled.[34] It is not clear which of the road's officers lived at the Shops. Superintendent Sumner was living there at the end of the war and presumably earlier.[35] The others probably did so too.

Virtually all southern railroads experienced a false prosperity during the war. Receipts and dividends reached levels hitherto undreamed of. Traffic was heavier than ever before and of course produced greater receipts. But much of the apparent prosperity was simply the product of inflated currency. Figured in terms of gold or prewar dollars, the bloated wartime profits often fell short of those before the war. The same was true of dividends. Moreover, maintenance costs were unavoidably being postponed to a day of reckoning after the war. What purported to be profit paid out to the stockholders was partly drainage of capital in the form of deteriorating track and equipment.[36]

Some, perhaps many, railroad leaders recognized the difference between appearance and reality. William Johnston of the C&SC pointed out to his stockholders in 1864 that if the large dividends being paid by many roads were spent instead on rails and rolling stock at the prevalent prices, they probably would not be sufficient for the purpose. But the impossibility of procuring these articles left no alternative to declaring dividends. While stockholders might receive nominally double the usual dividend, Johnston said, by that time it did not equal in value half of the prewar distribution.[37]

Thomas Webb seems either to have come to this truth more slowly or to have been less candid in voicing it. "I think the State and Stockholders may be congratulated that the success of their road is now beyond what the most sanguine of its friends ever anticipated," he told NCRR stockholders in 1863. "Its prospects for the future are very bright. Not only have they realized handsome dividends, but their . . . debt is but a trifle, with a sinking fund fully equal to discharge it, the day it falls due."[38] He went on to exaggerate grossly the physical condition of the road and its rolling stock.

NCRR receipts mushroomed as did those of other roads, from $791,000 in 1861–62 (almost twice the preceding year's figure) to $5,406,000 in 1864–65. Operating expenses went up in even greater proportion, as rate increases (especially those paid by the government, the road's greatest customer) failed to keep pace with rising costs. In three of the four war years, expenses reached or slightly exceeded 50 percent of receipts; the prewar median had been 45.5 percent. (See table 11.)[39] Real profits, therefore, were less than before the war. But that fact was masked by the massive inflation, producing exaggerated receipts and dividends in proportion. And they were amassed as the road found it impossible to make the usual repairs and replacements. Overhead costs thus were artificially low. These neglected expenditures would severely handicap the road (and virtually all other roads too) in the early postwar period when the repairs had to be made.

Six dividends were declared during the war at roughly six-month intervals from July 1862 to February 1865. With one exception they rose steadily from 8 percent to 25 percent. Those in 1863 and 1864 added up to about 20 percent each year. All were payable in Confederate currency, the last one amounting to $1 million and all of them totaling $2,960,000. (See table 3.) Their gold value at the times of issue came only to $446,540. In real (or gold) terms the largest dividend was actually the initial 8 percent distribution of 1862, representing 5.3 percent in gold; the $1 million dividend of 1865 was worth only $20,000 in gold, or 0.5 percent of the road's $4 million capitalization. One of the 1864 dividends was even smaller in real terms.[40] In each case the state received three-fourths of the dividend, no differentiation being made between the preferred and common stock. Much of its share was paid in kind, by transporting state troops and supplies. The remainder was paid in Confederate bonds and currency.[41]

As before the war, there was no active market for railroad stocks in the South, certainly not in North Carolina. NCRR shares sold in private transactions, sometimes being advertised in the newspapers. On one occasion a Charlotte auctioneer who also dealt in slaves, silver, livestock, and furniture advertised that he would sell sixty shares of NCRR stock at auction on the public square. Sometimes the price was reported by buyer or seller, as in

January 1863 when several shares sold in Raleigh at $93 including the current $10 dividend coupon, or $83 net. Over 100 shares sold at Salisbury in March 1863 at about $90.[42] Although editors approvingly noted the evident rise in value compared with previous years, they typically failed to recognize the role of inflation. Even in swollen dollars the price remained below the $100 par value at which the stock had been issued a decade before. And $90 in March 1863 equaled about $18 in gold.

One of the lessons that Civil War inflation eventually taught was its wonderful capacity to extinguish debt. The greater the inflation, the more awesome its power to nullify prior financial obligations. Some railroads, like the Raleigh and Gaston, took advantage of wartime conditions to retire their prewar debts, largely if not wholly.[43] The NCRR was not among them. The fault in its case lay partly in its management and partly in the restricted options it had available. Fortunately, its debt going into the war was at a reasonable level for a road of its size, only about $350,000.

When the road issued bonds in this amount in 1857, the legislature required that a sinking fund be created to provide for their retirement at maturity ten years hence.[44] The road complied and, after close calculation, mandated an annual appropriation of $25,000 to the fund, to be invested in state or NCRR bonds. That amount was expected to produce, with accrued interest, the required $350,000 by 1867. From 1858 to 1860 the appropriations were made accordingly. But in 1861 the treasurer reported an appropriation of only $15,000; even that amount was apparently never paid.[45] At their next meeting the directors appointed a special committee to manage (and presumably investigate) the sinking fund. If the committee members—Ralph Gorrell (chairman), Daniel M. Barringer, and Thomas Webb—ever knew why only $15,000 was appropriated during the previous year and why even it disappeared, they did not say publicly. They found only $76,000 and avoided any explanation of the deficiency.[46] The matter evoked silence on the part of other investigative groups as well in the next several years. Charles F. Fisher was ultimately and perhaps immediately responsible for the shortage. There is evidence that he borrowed $1,645 from the sinking fund account in April 1861. Three years later the stockholders' finance committee quietly settled one sum—overwritten and illegible in the treasurer's ledger, but probably less than $1,000—that had been charged to him from that fund.[47] No matter what Fisher might have done with the money by act of omission or commission, such as borrowing it to finance the raising of his regiment, his hero's death on the battlefield made recovery impossible and discussion inappropriate.

In 1862 the normal $25,000 payment plus accrued interest was invested in more state bonds, raising the total to a face value of about $113,000. The stockholders that year instructed the board to appropriate whatever sum was still necessary to bring the fund up to its proper level. They also permitted investment in Confederate securities as well as those of the company and state.[48] The committee set to work and by July 1863 reported a total of $214,000, almost half of it in Confederate bonds. The members looked forward with assurance to having more than enough to liquidate the debt in 1867.

Carried away by the paper profits dangling before their eyes, the committee made a further recommendation: to exchange $100,000 of prewar state bonds bearing 6 percent interest, which now sold at a $140 premium on the market, for new ones promising higher rates. By this means they could add to the sinking fund a premium of $140,000 over the face value of the old bonds, plus gather additional interest from the new ones. This one action would carry the fund beyond the $350,000 due in 1867. It might remove the need of any more $25,000 appropriations as well as cover much of the $28,000 annual interest on the company bonds, which the road had been paying on schedule all along.[49]

The Gorrell committee was replaced in 1863 owing to Governor Vance's change of directors. But a new committee—composed of Cyrus P. Mendenhall (chairman), Dolphin A. Davis, and John D. Flanner—was given essentially the mandate just requested.[50] Mendenhall and his colleagues proceeded at once to exchange the prewar North Carolina 6 percent bonds for new ones bearing 6 and 8 percent interest, on a basis of one for two. They continued to do so throughout 1864 despite the fact that the new bonds (dependent upon a Confederate military victory) were increasingly regarded as worthless. The exchanges occasioned such misgivings that the board ordered them stopped in January 1865.[51]

The committee did have the sense not to invest in any more Confederate bonds, which were under at least equal suspicion. But the Confederate government was by far the largest customer of the road and paid its bills in its own securities, when it paid them at all. Thus they were the only kind of payment Webb could make to the fund when the $25,000 appropriation came due in 1864. In July of that year the sinking fund amounted to $296,000, almost half of it still in Confederate bonds and most of the rest in the shaky wartime North Carolina bonds now being acquired.[52]

One of the committee's options all along had been to invest in the road's own 8 percent bonds, those that the sinking fund was created to redeem. Any of these bonds that the fund might acquire could be destroyed, thereby diminishing the company debt. It did acquire a few and erased $11,000 of the debt thereby, but most were not for sale. The road reasonably took this as evidence of a good credit rating.[53]

George W. Swepson, the budding financier, was the agent through whom many of the state bond exchanges took place. He was under contract to exchange the fund's last $23,000 in old bonds when the prohibition order came down in January 1865. Faced with that order and the generally perceived worthlessness of the new bonds, Mendenhall (who was in sole possession of the fund at this time) was reluctant to proceed with the deal. But

Swepson faced him down with a sermon on the sanctity of contract, and he acquiesced. The final exchange did not take place until after the Confederate surrender, when Swepson took the old bonds in return for new ones that he had picked up for about 3 cents on the dollar. A postwar legislative committee characterized this transaction as "equivalent to . . . a gratuitous donation."[54] It may or may not be significant that Swepson and Mendenhall were business partners at this time.[55]

In July 1865 Mendenhall and his committee solemnly reported that the sinking fund amounted to $379,871.90, an increase of over $83,000 from the preceding year. If those securities were available, they continued, there would be more than enough to cover the road's debt. But, as everyone knew, almost all of this sum was in wartime Confederate and North Carolina bonds that were now worthless. The committee also reported that no $25,000 appropriation had been made in the year just ended, the company lacking any means to make it. Yet Treasurer Ruffin listed in his own report for the year a payment of $25,000 to the sinking fund. This discrepancy, like that of 1861, was never explained. It no longer mattered. At war's end the road still had a bonded debt of $339,000 ($11,000 having been retired by the acquisition of its own bonds), and the sinking fund created to redeem it was to all intents and purposes empty.[56]

The final bond exchange of 1865 was so flagrant that in 1868 the company sued both Swepson and Mendenhall to recover its loss from that transaction. After two appeals to the state supreme court and a referral back down to a lower court, the suit was finally settled in 1877, with the two men ordered to pay the road $10,810, the estimated value of the old bonds in April 1865.[57]

Mendenhall's action seems not to have been generally known for some time, even among company directors.[58] He was popular enough with the stockholders in July 1865 to place first in the election of private directors, and he remained as chairman of the sinking fund committee until 1866. Until 1869 the worthless securities were still listed with apparent gravity as sinking fund assets.[59] Nothing was added to the fund after the war, and in 1867 the road issued new bonds to fund the previous debt.

THE NCRR MADE an altogether different kind of investment in the building of a new feeder road near Raleigh. In 1862 the Chatham Railroad was chartered to connect Raleigh with the state's only significant coalfields, on the Deep River near modern Sanford. The state and the Raleigh and Gaston subscribed liberally to the new company's stock; the NCRR made a belated subscription of $200,000 in 1864. Meanwhile it permitted the new road in 1862 to use the NCRR right of way for eight miles from Raleigh to Cary before it cut southward on its own course. NCRR locomotives were woodburners, but coal from the Deep River fields was used in its shops as well as in government workshops in Salisbury and Charlotte. The coal had to be carried by roundabout routes. One of these was down the Cape Fear by boat to Wilmington, then up the Wilmington and Weldon Railroad to Goldsboro, then westward along the NCRR. Having it brought directly to Cary promised to be a great improvement. After many difficulties the Chatham road was almost completed when Sherman invaded the region in March 1865. It played almost no part in the war, therefore, although it would figure importantly in postwar through railway development.[60]

Confederate taxation was minimal during the first half of the war. In August 1861 the Congress in Richmond enacted a war tax of one-half of 1 percent on certain kinds of property, including corporate stock. (Although the Confederacy could not tax state-owned stock, it could tax any owned by individuals.) In November President Cameron announced that the road itself would pay the tax owed by its individual stockholders.[61]

But by April 1863 financial needs had become more pressing, and Congress imposed a small ad valorem tax on money held and an income tax of 15 percent on all incomes over $500 other than salaries.[62] President W. J. Hawkins of the Raleigh and Gaston took the lead in mobilizing opposition to this law on the part of North Carolina railways. Webb agreed with him that these roads were tax exempt since most of them were owned in part by the state and the Confederacy was legally forbidden to tax state property.[63]

The Confederate government did not agree, however, and taxes continued to increase. An act of February 1864 added a 5 percent tax on the value of corporate stock, another of 10 percent on business profits, and an excess profits tax of one-quarter of all corporate profits exceeding 25 percent.[64] As in 1861, the NCRR decided to pay the 5 percent property tax for its individual stockholders, amounting to $50,000 in all. This time the road felt obliged as well to make a proportional in lieu payment of $150,000 to its largest stockholder, the state, for its $3 million holding. To meet these obligations the directors used $200,000 in Confederate bonds that had been received from the government in payment for transportation. Other railroads in the state made similar payments, more or less under protest, maintaining that they were exempt from both state and Confederate taxation.[65] Altogether, the road paid over $35,000 in its own tax payments for 1863–64 and over $68,000 the next year.[66]

Difficulties with the Confederate government were by no means limited to taxation. Increasingly, as the war dragged on, the government lacked the means to pay the bills it incurred, even at the preferential rates it commanded, and its payments fell in arrears. Besides raising taxes, it resorted to the printing press, progressively fueling inflation, and paid its bills either in paper currency or bonds. By 1864 both were so apt to depreciate that recipients were anxious to turn them into other, more solid assets as quickly as possible. And as the government was the railroads' largest customer by far, they experienced comparable problems in meeting their own obligations.[67]

Military transportation, of both men and materiel, was ordered by the states as well as the Confederacy. Early in the war particularly, it was hard to determine which government should pay the bill. The NCRR charged the state almost $43,000 for military transportation between April and August 1861. The state board of claims allowed the payment, but the legislature refused to appropriate it, arguing that the service was rendered for the common good and should be paid for by the Confederacy. That government too refused to pay, at least for a time, requiring a certification by some Confederate official that the transportation was done in its behalf.

By July 1862 the NCRR had received $96,000 from the Confederacy and nothing from the state. It had over $222,000 in outstanding claims against the two governments. Webb reported that about 5 percent of the road's claims against the Confederacy had been suspended because of faulty paperwork, and those it did allow it insisted upon paying in bonds. "We work for the government at half price," Webb growled, referring to the government's preferred rates, yet "it refuses to pay a portion of our claims although acknowledged just; it suspends others, and it should pay us in money or notes whatever is due." (The R&G got around the state's failure to pay its bills by withholding its dividend until the claims were settled in 1863.)[68]

By July 1864 the Confederate government was in arrears over $650,000, according to the road's account. Although payments were made on occasion, partly in money and partly in treasury certificates or other securities, the government's back was to the wall. Often its answer to repeated applications was that no money was on hand. This left the railroad in similar straits. "When it is considered that our monthly expenditures are now about $200,000," said Webb, "and that our duty to the Government requires us to give them almost the exclusive use of the road, thus depriving us of our ordinary revenue from private freights and passengers, it is not a matter of astonishment that we have not been able to pay our ordinary expenses without recourse to loans." Twice, he said, the road had been forced to borrow money to pay operating expenses. Although the treasurer's account of funds on hand looked impressive on paper, they consisted in reality of bonds that were almost useless in paying the road's own bills.[69] "I am completely at the mercy of the Government," Webb wrote State Treasurer Worth in August 1864, explaining the difficulty of paying that year's apparently lavish dividend. "But if begging will do any good I will soon be able to pay off the State as well as the Stockholders."[70]

Eventually Webb arranged a settlement of accounts with the central government every two months, at which times the road received partial payment of what it was owed. As quickly as possible it turned these payments into machinery and supplies before depreciation set in. Part of the state's bill, by contrast, was settled by subtractions from its stock dividend; but at the end of the war the road still had a claim of about $210,000 against the state. The Confederacy owed $1,380,000 shortly before the surrender, but

Webb was able to reduce this figure considerably by obtaining payments in kind from various agents of the collapsing government. Just before the fall of Richmond, he reported with pardonable pride, the road obtained forty-eight freight cars and other equipment, worth about $600,000, from the government. The road also acquired some government supplies in Raleigh and Greensboro shortly before Johnston's surrender to Sherman. These sometimes took the form of machinery or other railroad supplies; sometimes they were cotton or other goods that could be turned into money. The Confederate navy's machine shops at Charlotte with all of their equipment were turned over to the NCRR and two other roads in partial payment of sums owed to them. It was not yet clear in July 1865, when Webb reported these transactions, whether they would all be allowed by the United States authorities, but some, including the purchase of rolling stock, were approved.[71]

One way of hedging against inflation and, almost the same thing, hedging against the total collapse of Confederate money and securities in the event of defeat, was to invest in cotton or other commodities that could readily be sold later. This was also a means of acquiring foreign exchange for purchases through the Union blockade. In company with many other businesses and individuals, the NCRR did this, beginning in the fall of 1863. The stockholders, in fact, mandated it that summer to provide a fund for the purchase of necessary equipment and supplies. By July 1864 the road had acquired 862 bales of cotton and stored them in various places for safekeeping. Late in the war 118 of these bales were burned by Sherman's troops in South Carolina; others were lost, destroyed, stolen, or deteriorated under poor care. After the war 657 bales were sold, netting only $66,000, or about 25 cents per pound. Efforts to locate the remainder continued for some time after the war. The proceeds of these sales, as far as they went, helped to rebuild the road.[72]

Railroad employees were strategically placed to speculate in commodities in their own behalf. Many were known further to ship these goods without paying freight charges, placing their private shipments ahead of higher-priority government freight. Nothing was better calculated to infuriate the general public, who bore the brunt of the war without enjoying such perquisites. Editor D. K. McRae of the *Raleigh Daily Confederate* voiced this feeling in February 1865, accusing the railroads of "out 'Heroding Herod' in their sordid grasping and extortionate greed for money making." By making their trains available to speculators they often delayed troops as well as government freight. Railway officers who connived at these practices, said McRae, were no greater friends to the Confederacy than Sherman or Grant.[73]

Although a number of NCRR officers later denied any knowledge of such activity, President Webb testified that there was scarcely an agent or officer of the road "that did not buy or sell or both more or less during the war." But so far as he claimed to know, they all paid full freight.[74] One who was clearly involved in such traffic was Superintendent T. J. Sumner. There seems no question that Sumner used the road improperly, beginning in the fall of 1864 if not earlier. In fact, evidence of his wrongdoing was so plentiful that it seems impossible Webb did not know about it. No evidence has been found, however, that Webb himself profited from such transactions. Several employees testified after the war that Sumner had repeatedly shipped large amounts of flour, cotton, whiskey, brandy, and other commodities, using company employees at its expense and paying no freight charges except to other railroads. He was apparently acting as an agent if not partner of George W. Swepson and perhaps of Cyrus P. Mendenhall.[75]

Some of Sumner's dealings were on a large scale; in the fall of 1864 he shipped nine carloads (some 585 barrels) of his or his partners' flour to Richmond in expectation of selling it at $1,500 per barrel. When his agent (actually an NCRR purchasing agent) could not sell at that figure, the flour was stored, part of it in a house occupied by Swepson. Some of the flour was later traded for nails, the rest for furniture. The nine carloads of flour comprised a special train at a time when the road could not meet the military and other needs imposed upon it and when Lee's army in Virginia was going hungry. President Webb apparently knew of the train; what other knowledge or interest he may have had is problematical.[76]

At the end of the war there was a good deal of confusion (some of it contrived) as to whether substantial quantities of freight stranded along the railroad belonged to the road, to private individuals, including employees and other speculators, or to the Federal government as contraband of war. In February 1865 the authorities in Richmond had confiscated 190 bales of Sumner's cotton for official purposes. Late in April, as the Confederate government was fleeing southward through Charlotte, Sumner prevailed on Secretary of War John C. Breckinridge to order any Confederate agent with that much cotton in his control to convey it to Sumner.[77]

Meanwhile Sumner got the Confederate quartermaster at Greensboro, Major S. R. Chisman, to turn over a substantial quantity of cotton goods, steel, copper, brass, and other commodities in payment of NCRR claims against the Confederacy. Actually, as Sumner later testified, half the proceeds from the sale of the cotton goods were to be divided between Chisman and others, including an NCRR conductor. Sumner explained this arrangement to Webb's satisfaction with the story that rampaging Confederate soldiers prevented him from gaining possession of the goods but that two men whom he did not care to name had agreed to protect them in return for half of the cotton proceeds. The superintendent then had employees of the road surreptitiously place about a carload of these goods in his house at Company Shops. He later shipped them, with some other cotton that he claimed to be his, to Swepson, Mendenhall and Company in New York and reportedly had the proceeds placed to his own credit. (In fact, Sumner was a partner in that new commission house, built on such accumulations of cotton and tobacco by Swepson, Mendenhall, and Sumner at the end of the war.)[78]

According to one account, NCRR President Nathaniel Boyden (serving in 1865–66) learned of the transaction and had the proceeds returned to the railroad's credit. Boyden himself did not mention this incident when these matters were investigated by a legislative committee in 1867 and, like Webb, carefully disclaimed any personal knowledge of speculation by employees of the road. Sumner's predecessor and successor as superintendent, Edmund Wilkes, was almost as circumspect. Sumner admitted that he had been engaged in speculation but denied any wrongdoing. His examination does not seem to have been very searching.[79] In June 1865 the United States army turned over to the NCRR a quantity of miscellaneous freight that it had temporarily confiscated as contraband. Along with it were 5 carloads of loose and baled cotton and 139 bales of raw cotton, the personal property of T. J. Sumner.[80]

11

The Road and Its Workers

ECONOMIES AND ERRORS in the road's original construction returned to haunt it during the war, when routine maintenance became more difficult. The roadbed was in reasonably good condition at the war's beginning— better than a year before, according to President Fisher—although ditching had been neglected owing to persistent rains and heavy traffic.[1]

It is an occupational characteristic of corporate officials to paint the rosiest picture possible of the past year's accomplishments under their direction. Nonetheless, NCRR officials made a good case in 1862 for their contention that the roadbed had even improved during the first wartime year. The stockholders' inspection committee, having a smaller axe to grind, agreed. During the year the drainage ditches had been renewed all along the road except for the few miles from Concord to Charlotte. Gravel ballasting had also been done at points, helping very slightly to rectify another serious omission in the road's construction. The inspection committee recommended raising the roadbed and track by six to eight inches at some points to aid in drainage and maintenance. Over 93,000 crossties were replaced during the year (about one-fifth of the total); about as many more were still needed to put the track in sound condition. The rails were holding up reasonably well, although some of them were approaching the end of their ten-year normal lifespan. Repairs to the rails fell behind owing to the difficulty of obtaining necessary materials. New rails were unobtainable throughout the war. Replacements for those most badly worn were taken, as long as they lasted, from the seventeen miles of sidetrack.[2]

Winter was usually the most destructive season in railroad maintenance, owing to frequent rainfall, melting snow, and lack of evaporation. Although the road survived the winter of 1861–62 better than previous ones, Superintendent Wilkes had to report that heavy rains in May caused three washouts east of Raleigh, on the section built by the McRaes, in one case causing a derailment and fatalities.[3]

Deterioration was rapid in the months that followed. Unprecedentedly heavy traffic was unmatched by corresponding maintenance. Confederate conscription policy was eating away at the road's work force, skilled mechanics in particular. Equipment grew dilapidated from lack of men and materials to repair it. By November passenger cars were running without glass in the windows, water to drink, or wood to heat the stoves.[4] Lieutenant Colonel Frederick W. Sims, head of the Confederate Railroad Bureau, later recalled that the NCRR became almost impassable from fall 1862 to spring 1863. He rightly attributed this to government conscription policy although newspapers were still blaming company mismanagement. Ultimately the army was called in to help restore the road, using conscript labor.[5] Continuing government intervention seems to have permitted the road to increase its work force and keep the roadbed in better shape. This is barely apparent in the 1863 annual report, which catalogs another 92,000 sills installed, 1,500 rails replaced from sidings, and further ditching, ballasting, and widening of embankments. The worst sections of the road were divided, and additional section masters and hands were assigned to them. Rails were becoming a major problem despite the continued replacements, which could not continue much longer from the road's own limited sidings. About 2,000 more or less defective rails remained in the main line in July 1863. Nevertheless, President Webb could claim that, at least from Hillsboro west, the road had never been in better condition.[6]

In the following year two gravel trains worked full time, their crews ditching and ballasting a total of fifteen or twenty miles, especially in cuts. The work would continue, promised Webb, until the entire line had been ballasted. Except for bad rails, he claimed in 1864, the road as a whole was in better condition than ever before. He noted a decrease in derailments as a result. The inspection committee attributed the improvement to more favorable weather and a reduction in train speeds as well as to the increased work crews. In August 1864 Colonel Sims characterized the NCRR as one of the best roads in the Confederacy.[7]

The South contained only a few rolling mills capable of turning out iron rails. These were soon taken over by the government for other purposes. (One of the largest domestic suppliers of railroad iron to the South before the war was the Tredegar Iron Works in Richmond. Although it continued to sell iron to the NCRR and other southern roads, these products were not rails; it discontinued rail manufacture altogether during the war.)[8] Despite the imperative need of the railroads for continuing supplies of rails, some of these mills early in the war actually converted new rails into armor plate for gunboats when old iron would have served that purpose just as well. "There was not a road in the Confederacy but would gladly have exchanged its worn out iron and paid a handsome sum besides" for new rails, President Webb pointed out in 1863. Although the roads talked about establishing rolling mills for their own needs, virtually nothing was done.[9]

Once sidetracks had been exhausted, therefore, the major source of rails was minor roads that were judged nonessential to the war effort. By this means the Roanoke Valley Railroad northwest of Weldon and the Atlantic, Tennessee, and Ohio between Charlotte and Statesville were dismantled. The Atlantic and North Carolina sold a large part of its rails between

Kinston and New Bern to the government after Union forces captured the road from New Bern eastward.[10] The only recorded allocation of rails to the NCRR was in April 1865, courtesy of the United States Army under Sherman, which laid some rails east of Raleigh that had been taken from the Raleigh and Gaston.[11] Only the impending close of hostilities seems to have prevented the NCRR from receiving rails from a branch of the Western North Carolina Railroad in February 1865.[12]

Most of the bridges were in reasonably good condition in 1861. Only one, over Cate's Creek near Hillsboro, was a temporary trestle, still replacing the structure that burned in 1856 near Thomas Webb's home. The bridges required more or less constant maintenance, and enough work was done throughout the war to keep them passable if not in first-rate order. Once the lattice bridges had begun to sag, they could only be straightened by substantial bracing from below. Maintenance was ordinarily easier on the Howe truss bridges through periodic adjustment and the repair or replacement of individual members, but under wartime conditions it soon became impossible to obtain new iron rods. In both cases, therefore, additional piers, braces, or even trestlework were sometimes resorted to for further support. Trestlework was also used during the war to replace the several bridges that were destroyed by natural and human causes. As with maintenance of the road generally, great improvement was noticeable in bridge maintenance after the spring of 1863, probably the result of additional personnel permitted, if not supplied, by the government.

Some of the culverts east of Raleigh were still too small and contained defective masonry. In the spring of 1862 heavy rains and flooding washed out three embankments on this division and damaged three others. On May 22 a locomotive was "precipitated into the chasm" created by one of these washouts near Selma, killing two of the crew. Two culverts near Raleigh gave way in 1864.[13]

Rolling stock deteriorated as rapidly as rails, and opportunities for repair and replacement were scarce. The road possessed twenty-three locomotives when the war started. Even then, according to Webb, it needed several more engines as well as additional passenger and freight cars. Partial relief began appearing in May 1862 in the form of engines and cars rented from the Manassas Gap Railroad and other lines in Virginia, some of which had fallen into enemy hands.[14] Five more locomotives arrived by February 1863: another rented from the Manassas Gap Railroad and four purchased from the Confederate government, at least one of them captured from the Baltimore and Ohio.[15] These accessions were a product of the same government concern that resulted in more section hands and a greatly improved roadbed that spring. Although William Wadley, head of the army's railroad bureau, estimated in April that the NCRR needed yet another four engines to do its work properly,[16] these seem to have arrived only as replacements for engines that wore out altogether. Webb reported in July

1864 that the road was operating with the same number of locomotives as a year earlier.[17]

Another product of government intervention in 1863 may have been an improvement in locomotive maintenance. During the first two years of the war the engines deteriorated rapidly under the stress of pulling longer, heavier, and more frequent trains. As many as five were apt to be in the shops at a given time.[18] Some gave out altogether and were scrapped. Two were rebuilt at the shops ("from the ground to the top of the whistle," Webb boasted) and put back into service in 1864 and 1865, rechristened the Governor Morehead and the Charles F. Fisher.[19] In 1862 Quartermaster General Myers established a railroad shop in Raleigh for the repair of any locomotives and cars that the government might acquire.[20] Some of the engines acquired by the NCRR may have gone through that shop first, but most if not all of the NCRR's work continued to be done at its own shops with whatever materials it could bring to hand. Some of these materials may have been smuggled in through the blockade. The company records contain a copy of a contract in October 1862 with an importer of British supplies for a long list of items ranging from flanged wheel tires and boiler plate for locomotives to varnish and plush carpeting for cars.[21] The locomotives remaining in service in 1863 were pronounced to be in much better order, on average, than they were a year earlier.[22] The same was reported in 1864. Even in July 1865 Webb reported—at severe risk to his credibility, given other evidence—that the locomotives were generally in first-rate order, although two or three were virtually worn out.[23]

Although cars were cheaper to buy and easier to build than locomotives, they were needed in much greater quantity. The road possessed 313 (of all descriptions) in 1860. In 1862 the number was 285, to which were added 95 others rented from the Manassas Gap, Seaboard and Roanoke, and Richmond, Fredericksburg, and Potomac railroads in Virginia—all more or less in Federal hands—and perhaps 50 flatcars belonging to the Confederate government. During 1861–62, 34 new cars were produced in the shops, all but 1 of them freight and work cars. The road was still short by over 100 cars—mostly freight cars, given its traffic load.[24] Despite later acquisitions, the same would be true in 1863 and afterward. Most of the new cars were purchased, owing to the difficulty of obtaining construction materials.[25] They were likely bought from the army, and may have been captured Yankee cars. Late in March 1865 the road agreed to buy eleven army-owned freight cars that were already operating on the NCRR.[26]

Heavy traffic required that cars be in constant use, as compared with prewar times when they were taken out of service at regular intervals for inspection and overhaul. As a result, damage became more frequent, causing expensive and sometimes fatal accidents. Broken axles and trucks were among the most common and lethal causes of accidents, often leading to derailments.

Unaccustomed usage also accelerated deterioration. Owing to the shortage of passenger coaches, soldiers traveled chiefly in boxcars. These were often overcrowded and lacked ventilation, especially at the slow speeds mandated by deteriorating rails and equipment. Soldiers rectified the lack by kicking holes in the sides or pulling boards off altogether. They were replaced over and over again. At one point the NCRR remodeled forty-five boxcars for soldier use by installing windows and plank seats, but that hardly ended the problem. Broken and dilapidated cars left their freight cargoes open to weather damage, theft, and further vandalism. As for the passenger cars, the 1864 stockholders' inspection committee characterized them as even shabbier than the freight cars.[27]

The addition of cars from other roads in 1862 and later permitted somewhat better inspection, and the shops were constantly at work repairing and rebuilding passenger and freight cars. But they never caught up. Many of the cars that remained at war's end were in woeful condition.[28]

Wartime traffic about doubled the road's fuel consumption. By 1862 wood was in very short supply for both fuel and crossties. The same was true in large degree for all the state's railroads. The problem was less a shortage of trees than of the labor to cut and deliver them. Before the war the NCRR contracted with nearby landowners who furnished their own labor, usually slaves, to deliver a stipulated quantity of wood cut to the proper sizes. Now, however, labor became so scarce that it could often be employed more profitably in farming and other activities. The Confederate government, needing wood for hospitals and military installations, frequently added to the problem by commandeering a large share of the available supply or by offering such high prices that private suppliers were induced to violate their contracts with the railroad. Editor William W. Holden of the *Standard* was outraged at reports of military details appropriating all the cordwood they found along the railroad late in 1862, when Raleigh's poor were suffering from lack of wood and from extortionate prices on the supply that was available. He was no happier at hearing that the railroads themselves were unwilling to bring more wood to the city.[29]

In 1863 the NCRR, in self-protection it said, began demanding for itself half of any wood it hauled.[30] At about the same time it began (like other roads) to purchase woodlands of its own to assure a steady supply, particularly between Company Shops and Raleigh. It still had to find labor to cut the wood, and slave work crews were constantly under threat of conscription to build fortifications or to perform other labor for the army. If that practice went much further, Webb warned ominously in 1864, it threatened to cripple the railroad. But in March 1865 the NCRR was so vital to Confederate strategy and in such dire straits that the army actually conscripted laborers to cut wood for the railroad.[31]

The road also experienced water shortages, again particularly between Company Shops and Raleigh. Water stations or tanks were distributed evenly along the road. Where dependable streams flowed nearby, water was pumped from them. Where streams were not so dependable, reliance was placed on wells. Heavy wartime usage caused some of the wells to run dry. Train schedules were even interrupted as locomotives were temporarily immobilized. Blasting powder, often needed to dig additional wells, was unavailable. Nevertheless, new wells were dug at Raleigh, Durham, and elsewhere, and larger tanks were built at a number of places. Another solution was to procure additional pumps and employ creeks that had hitherto been bypassed. By these means the road ultimately seems to have satisfied its water needs.[32]

Depots and warehouses were another source of concern. At Raleigh, the NCRR and the Raleigh and Gaston had never agreed on the location of a joint passenger station. The temporary substitute was hardly worthy of the name. In February 1862 the *Raleigh Register* described the vicinity as a "hog-wallow" and pointed to the absence of even a proper platform from which to board NCRR trains. "Daily is presented the spectacle not only of men, but of delicate women and children wading over their ankles in red clay mire, in their entrance and departure from the cars. Such a railroad platform is a disgrace to the Company to which it belongs, and to the Capital of the State, while it is a most uncomfortable imposition on the traveller." Three weeks later there was a new platform, attributed by some to the change of presidents that month. But there was no accompanying building, and the surrounding mud threatened to mire even the horses that approached.[33] The stockholders' inspection committee was equally indignant: "It is a reproach both to the road and to the State, that the station at our Capital, where hundreds of passengers are passing and repassing daily, should be without a passenger shed to protect them and their baggage from the weather, and that a station where ladies and gentlemen are often compelled to wait for hours for the arrival of the cars, should not even have appropriate room for ladies or a water closet for gentlemen." A repetition of the complaint and a formal vote of the stockholders in 1863 could not procure the necessary building, although the drainage was improved.

When plans were finally made with the Raleigh and Gaston for a joint passenger shed, government demands for lumber were so great that, even possessing a sawmill of its own, the NCRR could not get the necessary lumber.[34]

Accommodations were not much different at Charlotte, where passengers also waded through mud while changing trains. Additional room for passengers was needed at Greensboro and Salisbury, also among the busiest stations and junctions where through passengers had to wait between trains.[35]

Freight warehouses were inadequate at a number of places, but particularly at the busiest depots. Both Charlotte and Goldsboro lacked proper facilities for housing the engines and cars that had to lie over at those termini.[36]

The road suffered fire losses of various kinds, some accidental, others the work of arsonists. Some were unconnected with the war, others directly related to it. On two occasions, in 1861 and 1863, woodpiles adjacent to the track were consumed, perhaps ignited by sparks from a locomotive. In the earlier case, near Selma, about 200 yards of crossties in the track burned also.[37] Similar events in that vicinity in 1857 and 1858 had been attributed to arson. In January 1865 a catastrophic fire—to be discussed later—destroyed the depot at Charlotte. In addition, both armies would be responsible for burnings in the final weeks of the war.

The road's wooden bridges were always in some danger from locomotive sparks. They were also an obvious target of arsonists seeking to hurt the railroad if not the Confederacy. Thus the road continued to hire watchmen for some of its bridges. The quality of service left something to be desired, as when the watchman at the Yadkin River bridge fell asleep on the track and was nearly killed by a passing train.[38] In time, soldiers were assigned to the duty in recognition that the road was vital to the war effort. But their performance was not always better. In May 1863 the bridge over South Buffalo Creek west of Greensboro was discovered to be on fire by the engineer of a train passing over it. The flames were put out and the guards who had been posted at the bridge to protect it were found some distance away, fishing.[39] Soon afterward, and perhaps coincidentally, the army decided that its bridge details were needed more urgently at the front and withdrew them. Governor Vance replaced them with North Carolina militia, but this proved unpopular with the public, who resented being drafted for this duty when the NCRR and other railroads seemed to wallow in swollen profits taken at the public's expense. Let the roads hire their own guards, was the cry.[40]

The need for protection of some kind was dramatically shown in July 1864 when two adjacent NCRR bridges in Davidson County were burned, apparently by incendiaries. They were the spans over Rich Fork and Abbott's Creek, near Lexington. It is unclear if guards were assigned to these bridges; one account had a sleeping watchman on duty.[41]

President Webb in 1862 pronounced the shops complex to have been the road's salvation. He thus paid tribute to his predecessors' controversial decisions in building it on such a large scale. At the same time he asked forcefully for authorization to build a new roundhouse for engines. "The present shed is for the purpose intended a miserable abortion. So great is the difficulty of getting an engine into it and out of it, that it is scarcely ever used." Instead engines were housed at one end of the car shed or outside, exposed to the elements. Although the stockholders granted this request in 1863, wartime material shortages prevented any action until after the war.[42]

Railway labor—all kinds of labor—of course was in short supply throughout the war. The problem was most acute with skilled mechanics, who were limited in number anyway and whose skills were valuable in the army. Some of the best workers enlisted in the army early in the war or were lured away by higher wages on other roads, in other industries, or even in working for the government. Thus the quality as well as quantity of workers diminished. The shortage extended also to common laborers and section hands—usually hired slaves—whose services were sought by urban and rural employers of every kind and by army work details.

The first Confederate conscription act of April 1862 specifically exempted all railway employees. But this law was supplanted in October by another that limited railroad exemptions to higher officials, conductors, engineers, station agents, section masters, mechanics, and two expert track hands for each eight-mile section.[43] In February 1864, as military manpower needs became increasingly desperate, a new law limited exemptions to one worker for each mile of railroad that was in actual use for military transportation. Presumably to compensate for the decreasing numbers of men exempted, the president and the secretary of war were permitted to detail military personnel to essential civilian jobs, including railroad work. The roads were shorthanded in almost every respect, but they perhaps experienced their greatest hardship in securing workers for fringe labor such as woodcutting. Slaves were sometimes commandeered temporarily for these tasks, as in the last hectic days of the war when General Joseph E. Johnston was using the NCRR to assemble an army below Raleigh to oppose Sherman.[44]

Early in the war the government was slow to recognize the impact of its conscription laws on the railroads, and the NCRR almost went to rack and ruin by the end of 1862. Detailed personnel from the army saved the situation the next spring, but the prospect of further tightening under the 1864 law brought protests from President Webb and other railroad officials and even from Colonel Sims, head of the railroad bureau. Webb, who seems to have earned a reputation as a complainer, now argued that his road could not operate with fewer men than it already had. If more were taken away, he threatened to prevent trains from other roads from operating on the NCRR. There were then six of these, he said in June, and wood could barely be found for them with the personnel at hand.

The head of the conscription bureau in Richmond believed that he had already been too lenient with the NCRR. He responded to Webb's threat by proposing a more drastic cutback on the NCRR than had originally been contemplated—a reduction of its employees by one-quarter at the end of a month and by one-eighth every fifteen days thereafter until the force was down to the new legal limit. Colonel Sims conceded that the NCRR's labor demands "have been always excessive and no doubt are so in this instance[.] But from my information as to the actual wants of a railroad doing so much work as the North Carolina company, I am satisfied that it is impossible to operate and keep it up with the one man per mile allowed by law." He called attention to the NCRR's previous deterioration and the work that had to be done a year earlier to bring it back. He urged at least a partial compliance with Webb's request, therefore, and this view seems to have prevailed.[45]

The wartime wages of railway workers lagged well behind the inflation rate. By 1863 those in North Carolina received less than half in real wages what they had gotten in 1860. Railwaymen in Atlanta nominally made six times as much in January 1865 as they had four years earlier, but their real wages were only one-third to one-half of the prewar level. Shopmen often fared best on account of their skills.[46]

The NCRR actually had the temerity in 1862 to lower the wages of its section masters, from $33 to $25 per month.[47] For white employees in particular, the road did not record its wages systematically until 1865, so wartime comparisons for them are impossible.

The road did a better job of recording Negro hand hire. As before the war, nearly all of the hands were slaves hired from masters to whom an account had to be made. In January 1862 the road hired 283 slaves, compared with 276 in 1856. Among the larger owners were Paul C. Cameron (then president of the road), with fifteen slaves; George W. Mordecai of Raleigh, ten; and Josiah Collins of Cool Spring, thirty-four. A number of the slaveowners were normally residents of New Bern and other coastal places experiencing or threatened with Union occupation. The hiring cost varied from $60 to $200 apiece for the year, with the average about $90 and the total $25,675. In each case the amount depended partly on the qualifications and responsibilities of the slave himself but (in the case of unskilled laborers) chiefly on the deal struck by each owner. Firemen (or rather, their owners) received from $80 to $150; an office boy was hired at $65.

In 1864 the number of hired slaves rose to about 318. Inflation by this time had raised the average annual cost into the $200 to $400 range. A sawyer at the shops drew $720 for his owner. J. W. B. Watson of Smithfield received $300 for each of his thirty-five slaves. In general, the road supplied food, clothing, housing, and medical care, although some owners made special stipulations. Jacob Mordecai of Raleigh required that his slaves be returned to him for a week at harvest time. Clothing still normally consisted of "two pair of Shoes, one Hat, one Blanket, or [as was stipulated in one case] a good substitute." The company itself often required that any runaway time be deducted from the amount owed the master.[48] By 1865 the road publicly offered $800 for ordinary laborers and $1,000 for mechanics. It paid these amounts as well as $2,000 for a blacksmith. The total cost of slave hire that year reached $179,079, compared with the $25,675 of 1862.[49] It became increasingly hard to find slaves for hire at any price, owing to the competition for their labor. Hence railroads began buying slaves of their own so far as they could find and afford them. By late 1864 few were for sale either.[50]

Despite appeals by President Fisher in 1856 and 1859 for the purchase of a substantial number of slaves, the NCRR seems to have bought only two before the war. President Webb renewed the appeal in 1862, urging the stockholders to buy enough men at once to supply at least the train crews.

From time to time, he said, more should be added until the company owned enough to work the whole road effectively. When the stockholders took no action, he asked again in 1863, citing the low cost of slaves at that juncture compared with what they would cost once the South had won the war and peace returned. This time he secured an appropriation of $100,000.[51]

For whatever reason, no purchases were actually made until December 1864. But in that month and the next, the road bought twenty-eight slaves for a total of about $138,000 in depreciated end-of-the-war currency. The great majority were young males between fifteen and twenty-four years old, bringing from $4,500 to $6,000 apiece. Also included was a girl of twenty and a woman named Margaret and her five children, including an infant not yet named. Twelve of the men were purchased in Augusta, Georgia, in December, just as Sherman passed by; the others appear to have been bought in Raleigh, Charlotte, and other places in North Carolina.[52] There is no record of what work these people did in the final months of the war. The road's financial investment in them was soon lost, of course, together with all the Confederate money and bonds that the road might have invested in slaves but did not.

12

Passenger and Freight Operations

WARTIME TRAVEL ON southern railroads became high adventure, and conditions got worse as the war progressed. Trains were overcrowded. Speeds were lowered to ten miles per hour, even to walking speed under some conditions as roadbed and equipment deteriorated, and it became almost impossible to adhere to schedules. The condition of prepared meals at the wayside eating places may well be imagined. Breakdowns were increasingly common. Troop trains usually consisted of boxcars fitted with plank seats or, increasingly, box- and flatcars with no seats at all. Many men chose to ride on top. One army officer estimated that a railway trip from Montgomery to Richmond was "as hazardous as picket duty on the Potomac."[1]

The NCRR was by no means spared these conditions. Passenger trains quickly increased in size to six to ten overflowing cars from the two partially filled ones before the war. Passenger train speeds, previously up to twenty-two miles per hour (including stops) were reduced to seventeen in the first year of the war.[2] Two daily passenger trains (one a mixed train including freight) were the rule throughout most of the war.

Schedules changed frequently, and eventually war-related interruptions became so common that regular schedules were impossible to maintain. In an effort to preserve a semblance of them, trains sometimes cut short their stops or even passed rural stations altogether without stopping.[3] In these circumstances the NCRR and other roads virtually gave up advertising their schedules—it seemed an exercise in futility.[4]

As before the war, there were complaints that trains on connecting roads did not actually connect, forcing through passengers to make long layovers. Faulty connections sometimes resulted from the complexity of coordinating schedules among several connecting roads but probably more often from delays attributable to military intervention and deteriorating roads and equipment.[5]

In January 1863 the *Greensboro Patriot*, no friend to the NCRR since Fisher's day, snapped that "the detentions, accidents and general mismanagement on the N.C. Railroad are becoming intolerable." Even the friendly

Raleigh *Standard* complained of "exceedingly vexatious" failures on the NCRR. "We are afraid the trains will stop altogether if something is not done soon." A frustrated Editor Holden repeated a current joke: "'Have you heard of the Railroad accident?'—'No—where was it?' 'The Central train left Charlotte and arrived at Raleigh in schedule time.'"[6] An army surgeon, trying to return to the front in September 1863 from High Point, found his train twelve hours late owing to troop movements. (Longstreet's corps was being shifted south from Virginia to reinforce Bragg near Chattanooga; the direct route through East Tennessee had just been cut by the enemy.)[7] At various times, and especially in spring 1864 and spring 1865, civilian traffic was virtually suspended as all available rolling stock was temporarily impressed for military service.[8]

When the trains did run, passengers experienced many discomforts. As early as June 1861, soldiers noted the absence of water on NCRR trains. The stockholders' inspection committee made the same complaint a year later, emphasizing the plight of sick and wounded soldiers without water.[9] By 1864 North Carolina and other states had passed laws requiring railroads to provide water, lights, and in some cases fire on every car. Despite such provisions, these amenities were often lacking, probably from a shortage of personnel to attend to them. A Raleigh paper referred in the spring of 1864 to robberies of passengers on darkened NCRR cars.[10]

Sick and wounded soldiers were carried in conventional cars—passenger coaches wherever possible. The Wilmington and Weldon reportedly fitted out a few ambulance cars early in the war, but there is no record of them on the NCRR.[11] Local women provided food, cheer, and clean bandages for wounded soldiers passing through Greensboro and Hillsboro, in the latter part of 1862 at least. Those at Greensboro would go to the Shops to meet westbound trains, even at midnight, then accompany them back to Greensboro in this voluntary service. At Raleigh the Ladies' Way Side Hospital was established and run by local women near the NCRR depot to care for wounded soldiers under the supervision of the surgeon general.[12]

Vendors continued to sell food, some of it cooked, to passengers at the stations. Apparently whites and blacks, free and slave, pursued this trade.[13] In October 1863 the hotel at Company Shops closed down as an eating house for passengers but remained as a boarding house for shop employees. "Many a weary traveler will thank the fates for this," wrote Editor J. L. Pennington of the Raleigh *Daily Progress*, "for now he will retain his money and his hunger will go unappeased, while before he parted from his money and still went hungry." An eating house remained at Durham, he added, that "furnishes a passable breakfast at $3."[14]

Railroads made little effort to inform or conciliate the public—the failure that did in Paul C. Cameron. Poor public relations extended from the top down. Announcements concerning higher rates, curtailed service, and the unacceptability at certain times of Confederate currency were couched in the most abrupt terms, with little or no attempt at explanation. Employees, diminished in numbers and coping with unprecedented traffic, lost much of the courtesy and deference that the traveling public remembered from prewar days. The Salisbury *Carolina Watchman* complained early in 1864 of the "train servants on the N.C. Road, who went swinging through the cars smoking their pipes with as much self-importance as some of the insolent conductors."[15]

These conditions were endemic by the latter part of 1864. "If any one wishes to pass through just that amount of torture that is insupportable," wrote Editor D. K. McRae of the *Raleigh Confederate* in February 1865,

> let him take a trip on the North Carolina Railroad, towards Greensboro', and, thence, over the Piedmont to Danville. Great allowance is to be made for the times, and the difficulties of keeping up the condition of the roads. But neither the times nor the condition of roads excuse a total abandonment of order, method, neatness, regularity and comfort. When an Engine comes from Goldsboro' towards Raleigh, broken down, and thence starts for Greensboro, there is neither reason or sense in the endeavor to force it through at the hazard of life to all aboard; certainly to the prolongation of their travel, when Engines are standing, in better plight, at Company Shops, and there are telegraph stations along the route.

McRae wrote, from personal experience, a few nights earlier:

> The train was long and full;—many soldiers returning to their commands. The Engine on leaving Raleigh was completely broken down, so that the speed attained averaged about two miles per hour. It was easy to telegraph from Raleigh so as to have a good Engine to meet the train at Durham's. Yet this simple act of justice, to a heavily taxed traveling public, was wholly ignored, and we were compelled to fret and worry along through the cold bitter night, consuming twenty four hours in reaching Greensboro, the better engine only reaching us near Haw river? [sic] As for cleanliness or comfort, they are gone out of date—out of recollection—and if any unfortunate passenger should desire to obtain information, and applied to the conductor, he might as well attack a bull dog.

The Piedmont was even worse. "God save the country," McRae concluded, "if its destiny in any wise depends on proper and conscientious performance of duty by Railroad corporations."[16]

If conditions were bad with the new presence of the telegraph, they would surely have been much worse in its absence. It was pretty well established during the 1850s that the use of the telegraph in dispatching trains virtually doubled the capacity of a single-track railroad. In addition, it brought company personnel closer together into a more effective unit; it reported weather conditions, and it helped to standardize time.[17]

By 1860 the American Telegraph Company stretched virtually without competition from Newfoundland to New Orleans. The Civil War temporarily tore this empire asunder. Early in 1861 the southern part of the system was organized as the Southern Telegraph Company, and it quickly dominated the industry in the new confederacy.[18]

Despite President Fisher's prewar efforts to acquire telegraph service along the line of the NCRR, it did not come until 1861 and 1862. In the former year Southern Telegraph built a line from Goldsboro to Raleigh. In spring and summer 1862 the Southern Express Company constructed a line from Charlotte to Raleigh. Both used the railroad right of way. Under the Southern Express contract the NCRR erected the poles and the express company strung the wires, provided the apparatus, and operated the service. Telegraph offices were established at Charlotte, Concord, Salisbury, Lexington, High Point, Greensboro, Company Shops, Hillsboro, Durham, and Raleigh. President Webb hoped for a similar agreement with Southern Telegraph permitting service on its line at Selma as well as at Raleigh and Goldsboro. Once opened, these offices were distributed along the road at roughly twenty-mile intervals. The railroad was to have free use of the telegraph for its own operations.[19] NCRR officials all lamented that the device had not been available to them earlier; the stockholders' inspection committee of 1863 cited it as an efficient means of preventing accidents.[20] The communities along the road were also eager to see its arrival.

The telegraph may well have diminished the number of collisions. These seem to have fallen off after its completion in 1862. But it could do little to prevent the frequent derailments occasioned by deteriorating track and equipment and an unprecedented volume of traffic. Amazingly, only one NCRR passenger was killed in a train accident during the war,[21] although injuries to passengers and crews were considerable. Not counted among these were the perennial cases of persons running to board moving trains then falling beneath the wheels or those where trains ran over persons walking, standing, or lying on the track in varying stages of inebriation. Brakemen and other workers continued to suffer injury or death while coupling or uncoupling cars and performing other tasks in a very dangerous occupation.

Altogether the accident rate was abnormally high. In the first year of the war, 1861–62, there were twenty-five derailments. By far the worst was occasioned by a washed-out culvert near Selma, killing the fireman and woodpasser and severely injuring the engineer. Another occurred when a train ran over a cow. Three resulted from defective track, twelve from broken axles, and eight from other mechanical failures on the cars. In addition, there were three collisions, two of them serious. Despite the single passenger fatality (and few injuries) during the war, most of these accidents involved passenger trains.[22]

Employee negligence was responsible for some of the most serious accidents. One of the derailments and one of the collisions were caused by

misdirected switches at or near Raleigh. A slave injured in the collision had
to have an arm amputated.[23] Another collision occurred in February 1862
when a northbound accommodation train ran head-on into the southbound
express about ten miles north of Charlotte. The fault lay with the engineer
of the accommodation train, whom Superintendent Wilkes accused of "extreme recklessness." The express train was carrying Georgia and South
Carolina soldiers home on furlough. Although there were no fatalities, four
or five persons (both soldiers and train crew) were seriously hurt, and one
had to have a leg amputated. A subscription of $120 was raised in Charlotte
to aid the injured soldiers. Both locomotives and several cars were lost.
Another collision resulted from a typographical error in a new timetable on
its first day in use.[24]

The first fatality among crewmen came in April 1862 when a car broke
down causing the death of the Southern Express messenger and several
injuries.[25] The Selma washout with its two deaths took place in May 1862. A
second head-on collision, between High Point and Thomasville in June,
seems to have resulted from army officers running an unauthorized train
despite warnings against it. There was one fatality and about $30,000 in
property damage.[26] All of this occurred before the completion of the telegraph west of Raleigh and in the absence of a telegraph office at Selma.

The *Concord Flag* declared in May 1862 that "the present condition of the
N.C.R.R. is absolutely frightful. Crashes, smashes up, collisions, broken
axles, running off the track, and accidents of every imaginable description, are of such frequent occurrence that, they are scarcely noticed by the
newspapers and [are] looked upon by the community as small matters of
course." One reason it assigned was poor track occasioned by rotten crossties. That same month the port of Norfolk fell into Union hands, and the
Confederate navy yard was being relocated to a trackside location in Charlotte. A train carrying navy equipment was involved in a collision at the
Concord depot and was delayed for several days.[27] The *Raleigh Register*,
commenting that "it is getting to be as much as one's life is worth to travel
on the N.C. Railroad," held up the Raleigh and Gaston as an example of a
well-run railroad, but several months later it had to report a head-on collision resulting in three deaths on that road.[28]

Derailments increased after 1862 despite the telegraph and slower train
speeds mandated that year. Some were serious, taking lives and damaging
or destroying scarce rolling stock.[29] And some continued to result from
negligence such as open switches rather than from wear and tear.[30] In the
last month of the war General Joseph E. Johnston was detained for the
greater part of a night "by one of the accidents then inevitable on the North
Carolina Railroad." He had gone to Greensboro to consult with Jefferson
Davis and the refugee Confederate government after Lee's surrender and
now was trying to rejoin his army facing Sherman near Hillsboro.[31]

Collisions probably diminished because of the telegraph. Nevertheless, two trains collided near Hillsboro in 1863, the result of an engineer's watch being twenty-six minutes slow.[32] The most egregious case of negligence came in July 1864 when conductor Wynn Robinson forced his train to stop and back up between High Point and Jamestown in order to retrieve his hat, which had blown off. He declared that he would find it if it took all night. In time a freight train, headed in the same direction, rounded a curve and rammed into the rear coach, killing a woman passenger and injuring several others. Having caused what proved to be the road's only passenger fatality of the war and the first in its history, Robinson "broke for the woods." A few weeks later he was arrested in Goldsboro and brought back to Greensboro to face trial.[33] Another collision, seemingly preventable by the telegraph, occurred at Morrisville, near Raleigh, in September 1864. The express or mail train collided with a freight train, badly damaging both locomotives and a number of cars. Among the injured passengers was a member-elect of the legislature, returning from the army, who lost a leg.[34]

One of the most spectacular accidents came in January 1865 with the explosion of the locomotive Rowan, pulling a freight train near Lexington. The engineer and two black firemen lost their lives. The Rowan, one of the road's two 4-6-0s (or ten-wheelers), had just been rebuilt in the shops—imperfectly, it seems—and the loss to the road was great.[35]

Prisoners of war seldom traveled on regularly scheduled passenger trains. Apart from the quality of personal service they received, it is unclear how typical were the engines and cars assigned to their trains. They were not apt to have been the best. Many Federal prisoners traveling on the NCRR were bound to or from the Confederate prison at Salisbury. Some passed through on their way to or from prisons at Danville, Richmond, Andersonville, Georgia, and other points at a distance.

The Salisbury prison was adjacent to the NCRR track (see fig. 17). Originally built as a cotton mill in 1839, it was converted to its wartime use in December 1861. The main building of three full stories measured about 40 by 100 feet. It housed all of the prisoners assigned there until October 1864, when a deluge of additional inmates arrived. For the next four months the facility was grossly overcrowded and became a death camp. At the end of 1864 it contained over 8,000 men, about three times its estimated capacity. They found what shelter they could in the surrounding stockaded compound. Up to 75 per day died from exposure and starvation.[36]

Over 5,000 prisoners were in residence in February 1865 when virtually all of them were sent off to Richmond and Wilmington for exchange. At this point Sherman was expected to advance northward toward Charlotte and Salisbury. Confederate officials were anxious to prevent their prisoners from falling into his hands, thereby destroying the possibility of a prisoner exchange. The railroad was thus faced with the extra assignment of moving these 5,000 prisoners, plus 6,000 more from South Carolina. Many were to go as far as Greensboro on the NCRR, many others all the way to Goldsboro. Rolling stock was in acutely short supply, so those prisoners able to do so were required to march fifty miles to Greensboro to board trains. Almost 2,300 were not able; they were moved the whole distance by rail.[37] This exercise took place just before the even greater confusion in March, when Confederate forces retreated by rail through Charlotte, Salisbury, and Raleigh in order to regroup before Sherman, who was now headed into eastern North Carolina.

After the war some of the involuntary passengers published accounts of their experiences. Nearly all of them recounted events of 1864 or early 1865, when the prisoner population at Salisbury and elsewhere was greatest and conditions on and off the railroad were at their most wretched. Their accounts tend to corroborate each other; in fact, two of the prisoners (Allen O. Abbott and Asa B. Isham) appear to have traveled in the same car between Greensboro and Charlotte on their way to Andersonville in May 1864. At Greensboro they were herded into rickety boxcars, sixty men to a car with a lucky few permitted to ride on top. It was impossible for more than a quarter of the men to sit, much less lie down, at once. Ten miles out of Greensboro the train stopped; the locomotive had run out of steam. It was uncoupled, went off to get up steam, and returned in an hour. Resuming, the train proceeded at about eight miles per hour, reaching Charlotte fourteen hours after leaving Greensboro. Despite numerous stops along the way, prisoners were forbidden to leave the train for any reason, and some were shot for doing so to relieve themselves. On other trains the men were crowded seventy or more per car, some of them again riding on top.[38]

Major Abner Small made the same trip as far as Salisbury in October 1864. Departing Greensboro on the morning of October 5, he recalled:

> Our progress was slow. The road was sadly out of repair, the rolling stock was worn out, and fuel was scarce. Often on an ascending grade the train would stop, and sometimes would run back in spite of brakes. The trainmen replenished the tender with fence rails, and themselves with corn whiskey. The firebox was crammed with pitch knots, the heat became fervent, the steam hissed; the engine would creak and groan in every joint when the throttle was pulled wide open at the head of a long, steep grade, and the cars with their living freight would gather speed and plunge madly down the uneven track. We were slatted from side to side, thrown down, and piled in heaps, groaning and cursing. Several of our number saw their opportunity and leaped from the rushing train, preferring the risk to an indefinite stay in a stockade. The guard fired at them dutifully, but the shots must have gone wide. At nightfall we reached Salisbury.

The fifty-mile trip took twelve hours.[39]

Several months later Benjamin F. Booth, one of those forced to march from Salisbury to Greensboro toward a prisoner exchange, found himself on a train of flatcars (for the most part) headed toward Raleigh. The cars were so crowded that some men nearly fell off. It was an overnight trip on a cold night in February, and most of the men lacked any protection from the elements. It took eleven hours to travel the eighty-one miles from Greensboro. After a five-hour stop in Raleigh they left for Goldsboro on another train of flatcars. This fifty-mile trip took about four hours. The track was out of repair, Booth recalled, and from the clatter of the engine and cars, they were in equally bad shape. Even in this relatively flat country the decrepit engine failed to make the grade on one occasion. It backed down and the prisoners waited an hour for sufficient steam to be made to take them up the hill. From Goldsboro Booth took a similar trip to Wilmington, the W&W train sometimes traveling at only a good walking speed.[40]

GIVEN THESE CONDITIONS, wartime mail service was less than regular. "Disrupted train schedules meant disrupted mails," as historian Robert C. Black remarked. "Diversion of rolling stock to military use brought chaos to many postal routes, and fantastic delays were experienced by even government dispatches. The army attempted to alleviate the situation in 1862 with a directive requiring troop trains to carry mail cars, but this was of little help, for such trains could hardly wait for connections." In general, southern railroads were underpaid by the government for carrying the mails, and increasingly so as inflation mounted. Postmaster General John H. Reagan met with a number of leading railroad presidents at Montgomery late in April 1861 in order to work out a system of mail contracts. The compensation agreed upon was $150 per mile per year on the major through lines "connecting important points and conveying heavy mails"; $100 per mile on roads carrying heavy local mail; and $50 per mile on short or unfinished roads with light mail. This scale remained generally in effect until February 1865, despite the catastrophic fall in the value of the Confederate dollar. Thus the roads carried the mails, to the extent that they were able to do so, increasingly as a public service. Even the revised rates of early 1865 were "ridiculously small," as Black says, amounting to only $225 per mile on the heavily trafficked lines.[41]

North Carolina did not secede until May 1861. The United States Post Office discontinued mail service on the NCRR at the end of that month, "till the same can be safely restored."[42] This came a month after the Montgomery meeting. Until that time the road had been receiving $22,300 per annum for carrying the mail, or $100 per mile. During the next two years it annually received $26,375 from the Confederacy and slightly more thereafter, averaging between $118 and $130 per mile.

Nineteenth-century newspapers disseminated the news by exchanging with and copying each other. Even after the advent of the telegraph they were largely dependent on the mails—and the railroads that carried the mails—for outside news in the form of out-of-town papers and for the circulation of their own papers. They were acutely sensitive to train schedules, therefore, sometimes changing publication times to anticipate the departure of the daily mail train.

Throughout the war, mail service along the NCRR was as irregular as its train schedules. Service was particularly bad at times of heavy troop movements or of crises in supplying the army, when the government impressed trains or even temporarily suspended civilian traffic altogether. Newspapers along the road sporadically noted, lamented, or exploded over interruptions, delays, and other inconveniences in the mail service. Often ignorant of the causes, they were inclined to blame the most visible target, the railroad. Sometimes they were right, as when the Charlotte *Daily Bulletin* charged the road's officers with "culpible [sic] neglect . . . in not giving notice of their intention to change the transportation of the Mails from the morning to the night train." The paper changed its publication time accordingly.[43]

Delays were particularly frequent in the winter of 1862–63. After several months of this, the *Greensboro Patriot* characterized "the detentions, accidents and general mismanagement on the N.C. Railroad" as "becoming intolerable," and the Raleigh *Standard* called its failures "exceedingly vexatious."[44] The Raleigh *Daily Progress* fired a more general blast: "No mail from the North last night, no mail from the West yesterday, and none from anywhere that anybody knows of save the Fayetteville [mail], which, being moved by horse power, is always on time. We print our paper as heretofore and send it to the post office, but we can't promise that subscribers will ever receive it, for we have no power over the mails." To this the editor added a postscript saying that the northern mail had just been interrupted by a derailment on the Raleigh and Gaston.[45]

Sometimes the train, mail car and all, would arrive more or less on schedule but without any mail, leaving editors to fume helplessly about "gross negligence somewhere."[46] In April 1864 and again in March 1865 government impressment of all available trains suspended mail service entirely for several days despite a requirement that troop trains had to carry mail cars whenever regular passenger service was interrupted. The failure of these special trains to make regular connections with those on other roads does not explain their failure even to carry mail from Raleigh to Charlotte. The Raleigh *Daily Confederate* finally suspended publication until further notice in March 1865 because of the current "derangement of the mails."[47]

Almost as frustrating sometimes, but much more remunerative to railroads during the war, was the express business. The Adams Express Company had become the dominant firm in the South during the 1850s. At the outbreak of the war its southern operations were sold to a newly organized Southern Express Company under Henry B. Plant, the later Florida railroad promoter. As superintendent of the company's eastern division, including North Carolina, Plant appointed Rufus B. Bullock, who would achieve fame after the war as Reconstruction governor of Georgia. The Confederate government made Southern Express the official custodian of all funds being transferred from place to place. Its agents were exempt from conscription.[48]

The NCRR had been under contract with Adams Express since 1859, and its agreement was one of many inherited by Southern Express in 1861. When President Cameron (along with the executives of connecting roads) renewed the contract with Southern Express in November 1861, he stipulated that it use its own cars on the NCRR and that they be carried in the daily accommodation train, which carried freight primarily.[49] Subsequently the express seems to have been carried on both passenger and freight trains.[50] The relationship with Southern Express was sometimes a rocky one, but it endured for many years.[51] As already described, Southern Express and the NCRR also agreed early in 1862 to construct a telegraph line from Raleigh to Charlotte, a task that was completed that summer.

Like so many other wartime business dealings, those with Southern Express fell afoul of the unprecedented wartime inflation and the widespread misunderstanding of its causes. As express rates mounted, Southern Express, like the railroads themselves, came to be perceived as profiteering at public expense. Its officers were suspected also of corruption and trading with the enemy.[52] There were unsuccessful efforts in the North Carolina and other legislatures to tax it out of the state. But Southern Express had its defenders. Its higher rates, they pointed out, usually sprang from its own rising costs, chiefly in the form of rates paid to the host railroads. And the company performed indispensable services. As the war progressed, shipping other kinds of freight became more and more difficult. If goods were of sufficient value to justify the higher cost, they were sent by express with some assurance that they would reach their destinations. "If speed, promptness, and certainty are required in the transmission of an article, from a lady's ring to a hogshead of molasses," said the *Greensboro Patriot*, "it is only necessary to put it on the Express and the safe and punctual delivery of it may be amply relied on." But once an item of value was "entrusted to the railroad companies, as common freight," agreed the Raleigh *Daily Progress*, "the chances are you will never hear of it again."[53]

Express receipts represented only a fraction of total freight receipts on the NCRR, but as Superintendent Wilkes pointed out in 1862, it was becoming the most remunerative branch of the road's business.[54] Amounting to only $4,000 per year before the war, express receipts climbed to nearly $24,000 in 1861–62, roughly equivalent to the the road's return from carrying the mails. Unlike the mail, express receipts mushroomed further, reaching 386,000 (inflated) dollars in the last year of the war. These dollars were received from Southern Express. Although that company seems not to have profiteered more than others, its own rates and receipts seemed so immense in swollen late-war currency as to attract the envy of the railroads who carried its business. Why not develop their own express services and thereby eliminate the middleman?

A sense of business opportunity was coupled with citizen resentment, therefore, when the NCRR stockholders in July 1864 authorized negotiations with other connecting roads to create a new joint express company of their own. President Webb himself moved that a local express service be instituted unilaterally on the NCRR, limiting Southern Express to through shipments involving other roads as well. This was soon instituted, with the railroad charging about double the regular freight rate instead of Southern's reported quintuple rate, but the experiment seems not to have lasted long.[55] When Webb contacted other railroads about a joint express service, the Western North Carolina Railroad stockholders were eager to cooperate and even terminated their contract with Southern, but the joint effort seems not to have borne fruit.[56] Soon the roads were too busy with elemental problems of survival to concern themselves with a new express service.

The more conventional freight service of the NCRR was second to none in its power to evoke public criticism. As usual, part of the comment was justified. From the beginning there were complaints about delays in moving freight. If the complaints ever subsided, it was owing to public resignation rather than improved service. Conditions got worse, in fact, as increasing traffic, deteriorating equipment, and insistent government needs and the resultant diversion of resources increasingly took their toll. Particularly late in the war, private traffic was interdicted altogether. The public—or at least the newspaper editors—came to accept these conditions with better grace than they did the postal disruptions.

One shortage that did attract sharp criticism was a lack of rosin to fuel the municipal gasworks in Charlotte and Raleigh. In 1864 and early 1865 both towns occasionally went in darkness owing to the seemingly inexplicable failure of the railroads to ship the four or five barrels needed daily (in the case of Raleigh) for gas illumination. It helped only slightly when President Webb declared after investigation that the NCRR had shipped every barrel of rosin brought to it. An editor forced to go to press by candlelight could be almost as eloquent a critic as one dependent for news and readership on capricious mail deliveries.[57] A decade of railroading had created new dependencies.

Theft was a major problem throughout the war. Webb reported in July 1862 that "from the insecure condition of our cars, caused by dilapidation, and injury from soldiers knocking off the boards, and the impossibility of procuring locks," large quantities of freight were being stolen from cars all along the line despite the posting of reliable watchmen. Warehouses were also broken into. Liquor and foodstuffs, being the chief items of freight carried, were the chief items stolen. In time both cars and buildings were better maintained, but theft remained a problem.[58]

Other losses were attributable to derailments and collisions and to fire and water. Leaky cars brought extensive rain damage. In 1862–63 fire caused by locomotive sparks consumed six cars loaded with cotton, another carrying manufactured tobacco, a baggage car, and a Southern Express car.[59] In the war's last days a boxcar carrying cotton actually exploded east of Greensboro. Traces of gunpowder from a previous shipment were ignited either by sparks from the engine or, more likely, by someone smoking. A similar event occurred in June 1865.[60]

The Charlotte station and its environs were long a potential disaster area. The Charlotte and South Carolina Railroad, sharing the depot, called attention in February 1864 to large amounts of cotton lying around the premises. It was apparently the property of private shippers and had been stranded there by the chaotic conditions existing at that transshipment bottleneck. The Charlotte newspapers warned on several occasions of the fire hazard as well as the waste of good cotton exposed to the elements. So did the NCRR stockholders' inspection committee.[61] The disaster finally came on 7 January 1865 when the cotton caught fire and was consumed along with the adjacent warehouses and thousands of bushels of grain and other military supplies bound for Virginia.[62]

As before the war, private (not governmental) passenger and freight rates were the product of both competition and agreement among the various roads. The trend of rates was of course upward, in nominal if not real dollars. In December 1861 the Raleigh and Gaston, NCRR, and Charlotte and South Carolina revoked their through freight rates for private shippers in favor of the higher local rate, no matter how far they intended to ship.[63] Three months later, representatives of these roads and those belonging to the competing coastal route met at Petersburg. In prewar fashion they agreed upon an identical through passenger fare between Weldon and Kingsville, South Carolina (the points at which the two routes diverged), regardless of which route a passenger chose. Each road received a pro rata share of the total, depending upon its proportion of the total mileage by its route. They also raised private freight rates by about 25 percent.[64]

The NCRR was presumably a party to this agreement, though not listed as a direct participant. In October 1862 it raised its private freight rates by another 25 percent, presumably the result of another agreement. NCRR passenger rates were 4 cents per mile until April 1862, slightly under the prewar southern average. Rates rose gradually thereafter to 10 cents in January 1864. In March both passenger and freight rates went up another 50 percent.[65]

These increases, like the rising cost of living generally, evoked public anger. The almost universal temptation, and sometimes with reason, was to ascribe the process to speculation and profiteering.[66] It was difficult not to view rate increases as a form of extortion when one saw the paper profits of railroads escalating simultaneously.[67] Thus Duncan McRae of the Raleigh

Confederate, viewing the rate increases, the profits, and the deteriorating service, saw the railway managers as equivalent to Grant or Sherman as friends of the Confederacy. But Colonel F. W. Sims, head of the Confederacy's railroad bureau and beneficiary of artificially low government rates, defended the railroads as holders of the line compared with other businesses.[68] Certainly their rates fell short of the inflation rate.

That phenomenon itself resulted from the central government's increasing resort to the printing press to pay its bills, lacking the ability (and to some degree the will) to cover them in other ways. To this was added the growing shortage of goods and services, forcing people to pay higher and higher prices for them. Inflation carried its usual dangers to persons on fixed or relatively fixed incomes. Voicing concern for farmers who might be driven to the wall by escalating freight rates, Governor Zebulon Vance and the state Board of Internal Improvements adopted a resolution in June 1863 opposing any further rate increases—unless necessitated by future events. They instructed the state proxies on the various railroads to pursue the matter at the respective stockholders' meetings.[69] When Ralph Gorrell, state proxy on the NCRR, asked its stockholders in July to endorse the resolution and to ask the board of directors to lower whatever rates they could, especially on salt and provisions, his request was tabled. Neither he nor (presumably) the governor felt strongly enough about the requests to cast the state's controlling vote for them.[70]

Although the war would vastly increase the traffic of southern railroads, the immediate effect of secession in 1861 was to curtail business activity and the freight shipments that served it. On the NCRR, freight receipts ran below the 1860 levels from January through September. Great increases in both government and civilian freight then reversed the pattern. Passenger revenues fell off initially too, but began to surpass 1860 levels in April as new recruits were transported to their camps.[71]

It is difficult to measure the actual increase in freight because the NCRR did not keep tonnage records. Freight receipts, reflecting inflation as well as increased business, rose every year, from $214,361 in 1860–61 to $2,395,929 in 1864–65. President Webb, reporting a good crop year in the summer of 1862, claimed that the road had never done so much freight business before, quite apart from the shipment of military stores: "The local business of the Road has kept our warehouses crowded with every species of freight seeking a market; and as fast as a car load was taken out there were three, or four, or more waiting to be put in."[72] Monthly receipts show that the seasonal distribution of civilian freight during the war did not diverge much from that in earlier and later years; military freight was not itemized by month.

The NCRR did record the numbers of passengers it carried. They rose steadily, from 90,247 in 1860–61 to 506,166 in 1864–65. Quite apart from military travel, civilian passengers increased at an astonishing rate until near the end of the war. From a prewar high of 85,733 in 1860–61, their number increased annually to 228,522 in 1863–64. The next year, during the last months of which the road barely operated, saw a decline to 176,276, still over twice the prewar rate. As before the war, local passengers continued greatly to outnumber through passengers, and the numbers going east and west remained roughly in balance. (Military passengers were not itemized in this fashion.) The proportion of total receipts attributable to passengers rose somewhat, from a median of 43 percent in prewar years to 53 percent during the conflict. (See table 11.)

Government transportation, both passenger and freight, increased every year during the war. Taking freight and passenger traffic together, government receipts (or at least the charges levied for government transportation, whether ultimately paid or not) amounted to from 29 to 53 percent of all revenues. Military passengers, numbering only 4,514 or 5 percent of the total in 1860–61, increased to 329,890 or 65 percent in 1864–65. Military passenger receipts increased to only 59 percent of all passenger revenues in the last year because soldiers rode at a lower fare and probably traveled longer distances on average than did the civilians. Government freight receipts rose from 1.3 percent of all freight receipts in 1860–61 to 57 percent in 1864–65. (See table 15.) As with military passengers, this figure understates the actual volume of government freight because it too traveled at a lower rate.[73]

The strikingly higher volume of traffic was carried with a comparatively slight addition of rolling stock, both in engines and cars. There was only a modest increase, therefore, in the number of train miles run. From 1859–60, the last recorded prewar year, to the highest wartime year, 1864–65, passenger locomotive mileage increased only from 278,197 to 288,280, an increase of less than 4 percent. By comparison, the number of passengers increased by 563 percent in those years. It is true that soldiers commonly traveled by boxcar or whatever conveyance was at hand and may not always have been included in the passenger train statistics. If only civilian passengers are considered, the increase from 1859–60 to 1864–65 was 131 percent. Lacking any measurement of freight volume beyond inflated dollar receipts, the same comparison cannot be made. But freight train mileage rose from 176,415 in the same prewar base year to 226,750 in 1863–64, the highest wartime year—an increase of only 29 percent. The increase in freight volume was almost certainly a great deal more. Clearly, wartime trains—passenger and freight—were longer and more crowded.

Passenger and freight receipts were almost in balance before 1861. During the first two years of the war, the growth in passenger revenue far outstripped that from freight. After 1863 the difference narrowed, but passenger trains continued to produce substantially more income. In terms of receipts per mile, freight trains had a considerable advantage in peacetime but lost much of it during the war. (See tables 11 and 12.)

The war affected the sources of freight shipments. Charlotte accounted for one-third of the freight shipped throughout the conflict, over twice its prewar share, reflecting the increased volume of through freight to Virginia. At the other end of the line, Raleigh supplanted Goldsboro as the main shipping point, only to be replaced by Greensboro as the Piedmont Railroad was completed to Danville in May 1864. (Raleigh's share in the first year of the war was 24.5 percent, gradually sinking to 6.8; Greensboro's rose rapidly from 4.3 in the first year to 29 percent in 1864–65.) No other station rivaled Charlotte, Greensboro, and Raleigh; only Goldsboro joined them in exceeding 10 percent in any year. (See table 16.)

13

Supplying Lee's Army?

DURING THE CIVIL WAR, few southern railroads were more strategically placed or played a greater role in determining the fate of the Confederacy than the NCRR. In this first modern war, railroads were the most striking innovation, enabling armies to shift from place to place, even from one theater to another as strategic needs required. Just as important, armies could now be supplied relatively quickly with reinforcements, armaments, and provisions over hundreds of miles.

In the South particularly, these potentialities were achieved only partially and with difficulty. A southern railroad system had begun to emerge by 1861. Although rails connected Richmond and New Orleans by three different routes, each was the product of alliances between relatively short roads more or less abutting each other, sometimes with different gauges or unfilled gaps between them. Often they had different interests to pursue. It was possible, therefore, but neither fast nor easy to travel or ship freight over long distances. Yet the military situation demanded long-distance transportation in great volume. As the Union naval blockade impeded communication by sea and treacherous dirt roads still forbade long-distance transportation by coach or wagon, the railroads bore the brunt of carrying soldiers where they could not march and of supplying their material needs.

In seeking to mobilize the southern railroads to that end, the Confederate government was both halting and inefficient. In fact, few things within its power handicapped the Confederacy's war effort more seriously than its failure to organize its rail network into a rational system. Emory M. Thomas and other recent historians have emphasized the war's impact in creating a new southern nation under a strong central government in Richmond. Jefferson Davis receives much of the credit.[1] This argument has merit, but it is easy to exaggerate. Government expansion was reluctant and often uncoordinated. In the case of railroad policy, officials differed sharply over how far the central government should go in interfering with private enterprise. President Davis in particular had to be dragged kicking and screaming to a number of the centralizing measures that were adopted. The most far-reaching and effective government controls were employed too sparingly and too late.

The mechanism of government control expanded gradually. In the summer of 1861 William S. Ashe, president of North Carolina's Wilmington and Weldon Railroad, was named an assistant quartermaster general with very limited powers of inspection and recommendation concerning the railroads. In December 1862 a special railroad bureau headed briefly by William Wadley and, after May 1863, by Frederick W. Sims, was established in the War Department. In addition, the government appointed transportation supervisors or agents to expedite the movement of troops and supplies within designated areas. John D. Whitford, president of the Atlantic and North Carolina Railroad, was placed in charge of North Carolina.[2]

State governors also took a more or less active role in railroad affairs. This was often done in cooperation with Confederate authorities, but sometimes independently or even in opposition to them. Zebulon Vance of North Carolina intervened repeatedly in this as other matters. Although a sincere supporter of the southern cause, he seldom let it override the narrower concerns of his native state.

One of the Confederacy's first actions, in April 1861, was to agree with the railroads on the rates it would pay for carrying government passengers and freight as well as the mails. That summer it supervised the construction of trackage through the streets of Petersburg and Richmond, linking roads that had not hitherto joined and making possible for the first time uninterrupted rail communication through those cities.[3] The government also adopted a priority system generally favoring military over civilian traffic whenever they conflicted. On occasion private travel or shipment was forbidden altogether; these occasions grew more frequent toward the end of the war. In addition, locomotives and cars were often requisitioned for military use or were impressed for use on other roads where the need was greater. Rails were taken up from secondary roads and sidetracks and relaid on deteriorating main lines. After May 1863 the government was empowered to seize railroads and operate them itself, a power it exercised very sparingly. It was on government insistence that the Piedmont Railroad between Greensboro and Danville was built, belatedly, in 1864.

Necessary as these measures were, other government actions were counterproductive. Military commanders sometimes took a narrow view of the general good, issuing commands without much thought to their broader consequences. Some commandeered trains or created special ones without informing railroad officials who had the task of scheduling traffic. This was apt to create exciting results on single-track roads (as most were) with trains operating in both directions.[4]

The government's rate policy was also dubious, keeping its own rates so low that the roads were led (often forced) to gouge their civilian customers in compensation.[5] At the beginning of the war some southern railroads carried troops and military supplies free; others charged lower than usual rates, and a few made no concession at all for government traffic. The situation required standardization. Choosing at the outset to negotiate with the railroads rather than impose orders upon them, the government called a meeting of their presidents at Montgomery late in April 1861. In the flush of early patriotism they agreed to carry soldiers at 2 cents per mile at a time when civilian fares averaged 4½ cents; military freight would travel at one-half of the local freight rate on each road.[6] But freight rates varied so much from one road to another that a further meeting was held at Chattanooga in October to produce greater uniformity for military freight.[7]

As inflation raised the roads' operating costs, they appealed individually to the government for relief, often successfully. In time the exceptions multiplied and uniformity vanished. A third conference at Augusta in December 1862 produced uniformity at higher levels. But as inflation soared, these rates too failed to cover costs. In May 1864 the Wilmington and Weldon received a military passenger increase to 5 cents per mile that was extended throughout the Confederacy. Despite widespread dissatisfaction as the inflation went unchecked, there were no further efforts to set uniform rates. Individual roads still asked for and sometimes got increases for themselves. In September 1864 troop fares were 5 to 7½ cents per mile, about double the prewar rates. Freight rates rose in about the same ratio— far less than the inflation rate, which by that time had advanced to about twenty-five times its prewar base. By April 1865, the multiple was ninety-two.[8]

Private rates climbed farther, eventually to 20 cents or more per mile for passengers and to well over three times the prewar level for freight. But these were still well below the inflation rate.[9] To the degree that the artificially low government rates failed to cover the costs of transportation, private travelers and shippers were subsidizing the government. To the degree, further, that railroads made a profit under these conditions, it was the private travelers and shippers who provided it. And to the degree that private shippers could only get access to the railroads at all by paying secret or extortionate rates—if not outright bribery—the low government fares encouraged such corruption. Indeed, low government rates encouraged railroads and their employees to defer some military shipments in favor of profiteers who paid higher rates.[10]

So far as the NCRR was concerned, the war accelerated a trend already evident by 1860: it was preeminently a north-south road rather than an east-west feeder of the state's own seaports as envisioned by many of its projectors. More specifically, it was a major link in one of the three railroad lines joining Virginia (including the Confederate capital at Richmond) with the rest of the Confederacy. (The others were the coastal route including the Wilmington and Weldon, and the newer East Tennessee and Virginia line west of the mountains.) The NCRR's role was further enhanced by the construction of the Piedmont Railroad (the long-sought Danville Connection) in 1864.

Had the Federals who occupied the North Carolina coast in 1861 been given the assignment, with resources to match, they might have driven westward across the state and, in cooperation with forces operating west of the mountains, cut all three of the rail arteries to Virginia. That effort, if successful, might have shortened the war substantially.[11] Although the high command in Washington chose instead to hammer away at Richmond from above, Union forces did manage to cut the eastern and western roads into Virginia. The central route, by contrast, was never broken or in serious danger until the closing weeks of the war. Thus the NCRR was the longest link in what proved to be the Confederacy's most dependable lifeline—a major carrier of the manpower and materiel for Robert E. Lee's Army of Northern Virginia.

Hardly had the shells fallen on Fort Sumter, and weeks before North Carolina's secession, her railroad presidents met to decide the most efficient means of carrying military troops and supplies. On 20 April it was announced that "all the Railroad companies of the State will transport troops and munitions of war for the use of the State *free of charge*, and *extra trains* will always be in readiness for any emergency." By 1 May the roads were described as busily moving troops and supplies "at all hours and at every inconvenience and expense, free of all charge."[12] The Greensboro papers noted that eastbound trains there daily were carrying hundreds of soldiers from the western counties and from Georgia and South Carolina to camps at Raleigh and beyond. Passenger trains, commonly consisting before the war of only two partially filled cars, now contained six to ten cars, fully loaded. In June the longest passenger train in NCRR history was noted—twelve coaches, all filled with soldiers en route to Virginia.[13]

The NCRR's annual passenger count rose from 90,247 in the year ending with May 1861 to 204,384 in the following year. The volume of freight was not recorded, but it seems to have risen comparably. The road managed to carry this increased load with the same prewar equipment; every car in active use traveled the length of the road daily. Reporting this achievement in his first report to the stockholders in June 1862, President Webb confessed that "we have not been able to satisfy the public" at the same time.

> Government officials, at many points on the road, have been clamorous for transporting their material and supplies, each one demanding that his own should be attended to immediately, the general government, at Richmond, demanding of us immediate transportation for all public freight in preference to that of private persons, the State authorities, at Raleigh, demanding the immediate transportation of provision and forage and lumber for Camp Mangum, the General in command at Goldsboro', needing our engines and cars to transport his troops even on other roads, the clamors of speculators to get off their

freight, and the urgent, but respectful application of private persons to bring them stores for the support of their families, have caused the officers of this road to be up and doing, to be instant in season and out of season, to spend sleepless nights and anxious days.[14]

One unpublicized service the NCRR performed early in the war was to help suppress Unionist resistance in Randolph and Davidson counties. Parts of those and neighboring counties became centers of opposition to the war, owing in large measure to the pacifist, antislavery Quaker and Wesleyan Methodist background of many of the local population. The opposition was best organized and most vocal in northwestern Randolph and eastern Davidson, around Thomasville. On two occasions, in July 1861 and March 1862, Governor Henry T. Clark sent troops by rail to put down the resistance and arrest the ringleaders. Thereafter, says William T. Auman, the historian of this movement, Unionism in that part of the state was driven underground, and it focused primarily in southeastern Randolph, relatively remote from the railroad and from the new telegraph.[15]

The escalating volume of freight eventually exceeded the ability to carry it. Freight piled up, particularly at transshipment points. One of these was Salisbury, the junction with the WNCRR. The difficulty here was self-inflicted, as the NCRR refused to allow WNCRR trains (of the same gauge) onto its road to relieve the congestion. These pileups were serious enough by November 1861 that Governor Clark had to ask the two roads to cooperate in clearing them up.[16] By the following summer WNCRR trains were going to Charlotte and even to Goldsboro and Richmond with troops and military supplies. This agreement seems not to have lasted long, however, and it did not extend to other roads of the same gauge.[17] The worst bottleneck on the NCRR, and perhaps in the South, was at Charlotte, where the gauge difference between the NCRR and the C&SC forced the unloading and reloading of every car. One South Carolina road refused to let its cars go to Charlotte because it could not afford to have them standing idle there as emergency warehouses. By January 1862 it was almost impossible to get local freight shipped to any point on the NCRR because of heavy government shipments. Soon the state government itself was utilizing the express company to forward some military supplies. At the same time stores in Wilmington were running out of such interior commodities as corn and flour.[18] Such conditions inspired the demands for President Cameron's resignation.

In the hope of getting Confederate government aid to alleviate these problems, the presidents of several North Carolina and Virginia roads met at Richmond early in January 1862. One of their requests was for the use of rolling stock captured from the Baltimore and Ohio Railroad. The presidents also agreed on a plan to establish rolling mills to make or recondition rails.[19] Subsequently a good deal of B&O equipment was turned over to southern roads, including the NCRR, but the rolling mills never came to pass. Only in May 1862 was the NCRR able to acquire additional rolling stock, most of it from Virginia roads that had been overrun by the enemy.

In a further effort to expedite through traffic, Superintendent Samuel L. Fremont of the Wilmington and Weldon called a meeting of the NCRR and other connecting lines at Goldsboro in April 1862. They provided tentatively for the exchange of cars and the running of trains on each others' roads, as arranged here or elsewhere between the NCRR and WNCRR. But support for the plan was half-hearted, and it did not endure.[20] "Foreign trains" did subsequently operate on the NCRR, at least irregularly. President Webb reported six of them doing so simultaneously in June 1864.[21]

Another agreement at Goldsboro was occasioned by the recent appearance of General George B. McClellan with a Union army near Richmond. The roads agreed to keep on hand at Goldsboro, Weldon, and Raleigh a temporary pool of 10 locomotives and 200 cars, each road being allotted a quota. This pool was supposed to be able to carry 10,000 men anywhere on these roads within twenty-four hours. The NCRR's quota was 1 engine and 30 cars, to be kept at Raleigh. The government was to be charged $20 per day for each locomotive and $3 per day for each car so reserved.[22] McClellan's peninsular campaign near Richmond never required the use of this equipment, and it may be questioned how long the roads actually kept so much of it out of regular use.

The emergency also evoked a temporary ban on all nongovernment freight. So much had towns become dependent on the railroads in the past decade that newspapers like the Raleigh *Standard* made special pleas for farmers to bring their foodstuffs to market by wagon.[23] Local military commanders throughout the Confederacy resorted to such bans frequently during the summer and fall of 1862. The resultant complaints finally brought President Davis to approve the appointment of a general railway superintendent to coordinate the government's policies—the position to which William Wadley was named in December.[24]

To the unprecedented traffic burden was soon added deteriorating equipment and roadbed. The road's decrepitude contributed directly to the dwindling of supplies reaching Lee's army during the winter of 1862–63. Late in January he had only an eight-day ration of meat left and had nearly exhausted his forage supply. The army continued on a hand-to-mouth basis into April. Meanwhile, railroad bureau chief William Wadley reported from Raleigh in February that "utmost confusion" reigned on the NCRR. Large quantities of government freight, much of it bacon and rice, were piled up along the road awaiting shipment. Everywhere provisions were spoiling for lack of protection or means of transportation.[25] Accompanying these troubles were widespread and well-founded reports that the roads (including the NCRR) preferred to use their limited resources to carry private freight at extortionate rates and that railroad employees were not above taking bribes in such cases.[26]

Zebulon Vance noted in February 1863 that the NCRR's inability to carry all the freight assigned to it was holding up the shipment of supplies for the army, corn for the civilian population, and cotton for foreign purchases through the blockade. He suggested letting the Atlantic and North Carolina Railroad operate that part of the NCRR between Raleigh and Goldsboro. The A&NC had both men and equipment available since much of its line was in Federal hands after the fall of New Bern and Morehead City. The only alternative, Vance said, was to let other roads operate their trains over the NCRR as a whole—a privilege its managers had previously extended only with great reluctance.

President Webb and his board were similarly reluctant to let another road work part of their line. They offered instead to rent equipment from the A&NC for use between Raleigh and Goldsboro. At the same time, Webb tried to appease the governor with a rosy prediction of acquiring enough additional locomotives to clear up the backlog of freight in short order. This was not to happen, and A&NC trains soon did run at least occasionally between Goldsboro and Raleigh.[27]

Several weeks later Colonel Wadley drew up a detailed list of the needs and capacities of every line of importance in the Southeast. Worst off were the NCRR, the Wilmington and Manchester, the Wilmington and Weldon, and the Richmond and Danville, none of which, he estimated, could carry more than 200 tons of freight per day. In fact, despite Webb's February projections, the NCRR was now limited to one freight train in each direction every other day with a capacity of only fifty tons. The W&W was in similar plight. To increase the efficiency of these two roads enough to meet the needs of the country, Wadley estimated that each needed an additional 4 engines and 100 cars. All of the principal roads, he added, urgently needed major repairs.[28]

That spring (1863) the government took his advice, with respect to the NCRR at least. Conscript labor was brought in to do extensive work on the roadbed, maintenance crews were enlarged, and at least four locomotives were added. Webb reported in July that the road was now in admirable condition, excepting bad rails for which there were no replacements. In 1864 Wadley's successor Sims described the NCRR as one of the best roads in the Confederacy.[29]

Early in September 1863 Union forces captured Knoxville and Chattanooga, severing the western rail line into Virginia. Thereafter "the feeding of the animals and men of the Army of Northern Virginia and of a large proportion of the city of Richmond depended on a shaky, rundown railroad system culminating in 85 miles of single track" between the capital and Weldon.[30] This last bottleneck would be relieved for a time by the opening of the Danville Connection in May 1864. But in August of that year the eastern route was cut by Union forces besieging Petersburg, and the Danville route itself became the bottleneck.

Meanwhile, the crisis of freight transportation was so general that the central government called a meeting of southern railway managers at Richmond in April 1863 to see what could be done cooperatively to stave off a general breakdown. The meeting brought little result. The railroads called for more captured or other rolling stock than the government could supply, while rejecting the idea of direct government control of operations. This unsatisfactory meeting, coupled with the desperate condition of Lee's army, encouraged Congress to pass a bill late in April greatly expanding the government's regulatory powers. The quartermaster general was empowered to arrange through freight schedules, form trains from the rolling stock of different roads, take rails and equipment from one road for use on another, and even seize uncooperative railroads and operate them in the public interest. The railroads further invited this measure by failing to deliver any meat to Richmond during the last week in April after promising to send 120,000 pounds per day. President Davis signed the bill on 1 May.[31]

Lee's condition improved enough during the summer that only he of all the Confederate commanders was free enough of supply worries to base his movements primarily on strategic considerations. But by fall, supply problems were again crippling his activities. Richard D. Goff, the historian of the Confederate supply effort, blames the railroads for this dilemma and also Jefferson Davis's persistent reluctance to use the regulatory powers that Congress had given him. Lee's army depended on the daily delivery of about twenty boxcars of corn from as far away as Georgia simply to feed their horses and mules. The railroads tended to assign a lower priority to corn than to other kinds of freight that might have seemed more pressing and certainly traveled at higher rates. And the barriers at Charlotte, Greensboro, and Danville were always an obstacle. Hence the required amounts did not reach the army, and Lee scattered his cavalry and artillery over Virginia and North Carolina to find subsistence. This problem was never solved, and weakened cavalry contributed to the military setbacks experienced in 1864.[32]

The soldiers' own needs were hardly better provided for. At the end of February 1864 they were down to a two-day bread supply and only a few days of meat. Yet there was an abundance of supplies in the Deep South awaiting shipment. Commissary General Lucius B. Northrop, estimating (incredibly) that only one-eighth of the railways' transportation resources had been used to carry government freight, urged that passenger trains be curtailed in order to facilitate the shipment of provisions. President Davis reluctantly agreed, and on 16 March the whole Augusta-Charlotte-Weldon railway line was put under military control. Only one passenger train was allowed per day; all other rolling stock was to be devoted to moving government freight. At Raleigh, mail (and presumably passenger-train) service in both directions was interrupted for several days early in April.[33]

These orders brought the desired results: in the next twelve days, fifteen days' supply of meat reached Lee's army plus 3,000 bushels of corn meal daily. But as soon as the worst of the emergency was over, the special orders were relaxed on 30 March, and shipments fell off again. On 12 April Lee reported that his army was back to a day's supply of food. Davis repeatedly refused to take full control of the railroads, preferring to rely on appeals for voluntary cooperation. Under additional promises from the railroads, he even relaxed the controls still in force. The promises did not avail much; food supplies still accumulated in Deep South depots while the army in Virginia subsisted in part on local forage and vegetables.[34]

Sporadic military controls continued on a local basis. Sometimes passenger travel was temporarily forbidden altogether on a given road. The public was resigned to such inconveniences when they brought tangible results, but they were not always convinced that the measures were effective.[35]

The situation improved somewhat with the opening of the long-awaited Piedmont Railroad between Greensboro and Danville in May. It was constructed as a wartime necessity over the now-muted objections of eastern North Carolinians who had opposed a direct link with the Richmond and Danville since the 1840s.[36] In November 1861 President Davis called attention to the limited routes into Virginia and asked Congress for money to fill in the forty-eight-mile gap. The bill passed in February 1862 after the North Carolina State Convention issued the necessary charter as a matter of national defense. The charter stipulated that the road should be built to the North Carolina gauge of four feet, eight and a half inches rather than the R&D's five-foot gauge.

The R&D had consistently advocated this project and, among the region's railroads, was to be its chief beneficiary. It subscribed 14,900 of the 15,000 shares of Piedmont stock, using a $1 million Confederate loan. Construction started quickly, but the work was handicapped by the dire shortage of labor and materiel. The government commandeered rails from several other roads deemed to be less important. But these requisitions were stoutly resisted, and the first rails did not arrive until April 1863. Tracklaying consumed the next year, with the first through train reaching Greensboro from Danville on 21 May 1864. The contractors for most of the project were Edmund Wilkes, recent superintendent of the NCRR, and his brother John, of Charlotte.[37]

The Piedmont became a major supply route even before its completion, as wagons traversed the narrowing gap between the tracks at either end. On completion, the quartermaster general routed the bulk of shipments from the Deep South over the new line, embracing the NCRR and R&D as well. The militarily endangered Weldon-Petersburg route was limited to goods originating in eastern North Carolina or imported by blockade runners in Wilmington and Charleston. Historian Robert C. Black was surely correct in venturing that "the Piedmont Railroad added months to the length of the Civil War."[38]

The advantage of the new road to the NCRR was less clear than it was to the Confederacy or to other roads. No one could predict with certainty whether the increased traffic brought to the western half of its line by the shorter route to Richmond would compensate for the loss of traffic that otherwise would have continued to Raleigh or Goldsboro. Prewar NCRR officials had tended to oppose the connection once their own road was in operation, although John Motley Morehead was always an enthusiastic advocate. (More than incidentally, he owned property and had mining and manufacturing interests in Rockingham County, near the proposed route.)[39] When President Davis officially broached the subject in November 1861, the NCRR joined the Raleigh and Gaston in sending a delegation to Richmond to voice their concerns.[40] But when the new road was completed, Webb was guardedly optimistic concerning its impact. He expected NCRR passenger receipts to decline as many through travelers would get on or off at Greensboro while the trains necessarily continued to run the length of the road. But freight traffic should sustain no loss, he thought, as freight trains could make two trips from Charlotte to Greensboro while making one to Raleigh. The eastern roads, by comparison, did suffer from the new route just as they had predicted. It is difficult to measure the degree because the Petersburg route became more and more perilous at the same time and was finally severed on 17 August. For both reasons through traffic fell off drastically on both the Wilmington and Weldon and the Wilmington and Manchester. The Raleigh and Gaston reported in July 1864 that its receipts had fallen by at least half.[41]

The Piedmont proved to be a worse bottleneck than the Weldon-to-Richmond line had been. The road was in poor shape, hastily built without adequate labor or equipment. It lacked proper grading, ballasting, depots, platforms, water stations, cordwood supplies, or sidings. Its rolling stock consisted mostly of R&D engines and cars modified to the North Carolina gauge. The parent road could provide no additional emergency stock because of the gauge difference, so the Piedmont frequently had to borrow from the NCRR, which had very little to lend. The road's weakness was apparent even before Union forces cut the eastern line below Petersburg in August. With that event the NCRR-Piedmont-R&D route constituted the only remaining lifeline to Richmond and the Army of Northern Virginia. Now the slightest overload brought paralysis, as Robert Black observed. In December 1864 it took three days to transport an army brigade over the forty-eight-mile road.[42] The NCRR on this occasion sent three engines to help bring the men down from Danville and kept all of its own trains waiting at Greensboro for at least two days to convey the troops toward their destination in Wilmington.[43]

In June, meanwhile, drought diminished Lee's sources of food and forage in Virginia. Supplies remained abundant in parts of Alabama, Georgia, and Florida, but they were reaching him in only a trickle. He asked therefore that the railways leading to Richmond be put under military control and that only government supplies be brought forward until the army had built up a reserve. In particular he asked for military control of the Piedmont Railroad. Again President Davis refused to go that far, although quartermasters were permitted to stop private trains in order to facilitate government shipments.[44] The Richmond and Danville and its southern connections (including the NCRR) were at least temporarily closed to civilian traffic in late December 1864.[45] Such measures plus local provender barely kept the army alive and functioning through the remainder of 1864. As historian Charles W. Ramsdell wrote, "It is hard to see how Lee could have maintained his army in Virginia for another year, even if Grant had been content to watch him peacefully from a distance."[46]

The Piedmont was by no means the only bottleneck. Freight continued to pile up in Charlotte and Greensboro, with the NCRR bearing some responsibility at both places, perhaps especially at Greensboro because of its refusal normally to run its trains on the Piedmont. As a result, goods had to be transferred from one train to another there as well as at the gauge barriers in Charlotte and Danville. One would never realize this from President Webb's glowing and self-congratulatory report in June 1864: "Your road and its equipment is in good order—inferior to none in the Confederacy. . . . Its importance to our country cannot be calculated. Being one of the main arteries by which the army is sustained, our destruction would be its destruction, and that gallant band of heroes, who now in Virginia are stemming the angry tide of battle and keeping from our immediate homes the desolations of war, would be forced into our midst, and the time of our redemption would be prolonged."[47]

No doubt aware of the political sensitivities in North Carolina that had created the Greensboro bottleneck, General Lee asked Governor Vance late in December to persuade the NCRR to let its trains continue onto the Piedmont.[48] A more far-reaching suggestion by General Robert F. Hoke was to place all Piedmont operations under NCRR control. This would make available the NCRR maintenance crews and equipment as well as its rolling stock. Superintendent Sumner favored this idea, not surprisingly, but the government in Richmond decided instead to take over the operations itself.[49] On 3 January 1865 Quartermaster General Alexander R. Lawton ordered the impressment of all trains reaching Greensboro for use on the Piedmont road.[50]

Theoretically, the Piedmont was run by the quartermaster general during the remainder of the war. Actually, the change was not carried out, and the road operated as before, subject to sporadic military orders. At one point in February, sixty-one R&D cars stood idle in the Danville yards awaiting supplies from the south, immobilized by the gauge barrier.[51]

Bad weather and bad luck combined to make the situation even worse. The Charlotte depot fire on 7 January consumed about 25,000 sacks of corn, oats, and flour plus other stores—a large part of the government supplies that had accumulated near the depot.[52] Another major loser was the Tredegar Iron Works of Richmond, a vital contributor to the Confederate war effort. Tredegar had bought several thousand bushels of grain in South Carolina to feed its employees and teams of draft animals. The provisions were caught in the clog at Charlotte. About 6,000 bushels of Tredegar corn and other supplies went up in flames. It almost put the company out of business.[53]

Then torrential rains and flooding across the state (dubbed Sherman's Freshet farther south) on 11 January washed out trestles and culverts on the Piedmont, putting it out of commission for ten days. The NCRR was also closed for a few days between High Point and Salisbury.[54] At this time the army in Virginia was down to two days' food supply, and the men were on half-rations. Lee managed to survive by personal appeals for donations from public-spirited Virginians, but the railroads were unable to deliver all of these.[55]

Union operations in January and February 1865, especially those of General William T. Sherman in South Carolina, cut off the major sources of supply for Lee's army. Sherman's capture of Branchville, South Carolina, broke the rail connection with central Georgia; the fall of Charleston and Wilmington ended the trickle of foreign supplies. Ironically, in the final month of the war, the food surpluses of North Carolina, Georgia, Alabama, and Mississippi were reported to be the largest on record, but nearly all of them were now out of reach.[56]

The gauge barriers at Charlotte and Danville were among the most serious, persistent, and remediable transportation problems of the Confederacy. It was almost impossible to prevent freight from piling up wherever it had to be transshipped from one railroad to another. By 1864, when the Piedmont road was opened, Congress had long since authorized President Davis to impose virtually any railroad regulations that he regarded as in the public interest. Only the direst emergencies, however, could force him to depart, and then only temporarily, from an ideological commitment to private management. His inflexibility stood in sharp contrast to General Lee's readiness to improvise and experiment. Perhaps the best that can be said in Davis's behalf is that nothing he could do—by 1864, at least—could have changed the war's outcome; greater activity would have lengthened it.

When the government did move to alter the gauge between Charlotte and Danville, it was a case of too little and too late. The first effort came in December 1864, when Secretary of War James A. Seddon urged Governor Vance and the North Carolina legislature merely to let the Piedmont change its own gauge to five feet. Taken alone, this would simply move the barrier from Danville to Greensboro, with little benefit except to permit surplus R&D rolling stock to cover fifty more miles of railroad. The Piedmont charter of 1861 specifically forbade this change, but the legislature, as a further grudging act of patriotic necessity, acceded in February 1865, stipulating that the gauge be changed back again within six months of the end of the war. The actual work did not commence until April, however, and was in progress when the war ended. At that point the original gauge was immediately restored.[57]

Work also began early in 1865 to widen the NCRR gauge from Charlotte to Greensboro. General Pierre G. T. Beauregard gave the order, apparently on his own volition, after the Piedmont change was authorized. This work (never completed) would have established a uniform five-foot gauge from Richmond to South Carolina and beyond—if Confederate trains could get that far. Moving northward from Charlotte in February, the work was quickly accomplished as far as Salisbury, using a thousand laborers. Many of these and much of the equipment were lent by the Charlotte and South Carolina Railroad.[58]

At the time this work began, Sherman was advancing northward toward Charlotte. The immediate impetus, therefore, was not only the supplying of Lee's army but also the retention of five-foot-gauge rolling stock from South Carolina that otherwise faced capture. But Sherman turned away, toward eastern North Carolina. When the army showed no sign of abandoning the project after that development, some NCRR stockholders asked Governor Vance to have it stopped. Their concern, they said, was for the safety of NCRR rolling stock, which then would be forced to stay at Greensboro and points eastward, in Sherman's new path.[59] Vance had already objected to continuing the work, out of concern for the Western North Carolina Railroad with its similar gauge, which faced isolation west of Salisbury. Secretary of War John C. Breckinridge and Generals Lee, Johnston, Lawton, and others told Vance that the gauge change was a military necessity. But failing to convince him of this point, they refused to override him. Although orders were issued as late as 19 March to conscript Negro laborers to continue the work at Salisbury, no work appears to have been done beyond that point, and the matter remained unresolved at war's end.[60]

Salisbury thus supplanted Charlotte as the greatest bottleneck after the Piedmont road. At this point, early in March, the NCRR suddenly found itself the major carrier for an army of men, animals, and supplies gathering as quickly as possible under General Joseph E. Johnston to meet Sherman in eastern North Carolina. (It remained the chief supply line as well for Lee in Virginia, but increasingly Lee's supplies were drawn from eastern North Carolina and taken westward by the NCRR to Greensboro, thence northward to Virginia.) Every train had to be unloaded and reloaded in Salisbury. Traffic backed up into South Carolina. After eight days, 120 carloads of men, artillery, and wagons were still in Salisbury; 65 more loads of soldiers were immobilized at Chester, South Carolina, waiting for transportation to take them to Johnston below Raleigh. In desperation, men were ordered to march alongside the railroad, to be taken up by any trains that came their way. Johnston complained that the NCRR "with its enormous amount of rolling stock has brought us only about five hundred men a day." The movement took over two weeks, and as a result of the delay, the Confederates were able to manage only a partial concentration against the enemy.[61]

Throughout March 1865 the war had been a distant presence, affecting almost everything the railroad did, but still out of sight. In April, destined to be the last month of the war, the NCRR was suddenly at the center of things. For the first time, and virtually from one end to the other, it found itself under enemy attack. It was the Union army's most important target, next to Johnston's army. The first blows came from the west, between 11 and 13 April. Major General George Stoneman led three brigades of Union cavalry, about 6,000 men, across the mountains from Tennessee late in March. His primary objective was to cut off Lee's escape routes in the event of his expected defeat in Virginia. This entailed cutting the Virginia and Tennessee Railroad in Virginia and the Piedmont and NCRR lines between Danville and Salisbury. From Greensboro southward these operations would also cut off the main supply and retreat route for Joseph E. Johnston's army near Raleigh. Moving through Boone and Wilkesboro, Stoneman veered northward into Virginia early in April to achieve his first objective around Christiansburg and Lynchburg. Riding hard, his men returned to North Carolina on 9 April, coincidentally the day of Lee's surrender.[62]

Next day, at Germanton, Stoneman detached one of his brigades under Colonel William J. Palmer to take Salem and then move eastward to cut the railroads north and south of Greensboro. Stoneman himself proceeded southward with the remainder of his command toward Salisbury.

At Salem Palmer divided his own command into four columns. One of these, consisting of 100 men, reached the Piedmont's bridge over Reedy Fork, ten miles north of Greensboro, on the morning of 11 April and burned it just after Jefferson Davis and his cabinet had crossed it fleeing southward from Virginia. Palmer's men missed capturing the entire Confederate government by perhaps as little as half an hour.

Palmer's second detachment, under Lieutenant Colonel Charles Betts, got to within two miles of Greensboro, defeating a South Carolina cavalry unit of about the same size. It then burned the NCRR bridge over South Buffalo Creek, about four miles west of town.

The third column, of eighty-six men under Captain Adam Kramer, was sent to Jamestown where they destroyed a gun factory and burned the NCRR bridge over the Deep River as well as some Confederate commissary stores at the depot. They were about to burn the station when a false alarm led them to retreat.

Palmer's fourth detachment, a Michigan battalion, was sent to High Point where it captured two trains loaded with commissary and medical supplies. These, the depot, and a warehouse containing 1,700 bales of cotton belonging to Francis Fries were put to the torch. The total damages were estimated at over $3 million. Still other forces sent to destroy NCRR bridges toward Lexington encountered stiff Confederate resistance and withdrew without accomplishing that mission.[63]

All of these events took place on 11 April. Next day the various detachments rejoined Stoneman at Salisbury. That town was an important military target for several reasons. It was the junction of the North Carolina and Western North Carolina railroads. It was also the site of the gauge barrier on the NCRR, where large quantities of materiel had piled up. Both the Confederate government in Richmond and the state government at Raleigh had sent quantities of military supplies there for safekeeping. Even more important, there was a Confederate ordnance depot, including a foundry and arsenal. All of these things had been brought to Salisbury by the railroads and were located adjacent to the station. Also nearby was the infamous military prison. And six miles north was the NCRR's Yadkin River bridge.

At Salisbury, therefore, Stoneman's men repeated the previous day's work on an infinitely larger scale. They burned the WNCRR's headquarters building, car shed, and machine shops as well as two freight depots and a joint passenger shed shared with the NCRR. About ten miles of NCRR track was partly burned. The troops captured and burned a WNCRR passenger train after removing the passengers. The contents of the Confederate supply depot were thrown into the streets for the benefit of the poor. Also consigned to flames during the day and night of 12 April and the following morning were the ordnance depot with its foundry and arsenal, some warehouses, a large tannery, a distillery, and four cotton mills, together with nearly all of their contents. One million rounds of small ammunition, 10,000 pounds of artillery ammunition, 10,000 pounds of saltpeter, 6,000 pounds of powder, and 10,000 stands of arms were destroyed, to say nothing of 7,000 bales of cotton and quantities of Confederate uniforms, blankets, and other supplies. Stoneman was unable to liberate any Union prisoners of war; they had been evacuated in February and sent off to Richmond and Wilmington for exchange. But he did burn the prison, which was now serving as a warehouse. In the course of the bonfire at the ordnance depot, shells and other ammunition went off in every direction. Great clouds of smoke were visible by day, and the flames that night could be seen for fifteen miles.

When Stoneman had first entered the state, late in March, Confederate authorities supposed that he might head for Salisbury and the Yadkin River bridge. Accordingly, General Beauregard sent a substantial contingent of troops there. But when Stoneman veered north into Virginia, they thought they had seen the last of him. Most of the soldiers were removed to Greensboro, which seemed nearer the scene of action. When Stoneman reappeared, his striking forces moved so fast and in so many directions that few Confederates could be mobilized to oppose him. By the time Stoneman reached Salisbury, the railroad breaks his men had just made between Greensboro and High Point prevented reinforcements from being sent back to oppose him. There were enough men left in Davidson County, however, to deter the raiding party sent toward Lexington and, more important, to defend the Yadkin River bridge. Unlike the relatively short spans over South Buffalo Creek and even the Deep River at Jamestown, this 660-foot-long wooden structure could not easily or quickly have been replaced. About a thousand Confederates entrenched themselves on heights along the northern, or Davidson, side of the river where they could command both shores. As expected, Stoneman sent a strong detachment from Salisbury to destroy the bridge. But after a sharp engagement it found the defenders too strong to warrant a major assault and withdrew, leaving the bridge intact.

With few exceptions, Stoneman's destruction was confined to legitimate military objectives. He made it a point to prevent looting and indiscriminate property destruction. Having accomplished nearly all he set out to do, he departed on 13 April, headed back to his base in Tennessee. It had been an eventful three days. Before returning to Tennessee, the raiders destroyed an 1,100-foot bridge over the Catawba River on the Charlotte and South Carolina Railroad.[64]

It was argued in hindsight that, even as Stoneman acted, the Confederacy was in process of collapse; thus his property destruction, especially at Salisbury, served no remaining military purpose.[65] But that view could not have been as clear at the time. The Confederates still had the capacity to fight if not to win, and their readiness to do so was still an open question. On 24 April Stoneman, back in Knoxville, noted the repudiation in Washington of Sherman's recent truce with Johnston. He issued orders to destroy Johnston's communication lines by attacking Charlotte, Greensboro, and as much of the NCRR as possible between them. Fortunately a new agreement two days later made this action unnecessary.[66]

The eastern end of the line, from Raleigh to Goldsboro, suffered at least equal damage. Responsibility here lay almost entirely with the retreating Confederates, seeking to slow Sherman's advance and to destroy anything of value to him. On 6 April, having evacuated Goldsboro, Johnston ordered that both the NCRR and the Wilmington and Weldon be torn up as close as possible to Sherman's army. Next day the order was broadened to include any rolling stock that could not be saved.[67] As the Confederates retreated toward Raleigh, therefore, they burned the NCRR bridges over the Little and Neuse rivers, tore up some eight miles of track (burning the ties and bending rails), and filled in cuts with trees, brush, logs, rocks, and dirt.[68]

The Federals, by contrast, had every reason to preserve the road; in fact they set to work at once repairing it for purposes of pursuit. Their destruction was limited to the careless burning of the Goldsboro depot a few days after taking that town.[69] The United States Military Railroads Construction

Corps under Colonel William W. Wright worked quickly to repair the Confederates' damage. Their trains would be running to Raleigh by 19 April, six days after its capture. The temporary trackage and trestles they built were adequate for present needs but (like much of the NCRR's own wartime repair work) would need to be redone after the war.[70]

For Johnston's part, the NCRR was as much his line of retreat as it was Sherman's line of advance. Knowing that his force was too small to stop Sherman, his task was to slow down the Federal advance as much as possible while preserving what was left of his own army. The only place left for retreat appeared to be western North Carolina and South Carolina, whence he had just come. The NCRR, having brought his army here, might well have to take it back again. And since fighting could be expected along the way, many of the troops might not be able to ride. In preparation for that eventuality, Johnston ordered that the Haw and Yadkin River bridges, crossing the least fordable streams, be made passable for horse-drawn artillery. That order came on 11 April, the day before Stoneman attempted to burn the Yadkin River bridge.[71]

Three days later Johnston issued new orders to destroy all railway bridges and the telegraph line to the rear, together with any stores that could not be taken by either the army or the local population.[72] His troops had already done this at Raleigh, burning the NCRR depot and warehouse as they evacuated the town on 13 April—the same day that Stoneman finished his work in Salisbury. The *Standard* waxed indignant at what it termed the useless destruction of a valuable building and of large quantities of foodstuffs stored within. It added, without sensing any incongruity, that the building also housed explosives which shot off in all directions. The Confederates made an unsuccessful effort to burn the Raleigh and Gaston shops as well.[73] They subsequently burned the station at Morrisville and a small bridge near Hillsboro, but apparently were unwilling or unable to do more.[74]

State officials had anticipated the evacuation of Raleigh and made the best arrangements they could for the safety of the state records, the treasury, the city, and themselves. State Treasurer Jonathan Worth loaded the treasury and the state archives onto a train and managed with considerable difficulty to convey them to Greensboro, then to Company Shops.[75] On the morning of the twelfth, Governor Vance sent former Governors William A. Graham and David L. Swain with a message to Sherman requesting a suspension of hostilities and lenient treatment for the capital city. Their special train proceeded only a short distance when it was intercepted by the Confederate rear guard under Wade Hampton and ordered to return to Raleigh. The train backed up slowly for a mile or two when it was stopped again, this time by Federal cavalry under General Judson Kilpatrick. It was the Yankees who took the emissaries to Sherman, who had set up headquarters near what is now Clayton. After being captured successively by two

contending armies and now taken before this general with the fearful reputation, the former governors appeared "dreadfully excited," as Sherman
later recalled. He agreed to their request, however, and promised no harm
to Raleigh or the state officials as long as no acts of hostility were committed
before the city was taken. When Graham and Swain returned to Raleigh on
the thirteenth, Vance had already left with the retreating Confederates, and
the Raleigh depot was in flames.[76] No resistance was made to Sherman, and
he left the town as he found it.

But prior to his arrival in eastern North Carolina, Sherman's approach
created a near panic among people who had heard of his exploits farther
south. Those who could fled westward. Those (like the state treasurer) with
merchandise or valuables to preserve desperately committed them to the
railroad. Bales of cotton, boxes of merchandise, even kegs of gold and
other currency were frantically entrusted to freight cars headed westward.

By mid-April the railroad operated only between Hillsboro and Greensboro; east of the former lay Sherman and west of the latter, Stoneman's
burned bridges. Between them chaos reigned. Goods of every description
and beyond any accounting accumulated in stations, warehouses, private
homes, on platforms, or just piled up along the track. A great deal of this
material was carted off and never heard of again. By general consensus the
worst predators were soldiers from Johnston's army, demoralized by lack of
pay and certainty of defeat. (At the end the Union army helped to feed
these men before their final disbandment.) Superintendent Sumner's excuse for hiding cotton goods in his home was that undisciplined Confederate soldiers would otherwise take them. By 19 April it became clear that the
state treasury and archives were in greater danger among Johnston's men
at Greensboro than they would be with Sherman at Raleigh, and upon the
latter's assurance of their safety, Vance and Johnston ordered them returned.[77] Soon afterward, Union soldiers occupying Company Shops reportedly uncovered $80,000 to $100,000 in gold belonging to a bank in
New Bern and divided it among themselves. Soldiers admitted seizing and
burying about $30,000 between the Shops and Hillsboro. Some of the sto-
len money was recovered—a farmer reportedly found a large number of
gold coins while plowing near the tracks—but to this day no one knows how
much was actually buried or subsequently recovered.[78]

Into this mess were precipitated Jefferson Davis and the Confederate
government. Fleeing southward after Lee's surrender, they reached Greensboro on 11 April, having just beaten Stoneman's raiders to the Reedy Fork
bridge north of town. They too brought treasure, about $500,000 in gold
and silver, the remains of the Confederate treasury and the private resources of the Richmond banks. Most of it preceded Davis and his cabinet
by several days and was taken to Charlotte and beyond before Stoneman
broke the railroad south. About $75,000 of the money was left in Greens-
boro to pay Johnston's men and for other purposes. The dignitaries re-

mained until the fifteenth. Davis took up quarters and held cabinet meetings in "an old leaky car on the Rail Road tracks." As Stoneman had just broken the railroad below Greensboro, they continued southward by road. The roads were muddy and progress was very slow; it took four days to reach Charlotte. Eventually Davis was captured near Irwinville, Georgia, on 10 May.[79]

Johnston's position had become hopeless. He met Sherman on 18 April near Durham, both of them traveling part of the way by train from their respective headquarters. The terms that Sherman stipulated that day contained political ramifications that were unacceptable in Washington. Technically the war resumed. No battles were fought, however, and on 26 April the two generals met again at the same place. The terms reached this time were approved, and the war came to an end. It is fitting to note that this event was delayed by two hours while Johnston, coming from Greensboro, was held up by an accident on the NCRR.[80]

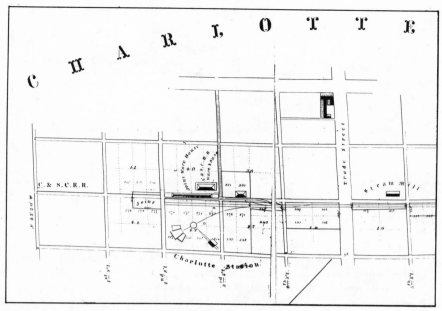

Fig. 1. The Charlotte depot area, 1850s. This plan is the last in a fascinating five-volume series of maps drawn at the time of the road's construction, some on a scale of 100 feet per inch, others 200 feet per inch, showing the entire route from Goldsboro to Charlotte, indicating every structure, road crossing, and property owner along the way. Note the turntable below the joint Charlotte and South Carolina Railroad and NCRR station, marking the NCRR's western terminus. (NCRR Records, North Carolina Division of Archives and History)

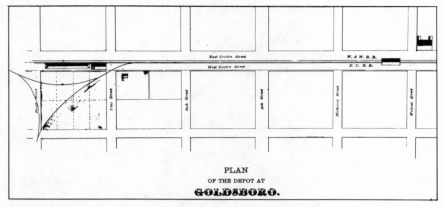

Fig. 2. The Goldsboro depot area, 1871. Unlike the Charlotte plan, this one was made in 1871, at the time of the Richmond and Danville Railroad lease. North here is to the left. Note the triangular wye at the left, for turning around locomotives or short trains without the use of a turntable. It marks the NCRR's eastern terminus. The long building in the middle of Center Street nearby is the joint NCRR and Wilmington and Weldon Railroad freight warehouse pictured in fig. 14. At right is the passenger depot, near where the trains are stopped in fig. 15. (NCRR Records, North Carolina Division of Archives and History)

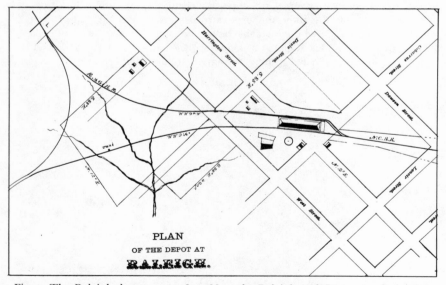

Fig. 3. The Raleigh depot area, 1871. Note the Raleigh and Gaston tracks joining the NCRR from the upper left, as well as the connecting link at left for nonstopping trains. An Amtrak station now occupies nearly the same location. (NCRR Records, North Carolina Division of Archives and History)

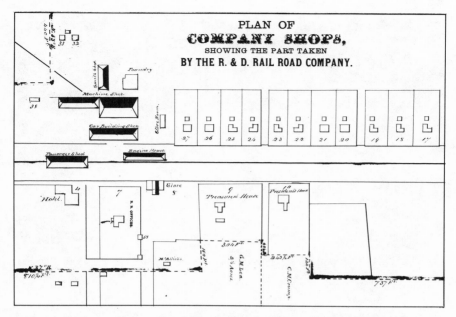

Fig. 4. Company Shops, 1871. Note the hotel, NCRR offices, and other NCRR buildings on the lower (south) side of the tracks as well as the more conspicuous shop buildings above. The small buildings to the right of the shops are employees' houses. Of all these buildings, the only survivals today are the engine house and foundry. See figs. 10 and 11 for views of the shop buildings and hotel. (NCRR Records, North Carolina Division of Archives and History)

Fig. 5. NCRR stock certificate. This certificate for ten shares was issued in 1854 to Robert G. Lindsay of Greensboro and sold by him in 1860 to John L. Morehead of Charlotte, son of John Motley Morehead and a major stockholder. (North Carolina Division of Archives and History)

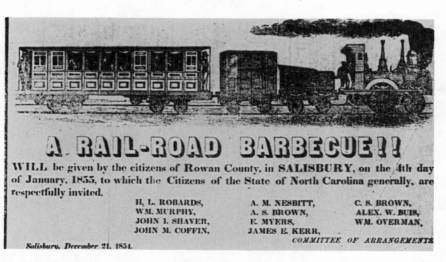

Fig. 6. Notice of a railroad barbecue, Salisbury, 1854. The western end of the NCRR was built northward from Charlotte. Several towns held celebrations in honor of its arrival. The Salisbury barbecue was held as advertised, on 4 January 1855. (Salisbury *Carolina Watchman*, 21 December 1854)

North Carolina Railroad.—On and after Monday, January 1st 1855, the North Carolina Railroad will be opened for the transportation of passengers and freights from Goldsboro' to Durham's 26 miles west of Raleigh.

Passenger train leaves Goldsboro' daily 3 00 A.M.
"   "   passes Raleigh   6 00 "
"   "   arrives at Durham's " 7 46 "
RETURNING.
Passenger train leaves Durham's daily 2 00 P.M.
"   "   passes Raleigh   " 3 30 "
"   "   arrives at Goldsboro' " 6 42 "

Connecting with the United States mail train on the Wilmington and Raleigh Railroad at Goldsboro'; the Raleigh and Gaston Railroad, and Messrs. Bland & Dunn's mail line of four horse post coaches at Durham's running daily via Hillsboro' Graham, Greensboro'. Jamestown, Salem and Lexington to Salisbury ; from which point to Charlotte, the North Carolina Railroad Company are running a daily train. A through freight train leaves Goldsboro' every Thursday for Durham's' returning every Friday. A way freight train will run every Thursday from Goldsboro' to Stalling's, and return same day, and will make extra trips when necessary.
WALTER GWYNN,
Chief Engineer N. C. R. R. Co.
Jan. 1, 1855.

The undersigned are running daily four-horse Post Coaches between Durham's and Salisbury, connecting with the Rail Road Cars at those places, as follows :

Leave Durham's for Greensboro', at 7 46, A. M.
Arrive at Greensboro' at 1, A M.
Leave Greensboro' for Durham's at 1, P. M.
Arrive at Durham's at 6, A. M.
Leave Greensboro' for Salisbury at 8, A. M.
Arrive at Salisbury at 10, P. M.
Leave Salisbury for Greensboro' at 8, P. M.
Arrive at Greensboro' at 12, M.

Going West, these stages pass through Salem, on Monday, Wednesday, and Friday; and returning East, they pass through Salem on Tuesday, Thursday, and Saturday. The other days in each week they go direct through by Jamestown.

The subscribers are now making arrangements to give through tickets to Weldon. N. C., Petersburg, Va., &c.   BLAND & DUNN.
Greensboro' Jan. 1855

North Carolina Rail Road.

JULY, 29TH, 1856.

Change of Schedule for
Mail-Train,
On and after MONDAY the 4th day of August, 1856.

WEST.	
Leaves Goldsboro', at	2.00 A. M
Arrive at Raleigh, at	4.00
" Hillsboro',	7.10
" Graham,	8.45
" Greensboro',	10.12
" Jamestown,	10.52
" Lexington,	12.22 P. M.
" Salisbury,	1.21
" Concord,	3.17
" Charlotte,	4.20

EAST.	
Leave Charlotte, at	5.30 P. M.
Arrive at Concord, at	6.38
" Salisbury,	7.54
" Lexington,	9.33
" Jamestown,	11.04
" Greensboro',	11.39
" Graham,	1.11 A. M.
" Hillsboro',	2.40
" Raleigh,	4.55
" Goldsboro',	7.45

Connecting both ways with the Charlotte and South Carolina Rail Road, and with the Wilmington and Weldon Rail Road.
THEODORE S. GARNETT,
Eng'r and Superintendent.
August 12, 1856—2w

Fig. 7. Advertisements for the NCRR and for Bland & Dunn's Stagecoach Line, 1855. While the NCRR was under construction from Goldsboro westward and from Charlotte northward, it operated trains as far as the tracks would permit, and Bland & Dunn provided stagecoach service in the middle. Early in 1855, the stages ran between Durham and Salisbury. Unlike the NCRR after its completion, they sometimes followed the old post road through Salem. (*Greensboro Patriot*, 31 March 1855)

Fig. 8. NCRR mail train schedule, 1856. Railroad schedules were commonly published in newspapers along the route. This one took effect about six months after the NCRR was completed and began through service along its entire length from Goldsboro to Charlotte. (Charlotte *Western Democrat*, 12 August 1856)

TIME TABLE.
North Carolina Rail Road.
EXPRESS TRAIN—SOUTH.

To go into effect on MONDAY, JULY 26, 1858.

Names of Stations.	Whole Distance.	Distance of Stations.	Time bet. Stations.	Time at Stations.	Arrive.	Leave.	Remarks.
Goldsboro',						1.20PM	
Boon Hill,	12	12	33	3	1.53PM	1.56 "	
Smithfield,	22	10	27	2	2.23 "	2.25 "	
Stallings',	34	12	33	3	2.58 "	3.01 "	Wood.
Raleigh,	49	15	44	15	3.45 "	4.00 "	Water.
Morrisville,	61	12	26	0	4.26 "	4.26 "	
Durham's,	74	13	33	0	4.59 "	4.59 "	
Hillsboro',	88	14	33	3	5.32 "	5.35 "	Wood & Water.
Mebane's,	98	40	23	0	5.58 "	5.58 "	
Haw River,	104	6	14	0	6.12 "	6.12 "	
Graham,	106	2	5	0	6.17 "	6.17 "	
Comp'y's Shops	108	2	4	5	6.21 "	6.25 "	Change Engines.
Gibsonville,	115	7	16	0	6.41 "	6.41 "	
McLean's,	122	7	16	0	6.57 "	6.57 "	
Greensboro',	130	8	19	3	7.16 "	7.19 "	Wood & Water.
Jamestown,	140	10	24	0	7.43 "	7.43 "	
High Point,	145	5	12	0	7.55 "	7.55 "	
Thomasville,	152	7	16	0	8.11 "	8.11 "	
Lexington,	163	11	26	0	8.37 "	8.37 "	
Holtsburg,	172	9	22	0	8.59 "	8.59 "	
Salisbury,	180	8	19	15	9.18 "	9.33 "	Wood & Water.
China Grove,	189	9	20	0	9.53 "	9.53 "	
Concord,	202	13	30	0	10.23 "	10.23 "	
Harrisburg,	210	8	19	0	10.42 "	10.42 "	
Charlotte,	223	13	33	—	11.15 "		

TIME TABLE.
North Carolina Rail Road.
EXPRESS TRAIN—NORTH.

To go into effect on MONDAY, JULY 26, 1858.

Names of Stations.	Whole Distance.	Distance of Stations.	Time bet. Stations.	Time at Stations.	Arrive.	Leave.	Remarks.
Charlotte,						12.55AM	
Harrisburg,	13	13	32	0	1.27AM	1.27 "	
Concord,	21	8	21	0	1.48 "	1.48 "	
China Grove,	34	13	32	0	2.20 "	2.20 "	
Salisbury,	43	9	23	3	2.44 "	2.47 "	Wood & Water.
Holtsburg,	51	8	20	0	3.07 "	3.07 "	
Lexington,	60	9	23	0	3.30 "	3.30 "	
Thomasville,	71	11	27	0	3.57 "	3.57 "	
High Point,	78	7	16	0	4.13 "	4.13 "	
Jamestown,	83	5	13	0	4.26 "	4.26 "	
Greensboro',	93	10	25	3	4.51 "	4.54 "	Wood & Water.
McLean's,	101	8	21	0	5.15 "	5.15 "	
Gibsonville,	108	7	17	0	5.32 "	5.32 "	
Comp'y's Shops	115	7	17	20	5.49 "	6.09 "	Change Engines.
Graham,	117	2	5	0	6.14 "	6.14 "	
Haw River,	119	2	5	0	6.19 "	6.19 "	
Mebane's,	125	6	15	0	6.34 "	6.34 "	
Hillsboro',	135	10	25	3	6.59 "	7.02 "	Wood & Water.
Durham's,	149	14	36	0	7.38 "	7.38 "	
Morrisville,	162	13	35	0	8.14 "	8.14 "	
Raleigh,	174	12	30	15	8.45 "	9.00 "	Water.
Stallings',	189	15	40	3	9.45 "	9.48 "	Wood.
Smithfield,	201	12	33	2	10.22 "	10.24 "	
Boon Hill,	211	10	30	2	10.54 "	10.56 "	
Goldsboro',	223	12	33	—	11.30 "		

This Train shall make no stops, except for Wood and Water, when behind time.

Engineers are forbidden to make up lost time beyond TEN minutes.

No Train, Engine or Hand Car is allowed to be on the main Track within FIFTEEN MINUTES of this Time.

The Standard Clock is at Raleigh.

S. W. James, Printer, at the " Watchman" Office, Salisbury, N. C.

Fig. 9. NCRR timetable, 1858. Showing all the stations along the road in 1858, this timetable indicates wood, water, and engine stops as well as those for passengers. Notice at the bottom which had priority. Under this schedule the run from Goldsboro to Charlotte or vice versa was about ten hours. (North Carolina Collection, University of North Carolina, Chapel Hill)

Fig. 10. Former NCRR repair shops, Burlington, 1906. The photograph shows the shops as they looked roughly half a century after their construction. Of the buildings shown, only the engine house (euphemistically called the roundhouse) at the far right still stands, the others having burned in 1918. (Courtesy W. T. Lasley)

Fig. 11. NCRR Hotel, Burlington, ca. 1900. Perhaps the most elegant building in Company Shops, the hotel was destroyed by an arsonist in 1904, about four years after this picture was taken. (Courtesy W. T. Lasley)

Fig. 12. Rock Creek culvert, Guilford County. Located in eastern Guilford County, this masonry structure was part of the NCRR's original construction in 1853. This photograph shows the culvert in 1989. (Photo by author)

Fig. 13. NCRR locomotives. The Astron (top). A Norris locomotive acquired new in 1855 and rebuilt in 1862 and 1870, it is shown here ca. 1880 in Company Shops. (Courtesy R. B. Carneal, W. T. Lasley) The Colonel Webster, later the Nathaniel Boyden (bottom). Built by Amoskeag for a New England road in 1856, it was acquired during the war by the United States Military Railroads and renamed the Colonel Webster. They sold it late in 1865 to the NCRR, which seems to have rebuilt it a year or so later as the Nathaniel Boyden. Shown here reportedly while in service for the USMRR in North Carolina. (George B. Abdill, *Civil War Railroads* [New York: Bonanza Books, Clarkson N. Potter, Inc., 1961])

Fig. 14. NCRR–Wilmington and Weldon Railroad joint warehouse, Goldsboro. In 1866, this freight warehouse replaced the original which had been accidentally burned by Federal troops the year before. It was built along the tracks in the middle of Center Street as shown in fig. 2, not far from the trains pictured in fig. 15. It was demolished after this shot was taken in 1971. (Courtesy John F. Gilbert)

Fig. 15. Passenger trains on Center Street, Goldsboro. This 1870 view looks south near the passenger depot pictured at the right of fig. 2. In the foreground is an Atlantic and North Carolina Railroad train about to leave for Morehead City, in the rear a Wilmington and Weldon Railroad train headed for Wilmington. The NCRR, ever shy in front of a camera, used the farthest track. (Manuscript Department, Duke University)

Fig. 16. Atlantic and North Carolina Railroad train at Little River bridge, 1865. The United States Military Railroads operated A&NCRR equipment on the NCRR between Goldsboro and Raleigh in 1865. Federal troops built this temporary trestle just west of Goldsboro to replace the structure burned by Joseph E. Johnston's retreating Confederates. (Library of Congress)

Fig. 17. Confederate prison at Salisbury, 1864. The military prison, housed in a former cotton textile mill, lay adjacent to the NCRR track. (North Carolina Collection, University of North Carolina, Chapel Hill)

Fig. 18. NCRR depot at Thomasville. Built about 1870, this depot was restored in recent years and moved to a new location not far from the original site, adjacent to the railway tracks. This shot was taken in 1981. (North Carolina Division of Archives and History)

Fig. 19. John Motley Morehead, NCRR president, 1850–55 (Greensboro Historical Museum)

Fig. 20. Charles F. Fisher, NCRR president, 1855–61 (Walter Clark, *Histories of the Several Regiments and Battalions from North Carolina in the Great War, 1861–65* [Raleigh, N.C.: State of North Carolina, 1901])

Fig. 21. Paul C. Cameron, NCRR president, 1861–62 (Samuel A. Ashe et al., *Biographical History of North Carolina* [Greensboro, N.C.: C. L. Van Noppen, 1905–17])

Fig. 22. Nathaniel Boyden, NCRR president, 1865–66 (Robert D. W. Connor, William K. Boyd, and J. G. de Roulhac Hamilton, *History of North Carolina* [Chicago: Lewis, 1919])

Fig. 23. Josiah Turner, Jr., NCRR president, 1867–68 (Samuel A. Ashe et al., *Biographical History of North Carolina* [Greensboro, N.C.: C. L. Van Noppen, 1905–17])

PART 3

After the War

14

The Road and Its Equipment

IN MAY 1865, with the guns barely stilled, the stockholders' inspection committee made its annual survey and report on the condition of the road. (Although no one was listed as chairman, John Motley Morehead was a member of the committee, and its prose style is like his.) The past year, the committee remarked, was the first in the road's history in which a passenger had been killed in a train accident and the first in which a locomotive had exploded. More broadly, the road had suffered unparalleled damage from rains and high water, and nearly the whole length of the line became the closing scene of one of the greatest wars in history. During the year, seven bridges were burned. The depots at Goldsboro, Raleigh, High Point, and Salisbury were in ashes, as were the passenger shed, offices, and half of the joint depot at Charlotte. And some ten miles of track near Salisbury had been partially burned by Stoneman's raiders. Elsewhere some of the track was so worn as to be nearly useless. (The committee did not examine the road east of Raleigh, which was now under government control.) The entire line had just been reopened although most of the repairs, such as trestle-work bridges, were temporary and would soon have to be replaced. Nothing had yet been done to replace the burnt depots.[1]

Actually, the NCRR suffered relatively little direct military damage; both President Webb and the committee noted their good fortune in this respect. Virtually all of the war-caused destruction had occurred in April 1865, and the road was closed for only ten days. Only the most basic repairs had been possible since the January floods, however; despite a basically sound roadbed (the work of slave section gangs), much ditching and ballasting was needed. The need for new rolling stock and rails at certain places was desperate. Edmund Wilkes, who returned as superintendent in July 1865, characterized the road as unsafe at over twelve miles per hour.[2]

Historian James F. Doster has pointed out that southern railroads in general were not destroyed by the war; rather they suffered from the dilapidation just described. Most made relatively quick recoveries.[3] Worst off, perhaps, were those short lines (like the Atlantic, Tennessee, and Ohio, between Charlotte and Statesville, and the Roanoke Valley Railroad, northwest of Weldon) that joined places of little economic or military importance and that were dismantled in order to supply rails and rolling stock for more strategic roads.[4]

The eastern end of the NCRR, from Raleigh to Goldsboro, had been the worst-constructed segment at the outset, and to make matters worse, it was hardest hit by military destruction. During March and early April 1865 the United States Military Railroads Construction Corps under Colonel William W. Wright rapidly rebuilt both the Atlantic and North Carolina Railroad from Morehead City to Goldsboro and the Wilmington and Weldon from Wilmington to Goldsboro. (Both roads were intended as supply routes for Sherman's army once it moved into the vicinity from South Carolina.) Then, as the outnumbered Confederates under Joseph E. Johnston retreated up the NCRR from Goldsboro, tearing up track and burning bridges behind them, Wright's corps followed close behind, repairing the damage enough to permit Federal pursuit. Most of the destruction and repair occurred east of Raleigh, but the process continued in some degree as far as Hillsboro until Johnston's final surrender at the end of April. During their pursuit, the construction corps relaid about eight miles of track near Boon Hill (now Princeton), rebuilt three bridges, and cleared cuts that Johnston's men had filled with debris. With the surrender, the Federal army relinquished to the NCRR control of its road west of Raleigh. But east of the capital it retained active management until October 1865, operating it as a unit with the A&NC to Morehead City.[5]

During that time the United States Military Railroads (USMRR) ran a quasi-civilian operation, carrying passengers and freight as well as military traffic. As a matter of fact, it carried a large portion of the NCRR's through freight to New Bern and Morehead City, since the Roanoke River bridge at Weldon was destroyed, blocking through trains to both Norfolk and Petersburg. (Never, perhaps, were the objectives of the NCRR's original projectors more fully carried out than at this time, under the auspices of the United States Army!) Service was very poor, however, partly from the worn condition of the road, partly from inefficiency by USMRR personnel, and partly from inattention of the New Bern and Morehead City mercantile communities.[6] In fact, these ports quickly got a bad reputation with interior merchants, fully rivaling their natural disadvantages. Once alternative routes were again open, the traffic followed them to Norfolk, Petersburg, and beyond.

The army deliberately operated in the most Spartan fashion, knowing it would turn the roads back to their owners before long and being anxious to spend as little money as necessary in the meantime. The quality of reconstruction and maintenance work done under these circumstances was well short of peacetime or permanent standards. The inspection committee of 1866 found the worst track on the road to be in the stretch near Boon Hill where the Federals "had relaid some eight miles with a very light T iron, upon small, round, (old-field pine) cross-ties, placed at such a distance part that their heavy trains passing over, bent the iron."[7] The committee neglected to mention that most of the rails taken up there by the retreating Confederates were already badly worn and in need of replacement. Although Wright's men found many of these near the track, he preferred to install others, despite their lighter weight, that he had taken from the Raleigh and Gaston and elsewhere.[8] Following its resumption of control in October, the NCRR found it necessary to make heavier repairs on the eastern end of the line than anywhere else on the road.[9]

The roadbed as a whole suffered primarily from the flood damage back in January, only partially repaired so far. Hardest hit at that time (besides the eastern end with its too-small culverts) were sections in Davidson County near Lexington. There flood waters washed away trestles over Rich Fork and Abbott's Creek (themselves replacements for bridges recently burned by incendiaries) and a section of track and embankment along Swearing Creek.[10]

Normal winter and spring rains tended especially to fill in cuts, which appear not to have been planted with vegetation or faced with stone to retard erosion, at least until 1869. The work of ditching and graveling or ballasting was therefore a perennial chore, particularly in summer and fall when the ground was most workable. Four gravel trains were assigned to this duty in 1865–67. President Webb, who had reported the roadbed to be in good condition in July 1865, pronounced it admirable in 1867 as a result of these efforts but admitted even then that there was still much to do.[11] In the same fashion Superintendent James Anderson reported in 1868 that some twenty-seven miles were ballasted at the most essential points and seventy-six miles of ditches were opened during the past year, but the ensuing severe winter required going over it all again. President William A. Smith reported in 1871 that 200 miles of roadbed had been ballasted in the past three years, much of that figure doubtless reflecting repeated work on trouble spots.[12]

Fuller reporting after 1869 permits a closer look at the task of road maintenance. In April 1870 the Eastern Division had a gravel train as well as a wood and lumber train; on the Western Division one train performed both functions. From twelve to twenty-eight hands were assigned to each. The wood and lumber train carried crossties, fuel, and lumber, presumably for construction work along the road. The gravel train hauled ballasting material, dirt dug from the roadside ditches, and the bricks and stone used in building bridge abutments and riprapping or dressing embankments.[13]

When the road was leased to the Richmond and Danville Railroad in 1871, a detailed survey of the roadbed was undertaken as part of a general inventory of the road and its assets. Ditching was reported as in good order for 142 of the road's 223 miles; cleaning out was needed on the remaining 81. This must have been close to the norm every year. Moreover, representatives of both the NCRR and the R&D agreed that the roadbed between

Raleigh and Goldsboro needed substantial widening after twenty years of erosion. The best segment was that between Greensboro and Charlotte.[14]

The greatest need for new crossties or sills in 1865 was near the eastern end, where USMRR personnel had hurriedly installed inferior ones. The wartime shortage was so far allayed by 1866 that the NCRR temporarily allowed the Raleigh and Gaston to buy sills already cut and available along the line and carry them away on its own trains.[15]

The most expensive phase of postwar reconstruction was the replacement of wornout rails. The NCRR, like other roads, needed more rails than it could afford—2,000 tons or 20 miles of them at the very least, according to President Webb and the inspection committee in the summer of 1865.[16] Accordingly, Webb's successor, Nathaniel Boyden, went to New York that fall, like many another southern railroad president, to buy new rails and equipment. There he purchased 1,200 tons of English rails (weighing 55 pounds per yard) and (relying on an incompetent advisor) another 1,000 tons of lightweight (50-pound) rails that before long had to be replaced. At least part of these purchases were made with cotton that the road had accumulated during the war for just such an eventuality.[17]

In 1867, after twenty-three miles of new rail had been installed, Superintendent Wilkes indicated that much more was still needed; he recommended relaying twenty-five miles per year. The sale of the old rails (for re-rolling) would defray about half of the $225,000 annual cost.[18] An alternate solution was to send the worst iron off to the Tredegar Works in Richmond to be re-rolled and brought back. With freight charges, this would cost slightly more than purchasing new rails, but Webb believed that the re-rolled iron was better in quality than what was available new.[19]

For reasons of economy or otherwise, this course was not followed, and the road appears to have bought only new iron. Webb's successors in 1867–68 made calculations of their own and authorized over $90,000 in purchases, partially on credit. About 1,000 tons, or 10 additional miles, were installed during that year. Another 2,337 tons followed in the three years from 1868 to 1871. This iron ranged in weight from 50 to 60 pounds per yard, most of it at least 55 pounds. (Sixty-pound rail had been used in the original construction.) Most if not all of the new rails were of British manufacture, as before the war.[20]

The NCRR dealt primarily with Tredegar in this period, which re-rolled old iron as formerly, manufactured new rails from 1866 onward, and engaged in the import business as well. The road also dealt with Soutter and Company of Richmond and other importing firms. In general the road paid about $80 per ton for British rails and traded in old ones for about half of that amount.[21]

Steel rail represented a major technological innovation on American railroads in this era. It was not produced domestically until 1867, but a few roads had begun to import British steel rails, at least in small quantities for high-wear places. They were estimated to last at least twice as long as iron—some said up to fifty times longer. By 1869, twenty-six American railroads used steel rails in some quantity, but all were in the North. The delay in transition resulted from steel's higher cost. It gradually became cheaper, falling below iron in 1883 and virtually superseding it thereafter. Where only 30 percent of the nation's track mileage was steel in 1880, it became 80 percent by 1890.[22]

The NCRR inspection committee of 1867 (William Murdoch and William R. Holt) suggested beginning the transition to steel at that time. While more expensive to buy, its durability, they argued, was sure to make it cheaper in the long run.[23] However appealing that view might have been in the abstract, the immediate need was for maximum mileage in new rails, and the directors continued to buy iron.

They were eager to acquire this as cheaply as possible. In August 1868 the NCRR joined most other roads in the state to obtain from the legislature a charter for a North Carolina Iron and Steel Rail Company, empowered to manufacture or re-roll rails and other metal railroad equipment.[24] By this means they hoped to produce or repair rails more cheaply, at the same time keeping their money in the state. The plan was to have each railroad purchase stock in the new enterprise, $100 for every mile of road. But when Silas Burns, an NCRR state director and one of the leaders in the effort, tried to obtain a subscription from the stockholders at their annual meeting in 1869, the matter was tabled on a motion by Paul C. Cameron. The Raleigh and Gaston soon did likewise, and the matter died.[25]

By 1871, when the NCRR was leased, it contained a diversity of rail weights from 50 to 60 pounds per yard, all wrought iron.[26] At the same time the road possessed between 10 and 13 miles of sidetrack, depending on which list one follows. Almost every section of the road (each of them 4 to 8 miles long) had a station, and every station had at least a single siding of 480 feet or more. Sidings varied in length and number in rough proportion to the business done at each station. Charlotte led with 5,466 feet and 7 switches (the latter probably approximating the number of parallel sidetracks). Following, in order, were Goldsboro (4,160 feet and 6 switches), Raleigh (3,790 feet and 6 switches), Greensboro (2,851 feet and 5 switches), and Salisbury (2,760 feet and 4 switches).[27]

The road boasted only three turntables in 1871, at Charlotte, the Shops, and Raleigh. A map of the road in the 1850s shows a turntable at Goldsboro as well, but by 1871 it had apparently been replaced by a triangular wye, which took more space but was cheaper to build and maintain.[28]

Of the seven bridges burned during the war, the two over Rich Fork and Abbott's Creek near Lexington were torched by unknown incendiaries in July 1864. Two others, over the Deep River at Jamestown and South Buffalo Creek near Greensboro, were destroyed by Stoneman's raiders in April 1865. The last three, over the Little River near Goldsboro, the Neuse

River near Selma, and Stony (Stone's or Flat) Creek west of Durham, were burned by retreating Confederates, also in April. The masonry abutments were all more or less intact, and each bridge was replaced immediately by a temporary trestle.[29] Those near Lexington were in turn washed out by floods and replaced with new trestles by the Confederate army early in 1865. Temporary trestling was also used to support weakened bridges elsewhere. The Neuse River trestle was once damaged and twice washed away altogether by floods during the winter of 1865–66.[30] It was therefore a prime candidate for replacement with a more permanent Howe truss bridge in 1866. Similar bridges were built by 1867 over the Little and Deep rivers and the creeks near Lexington. Roofs for these structures, as well as additional bridges elsewhere, followed in the next few years. So did extensive repairs to the long Yadkin and Haw River bridges. By 1870 the war damage was repaired and nearly all of the trestles were superseded with Howe truss bridges. In each case these were of wood, sometimes covered with sheet iron.[31] The few trestles that remained in 1871 were in the east, replacing inadequate culverts that had plagued the road since its first construction.[32]

Within two years of the war the roadbed, track, and bridges had been put in reasonably good repair. Early in 1867, in fact, they were pronounced to be never better by a legislative committee that was more than a little critical of the road's management in other respects.[33] This was also the view of state Superintendent of Public Works Ceburn L. Harris after his official inspection trip late in 1870. He pronounced most of the road to be in very good condition, if only fair on the troublesome segment from Raleigh to Goldsboro.[34]

At the end of the war the United States government confiscated all railway rolling stock that had belonged to the Confederate government and also any that had been captured from northern roads. The former it sold and the latter it returned to the previous owners. The buyers at government sales were generally southern railroads located in the vicinity of the sale. The prices they paid for locomotives were not greatly different from those charged by private sellers; cars, however, were often acquired very cheaply. The roads in greatest need of equipment were not always able to pay cash. Often, therefore, the government sold equipment on credit, with an eye both to its own revenue and to restoring the region's rail network and economy.[35]

Not surprisingly, the NCRR was among the roads buying this equipment, a small part of it on credit. Twice during the spring and summer of 1865 the road sought to borrow or rent two locomotives from the army in order (it said) to better transport military stores.[36] The government responded affirmatively in at least one case, on the understanding that the road contemplated purchase as soon as it was able.

The road possessed twenty-one locomotives in July 1865. Although President Webb characterized them generally as in first-rate order, this defies belief. Sidney Andrews, a northern journalist traveling through the Carolinas in September and October 1865, remarked that a careful inspection of almost any locomotive in that region was "calculated to vividly impress the traveller with the uncertainty of life."[37] Two or three were almost worn out, and another three were being rebuilt in the shops. Moreover, four engines captured from the Baltimore and Ohio Railroad during the war and purchased from the Confederate government had been returned to the B&O, and two others rented from the Manassas Gap Railroad of Virginia would soon be returned. With five engines normally in the shops for repair at a given time, the road was left with only sixteen in working order. Webb recommended buying at least three more.[38]

The road actually bought five during 1865–66, and at least thirty flatcars. The flatcars and four of the locomotives were secondhand, purchased from the government. Most of the payment was rendered in the form of military transportation rather than cash.[39] A fifth locomotive (named the General Washington) was purchased from the New Jersey Locomotive Works, which wanted to place one of its engines on a southern railroad and offered to do so on six months' approval at a reduced price of $15,000. The engine proved acceptable and was the NCRR's first new locomotive purchase since 1857.[40]

By July 1866 the road possessed twenty-five engines, about the same as before the war. The number remained nearly constant until the lease of 1871. In addition to those under repair at any time, at least one was usually being rebuilt. If that operation were basic enough, the engine reappeared under a new name, such as the Giles Mebane in 1867. Some of the oldest locomotives—the Cyclops and the Roanoke in 1866–67—were regarded as unreconstructible and were scrapped. In March 1868 the Pioneer was turned out of the shops, described as the first locomotive ever built from scratch in North Carolina.[41]

Less than a year later the Governor Holden was completed—rebuilt from an earlier locomotive and reflecting in its name the new state of political affairs in North Carolina. The Holden merits special attention because it received an inaugural fanfare and a fuller description in the press than any other engine on the road. On 11 February 1869 it drew its namesake and a party of forty government officials and friends in an elegant new coach (also built at the shops) on an inaugural ride from Raleigh to Company Shops. They toured the shops, were treated to dinner at the hotel, and returned to Raleigh late in the evening. As to the locomotive, its drive wheels were five and a half feet in diameter—normal for the road's passenger engines; it bore flags flying in the breeze, and on its sides were plates bearing the name "Gov. Holden" in brass letters. On either side of the "elegantly painted" tender was a likeness of the governor flanked by "fancy designs," probably scrollwork. Above all this was an eagle with a scroll in its beak bearing the inscription "North Carolina Railroad." Throughout this description there is no hint of color except for the brass letters. The road purchased another new engine in 1870–71, which it named the W. A. Smith for the sitting president of the road.[42]

In July 1865 the road had only 3 or 4 passenger cars fit for service; 6 or 7 others required complete overhaul. Edmund Wilkes, who returned as superintendent in July, later recalled that he found only 1 first-class and 2 second-class cars, all with seats in bad order and lacking lights and water; traveling accommodations could not have been worse, he said. Although President Webb characterized the freight cars as in fair condition overall, Wilkes recalled (more honestly) that not one of them really carried its contents safely. In July 135 boxcars and 35 flatcars were counted as fit for service, with 53 cars of both kinds so worn down as to be unusable. Another 18 cars were in Federal hands on the eastern end of the line.

The road performed something of a miracle in rehabilitating its cars and even adding to their number in the months that followed. As early as September, Sidney Andrews praised the NCRR's rolling stock, noting that many cars had just been thoroughly repaired and repainted.[43] The shops, now able to obtain the necessary materials, were constantly busy repairing and rebuilding old cars and constructing new ones. Finding that those built on the premises were of equal quality and cost only half as much as cars purchased elsewhere, Wilkes decided to rely on the shops entirely for new cars, using old parts wherever possible. In 1871, however, the road purchased three "most elegant new passenger cars" from the outside.[44]

Within a year after the war the road had resumed its prewar total of seventeen passenger coaches, including both first- and second-class cars. It maintained about that number thereafter. In keeping with national trends, these cars gradually increased in size: a coach dating from 1857 was forty-two feet long, two placed on the road in 1867 measured forty-four feet, and the three acquired in 1871 measured forty-eight feet. Often these new cars (that continued to be made of wood) carried fewer people than their shorter predecessors, but they provided greater comfort. Coaches of the 1860s commonly carried fifty passengers; the NCRR's reclining-chair cars of 1871 contained only forty-four seats.[45]

The numbers of baggage, mail, and express cars varied from one year to another, as cars were reassigned or remodeled for these uses. (Four mail cars were remodeled into mail and baggage cars in 1868–69, for example.)[46] Chronological comparisons are difficult, therefore, but these cars seem to have increased from about six before the war to at least ten afterward, probably reflecting a postwar increase in express business.

Boxcars and flatcars, which carried virtually all of the freight, gradually increased in number, in 1869 surpassing the immediate prewar totals of 142 and 83, respectively. Flatcars were used less after that year and declined in number while the total of boxcars continued to climb. Freight cars were in short supply early in 1867, but otherwise the number seems to have kept abreast of the road's needs.[47] The NCRR's business did not require—at least it did not possess—the specialized tank, livestock, or coal cars that were coming into use on other roads.

But several specialized service cars, by contrast, did appear after the war. Five cars variously called shanty, bridge, or dormitory cars were acquired in 1866–67, and the number increased to seventeen by 1872. A ration car appeared in 1870. These were apparently designed to accommodate construction workers repairing bridges and other parts of the road.[48] Fifteen gravel cars (gondolas, or flatcars with low sides) were built in 1868–69 and remained in use for several years. They were used by ditching crews and other maintenance workers. The road had possessed a larger number of these before 1860, but they disappeared from the roster during the war. Six conductors' cars made their debut in 1869. These forerunners of the later caboose, resembling boxcars, were designed for the use of freight-train crews and also carried the baggage of passengers traveling on mixed trains.[49] An office or business car appeared in 1867; judging by its value, comparable to passenger coaches, it was likely used by the superintendent and the president.[50] (For a list of all the road's cars, see table 9.)

One of the most pressing needs in the summer of 1865 was to rebuild the burnt depots at Goldsboro, Raleigh, High Point, Salisbury, and Charlotte. In addition, better joint passenger and freight accommodations were needed with the Piedmont Railroad at Greensboro. All along the line, stations, platforms, and other structures suffered from neglect. Some of the platforms were missing planks, even rotting away altogether. Quite apart from war-related damage, the inspection committee admitted that the road had hitherto done very little at its stations to facilitate the health, comfort, or convenience of its passengers; specifically they noted a lack of privacy for either ladies or gentlemen, presumably in providing separate restrooms. Such matters required attention, they warned, if the road expected to compete successfully as a passenger railroad.[51]

The more routine repairs were delegated to a force under Captain James E. Allen, who had done much of the original tracklaying and then served as road master until 1860. His party worked its way westward from Goldsboro, reaching Hillsboro in June or July 1866. It seems to have completed its work the next year. The larger rebuilding projects were undertaken separately. The joint warehouse with the Wilmington and Weldon at Goldsboro, accidentally burned by Union troops late in the war, was rebuilt in 1866.[52]

Facilities at Raleigh in particular had been inadequate for years. No passenger shed had ever been built there, first because it needed to be done in conjunction with the Raleigh and Gaston and the two roads had long disagreed on a location, then because of a wartime shortage of lumber. The freight depot at the juncture of Cabarrus and Harrington streets had therefore served passengers after a fashion until its destruction by the retreating

Confederates.[53] With the rapid development of through freight transportation, running cars from one road onto another without stopping for reshipment, the joint freight warehouse had become obsolete. Such was not the case with passenger travel, and the structure was therefore rebuilt as a joint passenger station in 1867. The NCRR refitted its engine house nearby as a freight depot for its own use.[54]

Since early in the war the mud surrounding the Raleigh depot had called forth the most eloquent denunciation and satire by the local press. The *Standard* warned early in 1865 that in another week wheeled vehicles would no longer be able to approach the place. Unless the streets were macadamized and lamps installed, "we fear that some worthy citizen, or member of the Legislature will sink in that awful mud some one of these dark nights and be lost to friends, to usefulness and fame, forever." A year later the city council ordered the NCRR to clean up the mess or face a lawsuit.[55] It seems to have been an empty threat; the complaint recurred every winter, and the council was still ordering the two roads to repair the surrounding streets in February 1870.[56]

The mud failed to deter townspeople from congregating around the station at train times. Some were vendors with business to transact, but the greater part were loungers of both races attracted by the excitement of arriving trains. They got in the way of passengers and train crews and were regarded as a public nuisance—a problem that existed in other towns as well.[57]

The construction of the Piedmont Railroad (in effect a continuation of the Richmond and Danville, which controlled it) required the erection of joint passenger and freight facilities in Greensboro. This too was done in 1866 and 1867. The "neat frame passenger building" contained both ladies' and gentlemen's waiting rooms, a baggage room, and ticket and telegraph offices.[58] The station was located adjacent to Elm Street, the main north-south thoroughfare in town, and trains sometimes blocked the street. A local ordinance of 1870 imposed fines of $50 to $100 on any railroad obstructing the public streets for more than fifteen minutes. Trains incurred another $100 fine for running more than four miles per hour inside the city limit.[59]

The station at High Point, burned by Stoneman's raiders, was quickly rebuilt, using brick from the old building.[60] At Salisbury, the "splendid and convenient buildings" erected with the Western North Carolina Railroad in 1859 and also torched by Stoneman were not fully replaced for several years. A joint passenger shed was delayed until 1870. Meanwhile temporary accommodations served both passengers and freight.[61]

Charlotte also suffered from poor accommodations for several years. A substantial proportion of the freight facilities there had burned in the January 1865 fire and were not rebuilt for at least a year.[62] Passenger accommodations were poor at the time of the fire and remained so, apparently because the NCRR and the Charlotte and South Carolina could not agree on plans for a joint station; the facilities in 1871 consisted of a wooden platform 284 feet long with a 12-by-25-foot ticket office in the center.[63] The Charlotte *Democrat* persistently complained of the lack of a shed to protect travelers from the rain. Locomotives and cars too suffered from exposure to the elements as they lay over for periods of time at the road's termini—both there and at Goldsboro. "Dimes spent in building a shed would save dollars on the stock," remarked the 1867 inspection committee—in vain.[64]

As business and travel patterns shifted over the years, new stations were built and others abandoned. Mitchener's Depot near Smithfield was moved to the new village of Selma, a mile and a half up the line, in 1867.[65] Two small stations were added on either side of Raleigh in 1867–68, Asbury and Wilson's Mills, bringing the total to twenty-eight. But the station at Asbury was dropped, while China Grove and McLeansville narrowly escaped that fate.[66] In 1870 the Holtsburg depot, midway between Lexington and Salisbury, was moved a short distance up the road to a place named Linwood, the future site in the 1980s of a massive Norfolk and Southern freight yard.[67] A short spur was built in 1870 into the grounds of the new state penitentiary then under construction in Raleigh.[68]

Every station had a variety of buildings or structures in addition to the depots and warehouses. These included woodsheds, water tanks, and commonly houses (of weatherboard or logs) for section hands. Occasionally there were also smokehouses, well or pump houses, and houses for bridge watchmen and other employees. Like the station buildings themselves, they were in various stages of repair at a given time. Leaking roofs and decaying wood were all too common.[69]

There was a perennial need to repair, rebuild, or enlarge water tanks and related equipment.[70] In 1871 some of these structures were described as tub tanks, round in shape; others were square. Many if not all were roofed over. All were made of wood and subject to decay. The "gum" (rubber) hoses also required periodic replacement.[71] The water supply seems to have been adequate everywhere along the line after the war.

The inspection committee of 1868 reported that the road owned in that year some twelve town lots and over 1,900 acres of land apart from its holdings in Company Shops. This property, estimated at about $12,000 in value, had no direct connection to the operation of the road and brought in very little income. It was unclear even then how the road had come to acquire some of it, and a number of the titles and boundaries were disputed.[72] In 1871, at the time of the lease, these properties were not included, and the directors ordered them sold.[73]

Some of the land had been acquired during the war as a source of wood for fuel and crossties. The road's need for wood was still staggering. Between 8,300 and 8,400 cords were annually consumed by the locomotives, apart from the 90,000 or so crossties requiring replacement each year.[74]

President Webb reported in July 1865 that the road was still getting much of its wood from its own lands. The wartime labor shortage persisted for a time afterward owing to the disruptions following the end of slavery, but outside wood supplies improved in quantity and price from 1866 onward. Even finished lumber was so easily obtained commercially that year that it was suggested the company get rid of the sawmill it had acquired earlier to ensure its lumber supply.[75] By 1867 the road obtained nearly all of its wood by contract from private parties, as before the war. It cost an average of $1.75 to $2.00 per cord, about 25 cents less than when it had paid workers to get the wood on its own lands.[76]

Most of the road's real-estate holdings were at Company Shops. The village, numbering about 300 persons in 1864, continued a slow growth to 817 at the time of its first census listing in 1880. The road had resumed construction of workers' homes in 1863 and continued to do so after the war. It owned over sixty houses of differing sizes and conditions in 1871, apart from the shops themselves.[77]

The wartime effort to sell town lots as a means of encouraging growth had not worked well and was soon suspended. In 1868 NCRR Treasurer William A. Caldwell and the stockholders' finance committee, chaired by Rufus Barringer, urged the road to divest itself of all properties at the Shops that were not actually required to run the railroad; too many of these buildings and lots returned an inadequate income or none at all. The committee rejected altogether the idea of an exclusive company town. Experience, it said, "has verified the prediction that the *Company Shops* would prove the '*Company Sinking Fund.*'" It urged instead that the NCRR promote the town's growth into "a large manufacturing or industrial centre," thereby increasing the road's business and assuring it a larger pool of cheap and reliable labor.[78] This advice was inspired in part by a laissez-faire mentality that was calling simultaneously for the state either to sell its railroad stocks or to turn control of the NCRR over to the private stockholders—all in the interest of greater efficiency.

The board of directors heeded the advice only to the point of resuming the sale of town lots and trying to sell the hotel and the houses built for the president and treasurer. These buildings were not sold, perhaps for want of purchasers, and continued to serve their original purposes.[79] The sale of lots began on a small scale in 1869, the road selling homesites primarily while leasing commercial lots. Every transaction had to be approved by the board of directors. Each conveyance, moreover, forbade use of the property as a tavern, gambling house, or "house of ill fame" on pain of reversion to the railroad. No liquor was sold in town. Under the leasing policy several stores and other small businesses were established. The largest store was a cooperative owned by NCRR employees. In 1869, and for some years to come, most of the houses in town were still owned by the road and were built of brick.[80]

The hotel was the largest and grandest building in town apart from the shops themselves. It stood alongside the depot and across the tracks from the shop buildings. Until 1862 the road had successfully rented it out. But train schedules were altered, and trains no longer stopped regularly at the Shops at mealtimes. Feeding passengers had been the hotel's main business; profits accordingly declined, and no one could be found to take over the enterprise. Since the hotel continued to perform a vital service in feeding shop employees and putting up occasional overnight guests, the road kept it open under a salaried manager. In 1867 the directors returned to a rental basis, but the hotel remained a losing proposition until after the arrival of Anna Troy in 1870. Her good management and—no less important—new train schedules making this a supper stop succeeded in revitalizing the business. She remained in charge for many years.[81]

Meanwhile, the town was formally chartered in February 1866, its limits forming a square one and a half miles in each dimension, centered on the hotel.[82] Most of the town council members for years to come were employed or otherwise associated with the NCRR. Superintendent Edmund Wilkes was a member of the original board. The first listed mayor, in 1869, was B. E. Sergeant, the foreman of the carpenter shop.[83]

The town still lacked some of the amenities that usually accompanied village life. Although "decidedly prepossessing" in appearance, with "good houses, neat places, everywhere," according to a writer in 1867 who echoed the prevailing opinion, most of its residents lived there for only a few years. He gave this as a reason why no churches existed.[84] Also, the townspeople belonged to different denominations, none of which could afford to build or maintain its own church. From the beginning, ministers of different faiths had come to the Shops from Graham and elsewhere and conducted services in various buildings. Then in 1868–69 the NCRR helped subsidize the erection of an interdenominational church with the gifts of a substantial lot and at least $1,100 in money. Local residents called it the only church in the United States built by a railroad. The road also gave land in 1869 for a freedmen's church.[85]

There was no school until 1866, when an academy was established through the efforts of a committee including Wilkes, Sergeant, NCRR Secretary Francis A. Stagg, and Master Machinist Rufus D. Wade. Two other schools followed, under Quaker auspices, teaching whites and blacks separately. In 1869 Ku Klux Klansmen burned one of these schools and flogged the teacher of the other. (Alamance County, nearly evenly divided among Democrats and Republicans, was the scene of more Klan activity in 1869 and 1870 than almost any county in the South.)[86]

The railroad of course remained by far the largest employer in this company town. The shops complex grew somewhat in size and was refurbished as need dictated and revenue permitted. Some of the machinery was aging under heavy use and needed replacement by 1868. A woodshed was remodeled into a shop for the repair of freight cars. A printshop was established to print tickets, timetables, handbills, stationery, and other supplies that had formerly been purchased from the outside. After years of planning for a permanent engine house, the plans frustrated by wartime shortages of materiel and postwar shortages of money, the structure was finally built by 1871. Made of brick like the other shop buildings, it was designed for the repair and housing of locomotives. Although it was commonly referred to as the roundhouse, it was in fact oblong in shape, with ingress and egress only at the ends. It was so difficult to remove engines parked near the center of the building that it partially defeated its purpose. But the structure served as long as the shops were open, and it was the only major building still standing in the 1980s.[87]

15

Labor and Operations

THE NUMBER OF WORKERS on the road fluctuated from day to day, but the totals captured on paper in the annual reports ranged from a high of 693 in 1866 to a low of 485 two years later; the 1865–71 average was 576.[1] (In 1857 and 1858, the only prewar years for which figures are available, the average was 428, free and slave.) The high employment immediately after the war reflected the temporary need to rebuild the road as well as to operate it; the low figure in 1868 resulted from an economy campaign instituted by President Thomas Webb in 1867 and continued by his successor, Josiah Turner. The latter reportedly saved between $13,000 and $14,000 through layoffs and pay cuts.[2] But the layoffs could not be sustained, and in 1869 the total labor force was nearly 100 higher.

Many, perhaps most, of the station agents were still part time, paid in rough correspondence to the business transacted at their stations. Their annual salaries in 1871 ranged from $100 at Wilson's Mills to $2,000 at Charlotte and $2,100 at Raleigh. Those at Raleigh, Greensboro, and Salisbury paid clerks and telegraph operators from their own salaries.[3] Especially at the smaller stations, these men were still associated with their localities; only occasionally did they move from one station to another. The agent at Wilson's Mills was named Wilson; at Cary he was a member of the locally prominent Page family; the Mebane agent was Stephen A. White, founder of the village and later of a furniture factory there. The agency at Haw River seems still to have belonged to the local textile mill; the agent replacing George W. Swepson there in 1865 or 1866 was Thomas M. Holt, the proprietor of the mill and destined in later years to be a (post-lease) president of the NCRR and governor of the state. Station agents generally had been insulated from political influences in the past, and with the probable exception of the agent at Raleigh, they seem not to have been affected by the political changes that occurred in 1865. But with the advent of congressional Reconstruction and Republican control in 1868, there was a wholesale turnover; nineteen of the twenty-eight were replaced. They included, but were by no means limited to, the largest and most lucrative stations.

Shortly before the war the road had been separated into two divisions for maintenance purposes, a single road master giving way to two division masters, east and west of Company Shops. In 1865–66 the number grew to four, in order to hasten the rebuilding efforts. It fell back to two the next year, and in 1868–69 a single road master was restored in the person of W. P. Raiford, a longtime division chief.[4] The maintenance force was also diminished that year, once the worst deficiencies in track and roadbed had been corrected.

The great majority of employees continued to be organized into three main departments, consolidated into two in 1867–68. The road department, under the road master, was concerned primarily with maintenance of way and employed two-thirds to three-quarters of the total force. The majority of these workers were section hands, and most of the remainder were gravel-train and station hands, equally unskilled. The road was divided after 1865 into thirty-five sections, almost double the original nineteen. Each section, averaging about six miles in length, was under the care of a section master and an average of five to seven laborers, or about one section hand per mile of mainline track. There were usually one or two gravel trains on each of the road's two divisions. Each crew consisted of about twenty-five laborers, an engineer, and a fireman—even a conductor (or overseer) in 1865–66.[5]

The machinery department, under the master mechanic, averaged 132 workers during the rebuilding period of 1865–66 and 86 thereafter—between 14 and 20 percent of the total. The majority of these shopmen were skilled as machinists, smiths, boilermakers, carpenters, painters, and the like, but there were also persons listed as helpers, apprentices, and laborers.

The third unit, called the transportation department before 1865 and the train department afterward, disappeared as a separate entity in 1867–68, when it was incorporated into the machinery department. Whether independent or not, it was headed by an official variously called the dispatcher of trains and the master of transportation. It consisted of the train crews, from engineers and conductors to brakemen and woodpassers. They averaged seventy-two in number during the postwar years—a little over 10 percent of the whole. The number of engineers, twenty-two in 1865, was cut back sharply to eleven or twelve after 1866. The same was true of conductors, firemen, and woodpassers. Generally speaking, one of each category was required per train, and peacetime traffic required fewer trains. In fact, only four conductors were listed on the payroll in 1868–70, when they were omitted altogether from freight trains. Brakemen, however, remained at about twenty throughout the period.

Two-thirds of the road's employees in 1857 and 1858 had been blacks, nearly all of them slaves. In 1865, 71 percent were black. But labor was unsettled, as whites often observed in the wake of emancipation. Measuring the bounds of their new freedom, blacks ceased to work like slaves. The stockholders' inspection committee promptly noted this tendency, displaying both indignation and satisfaction as to predictions come true: "Many of 'the freedmen' do not work as they have hitherto done; . . . no dependence can be put in them. They come to-day and engage to work for a month or three months, commence work, receive rations, and to-morrow they are gone." The problem might last for several years, the committee concluded, until blacks either learned to work responsibly or were replaced by white labor.[6]

The road's managers soon adopted the second alternative. In 1866 the same committee members noted "a great change in the character of the employees along the line. Hitherto nearly all the laborers employed were black, now, with but few exceptions, they are all *white*." Indeed, the 462 black employees of 1865 had shrunk to fewer than 150, and in 1867 perhaps to none at all. Even the section gangs were predominantly if not wholly white. These men commanded higher wages, receiving $1 per day for track work instead of the 49 cents (plus rations) received by blacks, but they were characterized as doing a better day's work.[7]

The experiment was not a success, however, for reasons that were not explained. Either blacks became more responsible or whites less so, or the change had been motivated more by philosophy than economics. In 1868, with much less commentary, the black labor force was back up to 70 percent of the total, where it remained through 1871. (Race is not mentioned in the employee lists after 1866, but in that and the preceding year only the black workers received rations in addition to money wages. No employees received rations in 1867, presumably in the absence of black workers, but rations reappeared in large numbers in 1868 in jobs that blacks had filled previously.)[8] There seem to have been no white section hands after 1867. The black restoration occurred in the Josiah Turner administration, before the advent of Republican control, presumably as part of his general economy drive: black labor was cheaper. Certainly Turner was not animated by compassion for the former slaves. He publicly attacked Freedmen's Bureau officials for intervening in behalf of blacks claiming money from the road, and he ignored summonses to appear in bureau courts. He was soon to be an apologist for and defender of the Ku Klux Klan and, as such, was briefly imprisoned when Republican Governor William W. Holden called out the state militia to combat the Klan in 1870.[9]

Racial discrimination in jobs and wages was constant throughout the period. Blacks were consistently excluded from the most prestigious positions, like engineer, conductor, and even section master and from most of the skilled trades. A few served as smiths and as carpenters and painters in the car shops in 1865–66, but these positions went to whites thereafter, even as blacks returned to other jobs. Train crews (apart from engineers and conductors) were substantially black in most years. About two-thirds of the firemen and woodpassers were black in 1865–66; following the hiatus they took over those jobs exclusively after 1868. Much the same was true of brakemen. In the road department, gravel-train and station hands, like the section gangs, were all black by 1870.

The comparison of wages, among NCRR employees and with workers on other roads, is uncertain because some were paid by the month and others by the day and because blacks received part of their compensation in rations. (In 1871 these rations were valued at 20 cents per day.) It is not always clear how many days were worked per month; the NCRR appears to have followed a six-day week and a ten-hour day, as before the war.[10] Other roads nationally had seven-day weeks of 70 hours. Rendigs Fels, writing about the Nashville, Chattanooga, and St. Louis Railroad from 1866 into the 1870s, says that workers' hours varied greatly, but the departures from a thirty- or thirty-one-day month often seem to have occurred because work wasn't available.[11] This was likely true on the NCRR as well.

The total compensation of blacks on the NCRR was usually (but not always) less than that received by whites in the same ranks. In 1866, for instance, the six white firemen received $40 per month, the twelve black firemen $30.20 ($25 per month plus rations valued at 20 cents per day during a twenty-six-day work month). White carpenters received from $2 to $3 per day, black carpenters $1.20 to $1.45 including rations. But in 1869 the nine white brakemen were paid $20 per month, the eleven blacks $20.20 ($15 plus rations). Among the unskilled section hands, those who can be identified as white in 1865–67 received 90 cents to $1 per day, or about $26 per month. The rest, almost certainly black, earned between $12.70 and $15.99 per month. The $10 per month and rations received by most unskilled black laborers during these years translated to $15.20 per month.

After the war as before it, southern roads faced a shortage of skilled mechanical workers and often had to pay a premium for their services. Nationally, locomotive engineers received an average of $3.19 per day, or $82.94 for a month of twenty-six workdays, according to a survey of railroad payrolls between 1868 and 1873. The average for conductors was virtually the same.[12] NCRR engineers were somewhat better paid, receiving from $80 to $100 per month; the yearly average from 1865 to 1871, with little annual fluctuation, was close to $90. (By 1871 engineers were being paid a stipulated rate per trip that averaged about $90 over a month.)[13] Conductors, somewhat easier to recruit locally, made $85 in most years, very close to the national average.[14] The wages of skilled shopmen on the NCRR varied considerably, but their average was not far from the national $2.60 per day. (The workers themselves seem to have regarded these wages as "tolerable" and competitive.)[15]

Among unskilled workers the sectional advantages were turned around. Freedmen were as numerous in the South as slaves had been, and with little more bargaining power in a white-dominated society. NCRR firemen, brakemen, and unskilled laborers earned less, often far less, than the national averages. Firemen nationally earned $1.80 per day or $46.80 monthly. On the NCRR, white firemen received $40 per month in 1865–66, $30 in

1867, and $20 thereafter; for the blacks who came to monopolize this labor, it fluctuated from $25 to $15 or $20 per month, always plus rations that added about $5 per month. (Those in Virginia were paid about the same: 99 cents per day.) Brakemen's wages approximated those of firemen nationally and locally. The national average for section and station hands was $1.55 per day, or about $40 per month. Whites performing this labor on the NCRR earned no more than $1 per day, and the blacks who dominated or monopolized it most years received a uniform $15 per month including rations.

On the NCRR as generally, labor was regarded as a commodity to be purchased as cheaply as possible and governed by supply and demand. Business slowdowns brought layoffs. Fluctuations in the supply of workers brought hikes or cuts in wages. One of the goals of the finance committee in seeking to open Company Shops to new business and new residents in 1868 was to "get good labor much easier and on better terms than . . . now."[16] Black firemen, brakemen, and woodpassers supplanted whites because they could be hired more cheaply. There was no consistent pattern of wage changes in this period beyond the fact that in many jobs wages reached a high point in 1866 and declined during the next two years as the result of economy measures. There was an accompanying drop in total employees for the same reason. The advent of Republican control in 1868 seems to have brought no significant changes in labor policy or compensation and few benefits to blacks beyond an expansion of the labor force to more realistic levels.

The great majority of workers were paid by the month, presumably including those listed at a daily rate.[17] Thomas Webb reported that when he resumed the presidency in July 1866 he found, among several hundred thousand dollars in pressing debts, that "the hands upon the road" had not been paid in three months.[18]

Labor costs were high in the first two postwar years as the road was being rebuilt. Along with other costs they were probably higher than necessary at that time, but the needs were extraordinary. Labor costs steadily declined until in 1868–69 they were only half of the 1865–66 level—$182,000 instead of $369,000. There was only a slight increase thereafter as the mounting business of the road required it. As a proportion of total expenses, labor costs varied between 37 and 47 percent between 1865 and 1871, without any clear pattern. As a proportion of total receipts they amounted to 53 percent in the first year, then declined rapidly to about 25 percent after 1868. The average for the six years was 35 percent, compared with a reported national norm in the nineteenth century of 40 percent.[19] In general, labor seems to have been a relatively lower item of expenditure on southern railroads, including the NCRR, than it was nationally.

In 1870, NCRR conductors were required to wear uniforms—apparently the first employees so directed.[20] The problem of conductors pocketing fares collected from passengers on the trains was a hardy perennial on almost every railroad. President Josiah Turner was not altogether facetious when he said in 1868 that "the best evidence of fidelity in a Conductor is that he keeps poor and not able to retire from so laborious a business." With only four conductors remaining in service that year, Turner promoted competition among them to see which would be first to make his monthly return to the road. "When Conductors are habitually behind in their monthly returns they should be suspected of negligence or playing false to the Company."[21]

There is every reason to believe that the NCRR recruited workers as other roads of the time did, hiring friends and relatives of existing employees wherever these came well recommended. There are scattered references to such relationships—Master Mechanic Emery Burns had a son in the company's service, for instance, and Master of Transportation William H. Green was (or became) the son-in-law of President William A. Smith. Political preference was also a factor, especially in the higher ranks and with the accession of the Republicans, who had been political outsiders previously. There was also continuing evidence of promotion from within: James Anderson rose from master mechanic to superintendent; occasionally a station agent was transferred from a smaller station to a busier and more lucrative one; and F. A. Stagg, who became something of a legend for his selfless and painstaking service as company secretary, was promoted to that position from general ticket agent and before that from station agent at Durham when that place could hardly be called a town.[22]

No suspicion ever arose on the NCRR of labor organization or of organized discontent. Management uniformly had its way without need of spies, blacklists, or strikebreakers and seemingly with general public acquiescence. Newspaper editors praised managerial policies that cut costs by trimming wages and laying off workers who were assumed to be superfluous because management said so.[23] That the lowest-paid and most vulnerable workers were only recently slaves until freed by the Yankee invader merely confirmed this ingrained conviction of the divine right of capital.

On the other hand, the road practiced a very limited paternalism in the form of housing at Company Shops and a long-delayed subsidy of the community church there, among other things. In keeping with general practice, the NCRR made no regular provision for disabled or retired workers and their families. Employees were warned that they worked at their own risk. But informal and at least occasional measures were taken in hardship cases. A gravel-train engineer who was held responsible for an accident in which he lost a leg in 1866 received two-thirds wages for six months.[24] The employee list of 1871 contains an entry of $10 per month and rations for two pensioned train hands, presumably black.[25] Often an employee's standing with the company was the major determinant of his treatment. After NCRR secretary and longtime employee F. A. Stagg fell ill in 1870, he retained his title and a reduced salary for several years while an assistant served in his place. President William A. Smith even summoned a physician from Richmond to treat him. In 1878 the stockholders voted him a $500 annual pension.[26]

The routine operations of the road after the war were not greatly different from those before it—with the significant addition of the telegraph in the interim. A large proportion of the trains—perhaps more than before the war—were mixed, consisting of both passenger and freight cars in varying combinations. The daily mail/passenger/express train often carried a few through freight cars, delivering them more expeditiously than the regular freight train could. In fact, the NCRR and the Wilmington and Weldon agreed in 1867 to run such cars regularly on their connecting passenger trains.[27] And the regular freight train (still called the accommodation train) routinely carried at least one passenger coach for local travelers who found it running at more convenient hours than the mail or express train.

In fact, it was not always easy to distinguish between passenger and freight trains. An accommodation train of 1870 consisted of four or five freight cars, a mail car, a second-class passenger coach, and a first-class coach, in that order.[28] Besides the local freight or accommodation trains, there were fast (or through) freight trains and some that carried both local and through shipments. When freight accumulated beyond the capacity of the regularly scheduled trains, as occasionally happened, extra trains were detailed to carry it. Dispatching cars to the stations where they were needed and when they were needed was one of the most complex tasks of railroading. It was commonplace, therefore, to have freight piled up awaiting cars to carry it off, or loaded cars on sidings awaiting a train to take them away, or empty cars on the sidings without any immediate employment. These delays were particularly apt to occur at the junction with other roads. Managers attempted to keep them brief.

Except for the new sleeping cars, introduced on the NCRR in 1866, passenger cars seldom ran through onto connecting roads in this period; through passengers were expected to walk across the platform to (and all too often wait for) the next train on a connecting road. Of course freight cars had been running continuously from one road to another since before the war—except at gauge barriers like Charlotte and Greensboro. The volume of through freight grew unprecedentedly with the postwar revival of commerce. It resumed on a large scale on the NCRR in 1866; by 1870 its cars were making over 200, occasionally over 300, round trips to Norfolk per month during the busiest seasons, using the Raleigh and Gaston and the Seaboard and Roanoke railroads. Those shorter roads in turn sent smaller but substantial numbers of their own cars onto the NCRR, in many cases as far as Charlotte. Similar exchanges were made with other connecting roads on a much smaller scale.[29]

The system was essential but complicated. Every road was expected to keep its own cars in repair; defective ones were regularly unloaded and returned home after routine inspections, interrupting the flow of traffic. Since every road charged a rental fee for the use of its cars on other roads—two and a half cents per mile per car in the case of the NCRR and its neighbors—every such instance involved a financial transaction. The bookkeeping duties expanded proportionately, along with the clerical staffs required to perform them. Given the financial incentives, roads were moved in dull seasons to keep their own cars busy and collecting rent on other roads while leaving the latters' cars sitting idle on sidings. There were frequent complaints of tardiness in returning cars. The NCRR developed the necessary record-keeping skills and facilities only gradually.[30]

Engines and cars, when they were not the same ones used in 1860, were similar in size and capacity. Passenger cars got somewhat larger and heavier, but there were seldom enough passengers to strain the capacity of the engines pulling them, unless freight cars were added to the train. Some engines were more powerful and some loads more heavy than others, but the maximum practical size of an NCRR freight train remained about fifteen to twenty loaded cars. The average was thirteen or fourteen.[31]

The number of trains per day varied according to the needs of the service. During some periods there were only two daily trains in each direction, the through mail or passenger train and a slower freight or accommodation train. At other times the effort to capture a larger share of the through passenger traffic brought two fast trains in addition to the slower freight. Traffic was particularly heavy in the fall of 1865; in September the NCRR ran two passenger and two freight trains daily in each direction.[32] In an effort to economize, however, the number of passenger trains was cut severely after 1866. Passenger train mileage declined to an annual average of 155,000, compared with about 275,000 before and during the war. Except in the first postwar year, freight train mileage remained about the same as before the war, though somewhat below wartime levels. As already indicated, most trains carried both passengers and freight in varying combination.

Train speeds and running times depended on the same factors and often fluctuated. On average they were about the same as before the war. The running times for the mail train from Goldsboro to Charlotte varied from eight hours and a quarter during two frenetic periods in 1867 and 1868 up to more than seventeen hours during a slow period in 1869. These involved average speeds of twenty-one and thirteen miles per hour, respectively, including stops. (In the dark days of July 1865 the mail train took over seventeen hours from Raleigh, not Goldsboro, for an average of ten miles per hour.) Actual running speeds reached twenty-five miles per hour, sometimes more. Freight trains were slower, of course, partly because their work required more and longer stops. They commonly took twenty to twenty-four hours between Goldsboro and Charlotte. A great deal of the through traffic never went east of Raleigh, thereby shortening the run on the NCRR by three to four hours on passenger trains and by nearly five hours on freight trains.[33] Trains still stopped at Company Shops, the midway point, to change locomotives and crews and to undergo routine inspection of the cars.[34]

The prewar debate over Sunday trains continued after the war, but sabbatarians had largely lost the battle. The NCRR, like most railroads, now ran at least its mail or through passenger trains on Sundays as a matter of course. The only exception in this period was a brief time from November 1868 to January 1869 when the road temporarily gave up the frustrating quest for through passengers, dropped Sunday service, and slowed down its trains to save operating costs.[35] The accommodation trains commonly were suspended on Sundays during 1865 and 1866; they were not mentioned thereafter in this connection.

The NCRR acquired telegraph service along its entire line in 1861 and 1862. From Raleigh westward the telegraph belonged to the Southern Express Company, which allowed the road free use of it. Before long Southern Express conveyed its telegraph operations to the Western Union Telegraph Company. In 1871 another firm, the Southern and Atlantic Telegraph Company, built a competing line along the NCRR right of way between Raleigh and Charlotte. The railroad played no part in this action beyond providing transportation service during construction.[36]

The worst deficiencies of roadbed and equipment were cured within a year of the war. But they contributed to more than a few accidents during that time. There were at least two derailments in May 1865, when the road was barely functioning. In one of these, near Company Shops, three cars were smashed, two lives were apparently lost, and several persons were injured. The accident was attributed to a broken axle, one of the commonest mechanical failures even in good times.[37]

In another accident that month, several passengers were severely injured by a gunpowder explosion on the freight train in which they were riding. In the next two years the road paid several thousand dollars in damages arising from this incident.[38] Three other passengers involved sued for $20,000 each; when their cases finally came to trial in 1869, one was awarded $10,000, the second $2,000. Judge Albion Tourgée dismissed the third man's claim on the ground that he was a Confederate soldier illegally returning to his post and therefore not entitled to damages. The NCRR attorney in these cases was Samuel F. Phillips, later solicitor general of the United States. He argued unsuccessfully that the Alamance County jury was improperly drawn, as it contained no blacks.[39]

Six other derailments followed by the end of 1865, four of them in December. They were variously ascribed to rotten crossties; broken axles, wheel, and rail; and (in one case) deliberate tampering with a rail. They caused two more fatalities besides considerable damage to equipment. A broken axle near Harrisburg shortly before Christmas took the lives of a baggage master and a young Southern Express agent.[40]

The Neuse River trestle, hastily built by Sherman's troops, was once damaged and twice washed away by floods during the winter of 1865–66. It was repaired each time, then replaced within the year by a Howe truss bridge. Meanwhile, as repairs were underway, trains ran to the place from Raleigh and Goldsboro, then waited to return until passengers and the mail were ferried across the river on flatboats. This crossing often occurred at night and was neither pleasant nor safe, as one of the newspapers observed. A railroad employee fell into the river and drowned in February while helping take the boat across the stream.[41]

Accidents were less frequent after 1865, but the few that did occur were apt to be lethal. In September 1866 a freight train and gravel train collided between Harrisburg and Concord, killing three of the gravel-train hands. President Webb, characterizing it as the worst accident in the road's history, blamed the gravel train engineer for failing to give way to the higher priority freight.[42] William B. Lewis, the engineer, who lost a leg in the accident, was reduced to two-thirds pay for six months. That he was not dismissed immediately raises the suspicion of mitigating circumstances. Lewis sued the road for damages, arguing that the freight train was not scheduled. The freight conductor and engineer testified that they were running six hours late, that their engine was so damaged that they could hardly control it, and that they had not wired this information to the station ahead where Lewis was based. The Davidson County court ruled in Lewis's favor and awarded him $2,000. A superior court jury later raised the award to $5,000. After the railroad appealed once more, to the state supreme court, the suit was settled out of court, Lewis accepting the original award of $2,000.[43]

Special trains were sources of danger. In October 1868, prior to the November elections, a special train that had just distributed details of soldiers to polling places in the Charlotte area collided head-on with a passenger train carrying Maginley and Carrol's Circus. A train hand lost a leg, and of course the engines and some of the cars were considerably damaged.[44]

The accident rate rose again in 1869 and afterward, for seemingly unrelated reasons. A brakeman lost his life after falling between two cars on a moving train near Goldsboro. Another was run over by the switching engine he was working on at Charlotte. Passengers continued to risk their lives by jumping onto or off of moving trains. In 1870 two men died this way in separate incidents.[45] A broken axle in 1869 near Jamestown caused the derailment of the passenger car attached to a through freight train. No one was killed, but Superintendent Albert Johnson himself was burned and bruised in the accident. He took charge of repairs, however, and in a few hours had a temporary track laid around the site to permit the passage of other trains.[46] Other derailments were caused by a broken rail and by a stick of wood falling from a tender. A boiler exploded on a gravel-train locomotive in January 1871 near Greensboro, critically injuring the engineer. Two months later a sleeping car turned over, landing on its roof as the passenger train was preparing to stop at the Salisbury depot. Although the car was full of passengers, miraculously none were seriously hurt.[47] There seem to have been fewer cases than before the war of trains running down persons as they walked or slept on the tracks. The only reported instance was that of an elderly bridge watchman near Hillsboro, asleep on the track as the mail train passed his post.[48]

The faulty equipment in use immediately after the war caused considerable freight damage. Sacks of grain and bales of hay and cotton were often carried on flatcars for lack of better conveyance, sometimes close enough to the locomotive to catch fire from its sparks. A car carrying twenty bales of hay was totally consumed in this fashion in May 1865. Sacks of grain and other cargoes were similarly consumed. Much of this damage could have been avoided if the cars had been placed farther back in the trains. Hence the road was open to charges of negligence.[49]

By far the most valuable commodity subject to fire damage was cotton. The NCRR had carried very little cotton before the war, and its locomotives were not yet equipped with the special spark arresters used on cotton-carrying roads farther south. Even closed boxcars were no proof against fire damage. In September 1865 two locked cars, one of them filled with cotton yarn, were consumed by fires that had smoldered undetected until too late to put them out. Both were attributed to locomotive sparks filtering through cracks in the cars.[50] Less than two weeks later more than forty bales were consumed in another spark-induced fire. In this case the burning car was deliberately derailed and precipitated down an embankment in order to save additional cotton piled along the track.[51] At least two more such fires followed in 1866. The problem was so great that the road not only refused to insure cotton shipments but offered half-fare to shippers who agreed beforehand to assume the liability for fire damage.[52] But equipment and operations were soon improved, and Superintendent James Anderson could boast that not a single bale of cotton was destroyed by fire or otherwise in 1867–68. The entire freight damage that year amounted to less than $1,800. This seems to have remained the case afterward.[53]

Dilapidated and insecure cars were an open invitation to robbery, especially given the social and economic dislocation, even destitution, that prevailed among people of both races for six months or so after the war.[54] In the summer of 1865 military guards were posted on trains carrying government shipments in order to protect against looting, but the guards themselves pilfered oats and commissary stores and traded them locally for liquor.[55] Recently disbanded Union soldiers were accused in October of organizing a robber gang around Raleigh and of waylaying passengers on trains and around stations and presumably stealing cotton as well.[56]

These conditions abated by the end of the year, but a certain amount of vandalism and violence continued. President Smith offered a reward in 1869 for the apprehension of persons throwing rocks into the passenger cars in Charlotte. Someone removed two rails from the track at Graham that year, derailing part of a train that was just leaving the depot.[57] No less than three NCRR conductors were either shot or shot at in separate incidents between 1866 and 1871. In one case it was done by a passenger, angry at being ejected from the train for lack of a ticket.[58]

The killing of livestock would remain a problem as long as the open range prevailed and animals were permitted to roam at large. NCRR policy remained basically the same as before the war. It allowed owners a month to make a claim.[59] In case of a claim, the animal was appraised, and the road automatically paid half of its value. Owners dissatisfied with this amount or procedure could and frequently did go to court. The road settled some, perhaps most, of these cases at higher figures before trial in order to save legal expenses and the time of employees called as witnesses. By this means and in court judgments, owners often received the full value of their animals, if not more. No doubt some of them succeeded in shaking down the road for larger sums than they were entitled to; a few may even have enticed worthless animals onto the tracks in order to collect damages. But the claims of justice were not easy to determine objectively, given the legal right of trains and animals to be in the same places at the same times.[60]

The road paid an average of $1,900 per year on this account, about double the prewar average. President Webb provided the specifications in 1867: $2,891.45 laid out for the deaths of 131 cows, 112 hogs, 4 yearlings, 19 sheep, and 9 pigs.[61] The total that year was higher than usual, and the board of directors tried briefly to make the locomotive engineers personally responsible for the value of stock killed by their trains. But this policy was unfair and evoked resistance. Engineers were personally at risk along with their trains every time they struck a large animal. They could nearly always be presumed to have done their best to avoid such accidents. After a month the board rescinded its order but continued to hold engineers responsible whenever personal negligence could be found.[62]

Both President Turner and the finance committee in 1868 waxed indignant at the financial imposition placed on the railroads by negligent stock owners. "In other countries when men or cattle trespass by walking on rail road tracks they are indicted for the trespass," said Turner. "In this country instead of indicting those who allow their cattle to run on rail road tracks, to the great danger of human life, we reward them by paying for the cow killed, although the cow may have been the means of killing a dozen men." Their solution was to change the law to make railroads liable only in case of gross negligence and to make the claimants prove that negligence. A less favored alternative, common in the other countries referred to, was to have the railroads fence in their own rights of way. The finance committee of 1870, after another expensive livestock year, seems to have entertained this idea along with securing more favorable laws.[63] But nothing was done in either respect.

Under the complicated formula by which the Post Office Department paid railroads to carry the mail, the NCRR's annual proceeds climbed from less than $8,000 in 1865–66 to nearly $19,000 in 1870–71. During much of that period it received $16,725, or $75 per mile. This was down from the $100 per mile it received before the war, but the higher rate was restored in the summer of 1871. In none of these years did mail receipts reach 3 percent of the road's total receipts.[64] (See table 11.)

Full mail service did not resume in North Carolina until August 1865, and it was irregular for some months after that. Even in the relatively normal times that followed, trains occasionally missed their connections or the mails were misdirected, causing delays. Newspaper editors, dependent on their exchanges with other papers, were still the most aggrieved and articulate reporters of these events.[65] One gets the impression, however, that service was much more reliable after 1865 than in years past.

Except in the first postwar year, express revenues were even less than those from the mails. (This had been true before but not during the war.) The Southern Express Company, born of Adams Express in the secession crisis, retained its hold on the South for many years to come. Its organizer, Henry B. Plant, was still president and majority stockholder at his death in 1899.[66] Although Adams and the National Express Company seem to have competed with it or even supplanted it on the NCRR for short times after the war, Southern Express remained a steady client.[67] Until 1869 it paid the road from 50 cents to $1.75 per hundred pounds, depending on distance. These rates, applying to the most costly freight items, were conventionally higher than the road's charges for regular freight, which traveled with less expedition or security. Beginning in 1869, Southern Express rented an entire car on the daily passenger train, at $1,000 to $1,300 per month.[68]

16

Passenger Service

TRAIN SERVICE immediately after the surrender was primitive, uncertain, and even dangerous. Captain Morris C. Runyan of the Ninth New Jersey Regiment was ordered to take a detail of men from Greensboro to Charlotte on 5 May—about three weeks after Stoneman's raids—in order to collect ordnance stores and equipment along the way. Their special train, consisting of a locomotive and some boxcars, seems not to have been delayed by the burned bridges near Greensboro and Jamestown; the temporary trestles were already in place. But on several occasions the locomotive came to a stop for lack of wood, which the men remedied by appropriating fence rails nearby. The fifty miles to Salisbury required five hours. Just beyond Salisbury they found the road closed on account of Stoneman's damage and telegraphed to Charlotte for another train to come get them. That train broke down soon after setting out, however, and Runyan's command ended up marching the rest of the way to Charlotte. After a week there (in which they unexpectedly captured the Confederate archives left by Jefferson Davis in his recent flight) they were able to return to Greensboro by train.[1]

At about the same time, Sarah F. Smiley, a northern visitor, was traveling with a companion from Raleigh to Greensboro. At Raleigh they mistakenly boarded an eastbound train. "Half the seats [in the passenger coach] had no backs—many no bottoms and the floor could hardly have been swept for years. The accumulation of hardened filth was about an inch in depth." When they found they were in the wrong train, they were shown to the right one, which seems to have had no passenger coaches at all. They boarded a boxcar filled with barrels but soon left it when some "drunken and profane" Irishmen climbed in after them. After "reconnoitering the length of the train," Smiley reported, "I found a retreat. A [flatcar] of hardtack, had a space in front nearly three feet wide." Seated here on her trunk and a box of hardtack and holding the brake wheel for support, they set off on the eighty-mile trip to Greensboro, which they reached in thirteen hours.[2] Under these conditions, and often a desperate need to return to their homes, some passengers, both military and civilian, refused to pay fares.[3]

In June the road was still using coaches with backless wooden seats that had been fitted out for the use of troops during the war. Other comforts and conveniences were lacking in proportion. But the travelers who noted these shortcomings reported that improvements were rapidly taking place.[4] By September, when northern correspondent Sidney Andrews came along, he reported the cars in relatively good shape, many of them having just been thoroughly repaired and repainted.[5] By June 1866 Superintendent Wilkes was boasting that every facility was given to make travelers comfortable and that the cars were kept clean and well supplied with water and lights. A year later President Webb pronounced the cars to be comfortable, some of them elegant; the process of refurbishing was still underway. And the trains ran so regularly, he claimed, that connections were seldom missed and people set their timepieces by the locomotive whistle.[6]

There was hyperbole in this, of course. A traveler in June 1867 reported "a good and almost exhilarating speed" from Raleigh to Greensboro (at twenty-three miles per hour), but this was offset by smoke, dust, cinders, and a shortage of ice water. When buckets of fresh water were brought aboard at station stops, passengers eagerly partook of it before it could be poured into the contrivance that passed for a cooler and mixed with the old water. This man noted that the road possessed better equipment than he was enjoying. Passing through Durham he observed a "very elegant" train stopped there; it had brought President Andrew Johnson from Raleigh to attend the commencement ceremonies at Chapel Hill and was waiting to take him back again. The traveler later took the Piedmont Railroad from Greensboro to Danville. That road, using Richmond and Danville equipment, provided a slower ride but more comfortable cars than the NCRR, he concluded.[7]

In general, the growing postwar competition between American railroads brought lower rates less than it brought faster schedules and more comfortable accommodations. The latter included sleeping cars and, in a few cases, dining cars. "Thus it is," observed an English visitor in 1869, "that railway travelling in America is assuming the form of luxury tempered by accidents." And faster advertised schedules did not always mean greater punctuality or surer connections, he added.[8] This was particularly true in the South, where the railroads, like the region itself, were poorer than the national average and lagged behind correspondingly.

The NCRR seems to have provided service and accommodations at least equal to the regional norms. Praise outweighed complaint after 1867, except for the service between Raleigh and Goldsboro, which was far inferior to that west of the capital.[9] Most of the through passengers entered or left the road at Raleigh or Greensboro. It did not pay to send every train to Goldsboro, and connections there were apt to be bad; in September 1870 a passenger complained of having to wait fifty-two hours for an NCRR train. Another critic facetiously reported that a stage line was being planned to ensure the public a "speedy and safe trip" from Raleigh to Goldsboro.[10]

Racial segregation remained the rule on southern railways after the war, but there were more exceptions than previously. Before the war, slaves or servants attending their masters were often permitted to ride in the first-class cars in order to perform their duties. Otherwise blacks were relegated to the second-class cars, which often did double duty as smoking cars for white men. These rules continued to prevail after the war whenever railroads were left to themselves or Conservatives were in political control. The "nigger cars" were invariably inferior, sometimes only converted boxcars.[11] Some military commanders before 1868, and some Republican policymakers afterward, enacted a policy of nondiscrimination and enforced it with varying degrees of zeal. This left a pattern of uncertainty or unpredictability, particularly for blacks traveling long distances on different railroads or through different political jurisdictions. The uncertainty could be as burdensome as the discrimination itself to blacks who wanted to avoid embarrassing or dangerous confrontations along the way.

Traditional mores prevailed everywhere in the Carolinas until the military commandant of the two states, General Daniel Sickles, issued general orders in May 1867 forbidding racial discrimination on public carriers. His order had the immediate effect, it seems, of permitting five Raleigh blacks to ride to Durham in the presidential car with Andrew Johnson a few days later. They thus enjoyed the "most elegant" car on the road, pulled by its newest engine at a speed of over thirty miles per hour.[12] The new dispensation did not last long. There is almost no evidence that blacks rode in first-class cars on the NCRR afterward, and evidence appears in 1870 that the custom was otherwise.

A few blacks took the risks and expense of suing for equality in the courts. Sometimes they won. Jessie Hill, a black woman, recovered damages in 1871 from the Chatham Railroad, running south from Raleigh, after a conductor made her move from the first-class to the second-class car.[13] More circumspect, perhaps because he had a job to protect, was J. W. Hoover, a black man associated with the office of the superintendent of public instruction in Raleigh. He wrote President William A. Smith of the NCRR in 1870 to say that, in traveling on public business, he had usually ridden in the second-class coach because of public prejudice against blacks and his desire to avoid controversy. He did this despite having been made sick by the tobacco smoke there, to which all black travelers were subjected. Recently, however, while escorting a lady from Washington, D.C., with a through first-class ticket to Charlotte, he accompanied her into the first-class car, only to be refused admittance by the NCRR conductor. What, he wanted to know, was his status? Smith's answer is not recorded, but two months later an NCRR employee in Charlotte implied that the road's rules had for some time permitted blacks in first-class cars and that he had followed that policy.[14] In July 1871 the road advertised the sale of first-, second-, and third-class tickets. Third-class tickets were to be sold only to colored persons, ministers of the gospel, and children between three and twelve years of age.[15] Such tickets obviously did not dictate where these quite separate categories of people could ride.

Very likely the Republican management of the NCRR, elevated to power in 1868 by the suffrage of the black population but economically dependent on a predominantly white clientele, found this question embarrassing. In the absence of fuller or more compelling evidence, the truth seems to be that blacks were expected to ride in the second-class coach and usually did so and that this expectation was often but not always enforced in 1867 and later. Those who wanted to be safe went second class.

One special category of passengers had plenty of wartime precedent. In June 1870, Governor William W. Holden was forced to employ a form of martial law in order to suppress Ku Klux Klan terrorism that had engulfed Alamance and Caswell counties. Under Holden's direction Colonel George W. Kirk recruited about 600 militiamen in the western mountains and adjacent Tennessee and brought them to the two affected counties in July. They made some 100 arrests before disbanding and returning home in September.[16] The great majority of these troops came via the Western North Carolina Railroad to Salisbury and thence on the NCRR to Company Shops. They returned the same way. For the most part they appear to have traveled in small units and did not require special trains. During the summer small detachments occasionally moved back and forth along the railroad, sometimes conveying prisoners. The NCRR seems to have charged 5 cents per mile for its services, which represented very little if any discount from the prevailing first-class rate. The total bill paid by the state came to a little over $5,000.[17]

Inevitably and unavoidably, through trains traveled overnight during much of their passage across the state. The same might be true of the accommodation trains, carrying local passengers as well as freight; they were slower, both on the road and in their necessarily longer station stops to load and unload freight. Local passengers had become inured to these inconveniences; complaints about them were much less frequent than in the road's early days. Overnight travelers on the NCRR were better served than before the war. Sleeping cars of various designs had come into use on a few northern roads before 1850. Their general adoption was delayed until after the war, particularly in the South. When most roads and most trips were short, these expensive cars were unnecessary and did not pay their way. The NCRR could have used them from the outset in cooperation with its connecting roads, but this required close cooperative scheduling. It also put a premium on long-distance through passage of the cars, which seemed impossible at Charlotte (or Greensboro, if headed to or from Danville) because of the gauge differences.

Some roads attempted to run their own sleeping cars, but most relied on independent companies (rather like the express companies) in return for a share of the proceeds. There were many small sleeping-car companies at first, but consolidation set in early. The first major operator was Theodore T. Woodruff. At the end of the war his firm was the largest in the country, and it moved into the South, forming the Southern Transportation Company. George Pullman developed a rival business in the 1860s, first dominating the Midwest. He competed with the Woodruff company in the South after 1867 then leased it in 1870. Going on quickly to acquire other independent companies, his Pullman Southern Car Company became the dominant force in the South in 1871. He promised greatly improved service between New York and New Orleans, using changeable-gauge trucks to accommodate the gauge differences at places like Charlotte and Greensboro.[18]

The simplest sleeping-car designs involved little more than reclining seats. More ambitious ones entailed the conversion of seats into bunks, with upper berths folding down from the ceiling. These cars were almost invariably larger, heavier, and more expensive than conventional coaches and held fewer people at night. Pullman cars of 1870 were sixty feet long, ten feet more than the typical daycoach, and held thirty-two passengers instead of fifty. The tendency was toward luxurious accommodations with lush upholstery, carpeting, and woodwork. Each car commonly had its own conductor, who collected the special fee for its use. The charge for a berth rose from the original 25 cents to $2 under Pullman.[19]

The Wilmington and Weldon was the first North Carolina road to acquire sleeping cars, in January 1866.[20] The NCRR followed suit in June. Its first two cars seem to have been comparatively simple reclining-seat cars operated by a small firm, Van Rensselaer and Van Nortwick of Bordentown, New Jersey. They were fifty feet long and seated forty-four persons. Each carried an attendant who was empowered to charge passengers a dollar beyond the normal rail fare. The road launched this service on a three-month trial basis; it is not clear what happened at the end of that period.[21] In March 1869 the road contracted with Woodruff's Southern Transportation Company for two reclining-seat cars, that firm charging only 50 cents per seat or whatever the competition might charge.[22] These cars gave way at the beginning of 1870 to more elaborate sleepers with upper and lower berths. They ran between Charlotte and Weldon, using the Raleigh and Gaston and the NCRR.[23] One of their first users pronounced them the finest cars he had ever seen. "To retire at Greensboro and wake up in Weldon, without having been shaken [a] half dozen times by conductors, or had your head knocked by some old lady's basket or your corns smashed by some awkward fellow—or any of the thousand annoyances that everyone experiences who tries to sleep on the ordinary passenger cars—oh, this was delightful." Nonetheless, he rather begrudged the extra charge of $2.[24]

George Pullman quickly tried to place his own cars on the competing line from Richmond to Danville and Greensboro and thence south to Augusta, using the new changeable-gauge trucks. President Smith of the NCRR initially resisted this overture, partly because he wasn't offered enough money but also because it entailed a closer relationship than he cared to develop at that point with the predatory Richmond and Danville Railroad.[25] He eventually fell into line, however, at an agreeable price, and the Pullman cars were placed in service. But in March 1871 Smith decided to discontinue them after an accident near Salisbury convinced him that they were unsafe. He substituted reclining-chair cars that an exuberant editor characterized as "magnificent palaces on wheels," comfortable "as art and genius could make them." Another writer preferred them to the preceding "box-up Sleeping Car"—more airy and comfortable, and more easily gotten out of in case of accident.[26]

Overnight accommodations along the road had not changed much since before the war. Travelers with overnight layovers or those unwilling to spend the night on the train had a very limited choice of hotels to choose from. Memoirist Frances Butler Leigh tells of having to spend a night in Greensboro in March 1866 at a "miserable tumble-down old frame house" that passed for a hotel some two miles from the depot. Her room, she said, was more fit for a stable than a human habitation.[27] Yet when John Motley Morehead died later that year, he left among his properties the American Hotel, fifty yards from the Greensboro station, including (in the not unbiased words of his heirs seeking to rent out the place) "commodious buildings, extensive grounds, and all necessary arrangements to a first class Hotel."[28]

The Wilmington and Weldon Railroad boasted "elegant and commodious eating cars" as early as 1867, but there is no record in this period of such accommodations on the NCRR, elegant or otherwise. Passengers apparently could buy food from vendors on the train. But for meals they still depended upon train stops along the way. Morehead's American Hotel was advertised as a potential eating house for passengers on both the North Carolina and Piedmont railroads.[29]

These establishments were apt to enjoy monopoly status; there wasn't enough business to keep more than one going in most locations. Their success or failure sometimes depended less on their own merits than on the caprice of train schedules, which connecting roads juggled frequently in order to maximize the through passenger traffic. Economic, personal, or political favor may have played a part as well in determining when and where stops were made. In September 1867 the NCRR and the Raleigh and Gaston advertised for rent an establishment at their joint depot variously called the "Hotel Department" and the "Rail Road eating House." They stipulated that the successful bidder "be required to keep a first-class Table." This person turned out to be the proprietor of Raleigh's Yarborough Hotel. But within three weeks a change in railroad schedules forced him to surrender the place. The winner by this change was the NCRR's own hotel at Company Shops, which the passenger train now passed at suppertime.[30] By 1871 the eastbound passenger trains were stopping at Thomasville for twenty or thirty minutes every evening to let travelers take supper at an eating house owned by John W. Thomas, the local patriarch. The road chose this over competing establishments at Salisbury, High Point, and Greensboro.[31]

Railroad traffic quickly resumed its prewar patterns in 1865, with the notable addition of the route to Danville and Richmond. Some through passengers now went that way rather than through Raleigh and Petersburg or by the coastal route through Wilmington. Each route had disadvantages that its member roads sought to rectify as quickly as possible. Some were war-induced: major bridges were destroyed over the James at Richmond, over the Roanoke at Weldon, over the Catawba below Charlotte, and there was a gap of fifty-one miles of track torn up around Columbia, South Carolina. (The NCRR had been very fortunate in the small scale of its war damage.) In some cases these breaks took many months to repair; the Roanoke and Catawba River bridges were not rebuilt and in use until April and May 1866. Meanwhile passengers spanned them by ferry.[32] But as war damage was repaired and facilities were restored, railroads improved their schedules and service. This, coupled with an improving economy and the return of cooperative alliances between connecting roads, brought an increase in through traffic. By northern standards, however, the volume of traffic was very slight in these years, and the competitors were, relatively speaking, scrambling for crumbs. The NCRR actually decreased its passenger train service after 1866, the annual mileage totaling about 155,000 compared with some 275,000 before and during the war. But as the volume of passengers about equaled that before the war, fewer trains seem to have carried the same numbers. (See tables 12 and 13.)

The route through Danville was at first almost identical in length with that through Wilmington, measuring about 418 miles from their common junctions at Kingsville, South Carolina, and Richmond.[33] But the coastal route involved (as it always had) ferrying across the Cape Fear at Wilmington. And a more direct line from Columbia to Augusta, completed in 1868, gave the interior route a twenty-five mile advantage into Georgia and beyond. This was so important to the NCRR that (despite its own financial problems) it helped to subsidize the new road by buying $100,000 of its bonds.[34] The Raleigh-Petersburg route was originally twenty-eight miles longer than the route through Wilmington; that difference virtually disappeared with the new link in South Carolina. The Raleigh route remained about twenty-eight miles longer than that through Danville, but it entailed only one gauge change instead of two.

Before the war, passengers through Richmond and Petersburg had been required to find their own way between the separate railroad stations in those towns. Military necessity bridged these gaps in the summer of 1861, but they returned after the war, partly a result of war damage. The interruptions in trackage were not wholly eliminated until August 1867.[35] For a time in 1865, through passengers in Raleigh too had to walk or hire rides from the Raleigh and Gaston's old depot to that of the NCRR—a necessity that had not previously existed since the NCRR's construction.[36]

All of the eastern Virginia and North Carolina roads (the Wilmington and Weldon, the Raleigh and Gaston, the Petersburg, the Richmond and Petersburg, and the Seaboard and Roanoke) shared a common gauge with the NCRR. The obvious next step toward faster and better through service was to provide continuous running of cars from one road to another without the necessity of changing trains at each junction. Running one's cars on other roads brought problems of bookkeeping and car recovery, and passengers could transport themselves across a platform more easily than freight could. Nevertheless the NCRR and the R&G initiated a through sleeping car from Charlotte to Weldon in April 1866. Soon it proceeded to Portsmouth as well on the Seaboard and Roanoke.[37]

The western route involved the gauge change from the NCRR's four feet, eight and one-half inches to the Richmond and Danville's five feet, with the necessity of changing trains. The break initially occurred at Danville, owing to North Carolina's insistence that the Piedmont have the same gauge as the NCRR. Although a change in the Piedmont gauge was authorized as a war measure early in 1865, it was not done. Local traffic along the fifty-mile line was negligible, and North Carolinians lost interest in the matter. Passenger and freight transfers in Greensboro might actually generate additional business there. So the state was persuaded in February 1866 to renew the authorization on a permanent basis. The work was done immediately. Henceforth the parent R&D was able to use its own equipment on the Piedmont, and it operated the road as an integral part of its own line. Trains now ran from Richmond to Greensboro.[38]

As the South Carolina and Georgia roads also operated on a five-foot gauge, the NCRR looked more and more like a bottleneck from their perspective. For the next five years the R&D sought unsuccessfully to get the NCRR to change its gauge, or at least to add a third rail from Greensboro southward, enabling trains to run on into Georgia and beyond. When the NCRR rejected these efforts, the R&D as well as the Pullman Company experimented with adjustable trucks allowing cars to cross the ninety-three miles of narrower gauge between Greensboro and Charlotte.[39]

Another competitor for through traffic was the Seaboard and Roanoke, running from Weldon to Portsmouth, Virginia, adjacent to Norfolk. It operated in conjunction with the Baltimore Steam Packet Company, or Old Bay Line. Passenger traffic on Chesapeake Bay revived after the war, but it failed to equal the increase in freight traffic.[40] Hence the S&R regarded itself as primarily a freight carrier and even rented the use of its vital bridge over the Roanoke River at Weldon to the rival Petersburg Railroad, which was only a slight threat in freight competition.[41]

Virtually no passengers to or from the North made connections at Goldsboro with either the Wilmington and Weldon or the Atlantic and North Carolina. These routes were so roundabout for the main north-south traffic as to be out of contention.

All other things equal, the NCRR preferred the route through Raleigh to that through Danville because it entailed longer travel on its own road. As early as August 1865 the NCRR, the Raleigh and Gaston, and the Petersburg Railroad jointly advertised themselves as "The Best, Most Expeditious and most Comfortable Route from Charlotte to the Northern Cities." (At Petersburg northbound passengers could choose between trains to Richmond and beyond or to nearby City Point where they changed to James River steamers headed for the North.) For over a year, therefore, the NCRR resisted efforts by the Richmond and Danville to get it to change its schedule to provide closer connections between their trains at Greensboro.[42]

Other things seldom were equal, however. In May 1866 the NCRR shifted policy somewhat as part of a new regional alliance. A convention of southern railroad presidents met in Richmond and adopted a system of through tickets and closer connections on all the major routes east of the mountains connecting New York with New Orleans.[43] This agreement emphasized both the coastal route through Wilmington and the comparable Richmond-Danville-Charlotte route over the slightly longer one through Petersburg and Raleigh. The NCRR therefore made the closer connections at Greensboro long sought by the R&D, and the two roads proceeded to enlarge their joint facilities there.[44] The new agreement also brought a sharp decrease in running time, which applied along the entire length of the road; the time between Charlotte and Goldsboro was cut from sixteen and a half hours to twelve.[45]

While these changes diverted many through passengers from the Raleigh and Gaston to the Richmond and Danville, they brought disappointing receipts as well as higher running and maintenance costs for the NCRR. Through passengers now rode some eighty miles less on the NCRR and at lower rates.[46] At the same time the road ran double passenger trains and sleeping cars in conjunction with the Raleigh and Gaston. Taken as a whole, and given the impoverished economy and the limited market, these services cost more than they were worth.[47] When the road ran a second successive annual deficit in 1866–67, the new president, Josiah Turner, concluded that the race for through passengers was a waste of money. The second passenger train must already have been discontinued, given the decline in passenger train mileage after 1866. Turner slowed down the mail train and added some through freight cars to it. The resulting increase in freight revenues more than compensated for the loss of passengers, he claimed.[48] But the new schedule worsened train connections in Raleigh. The local press protested so loudly that the connections were improved without materially increasing train speeds.[49]

NCRR policy continued to vacillate. The advantage of slow trains at the expense of through traffic was not so clear as Turner made it appear. Indeed he himself soon returned without explanation or fanfare to a policy of a single fast train per day and close connections with the R&D at Greensboro.[50] He even shortened by seven minutes the previous year's record schedule, involving train speeds of twenty-five miles per hour with an average of twenty including stops.[51] One solution was to arrange schedules so that the running time from Richmond to Charlotte was the same by either route. But competitive pressures made this hard to maintain. As soon as the NCRR made close connections with either the R&D or the R&G, the other and its remoter connections were sure to complain.

Turner's successor, William A. Smith, claimed to have returned to the Raleigh and Petersburg alliance in 1868. To a degree he did.[52] The NCRR ran a newspaper ad for "The Great Through Route" via Raleigh and Weldon in August, soon after his election. And he later made it a policy to sell through tickets only via Raleigh, thus securing passengers for a longer distance on the NCRR.[53] On the other hand, Smith also reestablished close connections with the Richmond and Danville early in 1869, to the discomfiture of the Raleigh interest.[54]

With some justification, presidents of connecting railroads in every direction accused Smith of fickleness and reneging on his agreements. Unlike the NCRR, many of their roads lacked the luxury or the burden of strategic options. Their positions were relatively fixed and their alliances obvious and unavoidable. Owing to the NCRR's multiple connections Smith had many suitors. Hence his frequent schedule changes and his shifting about for comparative advantage (like that of Turner before him) that caused such general frustration. No matter what he did, some other road could blame him (correctly) for its own lagging revenues.[55]

In December 1869 the board of directors authorized Smith to overhaul the rate and schedule agreements with all connecting railroads, especially those with the R&D. One of their stipulations—a sign of the NCRR's bargaining position—was that it receive the same amount for through freight and passengers whether they entered or left the road at Greensboro or Raleigh.[56] Smith quickly agreed with the Raleigh and Gaston to speed up their common schedule so as to equalize running time with the Danville route. Train speeds were raised to thirty miles per hour, and new sleeping cars were acquired to run through between Charlotte and Weldon—all designed to recapture some of the passengers who had been diverted to the R&D.[57]

Meanwhile the R&D was making arrangements to run its cars all the way through from Richmond to Atlanta, using a new "Air-Line" railroad from Charlotte to Atlanta, then under construction. The great fly in this ointment was the NCRR with its ninety-three miles of narrower gauge road between Greensboro and Charlotte.[58] R&D President Algernon S. Buford

intensely desired an agreement with Smith. Nevertheless he initially rejected the NCRR's inflated rate terms. But when the Pullman Company
requested permission early in 1870 to run adjustable-truck sleeping cars
from Richmond to Atlanta, passing through Danville, Greensboro, and
Charlotte, Buford was driven to visit Smith in person. They seem to have
reached an informal understanding in May, largely on Smith's terms.[59]

Soon the NCRR abandoned its close train connections at Raleigh in favor
of new ones in Greensboro. In return for this the R&D paid a bonus for
each through passenger almost equal to what the NCRR would have received if the passengers had traveled via Raleigh. This arrangement had
the desired effect of diverting most of Raleigh's through traffic to the
R&D.[60] That road went ahead with efforts to develop adjustable-truck cars
—largely unsuccessful—while the NCRR eventually discontinued altogether
its through passenger train east of Greensboro, citing lack of patronage.[61]

From the Richmond and Danville's perspective this new arrangement was
a mixed blessing. It was paying a high price for an expensive run over those
ninety-three miles of narrower gauge road. So Buford continued trying to
negotiate an end to that obstacle. In July 1870 the NCRR stockholders
formally authorized serious negotiations with the R&D regarding the use of
the road between Greensboro and Charlotte. They had in mind something
as momentous as a gauge change, perhaps even the lease of that section of
the road. The talks did not go well, however, and Buford's patience grew
thin. The creation of a common gauge from Virginia southward, he declared late in 1870, had become "a standing and clamorous want . . . that
must ultimately be responded to in the liberal and progressive spirit of the
age."[62] That goal would be achieved, but not without testing Buford's patience still further.

The postwar struggle for through passengers was based for several years
on hope more than reality. The NCRR's through traffic was very small in
1865–66, although receipts were probably higher than the negligible $1,700
that was reported. (See table 14.) They mounted to little over $34,000 in
each of the next two years, compared with an average of $46,000 in 1858–
61. Perhaps Josiah Turner's partial abandonment of the race for through
passengers in 1867–68 accounts for the lack of any rise that year. But the
numbers grew rapidly thereafter, reaching $85,000 in 1870–71. As before
the war, the larger share of through tickets on the NCRR was sold by other
railroads, and most of these were south- or westbound, implying northern
origins. Most of the through tickets sold on the NCRR itself were northbound.

As before the war, local passenger receipts dwarfed those from through
passengers. And they generally exceeded those before the war—an average
of $114,000 in 1856–61 and $160,000 in 1865–71, including the fares collected by conductors. Paradoxically, local passenger (and freight) revenues
were unusually high for some months after the war, owing to military traffic

and the continuation of abnormally high wartime rates.[63] Local passenger receipts then declined for about three years; rising thereafter, they exceeded $180,000 in 1870–71. There was no particular monthly or seasonal pattern, and they were fairly evenly divided between eastbound and westbound. During the five years, 1865–70, for which such data are available, Charlotte was the leading generator of passenger revenues in the first two years, Raleigh in the last three. Together with Salisbury, Greensboro, and Goldsboro they were responsible for an average of 45 percent of the identifiable passenger revenues.

Through passenger rates were unstable and highly competitive, the result of agreements between connecting roads. Meetings were periodically held and agreements were reached setting through rates and allocating the proceeds among the roads. (Sometimes these agreements extended to both passenger and freight service.) The general rule—or the point of departure—was to allocate to each road a fixed proportion of the proceeds from the sale of each through ticket corresponding to its share of the total mileage involved. From that point a road might use any superior bargaining power it possessed to increase its share. All this had been true before the war, but competitive pressures mounted after 1865 as never before. Sometimes through rates fell so low as scarcely to cover costs. In time, unbridled competition led to an almost irresistible demand to rationalize the system by consolidating the various units under a single management. In the meantime, roads commonly took what they could from the fickle through traffic, whether passenger or freight, while subsisting primarily on their local customers. These usually had little choice as to carrier and had to pay higher, noncompetitive rates.[64]

The NCRR's share of a $63 through ticket from New York to New Orleans via Danville in 1866 was $3.08, or about 3.3 cents per mile, based on its ninety-three miles between Greensboro and Charlotte.[65] By late 1867 its proportion fell to 2.1 cents, less than it was worth to cultivate the traffic.[66] Hence Josiah Turner's decision not to do so—for the time being.

Local rates by contrast were usually based on an estimate of the costs of transportation, with an added margin for profit. Although they were less competitive than through rates, they were anything but constant. The last prewar rate had been 3.5 cents per mile; it was considerably higher after the war. In October 1865 the first-class rate was increased from 5 cents per mile to 6 cents. For the next six years it fluctuated from 4 cents to 8 cents, usually remaining in the 5- to 6-cent range. Second-class and (at least sometimes) third-class tickets were available at proportionately lower rates.[67] In June 1871, for instance, the first-class rate was fixed at 5.5 cents per mile, second class at 4.5 cents, and third class at 3 cents—for colored only.[68]

There was perennial debate as to whether lower rates would increase the volume of traffic enough to compensate for the loss in revenue per passenger. Proponents of lower rates cited those of 2 cents per mile common in the Northeast, but they failed to note the higher population density, hence higher potential traffic volume there.[69]

The rate fluctuations that occurred every year or so on the NCRR were the product of sincere efforts to achieve profitable operations with as little public pain as possible. Unfortunately the experience did little to support proponents of lower rates. After the rate was lowered from 6 cents per mile to 5 cents early in 1867, the number of local passengers rose by 20 percent, but local passenger revenues fell by exactly the same amount. When the new Smith administration raised rates again in 1868–69, the number of passengers dropped 5 percent, but revenues increased by that same figure.[70] By the same token, when the R&D, upon leasing the NCRR in September 1871, lowered rates in accordance with its own previous policy, the number of local passengers burgeoned by 53 percent, but local receipts fell by nearly 15 percent.[71]

In October 1868 the NCRR experimented with a 500-mile ticket for $20, good for three months. This represented a rate of 4 cents per mile, a significant reduction from the regular 6 cents.[72] For whatever reason, it was not mentioned or repeated again.

As before the war, reduced fares were offered to a variety of persons because of personal status, organizational affiliation, or the function they were traveling to attend. The usual policy was to extend half-fare in the form of a roundtrip ticket for the full price one way. This courtesy was offered at one time or another to persons attending the commencements of the University of North Carolina, Trinity College, the Thomasville Female College, and all other schools and colleges along the line; the funeral of former Senator George E. Badger; the Raleigh speech of President Andrew Johnson; the state superior court clerks' convention; the state conventions of both political parties; the state fair at Raleigh and regional agricultural fairs at Henderson and Wilmington; a meeting of the Orange Presbytery; and a Baptist Sunday School convention in Raleigh. If the occasion were large enough, like the state fair or a Chapel Hill commencement, it might merit a special train. These special offers were a matter of frequent mention in the newspapers, as were special excursions.

Summertime railroad excursions gained popularity after the war. They too featured reduced roundtrip tickets—about 2 cents per mile—and were extended to all takers during the season. Special excursion trips were occasionally scheduled, as for a Raleigh hook and ladder company to the coast in 1869. These too might merit a special train if enough people were involved. A Greensboro Sunday School excursion to Company Shops (which was a minor tourist attraction) filled seven passenger cars attached to the regular eastbound freight. This trip was furnished by the road free of charge and featured speeches by President William A. Smith and others.[73] The favorite destinations were the coast, especially Morehead City, and the mountains, particularly the various "medicinal springs" resorts. The interroad ticket arrangements resembled those covering longer distances.

Roundtrip fares from Raleigh in the summer of 1870 ranged from $8 to New Bern and $10 to Morehead City to $16.75 for trips to Morganton or Cherryville.[74]

Many southern railroads offered special rates to attract new settlers to their regions. A convention of roads including the NCRR and its connections proposed them in July 1869.[75] The NCRR appears to have complied, although the special rates were not publicized within the state. In fact, it readily acquiesced in a request by the North Carolina commissioner of immigration to all the state's railroads in 1871 to allow bona fide settlers to pass over the road free.[76] Neither policy was very effective; most immigrants and others in search of new homes found greater opportunities in the North and West.

Indeed, railroads actively undercut the effort by offering reduced rates to current residents who wanted to leave the state. Despite the roads' long-term interest in population growth and the widespread public dismay at emigration, the pursuit of immediate revenues generally prevailed. Josiah Turner urged in vain in 1868 that the NCRR "should not be operated for corporate gains alone" and that emigrant tickets be abolished in favor of such inducements to local farmers as the transportation of fertilizer and agricultural implements at cost if not for free.[77] (The road did continue its prewar practice of carrying fertilizers at reduced rates.)

By the latter part of 1866 the NCRR was providing not only reduced emigrant rates but special monthly trains. Leaving from Greensboro, they connected at Raleigh with railroads leading eventually to Chicago and other places in the Midwest. Two emigration agents, Addison Coffin and Louis Zimmer, competed with each other in Greensboro, charging $2 or more per person to make arrangements and guide the passengers on their way. Zimmer worked for the Baltimore and Ohio Railroad, using its facilities so far as possible. Coffin, who was apparently a freelancer, said that he had made seven of these trips by January 1867. At least 300 persons departed on the November 1866 train, about 100 in December. The NCRR even provided circulars to prospective emigrants through the station agents at Hillsboro, Company Shops, Greensboro, High Point, and Lexington.[78] (These stations coincided with the areas of least population growth along the road.) The emigrant traffic continued, though at an apparently diminished rate, into the 1870s.[79] People were reportedly leaving Company Shops daily in 1870, using reduced-fare tickets procured from the local ticket agent.[80]

The antebellum problem of free passes (or dead heads) never went away. In fact they proliferated in the increasingly competitive postwar environment. Half-fare excursions and the like could be justified as generating at least marginally profitable business that would not otherwise have existed. Free passes required a different calculus. Usually it was expressed in terms of good will or public relations. Inevitably the practice was controversial. Stockholders (and taxpayers in the case of the state-owned NCRR) consid-

ered it a growing menace to company profits and the value of their investments.

When a legislative committee asked about the matter in 1867, President
Thomas Webb provided a list of the categories of people whom the board
of directors had decided were entitled to free passes: the governor, secretary of state, state treasurer, comptroller, state geologist (who later asked
for the use of a hand car as well), adjutant general, members of the board
of internal improvements, the literary board, federal tax officers, federal
military commanders and their staffs, the officers and employees of other
roads who extended the same favor, NCRR employees (in moderation),
commissioners of the NCRR sinking fund, general agents of each Christian
denomination in the state, and (finally) "persons in absolute charity." To all
of these had to be added express and telegraph company workers who
passed over the road under special contract.

Well over half of the free passes were given to employees of the road so
that they could visit their homes on weekends (meaning Saturday night and
Sunday), according to a tabulation made for a twenty-month period in
1865–67. About a third of the total were given by Master Mechanic R. D.
Wade to his shopworkers. Division masters and other supervisors were responsible for many others. The remainder were issued by the president and
superintendent at their discretion.[81]

The stockholders' finance committee of 1867 found the system unaccept-
ably lax and singled out especially the weekend fringe benefit for employees. It recommended that no one—officer, employee, or otherwise—be permitted to pass over the road for less than half-fare except when traveling on
NCRR business—or (the members were careful to add) to attend the annual stockholders' meeting.[82] When the authorities failed to heed the call,
the next year's finance committee, headed by Rufus Barringer, weighed in
more heavily. About thirty classes of people were allowed free passes, it said,
some of them numbering hundreds of persons. And as time passes,

> By habit and custom, and by hook and crook, others are gradually
> added to the list, and when a party once gets a free ride on a rail road
> the pleasure grows upon him and it is hard to get rid of him. See the
> result! Officials and ex-officials of the State and Federal governments,
> rail road men and ex-rail road men and their families (in many in-
> stances), politicians and ex-politicians, legislators, lawyers, and the lite-
> rati, divines and those who are past divining, objects of charity and
> hundreds who need no charity; not to add scores of others, many of
> whom refused to subscribe a dollar to the work, and never owned a
> share of stock, all manage to hold estates, more or less long, in the
> privileges of this Road, at the expense of its impoverished Stockholders
> and the suffering tax-ridden people of the State. It is an enormity
> which no President . . . or Board of Directors should tolerate a day.[83]

The stockholders as a whole were so moved by this appeal as to revoke all outstanding passes except those issued to the officers of reciprocating railroads and to the families of Calvin Graves and of Presidents Morehead and Fisher.[84]

But again there was little change. Incoming President William A. Smith seems if anything to have expanded the list of favored persons. Like his predecessors he was showered with requests for free passes—from clergymen, political friends, merchants who traveled and shipped a lot on the road, federal and state judges (George W. Brooks and Albion W. Tourgée), newspaper editors, a cattle judge at the state fair, and disabled veterans, including one who made his living vending food on the trains. Governor Holden requested a pass for the statewide leader of the Society of Friends, and Davidson College asked the same for members of the Salem Brass Band to come and perform at its commencement.[85] Some of these appeals were denied (among them the cattle judge); others were granted as a matter of custom or public relations. In December 1870 Smith offered a free ride to all members of the legislature going home for the holidays. He warmed Democratic hearts by furnishing Jefferson Davis with the finest car on the road as the former president traveled its length in May 1871.[86] And few stockholders objected when he ran special trains from Goldsboro and Charlotte to take them (presumably free) to the annual meeting at Greensboro that year.[87]

In November 1868 the Raleigh *Sentinel*, chief organ of the Democratic opposition, decried the "vast and sweeping system of *dead-headism* [that] prevails on the North Carolina Railroad, under its present management." Most of the beneficiaries, it charged, were Republican politicians.[88] A few weeks later, editorship of the *Sentinel* was taken over by Josiah Turner, the NCRR's immediate past president. In most respects he was an even harsher critic of the reigning Republican party than was his predecessor. But Turner, as past president, was the recipient of a lifetime free pass on the NCRR. And later being denied that pass and ejected from a train—not by William A. Smith and the Radicals, but by the management of the Richmond and Danville Railroad after the 1871 lease—Turner went to court, sued for its reinstatement, and lost.[89]

In fact, editors were an increasingly favored class of recipients, for obvious reasons. Democratic editors, so favored, were often profuse in their praise of Republican Smith and his management. One of them, James W. Albright of the *Greensboro Patriot*, openly requested a pass in his editorial columns.[90] Another quid pro quo, perhaps usually unspoken, was that editors run NCRR train schedules or advertisements without charge. When the *Sentinel* in 1871 billed the road $31.50 for such services, unsolicited by it, Smith refused to pay.[91]

17

Freight Service

ALTHOUGH Superintendent Edmund Wilkes recalled that not a single freight car carried its contents safely in July 1865, conditions began to improve by that month, and northbound shipments of cotton and tobacco were already heavy.[1] Freight receipts were abnormally large in the first postwar year, owing partly to a continuation of high wartime rates and partly to the clearing away of war-deferred backlogs. Freight trains in 1865–66 ran a total of only 84,000 miles, about half the prewar and subsequent postwar mileage. (See table 12.) In July 1865 the daily freight train consumed seventeen hours getting from Charlotte to Raleigh, an average of ten miles per hour including stops, but this run was only five minutes longer than the mail train's.[2] Federal military authorities continued to operate the road east of Raleigh until October.

By June 1866 the cars were secured with locks, and their contents were relatively safe from theft. But freight still took sixteen hours from Raleigh to Charlotte and twenty-one hours from Goldsboro. These times did not improve very much thereafter; there was even a period in 1869 when the freight train spent the night at Company Shops and took almost thirty-six hours running the length of the road. And owing to the vagaries of through freight arrangements with other roads that year, the NCRR cut back its service east of Raleigh to three days per week.[3]

Freight and passengers often took the same trains, but in large measure the services were separate. As with passengers, through freight got better service than local freight. This was especially true if the local freight was shipped in smaller than carload lots. Fast through freight cars were often attached to the mail trains or had comparably fast trains to themselves. Otherwise, carload shipments and through freight took the accommodation train; serving passengers as well, it stopped at most stations, picking up and dropping off cars as the occasion demanded and as the pulling capacity of the locomotive permitted. But small shipments, paying the highest rates, sometimes had to wait for a weekly local freight train.[4] Heavy business or special situations, like the piling up of cotton in Charlotte, could lead to additional trains.

Freight receipts in 1865–66 amounted to $462,000, more than twice the level in any prewar year. It was a temporary phenomenon, resulting from a backlog of war-deferred shipments, end-of-the-war military traffic, high rates, and perhaps the temporary closure of competing roads. It gives a highly misleading picture both of the road and of the country around it. Both experienced two years of grinding depression before times began to improve. Part of the road's salvation, especially in the second year, lay in the resurrection of cotton cultivation farther south and the rerouting of cotton shipments by rail instead of by sea, as before the war. For many months, President Thomas Webb confessed in 1867, the NCRR virtually "lived upon South Carolina," carrying her cotton north and her provisions south. As for North Carolina, "the condition of our people along the whole line of the Road . . . has been a deplorable one. It really seems as if the hand of an offended God was pressing heavily upon us. Four years of desolating war were succeeded by two more of drought and famine. The husbandman has reaped no reward from his labors; the garners that formerly were burdened with grain, and the barns that were crowded with forage, have both been empty. Man and beast alike have suffered, and many who never felt want before, have realized its presence most wofully." Hence few people had much to ship, and many of the freights were imported provisions. By this time the road had cut the number of trains to two, "and I am sorry to say that neither of these are doing much."[5]

Prewar freight receipts had gradually climbed to a high of $225,000 in 1859–60. They were consistently higher after the war. Following a low of $288,000 in the depression year of 1866–67, they gradually mounted, exceeding $420,000 in 1870–71. Except in wartime, NCRR freight revenue had always exceeded that from passengers; the margin now increased, freight accounting for 53.5 percent of all receipts from 1865 to 1871 compared with only 32 percent from passengers. (See table 11.) The prevalence of freight over passenger revenues was common to most American railroads from the 1850s onward.

Much the greater portion of freight traffic was through rather than local—the opposite of passenger service. Through tonnage increased every year, nearly doubling from 1867 to 1872. By the latter year it amounted to almost 70 percent of the total. Local tonnage, by contrast, fluctuated from year to year without any clear direction. Although we have no data on local versus through receipts (as opposed to tonnage), the through freight traffic was clearly more worth fighting for than was the through passenger. (See table 17.)[6]

Westbound freight receipts continued greatly to exceed eastbound, amounting to about 59 percent in four of the five postwar years for which there are data.[7] To a considerable degree this continued to reflect the greater value of northern manufactures shipped south compared with southern farm products shipped north. It was one of the signs of the South's underdevelopment.

Seasonally, the heaviest shipping months after the war (as before it, largely) were September, October, and November when (besides the usual southbound traffic) crops were sent to market. The lightest receipts came in June, July, and August. (See table 18.)[8]

From the road's beginning, six stations (Goldsboro, Raleigh, Greensboro, High Point, Salisbury, and Charlotte) had accounted for the bulk of the road's freight receipts. In general, their share had inched upward ever since; after the war it averaged about 85 percent. (See table 16.) All except High Point were junctions with other roads. In every postwar year but one, Charlotte and Raleigh together accounted for well over half of the road's freight receipts. (In that year—1867–68—Goldsboro replaced Raleigh as the result of a controversial through freight arrangement with the Wilmington and Weldon.) During the last three years for which data are available (1867–70), Goldsboro and Raleigh at the eastern end of the road were responsible for about 40 percent of the freight receipts; Charlotte at the other end brought in 25 to 30 percent, reflecting again the greater value of southbound goods over those proceeding in the other direction. Salisbury contributed another 9 or 10 percent, mostly heading northward. (By comparison with the NCRR's hazy and fragmentary traffic data, the Richmond and Danville, taking over the NCRR in 1871, was a model of record keeping. In 1871–72 it reported nearly two-thirds of Salisbury's tonnage to be headed northward.)

In 1871–72, the R&D lease helped Greensboro move up to 10 percent of the NCRR's total freight tonnage. But in the short run the lease did less for freight than for passenger connections with the R&D. Freight connections were much more dependent on continuous running of cars from one road to another with a common gauge, a condition that existed at Raleigh and Goldsboro but not at Greensboro before 1875. The experimentation with adjustable-truck cars was not very successful in either passenger or freight service.[9]

Local freight rates, like their passenger equivalents, were usually based on the cost of transportation plus a margin for profit. Through freight (like passenger) rates were determined by competitive factors, usually in collaboration with connecting roads and steamship lines. These arrangements were apt to become unstuck as temptations arose to undercut them, openly or surreptitiously, to attract additional business. Again, unbridled competition quickly led to efforts at consolidation.[10]

NCRR freight rates immediately after the war were abnormally high, presumably to generate money for reconstruction of the road. In June 1866 they were lowered to about prewar levels.[11] The long haul/short haul differential—charging lower rates per mile for long-distance shipments than for short ones—continued to generate the greatest public anger year after year. Through rates were almost invariably less per mile than local rates, given identical shipments. As a result a given commodity could often be procured more cheaply from a great distance than from nearer home.

(A Raleigh commission house early in 1867 reportedly had to pay freight charges of $19.95 for a small shipment of potatoes from Morganton via the NCRR and Western North Carolina Railroad, whereas the same shipment from New York by a combination of steamship and railroad lines cost only $14.40.)[12] Proponents of local and regional economic development were furious at such perversity on the part of local railroads, paying people to buy goods from New York rather than North Carolina.

No railroad president was more willing than Josiah Turner to change such policies for the benefit of local producers. As soon as he assumed control of the NCRR in July 1867, he lowered freight tariffs by 20 percent; in November the rate on local products was cut still further.[13] The new rates were credited not only with opening the North Carolina market to local farmers, but even letting them ship produce north to New York. One enterprising shipper, reported Turner, sent 1,000 chickens to Baltimore. "They cackle and crow, as if they were glad to die for forty and fifty cents apiece instead of ten and twelve and a half each" as formerly. And the bottom line, as he jubilantly announced a year later, was that freight receipts increased at the same time.[14]

The Wilmington and Weldon adopted the same policy in 1867, even encouraging farmers along its road to go into truck farming for the northern market.[15] But rates on the W&W and other local roads remained higher than the NCRR's, with resulting dissatisfaction by officers of the other roads and the public who were dependent on them.[16] A Raleigh *Standard* correspondent characterized the W&W as an aristocratic railroad, run by "broken-down politicians, West Point sappers, and degenerate sons of the former chivalry."[17]

Most railroads were besieged with requests for special rates from large shippers, actual or prospective. In 1869 Turner's successor, William A. Smith, was asked by some large cotton shippers in Chester, South Carolina, to better the rate they paid on cotton shipped to New York via Charleston, which had just increased. In return for a specified lower rate they promised to ship and receive all their freight via the NCRR. Smith's answer is not on record, but the next year he concluded a contract in behalf of the NCRR and connecting lines with these shippers, embodying about the same rates as they had requested.[18] Substantial local shippers of logs and bricks got special rates in 1871.[19] Smith, in fact, gained a reputation for violating general rate agreements and offering special rates if they paid. The presidents of the Old Dominion Steamship Line, the Seaboard and Roanoke Railroad, and the Raleigh and Gaston wrote him in May 1869 protesting his violation of their earlier agreement by setting lower through rates with the Wilmington and Weldon and the Atlantic and North Carolina. In this case Smith seems to have pulled back and amended his later cuts.[20]

Despite the generally lower rates that prevailed after 1867, there were some who complained; occasionally they won concessions. Complaints from

Salisbury obtained lower rates there in 1868. Later Smith offered publicly to make special rates for any shippers in western North Carolina who found the posted rates too high to justify shipment. On the other hand, complaints from Concord brought no redress even when they were conveyed by a member of the board of directors who lived there.[21] And persons sending goods northward from High Point regularly wagoned them to Greensboro for shipment on the Richmond and Danville rather than pay the NCRR's local rate to Greensboro.[22]

The NCRR joined many other southern roads in shipping fertilizers at very low rates, particularly in the slack summer and winter seasons when trains ran light. Between 1 July and 15 August 1869, for instance, it offered a special rate on guano and other fertilizers from Norfolk and other ports to any point on the road. Like other through rates these were made cooperatively by the connecting railroad and steamship lines. All regarded special fertilizer rates as an inexpensive way of promoting the economic development of the tributary territory.[23]

In 1859–60 the NCRR annual report itemized the kinds and quantities of freight sent from each station and in which direction. Unfortunately, that effort was never repeated. We have only fragmentary evidence of this sort after the war, some provided by the road and some by the newspapers, both rather episodically.

Unquestionably the most valuable commodity carried by the road was cotton, the bulk of it northward to Norfolk and beyond. This was distinctly a postwar phenomenon. Cotton production increased rapidly in the Southeast after the war, and larger proportions of it were shipped by rail. Previously, southern cotton had gone predominantly to Atlantic and Gulf ports adjacent to the cotton belt, thence by boat to the Northeast and Europe. The ultimate destinations remained much the same for some time after the war, but the flow of shipment rapidly shifted to railroads heading northward at least as far as Norfolk. That city now emerged as one of the nation's leading trade centers, connected by steamship with ports farther north, but direct overseas trade remained small until the 1870s. Railroad cars ran onto the wharves where they were unloaded onto ships.[24]

The NCRR carried in 1859–60 only 6,870 bales of cotton, virtually all of it going to local mills.[25] In 1867–68 (the first postwar year reported) the figure was 39,847 bales; in 1870–71 it was 75,092. About 60 percent of this cotton originated farther south and was received from the Charlotte and South Carolina Railroad; another 33 percent originated in the Charlotte area (both Carolinas), and nearly all of the remainder was shipped from Concord and Salisbury. Only about 14 percent of it appears to have been destined for mills within the state. The rest was headed northward, most of it to Norfolk.[26] Shipments were so large that cotton sometimes stacked up at Charlotte (still the transshipment bottleneck) in a fashion reminiscent of wartime days. Station Agent J. T. Ecton complained in December 1869 that forty to fifty carloads (over a thousand bales) had accumulated, with not a single car available to carry it away. Despite ever-increasing volume, the situation improved by 1871.[27] The published NCRR records permit no reliable estimate as to the proportion of total revenues attributable to cotton, but it must have been high.

Another commodity of large volume and considerable value was dried fruit. The NCRR had virtually created this as a commercial crop in the state before the war. Much of it was produced (in the case of blackberries, gathered in the wild) by women and children. The trade resumed quickly, encouraged by a combination of high prices, newspaper publicity, and the federal taxes on distillation of fruit. Newspaper support included not only glowing accounts of the annual crop and the proceeds from its sale, but editorial encouragement and instructions on how to dry the fruit.[28]

Salem remained the largest marketing center for the crop, drawing from Forsyth, Surry and other nearby counties. A writer in Mt. Airy reported in 1867 that nearly every farm in that area could boast a log drying kiln. Salem merchants bought and shipped over $60,000 worth of dried fruit in 1866, equal to Forsyth County's total tax revenue. One shipper alone, E. A. Vogler, sent 300,000 pounds of dried apples, 100,000 pounds of dried blackberries, and 10,000 pounds of dried peaches. (The sheriff remarked in 1867 that he could almost tell the day Vogler began buying fruit, because that was when people began paying taxes.) All of these figures increased in the following years.[29]

The fruit was shipped in barrels. High Point was the major shipping point, but soon a single Greensboro firm, Odell & Co., would be sending off thirty to forty carloads of dried blackberries per year, much of it finding a foreign market.[30] In 1866, the best season so far, the state's commercial production exceeded 1 million pounds, worth $300,000 on the northern market. In 1867 High Point alone shipped over 1 million pounds; the next year it sent 1,822,000 pounds, followed distantly by Salisbury, Lexington, and Greensboro. The NCRR shipped 3,151,000 pounds in 1868–69, virtually all of it from stations between Salisbury and Hillsboro.[31] The Seaboard and Roanoke shipped 2,385,000 pounds of dried fruit to Portsmouth that same year, most if not all of it likely originating on the NCRR. Much of the crop found its way northward on the Richmond and Danville as well.[32]

We get only the haziest glance at the road's other freight. Tobacco continued to be a major commodity on the NCRR, although most of it was still grown, marketed, and manufactured in Virginia. Small factories had existed in North Carolina for some time, but the state's first warehouse opened at Durham in 1871.[33] Tobacco was shipped from Durham, Salisbury, and doubtless most of the stations between. As before the war, the largest amounts appear to have been sent southward from Greensboro. That town's position was now enhanced by the Richmond and Danville, which tapped some of the largest sources of supply.[34]

The Gardner Mine at Jamestown and others around Thomasville and Lexington sent large quantities of copper ore to Baltimore, resuming a prewar trade.[35] Naval stores destined for Wilmington and Morehead City were shipped from stations east of Raleigh; they seem to have constituted the bulk of the shipments headed to those ports. Wilmington sent back salt and molasses.[36] There are scattered references as well to lumber, poultry, livestock, hay, corn, oats, brandy, and furniture—the last heading south from Salisbury.[37] There is little mention of wheat and flour, two of the road's major freight items before the war. The wheat crop was poor in the first two postwar years. But although conditions improved thereafter, middle western producers seem to have taken over much of the outside markets previously enjoyed by North Carolina producers and even shipped flour into the state.[38]

Most of the freight items so far mentioned were products of North Carolina and neighboring states being shipped to points along the road or to the North. So far as the NCRR and its connecting roads enumerated the kinds of freight they carried, they emphasized outgoing commodities produced in their own territories, despite the fact that incoming southbound shipments were usually of greater total value. Some importance attaches, therefore, to the Seaboard and Roanoke's report that it shipped to the Carolinas in 1866 chiefly dry goods, groceries, farm implements, and guano.[39] After 1866 most of the NCRR's through freight, coming and going, passed over that road between Portsmouth (next to Norfolk) and Weldon.

NCRR officials were seldom as reflective as William Johnston, the veteran president of the Charlotte and South Carolina (now enlarged and renamed the Charlotte, Columbia, and Augusta) Railroad. Johnston noted in 1870 the rise of cotton monoculture in his territory, occasioned by temporarily high prices of that commodity. The production of corn, wheat, and livestock as well as textile manufacturing was therefore neglected, and the South was developing a dependency on the North and West for these essential items. Johnston welcomed the resulting increase in freight tonnage, but his joy was mixed with regrets at the evaporation of southern self-sufficiency.[40] North Carolina grew little cotton, but the state too was being incorporated more and more into a national economy, even to the point of importing northern foodstuffs. In the process the NCRR also profited by the growth of through freight.

As the necessities of passenger and freight service sometimes differed, so did the through traffic agreements that railroads made to govern them. The NCRR often made separate agreements concerning the two. Sometimes it favored one connecting road in passenger service and another in freight service. In either case these agreements were frequently modified.

Although shipments picked up fairly quickly after the war, owing partly to deferred backlogs of supply and demand, it took about a year for trade patterns to resume on anything like the prewar basis. The Roanoke River bridge at Weldon was not rebuilt until April 1866.[41] Meanwhile through traffic to and from the North (not transshipped at Greensboro) was apt to go via New Bern or Wilmington.[42]

The NCRR had had through freight rates with the Wilmington and Weldon since 1855, and in February 1866 it made a new agreement with the Atlantic and North Carolina.[43] Unfortunately for the A&NC and despite its best efforts, that relationship produced very little traffic except during the temporary dislocation right after the war. The treacherous winds off Hatteras and the shallow approaches to Beaufort and New Bern harbors were severe deterrents. Josiah Turner—ever the booster of his native state—refused to admit that Beaufort harbor was not the equal of Norfolk, but the opposite impression was general outside the state, among insurance brokers as well as ship captains.[44]

Owing to the gauge barrier at Greensboro and the failure to develop satisfactory adjustable-truck cars to bridge it, no substantial freight traffic developed between the NCRR and the Richmond and Danville. Passengers could get out and cross the platform on foot, but efficient freight service required running the cars through.[45] Because of this difference in the NCRR's passenger and freight connections, its relations with connecting roads were apt to vary according to which service was involved.

In May 1866, with the Weldon bridge in service, a much broader agreement followed with all the connecting railroads running from Raleigh and Goldsboro to Petersburg, Norfolk, Morehead City, and Wilmington and with steamship lines running from those places to Baltimore, Philadelphia, New York, and Boston. Cars had already begun running through on these roads without breaking bulk, and NCRR rates were lowered to about their prewar levels.[46]

The great beneficiaries of this arrangement were the Raleigh and Gaston and the Seaboard and Roanoke, the connecting links between Raleigh and Norfolk. The NCRR soon joined with them and the Charlotte and South Carolina to form a fast freight line called the Through Freight Air Line. Newspaper ads proclaimed that it "gives more Despatch than any Express Company, and at about one-fourth the Cost."[47] President John M. Robinson of the S&R echoed the NCRR's Thomas Webb in rejoicing that their route had captured much of the through freight from upcountry South Carolina and virtually all of that from the western end of the NCRR, which had gone through Charleston before the war.[48]

The greatest loser was the Wilmington and Weldon, since most shippers preferred Norfolk to Wilmington and avoided the longer rail route via Goldsboro. (The difference was twenty-eight miles.) When that road, in some alarm, approached the NCRR about routing half of its freight through Goldsboro anyway, incoming President Webb refused. Early in 1867, therefore, the W&W opened a vigorous campaign to capture more of the through freight traffic.[49] One of the arguments made in its behalf was that the state had an economic stake in both that road and the NCRR; the state's interest would be advanced, therefore, if as much freight as possible passed over those two roads in preference to the privately owned Raleigh and Gaston. (The R&G had recently purchased all the shares of its stock previously owned by the state.)

Governor Jonathan Worth (President Fisher's old antagonist in 1859) was so impressed with this argument that he instructed his state proxy, Captain John Berry, to offer a resolution to that effect at the NCRR stockholders' meeting in July. Berry did so, and the resolution passed unanimously.[50] (Berry's resolution pertained to passengers as well as freight, but passengers were not as amenable to being forced to travel longer distances, and the policy was actually applied only to freight traffic.) The board of directors, also under pressure from Governor Worth, replaced Thomas Webb with a new president, Josiah Turner, who was already pledged to this course. The central purpose and result of the new policy was to carry the great bulk of through freight over the remaining fifty miles of the road and to collect proportionately more revenues. These were estimated at about $80,000 per year.[51] And there were some who hoped that, besides the additional benefit to the W&W, diverting the traffic through Goldsboro might benefit the state's own ports at Wilmington, New Bern, and Beaufort/ Morehead City.[52] This last effect proved to be negligible.

The new policy took effect in August 1867. Under it through freight went via the R&G only if shippers specified it. Few bothered to do so as the rates were the same either way. R&G President William J. Hawkins estimated that his road lost four-fifths of its through freight traffic to the W&W.[53] Of the NCRR's through tonnage going to and from Norfolk—and that was the vast majority—roughly two-thirds passed through Goldsboro in fiscal 1867–68. The proportion would have been much higher if the policy had extended through the year; it lasted only seven months. (Next year, with traffic restored to the Raleigh and Gaston, Goldsboro received less than one-quarter of this freight.)[54] Feelings ran high on both sides. Each accused the other of diverting traffic its way by subterfuge. At one point Turner was on the verge of terminating freight connections with the R&G altogether.[55]

At the same time, amid signs of a reviving economy, competition for through freight reached unprecedented levels. New cooperative agreements proliferated. The NCRR, with its central location, was party to nearly all of them. That with the Atlantic and North Carolina was publicized as the North Carolina Grand Trunk Railroad, three-fourths of whose profits would go to the state treasury, lightening the public tax burden proportionately. Another, calling itself the Baltimore and Carolina Grand Trunk Freight Line, embraced nearly every road in North Carolina plus the Petersburg Railroad and the Powhatan Steamboat Company in Virginia. It requested all shippers to mark their freight "Via Petersburg."[56]

The Raleigh and Gaston sued for terms by January 1868; agreement was reached late in February. In order to recover the traffic, it agreed to pay the NCRR a bonus equal to what the freight would have paid had it gone on to Goldsboro.[57] This arrangement would cost the R&G some $60,000 in 1868–69, a substantial part of its net income; even so, the road enlarged its freight receipts that year by more than $38,000.[58] Although Governor Worth was not pleased when he heard of the reversal in NCRR policy, it was confirmed at the July 1868 stockholders' meeting. Instrumental in that decision was a quite different state proxy, General Byron Laflin, recently of the United States Army, representing the new Republican state administration.[59]

Some of those in Raleigh who rejoiced at the R&G freight settlement were laissez-faire partisans who believed that forcing the longer Goldsboro route had violated "the great laws of trade and travel, which all experience and observation prove are insurmountable."[60] Turner and his colleagues seem all along to have been motivated primarily by financial considerations. They ran the freight to Goldsboro because it enhanced the road's revenue. They stopped when the opportunity arose to make the same amount of money without running the trains as far. This was also in keeping with the prevailing notions of economic law.

The arrangements of 1868 continued, at least in broad outline, during the remaining three years of the NCRR's independent operation. In fact, they were soon confirmed in a new rate agreement looking to the early completion of the direct railroad link between Columbia and Augusta, shortening the line. Turner's successor, William A. Smith, defended the arrangements on the same economic grounds: "If [the R&G] was a State Road I would object to gouging so deep; but it belongs to individuals, and I therefore, for the benefit of the North Carolina Railroad Company, and the State, take all I can get from them."[61]

Despite early efforts by the W&W to recover at least part of the through traffic, it dwindled to almost nothing when the NCRR announced in December 1868 that all freight going to or from the W&W would be charged local rates.[62] Regular freight trains between Raleigh and Goldsboro were discontinued the next month, and such freight as there was went on the accommodation train, three times a week in each direction. In February 1870 the NCRR would no longer exchange cars with the W&W; henceforth they had to be loaded and unloaded at Goldsboro.[63] Ensuing relations between the managers of the two roads were strained, to put it mildly.[64]

It could be argued that NCRR freight policy in this period was a model of constancy compared with its shifting passenger alliances rotating between the Raleigh and Greensboro connections. The only serious infidelity in freight relations was Turner's brief fling with the W&W. Nevertheless the Raleigh and Norfolk alliance was a troubled one, particularly under William A. Smith. It was impossible as a practical matter to separate freight and passenger relations all of the time, as this chapter and the preceding one have sought to do. The same persons were involved simultaneously with both concerns. In its freight relations as in passenger service, the NCRR enjoyed a desirable strategic position with various options. Other roads were not so fortunate. Any president of the NCRR was apt to incur some hostility as he sought the greatest advantage for his road. But again, Smith was widely regarded as fickle if not untrustworthy. Celebrated at home (in spite of his active and vocal Republican politics) for making the road pay better than any previous administration, he seems to have been distrusted, if not disliked, by virtually every other railroad manager. Most of them probably resented his Republican politics and, even more, the uncouth combative manner in which he carried on public debate. (He was a stump politician reminiscent of Andrew Johnson.) They also disliked his managerial style.

Leaders of the Raleigh and Gaston resented paying blackmail for their through freight and were under no illusion concerning Smith's ultimate motivation or constancy. In an effort to free themselves from dependence upon the NCRR and to strengthen their own bargaining stance with other roads, they tried unsuccessfully to lease the NCRR in 1869. Officials of both the R&G and the Seaboard and Roanoke were convinced in 1870 of the NCRR's bad faith in surreptitiously extending lower special rates than the agreements permitted, but they were more inclined to attribute it to Master of Transportation William H. Green (the official most directly in charge of rate management) than to Smith.[65]

The Richmond and Danville lamented Smith's reluctance to connect with it for either passengers or freight; then it grudgingly paid similar extortion money for through passengers in 1870. For years that road's managers had regarded it as their heaven-sent destiny to control the major north-south transportation route between Richmond and Atlanta or beyond. Now the NCRR, and specifically William A. Smith, was the greatest remaining obstacle in their way.

President William Johnston of the Charlotte, Columbia, and Augusta Railroad was as close to a natural ally as the NCRR could reasonably expect to find. But he was among those who regarded Smith personally as shifty and unreliable.[66] Their personal relations may be judged from the gratuitous announcement that Smith placed in the Charlotte *Democrat* in February 1870 calling public attention to a backlog of southbound freight at the depot there and blaming it on the CC&A. In a letter published in the Charlotte *Observer* several months later, he referred to Johnston as "Old Billie."[67]

The Atlantic and North Carolina Railroad, seeking to merge with the NCRR in 1869 as a matter of economic survival, encountered both opposition and sarcasm from Smith. (See discussion of the consolidation issue in Chapter 20.)

The Western North Carolina Railroad also regarded him as an extortion-ist. That road, still incomplete beyond Morganton, was dependent upon the NCRR for virtually all of its through traffic. Some of its board members wrote Smith in October 1869 protesting the NCRR freight rates, which seemed deliberately to discriminate against their road. Most eastern or northern shippers intending freight for points along the WNCRR, they said, sent it on past Salisbury (the junction) to Charlotte. It was cheaper to do that and wagon the goods to their destinations in western North Carolina than it was to transfer at Salisbury, where the NCRR charged higher rates. The NCRR, they advised, could save itself the needless expense of carrying these goods on to Charlotte by fixing the same rate to Salisbury.[68] In this case the NCRR seems readily to have complied with the request. It was included in the next general rate agreement, reached in February 1870.[69]

That agreement embraced the NCRR, R&G, S&R, and two steamship lines running from Norfolk to Baltimore and New York. It did not include the W&W, R&D, or roads south of Charlotte. (The connecting roads in South Carolina were still included in a previous and apparently continuing 1868 agreement.) The NCRR now gave up the R&G bonus and collected mileage only on the basis of the 175 miles it actually carried freight from Charlotte to Raleigh. But it got instead of the bonus a 10 percent surcharge on the receipts it collected for carrying most kinds of through freight. The new compact involved more than rates; it institutionalized the partnership more than ever before. The respective presidents themselves constituted a board and agreed to meet on a continuing basis. They also provided for a joint trace and claim agency to be located at Portsmouth, Virginia, with the duty of locating missing freight and paying for losses or damage. The agreement was to last until August 1873.[70] By 1871, therefore, the NCRR had cemented its freight relationship with the railroad and steamship lines on the Norfolk route at the same time that it was establishing a new passenger agreement with the Richmond and Danville.

18

Management and Finance: Boyden, Webb, and Turner

RECONSTRUCTION BROUGHT a revolution unmatched in southern (or American) history. Politically, the greatest changes came in 1868 with the advent of congressional reconstruction. But North Carolina had a foretaste of the new era immediately after the war. It was owing largely to William W. Holden, the secessionist-turned-unionist and wartime peace advocate who was Andrew Johnson's choice as provisional governor of the state in May 1865. Holden's assignment, ardently assumed, was to promote North Carolina's adherence to the postwar Union by favoring those who had opposed secession. But he went farther than that. Most Unionists of 1861, having lost that battle, went on to support the Confederacy (with varying degrees of zeal) for the rest of the war. Among these were Zebulon Vance, Jonathan Worth, Josiah Turner, and a large proportion of the antebellum Whig party leadership. Only a small minority, drawn from both parties, turned against the war so strongly as to organize publicly and privately in favor of a negotiated peace with the North. When Holden, as leader of the peace movement, ran against Vance for governor in 1864, he was badly beaten. But now he made support of the peace movement his litmus test of Unionism. In appointing such persons primarily to office, he was also building a political party in his own behalf.[1] Holden thus polarized state politics. As prewar secessionists temporarily went underground, the issue was often less one of Unionism than of pro- or anti-Holdenism.

His own appointment in May came just in time to let Holden make the annual directorship and state proxy appointments on the NCRR and the other railroads owned in part by the state. In an era of small government these were among the most important patronage positions at his disposal. As disgruntled opponents pointed out, far greater preference went to men who had previously supported Holden politically and personally than to men who had railroad experience. Some had that experience, but most did not.[2] Some did not own stock in the roads they were appointed to govern and were thus ineligible under company regulations. But for Holden these were emergency times, and Unionism (of his variety) overbore every other consideration. He had the virtue of consistency so far as stock ownership was concerned. Back in 1858, as editor of the *Standard*, he had opposed such a requirement as aristocratic. It did not matter whether an honest man owned stock or not; the state needed "practical, working men" as directors and officers of its public works.[3]

In the case of the NCRR board, Holden made a clean sweep, although two of his eight appointees had served in earlier years. Albert Johnson, the veteran master machinist of the Raleigh and Gaston—a "practical working man"—had been named to the board by Vance in 1863 and then dumped the next year for supporting Holden for governor. (Holden's influence would make Johnson superintendent of the R&G in 1865 and of the NCRR in 1868.)[4] Robert P. Dick of Greensboro was one of the first NCRR state directors, serving from 1853 until dropped in 1861, presumably for having supported Stephen A. Douglas for president. Other new directors included Nathaniel Boyden of Salisbury, William A. Smith of Johnston County (who would become president of the road in 1868), and the soon-to-be notorious George W. Swepson of Alamance. Four of Holden's directors, including Dick and Smith, owned no NCRR stock and were therefore ineligible under the charter amendment of 1855. Dick was a former stockholder and soon reacquired the minimum five shares; Smith owned no stock until after his election as president.

The private stockholders reelected to the board President Thomas Webb and John L. Morehead, son of the first president and a major stock owner. The other two private members, Giles Mebane and former President Paul C. Cameron, were so antagonized by Holden's appointments that they refused to attend the annual meeting or to accept reelection.[5] In their place the stockholders chose two sitting state directors whom Holden had passed by, Dolphin A. Davis of Salisbury and former NCRR Secretary (and presently sinking fund committee chairman) Cyrus P. Mendenhall of Greensboro.

Holden and the state directors determined from the beginning that the Webb administration had to go; it was not so clear who should succeed Webb. On the eleventh ballot and over the objections of the private directors, they elected—perhaps drafted is the better term—Nathaniel Boyden. This was the first time the public and private directors had divided in this fashion and only the second time that a state director had been elected president. (Paul C. Cameron had been a state director in 1861 but was chosen by general consent.)[6] By the same token the state proxy (Henderson Adams of Davidson County) for the first time in the road's history cast his 30,000 votes to elect a new finance committee, replacing the three incumbents for years back (including textile magnate Edwin M. Holt) with candidates put forward by Boyden and Dick. The division between the state and the private stockholders was very clear: the vote was 30,298 to 4,127.[7]

Sixty-nine years old, Nathaniel Boyden was a Massachusetts native and veteran of the War of 1812 who had moved to North Carolina in 1822.

Turning to the law, he eventually built up one of the largest practices in the state. He served a term in Congress as a Whig in the 1840s. Boyden had opposed secession and was an unwilling supporter of the Confederacy.[8] He now accepted the presidency with the greatest reluctance, on condition that he would serve only part time, devoting the rest of his time to his law practice, and that he might resign before the end of the year.[9] His service was indeed part time; in fact, he took a leading part in the state constitutional convention that met in October 1865 and again in May and June 1866. Boyden did not resign, but he made it clear that he would decline a second term in 1866.[10] (Subsequently he served another term in Congress, 1868–69, as a quasi-Republican and was appointed to the state supreme court in 1871. He died two years later.)

Boyden could hardly have been reelected in any case; the perception was almost universal that he had neglected his duties. Thomas Webb wanted the job back and was a favorite of many private stockholders. Josiah Turner and former Governor Zebulon Vance were also candidates. Political winds had shifted by 1866, else the hopes of all three would have been vain. When Governor Holden ran to succeed himself in the first postwar elections late in 1865, he was defeated by Jonathan Worth. The new governor, an opponent of secession, had gone on to serve as state treasurer throughout the war. He was closer than Holden to the state's political mainstream and was more likely, therefore, to look there for new appointees. He did so but made it a policy to keep one Holden appointee on each board.[11] Nathaniel Boyden was that man on the NCRR board; he was probably the least obnoxious to Worth politically.

But Worth did not favor returning either Boyden or Webb to the presidency. He noted the road's deficit in 1865–66 and Boyden's reputation for neglect of duty. Webb was a personal friend, but Worth regarded him as too weak and too much under the influence of a clique of large stockholders who were also interested financially in the Raleigh and Gaston Railroad. Worth thought the NCRR needed a new orientation. At the same time he owed a large political debt to Josiah Turner, a key supporter in the late election. As Turner agreed on the need for change and promised to give the job his full attention, Worth promised to support him. When Zebulon Vance subsequently expressed interest in the position, Worth politely turned him down. However, Turner had two disqualifications. He rectified one by acquiring five shares of stock from his father, an original stockholder.[12] The governor rectified the second by securing from Andrew Johnson a presidential pardon for Turner, who had served in the Confederate Congress and army; this effort required a year of letter writing. (Before long Worth confided, "My friends and enemies have cooperated to make this nomination of R.R. Directors the most infernal ordeal through which I have ever passed.")[13]

Apart from Boyden and Turner, Worth's appointees included John A.

Gilmer of Greensboro, John Berry of Hillsboro, Robert Strange, Jr., of Wilmington, and William C. Means of Concord, all former directors whose service went back to the road's early days. Worth adhered (as Holden had) to the tradition of appointing a man from nearly every county along the road; Wilmington was occasionally substituted for one of these counties. The stockholders reelected three of the men they had chosen in 1865.[14]

Although Worth made clear his preference for Turner as president, he refrained as a matter of principle from extracting pledges from his new directors. For a number of them Turner was a hard pill to swallow. Brilliant but erratic and temperamental, he had made political enemies ever since the 1850s. There appears to have been intense political maneuvering behind the scenes among both the state and private directors. The result was that four of the state directors, including Boyden and Strange, apparently joined the private directors to restore Thomas Webb as president.[15]

Worth and Turner returned to the fray in 1867, still smarting from their defeat. Six of the previous year's eight appointees were replaced, leaving only Turner and Means. Worth was reluctant to admit that he removed directors for exercising their independent judgment in voting for president. In the cases of Boyden and Strange he determined that both had exceptionally poor attendance records at board meetings, and he replaced them for that reason. The governor again refused to extract formal pledges, but he and Turner made even greater efforts to find men who could be expected to vote the right way and then made sure they did so.[16] One of the new appointees was James E. Allen, the NCRR road master from the completion of the road until 1860 and more recently involved in its reconstruction.

At the annual meeting in Greensboro the private stockholders again reelected three of their four directors. The same political maneuvering occurred as in 1866. At the ensuing board meeting, Worth and Turner finally prevailed by a narrow margin; Turner secured his election only by voting for himself. Webb's partisans immediately laid plans for a comeback in 1868.[17] But they reckoned without the political revolution that came that year, sweeping Republicans into control of the state and its railroads.

Josiah Turner was a native of Orange County, where his father was the largest landowner, with the considerable exception of the Camerons. A lawyer and an ardent Whig—Turner was always ardent—he waged two bitter and close election campaigns against Paul C. Cameron for the state senate in 1856 and 1858, losing the first and winning the second. Some of the wounds engendered at that time never healed. George W. Mordecai, a brother-in-law of Cameron and an NCRR director in 1866, was credited by Holden with defeating Turner for president that year and for that reason.[18] As state senator in 1859, Turner was a vocal (even violent) supporter of Jonathan Worth's partisan investigation of the Fisher administration. He subsequently opposed secession but nevertheless entered the army and served until badly wounded in 1862. Next year he was elected to the Confederate Congress, where he became a thorn in the side of the Davis administration.

In December 1868, several months after his year as NCRR president, Turner took over the Raleigh *Sentinel*, which he turned into the scourge of the Republican Holden administration. Turner encouraged the Ku Klux Klan insurgency and was briefly arrested by state militiamen called out to suppress it. Brilliant, erratic, and obstreperous throughout his public life, Turner did not submit well to party (or any other) discipline. He was virtually read out of the Democratic party and was expelled from the 1879 legislature for disorderly conduct. He died a political outcast in 1901. Perhaps the greatest exception to this career of anarchy was the short year Turner served as president of the NCRR. In that position he was credited, even by his enemies, with a rare record of constructive achievement.[19]

Party or factional politics had always influenced governors' choices of NCRR directors. And Turner, like Morehead and Fisher before him, was actively engaged in political campaigning during his presidency, especially in opposition to the Republican party in the spring of 1868. But politics played little part in personnel matters or the operations of the railroad before 1868.[20]

Company Shops was by now well established as the corporate headquarters. The offices and books were there. Most company officers lived there; the finance committee recommended in 1867 that all do so and keep regular hours. Bylaw revisions that year called for the board of directors' meetings to be held there bimonthly unless specified otherwise. But the stockholders rebelled at a recommendation that their own annual meetings be held there too; these continued to rotate between Greensboro, Raleigh, Salisbury, and Hillsboro.[21] President Boyden seems to have spent most of his time in Salisbury as Fisher had done. That experience likely prompted the subsequent effort to centralize everything at the Shops. Presidents Webb, Turner, and Smith appear to have worked and lived there most of the time. Turner's family apparently remained in Hillsboro, and he kept a room at the Shops from which he commuted home on weekends.[22] Webb, also from Hillsboro, may have done the same. Smith lived at the Shops in a house provided by the road and moved back to his Johnston County farm in 1871 only after the lease removed most of his duties as president.[23]

Thomas J. Sumner was narrowly defeated for reelection as superintendent in 1865, his reputation clouded by his wartime use of the office for personal gain. The road was fortunate in the three men who successively took his place, although for political reasons in part, none of them lasted long. The first, Edmund Wilkes, returned to the post that he had vacated in 1862. Wilkes appears to have performed prodigies in rebuilding and restocking the road during the first two years after the war. These years brought operating deficits, only some of them avoidable, and he received blame along with President Boyden. He departed in February 1867 after a legislative committee criticized the road's management.[24] His successor, James Anderson, was a former NCRR master machinist who since 1864 had been superintendent of the Charlotte and South Carolina Railroad. Anderson was also highly capable, but his service terminated with the Republican takeover of the road in 1868. He was replaced by Albert Johnson, the Holden protégé and longtime master mechanic of the Raleigh and Gaston.[25]

The master mechanic succeeding Anderson in 1864 was Rufus D. Wade. He gave way in 1868 to Emery Burns, probably another Holden supporter. After a year and a half Burns was denounced as incompetent by an investigating committee of the board of directors. The board fired him and recalled Wade in February 1870, to general acclaim.[26]

Secretary Francis A. Stagg became an institution, regarded as almost indispensable to the company's operations. He was a tireless worker and a fount of information about the road and its inner workings. Starting in 1856 as station agent at Durham (then one of the more inconsequential depots on the road), he came to Company Shops in 1861 as general ticket agent. He was promoted in 1864 to secretary. Josiah Turner said of Stagg in 1868: "He knows more of the orders, contracts, books, accounts and liabilities of the Company than *any* other, (I came near saying than *all* other persons.) I have never known a more indefatigable worker or a better man."[27] Stagg remained when the Republicans took over, but his health soon broke down and he became an invalid; colleagues believed he had destroyed his health in the service of the company. It had no established provision for disability retirement; Stagg was nominally retained as secretary at somewhat less than half-pay ($1,000) until 1873. In 1878 he was voted a $500 annual pension. By 1871 his assistant, Charles M. Crump, was performing the duties of the office.[28]

Prewar NCRR secretaries had been bookkeepers, subordinate to the treasurer. During Stagg's time the two positions were usually reversed in status. Under the 1867 bylaws the secretary was to keep the company accounts as well as to record the proceedings of the directors' and stockholders' meetings. The treasurer was in charge of collecting receipts and paying bills, a position requiring less judgment or authority.[29]

Peter Brown Ruffin, who had been treasurer since 1859, was dropped in the upheaval of 1865; a son of Judge Thomas Ruffin, his family and political ties were too strong for Holden. But he came back with President Webb for another year in 1866 and would serve as treasurer again for many years after Reconstruction. Gabriel M. Lea replaced Ruffin in 1865–66 and again after 1868. Both men were regarded as competent officials, if not in the same league with Stagg. William A. Caldwell of Greensboro, who served as treasurer under Josiah Turner in 1867–68, was also in a different category. Turner referred to him as "one of the first financiers of the State."[30] He was an active and influential stockholder, chairman of the finance committee for the two previous years, and a sharp critic of the road's accounting system.

Until 1867 Stagg was listed as both secretary and auditor. The bylaws that year provided for a separate auditor, but none was appointed for the time being, probably for reasons of frugality. In 1869, responding to another recommendation, a company attorney was appointed who doubled as auditor. E. S. Parker, the first incumbent in this office, proved unsatisfactory and was replaced in 1871 by J. H. Abell, only as attorney. So the stockholders' finance committee continued to make regular (now bimonthly) audits of confessedly dubious value, hampered by what it always regarded as a deplorable accounting system.[31]

The inflated wartime salaries were restored to about their prewar levels in 1865. The president's salary was returned to $2,500. With improving times and profits this was raised in 1869 to $3,500 and the next year to $5,000. In both of the latter years (but not explicitly before) President Smith was furnished with a house in Company Shops. Until 1869 superintendents were paid more than the presidents, as had been true of Walter Gwynn. Edmund Wilkes earned $4,000, his successors James Anderson and Albert Johnson $3,000, when their presidents were making $2,500. The master machinist received $2,000. The secretary and treasurer earned $1,500 each for several years; by 1870 Secretary Stagg was receiving $2,500 and Treasurer Lea $2,000.[32]

The financial outlook of the NCRR at war's end was not bright.[33] The regional economy was in a shambles as a result of the war and two successive crop failures in 1865 and 1866. Both passenger and freight traffic would necessarily be light for some time to come. Despite its good fortune in avoiding the worst ravages of military attack, the road faced large reconstruction costs, variously repairing or replacing roadbed, track, bridges and other structures, and equipment. There were $339,000 in NCRR mortgage bonds issued in 1857 that were due to mature on 1 March 1867. Another $50,000 or more in additional debts appeared every year, some of them unrecorded and therefore unknown until the bills came.[34]

The NCRR had precious few resources with which to meet these expenses. Of the $356,000 in cash and securities it had on hand at the end of May 1865, all but $3,620 was of Confederate issue and thus worthless. The Confederate government expired still owing the road about $700,000 for transportation. The state of North Carolina owed $210,000 similarly, and there was little likelihood of collecting this soon, if ever.[35] During the war the company had bought 862 bales of cotton. As recounted in Chapter 10, it retained 657 bales in 1865. These were eventually sold at well below the market price for $66,000.[36] The road also acquired some 15,000 pounds of tobacco at the end of the war. It was entrusted in 1866 to an agent, James V. Moore, who went as far as Mississippi selling it along the way. Unfortunately for the road, he seems to have sent back only about $1,400 from these sales.[37]

The exact cost of reconstruction is unknown, for the same reason we cannot know the cost of the original construction. As President Webb explained it, superintendents, road masters, section masters, and other officials were commonly entrusted as a matter of convenience and efficiency to let contracts for laborers, fuel, crossties, and supplies of all kinds whenever and wherever these were needed along the road. They were supposed to report these transactions at headquarters for approval and entry in the books, but they often neglected to do so.[38] Many financial obligations thus were unknown until demands were made for payment, sometimes years later. Little fraud seems to have been involved, just slipshod procedure. Intense criticism of these practices brought record-keeping reforms after 1866.

Nor is it always possible to distinguish between reconstruction costs and routine operating expenses. The best estimate was that, of the road's total expenses of $984,000 in 1865–66, $549,000 was spent on reconstruction. This year brought a deficit of $94,000, the first since the road began operating. The picture would have been worse but for the remarkably large receipts that year, having several causes: abnormally high wartime rates not yet lowered to peacetime levels, heavy military traffic, and an apparent backlog of civilian traffic previously interdicted by the war. The next year brought sharply lower expenses matched by equally lower receipts, resulting in a further deficit of $92,000. The total debt in 1867 was estimated at $750,000.[39]

President Boyden turned over management of the road, for all practical purposes, to Superintendent Wilkes. Boyden looked in from time to time, even went to New York on company business, but nearly all of the financial dealings as well as daily operations were entrusted to Wilkes.[40] The superintendent was a skilled railroadman who did a superb job of rebuilding the road during the period he was in charge.[41] But he was overworked and inexperienced in some financial matters. He delegated money-spending authority to incapable (probably not dishonest) subordinates; too much money was spent unwisely. In one instance a purchasing agent whom Wilkes had sent to New York without proper authorization or control cost the company over $7,000 by purchasing rails that turned out to be too light for use on the road. Eventually the board of directors held Wilkes personally accountable for further debts incurred by this man.[42] In another case, Wilkes, to meet pressing claims, borrowed $25,000 at 8 percent interest from the Raleigh National Bank, whose president was the unsavory George W. Swepson. Later, owing to the federal government's tardiness in paying its own bills to the road, Wilkes was overdue in repaying the bank. Swepson (then an NCRR director) charged the road $975 in penalties.[43] The Boyden-Wilkes management was to incur scathing criticism for its wastefulness. The waste was well established, but critics nevertheless underestimated the necessary costs of reconstruction.[44]

When Webb resumed control in 1866, he found the road on the verge of bankruptcy. Debts amounting to several hundred thousand dollars were due. Most were urgent and suits were threatened. Laborers had not been paid for three months, and payments were due to furnishers of ties, wood, and other supplies. Webb cut expenses wherever possible. Over 100 employees were laid off. (Fewer were needed after the road was rebuilt.)[45] To meet the most pressing needs, he went to New York and borrowed $50,000 in short-term loans at 1½ percent monthly interest. These notes were promptly repaid at maturity. Soon the board of directors authorized him to borrow $250,000 more. In January 1867 the NCRR ran a newspaper ad headed, "Money Wanted!," soliciting loans up to a total of $100,000 at 8 percent annual interest. Ultimately Webb got $182,000 at 8 percent, nearly all of it from members of the Cameron and Holt families.[46] These temporary loans enabled the NCRR to survive the immediate crisis, but no funds were available to repay the $339,000 in bonds maturing on 1 March 1867. In January the board notified bondholders that the company could not redeem the bonds, probably for another five years. But it promised to continue semiannual interest payments as before.[47]

Webb's policies in 1866–67 were only temporary expedients. He recommended to the stockholders in 1867 that the entire debt, then estimated at $750,000, be funded by issuing new bonds. These could be made more attractive by securing them with a mortgage on the road. He believed that with a fair crop and an increased money supply next year, the company could pay interest, set up a sinking fund to retire the bonds at maturity, and still pay the stockholders an annual dividend of 6 percent. The stockholders accepted the recommendations, approved a mortgage of the road for $1,500,000, and authorized the president and directors to issue up to $800,000 in bonds backed by the mortgage. They were to be issued in sums of $500 and $1,000 at 8 percent interest, payable in five, ten, fifteen, and twenty years. Webb's estimate of a $750,000 debt was based on the belief that about $50,000 in unrecorded old debts were outstanding. Experience taught that such beliefs could not be relied on, so the stockholders provided for an extra $50,000 in bonds. A year later President Turner confirmed at least this amount by reporting the unrecorded debt at $97,000.[48]

When Josiah Turner, Webb's successor, went to New York to sell the bonds, he could get no better offer than 80 cents on the dollar. He refused to sell below par and came home. He persisted in this refusal even after a majority of the board appear to have directed him to sell. Instead he persuaded many of the current bondholders to exchange their old bonds for the new. He also persuaded some of those who had lent money the year before to accept $95,000 of the new bonds in repayment. By these means $300,000 of the new bonds were issued, all at par, by July 1868.[49] George W. Mordecai, and presumably other holders of the prewar NCRR bonds, would have preferred to invest their money elsewhere. But he agreed to the exchange because there seemed no chance of redeeming the old bonds anytime soon and the new ones had the added security of the mortgage lien.[50]

Meanwhile, with improving times and leadership the road showed a profit for the first time since the war. On the eve of the annual meeting in July 1868 the outgoing board of directors voted a 6 percent dividend. It was a peculiar dividend, payable not in money but in the new mortgage bonds or in company scrip. The latter was convertible into bonds if held in quantities of $500, the smallest denomination bond. The board's justification for the dividend was that the road had shown a "profit" of $316,000 in the preceding year. This was a selective reading of the balance sheet, as it included all the receipts but only part of the expenditures. The surplus was actually about $77,000. In any event the dividend increased the already high company debt by another $240,000 plus 8 percent interest carried by the bonds. It was enacted over the opposition of outgoing president Turner, Treasurer Caldwell, and other company officials.[51]

To make matters worse, the stockholders were far from receiving $240,000 in real dividends. The largest stockholder, the state, received $180,000 in NCRR bonds, face value—equal to its three-quarters share. The new Republican state treasurer, David A. Jenkins, accepted them as manna from heaven at a time when the state's financial condition was not much different from the NCRR's. But when he sold them, he could get no more than $117,600, or 65 cents on the dollar. (The purchaser of nearly all of these bonds was George W. Swepson, who made a special trip back from New York for the purpose.) Even this amount represented more than 35 percent of the state's anticipated revenue that year.[52]

Several months later Josiah Turner, now editor of the Raleigh *Sentinel*, derived what political capital he could from the event, lambasting the "Radicals" for destroying the value of NCRR bonds.[53] (The old 1857 NCRR bonds had fluctuated between 75 and 95 cents on the dollar since late 1865, even when the road was temporarily unable—as in November 1865—to make more than half of the interest payments on time. Most often, quotations had been close to 90 cents.) Very soon the new bonds too would rise to par or just below.[54] The reduced price in 1868 may have resulted from the state's well-recognized need to sell quickly and Swepson's readiness to exploit it.

Presumably, individual stockholders received about the same discount as the state if they tried to sell their bonds. But most stockholders owned too little stock to receive a $500 bond. Their dividend came in the form of company scrip that they sold as best they could. John L. Morehead and George W. Swepson were later said to have bought it at 65 to 70 cents on the dollar, the same as the bonds were bringing. It too rose to par by 1870, so far as there was any left by that time.[55]

NCRR bonds were a gilt-edged investment compared with the company stock. It had never been traded widely, but a few shares were sold from time to time, and the transactions were sometimes noted in the newspapers. Some brokers, like Wilson & Shober in Greensboro or John G. Williams & Co. in Raleigh, occasionally listed nominal prices but indicated that they had no shares currently for sale. Several shares sold in Salisbury in January 1866 at $56 and $57. (They had been issued at a par value of $100.) From there it was downhill. In 1867 and 1868 the stock was usually advertised and sold at $15 to $20. This did not change after the 1868 dividend, perhaps from fears for the future under the "Black Republicans."[56]

"Retrenchment and reform" became the watchwords of the NCRR's postwar critics. Nothing cried out for reform more than the road's perennially wretched accounting system. The stockholders' finance committee of 1858 had arraigned the Fisher administration for its "entire want of system" in keeping the company books. The primary problem then as later was the unrecorded contracts that turned up unexpectedly for years afterward as bills to be paid.[57] The finance committee of 1866, under William A. Caldwell, found conditions virtually unchanged. No one yet knew what the total liabilities of the road were at any given time. Only F. A. Stagg came anywhere near approximating that knowledge, and his very indispensability was a measure of the institutional deficiency. Every succeeding administration, said Caldwell and his committee, had been able (with some truth) to blame its own disappointing performance on the perennial unanticipated debts. In 1865–66 old debts amounted to $167,000, of which $70,000 had never been entered on the books and were therefore unknown until the bills came. So it would remain, the committee warned, until one person alone approved every contract and saw that it was promptly recorded. No secretary or treasurer had that power; overall policy decisions were involved, and the most obvious person was the president. The committee specifically exonerated Secretary Stagg and Treasurer Lea: "They have kept their Books and Accounts as well as it is possible for any one to do under the [prevailing] system."[58]

This strong language, coupled with the postwar deficits, led to further efforts at reform of the road's management and operations. Two directors were added to the stockholders' finance committee in 1866, which now met more often to examine the books and the activities reflected in them. (The finance committee in 1866–67 consisted of Caldwell, again as chairman, Rufus S. Tucker, and Rufus Barringer; the directors who sat with it were the veteran Dolphin A. Davis and newcomer Burwell B. Roberts.) On their recommendation a number of changes were instituted. The hotel was rented out rather than operated directly by the road at a loss. Over 100 employees were laid off, and virtually all of the rest suffered wage cuts. Free passes were curtailed. Passenger and freight rates were lowered in the hope of encouraging more traffic and larger receipts. Edmund Wilkes was forced out as superintendent early in 1867. And by no means least—though hardest to implement—the board required the approval of all contracts by either the president or itself.[59]

Reform was made all the easier, and more urgent, by the Robins committee investigation of early 1867. This legislative inquiry was reminiscent of Jonathan Worth's investigation back in 1859, but this time there was less political sharpshooting. It came about because of pressure for reform among some of the leading NCRR stockholders. At their annual meeting in July 1866 they had created a committee, consisting of George W. Mordecai, Rufus Barringer, and William A. Caldwell, to propose revisions in the by-laws and to ask the legislature for a greater stockholder voice in the road's management. (That effort will be discussed later.) In its memorial the committee alleged a variety of shortcomings in the road's management that, it said, were largely the product of state control. Its request for charter amendments limiting that control led to the creation on 21 December 1866 of a joint investigating committee of two members from each house. The committee organized the next day and arranged for hearings to be held at Company Shops in January.[60] Chairman Marmaduke S. Robins was (like Worth in 1859) a state senator from Randolph County. Party divisions were less rife in this legislature, and there seem to have been no public differences among the four committee members. All signed the final report.

The committee started with written inquiries to the road's recent and present officers and any others who were expected to be knowledgeable. It used their responses as the basis for later hearings.[61] The inquiry lasted about a month and was as extensive as that time limitation permitted. The committee could not investigate all of the company books, but it examined the entries concerning particular subjects drawn to its attention. These included the sinking fund bond exchange, the lost cotton, the irresponsible purchasing agent in New York, and perhaps particularly the lack of adequate financial records. (Related to this last was the company storekeeper at Company Shops, James G. Moore; it was guessed that he handled at least $50,000 in supplies every year, but nobody knew for sure because he had kept no books until Webb and Wilkes required it late in 1866.) Also included in the inquiry were a probable overpayment of damages to John Motley Morehead for the accidental burning of some cotton shipped by him; an apparent overpayment for a wooded lot near Greensboro, acquired to provide the road with fuel; the proliferation of free passes; and a few other matters of apparently small consequence. Of all these subjects, the storekeeper and the sinking fund exchange seem to have excited the greatest indignation. Yet even in those cases the committee refrained from explicit charges, especially of fraud. Moore was not really suspected of it, and it was debatable even in the case of Mendenhall.

Taken as a whole, however, these matters created an inescapable picture of administrative laxity. The committee pronounced itself "satisfied that gross abuses exist and have probably existed from the commencement of the road." It implicitly or explicitly taxed Boyden, Webb, Wilkes, and others with carelessness or poor judgment on a number of occasions. But it agreed with the company's own finance committee that responsibility was so loosely distributed, particularly in financial matters, that it was virtually impossible to assign individual guilt. In effect, the "gross abuses" were ones of administrative disorganization that had been institutionalized on the road from the beginning. The committee noted that a number of these matters had already been addressed by the road's managers before the investigation began. By implication it complimented Wilkes on the excellent physical condition of the road, rejoicing that so much of the "profuse expenditure" had been directed to that end.[62] Nevertheless it was surely more than coincidence that Wilkes left the road immediately after the committee issued its report.

Some persons, like Director John Berry, were readier than the committee itself to level charges of dishonesty, at least in private. Governor Worth's reaction to the findings was not much different from the committee's or from his own findings in 1859, for that matter: radical changes were needed in the road's management. Josiah Turner was credited with drawing many of the abuses to the committee's attention, and Worth pushed harder to have him chosen president.[63]

At the ensuing annual meeting the NCRR finance committee pointed with some pride to the various reforms enacted on its recommendation by the board of directors. Expenses in 1866–67 fell by almost $300,000. However, receipts fell by the same amount, leaving another deficit of over $90,000. The reforms to date were not enough. Money was still being wasted, the committee felt, and it remained difficult to determine who was at fault. Lack of coordination between the secretary and treasurer still caused their books to disagree, and neither differentiated properly between old debts and new. The committee recommended the appointment of an auditor to examine the books on a regular basis.[64]

More broadly, the finance committee called for a thorough reorganization of the road's management. Officers' duties were not clearly defined, and department heads were not required to make regular reports.[65] Of the three committee members, Caldwell and Barringer at least were advocates of private stockholder control. Both were also on the committee chosen in 1866 to ask for charter amendments to that end and to propose new bylaws. The legislature did not pass any charter amendments, but the stockholders in 1867 did adopt a new set of bylaws. These were not radically different from the ones previously in force, but they embodied a number of the finance committee's recent recommendations: provision for an auditor, monthly financial reports from all officials, expansion of the finance committee by adding two directors (as done the previous year on an ad hoc basis), and again, "no contract shall be considered as binding . . . unless . . . approved by the President or Board of Directors."[66]

Under these rules, and with the new president, Josiah Turner, committed to retrenchment and reform, Caldwell himself agreed to serve as treasurer in 1867. He brought greater stature to the post than it had ever had before.

Passenger and freight rates were lowered, again in the hope (which was realized) of increasing traffic and revenues. More employees were laid off. Greater care was taken to estimate the road's needs in advance, to purchase supplies at the best rates, and to ascertain and pay the unrecorded debts. Caldwell made a public announcement in February 1868 warning that all persons having claims against the road and failing to present them for adjustment by 1 April "will find their demands resisted by every means in the power of the Board of Directors."[67] At the end of the year the finance committee, now under Rufus Barringer, credited Caldwell with introducing new order and efficiency and significantly reducing the company debt. "Amid many great difficulties, he has not only maintained but elevated the credit of the corporation, and has inspired a well-founded confidence in its ultimate pecuniary success." But the ghost of past practices remained to haunt the company. Old debts from earlier years continued to pop up; as late as 1871 the year's accumulation exceeded $52,000. As a result no one ever knew the road's true indebtedness.[68]

To an important degree, continuity prevailed over change in NCRR affairs, even during the political instability and tumult of Reconstruction. Much as they always had, the public and private directors customarily united in determining company policy—or sanctioning that of the president—without any discernible difference between them. Presidents Boyden and Webb are both on record to this effect, Webb excepting only Boyden's election as president in 1865, accomplished by the state directors.[69] Superintendents Wilkes and Anderson were chosen by the votes of public and private directors alike.[70]

But in other respects governmental intervention in NCRR management and operations exceeded by far anything that had occurred before. If the private stockholders and directors had been left alone they might have reelected Thomas Webb to the presidency indefinitely. He was a creature of the larger stockholders, was competent, and did not rock the boat. But they were three times disappointed by gubernatorial intervention, in 1865, 1867, and 1868.

There was nothing very new about the political choice of directors by Governors Holden and Worth; Reid, Bragg, and Vance had done the same. But Worth in particular set out to impose a specific man as president and shuffled the board of directors in two successive years to get him elected. He did this, moreover, to achieve an administrative reorganization of the road and a specific reorientation of its policy: the diversion of through traffic so far as possible from the Raleigh and Gaston to the Wilmington and Weldon at Goldsboro. The quality of Worth's appointments was high, and there was at least arguable merit in his policy initiative. He was quite within his legal and political rights as governor. But the fact remains that he far surpassed any previous executive in the degree of his intervention.

Worth came to the conclusion that the NCRR management was too much under the influence of the prominent men in and around Raleigh who controlled the Raleigh and Gaston Railroad. This subservience was a mark of both the Webb and Boyden administrations, he believed, going back for some years. He did not make it clear how this thralldom was manifested, except in the close connections that the two roads maintained, resulting in through passengers and freight entering and leaving the NCRR at Raleigh rather than at Goldsboro. In fact the two roads reached a new accord for this purpose in the spring of 1866, at about the time Worth was making his railroad directorship appointments. (The new passenger agreement that year actually tended to divert travelers to Greensboro—even less advantageous to the NCRR.) Thus, as the governor saw it, three railroads in which the state had a financial interest (the Wilmington and Weldon, the Atlantic and North Carolina, and the NCRR) were deprived of large revenues, and the state was denied potential dividends from traffic that entered or left the road at Raleigh. (The state owned stock in the R&G as well, but later in 1866 its managers bought out the state's shares, and it was henceforth wholly in private hands.) Worth believed that Josiah Turner had the nerve and capacity to end this subservience as well as to clean up the abuses in management that Worth had noted since his own investigative days in 1859.[71]

It was the state proxies who elected the NCRR finance committees in 1865 and 1867, presumably at their governors' behest. With Josiah Turner finally installed in 1867, State Proxy John Berry carried out a second mandate from the governor by introducing a resolution to carry through traffic so far as possible along the entire length of the road.[72] As already seen in Chapter 17, this resolution was approved by the stockholders and implemented by Turner and the directors soon afterward. It had the desired effect but came to an end several months later (without any prior consultation with Worth) when the R&G, to regain its lost traffic, offered to pay the NCRR sums equal to the revenues it would lose by not going on to Goldsboro. Next year the new Republican state proxy killed an effort by the W&W to resurrect the Goldsboro policy.[73] Republican intervention in the road's affairs would be more startling politically but hardly more fundamental to its operations than Worth's had been.

19

Management and Finance: W. A. Smith

THE REPUBLICAN PARTY had no organized existence in North Carolina until it formed in support of the congressional Reconstruction acts of March 1867. It was a coalition of the newly enfranchised blacks, white Unionists primarily from the western half of the state, and a small number of northerners who had settled primarily in the eastern half during and right after the war. Republicans controlled the state constitutional convention that met early in 1868, and they won the April elections that ratified the constitution and chose state officials for the next four years. William W. Holden, who had abandoned Andrew Johnson in favor of Congress and gone on to lead the new party, was elected governor.

Most of those who had previously held power in the state—regardless of their stance on secession in 1861—either held themselves aloof from the new movement or actively opposed it. They expected Holden's previous term in 1865 to be a garden party compared with this one, supported as it was by a political party committed not only to Unionism but to Negro suffrage and civil rights. At the very least they expected a turnover in patronage positions comparable to that of 1865. President John D. Whitford of the Atlantic and North Carolina Railroad wrote facetiously to Samuel McD. Tate, president of the Western North Carolina, predicting a Negro president on the latter road while his own got "a white man meaner than a Negro." More seriously, he predicted that he and Josiah Turner would go but that Tate had a fair chance of surviving.[1] As it happened, all three were replaced.

Jonathan Worth was not blessed with a sense of humor; his effort to appoint all of the state's railway directors on 30 June was intended in all seriousness despite the election of his successor more than a month earlier. This proved to be his last act as governor. On the same day, General E. R. S. Canby, the military commandant in the Carolinas, removed Worth from office and appointed Holden in his place. On 2 July Canby revoked Worth's railroad appointments.[2] Holden went ahead to appoint a wholly new board although two of his appointees (William A. Smith of Johnston County and

Dr. William Sloan of Mecklenburg) had served in 1865. Sloan would soon become president of the Wilmington, Charlotte, and Rutherford Railroad. Willie D. Jones was a state senator from Raleigh, an assessor of internal revenue, and later a major general of militia under Holden. John McDonald was a textile manufacturer in Concord.[3] Two others, John R. Harrison and Silas Burns, were among the "practical working men" whom Holden believed should serve on railroad boards. Both were prewar builders of railroad cars, and Harrison was president of the Raleigh Workingmen's Association in 1859.[4] William F. Henderson and George W. Welker were Republican leaders in Davidson and Guilford counties, respectively. Four of the eight were delegates to the convention that had organized the state Republican party a year earlier.[5] Most would continue to serve until 1871. The state proxy was General Byron Laflin of Pitt County, a Union Army veteran who had only recently settled in the state; to Conservatives, Laflin was the quintessential carpetbagger.

A number of the stockholders thought to prevent the new regime from taking control by preventing a quorum at the annual meeting in July. But the state directors and Laflin were determined to organize anyway, and the boycott did not materialize.[6] The stockholders reelected Thomas Webb, Dolphin A. Davis, and John L. Morehead in addition to the outgoing treasurer, William A. Caldwell.

The meeting was a donnybrook the like of which the road had never seen. Josiah Turner was temperamentally incapable of retiring quietly. His presidential report contained two political barbs, one of them an attack on Governor Holden that drew the fire of the few Republicans present. State Proxy Laflin in particular rose to the bait, moving to strike out the offending passages. When Chairman George W. Mordecai ruled him out of order, Laflin offered a motion to condemn them. Lengthy and heated debate ensued, Turner on one occasion referring sarcastically to Laflin's recency on the North Carolina scene. On another occasion Turner refused to hear any more about loyalty to the Union from William A. Smith, whom he accused of hunting down Confederate deserters with dogs during the war. Eventually Laflin's motion carried on a stock vote of 30,402 to 4,188, he of course casting 30,000 of the affirmative votes. On the other side were virtually all of those who had guided the road in days past, including William A. Graham, George W. Mordecai, members of the Holt, Morehead, and Caldwell families, and former Presidents Cameron, Webb, and Boyden. (It is worth noting that only twenty-nine stockholders were present at this meeting; they cast many of the votes as proxies for absentees.) A large proportion of the stockholders later entered a formal protest against Laflin's "arbitrary and unnecessary" behavior.[7]

When a bipartisan committee strongly commended the performance of Superintendent James Anderson, William A. Graham offered an extraordinary motion to suspend the bylaws, bypass the board of directors, and elect

Anderson for another year forthwith. Laflin was instrumental in defeating this motion. Later he voted for and thus passed a motion authorizing the road to issue the remaining $700,000 in company bonds permitted under the previous year's $1,500,000 mortgage. This time he got only 78 additional votes, most of the Republicans also voting on the other side.[8]

At the subsequent board meeting William A. Smith was elected president with eight votes to one each for Thomas Webb and John L. Morehead. Albert Johnson was chosen superintendent by eight votes to four, the state directors outvoting the private ones. Secretary F. A. Stagg was reelected, and G. M. Lea returned as treasurer, both unanimously.[9] All four men would serve during the next several years.

William A. Smith was a self-made man, well out of the tradition of NCRR and other railroad presidents. Reconstruction was to some degree a plebeian movement, bringing forth men who would never have realized their potential otherwise. This was most obviously true of blacks, but it elevated many lower-class whites as well. Smith was born in Warren County in 1828, the son of a plantation overseer.[10] He received only an old field school education before going to work at age fourteen as a day laborer on the Raleigh and Gaston Railroad. Hoping to better his fortunes, he migrated to Alabama, Louisiana, and Texas but returned to North Carolina and settled down as a farmer in Johnston County. By 1860 he owned twenty-four slaves.

Smith entered local politics as a Whig or Constitutional Unionist. He was elected to the state convention of 1861–62 as an opponent of secession, but he later did (as Turner said) serve as major of the Johnston County home guard, arresting Confederate deserters.[11] At the same time he was an early adherent of Holden's peace movement and was instrumental in carrying his county for Holden in the 1864 gubernatorial election.[12] Smith was elected to the legislature that year and to the state convention in 1865 as a Holden supporter. Holden named him to the NCRR board in 1865. In 1868 he was Holden's choice as president.

Smith was actively engaged in Republican politics throughout his presidential years and afterward. He was a gifted stump speaker, convulsing audiences with homespun humor and witty jabs at his opponents. Like Holden he accepted Negro suffrage only when Congress required it. In 1870 he took over management of the *Standard*, the party organ in Raleigh, but he gave it up after the fall election, reportedly with the remark, "What in hell is the good of running a Republican paper when none of the party can read?"[13] Smith was also elected to the state senate from Alamance County that year, only to be unseated by the Democratic senate majority as a step toward the impeachment and removal of Governor Holden. After the Richmond and Danville lease in 1871 Smith moved back to his Johnston County farm. He retained the much-abridged NCRR presidency (with the exception of one year) until 1877. He served a term in Congress, 1873–75, and was the unsuccessful Republican candidate for lieutenant governor in 1876. He soon afterward retired from public life and died in 1888.[14]

Superintendent Albert Johnson came to his job with more obvious railroad credentials than Smith, but his political credentials were in order too. He had been a locomotive engineer on the Richmond and Fredericksburg Railroad in Virginia in 1836, master machinist of the Raleigh and Gaston for over twenty years, and for one year (under Holden) superintendent of that road. As a follower of Holden he had also been appointed to the NCRR board in 1863, removed in 1864, and reappointed in 1865.[15]

When Smith assumed office in July 1868, stockholders and others expected the worst. Some threatened to sell if not give away their stock. This was not wholly the product of political bias. One previous year on the board was not enough to dispel the notion that he was a political hack who would soon run the road into bankruptcy—a redneck Nathaniel Boyden.[16] Smith smarted under these predictions and set out to prove them false. Although patrician President William Johnston of the Charlotte, Columbia, and Augusta Railroad continued to regard him as "an ignoramus & knave," Smith cultivated and soon won over a significant number of the NCRR stockholders and directors.[17] Longtime director Dolphin A. Davis reportedly incurred some partisan ire by switching his support to Smith in 1869,[18] but in fact the board reelected Smith unanimously that year. He went out of his way to cultivate William A. Graham, Paul C. Cameron, and other members of the old guard.[19] In June 1871, for instance, Smith arranged a junket for the directors and others, labeled an inspection of the road, from Charlotte to Goldsboro. David F. Caldwell preserved a printed invitation to this affair with a handwritten message from Smith at the bottom: "Cold ham—pickles—crackers—& *whiskey*." Though not a director, Caldwell was an important stockholder.[20]

To an increasing degree, these men responded favorably.[21] They always found Smith's Republican politics obnoxious, but before long he established himself as a moderate who condemned the lavish railroad aid schemes of his party colleagues in the legislature. Not only did this position make sense in terms of the state's financial resources, but the NCRR already had its share of state aid. In time Smith even criticized political interference in the road's management and advocated stockholder control, at least in the abstract. In November 1869 he told William A. Graham that "the road has allways [sic] been controlled by party and as long as it is, it will be impossible for it to pay the stockholders long at a time."[22]

Smith turned out to be a surprisingly capable president, greatly aided by improving business conditions. He made the road pay. His views seem to have evolved gradually as he gained experience. He was not in a position to express or act upon all of them in 1868. The Republican party was new; most of its members and many of its leaders were (like Smith himself) men of humble origin who lacked family estates and independent incomes. Party leaders, workers, and voters needed paying jobs. Nowhere could they be found in greater abundance than on the state-controlled railroads. Thus Governor Holden, Superintendent of Public Works Ceburn L. Harris, and the presidents of the various railroads were inundated with applications.[23]

Smith was in no position to resist this tide. He may not even have wanted to at first. There ensued in 1868–69 a turnover in NCRR employment far greater in proportion—because it extended much deeper into the ranks—than ever before. Most jobs on the road involved unskilled labor and were held by blacks. Previous administrations had hired slaves and then freedmen before anyone thought of their voting. The Smith administration continued to do so, apparently without much thought of politics beyond seeing to it that they could get to the polls on election day. Black votes were the foundation of Republican power in the counties along the railroad as in most of the Reconstruction South. Black employees constituted about the same proportion of the work force under Smith (70 to 72 percent) as under his predecessors, except for the two years (1866–67) when the road tried to dispense with them altogether.[24] The specifically white jobs, so to speak, were very much subject to political influence in 1868. It extended to supervisory positions from the president down and perhaps especially to the station agents. Nineteen of the twenty-eight agents were replaced this year. (One of the new appointees, Dr. H. M. Pritchard, found the agency at Charlotte more desirable than the mayoralty there, which he resigned.)[25]

Some of the new appointees did not perform acceptably. Defaults by station agents were about three times greater in 1868–69 than in previous years. In such cases Smith replaced the offenders, sometimes taking political heat from Republicans in the process.[26] Calvin J. Rogers, the new agent at Raleigh, lasted only one month before he was sacked for incompetence and for defaulting in his accounts to the tune of $3,000. Rogers soon became postmaster of Raleigh. Smith allegedly fired another agent with the message: "To Nathan Gully, Clayton, bully Republican but d—n poor Agent."[27] In 1871 the road sued seven former agents (including Gully) for default. Some of them were men who had served for years before 1868, others were recent appointees.[28] When complaints multiplied concerning shoddy workmanship at the shops, Smith blamed Master Mechanic Emery Burns and handed the problem to the directors, saying that Burns had been their choice. Their own investigation confirmed Smith's diagnosis; as a result Burns was discharged and Rufus D. Wade was reinstated. In general, Smith appeared to be replacing discharged workers with the best men he could find, regardless of party.[29] Before long, political considerations played about as minor a role in NCRR personnel policies as they had in earlier years.

During the 1868 fall campaign, the Smith administration permitted Republican speakers to travel free and persons attending Republican meetings to go at half-fare or less, while denying such privileges to the opposition.[30]

Conservative papers reacted sometimes with fury, sometimes with humor. The *Milton Chronicle* told of a man who observed another traveler securing roundtrip tickets at half fare. When asked how he did this, the second man simply held up his carpetbag. The first man then bought a carpetbag himself. This aspect of operations seems not to have lasted beyond 1868. However, Smith offered free passes home to all legislators (regardless of party) when they adjourned in April 1869.[31] And he was reported to have provided financier George W. Swepson with a special train in March 1870, enabling Swepson to avoid testifying before a legislative committee and possible arrest.[32]

Smith alienated some Republicans as well. At the 1869 stockholders' meeting he delivered a blistering attack on the Republican legislative majority, which had recently voted far more aid to other railroads than the state could possibly afford. The legislature lacked men of property and character, he charged. This played well with the stockholders, but it infuriated other Republicans, who accused him of going over to the enemy. State Senator Abraham Galloway of Wilmington offered a resolution asking the governor to remove Smith as a state director and thus as president.[33] In the end, Smith won over the stockholders while retaining his Republican credentials.

Smith's good-old-boy mannerisms, rustic humor, and uninhibited campaign style were both strengths and weaknesses. Josiah Turner in particular had a field day with them after taking over the Raleigh *Sentinel* in December 1868. He coined the name Blow Your Horn Billy Smith as part of a larger repertoire of nicknames for prominent Republicans. After Smith allegedly promised in 1868 to run the NCRR in such a fashion as to create 10,000 Republican votes, opponents accused him of keeping his promise by firing any employees who voted Democratic that fall.[34] Much later, Turner published the names of over thirty such people; almost half were station agents.[35] Smith was also charged with manipulating train schedules on election day so as to get the crews to the polls on time. Conservatives said he voted his black employees at whatever polling place Republican votes were most needed and even imported black laborers from South Carolina and elsewhere in order to vote them in his 1870 state senate campaign.[36] Most extravagant of all, he reportedly claimed to have masqueraded 200 black women as men in Johnston County, marched them to the polls on election day, and voted them. Smith of course denied this story as he did most of the others.[37]

He was in fact about as combative as Turner and gave almost as much as he received. Readers of the *Standard* and *Sentinel* were treated to an entertaining if not edifying verbal battle of several years' duration. Smith wrote on one occasion that when he inherited the NCRR presidency from Turner, the road was in deplorable condition, "running along without a head, broken down, almost insolvent, crushed by a debt of nearly a million dol-

lars, with less than twenty thousand in the treasury. I found in the office
when I took charge an old pine table, a sort of cupboard containing one
empty jug and several empty bottles, an old bedstead and mattress, full of
chinches, and covered with old dirty sheets. All was dirt and confusion.
A majority of the officers and employees were drunkards and unreliable
men."[38] By contrast, Smith loved to recall the initial Democratic prognosti-
cations of doom for the NCRR under his redneck/radical leadership and
then to recount the increasing profits and dividends that actually ensued.

In general, Smith accepted the reforms of the Turner/Caldwell administration and proceeded with them. Political hirings and firings as well as
politically oriented operations were always exaggerated and were largely
limited to his first year.[39] The criticism of partisan Republicans was over-
borne by the rising revenues and dividends as well as growing stockholder
support.

Calls for government regulation of the railroads in this era, whether for
rate regulation or otherwise, were few and far between in North Carolina
and the South generally. The Granger laws of the 1860s and 1870s were a
midwestern phenomenon.[40] In fact, the very state ownership and control
exercised in North Carolina and other states over such roads as the NCRR
obviated some of the need for state regulatory legislation. To make that
control more effective, Governor Worth and his board of internal improvements called in 1866 for standardizing the powers of the various state proxies and giving them investigatory powers. Holden's alternative, also put
forth in 1866, was to create a superintendent of public works empowered
to direct the operations of the state-controlled railroads in the public
interest.[41]

That suggestion was incorporated into the constitution of 1868. It provided for a publicly elected superintendent but left his duties to be defined
by the legislature.[42] That body in April 1869 placed the superintendent in
charge of the state's interest in all railroads and other public improvements.
They were to report annually to him, as he to the legislature, concerning
their status. More importantly, the law empowered him "to vote either in
person or by proxy, in behalf of the State, at all elections of directors of
corporations or joint stock companies, at which the State is entitled to
vote."[43] The wording is muddy, but it appeared to give the superintendent
the power to name railroad directors and state proxies and thus take from
the governor some of the most valuable patronage positions at his disposal.
Why this was done is unclear. The bill appears to have originated with a
special code commission composed of three eminent jurists, although an
opponent later characterized this provision as the work of the legislature's
"railroad ring," pulled off during the turbulent closing hours of the session.[44] The beneficiary of the measure, Superintendent of Public Works
Ceburn L. Harris, had been elected with Holden in 1868. A fellow Republican, Harris was closely affiliated politically and by marriage with Judge

George W. Logan of Rutherford County, an emerging factional rival of Holden's. The ensuing dispute between Harris and Holden over control of the railroads was therefore part of a larger contest for control of the state's Republican party.[45]

Harris wasted no time in trying to assume his new duties at the ensuing stockholders' meetings around the state. He was accepted by the Atlantic and North Carolina stockholders at Beaufort in June. (Harris seemed more amenable than Holden to consolidating that road with the NCRR, something the eastern road desperately desired.)[46] Governor Holden had no intention of giving up his powers over the railroads, however, and fought back. President Smith and state Attorney General Lewis P. Olds were firmly in his camp. Both assured him that the NCRR charter specified the governor as the appointing power over the road and that the legislature had no power to modify the charter without stockholder consent; charters were contracts whose obligations states were forbidden to impair.[47] The NCRR meeting at Salisbury in July promised to be fully as exciting as the one a year earlier, when the Republicans had taken control of the road.

Smith anticipated the meeting by securing an injunction from a friendly judge, Samuel W. Watts of Raleigh, restraining Harris from serving as state proxy pending a judicial settlement of the case. As soon as Harris arrived, he obtained a similar order from his brother-in-law, Judge Logan, restraining Holden's appointee, Byron Laflin. Holden himself came to Salisbury on a special train furnished by Smith (bringing Watts, Laflin, and a big supply of whiskey, according to Turner's *Sentinel*) in order to be on the scene, although he did not actually attend the meeting. Both Harris and Laflin attended and stated their claims. When a resolution was offered in support of Harris, Paul C. Cameron and other leading stockholders opposed it. Their dislike for Holden was exceeded by distrust of Harris and their growing support of Smith's leadership of the NCRR. When the question came to a vote, Laflin attempted to cast the state's 30,000 votes against it, in effect voting on his own case. Stockholder Josiah Turner was thus offered a golden opportunity to berate Laflin and Holden, his antagonists the year before. It was, said he, yet another case of carpetbaggers with loose northern morals attempting to corrupt the South. Turner supported Harris, less from love of him than hatred of his opponents. Ultimately the resolution in favor of Harris was tabled by a vote of 7,154 to 1,904, the state not voting.[48]

Holden's victory (subject to a judicial review) was repeated with the stockholders of the Wilmington, Charlotte, and Rutherford and the Western North Carolina railroads. By December the matter was before the state supreme court. Harris lacked money to conduct the suit and suggested further legislation to clarify the assembly's intent.[49] Holden supporters also endorsed a legislative solution, according to one report, when it leaked out that the supreme court was going to rule in favor of Harris.[50] In March 1870, still before the court had been heard from, the legislature modified the previous law to permit the governor to continue to name directors and proxies on all railroads chartered before the 1868 constitution was adopted.[51] As all the functioning railroads in the state had been chartered before that time, the result was a triumph for the governor.

A comparable dispute arose in 1871, after the Democrats had captured control of the legislature. In April of that year they passed a law removing the railroad appointive power from the governor and conferring it on the Speakers of the two houses of assembly. (This bill was originally intended to apply only to the NCRR, but it was amended on the floor to include all the railroads in which the state owned stock.)[52] The argument that this violated the preexisting charters was just as clear as in 1869, but Democrats in effect adopted Harris's argument, not ruled upon by the court and now buttressed by their power to change legislation to suit their own needs.[53] House Speaker Thomas J. Jarvis and acting Senate President Edward J. Warren went ahead to make proxy and directorship appointments for the various railroads. (Josiah Turner was one of those named to the NCRR.)[54] Meanwhile Governor Holden had just been impeached, convicted, and removed from office for calling out militia to suppress the Ku Klux Klan. His Republican successor, Tod R. Caldwell, also made appointments, reportedly swearing that "he'd see 'em d——d before he'd yield."[55]

As in 1869, William A. Smith was wholeheartedly on the side of the governor. He quickly prepared for a lawsuit challenging the April enactment, the board of directors voting him $1,000 for expenses.[56] In his behalf attorney Samuel F. Phillips approached a number of state judges for an injunction, but all of them refused to risk any further conflict with the legislature. Phillips then approached United States Circuit Judge Hugh Bond, who responded with what amounted to a temporary injunction on 3 July, just ten days before the scheduled stockholders' meeting; he ordered a full hearing in September. (Bond would gain national fame in September as he presided over the trials of North Carolina Ku Klux Klansmen in Raleigh.) The plaintiff of record was Joseph B. Stafford of Baltimore, a small stockholder who was solicited for this purpose because his residence in another state would help to establish federal jurisdiction over the case.[57]

Democrats were concerned over more than political control of the NCRR. Some were hoping to head off an impending lease of the road to the Richmond and Danville Railroad, which they knew Smith and many other Republicans favored. Accordingly they procured two injunctions of their own from state judges, one restraining Governor Caldwell's appointees from serving and the other forbidding the private stockholders to lease the road.[58]

Both sides looked to the July stockholders' meeting, just as in 1869, to seat their respective candidates for director. The stockholders were in a quandary as to what they could do without violating one or another of the court orders just handed down. Reportedly it was John L. Morehead who suggested that they prevent a quorum and thus avoid a meeting altogether. In such a case the charter decreed that the preceding year's directors (Holden's 1870 appointees plus the four elected that year) carry over until new ones could be chosen at a legal meeting. Under the bylaws a quorum required at least 100 individual stockholders, present or by proxy, holding a majority of the privately owned stock.[59] Smith and about ten of the major stockholders agreed to do this. More than enough stockholders or their proxies to form a quorum came to the meeting in Greensboro. In fact Smith had arranged special trains from either end of the line for their convenience, and they converged on the town at 11 A.M. with at least 1,100 persons aboard, according to the *Patriot*. But Smith and his collaborators now refrained from formally listing their stock. As a result only 1,889 of the 10,000 privately owned shares were officially represented. Their success in this maneuver was probably the supreme evidence of Smith's ascendancy with the larger stockholders, virtually all of them Democrats. They were not recorded by name, but they included Morehead, Dolphin A. Davis, John I. Shaver, and Rufus Barringer. William A. Graham and Josiah Turner were among those opposed.[60]

The old board continued to function, therefore, in accordance with the charter. (In fact it would be they who leased the road on 11 September, before any court determined who were the legal appointees for 1871.) An effort to hold another stockholders' meeting on 20 September failed again for lack of a quorum.[61] The Stafford case finally came to trial late in 1871, only to be dismissed on technical grounds. Early in 1872 the state supreme court heard a parallel case arising from the Atlantic and North Carolina Railroad. It ruled in favor of the governor's appointive power and declared the 1871 act unconstitutional. This laid the question at rest for the NCRR as well.[62]

Financially, the years from 1868 to 1871 were the most successful in the road's history to that point. Passenger and freight receipts both increased each year, reaching a total of $765,000 in 1870–71. At the same time expenses continued to decline, amounting to only $404,000 in 1870–71. The operating ratio (expenses as a percentage of receipts) thus fell steadily, amounting in 1870–71 to a quite acceptable 53 percent. (Before the war, when track and equipment were new, the ratio had been an even better 45 to 47 percent.) (See table 11.) Although improving economic conditions contributed to the 16 percent increase in receipts between 1868 and 1871, economical management accounted for the concurrent 14 percent drop in expenses despite growing business. The physical condition of the road was good in 1871; it was generally agreed that the increasing profits did not come at the expense of maintenance. (Josiah Turner, smarting under Smith's annual reports citing his own more successful performance, accused Smith of spending too little on new rails, thus letting the track deteriorate; but there is no real evidence that this was true.)[63]

The road's rate of return on its capital investment was 7.3 percent in 1870–71, up from 4.8 percent in 1859–60.[64] President Smith could report in 1871 that net earnings totaled $925,000 during his three years of stewardship; of that amount $445,000 had been applied to the company debt, and $480,000 had been paid to the stockholders as dividends.[65]

Only slightly offsetting this prosperity was the company debt. Despite the procedural and bookkeeping reforms of 1867, no one yet could say exactly what the debt was at a given time. Old debts continued to pop up without advance notice, amounting to $73,000 in 1870.[66] Successive finance committees after 1868 praised the bookkeeping, and no one suggested that the unrecorded debt was fraudulent or out of line beyond the fact of its being unrecorded. The road now found this debt to be manageable and, unable to prevent it, had learned to live with it.

The bonded debt was also manageable and easier to document. The 1857 debt, still amounting to $339,000 when it fell due ten years later, was reduced to $54,500 by 1871; it would have disappeared altogether but for the reluctance of some owners to turn in their bonds. The road redeemed the bulk of these securities partly in cash and, so far as possible, by exchanging them for new bonds issued in pursuance of the 1867 mortgage loan. The stockholders had authorized $800,000 of new bonds in 1867. Next year they authorized an additional $700,000, bringing the total to the $1,500,000 allowable under the mortgage. The reason given for this increase was that much of the original amount was to be paid out in the controversial bond dividend that year. State Proxy Byron Laflin voted the state's 30,000 shares in favor of the increase, and it passed by 30,078 to 5,101. Only two private stockholders, with 78 shares, voted with Laflin.[67]

The additional $700,000 was not needed, however, and was never issued. In fact, the original $800,000 was not all used. Turner had issued $300,000 of the bonds by July 1868. The Smith administration issued another $470,000 by 1871. But only $492,000 of them were still outstanding at that time; Treasurer Lea reported the total bonded debt that year, both old and new, at $546,500.[68] The net earnings in 1870–71 amounted to two-thirds of that figure, and without the $480,000 in dividends paid in the past two years, the debt would nearly have been retired in 1871. There was no reason to doubt the road's ability to redeem the bonds well before the last of them reached maturity in 1887. William A. Graham was the trustee of a new sinking fund created to assure it. Unlike the original sinking fund, it received the appropriate payments on schedule, mostly in the form of the new bonds themselves.[69] Railroad historian John F. Stover lists the NCRR among the five major southern railroads that were operating profitably before the panic of 1873. All paid fairly regular dividends, had a low debt compared with net earnings, and enjoyed a low operating ratio of expenses compared with receipts. The NCRR ratio of 53 percent (in 1870–71) was better than the group's average of 59 percent.[70]

Returning prosperity was reflected in the quotations on NCRR stock and bonds. Although Josiah Turner accused the Republicans in January 1869 of destroying the value of NCRR bonds when the state had to cash in its bond dividend at 65 cents on the dollar, the facts soon proved otherwise. Five days later his own paper printed a quotation of 93 cents, and there or at par (100) it remained.[71] The reduced price in 1868 may have resulted from the state's well-recognized need to sell quickly. Similarly the scrip issued with the dividend started at 65 to 70 cents on the dollar, fell to 60, then remained at 75 or 80 through most of 1869. Secretary Stagg said it readily sold at face value in 1870.[72]

NCRR stock had sunk to $15 or $20 per share by 1867, and it remained there well into 1869. Then, buoyed by news of an impending lease to the Raleigh and Gaston, it climbed to $50 in October 1869.[73] When that arrangement fell through, the stock dropped to $33 in 1870, where it remained for some time after the Richmond and Danville lease in 1871.[74]

The 6 percent dividend of 1868, voted by the Worth/Turner board (though personally opposed by Turner), was somewhat fraudulent in that the stockholders received bonds and scrip that netted them only about 65 cents on the dollar if they tried to cash them right away. At the same time the road indebted itself for the full face value of the bonds, $240,000, plus 8 percent accrued interest over the years until the bonds reached maturity or were called in. Few people could be found to justify this dividend after it was declared. The Smith administration declared no dividend in 1869, but Smith that year promised one in 1870, "or he would forfeit his ears, and agree to be dismissed the service of the Company."[75] When the dividends did come, beginning in 1870, they were paid in cash.

Since 1855, when the legislature stipulated that its additional $1 million of stock should receive a 6 percent dividend before any other distributions were paid, many of the private stockholders had smarted under that discrimination. (In the first two dividends in 1859 and 1860 the road had paid 6 percent on the preferred stock and only 2 and 3 percent on the remainder.) In 1869, believing that the road could sometimes afford to pay smaller dividends and would do so but for that restriction, the stockholders requested that the state remove the obstacle by converting its preferred stock to common stock.[76] When a bill to that effect was introduced, the board decided that in case of passage it would declare a 3 percent dividend; but the bill did not pass.[77]

What the legislature did do, in spectacular fashion, was pass a law in February 1870 ordering the state directors to call a board meeting within ten days and to vote a dividend of all surplus earnings for the past year; the road was not to divert any of these earnings to pay debts not yet due.[78] This was an act of desperation. The Republican state government, having committed itself since 1868 to unprecedented expenditures for education, railroad construction, and other purposes, found itself on the verge of bankruptcy. Under this command the board assembled the very next day and declared a cash dividend of 6 percent, payable in two equal installments in April and July. The state's share was $180,000; it represented 24 percent of the state's expendable revenue that year.[79]

Democratic newspapers accused the legislators of forcing the dividend so as to receive their own per diem allowance, supposedly otherwise in jeopardy.[80] Over a decade later, Governor Holden wrote that his militia campaign against the Ku Klux Klan that year was delayed at least a month by the barrenness of the state treasury. Only after receiving the NCRR's July dividend installment could he proceed with the operation.[81] Soon part of the dividend would be returned to the road as compensation for transporting the state troops.

When a new Democratic legislature—partly a result of Holden's militia campaign—assembled late in 1870, the state was still in dire financial straits. Suggestions were therefore made that it borrow $180,000 from the NCRR in anticipation of the road's next dividend. A law authorizing such a loan was passed in January 1871, but it was not implemented.[82] The NCRR directors had already declared another 6 percent dividend for 1871, payable again in two installments. These promised the state $90,000 in March and again in July.[83] Under these political pressures the road may have declared dividends slightly in advance of its capacity to afford them. (According to Josiah Turner, bonds were issued at this time—among the last ones authorized under the 1867 mortgage—in order to pay company debts because the road's earnings were committed to dividends.)[84] This time circumstances intervened to prevent the state from collecting its dividend.

The state's cupboard was so bare that it stopped paying interest after October 1868 on the bonds it had issued in the 1850s to finance its contribution to the NCRR. This default was made easier, no doubt, by the fact that nearly all of the bondholders lived out of state. But one of them, Anthony H. Swasey of New York, obtained early in 1871 a federal court order sequestering all NCRR dividends to the state, beginning with those payable in March, in order to ensure payment of the interest due to the bondholders, which had legal priority. The Swasey case dragged on in the courts for years, and until 1882 the state received no further dividends from the NCRR.[85] In the postwar years before the lease, therefore, the state collected only the $117,600 from the sale of NCRR bonds in 1868 and $180,000 in cash in 1870.

20

To Sell, Merge, or Lease?

A GROWING BODY of thought around the country condemned government participation in business as inefficient if not downright immoral. Before the war, state and local governments in particular had invested in turnpikes, canals, river improvements, and railroads as a matter of public service and almost of necessity. In many areas, particularly the South and West, private capital was simply inadequate to finance the internal improvements that society demanded. But there were strings attached. Once public aid was extended, the public interest seemed to require some measure of government control or even participation in the projects it helped to finance. That in turn brought political influence in management, which businessmen regarded as intrusive, even disruptive.

As private capital became more widely available and businesses better able to manage themselves, the yoke of government control grew increasingly burdensome. Demands for government aid by no means ceased; on the contrary, the clamor for aid to railroads reached unprecedented levels in the Reconstruction era. But it was a demand for aid without significant strings attached. Governments were expected to act more nearly as investors than managers. Even where government had contributed the larger share of capital, it was widely believed that the private sector should remain dominant. Thus in Virginia, where state aid to railroads reached three-fifths of the total investment, the commonwealth deliberately limited its stock voting rights to two-fifths.[1] Whether active government participation was a benefit or a curse depended on individual circumstances that could vary from time to time on the same public work.[2]

So far as the NCRR was concerned, demands for change began early and took different forms. Serious efforts were made to lessen the state's stock voting rights in 1852–53 and its representation on the board of directors in 1858–59. As noted in Chapters 8 and 9, these were defeated by the stockholders in the one case and the legislature in the other.[3] Such efforts gained greater attention and support after the war.

The most drastic suggestion was that the state sell all of its railroad stock outright, including that in the NCRR. The state convention (acting as a legislature) actually provided for this in June 1866, not so much from philosophical conviction as to stave off state insolvency. It permitted the state to exchange its railroad stocks for outstanding state bonds, thereby canceling that much of the state debt.[4] The plan was supported by the Raleigh *Sentinel* and others who already had a predisposition against state involvement in railroad operations.[5]

There were legal complications in the case of the NCRR. Its charter pledged the state-owned stock and any dividends derived from it to repay the principal and interest on the state bonds that had been issued to finance the road's construction.[6] The state, then, might not have had a legal right to sell. In addition, the law required that the stocks be exchanged at their par value—far in excess of their market value. For these reasons, no doubt, there were no takers when the state advertised its $3 million in NCRR stock for bids. (This was the occasion on which the state's Raleigh and Gaston stock was sold, however, most of it to the road itself.) A month later the legislature put up its NCRR stock as collateral for state bonds issued to aid in extending the Western North Carolina Railroad.[7] That imposed a further obstacle to the state's selling it anytime soon.[8]

An exchange might have had other drawbacks as well. Neither the NCRR nor its private stockholders were in a position to purchase a significant share of the state's stock. Moreover a large proportion of the state bonds issued since the 1850s had been bought and were still held by northerners with little or no other tie to the state. Most North Carolinians, including the private stockholders, would not have rejoiced at the prospect of a controlling interest falling into the hands of outsiders, despite a remarkable effort at reassurance by the Raleigh *Sentinel*: "All experience proves that one Northern business man, in foresight, energy and frugality, is generally equal to half a dozen Southern men."[9]

The NCRR stockholders therefore mounted a simultaneous effort to increase their own power without affecting state ownership. In July 1866 they chose a committee (George W. Mordecai, Rufus Barringer, and William A. Caldwell) to formulate appropriate changes in the company charter and bylaws and to petition the legislature for the desired charter amendments.[10] These efforts were seen as part of a much-needed overhaul of the road's management.

With an eye on the recent Boyden administration and the almost annual turnovers among the state directors since 1863, the committee drew up a series of four charter amendments designed to transfer control of the road to its private stockholders:

1. Reduce the number of directors to nine, with the stockholders naming six of them. This change, they said, should ensure better management, as "all experience has proved that a divided responsibility between the State and individuals . . . has uniformly worked injuriously to both interests."

2. Limit the state proxy to casting one-third as many votes as the private stockholders were entitled to cast.

3. Require all directors, state or private, to own at least twenty shares of

stock instead of five shares, the existing requirement. "No person who has not some decided pecuniary interest in the Company, will be willing to devote sufficient of his time and attention to the details of its management."

4. Broaden into a total exemption the existing exemption of NCRR property from state and local taxation as long as the road paid dividends of no more than 6 percent. Under existing taxation, the state itself as three-quarters owner of the road would be paying three-quarters of the taxes, an absurdity. In return for the broader exemption the individual stockholders' dividends would become taxable.[11]

A special stockholders' meeting was called at Raleigh on 12 December 1866 to consider these proposals. The absence of the state proxy (which could hardly have been inadvertent) prevented any legal action. But the private stockholders approved the suggested amendments informally and authorized the committee to take them before the legislature, which was about to convene.

In explaining their proposals to the legislature, the committee argued that their sole object was to secure such management as would guarantee a dividend and enhance the value of company stock. This could only benefit the state's interest. As it was, they continued, state control discouraged efforts at reform: "The Governor, from the nature of his engagements, however much disposed, is utterly unable to make the best appointments [as directors], and after these appointments are made, whether wisely or unwisely, the history of the past, warrants the assertion, that little hope can be entertained of their being permanent. Owing to these frequent changes, the Company can adopt no fixed and permanent policy; and instability has consequently marked the government of the Road from its commencement."[12]

At almost the same time Governor Worth and the state board of internal improvements issued a report agreeing that the railroads in which the state had an interest would be better managed by their private stockholders, free of partisan influences. Their recommendation, to be implemented on an experimental basis, was that the legislature instruct the governor to cease appointing railroad directors altogether, leaving month-by-month control to the private directors. But at the same time they asked that the powers of the state proxies be standardized on the various roads and broadened to include a power of investigation in behalf of the state.[13] This plan was to be applied on all of the roads in which the state owned stock, including the NCRR. Whatever its merits, it certainly ran counter to Governor Worth's continuing efforts to redirect the leadership and policies of the NCRR.

William W. Holden's *North Carolina Standard* had another suggestion. It argued early in 1866 that the state had too little power to regulate the railroads in which it had an interest. If the state chose to retain that interest, the *Standard* urged that a superintendent of public works be created with general oversight over all the internal improvements in which it had a voice. The superintendent could then establish some uniformity in their management and direct their operations so as to promote the public interest.[14] That office was created by the constitution of 1868, but Holden as governor in 1869 clashed with the superintendent when he tried to assume the duties that Holden as editor had described in 1866.

The absence of the state proxy from the December stockholders' meeting probably reflected Worth's unwillingness for the moment to commit himself or the state to the proposals of the stockholders' committee, which were more drastic and permanent than his own. Or perhaps he was not charmed with the unflattering characterization of gubernatorial appointees to the board. The legislature was not ready to commit itself either. Its immediate response to the stockholder proposals was the Robins committee investigation in January 1867.

The most articulate opponent of giving up state control turned out to be Josiah Turner, who never bothered to reconcile this position with his opposite view in 1859, when he said that "politicians were not the right sort of men to manage public works—they did not get up early enough in the morning."[15] He was now about to launch his second campaign for the NCRR presidency. Turner freely conceded that there had been mismanagement in the NCRR but declared that this was not the state's fault. "Now that we stand upon the verge of bankruptcy and ruin by reason of our own indifference, neglect and bad management," he told the stockholders at the special meeting in December 1866, "instead of facing the difficulty like men, instead of correcting our errors and abuses, gentlemen are looking out for a scapegoat, and they have found him in the person of the State." In effect, said Turner, echoing previous presidents of the road, the NCRR had been under the control of the stockholders from the beginning, with state directors and proxies uniting behind the presidents who had been chosen primarily from and by the private directors. More economical management under existing auspices was needed. (This was a rare issue on which Turner and William W. Holden agreed.)[16]

The publication of Turner's remarks set off a newspaper debate between him and Rufus Barringer, a member of the stockholders' committee. In a series of letters to the Raleigh *Sentinel*, Barringer argued that Turner's cry of "retrenchment and reform" was not enough; it had been called for repeatedly in the past and ignored. He praised the state for its generosity in getting the road started and conceded that the public and private directors had usually been in agreement. The real problem was the system of joint authority, which by its nature led to joint evasion of responsibility. "It is under the shelter of this mongrel management, this divided responsibility, that all of the abuses of this Road are covered up." The system "inspires no zeal, no pride, no energy, no confidence, no hope." Capitalists saw this and refused to invest wherever the state was involved.[17]

The NCRR, Barringer continued, "is erroneously regarded as a public work. . . . In point of fact, it is a private corporation, intended to make money for the Stockholders—the State included. The best service a railroad can render a community, is to pay dividends to its Stockholders. This is a sure index of efficiency. Efficiency secures safety, dispatch and fair dealing." But in the case of the NCRR that was impossible; it was subjected to every local, personal, sectional, and political influence. The controlling state directors were always influenced in some degree by party politics. As soon as their appointments were known in the spring,

> their predilections in public life are canvassed, combinations are formed to influence the election of the four Stockholders' Directors, and thus control the choice of officers and the policy of the Road. If the State appointments are not made on party grounds, they are certain to be selected on account of mere personal or local considerations. Thus the Board is invariably made up, in great part, of men, selected, not because of their pecuniary interest in the work or peculiar fitness for the duty; but for reasons and motives positively adverse to the interests of the Company. They are all apt to be politicians, who have friends to make or enemies to punish; prominent lawyers, who have neither time, taste or talent for the dull routine of figures and statistics; or shrewd wire workers, who are always selfish, and prove dangerous men, where public interests are involved. The grand result is an army of officials, employees, contractors and 'dead heads,' no dividends, a rapidly increasing debt, a constantly depreciating stock, destitute stockholders and a bankrupt State! . . . [Only] the love and hope of private gain, that mighty principle of human action, can resist, overcome and conquer the tendencies of this corporation to demoralization and ruin.[18]

To this onslaught Turner replied that the sins of the Boyden administration (Barringer's most salient examples) were as much attributable to the private directors that year as to the state directors. These four men (Thomas Webb, Cyrus P. Mendenhall, Dolphin A. Davis, and John L. Morehead) were all substantial stockholders with a long interest in the road. In fact, Turner observed, all roads are governed by their presidents and superintendents, not by their boards of directors.[19]

This exchange took place very shortly after the Robins committee finished its investigation. As with Worth's inquiry in 1859, the Robins report brought criticism of the road's management but no charter amendments or other legislation to modify its organic structure. Nor did the legislature implement Governor Worth's proposal to cease appointing state directors and thereby turn the railroads over to their private stockholders de facto. Legislators did not explain why they neglected or refused to make any of these changes. Turner's arguments probably carried weight, and there must have been a reluctance to give away the state's powers when the merits were so debatable.

Another consideration had not gotten much publicity: what persons and policies would prevail on the NCRR if the state withdrew? Political maneuvering on the road had not been limited to the state directors. Some observers like Veritas, (David F. Caldwell?) writing in the *Greensboro Patriot*, charged a clique of major stockholders with trying to run the road in their own interest. Veritas did not name names, but he clearly had in mind George W. Mordecai, Paul C. Cameron, John L. Morehead, and members of the Holt family, among others. He accused them of buying stock at the cheap prices for which it was currently selling, voting themselves or their favorites into directorships, and then trying to award the presidency to the man with the largest vote.[20] Their favorite seemed still to be Thomas Webb. This was the group (tied in some measure to the Raleigh and Gaston) whom Worth had been trying to overthrow. Casting the road into their hands was not quite the reform that Worth, and probably many legislators, had in mind. Better retain the present system and try to reform it from within through a new president imposed by the state. The ensuing Turner administration appeared to do just that.

Then the political revolution of 1868 swept in with a new set of actors and policies. Republicans came to power full of enthusiasm for building railroads and rejuvenating the economy. Their enthusiasm quickly outpaced their capital, their credit, and their sense of discretion. The legislature of 1868–69 threw caution and the constitution to the winds in extending state credit to a variety of actual or prospective railroads across the state. Public reaction and sober second thought led the same legislators in 1869–70 to withdraw much of that aid, which had not actually been granted.[21]

Meanwhile minor-league Vanderbilts, Drews, and Fisks (lesser figures if only because they commanded less capital) had a speculative field day. The biggest operator in North Carolina (and for a time, in Florida) was George W. Swepson, whose railroading career had begun in 1859 as NCRR station agent at Haw River. Closely allied with him was General Milton S. Littlefield, formerly of the United States Army, who became the chief lobbyist in Raleigh for the "railroad ring." The reputed ringmaster within the legislature was Representative (and former Union General) Byron Laflin of Pitt County, who doubled as Governor Holden's proxy on the NCRR. Other members were Samuel McD. Tate, sometime president of the Western North Carolina Railroad, and Dr. William Sloan, president of the Wilmington, Charlotte, and Rutherford Railroad and sometime state director on the NCRR. Lacking investment capital for their schemes, Swepson and his allies sought to create it by issuing bonds—railroad bonds from the roads they controlled and state bonds issued in behalf of those roads—and then manipulating their value on the market.

Swepson had the further idea in 1868 of buying the state's share of the NCRR, probably using state bonds already issued in behalf of the WNCRR, which he and his friends controlled. A bill was introduced in the legislature to that end and was pushed vigorously by his lobbyist, former Senator Thomas L. Clingman. The same argument was used as in 1866: have the state exchange its NCRR stock for outstanding state bonds that it could cancel and thereby retire so much of the intimidating state debt. With the NCRR in their grasp, Swepson and company would control the centerpiece in the state's railway system and further their efforts to acquire more. He seems also to have hoped for Conservative support, aimed at removing the Republicans' largest patronage outlet. But the bill meant dismantling the state's railroad system, which to many seemed a retrograde step. Josiah Turner, newly installed as editor of the Raleigh *Sentinel*, bitterly opposed the bill. So did most other Democratic editors. On top of this, Swepson and his friend Littlefield fled Raleigh while the bill was under consideration in order to avoid testifying about their activities. The House defeated the measure in April 1869 by a bipartisan vote of 65 to 19.[22]

William A. Smith's successful management of the road went far to stave off such efforts. More than a few suspicious and fearful Democrats, and some Republicans too, had advocated private management if not ownership at the time the Republicans took over in July 1868.[23] Much of that sentiment faded as Smith's administration began to produce dividends. The Raleigh *Standard*, which had shared the sentiment for private control a year earlier, rejoiced in June 1869 at Smith's management "because it gives us a practical illustration of a paying railroad in which the State has an interest."[24]

Nevertheless some sentiment remained for selling the state's stock. Proposals to this effect were made in the legislature and the press every year. To some it seemed the least painful way to bring the state debt down to manageable proportions. Former NCRR Treasurer William A. Caldwell suggested late in 1869 that the state sell its $2 million in common stock, retaining only the $1 million of preferred stock. President Smith himself favored this plan if, as he feared, legislators were determined to sell in some fashion.[25] Smith also showed interest in a suggestion that the NCRR buy its own stock from the state, much as the Raleigh and Gaston had in 1866.[26] The *Raleigh Telegram* tried to refute the argument that if the state sold its railway stocks they would fall into the hands of outsiders, meaning Yankee capitalists. These people already held the state debt and would have to improve the railroads to make them profitable, thereby helping North Carolinians as well.[27]

Josiah Turner fought valiantly against every attempt to alienate the road, but at times his opposition shaded into paranoia. He persisted in calling Holden an advocate of sale despite the governor's clear statements to the contrary. In February 1870 he facetiously advised legislators to sell their votes in this matter for no less than $10,000; some of the more articulate might get $50,000. "Hands [his term for Republican members], we tell you, this is the last chance for a fortune, let no man value himself too low."[28]

Ultimately there was no sale, partly because Governor Holden too opposed any change in the road's status, citing Smith's record, and partly because other alternatives, like a lease, seemed more attractive.[29] Moreover the ring was less powerful in this session, which repealed a goodly share of the previous year's railway largesse.

There was a distinct possibility for some years that the state would be forced to sell its NCRR stock by a federal court order in the Swasey case, mentioned in Chapter 19. This stock was pledged by the 1849 charter to pay the interest due on the state bonds issued to help finance the NCRR's construction. Bondholder Swasey asked the court for such an order, but instead it ordered that the bondholders be paid regularly from the state's NCRR dividends, which was done. In 1882 most of the bondholders agreed to accept new state bonds for the old. The threat to the state's stock receded, and it began again to collect its NCRR dividends.[30]

Simultaneous with the debate over sale of the state's NCRR stock was another over merger with the Atlantic and North Carolina Railroad. This too was a hardy perennial with roots in the prewar period. The NCRR had been chartered as the centerpiece of a railroad system that was to extend from the mountains to the sea. The state could not afford to build this all at once, and the system was created in three separate pieces with the NCRR first and the two flankers following. The A&NC and the Western North Carolina Railroad were both chartered in 1854, with the state providing two-thirds of the capital. Four years later the eastern road was completed from Goldsboro through New Bern to Morehead City, a distance of ninety-six miles. It was always dependent, for more than local traffic, on the ports of New Bern and Beaufort/Morehead City. Neither developed very much, owing to shifting sands, shallow waters, and the treacherous winds off Hatteras. The A&NC was thus a marginal road financially despite the best efforts of its managers and local boosters.

Those efforts increasingly took the form of advocating merger—people generally called it consolidation—with the NCRR. Only by bringing the two roads together under common management, so the argument went, could the real potentiality of the eastern road and its seaports be realized. Only then would the NCRR find it to its own interest to send its traffic to the state's own seaports instead of those in Virginia. It was an emotional argument, for the most part, stronger in state pride than economic analysis.

To a lesser degree, consolidation efforts also embraced the Western North Carolina Railroad, which remained a dead-end road running from Salisbury to the foot of the mountains. (It was extended from Morganton to Old Fort by the end of 1869.) Also marginal, the WNCRR had at least theoretically a shining future once it surmounted the topographical barrier and connected with roads in Tennessee and beyond.

The A&NC had no such future, except in combination with the NCRR. As a result, consolidation was pushed most strongly by the eastern road and its supporters. Legally such a measure required approval by the legislature as well as the stockholders of both roads. Efforts were made in the legislature in 1858 and again in early 1866 to merge the NCRR with the A&NC or with both of the other two state roads. Both attempts failed, but efforts would continue.[31]

Within months of the most recent defeat, John Motley Morehead entered the fray in July 1866 with a long communication addressed to the NCRR stockholders. The former governor and NCRR president was a lifelong champion of North Carolina's economic development and particularly of its mountains-to-sea railroad system. There is no question of his dedication to the completion of that system as a matter of state pride and deeply held conviction. But he had a clear economic interest as well. From the beginning Morehead had been a heavy investor in the A&NC and in Morehead City. In fact, he was a principal contractor in building that road and had not been fully paid. He was involved in a running dispute over the amount of the debt, which was unresolved at his death later that year. Along with the A&NC's other creditors Morehead stood to lose the greater part of his investment if that road went into bankruptcy and was reorganized by means of scaling down its debt, as usually happened. For a mixture of reasons, therefore, and in what proved to be his last political effort, Morehead pushed for consolidation of the roads that he had been so instrumental in creating. In this effort he included the WNCRR as well as the central and eastern roads. His letter to the NCRR stockholders eloquently set forth the history of the three roads and their common purpose. Now, he concluded, was the time to bring about their long-deferred consolidation.[32]

There was no lack of opposition. Wilmington saw consolidation as a threat to itself and its Wilmington and Weldon Railroad. Western North Carolinians favored strengthening the WNCRR but shied away from any measure forcing them to pay the unavoidably higher shipping rates encountered at New Bern and Morehead City.[33] The perception was widespread that the existing north-south trade routes had developed for good economic reasons; North Carolina's ports were not well favored by nature. Thus efforts to change these traffic patterns would be both expensive and doomed to failure. The Raleigh *Sentinel* equated the channels of trade with laws of nature. It also feared, with the Charlotte *Democrat*, that a combination of all three railroads would become too large to function efficiently and perhaps too powerful politically for the public good.[34]

Most NCRR stockholders, finally, saw little benefit in tying their road to such an unprofitable venture as the Atlantic and North Carolina. The merit of consolidation rested ultimately on the prospects of making New Bern or Morehead City into rivals of Norfolk. Given their disadvantages, that expectation was unrealistic. As one person put it, the only way to increase the through traffic via New Bern and Morehead City would be to make it a criminal offense to go by any other route.[35] Much the same consideration applied to the western road as long as it remained stalled east of the mountains. The chance of surmounting that barrier anytime soon seemed dim; certainly it was beyond the present capacity of the NCRR.

When Morehead's communication reached them, therefore, the stockholders discussed it, voted respectfully to receive and print it, then ignored it.[36] Morehead died in October, his goal unrealized. Consolidation was an external issue introduced for the most part by parties outside the NCRR with their own interests to advance. It seems not to have come up at the special stockholders' meeting in November, called to deal with what was to them the much more appealing question of private stockholder control.

Consolidation lay dormant until 1868. The A&NC worked valiantly to improve through traffic facilities with the NCRR and other railroad and steamship lines, but to little avail. Josiah Turner's policy in 1867–68 of sending NCRR freight through Goldsboro benefited the W&W far more than the A&NC. The coastal road, in desperation, even thought of abandoning its own ports in favor of close traffic arrangements to Norfolk.[37]

Before doing that, it once more appealed for a merger with the NCRR. This time both roads, like the legislature, were under Republican control; perhaps that would make a difference. Proponents pushed even harder than in 1866. There were reports that the railroad ring had taken it up. (The ring was in its heyday during the sessions of 1868 and 1869.) This seems unlikely, as Josiah Turner and other enemies of the ring and its railroad aid measures were in favor of consolidation.[38] In any event, a consolidation bill approving the matter and referring it to the stockholders of both roads sailed through both houses early in 1869. The state proxies would then be entitled to cast the determining votes.[39] How they might vote would depend in part on a resolution of the impending controversy over who had the power to appoint them—the governor or the superintendent of public works. In either case, there might be a readiness to listen to the private stockholders.

President Smith was an outspoken opponent of consolidation and worked actively to mobilize the NCRR stockholders against it. He sent communications to them and to the newspapers charging that it would impose a dead weight on the newly profitable NCRR. "Our true policy," he argued, "is to work with the shortest, quickest, and the cheapest lines North and South, both as regards passengers and freight. This has been my policy the present year, and has thus far proved successful. Any combination or consolidation with other roads which would tend to make your line longer from South to North, or . . . try to force the freight and passengers out of their natural channel, or to inferior ports and over longer lines, will certainly destroy your present bright prospects for the future."[40]

The consolidation issue generated a substantial body of literature through the greater part of 1869. Except for eastern papers that favored (or in the case of Wilmington opposed) it warmly, newspapers were much less committed on this issue than they were on the questions of sale or lease. The

Sentinel under Turner mildly favored consolidation as a means of unifying the state and frustrating ring efforts to sell the NCRR. The Republican *Standard* mildly opposed it as impractical. The *Greensboro Patriot* was on both sides of the issue and then in the middle within a period of five months.[41]

Attention was now focused on the NCRR stockholders. (The A&NC shareholders were firmly committed to merger.) President Edward R. Stanly of the A&NC invited the stockholders of both roads to a meeting in New Bern on 2 June to discuss the merits of consolidation; there would also be an opportunity, the invitation stated, to examine the shipping facilities at New Bern and Beaufort. As everyone recognized, this was actually to be a sales meeting combined with a seashore excursion. Stanly invited Governor Holden as well, but there is no evidence he attended.[42] Many NCRR stockholders, their families, and the newspaper press availed themselves of the free passes offered by the two railroads—very grudgingly in the case of the NCRR. Once at New Bern some of them were treated to a steamboat ride, and at least 600 were taken by rail to Beaufort harbor where they viewed the commercial facilities and enjoyed an evening dance. How many stockholders were converted is not known, but a number of newspaper editors clearly were. It was a public relations triumph.[43]

Anticipating as much, Smith countered with an excursion to Norfolk two weeks later. This was also free to stockholders and newspaper editors but open to the general public as well at a reduced fare amounting to $8 roundtrip from Charlotte. The Raleigh and Gaston and the Seaboard and Roanoke railroads were only too happy to cooperate. So was the Norfolk board of trade, which promised a banquet and a steamboat trip to Old Point Comfort and the capes.[44] On the appointed day, a special train left Charlotte, picked up additional cars at Company Shops, and joined a waiting R&G train at Raleigh. About fifteen cars long with at least 900 passengers, it headed northward with Smith and officers of the other two roads serving as hosts. At Norfolk they were met by the mayor, and two steamboats took them to Fortress Monroe (at Old Point Comfort) where the army treated them to a military dress parade. After the promised banquet in Norfolk, the travelers returned to Raleigh for closing ceremonies including "an appropriate and neat little speech of about ten minutes" by President Smith.[45]

Governor Holden seems to have leaned against consolidation. But the issue was so divisive within the Republican party and across the state that he refused to take a public stand. He reappointed all of the sitting directors on both roads, those on the A&NC known to favor consolidation and those on the NCRR opposed. He preferred to leave the decision to the private stockholders and gave no instructions to the state proxies, except perhaps not to vote on the question. It was foreordained that the A&NC stockholders would favor consolidation; they did so at their June meeting by 1,228 to 73.[46] Actually Holden was much more concerned with the simultaneous contest between him and Superintendent of Public Works Ceburn L. Harris for control of all the state-owned railroads. Harris was widely perceived to favor consolidation, hence the A&NC stockholders' vote to accept him as the state proxy.[47]

The NCRR stockholders were scheduled to meet at Salisbury on 8 July. They were thought to oppose consolidation, though it was by no means certain. That issue, coupled with the Holden/Harris dispute featuring rival court injunctions, promised an exciting meeting. Stockholders and their families, enjoying free passes, flocked to Salisbury. The governor himself arrived on a special train, though he remained in the background. Smith prepared to do battle on the front lines against both Harris and the consolidationists. He was in rare form as he delivered his major speech, and the audience was vastly entertained. In the process he antagonized many fellow Republicans around the state with his remarks about the current legislature, but his immediate constituency was the predominantly Democratic stockholders. His management during the past year, if not this speech, went far to win them over to his leadership.

Smith assailed the Republican legislature for its profligate railway policies in the last session, creating new roads that threatened the existing ones with ruinous competition while grinding the taxpayers into poverty to pay for them. The measure to make Harris state proxy on all the roads was sneaked through as a trick, he said, presumably because the ring could control him. And the consolidation bill was a piece of hypocrisy. Its backers' cry of "Good old North Carolina" was a mask to enhance their own property around New Bern and Morehead City. Smith ridiculed the Morehead City excursion. First-class ships had been advertised to convey the visitors around the deep and spacious Beaufort harbor; what they actually got was a fishing smack that ran aground. Otherwise the only things they saw were sand banks and banker ponies. "The truth is, this Atlantic Road is a humbug. Its real name is the Mullet Road, for its principal freight consist in fish, and occasionally oysters. . . . Our freights in one month are equal to a whole year's earnings of this Mullet Road." Why hang it around the neck of the NCRR?

Josiah Turner was so delighted with this performance that he forgot his own advocacy of consolidation and, for the moment, his hatred of Smith. When the question of consolidation came to a vote, it was defeated, 6,594 to 2,045, the state proxy not voting.[48]

Consolidationists renewed the attack at the next legislative session, this time with a bill to merge all three railroads and instructing the state proxies to vote in favor. When that bill failed they took up another empowering the A&NC to buy that part of the NCRR between Raleigh and Goldsboro. If the A&NC could not merge with the NCRR, at least it would be in a better position to compete with the R&G if it ran to Raleigh.[49] The NCRR board passed a resolution in February 1870, while this measure was pending, unanimously rejecting it as injurious to the state and the stockholders.[50] Although the eastern section of the road had never paid well, something Smith now chose to dispute, he argued cogently that losing it would lessen the NCRR's access to Wilmington by removing its connection with the W&W and would limit its bargaining power with the other two roads.[51]

This bill too failed. It was renewed in 1871 and this time passed, but in a form that left the decision to the NCRR private stockholders. They were authorized to sell the Raleigh-Goldsboro section to the A&NC in return for $650,000 of the latter's stock.[52] Smith exaggerated only slightly when he characterized this as an act to give away that section of the road, since the A&NC stock was worthless.[53] The NCRR stockholders deliberately aborted their meeting in 1871 during the crisis over legislative versus gubernatorial control. But a legal meeting would surely have rejected the A&NC purchase. The NCRR stockholders actually approved a three-way merger with the A&NC and the WNCRR in 1874. But the Richmond and Danville lease seemed to make the issue passé, and it was not pursued then.[54] The question of merger with the A&NC would continue to surface occasionally in later years and would finally triumph in 1989. (See Chapter 21.)

When the lease issue first arose, it came not from the Richmond and Danville but from the Raleigh and Gaston. Located along one of the major north-south traffic lines (unlike the A&NC), the R&G nevertheless suffered because it formed one side of a triangle, and freight (more easily than passengers) could be forced around the other two sides via Goldsboro as Turner had done in 1867. In addition, its partners could extort financial concessions from it, using that same threat. By 1871, in the allocation of through freight receipts, the NCRR received a share equal to its full length of 223 miles despite the fact that it actually carried most of that freight only 175 miles from Charlotte to Raleigh; the R&G had to pay the difference to the NCRR according to its agreement with Turner in 1868. Similarly, the Seaboard and Roanoke, 79 miles long, and the Petersburg Railroad, 62 miles long, each managed to get a pro rata share based on a length of 97 miles. The R&G was actually 97 miles long and was allotted precisely that amount, equal to its two shorter partners. It smarted under these discriminations.[55]

The R&G had been credited with good management ever since its reorganization in the 1850s. For a road of its size and circumstances it was in sound financial condition. Faced with the prospect of disaster if it did not reverse Turner's Goldsboro policy, it actually offered to buy the NCRR in July 1867 although the latter was more than twice as long. The NCRR board, recovering from its shock, declined the offer as it did later proposals to lease the road.[56] The R&G now turned to reversing Turner's policy. It accomplished this early in 1868 by offering the NCRR cash payments to regain the lost freight. These amounted to $60,000 in 1868–69 and were expected to be $80,000 the next year.[57]

But in October 1869, as soon as the danger of consolidation with the A&NC had receded, the R&G returned with an offer of a twenty-year lease at 6 percent, or $240,000 per year—more than the previous offers. The NCRR board found this proposal much more interesting. By a vote of 9 to 1, they empowered President Smith to negotiate a lease—with anyone—on terms at least as favorable as those offered by the R&G, and they called a special stockholders' meeting for 11 November to ratify whatever agreement was made.[58] Smith solicited higher bids from other sources, but none came forward until the last minute.[59]

Smith was as emphatically in favor of this lease as he had been opposed to consolidation with the A&NC. The NCRR had never yet been able to pay a peacetime cash dividend of 6 percent, and the offer of that amount every year was highly attractive. The very prospect of this income was said to have doubled the price of NCRR stock from about $25 to $50 per share.[60] In a different vein, Smith argued that without an arrangement of this sort the NCRR was condemned to perpetual instability. The plaything of politicians, it was subject to perennially shifting political winds, resulting in changing directorships and administrations as well as threats of consolidation with the doomed Atlantic road. And it burned a hole in the pockets of legislators and others who could think of nothing else than selling off the state's share in order to lessen the public debt. The lease would help to preserve, if it did not altogether assure, continued state ownership. At the same time it guaranteed a steady profit of 6 percent to the stockholders, including the state, once the debts were paid.

Still further, Smith argued, the lease might avert a grave danger to the NCRR in the form of a new railroad running directly from Raleigh to Columbia, South Carolina—sixty miles shorter than the existing route via the NCRR. During the war the state had chartered, and the NCRR helped to support, the Chatham Railroad, intended to run southward from Raleigh to the coal fields along the Deep River in southern Chatham (now Lee) County. Construction had not progressed very far, but in 1868 an extension to Columbia was chartered as part of the railroad fever that dominated that legislature. Were this plan consummated, the NCRR could expect to lose a great part of its through traffic. The R&G controlled the Chatham Railroad, and the lease might deter completion of the extension.[61] Other lines in contemplation or actually under construction—from Statesville to the Virginia-Tennessee line, from Wilmington to Charlotte, and from Fayetteville to either Salisbury or Greensboro—would further drain business from the NCRR. With all that competition, Smith asked, how could the road ever achieve a profit level equal to what the R&G was offering?[62]

Opposition to the lease surfaced quickly and overwhelmingly. Almost overnight it became, in the *Standard*'s words, "the absorbing subject of interest in the state." Josiah Turner turned against it as forcefully as he had against the road's sale. Editorials or communications from like-minded persons appeared in the *Sentinel* virtually every day during the three weeks between the announcement of the offer and the special stockholders' meeting. Typically, Turner was not always careful in either facts or fairness. He grudgingly admitted—because it served his present purpose—that NCRR income was rising under Smith's management; hence $240,000 was not nearly enough rental. If the road had to be leased, he said, then auction it off to the highest bidder. (That is close to what Smith and the board were trying to do.) A number of opponents feared that the lease would create a monopoly strong enough to dominate the state. Turner originally characterized it as a ring measure fobbed off by Smith and his colleagues in a secret meeting without advance notice. He even accused R&G President W. J. Hawkins of bribing unnamed parties on the NCRR (who else but Smith?) to accept the lease.

Much of this argument was hard to take seriously. Turner produced no evidence of ring involvement, much less bribery, and he eventually reversed that argument, saying that the ring opposed the deal as an obstacle to its own efforts to buy the NCRR. As usual, Turner found Holden's hand in the deal although the governor never publicly favored the lease, did nothing to forward it, and eventually helped to kill it. Holden's mouthpiece, the *Standard*, came close to favoring the measure initially but quickly joined the opposition. Most other papers seem to have opposed it from the outset while praising Smith's management of the road.[63]

On 11 November the NCRR stockholders assembled in the senate chamber of the capitol building in Raleigh. Richard C. Badger was seated as state proxy in place of Byron Laflin, who had served during the two previous annual meetings. It was becoming clear by now that opinion around the state and among the stockholders opposed the lease. Smith tried to salvage it by suggesting postponement to the next annual meeting. At this point the picture was complicated by the unheralded appearance of a new bid similar to the R&G's but for an additional $25,000 per year. The bidder was A. K. McClure of Philadelphia, heretofore unknown to the vast majority of stockholders but soon identified as an agent of the Pennsylvania Railroad. In the ensuing discussion some of the most influential stockholders, including William A. Graham, William A. Caldwell, and Rufus Barringer, spoke out against any lease. But if we are going to market, observed Graham, he preferred McClure as the higher bidder. Few spoke in favor. The meeting ended with a vote (by Badger as well as most of the private stockholders) to postpone the question indefinitely. McClure thereupon withdrew his offer. Badger announced that the governor had instructed him to oppose the lease; in agreeing to postpone he understood it as tantamount to rejection.[64] A few days later, in his annual message to the legislature, Holden confirmed his opposition to any lease or sale of the road.[65]

A new merger issue arose in 1870, this time favored by the NCRR management. In response to longstanding desires by the northwestern counties of the state for railroad service, the constitutional convention of 1868 had chartered a Northwestern North Carolina Railroad (NWNCRR) to run from some point on the NCRR to Salem. Later legislation authorized its extension either northward to Mt. Airy or westward to Wilkesboro and beyond. The company quickly organized, and by the end of April 1868 Cyrus P. Mendenhall, David F. Caldwell, and other Greensboro residents had secured its eastern terminus for their town by agreeing to finance the grading as far as the Forsyth County line.[66] In 1869 the NCRR bought $20,000 of the new road's stock and arranged with it for joint terminal facilities in Greensboro. Grading was completed to Salem by the summer of 1870, but funds gave out before any track could be laid. (The proffered state aid carried too many strings and was not accepted.)[67] Hence President Edward Belo of the NWNCRR in July 1870 proposed a merger with the NCRR. His terms were not acceptable, but the NCRR stockholders authorized the board to negotiate an agreement subject to later stockholder ratification.[68]

The Northwestern road seemed to offer great potential for the NCRR. Beyond its value as a local feeder line, enhancing and bringing in the produce of the upper Yadkin valley, it might be extended across the mountains to connect with the profitable East Tennessee and Virginia road.[69]

William A. Smith fortuitously was elected to the state senate at this time and saw his opportunity to kill two birds with one stone. As soon as the new legislature assembled in November 1870, he introduced a bill to merge the NCRR and the NWNCRR, extending the latter to the Tennessee border. The bill also proposed giving the private stockholders a majority of the stock in the combined road, thus assuring private stockholder control. (Smith had confided to William A. Graham a year earlier that the NCRR "has allways [*sic*] been controlled by party and as long as it is, it will be impossible for it to pay the stockholders long at a time.")[70] That provision ensured the opposition of Josiah Turner and others who valued state control of the NCRR. And protagonists of the Western North Carolina Railroad feared that the merger would divert attention from their road and defer even longer the hopes of reaching Tennessee and the Great West by that route. The bill died, therefore—even as Smith himself was deprived of his senate seat by the Democratic majority as a prelude to impeaching Governor Holden.[71]

The legislature did, however, pass a less controversial bill on this subject. Avoiding the question of stockholder control, it allowed the NWNCRR to merge with any connecting road that would complete its track to Salem.[72] The NCRR accordingly resumed negotiations with it. The directors actually approved a contract for its purchase in August 1871. At that point simultaneous and more urgent dealings with the Richmond and Danville intervened, culminating in the NCRR's own absorption by lease. Negotiations with the Northwestern road had probably continued to this point because of the possibility that the R&D agreement might result in a lease only of that part of the NCRR between Greensboro and Charlotte. In such a case, with the NCRR still operating from Goldsboro to Greensboro, the prospective road to Salem and beyond would have remained highly desirable. As it was, the NWNCRR contract was canceled. But the R&D soon acquired that road too and completed it to Salem in 1873.[73]

21

The Lease and Beyond, 1871–1990

THE OUTSIDE WORLD was rapidly closing in on the NCRR. The road had never existed in isolation; through traffic arrangements were anticipated at the time of its charter. From the beginning these relationships grew in volume, value, and complexity. An expanding economy created a demand for faster and cheaper transportation over longer distances and supplied the means of attaining it. Wartime requirements intensified the demand. Continued profits, even continued existence, required ever-greater efficiency on the part of every individual road. In time individuality itself became an obstacle to efficiency and economy. In 1850 hardly any railroad could afford to build or operate a line more than 200 miles long. In 1880 hardly any railroad could afford not to. Those that could not grow were absorbed by those that could.[1]

As it turned out, the NCRR was among the great majority that were absorbed. Owing to its quasi-political nature, it may have lacked the flexibility required to survive in the competitive jungle that flourished after the Civil War. Two-thirds of the board, the state proxy, and sometimes the president and other officers were chosen in part for political reasons. Shifting political winds hampered continuity and planning, particularly in the crucial years from 1865 to 1868 when competitive pressures on the road were multiplying. On the other hand, there is ample testimony that the state's voice in NCRR management was minimal and that the public and private directors almost invariably acted in unison, supporting policies set forth by the president and superintendent.[2] First and foremost, the NCRR failed to survive as an independent operation because it lacked the capital to do so. So did most other railroads. One by one, they were taken over, reorganized, and amalgamated by those organizations, chiefly in the North, who had the necessary resources. Large northern roads led the way, sometimes using southern roads as their agents. But in time they too were taken over or forced aside by investment banking firms with still greater resources.

The Richmond and Danville was a well-managed railroad. Although the state of Virginia owned 60 percent of its stock, it remained under private control and prospered under the leadership of Algernon S. Buford after 1865. Even before Buford's time, the R&D managers were uncommonly aggressive. Their future was so obviously dependent on developing through connections with the NCRR and roads farther south that it became a fix- ation. They built the Piedmont connection to Greensboro with this end in mind and pursued it relentlessly thereafter.[3] It was in the NCRR's interest to carry freight and passengers as far east as possible. Yet every through traffic agreement it made with the Raleigh and Gaston or the roads farther east tended to restrict the R&D to serving as a local carrier in the southern side of Virginia. Buford's efforts to reach comparable agreements with the NCRR had so little success that he set out to lease that part of the road between Greensboro and Charlotte—the only part that really interested him. Leasing the entire road came only on the insistence of the NCRR management.[4]

By the time of the lease, the R&D itself was no longer operating as an independent agent. The Pennsylvania Railroad, under J. Edgar Thomson and Thomas A. Scott, was one of the giants of American railroading. Enjoy- ing a prosperity well established before the war, it was now paying cash dividends of 8 to 10 percent. Its gross earnings of $22 million in 1872 were half as great as the total of the seventy major railroads in the South.[5] In 1869 the Pennsylvania embarked on a massive expansion campaign that would soon take its lines into New York, Chicago, and Washington. It then turned southward, acquiring control of existing roads by lease if possible, by purchase if necessary. Until the panic of 1873 forced a gradual with- drawal, it constructed a kind of satellite empire extending from Washington to Atlanta. One of the first tentative steps in this southward expansion was A. K. McClure's effort to lease the NCRR in November 1869 in the wake of the Raleigh and Gaston attempt. Between May and August 1871 the Penn- sylvania bought the state of Virginia's 60-percent share of stock in the Rich- mond and Danville Railroad. (Virginia was doing what North Carolina had attempted to do in 1866: exchange its state-owned railway stock for out- standing state bonds, thereby reducing the state debt.) This purchase and some of those that followed were actually made by a holding company— probably the first of its kind—the Southern Railway Security Company, controlled by Scott in the interest of the Pennsylvania Railroad.[6]

The Pennsylvania's interest was identical with the R&D's to create a through railroad line to Atlanta. Sometimes using the R&D as its proxy, it gained control of about a dozen southern railroads in rapid succession by the end of 1871. Collectively, they comprised a large part of the world the NCRR had operated in from its birth: the Richmond and Petersburg; the Charlotte, Columbia, and Augusta; the Atlanta and Richmond Air Line (an overnamed road then being constructed between Atlanta and Charlotte); the NCRR's old rival, the Wilmington and Weldon; its southern connection, the Wilmington, Columbia, and Augusta (formerly Wilmington and Manchester); the Northeastern Railroad and the Cheraw and Darlington, both in South Carolina; their trans-Appalachian rival, the East Tennessee, Virginia, and Georgia; and the little Northwestern North Carolina Railroad from Greensboro to Salem. The Pennsylvania also tried and failed in 1871 to buy a controlling share of the Raleigh and Gaston. The roads it did acquire provided three major through routes between the Northeast and the Deep South: a coastal line from the Potomac to Charleston, a piedmont route from Richmond to Atlanta, and a transmountain line from Bristol, Tennessee, to Atlanta and Memphis.[7]

In May 1870, a year before his road passed under control of the Pennsylvania, President Buford of the R&D met with NCRR President Smith, who invited him to submit an offer for a long-term lease of that part of the NCRR from Greensboro to Charlotte. Buford soon did so, attending the NCRR stockholders' meeting at Hillsboro in July.[8] Smith was still trying to keep his options open. In his annual report presented at this meeting, he himself noted the need for bringing the through route under common management. But the route Smith specified was that from Augusta to Norfolk, not Richmond. As a necessary step in that direction he now recommended that the NCRR itself purchase the Charlotte, Columbia, and Augusta Railroad, change its gauge, and put an end to the irksome and expensive transshipment required at Charlotte. He estimated that this would double the income of the road. The stockholders made no recorded response to this bold proposal, but they did authorize further negotiations with the R&D.[9]

Although Buford had been authorized by his own board to pay up to $240,000 in annual rent for the section between Greensboro and Charlotte, he now offered only $200,000 while demanding the right to change it to the five-foot gauge.[10] This offer carried grave and possibly permanent implications for the NCRR, and the board was hesitant to accept it without broader consultation. Another board meeting was scheduled in November to which William A. Graham, Paul C. Cameron, Rufus Barringer, John L. Morehead, and other leading stockholders were invited. Graham was even retained as counsel to draw up a contract.

Meanwhile Smith publicly opposed the R&D request, saying he had not heard a single board member favor it. He himself adhered to his own NCRR expansion plan. Apart from an unwillingness to forsake the Norfolk-oriented alliance, the NCRR managers feared that the road would lose its economic viability if it were restricted to the section east of Greensboro. They might retain operations to Charlotte by laying a parallel track, but the benefits seemed unlikely to match the cost. In fact, they might have rejected Buford's offer out of hand but for his threat to build a parallel line of his own from Greensboro to Charlotte. This was probably more than an empty threat; the moribund Atlantic, Tennessee, and Ohio from Statesville to Charlotte already offered part of such a road; charters now in existence authorized construction of the remainder. Furthermore, other projected roads threatened to compete with the NCRR. In particular, the Raleigh and Gaston was eager to extend its Chatham Railroad from Raleigh to Cheraw or Columbia, South Carolina, creating a shorter line than any in existence. If his own proposal to buy the Charlotte, Columbia, and Augusta should not materialize, Smith wrote Graham privately, the NCRR might have to make a deal with the Richmond and Danville. He also favored acquiring and constructing the Northwestern North Carolina Railroad to Salem and extending it beyond to Tennessee. "We cannot remain stationary while the whole railroad world is in motion. We must buy or lease roads, consolidate with short lines north & south, or build to connect with roads to give us business, or we must go down to local business alone. . . . Will it be wise to wait until our oil is exhausted before we replenish our lamps?"[11]

The November meeting at Company Shops was inconclusive. The participants voted down a motion to reject the R&D offer altogether, then created three committees to deal with the leading questions before the road. Five directors including Smith were authorized to confer with the officers of the CC&A, the R&G, and the Seaboard and Roanoke about a possible consolidation of the roads between Norfolk and Augusta—an expansion of Smith's proposal to purchase the CC&A. Three directors including Smith were to confer with the Northwestern road about merger. Finally, a supercommittee of seven stockholders, including Smith, Graham, Cameron, and Morehead, was appointed to consider all lease or consolidation proposals, including those presented by the first two panels. If it wished, it could ask the president to summon a special stockholders' meeting in January.[12]

Although veteran President William Johnston of the CC&A branded Smith as a knave and ignoramus whose mismanagement cost all the connecting roads thousands of dollars a year, he agreed with Smith on almost every substantive question before them. Writing privately to his son-in-law, Superintendent A. B. Andrews of the R&G, Johnston favored a merger of the roads between Augusta and Norfolk; failing that, he supported the alternative form of consolidation effected by a lease of the NCRR to the Richmond and Danville. Any change in the NCRR management, he said, would be an improvement.[13]

Conversations ensued between Smith and President William J. Hawkins of the R&G. A merger would require a new charter from the legislature. The other roads would insist, and Smith would surely agree, that the state could not have a controlling voice in the new road, much of which would lie in South Carolina and Virginia.[14] Perhaps for that reason the talks broke down. Governor Holden on 22 November reaffirmed his opposition to any lease or sale of the NCRR, and he instructed the state proxy to vote accordingly.[15] Although the merger did not fall strictly within either of those categories, it seems likely that state pride and perhaps more specifically political concerns prevented it from going forward. The NCRR would have been the centerpiece and largest component in any merger of the four roads from Augusta to Norfolk. Smith was probably right in saying that this union, or something like it, represented the NCRR's last real chance for continued operation on anything like an independent basis. But in the long run this combination, had it come to fruition, would likely have fallen prey to an even larger one.

As to the R&D lease offer, the stockholders' committee met in Raleigh in January 1871 and voted against it. They issued no explanation. The governor's opposition to any lease probably carried less weight under the circumstances—he was now on trial before the Senate for his role in suppressing the Ku Klux Klan—than the considerations that had bothered Smith from the beginning. A lease of the road from Greensboro to Charlotte, coupled with a gauge change on that section, would in effect dismantle the road. It would deprive the remaining portion of through traffic and consign it to poverty and irrelevance.[16] If the road were to be leased, and that seemed increasingly probable, the lease would have to cover the entire road.

It was not yet inevitable that the lease would go to the R&D. In June 1871 the Raleigh and Gaston was back again, trying to persuade its Norfolk-Augusta partners to join it in leasing the NCRR. But the Seaboard and Roanoke feared a long commitment. It could see the Baltimore and Ohio, an old rival of the Pennsylvania, penetrating western Virginia with apparent hopes of developing its own southeastern empire. The B&O already had a line to Lynchburg and was now extending it to Danville. With two major roads in Danville seeking a southern extension and the NCRR no longer available because of this proposed R&G lease, one of them at least would likely be moved to build the threatened parallel line to Charlotte. With that kind of competition it was far from sure that a lease of the NCRR would continue to be profitable.[17] The CC&A also withdrew from the effort, citing its heavy debt load, but that road was in fact selling out to the R&D itself.[18]

Thus the Pennsylvania was busily buying railroads, using the Richmond and Danville as its proxy. Failing to buy a controlling interest in the Raleigh and Gaston (which was sought primarily to silence its opposition to an NCRR lease), it easily prevailed with the more important CC&A stockholders, including President William Johnston.[19]

Meanwhile, in advance of the NCRR stockholders' meeting in July, President Smith laid out for them the confluence of events that was fast overtaking the road. The need for difficult decisions was at hand, he warned. It would be suicidal to sit still and watch both the B&O and the Pennsylvania build parallel lines to Charlotte without trying to stop them or at least to reach some agreement with one or the other to salvage as many benefits as possible. Without quite saying so, Smith had come to favor a lease if the terms were right.[20]

Josiah Turner was as opposed to a lease now as to the R&G's offer back in

1869. Smith, he said, was "the most thorough going 'selling out' Railroad President we have ever heard or read of." No sooner did one lease fail than he sought another. The NCRR was a paying road with improving prospects. Why sell out now? If a lease were inevitable, it was worth far more than the rentals that had so far been mentioned. And in that case it should go to neighbors like the R&G rather than Yankee monopolists with no concern for the welfare of North Carolina.[21]

The stockholders assembled at Greensboro in July 1871. But this was the meeting that never met, owing to the struggle between the Republican governor and Democratic legislature over who could appoint the NCRR directors and proxy. With conflicting court orders barring the stockholders from recognizing either set of appointees, a number of them refused to register their stock, and the meeting failed for lack of a quorum. (See Chapter 19.) How much the lease issue may have played in this action is hard to say. There was some feeling that the legislative appointees were opposed to a lease and might prevent it. Anything done to thwart their seating could thus be interpreted as favoring a lease.[22]

Opponents of a lease had procured an injunction against it shortly before the aborted meeting, but it was soon withdrawn.[23] Paul C. Cameron, elected to the R&G board at this time, seemed to regard a lease as inevitable even as he sought to have that road go to court to prevent it. Like Graham, Turner, and others who had labored to get the NCRR chartered, built, and on its way in the very different world of the 1850s, Cameron had developed a strong emotional attachment to it over the years. It was an object of state, local, and personal pride. If North Carolina was no longer called the Rip Van Winkle State, it was primarily because of this railroad. Leasing it away was a very bitter pill to swallow. "Those who built the Road no longer have any controul [sic] of it," wrote Cameron to his sister in July, "and the prospect is that it will pass into the hands of outsiders and strangers!!"[24]

But the efforts of the R&G to produce an acceptable counter offer had not been and would not be successful. Together with the Old Bay Line and perhaps others, it apparently did offer to lease the road at a rental of 7 percent ($280,000) per year, but only for three to five years. Smith and the board turned this down as virtually inviting construction of an alternate road from Greensboro to Charlotte, which they felt had to be avoided. Such a short lease would expire just as that road became operational, leaving the NCRR to face ruinous competition.[25]

By the time of the Greensboro meeting a growing proportion of the stockholders seemed resigned to a Richmond and Danville lease if favorable terms could be gotten.[26] The board of directors had apparently come to that conclusion already. There might well be a political and legal struggle over this issue in the state at large, but so far as the road's own managers were concerned, it had now reduced itself chiefly to a question of terms, and then of the means to see it legally effected.

President Buford, sensing victory, redoubled his own campaign during

July and August. Realizing the political and legal implications of the issue in North Carolina, and armed with an expense fund of $150,000, he sought as lawyers the most influential figures he could find in the state. He told William A. Graham that he wanted the former governor's services first as a lobbyist to get the lease enacted and then as a lawyer to defend it afterward. But Graham had mixed feelings about the issue. He eventually refused the offer and opposed the lease. Former Governor Thomas Bragg and three others were retained instead. For the NCRR, Ralph Gorrell of Greensboro, a former director, provided a legal brief also supporting the right of the 1870 board to carry over after the failed stockholders' meeting, with full power to make contracts.[27]

By now it was clear to Buford that if he wanted to lease the road, he would have to take it all. The chief remaining question was money. In July or August he offered an annual rental of $240,000, equivalent to a 6 percent dividend, for the entire road. (He was authorized to promise $280,000.) The board turned this down as too little.[28] Early in September Buford raised the bid to $260,000, or 6½ percent, for a term of thirty years. Smith called a special board meeting to discuss it.

Josiah Turner had threatened to enjoin the board legally from making any lease agreement. To avoid such a preemptive action Smith hastily summoned the directors to a meeting at Company Shops on 11 September, only four or five days distant, without indicating its purpose. Nine of the twelve appeared. So did Governor Bragg and others in behalf of the R&D. Bragg had already drawn the contract and read it to the board. When asked, he assured the board (all of whom had been appointed or elected back in 1870) that the charter empowered them to make the contract; those present later differed as to whether he added that there was no legal requirement to consult the stockholders. When a motion was made to accept the lease, it was approved 8 to 0, Smith as president not voting.[29]

The lease provided for a thirty-year rental of the NCRR's roadway, rolling stock, and operational facilities, beginning the very next day. Allowing for necessary replacements, the R&D contracted to keep all of this property in as good condition as when it was acquired, with an eye to its eventual return. To that end, provision was made for a massive inventory of the road's property, which was to be repeated in some degree every year thereafter. Finally, the R&D was allowed to change the NCRR gauge if it desired. (The inventory was to be made by a qualified "expert" on the part of each company, with provision for an impartial umpire if they disagreed. As this was an annual occurrence, the position of "expert" was added at least unofficially to the NCRR's roster of officers in the years ahead. The first inventory was taken soon after the lease. As preserved in the NCRR records, it provides invaluable information concerning the road's physical characteristics.)[30]

Next day Smith issued a public letter to the stockholders notifying them of the action and rehearsing the reasons for it. The NCRR, he said, simply could not cope with the capital that the R&D, backed by the Pennsylvania Railroad, threatened to mobilize against it. When the R&D offered a good bargain, it seemed the better part of wisdom to take it. As a result, he continued, the danger of a parallel road from Greensboro to Charlotte was now averted. The stockholders would be assured of dividends, and the value of their stock would double. Freight rates would drop, immigration and investment would follow, and towns and cities would flourish.[31] The justification that Smith provided was hard to refute, and even his predictions for the future were not far from the mark. Buford, in reporting to his own stockholders in December, said the terms had been favorable to the NCRR, but they were preferable to the "only probable alternative," a parallel line from Greensboro to Charlotte costing at least $2 million.[32]

Nevertheless the announcement created a furor in North Carolina. Newspapers lined up on both sides, with Turner and his *Sentinel* predictably hostile. To the previous arguments against a lease were added charges of undue haste and secrecy, probably masking fraud and corruption. William A. Graham wrote indignantly that the action was "a pure coup d'etat [by] A set of directors whose term had expired . . . and held over by usurpation." For one who had been regularly consulted by Smith and courted by Buford, Graham's anger is surprising; so was the fact that he wrote this to Ralph Gorrell, whom he apparently did not identify as an agent in the proceedings. No lease was valid, said Graham, until ratified by the stockholders.[33]

Certainly that had been the understanding previously. The charter gave the company the right to "farm out" its road but did not grant this power specifically to the board of directors. Smith himself felt the strength of this objection, and in October the board voted to submit the matter to a special stockholders' meeting, whenever expedient.[34] No time would be expedient until the state supreme court decided who had the right to choose state directors and proxies—the cause for breaking up the last meeting. That question was not settled until early in 1872.[35] By that time it may have seemed better to wait until the regular meeting in July, especially as the lease would then have been in effect for ten months and possibly harder to overthrow.

Meanwhile, in January the Democratic legislature appointed a joint committee to investigate the lease. It summoned Smith and most of the NCRR directors and secured statements from Buford and his lieutenant William T. Sutherlin of the R&D. In its report the committee sanctioned the 1870 directors' action in holding over, given the stockholders' failure to organize. It condemned the lease, however, and emphatically denied the board's right to make it without stockholder approval.[36]

The cries of corruption were hardly allayed when Smith, asked by the committee if anyone had received money for procuring the lease, refused to answer for fear of incriminating himself. Another board member reported Smith saying in jocular fashion that he expected a good job with the R&D, or something of the sort. The truth in this matter never appeared.

Buford and Sutherlin both denied any fraud, of course, and at the 1872 annual meeting Smith did so too, with some bitterness. He asked for a formal investigation to be headed by his chief accuser, former President Thomas Webb, but none was held. Later he lamely explained his self-in-criminating answer as a denial of a legislative committee's right to probe into one's personal affairs.[37] Smith got no job with the R&D; he remained as part-time president of the NCRR for several years while living on his Johnston County farm.

In his annual report for 1872 Smith once more defended the lease as a business necessity. More than that, "It purges from a great business interest of the State the poison of politics, and leaves it to be directed by business men for purposes of business only—to develope trade, increase population and thereby create wealth and help to restore prosperity to the people." At the annual meeting in July, with the governor's appointive powers now confirmed, the stockholders approved the lease by a vote of 36,269 to 752. Even without the state proxy's 30,000 votes the margin was overwhelming.[38]

The lease specifically granted the R&D the right to change the NCRR gauge to its own five-foot width. If done between Greensboro and Charlotte, that would eliminate the tedious, time-consuming, and expensive transshipments at both places and would permit continuous running from Virginia to Georgia and beyond. The change would cost a good deal of money, however, and controversy over the legality of the lease discouraged efforts at implementation before 1873. When the R&D signified its intention to make the change from Greensboro to Charlotte early that year, it evoked two lawsuits seeking to prevent the action and to invalidate the lease altogether. The plaintiff in one case was the state of North Carolina, which alleged that the gauge change would injure the state and its citizens' interest in the NCRR. Thomas Webb was the other plaintiff. Injunctions were issued to prevent the change until the issue could be resolved in the state supreme court. That did not occur until January 1875, when both the lease and the gauge change were upheld. The R&D started at once to adjust the track. The legislature passed an act in March to forbid the change; but the high court quickly declared the law unconstitutional, and the work was completed from Charlotte to Goldsboro—the length of the road.[39]

The shops complex was less in demand as the R&D increasingly used its own shops near Richmond. Although Company Shops remained the official headquarters of the NCRR until 1929, most officials and employees were gradually transferred to other places or left the road's service altogether. An act of the legislature in 1879 authorizing taxation of the road's nonoperational real estate at Company Shops induced the NCRR to sell much of it.[40]

By 1886 the five-foot gauge, which had become standard across the South, was at odds with the rest of the country; elsewhere the NCRR's original four feet, eight and a half inches had become standard. In that year a further step was taken toward creating a national railway network. During a few days in May and June most southern railways, including the R&D, moved one rail the few required inches, and the northern standard gauge—once the NCRR's—became national. This created some short-term employment for the NCRR shops in changing over rolling stock. That done, the entire maintenance operation was moved to the R&D shops near Richmond.

The village of Company Shops was already in danger of becoming a ghost town. In 1887 it changed its name to Burlington. Under that more refined designation it gradually attracted textile mills and other industries that more than replaced the railroad shops as a source of employment. Some of the shop buildings were taken over by other businesses. The hotel and depot were burned by an arsonist in 1904, and most of the others burned in a gigantic fire in 1918. Only the engine house and a few small structures remain today.[41]

In the 1890s, after the Southern Railway absorbed the Richmond and Danville, it built massive new shops at Spencer, just outside of Salisbury. Located midway between Washington and Atlanta, they served the road for many years before falling into obsolescence themselves. They are now the site of a state transportation museum. A few miles away, near the former NCRR station at Linwood in Davidson County, the Southern built in the 1970s a large, computerized switchyard that serves as a hub for tracks leading to Washington, New Orleans, and Knoxville.[42]

The physical condition of the road gradually improved under the lease. Heavier equipment and faster speeds required stronger rails. By 1891, sixty-pound steel rails had replaced the iron ones on the main line between Greensboro and Charlotte; three years later the entire road was equipped with steel. By 1982 the main line boasted welded steel rail from Greensboro to Charlotte. Iron bridges soon replaced the wooden structures, only five of which remained in 1891.[43]

As on other roads across the country, the traffic nowadays is virtually all freight. Passenger service has nearly disappeared in favor of automobiles, planes, and buses. Save for the Carolinian, a new train from Charlotte to Raleigh and thence northward, passenger service had been restricted in recent years to the Crescent, a single train traveling in each direction nightly on the main line between Washington and New Orleans.

Railroad consolidation also went on apace. In 1880 the Pennsylvania Railroad, in full retreat from its southern involvement, sold its Richmond and Danville stock to a northern-dominated syndicate headed by William P. Clyde of New York City. That group in turn organized a holding company known as the Richmond and West Point Terminal Railway and Warehouse Company. In five years it won control over a railway system of nearly 2,700 miles stretching from tidewater Virginia to central Alabama. Most of this system had been part of the Pennsylvania Railroad empire, but it included other roads as well, such as the Western North Carolina Railroad, sold by the state in 1880. By 1890 the Richmond and West Point Terminal controlled over 8,000 miles of road extending to the Ohio and Mississippi rivers. Two years later it went into receivership, the product of overexpansion. J. P. Morgan took over the combination in 1893 and reorganized it into the Southern Railway Company. The Southern remained thereafter under the control of the House of Morgan.[44]

With the NCRR lease due to expire in 1901, the Southern sought a more permanent arrangement to safeguard the vital link that the NCRR continued to provide in the main line between Washington and Atlanta. In 1895 a new ninety-nine-year lease was negotiated at an annual rental of $266,000 for the first six years and $286,000 thereafter. This lease was at least as controversial as the first. Republican Governor Daniel L. Russell, elected in 1896, believed that the rental was far too small. So did many of the Populists with whom he shared power in the fusion movement of that decade. They attempted in the 1897 legislative session, the first since the lease was signed, to have it annulled. The effort failed amidst tumultuous debate and parliamentary maneuvering. The lease was also upheld in the courts. It remains in effect after nearly a century, due to expire on 31 December 1994.[45]

NCRR ownership, both public and private, has remained virtually unchanged in character. The state has so far resisted every pressure to sell its stock, although there have been some hairbreadth escapes over the years and arguments are still made that the state has better employment for its funds. A forced sale was narrowly averted in the Swasey case of the 1870s by the legislature's funding the state debt and providing in another fashion for the bondholders who had invested in the road's original construction.[46]

Succeeding governors thus continued annually to appoint—usually from their own political parties—eight state directors as well as a state proxy. The private stockholders—many of them descendants of the original shareholders—continued to elect four directors, and in later years they have been empowered to choose a vice-president, unknown to the original charter. Until very recently, none of the officers has had many duties to perform under the successive leases. A particular irony lies in the fact that the president of the road from 1985 to 1987, Robert J. Brown of High Point, was the great-grandson of a slave who helped lay its track in the 1850s.[47]

There were sporadic suggestions over the years to convert the state's $1 million in preferred stock to common stock, since the former was entitled to a dividend of 6 percent before other dividends could be paid. This conversion took place without fanfare in 1897. Dividends have been virtually unbroken under both leases, and by 1980 the state, as three-quarters stockholder, had received over $26 million in dividends.[48]

It is inconceivable that the NCRR stockholders (including the state) could have bettered this record by continuing independent operations. The Richmond and Danville itself paid only eight dividends between 1865 and 1893.[49] The rent that it paid the NCRR year in and year out was a fixed obligation that had to be met before any profits could be distributed to its own stockholders. That rental was in turn the source of the NCRR's own unbroken dividend record as well as the means by which it gradually paid off its debt by 1895.[50] And the Southern rendered a good deal more than rent to the NCRR over the years. Its total return in 1981 for federal, state, and local taxes, for capital expenditures on the road, and for rent amounted to about $1,487,000.[51]

As the years passed, however, the value of the NCRR property came to exceed by far the original capitalization, which was the basis for the $286,000 annual rental stipulated in 1895. It was estimated in 1982 to be worth about $70 million, much of the increase attributable to improvements by the Southern. A 6 percent annual return on that amount would yield $4.2 million; the state's three-quarters share would be $3.15 million.[52] The state, as principal stockholder, has long anticipated the expiration of the lease and has begun studying its options. If, as seems likely, the lease is renewed with the Norfolk Southern Corporation (the product of a recent merger of the Southern with the Norfolk and Western Railroad), it will be at a much higher rate, quite likely with provision for built-in increases over the years.[53]

Merger with the Atlantic and North Carolina Railroad finally came to pass in 1989. The A&NC had a more checkered career than the NCRR, having been leased to various parties over the years. But the state also retained about three-quarters ownership of that road, and by the 1980s it too was under lease to the Norfolk Southern, timed to expire simultaneously with the NCRR lease. Proponents of a merger argued that it would strengthen the hands of the state and of both roads in the upcoming lease negotiations. Opponents, as of old, feared that merger would diminish the value of the NCRR and its stock. But NCRR stockholders (including the state) voted overwhelmingly for the proposal; and as before, A&NC shareholders were all but unanimous.[54] (The former Western North Carolina Railroad, sold by the state in 1880, also remains a part of the Norfolk Southern system but no longer exists as a separate entity.)

In the century following the 1871 lease the price of NCRR stock seldom reached the original par value of $100 per share. In the mid-1970s it ranged between $50 and $125. But in 1986, spurred by the approaching lease termination and the probability of a new lease at a much higher rental, producing higher dividends, the price shot up to $5,500 per share. Private individuals had trouble buying or selling shares at that rate and the road decided (with state acquiescence) to make a 100-for-1 split, creating 4,000,000 shares.[55] The state's position as three-quarters owner remained unchanged.

22

Forward or Backward: The Effects of the NCRR

RAILROADS BROUGHT remarkable changes to the territories they served and to the world beyond. Some of the changes were predictable and eagerly sought; others were unforeseen and even dismaying to the roads' promoters. In general, the early railroads commercialized existing local economies and broadened them into regional economies. They largely accomplished this in the 1850s. After the Civil War the railroads forged the regional economies into a national one.

This process brought both benefits and losses. Crops that had little or no local market now came to be raised for larger markets—for example, the gathering, growing, and drying of fruit along the NCRR. Trade and manufacturing expanded as railroads brought energy, labor, raw materials, and markets closer together, thereby lowering costs. Cheaper transportation meant both lower prices and greater variety of consumer goods and commodities. These in turn generated greater demand, production, sales, and ultimately economic growth.[1]

But cheaper transportation was a two-way street. If it stimulated greater production at home, it also facilitated the importation of goods and commodities from a distance. As farmers turned increasingly to cash crops for more distant markets, they no longer patronized local mills, merchants, and artisans as much. Such local businesses and crafts as tailoring, shoemaking, and coopering declined or disappeared.[2]

The Northeast was the greatest gainer from the expanding railway network. Northern products, chiefly manufactures, flooded the South and West. They were often cheaper and sometimes better than the products of the generally smaller and shakier firms in the hinterland. (Southern consumers helped the invasion by turning up their noses at southern-made goods even when they were as good or better in price and quality.) The industries that southern railroads generated most along their routes were small-scale producers of inexpensive goods made from nearby raw materials. They could not be shipped profitably over a great distance and therefore found only a local or regional market.

The sectional disparity between North and South had a variety of causes. The North benefited from superior financial resources and expertise gained over generations of time—an expertise that extended to skilled workers as well as to bankers and captains of industry. It possessed a larger and more lucrative home market by virtue of its greater population density and disposable income. Its coal supplies exceeded in quality and quantity any other fuel resource in the country. Least in importance, perhaps, but still tangible, was a widespread reluctance in the South to invest in manufacturing when agriculture (the more accustomed activity) paid so well.[3]

The railroads accentuated the sectional disparity in two ways. Not only did they carry goods more efficiently and cheaply, but their freight rates almost invariably discriminated in favor of long-distance traffic. Generally competing with each other for through traffic while monopolizing their own local traffic, they tended to charge the latter whatever it would bear. Southern railroads adopted this nationwide practice well before they were taken over by Yankee financiers. The *Raleigh Telegram* castigated it in 1871, saying that it encouraged cotton monoculture for distant markets, discouraged economic diversification, and generally stifled southern economic development.[4]

This went to the heart of the matter: American railroads brought better and cheaper goods to the consumer by encouraging mass production through specialization. The nation's carriers, southern as well as northern, helped confirm the South's specialty as a producer of staple crops for the world market. They carried southern cotton and tobacco away and brought northern (and European) manufactures, even western farm products, in return. In 1899 the *Greensboro Patriot* deplored the importation of meat from Chicago and flour from Minnesota when North Carolina could raise these things for itself. They were purchased with 5 cent cotton and 8 cent tobacco, the editor said, blaming the situation in part on the proliferation of railroads.[5]

Thus the southern railway promoters of the 1850s who had hoped to defeat the North's commercial, industrial, and financial dominance by erecting a southern rail network more nearly advanced that dominance; in seeking to achieve southern economic independence they helped confirm her tributary status.[6] Much the same happened in late nineteenth-century Mexico, where railroads reinforced that country's role as a supplier of raw materials—minerals and fibers—for the outside world and magnified the power of wealthy land and mine owners over the peasantry.[7]

Up to a point, commercial agriculture and the distribution of goods (of whatever origin) encouraged the growth of local and regional market towns. Those to which the railroad had been attracted in the first place now grew in size. Others arose where none had existed before. Small industries generated small towns. The southern mill village, before and after the railroad, was something of an urban plantation, deliberately isolated from outside distraction.[8] The earliest of them were located at waterpower sites, often isolated by necessity. Later steam-powered mills could be situated more freely. They were usually established adjacent to railroads but often on the outskirts of existing towns, where the paternal atmosphere might still be maintained.

Urbanization thus took place in the South, enhanced by the railroad. But it was "urbanization without cities," as David R. Goldfield puts it—the proliferation of small towns, usually of less than 4,000 people. In the absence of major industries and in the presence of staple-crop agriculture, towns rarely grew beyond local or regional marketing centers—way stations on the road to Philadelphia, New York, and Boston, as one man put it. The economy of these places was more dependent on the price of cotton or tobacco than on industrial conditions.[9]

This pattern actually intensified after the Civil War. Northern penetration so retarded southern industrial and commercial development that the proportion of southern urban dwellers living in cities of over 25,000 markedly declined between 1850 and 1900. Despite the urbanization of piedmont North Carolina in the late nineteenth century—wrought in large measure by the NCRR—no city in the state exceeded 25,000 in 1900; only six surpassed 10,000.[10]

As the nation's first big business, railroads pioneered in corporate organization, management, and finance. The early railroads usually represented the greatest concentrations of economic power so far seen in their localities.[11] Economic power brought political power and social status for railroads and their managers. Chartered by the state, sometimes subsidized by the state, and eventually regulated by the state, they in fact magnified and strengthened the state. Neither could ignore the other. Railroads pleaded, bribed, threatened, and otherwise lobbied legislators and other public officials. With the power to allocate unprecedented sums and influence unprecedented numbers of people, they raised the stakes of the political process.

When the NCRR was first projected, with its outrigger lines to Morehead City and the mountains, the idea was to build part of a *southern* coast-to-coast railroad, independent of the North and of the state's immediate neighbors north and south. As it soon turned out, the NCRR became a predominantly north-south road, a link in the tributary southern rail network pointed at New York and the Northeast. Therein lay much of its income as well as its value to the postwar consolidators.

NCRR promoters saw themselves also as the heralds of progress in rejuvenating backward North Carolina. The whistles, bells, and escaping steam of NCRR locomotives, they trusted, would finally wake up the old Rip Van Winkle State. Commercial farming, trade, and manufacturing would flourish as the railroad connected hitherto isolated localities and then linked all of them with the outside world. Property values would soar and towns would multiply in size and number—especially the state's long-neglected seaports. Westward emigration, then sapping the state's vitality by spiriting away some of her best and brightest, would come to a halt as opportunities increased at home. And in a time of increasing sectional friction the state would depend less on the North for her manufactures and even food supplies. North Carolina products would supply North Carolina markets, if not those of the world.

Less tangible benefits would also ensue. Cultural isolation would go the way of economic isolation as the railroad brought easier travel, the telegraph, and better newspaper and mail service. As future President Charles F. Fisher put it in 1852, the NCRR "was the sign of a new age . . . the token of a progress about to commence."[12]

Some of these benefits were observed almost immediately. As early as December 1855, the *Lexington and Yadkin Flag* credited the road with instilling a new spirit of enterprise in North Carolina. People who used to cringe at taxes now demanded new improvements. "Situated as we are, immediately on the N.C.R. Road, we can fully appreciate the blessings of these improvements. Having been all our lives shut up in the interior, with no traveling or commercial facilities, we begin now to feel that we live in a great and populous world, that we are not situated on a little island at least three thousand miles from any other part of the habitable globe." Four years later President Fisher boasted that the road's "effect . . . on the country and the people, has been marvellous; life, energy and thrift, have taken the place of a general stagnation." And, he added, "a grateful return comes to the agent of this change" in the form of increasing shipments along the road.[13]

All of these things happened, and more. The NCRR left its mark politically and even ideologically. It was far more than a patronage machine. As the longest road in the state and virtually a property of the state, managed indirectly by its governor, the NCRR conferred upon the state an opportunity and responsibility it never had before. The state was no longer just a keeper of the peace with minimal functions and costs. It was the majority owner of the largest business corporation in North Carolina, a corporation that might, if all went well, supply the state with revenue while rejuvenating the state's economy and society. Some governors—Jonathan Worth comes first to mind—took the opportunity and responsibility more seriously than others as they appointed and counseled their state directors and proxies. But all regarded it as a public resource not to be squandered. Most legislators agreed. When laissez-faire predilections combined with postwar poverty to evoke proposals to sell the state-owned railroads, thereby lessening the public debt and tax burden, only the Western North Carolina Railroad was actually sold. The NCRR emerged as a kind of public trust as well as a financial resource.

The growth of a commercial economy bred a growing class of merchants, professionals, and white-collar workers. Commonly more articulate and educated than their fellows, they tended to promote education and the arts, partly from need and partly for pleasure. In her study of Greensboro during the Civil War era, Gail O'Brien finds the most significant change in that community to have been the unprecedented rise in the status and influence of merchants and lawyers. Although their rise accelerated in the 1860s and 1870s, it was visible before the war, owing in large measure to the market economy ushered in by the NCRR.[14] Such persons existed in every community along the NCRR; they chartered and built the road, managed it, and used it to advance their state, their communities, and themselves. They comprised a large proportion of its presidents, directors, and major stockholders.

There is no question that the railroad lessened the cultural isolation of central and western North Carolina. Every year it granted half-fares to hundreds or thousands of persons attending state fairs, religious and educational meetings, or simply taking excursions, who would not otherwise have left home. The mere projection of the NCRR led postal authorities to establish daily mail service westward to Greensboro and Charlotte.[15] That in turn meant more frequent newspaper deliveries, not just to individual subscribers but to local editors who culled most of their own news items from distant papers. Nobody developed a quicker dependence on daily mail service or voiced greater outrage at interruptions in it than the fourth estate. When the telegraph came several years later, it provided a further and faster tie to the outside world, but one almost as dependent on the railroad whose track it followed.

Historians of Raleigh, Salisbury, and Charlotte note the arrival of ready-made clothing, expensive furniture, Parisian fashions, fancy groceries, and other consumer goods in the wake of the railroad. Raleigh soon boasted a soda fountain as well as the visit of a traveling circus and menagerie.[16]

The NCRR unquestionably transformed much of the farming in its tributary region. Although the number of improved acres in the NCRR counties increased little more than 20 percent from 1850 to 1900, the value of farms and buildings along the road more than doubled between 1850 and 1860 and nearly tripled by 1900 as subsistence crops gave way to commercial crops. The greatest proportional increases were in Mecklenburg, Cabarrus, Johnston, and Davidson. One of the first signs of commercial farming was the use of imported fertilizers to enhance productivity. As early as August 1855 the Charlotte *Democrat* noted bags of guano at the depots between there and Lexington. Like many roads, the NCRR carried fertilizers at special rates, particularly during seasons when westbound cars might otherwise be running empty.[17]

Throughout this period the estimated market value of farm lands and buildings in North Carolina was among the lowest in the nation. It averaged only $3 an acre in 1850 and 1870 and $6 in 1860 and 1880. But as the

NCRR's promoters had predicted, the eleven counties along the road, from Wayne to Mecklenburg, consistently exceeded the state average from 1850 through 1900.[18] In 1850 and 1860 all but Johnston exceeded the state average; by 1880 all of them did so. (See table 19.) Maps of 1850 and 1860 showing land values clearly depict a crescent-shaped band roughly including and parallel to the line of the NCRR. (It was matched by a similar band adjacent to the Wilmington and Weldon Railroad through most of its length.)[19] Although this phenomenon dated from before the NCRR's construction, the counties along its line subsequently increased their advantage. Their average land value more than doubled between 1850 and 1860. Amounting to 123 percent of the state average in 1850, it rose to 128 percent in 1860 and 177 percent in 1870. The advantage gradually declined to 117 percent by 1900 as the state's transportation network improved.[20] The growth of land values was not an unmixed blessing, as a landowner pointed out in 1858; it brought higher assessments and taxes for the majority who had no desire to sell.[21]

As historian Paul Escott has recently shown, the NCRR brought increased production of cash crops, especially wheat, cotton, and tobacco. At least three-quarters of the farmers in the counties along the route increased their production of these crops after 1850. It was remarked in 1848 that no wheat was grown around Salisbury for more than the local market because "it would take one bushel to pay the freight on another." But in 1856, the year of the NCRR's completion, the *Lexington and Yadkin Flag* reported Davidson County farmers as receiving $1 per bushel compared with 60 cents formerly.[22] Production more than doubled in Davidson between 1850 and 1860. Together with Guilford and Rowan it raised almost half of the wheat grown along the NCRR in 1860. Of course the increase was not limited to counties directly on the road. The *Winston Sentinel* reported in 1858 that a steam-powered flour mill established in Forsyth County after the NCRR's completion was paying local farmers $20,000 annually for wheat; ten years earlier the entire county hardly raised that much.[23] Wheat production increased by 85 percent in the NCRR counties in the 1850s, major gains being registered by every county from Raleigh westward. The gains were not sustained, however; along the NCRR and statewide, no succeeding census year to 1900 showed a wheat crop equaling that of 1860. Increasingly, commercial farmers turned their attention to cotton and tobacco as the railroads brought in midwestern flour.

Similarly, the value of livestock in the NCRR counties grew by 62 percent in the 1850s, but like wheat production it failed by the turn of the century to equal 1860 levels. Mecklenburg stood out by doubling its production between 1850 and 1890.

Cotton was by far the most valuable crop grown along the road after 1860. Commercial fertilizers stimulated cotton production not only by increasing the yield per acre but by hastening the crop's maturity, thus shortening its growing season and making it feasible to grow in places (like eastern and southern North Carolina) where it hitherto had been marginal.[24] North Carolina was never a leading cotton state, but in the 1850s its production increased at a greater rate than in the South as a whole. The NCRR counties, in turn, far exceeded the state's growth rate. Their production more than doubled in the decade, from 15,000 to 32,000 bales. After a decline in the 1860s it rose to 94,000 bales in 1880 and 107,000 in 1900. The greater part of this production (over 80 percent after 1870) was in four counties at opposite ends of the line: Wayne, Johnston, Wake, and Mecklenburg. The importance of cotton is reflected in the fact that the value of all farm products along the NCRR was greatest in those counties after these data came to be reported in 1870. (See table 20.)[25]

In 1850 tobacco production along the route of the NCRR was negligible—a mere 272,000 pounds in a statewide total of nearly 12 million. (Orange County accounted for about three-quarters of the former figure.) But the NCRR counties increased their production to well over 3 million pounds in 1860. Orange remained far and away the chief producer, followed by Guilford, Alamance, Rowan, and Wake. Following the general decline during and right after the war, production along the road increased to over 5 million pounds in 1890 and an incredible 17 million in 1900. By the turn of the century Wake, Wayne, Guilford, and Johnston were the leading producers. Virtually no tobacco came from the western end of the road between Salisbury and Charlotte. The NCRR counties as a whole increased their share of the state production from 2 percent in 1850 to 10 percent in 1860 and about 15 percent by the end of the century. (See table 20.) But never between 1850 and 1900 did the value of tobacco production along the road (and statewide) approach that of cotton.

A clear but transitory product of the NCRR was commercial fruit cultivation. Chapters 7 and 17 discussed the growth of the dried fruit trade. Called into existence after the road's construction, this rural industry lasted until the invention of refrigerator cars made possible the safer shipment of fresh fruit. Orchard products from the NCRR counties jumped in value from only $1,000 in 1850 to $120,000 in 1860 and $233,000 in 1880. Although these figures do not include the banner county of Forsyth and others at a distance that used the NCRR, they reflect a much greater increase after 1850 than the state at large. The NCRR counties produced only 3 percent of the state's orchard products by value in 1850; they accounted for 19 percent in 1860 and 26 percent in 1880. (See table 20.) Among them the chief producers were Guilford, Davidson, and Alamance. In 1880 the value of the fruit crop in the NCRR counties virtually equaled that of tobacco, although it fell well short of wheat and cotton. That situation soon changed. Fruit production in the NCRR counties (unlike the state as a whole) fell by more than two-thirds between 1880 and 1900 while tobacco production skyrocketed.

The 1880 and earlier censuses gave the amounts of wheat, tobacco, and cotton production by county but (unlike fruit) not by their value. Based on the average national commodity prices that year, the NCRR counties' wheat crop was worth about $858,000; cotton, $3,696,000; and tobacco, $234,000.[26]

As commercial crops, particularly cotton and tobacco, grew in importance, the old standbys like corn remained stationary or even fell. Never an important item of commerce or of shipment on the NCRR, corn dropped in production by 11 percent in the 1850s in the counties adjoining the road. It rose and fell in ensuing decades but always remained at about 16 percent of the statewide total.

The growth of commercial agriculture in the 1850s might have been expected to strengthen the hold of slavery along the road. Indeed the slave population there did increase by 9 percent in that decade. But the census provides some surprises. In every one of these counties the increase was less—often much less—than in the 1840s, when it was 17 percent. Moreover the *statewide* increase in the 1850s was 15 percent. Natural population growth can easily explain the slight gain along the NCRR. Pretty clearly the great majority of slaves raising the new cash crops there in 1860 were already on the scene in 1850.

The NCRR seems nevertheless to have encouraged a modest expansion of the plantation along its route. As the number of slaves rose very slowly, both slaveholding and landholding became more concentrated. Such, at least, was the case in Guilford. As Gail O'Brien reports, slaveowners there declined from 20 percent to 12 percent of all households between 1850 and 1860, while the average number of slaves they owned increased. Owners of at least twenty slaves increased in number from eighteen to forty during the decade. At the same time the number of farms in the county declined from 1,668 to 1,503, and the average farm size grew from 224 to 251 acres.[27]

Until 1870 the NCRR counties had somewhat fewer blacks than did the state in proportion to total population. From 1870 to 1900 they slightly exceeded the state average, with a black population that, like the white, was more and more urbanized. The largest proportions of blacks along the NCRR were in the leading cotton counties of Wayne, Wake, and Mecklenburg; each was between 40 and 50 percent black in nearly every census after 1850. The smallest proportion was in Davidson, the premier wheat county, never more than 21 percent black.

In many respects the NCRR counties merely kept abreast of statewide development. Consistently embracing about 18 percent of the state's population from 1850 to 1900, they accounted for about that proportion of the state's improved acres, of corn and livestock produced, and of the value of farm lands and buildings—unlike the average value per acre, which was well ahead of the state. Other indices, while above or below 18 percent, also tended to remain relatively constant in relation to statewide levels. This was true of cotton and tobacco production, once cultivation of the leaf was widely introduced along the road in the 1850s. Wheat production along the NCRR jumped by 85 percent in that decade, but it failed to match a 123 percent increase statewide; after 1860 the NCRR counties produced about 27 percent of the state's crop. Only orchard production grew consistently faster than statewide, until 1880, after which it dropped. The NCRR clearly helped to transform the agricultural development of its tributary region. But much the same thing was happening in other parts of the state.

The NCRR counties contributed a larger share of the state's manufacturing activity. But in this respect too the state sometimes grew faster. In the 1850s the annual value of manufactured products increased 46 percent in the NCRR counties and 83 percent, nearly twice as much, statewide. These counties thus fell from 25 percent of the state total to only 20 percent in 1860. But the situation was reversed in the war decade, and their share climbed to 34 percent by 1900. From 1880 to 1900 the NCRR counties generally equaled or surpassed state growth in capitalization and number of employees. At the same time, their factories grew larger in average size than those in the state as a whole.

Industrialization came very gradually, and for the most part after 1880. This was true in the South as a whole.[28] As late as 1880 the value of farm products along the NCRR exceeded that of manufactures by two to one. In none of these counties did manufactures prevail over agriculture until Orange and Alamance crossed that divide in 1880. Guilford, Cabarrus, and Mecklenburg followed (as did the NCRR counties as a whole) in 1890; Wake and Rowan trailed (with the state as a whole) in 1900. The premier industrial county along the NCRR after 1880 was Durham (formed in 1881 primarily from Orange). By 1900 it employed over 4,000 industrial workers and turned out almost $8.5 million in products. It was followed that year by Mecklenburg with $5.7 million and by Alamance and Guilford, each with about $3.7 million. (See table 21.)

The dominant industry in Durham was, of course, tobacco. In 1850, at the NCRR's commencement, the town of Durham hardly existed, and the tobacco industry along the road was minuscule. But two factories were operating there in 1860, fourteen in 1880. Until 1871 most of the tobacco was purchased (and presumably brought by railroad) from the major markets in Richmond, Petersburg, and Danville, Virginia. A market was established at Durham, and in 1872, its second year, two million pounds were sold there. Thus Durham became a warehousing center as a prerequisite to its emergence as a manufacturing center. In 1874 the William T. Blackwell Company, by far the largest manufacturer in town, built an imposing brick factory; that was also the year that Washington Duke sold his farm and moved to town.[29] Between 1860 and 1880 the average capitalization in Orange/Durham County's tobacco factories jumped from $8,500 to $46,000, the average work force from twenty to sixty-two, and the average value of product from $17,000 to $71,000. Total tobacco production in the county approached $1 million in 1880.[30]

Tobacco factories in other counties along the line were scattered and, by 1880, much smaller. In 1860 the NCRR counties grew 10 percent of the state's leaf and produced 12 percent by value of the state's manufactured tobacco. In 1880 they still grew only 11 percent but manufactured 47 percent of the state total; Orange/Durham alone produced 44 percent.[31]

The textile industry along the road went back to Edwin Holt's mill on Alamance Creek in 1837. The industry was retarded by the panic of 1857, coming just after the NCRR's completion. (One of the casualties was the Salisbury Manufacturing Company, whose buildings and grounds along the railroad track were converted a few years later into the Confederate prisoner of war camp.)[32]

Alamance County was the leading textile center along the NCRR. It boasted five of the eight mills in counties along the road in 1860 and seven of eleven in the next two census years. Four were controlled by the Holt family.[33] In 1869 the Granite factory at Haw River employed thirty to forty persons, mostly girls. It consumed about 1,000 pounds of raw cotton per day, making yarns that were sent to weavers within the state and as far away as Philadelphia and Ohio.[34]

Most new mills used steam power after 1880 and electricity after 1900. No longer needing waterpower sites, they commonly located along railroads, often on the outskirts of existing towns. (Older mills at a distance from the road, as George W. Swepson's at Swepsonville, had all along used the NCRR and wagons to obtain raw cotton and to ship finished products.) The NCRR and its successors were a focal point in such locations well into the twentieth century.[35] (Geographer Coy T. Phillips writes that later mills, and the towns around them, tended to locate at intervals of ten to twenty miles, thus drawing on the surrounding countryside for labor without competing with each other.) About half of the entire South's looms were located within a 100-mile radius of Charlotte by 1900.[36] The northern half of that circle was in North Carolina, barely including Burlington and vicinity.

Most of the late nineteenth-century North Carolina cotton mills scattered across the piedmont were small.[37] But those in Alamance and the other NCRR counties were generally larger and considerably outdistanced the industry's growth statewide. Between 1860 and 1880 they doubled their average work force and much more than doubled their capitalization and value of product. Their production grew from $204,000 to $720,000, or from 20 to 28 percent of the state's total; their share of capitalization and labor force grew even more. Alamance mills led the way, exceeding the average mill statewide in 1880 by one-third in number of employees and by more than half in capitalization and value of product.[38]

Paradoxically, given the later primacy of textiles and tobacco and its own primitive character, flour and grist milling was still the largest industry statewide and along the NCRR as late as 1880. In both 1860 and 1880 its annual product exceeded that of the tobacco factories; it was seven times more valuable than cotton textiles in the NCRR counties in 1860 and twice as valuable in 1880. There were hundreds of small mills, some employing no more than a single person. By a conservative estimate, more than 150 operated in the NCRR counties in 1860, and nearly 300 in 1880. Despite that increase, production actually declined slightly along the road during that period (while growing statewide), indicating that the mills were getting smaller. Wheat production fell even more drastically—by half—the NCRR counties producing only a fifth of the state's total in 1880 compared with nearly a third in 1860. Davidson and Guilford were the leading producers along the road in 1880, each with at least thirty-five mills and well over $200,000 in output. NCRR freight reports do not tell us much about wheat or flour shipments after the war, but there is every reason to believe that they fell sharply as midwestern producers took over the outside markets that North Carolina had briefly supplied before the war. Some of the postwar shipments were actually incoming, from the Midwest.

Household manufactures declined with the rise of the factory system. North Carolina was one of the last states to reflect this trend, showing a per capita increase until 1860. The NCRR counties seem to have fallen off after 1850, sooner and much faster than the state as a whole. They produced 13 percent of the state's total in 1840, 16 percent in 1850, then 8 and 9 percent respectively in 1860 and 1870. That decline mirrors the rise of industrialization at home and elsewhere, fostered by the railroads. (See table 22.)[39]

Emigration continued to take North Carolinians away to the West. Back in September 1850 the *Greensboro Patriot* had noted that numbers of people from that vicinity were moving West, "where industry meets a more prompt and full reward. And multitudes more would go," it added, "were it not for the prospect of the Railroad." In a countryside filled with "pictures of decay and dilapidation in houses, barns, fences and fields," the NCRR "affords the *last hope* for the prosperity of western Carolina."[40] But if the railroad even slowed this trend in Guilford County, it does not appear in the census reports before 1880. The white population of Guilford, having risen by only 1 percent in the 1830s, actually fell slightly during each of the next three censuses. (Black population gains partly masked the white flight, particularly after the war.) The case was similar in Orange County, and gains were minimal before the 1870s in Alamance, Rowan, and Cabarrus. Among the NCRR counties as a whole, the total population growth rate of the 1850s, 9 percent, barely equaled that of the 1840s. The NCRR's ready facilitation of postwar emigration was mentioned in Chapter 16. The stations between Hillsboro and Lexington (where that traffic was greatest and station agents offered information and special fares) coincided with the areas of least population growth along the road.

Urbanization like industrialization came gradually, and particularly after

1880.[41] When the population began to increase along the NCRR after 1860, it occurred primarily at the two ends of the road. The central counties did not equal the state's rate of growth until the 1880s, and the NCRR counties as a whole began to exceed the state rate only in the 1890s. With just under 19 percent of the state's population in 1840 and again in 1900, they were closer to 17 percent during the interval. Among the NCRR counties, the most consistent gainers through 1880 were the cotton counties of Wayne, Johnston, Wake, and Mecklenburg. (All but Johnston were served by other railroads as well as the NCRR.) The chief gainers after 1880 were the industrializing counties of Mecklenburg, Cabarrus, Rowan, Guilford, Alamance, and Durham—counties that in some cases had lagged most in the rural past.

However modest, urbanization was real in the eyes of a still rural populace. From the beginning, new towns were founded along the road, and old ones grew perceptibly if not spectacularly. Goldsboro, called into existence by the Wilmington and Weldon during the 1840s, was described in 1854 as a burgeoning town with three newspapers, a female college, and over 1,500 people.[42] But the 1860 census listed only 885; by 1900 it had yet to reach 6,000. In 1870 the Goldsboro *Carolina Messenger* lamented the town's lack of industry and enterprise. "North Carolina furnishes no another [sic] town of equal size, population and intelligence, so destitute of public spirit as Goldsboro. With every geographical advantage, and possessed of unsurpassed railroad facilities, in the midst of one of the finest agricultural sections of the South, it is a lasting reproach to every man in the community, that we have no enterprise of a public character going on in our midst except one hotel, two newspapers, one buggy factory, nine bar-rooms, and a blacksmith shop." In 1880 the town's industries were said to consist of a machine shop and a planing mill.[43]

Johnston County contained no town to compare with Goldsboro. The NCRR bypassed the county seat of Smithfield in favor of a more direct route four miles north, where Selma was established. Neither town had attained a thousand inhabitants by 1900.

Wake County boasted Raleigh, the state capital. Already served by the Raleigh and Gaston Railroad since 1840, it could claim only 4,518 people ten years later. Yet it would be the largest town on the NCRR until 1900, when it could boast a population of 13,643. Residents and visitors alike were conscious of the city's postwar growth. The *Raleigh Telegram* noted in 1871 that the city was becoming a wholesale trade center; country merchants now came there to buy dry goods and groceries rather than to Petersburg and Norfolk as before the war.[44] It was no industrial center, however. In 1880 (the last year of the century for which county data are available) Wake County's thirty-one flour and grist mills were its largest industry in value of output, amounting collectively to $111,000. Next were three sash, door, and blind factories whose combined product was estimated at $96,000.

Cary, the modern bedroom community for Raleigh and the Research Triangle Park, was the first station stop west of Raleigh. Lumberman Allison F. Page, the father of Walter Hines Page, was the chief landowner and by 1861 the NCRR station agent. The place could hardly be called a town until after the Chatham Railroad branched off here to the southwest in 1868. Even in 1900 it numbered only 333 people.[45]

Durham's Station was best known originally for its proximity to the university at Chapel Hill; students and distinguished visitors detrained there. Sherman rode that far on his way to meet Johnston in 1865. In the late 1860s, while the tobacco industry was yet small, Durham was known also as the home of "J. A. McManner's celebrated Smut and Screening Machine," a device to clean wheat. In 1874 the tobacco industry accounted for only one in four of the town's business firms.[46] But all of them were as likely attributable to the railroad as was the town itself. Durham's 1869 charter defined the town's boundaries as lying one-half mile in all directions from the NCRR depot. For all of its industrial growth, Durham loomed large only in its local environment. Not listed in the 1850 or 1860 censuses, it numbered 256 persons in 1870, 2,041 in 1880, and 6,679 in 1900. By 1910, however, it had multiplied nearly three times, almost equaling Raleigh.[47]

Historic Hillsboro stood in stark contrast to its brash new neighbor. A visitor described the town early in the 1850s as looking old and down at the heel. While that appearance improved by 1860, the place remained hardly more than a village.[48] Its population was nearly stationary throughout the period: 582 in 1850, 707 in 1900. The same was true of its business community; while the number of business firms in Durham grew from 5 in 1866 to 100 in 1880, Hillsboro's remained at about 30. In fact, the new town seems to have taken businesses away from the old. Hillsboro's failures were not for lack of trying. Contemporaneously with Durham, it acquired a tobacco factory in 1859 and a tobacco market in 1871, but little came of them.[49] Its industries relied on local farm products and involved little more investment than a middle-sized farm. In truth, Hillsboro was a planters' and lawyers' town with a small contingent of educators and other professionals like architect/builder John Berry to serve the elite. Were it not for the intimate and powerful role that several Hillsboro residents played in creating and managing the NCRR—particularly Berry, William A. Graham, Paul C. Cameron, Thomas Webb, and Josiah Turner—one could almost say that the road's impact on the town was negligible.[50]

Alamance was one of the more industrialized counties on the road. But until the turn of the century none of its mill towns was more than a village. Mebane (or Mebanesville) and Haw River were two such places, directly on the railroad. Although Mebane was called into existence by the railroad in 1854, the Granite mill at Haw River dated from 1844; if anything, it attracted the railroad. Subsequent steam-powered mills were built along the NCRR, however, in the 1880s and later.[51] Graham, the county seat, was as new as the county, both of them (like the NCRR) dating from 1849. It contained 379 people in 1880 and barely 2,000 in 1900. Company Shops, the NCRR's own company town, was not listed by the census until 1880, when it had 817 people. As Burlington in 1900, after the railroad shops had closed down and textile mills took over as the major employers, it had grown to 3,692. The railroad had a great deal to do, directly and indirectly, with the town's continuing development. In general, the new mills along the road were larger than the early ones, and they created larger towns.[52]

Greensboro gave the impression in the mid-1850s of a bustling town destined for bigger things.[53] It boasted several small industries that did indeed grow, if slowly. There was a tobacco factory and (soon after the NCRR's completion) a new tobacco warehouse where the American (or Whig) party held its state convention in 1856. Near the depot was a foundry that made tools and plows before the war, guns during the war, and stoves and farm implements afterward. Soon after the war a distillery was established and a maker of dyestuffs, primarily for foreign export. Another iron works appeared west of town in 1869.[54]

The industry that attracted the greatest attention from visitors was the manufacture of wooden spokes and handles. At least two firms were established in Greensboro soon after the war. The president of the second was for a time Judge Albion Tourgée, Greensboro's most famous carpetbagger and, later, novelist. In the early 1870s it employed over sixty workers in the plant and another seventy-four cutting timber. Calling itself the largest handle maker in the country, it shipped virtually all of its products to the North and beyond. It sent pick handles to the gold fields in California and as far away as Australia. It even helped equip the French army with spokes for cannon wheels during the Franco-Prussian War. Tourgée's connection with the enterprise ended with the crash in 1873–74, but the firm carried on afterward.[55]

For all of the hopes invested in these businesses, they were small by all but local standards. Greensboro residents and visitors reported what clearly was to them a boom in 1869 and 1870; local papers repeatedly and happily declared that there was not an empty house, store, or office building in town. Yet Greensboro in 1869 contained only fifteen stores and perhaps 1,500 people.[56] In 1880 it numbered 2,105 with another 615 in Warnersville, an adjacent black community. Presumably including Warnersville, the population reached 3,317 in 1890, then jumped to 10,035 in 1900. Samuel M. Kipp, in an excellent unpublished study of Greensboro between 1870 and 1920, attributes much of its industrial and population takeoff to the advent of further railroad facilities—westward, northward, and southward—by 1890. Woodworking, tobacco, and textiles were the major industries. A major contributor was the Cone Mill textile complex established after 1890 in industrial suburbs just north of town.[57]

High Point became in time the largest of those towns created by the NCRR. In 1859, six years after its establishment at the road's highest elevation, where it crossed the plank road connecting Fayetteville and Salem, High Point was described as a thriving place with 205 buildings, 3 doctors, 2 churches, and 2 hotels—with a third under construction. Its early business and growth derived largely from the fact that it was the best shipping point, via the plank road, for Salem and Forsyth County. First listed in the census of 1870, High Point then had 1,627 people. It claimed just over 4,000 at the turn of the century but was destined to double by 1910. The town's major growth came with the advent of the furniture industry, beginning in 1889.[58]

The High Point station handled more than dried fruit. Francis Fries began operating woolen and cotton mills in Salem in the 1840s. Seeing the opportunities for business expansion offered by a railroad, he became one of the NCRR's earliest promoters and directors. His expectations were realized in large measure and his firm maintained a warehouse near the High Point depot. Stoneman burned both buildings in 1865.[59]

Nearby Thomasville was also a creature of the NCRR. An earlier chapter described the solicitude with which State Senator John W. Thomas followed the railroad surveyors throughout northern Davidson. When the route was determined he bought land at an appropriate distance below High Point for a station and built a town. Thomasville attracted a number of small industries, some of them established by Thomas himself. A leather-working business moved there within a year of the railroad's completion. This soon led to a shoe factory that specialized in cheap brogans for slaves. Depending largely on leather shipped from the North, it claimed to be the largest shoe factory in the South. Other shoe factories followed, serving different clienteles. With four in operation in 1869, Thomasville called itself "the Lynn of North Carolina," and even of the South. Its modern designation, the "Chair City," derives from the establishment of two small chair factories after the war. A much larger factory came in 1879.[60] These developments too must be taken in perspective. With only 308 people in 1860, Thomasville hardly more than doubled that number by 1900; it would jump to nearly 4,000 in 1910.

Where Thomasville impressed visitors as new, well scrubbed, and dynamic, the older, county-seat town of Lexington was described by observers in 1857 as shabby and needing paint. The NCRR was built a short distance west of town. Perhaps owing to the region's agricultural prosperity, few industries were established there, even by the standards of the time and region. Lexington barely led Thomasville in population throughout this period.[61]

Salisbury was celebrating its centennial when the NCRR arrived in 1855. Although a biased Charlotte editor remarked that Rip Van Winkle still slumbered in Salisbury despite the railroad, another visitor noted a spirit of improvement a year later.[62] One of the first effects of the railroad to be noted was inflation—higher consumer prices, rents, and real estate. Businesses opened and artisans moved to town.[63] Among the new industries in 1857 were a manufacturer of wheat fans, two farm implement factories (one of them owned in part by Nathaniel Boyden), a railroad car shop for the new Western North Carolina Railroad, and a distillery. In addition there was the cotton mill (alongside the railroad but antedating it by several years) that would later become a military prison.[64]

Nine-tenths of the workingmen thereabouts found employment in the various mechanical operations in town. These mechanics numbered about 500 according to a visitor in 1858 who said he had never seen such industry in a place of its size. The Salisbury *Carolina Watchman* freely attributed the town's prosperity to its two new railroads. Salisbury's business foundation was firm enough that the town seems to have rebounded very quickly in the wake of Stoneman's raid and the burning of some of these industries at the end of the war.[65] But none of the industries was very large. According to the census, the railroad car shop employed 29 men in 1860. The distillery hired 8. The foundry (Boyden's or another) employed 20. There was 1 tobacco factory in 1860 with 40 workers and 2 in 1880 with 110 workers.

Like editors at the time, local historian James S. Brawley credits the NCRR with lifting Rowan County from depression to prosperity. But by his own evidence, most of its growth came after 1880, a generation after the railroad's arrival. Even then the growth was modest. After doubling in population from 1,086 in 1850 to 2,420 in 1860, Salisbury virtually stopped growing until the 1880s. It reached only 6,277 in 1900. By that year the two largest industries were new textile mills and the massive new repair shop complex built by the Southern Railway next door at Spencer, a larger version of Company Shops named for Samuel Spencer, the Southern's president. Each industry employed about 800 workers.[66]

More remarkable in terms of numerical growth, though still modest, was the rise of Concord. The Cabarrus County seat had 878 residents when it was first listed in the census of 1870. It exceeded 4,000 in 1890 and ten years later had left Salisbury behind with nearly 8,000. A long-established cotton mill (owned by John McDonald, a sometime NCRR director) employed 114 persons in 1880; others would follow by 1900. The mill towns of China Grove, Landis, and Kannapolis, lying along the railroad between Salisbury and Concord, were clearly dependent on it. China Grove antedates the railroad; the others were established just after the turn of the century.[67]

Charlotte was a muddy village with barely a thousand people when its position as the junction of two railroads became clear in 1850. That prospect created a building boom as early as the fall of 1851, a full year before the Charlotte and South Carolina made its appearance. In February 1852 the Charlotte *Whig* noted a rapid population growth: every day brought some new artisan, tradesman, merchant, or professional attracted by the approaching railroads. In June 1854, soon after the NCRR began construction at this end of the line, a local brickyard turning out 40,000 bricks a day still could not fill the demand. After a visit to Charlotte in 1860 William W. Holden called it the most enterprising and growing inland town in the state, with a population between 3,000 and 4,000.[68] The census that year listed only 2,265, however.

One of the early businesses was a steam-powered flour mill built along the NCRR tracks. By 1858 its chief proprietor was John Wilkes, the brother of NCRR Superintendent Edmund Wilkes. It shipped flour to eastern North Carolina as well as to Charleston and beyond. Soon finding that eastern and northern buyers would pay more for flour shipped in barrels rather than in sacks, Wilkes built a barrel factory next door. Ironically, another rail-oriented industry was the Confederate navy yard, which moved to a trackside location in Charlotte after being forced from Norfolk in 1862.[69]

Charlotte grew rapidly after the war. The marginal gold mines nearby were reopened. The Rock Island Woollen Mills moved into town from the Catawba River and were soon employing a hundred workers. A cotton mill was established in 1881. Other railroads were built or rebuilt to Atlanta, Statesville, and Wilmington. The city became an important cotton market, and stores and banks proliferated. In July 1869 the Charlotte *Democrat* contrasted the muddy village of twenty years earlier with what it now characterized as "a flourishing young city with macadamized streets and pavements."[70]

No doubt all this was true. But in Charlotte, too, growth appeared all the greater against small antecedents. Again the census was remorseless in cutting down the enthusiastic claims of contemporary boosters. Mecklenburg County's gold smelters employed only nine people in 1870 and none in 1880. By 1880 the woolen mill was closed, and Mecklenburg's largest industry in terms of employment was eighteen sawmills with a collective total of sixty-two workers. The largest industry in value of products consisted of twenty-two flour and grist mills employing little over one person each and producing $91,000 worth of flour and meal. With 2,265 people in 1860, Charlotte grew to only 7,094 in 1880. But growth came faster thereafter. The city had 11,557 residents in 1890, 18,091 in 1900, and then nearly doubled to 34,014 in 1910. As elsewhere along the NCRR, the city's industrial and commercial takeoff came a full generation after the advent of its earliest railroads.

By 1900 Charlotte was the largest city along the NCRR, having recently passed an almost standstill Raleigh. At that time, some forty-five years after the NCRR's construction, only seven towns along the road could yet claim more than 5,000 people: Charlotte, with 18,091; Raleigh, 13,643; Greensboro, 10,035; Concord, 7,910; Durham, 6,679; Salisbury, 6,277; and Goldsboro, 5,877.

Increasingly after the war, American railroads undertook "programs of creative traffic generation," as historian Roy V. Scott phrased it. In other words, they tried to promote economic development in their territories so as to generate additional traffic. The Wilmington and Weldon actively encouraged truck farming for the northern market among farmers along its route. Like many other railroads, the NCRR carried fertilizers at preferential rates. Like them it granted lower rates individually to large shippers of every description. It offered reduced fares to immigrants (at the same time it offered them to emigrants). These were the most minimal development policies, common to all railroads. Beyond them the NCRR had no systematic development program by 1871, when it ceased independent operations. In fairness, most such programs around the country came later. The successor Southern Railway had a development officer from the time of its organization in 1894.[71]

The Southern also promoted tourism, more in the mountains than along the route of the NCRR. But late in the nineteenth century and well into the twentieth, Guilford, Randolph, and Davidson counties became a kind of sportsman's paradise as tens of thousands of acres of farmland were leased every winter by exclusive hunting clubs. Beginning in November, "a succession of tweedy financiers, bankers, railway magnates and assorted millionaires detrained at High Point, Greensboro and Thomasville with their guns and valets." More than a few came in private cars, expedited by the Southern Railway. Quail was the favorite game. J. P. Morgan, Jr., the most prominent visitor, returned to Climax Lodge in southern Guilford for nearly forty years before his death in 1943.[72]

THIS ASSESSMENT OF the NCRR's impact has been confined largely to the counties and communities directly on its route, until the turn of the twentieth century. Within that time the NCRR may legitimately claim credit as well for much of the development in counties not directly on the road. Forsyth County is an obvious example. Those served by the Western North Carolina Railroad might also be included, as that road, tributary to the NCRR, was built through Iredell, Catawba, and Burke counties before the war, then later through the mountains to Asheville and beyond. Edward Phifer, in his history of Burke, points out that commercial lumbering in that area depended on the arrival of the railroad. Larger lumber companies coming to the county after 1900 built their own shortline railroads, connecting to the main line. The first cotton mill in Morganton was built across the street from the WNCRR depot in 1888.[73] Similarly Wilmington, New Bern, Morehead City, and other places in eastern North Carolina, well away from the route of the NCRR, derived business from it. So did Norfolk, Richmond, New York, and Liverpool.

Even in its own territory, the NCRR never existed in a vacuum. The communities immediately adjacent to it were influenced in varying measure by other transportation facilities and by considerations altogether different. The farther away from the road, the greater these other influences were apt to be. And in the fullness of time, as the national railway network developed and new technologies brought the automobile, bus, truck, and airplane, the harder it is to assess the impact of a single railroad.

It is obvious from the map that the Piedmont Crescent, so visible a part of contemporary North Carolina, was a product of the NCRR. Clearly apparent by 1910, it developed along the same semicircular route from Raleigh through Burlington, Greensboro, and High Point to Salisbury and Charlotte. (The NCRR bypasses only Winston-Salem among the later Crescent cities although Salem had been on the earlier stagecoach route from Greensboro to Salisbury.)[74]

Geographer D. Brooks Cates argues that "an incipient crescent" already existed when the route of the NCRR was chosen. Using modern location theory, he justifies the chosen route because the existing concentrations of people in 1850 point to it as offering the greatest potential traffic.[75] Indeed the NCRR charter required it to go from the capital at Raleigh to the already established towns of Salisbury and Charlotte. Walter Gwynn chose the longer intermediate route through Hillsboro and Greensboro rather than that through Pittsboro and Asheboro because of smoother terrain and easier grades and surely also because more people promised greater financial and political support and greater traffic through the chosen counties.

Its route thus determined by three existing towns and influenced by several others, the NCRR subsequently enlarged those places as it summoned still others like Durham, Burlington, and High Point into existence for the first time. Money was scarce, and this development came very gradually. But as Coy T. Phillips, another geographer, pointed out, the road roughly paralleled the northern edge of the cotton belt, touched the old bright tobacco belt in the Virginia and North Carolina piedmont, and penetrated the coastal plain where the new bright belt was to develop later. It also bisected the piedmont hardwood forest. So the towns that grew up along the road were well fixed to develop the state's three major manufacturing industries of the late nineteenth century and afterward: cigarettes, cotton textiles, and furniture.[76]

The Crescent became the most industrialized and urbanized region of the state. Ten counties from Wake to Mecklenburg (including Forsyth) contained in 1955 over 25 percent of the state's population on just 9 percent of its land. Those counties employed about 45 percent of the state's industrial workers and accounted for over half of the value added by manufacturing. Retail sales volume was near the national average and well ahead of that in the rest of the state. About 60 percent of the state's wholesale trade centered there.[77] Since the 1950s, the Crescent cities have grown faster than southeastern cities generally—similar on a much smaller scale to the megalopolis of the Northeast.[78]

On balance, the NCRR clearly moved piedmont North Carolina forward more than backward. As part of the Southern Railway, its role in retarding diversification and perpetuating a colonial economy proved less enduring than its role in fostering growth and lessening isolation. Its monuments are to be found not only in the Piedmont Crescent but in areas farther afield that it serves less directly. Nowadays highways and airlines also fuel southern growth. But they respond to established patterns. As the state's major airports are Raleigh/Durham, Greensboro/Winston-Salem/High Point, and Charlotte, so Interstate 85 parallels the North Carolina Railroad from Durham to Charlotte, at once reflecting and reinforcing its Piedmont Crescent.

The North Carolina Railroad remains a prime resource of the state that so largely built the road, oversaw its operations for more than fifteen years, and continues now to choose its presidents and boards of directors. Over the years it has become for many a public trust as well as a financial resource. What benefits it may continue to offer its ultimate owners, the people of North Carolina, deserve to be a matter of perennial interest.

APPENDIX

Table 1
NCRR Stock Subscriptions by County, 30 March 1850

Counties along Expected Route: Shares		Other Counties or Places: Shares	
Wayne	160	New Hanover	502
Johnston	52	Craven	340
Wake	1,340	Davie	260
Orange	977	Caswell	33
Alamance	400	Petersburg, Va.	173
Guilford	1,174		
Davidson	850	Total	1,308
Rowan	1,530		
Cabarrus	807		
Mecklenburg	80		
Total	7,370	Grand Total	8,678

Sources: Raleigh *North Carolina Star*, 3 April 1850; *Greensboro Patriot*, 6 April 1850.

Table 2
Twenty-five Largest NCRR Stockholders, 1859 and 1870

1859 Stockholders/Shares		1870 Stockholders/Shares	
John C. McRae & Co.	885	John I. Shaver	503
Shaver & Simonton	314	John L. Morehead	302
Cyrus P. Mendenhall	157	Thomas Branch	288
Charles F. Fisher	143	William R. Myers	224
William Murdoch	140	North Carolina Railroad	215
Michael Brown	133	Zebulon Latimer	182
Francis Fries	114	John C. McRae	178
Richard J. Ashe	110	Alexander McRae, Sr.	173
John B. Lord	106	John W. Thomas	166
John H. Caldwell	105	Francis Fries	137
Richard Smith	100	Moses L. Holmes	131
Philemon B. Hawkins	92	L. W. Humphrey	127
John Motley Morehead	88	Wilson & Shober	124
John A. Gilmer	81	Robert W. Foard	114
John Milton Coffin	80	George T. Barnes (Trustee)	113
Samuel Kerr	80	Reuben J. Holmes	109
George W. Mordecai	80	S. H. Wiley	105
John E. Patton	80	Myer Myers	104
Dabney Cosby	79	P. K. Dickinson	100
Joel H. Jenkins	78	Joseph Graham	100
John W. Thomas	75	Penelope Smith	100
Alonzo T. Jerkins	71	B. B. Roberts/D. A. Davis (Execs.)	98
John Finley McCorkle	71	R. W. Foard	86
Edward Strudwick	70	Joel H. Jenkins	78
Frederick J. Hill	50	Edwin M. Holt	72

Sources: NCRR, *Report of the President, January 20, 1859*; NCRR, *Annual Report*, 1870.

Table 3
NCRR Stock Dividends Paid, 1859–1872

Year	Number	Date Payable	Amount
1858–59	1	Jan. 1859	3% on state's preferred stock
		1 Aug. 1859	Same, plus 2% on common stock
1859–60	2	10 July 1860	6% on state's preferred stock, 3% on common stock
1861–62	3	2 July 1862	8% (in Confederate currency)
1862–63	4	2 Feb. 1863	10% (in Confederate currency)
	5	15 July 1863	10% (in Confederate currency)
1863–64	6	1 Feb. 1864	6% (in Confederate currency)
1864–65	7	19 Sept. 1864	15% (in Confederate currency)
	8	1 Feb. 1865	25% (in Confederate currency)
1867–68	9	1 Oct. 1868	6% (in NCRR 8% bonds or scrip)
1869–70	10	1 Apr. 1870	3%
		1 July 1870	3%
1870–71	11	1 Mar. 1871	3%
		1 July 1871	3%
1871–72	12	1 July 1872	3%
		31 Dec. 1872	3%

Sources: NCRR annual reports; N.C. *Senate Documents*, 1874–75, #18, p. 6.

Table 4
NCRR Directors with at Least Five Years' Service, 1850–1871

Director	Home County	Party Affiliation	Years of Service State	Private	Total	Shares Stock[a]
Dolphin A. Davis	Rowan	Whig/Cons.[b]	2	9	11	22
Paul C. Cameron	Orange	Democrat	8	2	10	65
Samuel Hargrave	Davidson	Democrat	10		10	27
Giles Mebane	Alamance	Whig	4	6	10	49
John I. Shaver	Rowan	Whig/Cons.	7	3	10	324
Robert P. Dick	Guilford	Dem./Repub.[c]	9		9	12
William T. Dortch	Wayne	Democrat	9		9	20
John D. Bellamy	New Hanover	Democrat	8		8	5
Charles F. Fisher	Rowan	Democrat	2	6	8	79
Philemon B. Hawkins	Franklin	Democrat	8		8	38
Romulus M. Saunders	Wake	Democrat		8	8	35
Thomas Webb	Orange	Whig/Cons.		8	8	40
Francis Fries	Forsyth	Whig		7	7	97
Alexander McRae	New Hanover	Whig		7	7	175
William C. Means	Cabarrus	Whig/Cons.	4	3	7	29
John L. Morehead	Mecklenburg	Conservative		6	6	257
Daniel M. Barringer	Wake	Democrat	5		5	5
Ralph Gorrell	Guilford	Whig	2	3	5	15
John Motley Morehead	Guilford	Whig		5	5	120
William A. Smith	Johnston	Republican	5		5	28

Source: NCRR annual reports.

[a] In some cases an estimated average over a period of years.
[b] Whig before the war, Conservative afterward.
[c] Democrat before the war, Republican afterward.

Table 5
Officers of the North Carolina Railroad, 1850–1872

President	John Motley Morehead, 1850–55
	Charles F. Fisher, 1855–61
	Paul C. Cameron, 1861–62
	Thomas Webb, 1862–65, 1866–67
	Nathaniel Boyden, 1865–66
	Josiah Turner, Jr., 1867–68
	William A. Smith, 1868–72
Superintendent/ Chief Engineer	Walter Gwynn, 1852–56
	Theodore S. Garnett, 1856
	Edmund Wilkes, 1861–62, 1865–67
	Thomas J. Sumner, 1862–65
	James Anderson, 1867–68
	Albert Johnson, 1868–71
Secretary-Treasurer	Jeduthun H. Lindsay, 1850–51
	Cyrus P. Mendenhall, 1851–55
Secretary	Julius D. Ramsey, 1855–58
	R. W. Mills, 1858–61
	John H. Bryan, Jr., 1861–64
	Francis A. Stagg, 1864–72
	Charles M. Crump (acting), 1871–72
Treasurer	Cyrus P. Mendenhall, 1855–59
	Peter B. Ruffin, 1859–65, 1866–67
	Gabriel M. Lea, 1865–66, 1868–72
	William A. Caldwell, 1867–68
Master Machinist	Thomas E. Roberts, 1854–60
	E. H. Marsh, 1860–63
	James Anderson, 1863–64
	Rufus D. Wade, 1864–68, 1870–71
	Emery Burns, 1868–70
	William R. Blake, 1870
Master of Transportation (General Transportation Agent; Dispatcher of Trains)	N. E. Scales, 1854–56
	Edmund Wilkes, 1859–61
	William A. Dunn, 1861–62
	Charles Parmenter, 1864–65
	John A. Wilson, 1865–69
	William H. Green, 1869–72
Road Master	Thomas J. Sumner, 1854–55?
	James E. Allen, 1855–56, 1859–60
	W. P. Raiford, 1868–71

Source: NCRR annual reports.

Table 6
NCRR Workers, 1857, 1858, and 1865–1871

Occupations	Race	1857	1858	1865	1866	1867	1868	1869	1870	1871
Train department										
Engineers	W	17	20	22	18	11	13	11	10	11
Conductors	W	8	9	11	12	7	4	4	4	6
Firemen	W		3	8	6	12	3	1		
	Free B		6	12	12		10	11	11	12
	Slaves		21							
Woodpassers	W			10	3	12				
	B			9	15		15	11	10	11
Brakemen	W			2	21	20	11	9	4	
	B			18			10	11	15	19
Baggage										
masters	W				4	3		4	3	2
	B								1	2
Watchmen	W						3			
Hands										
Passenger	W	6	3							
	Free B	12								
	Slaves	14	6							
Freight	W	3								
	Free B	5	4							
	Slaves	6								
Lumber	Slaves	9	6							
Pensioned	B									2
Total		80	78	92	91	65	69	62	58	65

Table 6 (continued)

Occupations	Race	1857	1858	1865	1866	1867	1868	1869	1870	1871
Road department										
Station										
Agents	W	26	26							
Hands	W	12	12	6	28	70	4	5		
	B			44	30		49	49	53	53
	Slaves	46	43							
Watchmen	W	3	3							
Mail carriers	W						4	4	5	4
Gravel train										
Engineers	W			2	4	4	2	3	2	2
Conductors	W			2	3					
Firemen	W						1	3		
	B						1	2	2	2
Hands	W	1			115	81				
	Free B	1		10			47	74	57	55
	Slaves	27	27							
Section										
Masters	W	19	20	28	35	35	35	35	35	35
Hands	W			15	215	212				
	Free B	1		241	25		192	239	200	194
	Slaves	162	140							
Wood										
choppers	B			75						
Greasers	W						1	1		
Switching										
engineers	W					2	2	1	1	1
Switchmen	W							1	1	1
Bridge										
Builders	W								1	1
Carpenters	W			6		20	1	2		
Watchmen	W	12	4	2	7	6	7	8	11	11
	B							7	1	
Hands	W								7	7
Total		310	275	431	462	420	346	434	376	366

Table 6 (continued)

Occupations	Race	1857	1858	1865	1866	1867	1868	1869	1870	1871
Machinery department										
Shopmen (undifferentiated)	W	39	39							
	Free B	1	2							
	Slaves	12	20							
Foremen	W			5	5	5	4	5	6	6
Coppersmiths	W				1	1	1	1	1	1
Boilermakers	W			2	2	2	2	2	1	1
Machinists	W			29	14	15	5	7	13	8
Laborers	W					12	1	4	4	3
	B			34	26		12	9	14	7
Moulders	W			2	1	3	1	2	1	1
Smiths	W			7	6	6	4	4	5	5
	B				3					
Watchmen	W			2	3	3		3	3	
Helpers	W				5	11	4	8	7	4
	B			11	11		4	1	4	12
Apprentices	W				6	10	12	12	10	12
	B								1	
Bolt cutters	W				1	1				
Patternmakers	W			1	1	2	1	1	1	1
Carpenters	W			24	36	21	11	15	16	14
	B			8	4					
Tinners	W				1	2	1	1	1	1
	B				1					
Trimmers	W				1	1	1			
Millers	W				1					
Core makers	W				1	1	1	1	1	1
Painters	W				4	1	1	2		2
	B				1					
Car cleaners	B				2					
Car greasers	W				1	1	1	1	1	1
Pump makers	W					1	1	1	1	1
Stationary engineers	W				1	1	1	1	1	1
Firemen	W						1		1	
	B					1		1		1
Total		52	61	125	140	101	70	82	93	82

Table 6 (continued)

Occupations	Race	1857	1858	1865	1866	1867	1868	1869	1870	1871
Grand Total		442	414	648	693	586	485	578	527	513
Workers per mile		1.98	1.86	2.91	3.11	2.63	2.17	2.59	2.36	2.30
Total blacks		296	275	462	131	0	341	414	370	369
Percent of Grand Total		67	66	71	19	0	70	72	70	72

Source: NCRR annual reports.

Note: Racial identification was not given after 1866. In later years blacks are identified here as those receiving part of their pay in rations; that practice was usual but not invariable with black employees.

Table 7
NCRR Bridges, 1859 and 1871 (All of Wood Construction)

Location	Lattice (L) or Howe Truss (HT) 1871	Deck (D) or Through (T) 1859	1871	Length (feet) 1859	1871	Number of Spans[a]	Length of Span (feet)[a]
Rocky River	L	T	T	117	117	1	100
Caudle Creek	L	T		136	136	1	115
Irish Buffalo Creek	L	D		67	77	1	57
Yadkin River	HT	D		658	660	4	150
S. Potts Creek	L	D	D	60	68	1	50
N. Potts Creek	L	D	T	54	56	1	40
Swearing Creek	L	D	D	70	72	1	60
Leonard's Creek	L	D	D	123	126	1	106
Abbott's Creek	HT	T	T	223		2	100
Rich Fork	HT	T	T	124	110	1	110
Jimmie's Creek	L	T	T	54	55	1	39
Deep River	HT	T	T	117		1	100
W. Buffalo Creek	HT	D	T	40		1	30
E. Buffalo Creek	L	T	T	130	134	1	118
Haw River	L	D	D	260	252	2	100
Back Creek	L	D	D	115	126	1	104
W. Eno River	HT	D	D	112	130	1	100
E. Eno River	HT	D	D	112	111	1	100
Cate's Creek	HT	Trestle	D		61		
Stony Creek	HT	D	D	54	61	1	40
Crabtree Creek	L	D	D	56	68	1	42
Walnut Creek	L	D	D	64	78	1	50
Neuse River	HT	T	T	264	360	2	100
Little River[b]	HT	T	T	130	150	1	115

Sources: NCRR, *Report of the President, January 20, 1859*; Property Inventory, September 1871, XV., v. 93–95, NCRR Records, North Carolina Archives.

[a] The number and length of spans in 1871, where given, were the same as in 1859.
[b] The Little River Bridge was described in the Goldsboro *Republican and Patriot* (17, 24 May 1853) as a through Burr truss with a single 150-foot span, to be covered.

Table 8
NCRR Locomotive Roster, 1854–1871

Name	Later Number	Builder	Type	Uses[a]	Year Acquired	Year Out of Service	Comments
Ixion		Norris	4-4-0	F	1854	1864	Rebuilt as the Col. C. F. Fisher.
Traho		Norris	4-2-0	G	1854	1859	Rebuilt with the Pello as the Carolina.
Pactolus	16	Norris	4-4-0	F,G	1854		Rebuilt 1871.
Pello		Norris	4-2-0	G	1854	1859	Rebuilt with the Traho as the Carolina.
Cybele		Norris	4-4-0	F	1854	1865/66	Probably rebuilt as the Thomas Webb.
Ajax		Norris	4-4-0	P	1854	1861/62?	Probably rebuilt as the Roanoke.
Sisyphus		Norris	4-4-0	P	1854	1865	Wrecked in collision.
Midas		Norris	4-4-0	F	1854	1867?	Probably rebuilt as the Giles Mebane.
Apollo	14	Norris	4-4-0	F,P	1854		Rebuilt 1861.
Ulysses		Norris	4-4-0	F,G	1854	1869?	Probably rebuilt as the E. M. Holt.
Cyclops		Norris	4-4-0	P,G	1854	1866/67	Scrapped.
Excelsior	7	Norris	4-4-0	P,G	1854	1869	Scrapped.
Astron	1	Norris	4-4-0	P	1855		Rebuilt 1862, 1870.
Aristos		Norris	4-4-0	F,G	1855	1866/67	Scrapped.
Helios		Norris	4-4-0	P,G	1855	1868	Rebuilt as the Gov. Holden.
Kratos		Norris	4-4-0	F	1855	1863/64	Probably rebuilt as the Gov. Morehead.
Yadkin	5	B&K[b]	4-4-0	P	1856		
Guilford	21	Norris	4-6-0	F	1856		Rebuilt 1865/66.
Watauga	6	Norris	4-4-0	P	1856		
Rowan		Norris	4-6-0	F	1856	1865	Rebuilt then wrecked in explosion.
Alamance	9	Norris	4-4-0	P	1857		

Table 8 (continued)

Name	Later Number	Builder	Type	Uses[a]	Year Acquired	Year Out of Service	Comments
Neuse	10	Norris	4-4-0	P	1857		Rebuilt from the Traho and the Pello.
Orange	11	Rogers	4-4-0	P	1857		Probably rebuilt from the Ajax.
Carolina	19	NCRR	4-4-0	F,G,S	1859	1872	Scrapped.
Roanoke		NCRR	4-4-0	P	1861/62	1865/66	
Manassas Gap #2					1862	1865	Rented from Manassas Gap RR. Returned 1865.
Manassas					1861/62	1862/63?	Rented from Richmond, Fredericksburg & Potomac RR?
Croatan		Norris		G,S	1862	1869/70	Probably rebuilt as the Phoenix.
#76		Denmead		F	1862	1864/65	Property of Confederate Govt.?
#225		Denmead		F	1862	1863/64	Property of Confederate Govt.?
Col. Myers		Mason		F	1862/63	1863/64	Rented from Richmond, Fredericksburg & Potomac RR?
Manassas Gap #9					1862/63	1865	Rented from Manassas Gap RR. Returned 1865.
Vulcan		Baldwin		F	1863	1865	Purchased from Confederate Govt. Reclaimed by B&O RR.
Hercules				F	1863	1865	Purchased from Confederate Govt. Reclaimed by B&O RR.
Orion		Norris		F	1863	1865	Purchased from Confederate Govt. Reclaimed by B&O RR.

Gen. Pettigrew		Hinkley		F	1863	1865	Purchased from Confederate Govt. Reclaimed by B&O RR.
Calvin Graves	22	Taunton		F	1863/64		Probably rebuilt from the Kratos.
Gov. Morehead	12	NCRR		P,F	1864		Rebuilt from the Ixion.
Col. C. F. Fisher	15	NCRR		P,F	1865		Purchased secondhand from U.S. Govt.
Paul C. Cameron	24	S&J[c,d]		F,G	1865		Built 1862. Purchased secondhand from U.S. Govt.
Jos. Caldwell	25	Taunton[d]		F	1865		
Mecklenburg		Taunton		F	1865	1866/67	Purchased secondhand from U.S. Govt.
Col. Webster		Amoskeag		L	1865	1866	Built 1856. Purchased secondhand from U.S. Govt.
Thomas Webb	17	NCRR		F	1866		Probably rebuilt from the Cybele.
Gen. Washington	26	Grant		F	1866		First new purchase since 1857.
Nathaniel Boyden	27	Amoskeag		F,G	1866		Probably rebuilt from the Col. Webster.
Giles Mebane	18	NCRR		F	1867		Probably rebuilt from the Midas.
Pioneer	8	NCRR		P	1868		First locomotive built wholly in North Carolina.
Gov. Holden	2	NCRR		P	1869		Rebuilt from the Helios.
Phoenix	20	NCRR		P	1869/70	1870	Probably rebuilt from the Croatan.
E. M. Holt	13	NCRR		P	1870		Traded to WC&R RR.[e]
W. A. Smith	3	Rogers	4-6-0?	F	1870		Probably rebuilt from the Ulysses.

Principal Sources: NCRR and R&DRR annual reports, 1854–74.

[a] Uses are abbreviated thus: F: Freight, G: Gravel, P: Passenger, S: Switching, L: Lumber
[b] Breese, Kneeland & Co.
[c] Smith and Jackson.
[d] Manufacturers of the Cameron and Caldwell may be reversed.
[e] Wilmington, Charlotte, and Rutherford Railroad.

Table 9

NCRR Passenger, Freight, and Work Cars, 1854–1872

Year	First-Class Coach	Second-Class Coach[a]	Total Coaches	Mail, Smoking, Baggage, Servants' Cars	Express, Mail Cars	Box-cars	Flat-cars	Stock Cars	Gravel Cars	Dump Cars	Conductors' Cars	Shanty, Dormitory Cars	Office Cars	Hand, Pole, or Crank Cars	Lumber Trucks
1854							35		11					4	
1855			7		4	39	100		20					15	
1856			8		8	102	66	6	30						
1857	13	4	17		5	114	87		30					39	
1858	14	3	17		5	121	92		30					33	
1859	14	3	17		7	138	81		24					41	
1860	13	4	17	4	6	142	83		20						
1861	—	—	—	—	—	—	—	—	—	—	—	—	—	—	—
1862[b]	13	3	16	4	6	147	56			12				44	
1863	—	—	—	—	—	—	—	—	—	—	—	—	—	—	—
1864	—	—	—	—	—	—	—	—	—	—	—	—	—	—	—
1865[c]			4		3	135	35							—	—
1866	11	6	17	4	4	108	60								
1867			15		13	121	70					5	1		
1868			18		13	134	76					5	1		
1869	10	10	20		13	142	105		15			5	1	42	
1870	5	13	18		10	155	80		15		6	10	2	42	
1871			18?		12	154	71		15		6	8	1	40	
1872	8	10	18		10	174	53		15		6	17			4

Sources: NCRR and R&DRR annual reports, 1854–72; NCRR Reports to State Supt. of Public Works, 1869–71, in Treasurers' and Comptrollers' Papers, Internal Improvements, North Carolina Archives.

a Includes combination cars. b The NCRR also rented cars from other roads during the war. c These figures do not include many cars listed as unusable. The inspection committee of 1866 said that even these figures were too high.

Table 10
NCRR Running Times and Speeds, 1856–1871

Effective Date	Kind of Train	Origin	Destination	Miles	Time (Hr:Min)	Average M.P.H. Including Stops
1/31/56	Mail[a]	Goldsboro	Charlotte	223	15:54	14
4/21/56	Mail	Charlotte	Goldsboro	223	13:35	16
April 1858	Express	Goldsboro	Charlotte	223	10:20	22[b]
April 1858	Mail	Goldsboro	Charlotte	223	12:45	17
7/28/65	Mail	Raleigh	Charlotte	174	17:20	10
1/7/66	Mail	Goldsboro	Charlotte	223	16:40	13
1/7/66	Mixed[c]	Goldsboro	Charlotte	223	20:45	11
6/10/66	Mail	Goldsboro	Charlotte	223	12:05	18.5
	Same	Raleigh	Charlotte	174	8:50	20
6/1/67	Mail	Goldsboro	Charlotte	223	11:12	20
6/1/67	Mixed	Goldsboro	Charlotte	223	24:30	12
4/1/68	Mail	Raleigh	Charlotte	174	8:15	21
1/15/69	Mail	Goldsboro	Charlotte	223	17:20	13
1/15/69	Mixed	Goldsboro	Charlotte	223	35:40	6
6/4/71	Mail	Goldsboro	Charlotte	223	16:15	14
6/4/71	Express	Raleigh	Charlotte	174	11:15	15.5

Sources: Newspaper advertisements of train schedules.

[a] Mail and passenger train.
[b] 26 m.p.h. between stops.
[c] Accommodation (freight and passenger) train.

Table 11
NCRR Receipts and Expenses, 1854–1871

Year	Passenger	Freight	Express	Mail	Other	Total
1854–55	$ 28,161	$ 28,702		$ 5,121		$ 61,984
1855–56	90,109	120,300		19,892		230,301
1856–57	132,016	146,134		22,300		300,450
1857–58	146,412	168,282		22,300	$ 2,315	339,309
1858–59[a]	145,452	184,640	$ 1,000	20,442	5,198	356,732
1859–60	174,847	225,755	4,000	22,300	203	427,105
1860–61	194,286	214,361	4,000	22,300	10	434,957
1861–62	460,504	272,398	23,765	26,375	8,024	791,066
1862–63	982,064	509,502	124,921	28,882	4,567	1,649,936
1863–64	1,547,192	1,352,898	292,176	26,375	28,439	3,247,080
1864–65	2,554,054	2,395,929	386,028	29,113	40,651	5,405,775
1865–66	279,628	462,557	47,657	7,994	92,088	889,924
1866–67	201,686	287,956	13,974	14,867	79,641	598,124
1867–68	172,770	336,512	7,847	16,725	51,552	585,406
1868–69	195,612	355,657	8,485	16,725	81,638	658,117
1869–70	233,409	391,466	13,600	16,725	64,196	719,396
1870–71	266,434	420,088	14,875	18,725	44,984	765,106
1871–72[b]	68,410	101,520	5,677	6,179	22,405[c]	204,192[c]

Source: NCRR annual reports.

[a] Eleven months.
[b] Prior to lease in September 1871.
[c] Omits $78,000 rent from Richmond and Danville Railroad.

Civilian Passenger Receipts as Percentage of Total Receipts	All Passenger Receipts as Percentage of Total Receipts	Civilian Freight Receipts as Percentage of Total Receipts	All Freight Receipts as Percentage of Total Receipts	Military Receipts as Percentage of Total Receipts	Expenses	Receipts over Expenses	Expenses as Percentage of Receipts
45	45	46	46		$ 48,678	$ 13,306	79
39	39	52	52		108,209	122,092	47
44	44	49	49		137,525	162,925	46
43	43	50	50		151,791	187,518	45
41	41	52	52		164,194	192,538	46
41	41	53	53		192,938	234,167	45
42	45	49	47	3	—	—	—
34	58	19	34	40	440,420	350,646	56
43	60	19	31	29	631,192	1,018,744	38
26	48	19	42	44	1,627,658	1,609,422	50
19	47	19	44	53	3,108,909	2,296,866	58
22	31	46	52	15	984,376	−94,452	111
33	34	48	48	1	690,456	−92,332	115
28	30	55	57	5	508,526	76,880	87
28	30	53	54	3	470,084	188,033	71
32	32	54	54		466,649	252,747	65
35	35	55	56		404,043	361,063	53
34	34	50	50		197,201	6,991	97

Table 12

NCRR Receipts and Expenses per Mile, 1856–1871

Fiscal Year	Passenger Trains			Freight Trains			Total (Passenger + Freight)				
	Receipts[a]	Miles Run	Receipts per Mile	Receipts	Miles Run	Receipts per Mile	Receipts	Miles Run	Receipts per Mile	Expenses[c]	Expenses per Mile
1856–57	$ 154,316	205,984	$ .749	$ 146,134	94,156	$ 1.552	$ 300,450	300,140	$ 1.001	$ 137,525	$ .458
1857–58	168,712	293,592	.575	168,282	122,820	1.370	339,309	431,773	.786	151,791	.352
1858–59[b]	166,894	266,138	.627	184,640	130,190	1.418	356,732	406,652	.877	164,194	.404
1859–60	201,147	278,197	.723	225,755	176,415	1.280	427,105	454,612	.939	192,938	.424
1860–61	220,586	—	—	214,361	—	—	434,957	—	—	—	—
1861–62	510,644	—	—	272,398	—	—	791,066	460,126	1.719	440,420	.957
1862–63	1,135,867	259,620	4.375	509,502	222,260	2.292	1,649,936	481,880	3.424	631,192	1.310
1863–64	1,865,743	273,600	6.819	1,352,898	226,750	5.966	3,247,080	500,350	6.490	1,637,658	3.273
1864–65	2,969,195	288,280	10.300	2,395,929	186,020	12.880	5,405,775	474,300	11.397	3,108,909	6.555
1865–66	335,279	206,477	1.624	462,557	84,255	5.490	889,924	362,846	2.453	984,376	2.713
1866–67	230,527	163,033	1.414	287,956	150,661	1.911	598,124	371,012	1.612	690,456	1.861
1867–68	197,342	140,283	1.407	336,512	175,982	1.912	576,131	350,965	1.642	508,526	1.449
1868–69	220,822	160,913	1.372	355,657	154,297	2.305	658,117	343,578	1.915	470,084	1.368
1869–70	263,734	154,237	1.710	391,466	180,143	2.173	719,396	342,792	2.099	466,649	1.361
1870–71	300,034	—	—	420,088	—	—	765,106	—	—	404,043	—

Source: NCRR annual reports.

[a] Includes receipts from passengers, express, and mail.
[b] Eleven months.
[c] Passenger and freight expenses not available separately.

Table 13
Number of NCRR Passengers, 1855–1871

Year	Local	Through	Tickets Sold by Conductors	Military	Total	Military as Percentage of Total
1855–56					51,190	
1856–57	59,077	7,672			66,749	
1857–58	64,606	10,051			74,657	
1858–59[a]	54,315	10,524			64,839	
1859–60	64,206	12,173			76,379	
1860–61	75,726	10,007		4,514	90,247	5.0
1861–62	83,849	5,679	27,799	87,057	204,384	42.6
1862–63	157,678	16,717	36,592	102,526	313,513	32.7
1863–64	162,865	9,150	56,507	166,172	394,694	42.1
1864–65	88,263	970	87,043	329,890	506,166	65.2
1865–66	45,162	170			45,332	
1866–67	43,352	7,440	14,396	3,484	68,672	5.1
1867–68	62,289	8,008	6,908	3,857	81,062	4.8
1868–69	60,873	10,259	4,576	3,242	78,950	4.1
1869–70	70,114	17,005	6,278	164	93,561	
1870–71	71,998	19,148	5,844		96,990	

Source: NCRR annual reports.

[a] Eleven months.

Table 14
NCRR Passenger Receipts, 1854–1871

| Year | Local | | | Through[a] | | |
	Eastbound	Westbound	Total	Eastbound	Westbound	Total
1854–55						
1855–56						
1856–57	$ 46,615	$ 46,411	$ 93,026	$16,941	$15,308	$32,249
1857–58[b]	51,913	48,329	100,242	20,445	19,062	39,507
1858–59	40,952	47,679	88,631	23,333	21,982	45,315
1859–60	49,392	53,557	102,949	26,029	24,434	50,463
1860–61	57,065	60,315	117,380	20,758	22,577	43,335
1861–62	77,527	92,418	169,945	14,428	11,430	25,858
1862–63	230,780	224,815	455,595	41,449	51,217	92,666
1863–64	289,359	269,055	558,414	26,618	31,278	57,896
1864–65	256,536	229,721	486,257	2,500	6,318	8,818
1865–66	80,398	59,226	139,624	1,284	420	1,704
1866–67	67,972	58,166	126,138	17,366	17,377	34,743
1867–68	58,218	55,855	114,073	15,525	18,969	34,494
1868–69	61,948	60,768	122,716	23,377	22,936	46,313
1869–70	71,272	64,803	136,075	34,430	43,085	77,515
1870–71			160,651			85,438

Source: NCRR annual reports.

[a] Includes tickets sold by other railroads.
[b] Eleven months.
[c] Includes east- and westbound tickets sold by conductors, undifferentiated in other years.

| Totals | | Sold by | Total | | Total Passenger |
Eastbound	Westbound	Conductors	Civilian	Military	Receipts
			28,161		$ 28,161
			90,109		90,109
$ 63,556	$ 61,719	$ 6,741	132,016		132,016
72,358	67,391	6,663	146,412		146,412
64,285	69,661	11,506	145,452		145,452
75,421	77,991	21,435	174,847		174,847
77,823	82,892	22,084	182,799	$ 11,487	194,286
122,151[c]	143,457[c]	69,805	265,608	194,896	460,504
335,966[c]	368,046[c]	155,751	704,012	278,052	982,064
315,977	300,333	235,173	851,483	695,709	1,547,192
259,036	236,039	545,607	1,040,682	1,513,372	2,554,054
81,682	59,646	56,778	198,106	81,522	279,628
85,338	75,543	34,872	195,753	5,933	201,686
73,743	74,824	14,928	163,495	9,275	172,770
85,325	83,704	13,235	182,264	13,348	195,612
105,702	107,888	19,358	232,948	461	233,409
		20,345	266,434		266,434

Table 15
NCRR Freight Receipts, 1854–1871

Year	Civilian Freight East-bound	West-bound	Miscel-laneous	Total	Military Freight	Total Freight Receipts
1854–55				$ 28,702		$ 28,702
1855–56				120,300		120,300
1856–57				146,134		146,134
1857–58	$ 61,484	$104,172	$2,626	168,282		168,282
1858–59[a]	81,205	103,435		184,640		184,640
1859–60	84,278	138,984	2,493	225,755		225,755
1860–61	70,803	140,665		211,468	$ 2,893	214,361
1861–62	59,983	88,880		148,863	123,535	272,398
1862–63	87,324	227,881		315,205	194,297	509,502
1863–64	245,945	363,372		609,317	743,581	1,352,898
1864–65	565,288	464,621	2,926	1,032,835	1,363,094	2,395,929
1865–66	277,829	134,483	528	412,840	49,717	462,557
1866–67	104,382	180,923	858	286,163	1,793	287,956
1867–68	135,794	183,369	274	319,437	17,075	336,512
1868–69	146,797	202,007	685	349,489	6,168	355,657
1869–70	163,606	227,518	325	391,449	17	391,466
1870–71				420,088		420,088
1871–72[b]				101,520		101,520

Source: NCRR annual reports.

[a] Eleven months.
[b] Prior to September lease.

Table 16
Six Leading NCRR Stations:
Percentages of Civilian Freight Receipts, 1855–1870

Year	Golds-boro	Raleigh	Greens-boro	High Point	Salis-bury	Char-lotte	Total
1855–56	15.9	3.4	5.5	4.5	24.4	14.4	68.1
1856–57	13.0	5.3	7.8	11.6	21.1	12.9	71.7
1857–58	—	—	—	—	—	—	—
1858–59	—	—	—	—	—	—	—
1859–60	19.3	10.7	5.1	10.9	18.1	14.2	78.3
1860–61	—	—	—	—	—	—	—
1861–62	12.6	24.5	4.3	5.5	4.3	33.0	84.2
1862–63	4.2	19.9	10.7	7.0	8.4	35.7	85.9
1863–64	9.4	16.2	13.3	4.5	6.9	35.0	85.3
1864–65	12.1	6.8	29.0	1.5	3.4	32.6	85.4
1865–66	8.7	10.6	4.8	2.6	9.3	47.4	83.4
1866–67	7.7	23.4	4.9	4.7	9.7	33.3	83.7
1867–68	30.4	14.4	2.7	4.4	9.3	24.8	86.0
1868–69	10.1	30.7	2.6	5.1	10.7	27.9	87.1
1869–70	5.3	35.0	3.1	4.5	10.1	29.3	87.3

Source: NCRR annual reports.

Table 17
NCRR Freight Tonnage, 1867–1872

Year	Through To and from Norfolk[a]	To All Points	Local	Total	Eastward	Westward	Through as Percentage of Total
1867–68	27,116	43,155	22,697	65,852			65.5
1868–69	31,767	45,351	37,932	83,283			54.5
1869–70		53,882	36,955	90,837			59.3
1870–71		62,522	27,470	89,992			69.5
1871–72[b]		78,982	34,145	113,127	47,413	65,713	69.8

Sources: NCRR and R&DRR annual reports.

[a] Actually Portsmouth, Va.
[b] October to September, after lease to Richmond and Danville Railroad.

Table 18

Median Monthly Percentages of Annual NCRR Freight Receipts, 1855–1871

Month	1855–1860	1861–1865	1866–1871	Overall
January	5.7[b]	6.9	7.5	6.8[b]
February	6.4[b]	8.8	8.85	7.9
March	9.1	12.4[a]	9.75	9.75[a]
April	10.9[a]	10.5[a]	8.15	9.2
May	8.2	7.5	7.0	8.0
June	7.8	4.8[b]	5.1[b]	5.2[b]
July	6.05[b]	4.1[b]	4.9[b]	5.15[b]
August	8.75	5.8[b]	6.4[b]	7.2
September	10.75[a]	7.4	10.0[a]	10.1[a]
October	10.35[a]	8.4	11.1[a]	10.35[a]
November	7.85	10.3[a]	9.9[a]	9.15
December	7.1	8.0	9.3	7.55

Source: NCRR annual reports.

[a] Three highest months in each group of years.
[b] Three lowest months in each group of years.

Table 19
Value of Farm Lands and Buildings:
NCRR Counties and the State, 1850–1900

| County | Average Value per Acre | | | | | |
	1850	1860	1870	1880	1890	1900
Wayne	$5	$10	$ 6	$10	$10	$10
Johnston	2	5	2	7	7	10
Wake	3	6	5	9	10	10
Durham					12	10
Orange	3	6	4	7	7	7
Alamance	4	7	3	7	10	9
Guilford	4	9	6	6	9	10
Davidson	4	6	5	8	10	11
Rowan	4	9	5	8	9	10
Cabarrus	4	9	7	11	12	12
Mecklenburg	4	10	10	12	16	17
Average of above	$3.7	$ 7.7	$ 5.3	$ 8.5	$10.2	$10.5
State	3	6	3	6	8	9
NCRR counties' average as percentage of state average	123	128	177	142	128	117

Source: Pressly and Scofield, *Farm Real Estate Values*, pp. 44–46.

Table 20
Population and Agriculture:
NCRR Counties as Percentage of the State, 1850–1900

	1850	1860	1870	1880	1890	1900
Population						
White	19	18	18	18	18	19
Black	16	15	18	18	18	19
Total	18	17	18	18	18	19
Improved						
acres, number	21	19	19	18	18	17
Farm lands						
and buildings,						
average value						
per acre[a]	123	128	177	142	128	117
Farm lands and						
buildings, total						
value	17	17	19	20	18	18
All property,						
assessed value	—	—	22	24	24	—
All farm						
products, value	—	—	18	20	20	18
Livestock						
produced, value	19	17	18	17	17	17
Corn						
produced	19	16	16	17	16	16
Wheat						
produced	32	26	29	27	27	27
Orchard						
products, value	3	19	14	26	—	6
Tobacco						
produced	2	10	9	11	15	14
Cotton						
produced	20	22	18	24	25	23

Source: U.S. Census.

[a] Percentages of state average per acre.

Table 21
Value of Manufactures and Farm Products (in thousands of dollars):
NCRR Counties and the State, 1850–1900

	1850	1860	1870	1880	1890	1900
Wayne						
Manufactures	$169	$212	$ 56	$ 335	$ 538	$1,232
Farm products	—	—	1,433	1,241	934	1,679
Johnston						
Manufactures	598	202	136	156	177	477
Farm products	—	—	614	1,270	1,127	1,820
Wake						
Manufactures	263	646	808	713	1,034	2,612
Farm products	—	—	1,741	2,044	1,529	2,164
Durham						
Manufactures					3,437	8,444
Farm products					446	492
Orange						
Manufactures	64	337	421	1,237	107	363
Farm products	—	—	737	694	494	661
Alamance						
Manufactures	221	501	631	769	1,609	3,738
Farm products	—	—	810	471	559	783
Guilford						
Manufactures	154	287	598	499	1,413	3,691
Farm products	—	—	1,056	797	744	1,126
Davidson						
Manufactures	87	188	993	453	599	1,047
Farm products	—	—	1,126	778	759	1,141
Rowan						
Manufactures	359	384	358	294	681	2,321
Farm products	—	—	822	789	760	1,287
Cabarrus						
Manufactures	250	258	400	314	667	2,232
Farm products	—	—	831	764	655	908
Mecklenburg						
Manufactures	81	258	1,183	350	2,166	5,736
Farm products	—	—	1,353	1,451	1,821	1,859
NCRR counties, total						
Manufactures	$2,246	$ 3,273	$ 5,584	$ 5,120	$12,428	$31,893
Farm products	—	—	10,496	10,299	9,828	14,010
State						
Manufactures	9,111	16,679	19,021	20,095	40,375	94,920
Farm products	—	—	57,846	51,721	50,071	79,201

Table 21 (continued)

	1850	1860	1870	1880	1890	1900
NCRR counties as percentage of state						
Manufactures	25	20	29	25	31	34
Farm products	—	—	18	20	20	18

Source: U.S. Census.

Table 22
Value of Household Manufactures (in thousands of dollars):
NCRR Counties and the State, 1840–1870

County	1840	1850	1860	1870
Wayne	$ 29	$ 26	$ 18	$ 18
Johnston	35	61	29	16
Wake	29	57	39	280
Orange	3	44	19	24
Alamance		30	13	2
Guilford	7	54	25	36
Davidson	38	53	23	30
Rowan		38	11	8
Cabarrus	41	15	12	.3
Mecklenburg	33	18	10	5
Total	216	396	200	419
Less Wake	187	339	161	139
State	$1,413	$2,087	$2,045	$1,604
NCRR counties as				
percentage of state	15	19	10	26
Less Wake	13	16	8	9

Sources: Tryon, *Household Manufactures in the U.S.*, pp. 309, 326–29; U.S. Census, 1870, 3:214, 218.

NOTES

Abbreviations Used in the Notes

A&NCRR	Atlantic and North Carolina Railroad
Archives	North Carolina Archives, Division of Archives and History, Raleigh, N.C.
C&SCRR	Charlotte and South Carolina Railroad
CC&ARR	Charlotte, Columbia, and Augusta Railroad
ECU	East Carolina University Manuscript Collection, University Library, Greenville, N.C.
N.C.	North Carolina Official Publications
NCRR	North Carolina Railroad
NWNCRR	Northwestern North Carolina Railroad
NCRR Office	North Carolina Railroad Company Office, Raleigh, N.C.
Official Records	*The War of the Rebellion: The Official Records of the Union and Confederate Armies.* 128 vols. Washington, D.C.: Government Printing Office, 1880–1901.
R&DRR	Richmond and Danville Railroad
R&GRR	Raleigh and Gaston Railroad
S&RRR	Seaboard and Roanoke Railroad
SHC	Southern Historical Collection, Wilson Library, University of North Carolina, Chapel Hill, N.C.
VPI	Virginia Polytechnic Institute and State University Library, Special Collections Department, Blacksburg, Va.
W&MRR	Wilmington and Manchester Railroad
W&WRR	Wilmington and Weldon Railroad
WNCRR	Western North Carolina Railroad

Chapter 1

1. Olmsted, *Cotton Kingdom*, pp. 128–29.
2. Ibid., pp. 137–40, 143.
3. Salisbury *Carolina Watchman*, 13 Jan. 1853.
4. *Hillsborough Recorder*, 27 July, 10 Aug. 1853.
5. Ibid., 11 Feb. 1852, 12 Jan. 1853; Olmsted, *Cotton Kingdom*, p. 142.
6. D. L. Swain to J. M. Morehead, 13 July 1849, in Caldwell Papers, SHC; J. Hayden Boyd and Walton, "Social Savings," pp. 246–47.
7. Advertisement dated April 1853, in *Greensboro Patriot*, 21 Jan. 1854.
8. Olmsted, *Papers*, 2:113.
9. Olmsted, *Seaboard Slave States*, pp. 321, 338–39.

10. Olmsted, *Cotton Kingdom*, pp. 141–42.

11. Olmsted, *Seaboard Slave States*, pp. 363–64; Fogel, "Social Saving Controversy," p. 30.

12. Cecil K. Brown, *State Highway System*, pp. 16–17; Starling, "Plank Road Movement," pp. 167–69.

13. Switzler, *Internal Commerce of the United States*, Appendix, pp. 215–16.

14. *Hillsborough Recorder*, 15 Oct., 12 Nov. 1851. For an account of this movement, see Williams, "Emigration from North Carolina."

15. [Joseph Caldwell], *The Numbers of Carlton* (New York: G. Long, 1828); Cecil K. Brown, *State Movement*, pp. 15–16.

16. Cecil K. Brown, *State Movement*, pp. 16–48.

17. Quoted in Raleigh *North Carolina Standard*, 30 July 1851.

18. See Cecil K. Brown, *State Movement*, pp. 48–62.

19. Graham, Message of 4 Dec. 1848, in N.C. *Public Documents*, 1848–49, #4, pp. 12–19.

20. North Carolina Railroad Charter, in N.C. *Public Laws*, 1848–49, chap. 82, or in NCRR, *Annual Report*, 1850, pp. 3–21. The legislative debates can be followed in the *Raleigh Register*, 6–27 Jan. 1849. See the discussions of the antecedents of the charter bill, its provisions, and its passage, in Cecil K. Brown, *State Movement*, pp. 63–69, 279–80; Jeffrey, "Internal Improvements and Political Parties," pp. 138–41, 150 (who credits the west primarily); and Kruman, *Parties and Politics*, pp. 67–68 (who credits the Whigs).

21. NCRR Charter, in *Annual Report*, 1850; Cecil K. Brown, *State Movement*, pp. 40–42, 57.

22. *Raleigh Register*, 27, 31 Jan. 1849.

23. Raleigh *North Carolina Standard*, 31 Jan., 7, 14 Feb. 1849, 27 March 1850; Norton, *Democratic Party*, pp. 126–27. See also Kruman, *Parties and Politics*, pp. 68–73, and Jeffrey, "Internal Improvements and Political Parties," pp. 140–42.

24. *Raleigh Register*, 30 Nov., 4, 14, 21 Dec. 1850; *Greensboro Patriot*, 30 Nov., 14, 21 Dec. 1850; Jeffrey, "Internal Improvements and Political Parties," p. 142.

25. Heath, "Public Railroad Construction," pp. 40–43, 46–48.

26. See Redlich, *Molding of American Banking*, 2:353; Chandler, "Patterns of American Railroad Finance," pp. 262–63.

27. NCRR Charter, in *Annual Report*, 1850, pp. 5–10.

28. The small number of active promoters is emphasized in the (Philadelphia) *Railroad Journal*, quoted in *Greensboro Patriot*, 27 Apr. 1850.

29. See Douglas L. Rights, *A Voyage Down the Yadkin–Great Peedee River*, 1928, reprinted with Floyd Rogers, *Yadkin Passage* (Winston-Salem: *Winston-Salem Journal*; Raleigh: N.C. Department of Natural Resources and Community Development, 1982), pp. 46–47.

30. Lillington et al., *To Our Constituents*.

31. *Raleigh Register*, 31 Jan., 12 May 1849; Salisbury *Carolina Watchman*, 28 June 1849; *Greensboro Patriot*, 21 Sept. 1850.

32. Raleigh *North Carolina Star*, 15 Aug. 1849, 10 July 1850.

33. See *Hillsborough Recorder*, 10 Oct. 1849.

34. Quotations from Salisbury *Carolina Watchman*, 8 Mar. 1849; *Raleigh Register*, 22 Sept. 1849.

35. Letter of Swain in *Raleigh Register*, 25 July 1849, corrected in issue of 3 Aug. 1849. Hinton in *Raleigh Register*, 28 Mar. 1849.

36. Raleigh *North Carolina Star*, 5 Sept. 1849; Salisbury *Carolina Watchman*, 23 May 1850.

37. *Raleigh Register*, 28 Mar., 1 Sept. 1849.

38. *Hillsborough Recorder*, 8, 22 Aug. 1849; Salisbury *Carolina Watchman*, 16 Aug., 6 Sept. 1849.

39. Cadwallader Jones in *Hillsborough Recorder*, 8 Aug. 1849.

40. Letter of Swain in *Raleigh Register*, 3 Aug. 1849.

41. *Raleigh Register*, 22 Sept. 1849; *Greensboro Patriot*, 24 Feb. 1849.

42. See Raleigh *North Carolina Star*, 29 Aug. 1849; *Hillsborough Recorder*, 22 Aug. 1849, 6 Feb. 1850; *Greensboro Patriot*, 26 Jan. 1850.

43. Raleigh *North Carolina Standard*, 14, 21, 28 Feb, 7 Mar. 1849; *Raleigh Register*, 14, 24 Feb., 3 Mar. 1849.

44. *Raleigh Register*, 28 Mar. 1849. See also W. A. Graham to James Graham, 24 Mar. 1850, in Graham, *Papers*, 3:318.

45. *Greensboro Patriot*, 16 June, 21 July 1849.

46. *Raleigh Register*, 21 Apr., 26 May 1849.

47. Ibid., 6, 9, 13, 16 June 1849.

48. Ibid., 20 June 1849. For accounts of the convention, see ibid., 20, 23 June, and the Raleigh *North Carolina Standard*, 20, 27 June 1849.

49. For Watson's suggestion, see Raleigh *North Carolina Standard*, 30 May 1849.

50. *Raleigh Register*, 10 Mar. 1849; *Greensboro Patriot*, 2 Feb. 1850; Heath, "Public Railroad Construction," pp. 51–52.

51. *Greensboro Patriot*, 30 June 1849.

52. Raleigh *North Carolina Star*, 29 Aug. 1849; Salisbury *Carolina Watchman*, 16 Aug. 1849; *Greensboro Patriot*, 25 Aug. 1849; Raleigh *North Carolina Standard*, 29 Aug. 1849.

53. *Raleigh Register*, 11, 29 Aug., 17 Oct. 1849; quotation from *Greensboro Patriot*, 1 Sept. 1849.

54. Raleigh *North Carolina Standard*, 10 Oct. 1849; *Greensboro Patriot*, 13, 20 Oct., 24 Nov. 1849.

55. See accounts of the Greensboro meeting in *Greensboro Patriot*, 1 Dec. 1849, and *Raleigh Register*, 5 Dec. 1849.

56. The *Raleigh Register*, Raleigh *North Carolina Standard*, and other papers carried accounts of these meetings during December and January.

57. Salisbury *Carolina Watchman*, 17 Jan. 1850; *Raleigh Register*, 23 Jan. 1850; *Watchman*, quoted in *Register*, 6 Feb. 1850.

58. *Raleigh Register*, 9 Feb. 1850.

59. Proceedings of the Hillsboro meeting are in *Raleigh Register*, 6, 13 Mar. 1850; *Greensboro Patriot*, 9 Mar. 1850.

60. *Greensboro Patriot*, 6 Apr., 11 May 1850.

61. *Raleigh Register*, 15 June 1850.

62. NCRR, *Report of the President and Directors*, 1852, p. 281. See also *Greensboro Patriot*, 23 Mar. 1850, and *Goldsboro Telegraph*, 21 Mar. 1850, each making the same point relative to stock subscribers in their regions.

63. Individual subscribers and their holdings are listed by county in the Stock Subscription Book, XVIII. v. 82, NCRR Records, Archives.

64. NCRR Charter, in *Annual Report*, 1850, pp. 8–9.

65. J. M. Morehead to G. W. Mordecai, 24 June 1850, Mordecai Papers, SHC; NCRR, *Annual Report*, 1850, pp. 28–29; Salisbury *Carolina Watchman*, 18 July 1850.

66. The Graham committee formula was not given in the 1850 annual report, but it was referred to two years later. See NCRR, *Annual Report*, 1850, p. 28; 1851, pp. 9–11; 1852, pp. 11–12; Salisbury *Carolina Watchman*, 18 July 1850.

67. NCRR, *Annual Report*, 1850, p. 28; 1851, pp. 10–11; 1852, p. 12. For stockholdings see N.C. *Public Documents*, 1858–59, #71, pp. 51–53.

68. NCRR By-Laws, in *Annual Report*, 1850, pp. 24–25.

69. Salisbury *Carolina Watchman*, 18 July 1850; *Raleigh Register*, 31 July 1850; Raleigh *North Carolina Standard*, 31 July 1850.

Chapter 2

1. See Hill, *Roads, Rails, and Waterways*, esp. pp. 96, 101–2, 105, 123, 128, 143, 146–47; Ward, "Antebellum Southern Railroad Development," pp. 416–17.

2. Gwynn's rank of colonel was earned in the Virginia militia. For his career, see Cullum, *Biographical Register*, 1:224; Charles W. Turner, "Early Virginia Railroad Entrepreneurs," pp. 328, 330; Sanderlin, *Great National Project*, 154–57; Dunaway, *James River and Kanawha Canal Company*, pp. 155, 157.

3. Cullum, *Biographical Register*, 1:224. For the newspaper controversy, see Salisbury *Carolina Watchman*, 1, 8 Aug. 1850, 6 Mar. 1851; Raleigh *North Carolina Standard*, 7, 24 Sept., 30 Nov. 1853. Editor William W. Holden of the *Standard* led the attack on Gwynn's salary and Virginia residence in 1853; two years later he had nothing but praise for the engineer's ability, experience, and dedication. See *Standard*, 12 Sept. 1855.

4. NCRR, *Report of the Chief Engineer on the Survey, 1851*, pp. 5–6; NCRR, *Annual Report*, 1851, pp. 4–5, 8–9.

5. NCRR, *Annual Report*, 1850, p. 30.

6. NCRR, *Report of the Chief Engineer on the Survey, 1851*, pp. 6–8. See the similar arguments of "A Farmer" in *Greensboro Patriot*, 17 Mar. 1849, and of President Alexander McRae of the Wilmington and Raleigh Railroad, in *Raleigh Register*, 1 Sept. 1849.

7. I am indebted to D. Brooks Cates, "The Piedmont Crescent and the North Carolina Railroad," pp. 1–9, for this argument. The 1850 census shows a combined population of 48,253 for Orange, Alamance, and Guilford, compared with a total of 34,281 for Chatham and Randolph. See also Phillips, "North Carolina's Rich Crescent," pp. 182–86, for the NCRR's role in creating the Piedmont Crescent.

8. This view was expressed by C. C. Raboteau in a letter to D. F. Caldwell, 18 Aug. 1849, in Caldwell Papers, SHC.

9. See the different interpretation, stressing the power of money and politics over topography and population, in Cecil K. Brown, *State Movement*, pp. 70, 74–77.

10. See *Greensboro Patriot*, 30 Nov. 1850. For evidence of Thomas's interest in the route, see ibid., 29 Mar. 1851; *Raleigh Register*, 30 May 1849; Nereus Mendenhall Diary, 3 Mar. to 1 Apr. 1851, in Hobbs-Mendenhall Papers, SHC; Sink and Matthews, *Pathfinders*, p. 230.

11. *Greensboro Patriot*, 1 Mar. 1851; *Hillsborough Recorder*, 19 Mar. 1851. Cf. Whitaker, *Centennial History of Alamance*, pp. 96, 107, and Harden, *Alamance County*, p. 16, who say that Graham residents opposed the NCRR's passing through the town. The town passed an ordinance forbidding the railroad to lay tracks within a mile of the courthouse or to build shops within the town limits. The track was laid just beyond

Graham's northern limit, about a mile from the courthouse. The shops were subsequently built about two miles northwest of Graham.

12. NCRR, *Report of the Chief Engineer on the Survey, 1851*, p. 12; Pierpont, "Development of the Textile Industry in Alamance," pp. 85–86; Hughes, *Development of the Textile Industry in Alamance*, p. 5; Whitaker, *Centennial History of Alamance*, pp. 139–40.

13. *Hillsborough Recorder*, 19, 26 Mar., 9 Apr., 7 May 1851; D. L. Swain to W. A. Graham, 27 Dec. 1854, in Graham, *Papers*, 4:584.

14. J. M. Morehead to W. A. Graham, 28 Dec. 1850, in Graham, *Papers*, 3:503; D. L. Swain to Graham, 27 Dec. 1854, in ibid., 4:584; NCRR, *Report of the Chief Engineer on the Survey, 1851*, pp. 12–13. Cf. Chamberlain, *This Was Home*, p. 95, who says that "the sober authorities of the day" would not let the NCRR pass through Chapel Hill for fear of distracting the students.

15. Charles Phillips to Governor D. S. Reid, with petition, 18, 19 Dec. 1855, in Reid Papers, Archives; Raleigh *North Carolina Standard*, 7 Mar. 1856, 8 June 1859; land notice by Thomas Webb, Clerk and Master in Equity, in *Hillsborough Recorder*, 14 May 1856.

16. William Kenneth Boyd, *Story of Durham*, p. 27; Paul, *History of Durham*, p. 29.

17. NCRR, *Report of the Chief Engineer on the Survey, 1851*, pp. 9–10; Raleigh *North Carolina Star*, 29 Oct. 1851.

18. Raleigh *North Carolina Standard*, 30 Oct. 1850, 15 Oct. 1851; Charlotte *Hornet's Nest*, quoted in *Standard*, 19 Apr., 3 May 1851; R&GRR, *Annual Report*, 1852, p. 10; Raleigh *North Carolina Star*, 8, 29 Oct. 1851, 26 May, 9 June, 21 July 1852; *Greensboro Patriot*, 6 Nov. 1852.

19. Raleigh *North Carolina Standard*, 31 July 1852, 2 Apr., 14 Dec. 1853; *Hillsborough Recorder*, 12 Apr. 1854.

20. NCRR, *Report of the Chief Engineer on the Survey, 1851*, p. 9; *Raleigh Register*, 11 June 1851; Raleigh *Daily Sentinel*, 4 Apr., 19 Sept. 1867; William Marsh Sanders, *Johnston County*, p. 14.

21. NCRR Charter, in *Annual Report*, 1850, p. 4.

22. NCRR, *Report of the Chief Engineer on the Survey, 1851*, pp. 8–11; Bob Johnson and Norwood, *History of Wayne County*, pp. vi, 4.

23. Raleigh *North Carolina Standard*, 24 Jan., 7 Feb. 1852; New Bern *Newbernian*, in *Raleigh Register*, 11 Feb. 1852; Goldsboro *Republican and Patriot*, 17, 24 Feb., 2 Mar. 1852. Perhaps the clearest explanations of the situation appeared in the *Hillsborough Recorder*, 18 Feb. 1852, and *Greensboro Patriot*, 21 Feb., 6, 13 Mar. 1852. The legislature had created a Neuse River Navigation Company, entitled to receive state financial aid once the NCRR began construction. Efforts were begun in the summer of 1851 to activate this company and proceed with the contemplated navigational improvements (*Standard*, 18 June 1851; Goldsboro *Republican and Patriot*, 31 July 1851).

24. *Raleigh Register*, 18 Feb., 7 Apr., 27 Nov. 1852; Raleigh *North Carolina Standard*, 6 Mar. 1852; Goldsboro *Republican and Patriot*, 9 Mar. 1852; Raleigh *North Carolina Star*, 28 Sept. 1853.

25. Raleigh *North Carolina Standard*, 19 Apr. 1854; NCRR, *Annual Report*, 1854, p. 5. In 1891 the legislature passed an act amending the charter to reflect the construction undertaken in 1854, although the stockholders (for other reasons) did not meet for several years afterward to ratify it. N.C. *Public Laws*, 1891, chap. 392.

26. Bob Johnson and Norwood, *History of Wayne County*, p. 80; Goldsboro *Tribune*, quoted in Salisbury *Carolina Watchman*, 13 Jan. 1862.

27. Table of elevations [1859], in Fisher Family Papers, SHC.

28. *Raleigh Register,* 12 Feb. 1851; NCRR, *Annual Report,* 1851, p. 5; 1854, p. 9; *Hillsborough Recorder,* 10 Mar. 1852.

29. NCRR, *Report of the President, January 20, 1859,* p. 32.

30. Wake County Railroad Records, 1837–73, Archives. The sparsity of such records, from Wake and the other counties through which the road passed, tends to confirm that nearly all owners settled with the railroad privately, whether donating or selling.

31. *Raleigh Register,* 4 Apr. 1849. In the North especially, large contractors, able to operate more economically, were beginning to drive smaller ones out of business in the 1850s. See Jervis, *Railway Property,* pp. 51–52; Chandler, *Visible Hand,* pp. 93–94.

32. See statement by Romulus M. Saunders in *Greensboro Patriot,* 2 Feb. 1850.

33. *Raleigh Register,* 30 May 1849; see also *Greensboro Patriot,* 16 June 1849.

34. *Greensboro Patriot,* 1 Mar. 1850; NCRR, *Annual Report,* 1850, pp. 29–30.

35. See *Raleigh Register,* 10 Mar. 1849, 23 Feb. 1850; *Greensboro Patriot,* 10 Feb. 1849; Salisbury *Carolina Watchman,* 22 Feb., 21 June 1849. The state supreme court upheld the half-and-half arrangement in 1855, in the case of *Ashe v. Johnson's Admr.,* 55 *N.C. Reports* 149. See Cecil K. Brown, *State Movement,* p. 78n.

36. NCRR, *Report of the Chief Engineer on the Survey, 1851,* p. 3; NCRR, *Annual Report,* 1851, p. 4. See Raleigh *North Carolina Standard,* 28 May 1851, for an NCRR advertisement inviting contractors to submit bids.

37. NCRR, *Report of the President and Directors,* 1852, p. 280; *Report of Col. Walter Gwynn, Jan. 10, 1856,* p. 8.

38. Graham was now secretary of the navy and resided in Washington. His partner, Charles W. Johnston, gave him an interesting report on the awards and their own prospects. See Johnston to Graham, 26 June 1851, in Graham, *Papers,* 4:127–28. See also Graham to James Graham, 20 July, 18 Aug. 1851, in ibid., pp. 155–56, 190. For evidence of the Cameron family's participation, see Rail Road Contract Account Book, v. 125, Cameron Family Papers, SHC.

39. *Greensboro Patriot,* 19 July, 22 Nov. 1851; Salisbury *Carolina Watchman,* 3 July 1851.

40. McRae, *Defence of John C. McRae,* pp. 3–7; NCRR, *Report of the President and Directors,* 1852, p. 278.

41. See NCRR advertisement for bridge and masonry contracts in *Raleigh Register,* 29 Oct. 1851. The *Greensboro Patriot* reported the letting of many of these contracts in December (*Patriot,* 20 Dec. 1851). For Gwynn's announcement see Goldsboro *Republican and Patriot,* in Raleigh *North Carolina Star,* 21 Jan. 1852.

42. *Greensboro Patriot,* 12 July 1851; Arnett, *Greensboro,* p. 148. The box was not sealed for some time, as the *Patriot* was soliciting newspapers and other publications for it in October (*Patriot,* 4 Oct. 1851). The box was later lost. See *Greensboro Daily News,* 29 Jan. 1956, Feature section, p. 1.

43. NCRR, *Report of the President and Directors,* 1852, pp. 280–82; NCRR, *Report of Col. Walter Gwynn, Jan. 10, 1856,* p. 8; Special Message of Governor David S. Reid, 9 Dec. 1852, in Governors' Letterbooks #40, Archives; NCRR, *Annual Report,* 1853, pp. 3, 6.

44. Raleigh *North Carolina Standard,* 6 Apr. 1853. The final installment was set for 1 May 1854. *Greensboro Patriot,* 7 Jan. 1854.

45. NCRR, *Report of the Chief Engineer on the Survey, 1851,* pp. 17, 19.

46. Stover, *History of the Illinois Central,* p. 49; Lightner, *Labor on the Illinois Central,* pp. 29–30.

47. Cotterill, "Southern Railroads, 1850–1860," p. 404; Dozier, "Trade and Transportation," p. 238.

48. Letters of C. W. Johnston and S. A. White to W. A. Graham, 21, 27 Jan., 6 Apr. 1852, in Graham, *Papers*, 4:236, 243, 287–88; Charlotte *North Carolina Whig*, 17 Mar. 1852; Charlotte *Western Democrat*, 8 Jan. 1856.

49. Letters of C. W. Johnston and S. A. White to W. A. Graham, 21, 27 Jan. 1852, in Graham, *Papers*, 4:236–38, 242–43; Raleigh *North Carolina Standard*, 10 July 1852. The Illinois Central paid its unskilled construction workers $1.00 to $1.50 per day. Skilled workers got up to twice as much. Stover, *History of the Illinois Central*, p. 49; Lightner, *Labor on the Illinois Central*, pp. 22–30. For Louisiana, see Earle and Hoffman, "Foundation of the Modern Economy," pp. 1074–75.

50. Raleigh *North Carolina Star*, 29 Oct. 1851.

51. *Greensboro Patriot*, 4 Oct., 22 Nov. 1851.

52. *Raleigh Register*, 17 Jan. 1852; Goldsboro *Republican and Patriot*, 3 Feb. 1852. For crosstie advertisements, see Salisbury *Carolina Watchman*, 12 Feb. 1852 and other issues.

53. Charlotte *North Carolina Whig*, 3 Nov. 1852; NCRR, *Report of the President and Directors*, 1852, p. 286; *Raleigh Register*, 24 Nov. 1852; NCRR, *Annual Report*, 1853, p. 14.

54. Goldsboro *Republican and Patriot*, 17, 24 May, 28 June 1853; Raleigh *North Carolina Standard*, 31 Dec. 1853.

55. Charlotte *North Carolina Whig*, 18 Oct. 1853, 7 Feb. 1854; Raleigh *North Carolina Standard*, 31 Dec. 1853. For the crosstie problem, see NCRR, *Annual Report*, 1854, p. 6.

56. Raleigh *North Carolina Standard*, 19 Apr. 1854; *Raleigh Register*, 10 May 1854.

57. NCRR, *Annual Report*, 1854, p. 6; 1855, p. 8.

58. *Banner* cited in Raleigh *North Carolina Standard*, 3 June 1854; Salisbury *Carolina Watchman*, 2 Nov. 1854; *Hillsborough Recorder*, 12 July 1854.

59. Raleigh *North Carolina Standard*, 15 July 1854; Salisbury *Carolina Watchman*, 14 Dec. 1854; C. F. Fisher to J. D. Whitford, 29 May 1855, Whitford Papers, Archives; *Greensboro Patriot*, 7 Dec. 1855.

60. NCRR, *Annual Report*, 1855, p. 8; 1856, p. 9; *Raleigh Register*, 9 Dec. 1854; *Hillsborough Recorder*, 4 Apr., 2 May, 6 June 1855.

61. *Raleigh Register*, 10 Jan. 1855; Salisbury *Carolina Watchman*, 11 Jan. 1855.

62. *Raleigh Register*, 14 July 1855; Raleigh *North Carolina Standard*, 14 Nov. 1855; *Greensboro Patriot*, 16 Nov. 1855; Salisbury *Carolina Watchman*, 20 Nov. 1855.

63. *Greensboro Patriot*, 14, 21 (quotation) Dec. 1855, 18 Jan. 1856; *Raleigh Register*, 15 Dec. 1855.

64. NCRR, *Annual Report*, 1856, p. 10; *Greensboro Patriot*, 18 Jan., 1 Feb. 1856; quotation from Greensboro *Times*, 31 Jan. 1856.

65. NCRR, *Report of Col. Walter Gwynn, Jan. 10, 1856*, pp. 14–15; Raleigh *North Carolina Standard*, 8 Mar. 1856.

66. *Greensboro Patriot*, 18 Jan., 13 June 1856; Greensboro *Times*, 17 Jan., 28 Feb., 13 Mar. 1856; *Patriot*, quoted in Salisbury *Carolina Watchman*, 26 Feb. 1856.

67. Charlotte *Western Democrat*, 17 June 1856; Salisbury *Carolina Watchman*, 1 July 1856.

68. NCRR, *Annual Report*, 1857, p. 7.

69. Ibid., 1856, p. 11.

70. For the directors' decision, see ibid., 1854, p. 9; 1856, p. 11; NCRR, *Report of*

the President, January 20, 1859, pp. 10–11. For Hillsboro and Greensboro interest, see *Hillsborough Recorder*, 31 Aug., 14 Sept. 1853, 1, 22 Feb. 1854; *Greensboro Patriot*, 10 Sept. 1853, 7 Jan. 1854, 7 Jan. 1859; Greensboro *Times*, 7 Feb. 1856.

71. Whitaker, *Centennial History of Alamance*, pp. 96, 107. Cf. the earlier desire of Graham residents to have the road pass through town.

72. NCRR, *Annual Report*, 1854, p. 9; Stokes, *Company Shops*, pp. 9–11.

73. *Hillsborough Recorder*, 23 Sept. 1853; NCRR, *Report of the Chief Engineer on the Survey, 1851*, pp. 18–19; NCRR, *Annual Report*, 1851, pp. 5–6; 1856, p. 18; NCRR, *Report of the President, January 20, 1859*, pp. 7, 23.

74. NCRR, *Annual Report*, 1867, p. 24; Report of President Josiah Turner to Bureau of Statistics, Treasury Department, 31 Aug. 1867, in XXIII. Correspondence, v. 22, NCRR Records, Archives.

75. Based on figures in Wicker, "Railroad Investment," p. 511. The Illinois Central cost $23,700 per mile (Stover, *History of the Illinois Central*, p. 41).

76. NCRR, *Report of Col. Walter Gwynn, Jan. 10, 1856*, pp. 10–13; NCRR, *Report of the President, January 20, 1859*, pp. 7–8.

77. For examples of such criticism, see Charlotte *North Carolina Whig*, 3 Apr. 1855, and the charges of Jonathan Worth's legislative investigating committee of 1859, in N.C. *Public Documents*, 1858–59, #71. For a defense of the road's management, no doubt inspired if not written by Morehead, see *Greensboro Patriot*, 17 Mar. 1855.

78. Raleigh *North Carolina Standard*, 24 Sept. 1853; *Greensboro Patriot*, 15 Oct. 1853; NCRR, *Annual Report*, 1854, pp. 7–9; J. M. Morehead to W. A. Graham, 27 Mar. 1855, in Graham, *Papers*, 4:595.

79. J. M. Morehead to W. A. Graham, 28 Dec. 1850, in Graham, *Papers*, 3:503; NCRR, *Annual Report*, 1852, p. 8; 1853, p. 5; 1854, p. 7; Baltimore *American*, in Raleigh *North Carolina Star*, 14 July 1852. According to North Carolina Senator Thomas Clingman in December 1853, the price of British railroad iron had doubled, from $40 to $80 per ton, within the past eighteen months (*Star*, 28 Dec. 1853).

80. NCRR, *Annual Report*, 1854, p. 7; *American Railroad Journal*, 25 Feb. 1854, p. 121. In 1854 the price fell again, and Morehead was able to buy 9,000 tons at $42.50 per ton (*Annual Report*, 1855, p. 8).

81. J. M. Morehead to Governor Thomas Bragg, 6 Mar. 1855, in Governors' Papers, Box 138, Archives.

82. Temin, *Iron and Steel*, pp. 21–23; Cotterill, "Southern Railroads, 1850–1860," p. 404.

83. Adler, *British Investments*, pp. 25, 32, 34.

84. NCRR, *Report of the President, January 20, 1859*, pp. 8–9; *Greensboro Patriot*, 18 Nov. 1859; Raleigh *Daily Sentinel*, 18 Dec. 1866; letter of Walter Gwynn, 19 Dec. 1866, in *Sentinel*, 21 Feb. 1867; Gwynn to M. S. Robins, 26 Dec. 1866, Robins Papers, SHC. See the discussion in Cecil K. Brown, *State Movement*, p. 78.

85. Report of the Joint Select Committee, in N.C. *Public Documents*, 1858–59, #71, pp. 17–21; NCRR, *Report of the President, January 20, 1859*, pp. 13–14.

86. *Hillsborough Recorder*, 9 June 1855.

Chapter 3

1. Kirkman, *Railway Expenditures*, 1:86–88 (including quotation); Black, *Railroads of the Confederacy*, pp. 12–13; Jervis, *Railway Property*, pp. 74–77, 118–19, 225–26.

2. See the letters by "H" in *Greensboro Patriot*, 3, 10 July 1862. For the conflicting accounts of the maximum grade, which were more typical than exceptional in that day, see NCRR, *Report of the Chief Engineer on the Survey, 1851*, p. 17; NCRR, *Annual Report*, 1868, p. 26; 1869, p. 16. In 1869 Ceburn L. Harris, then state superintendent of public works, criticized some of the grades as being unnecessarily steep (Report of Superintendent of Public Works, 9 Dec. 1869, in N.C. *Public Documents*, 1869–70, #5, p. 9). For comparative information on railroad grades at that time and later, see Flint, *Railroads of the United States*, pp. 27–28, and Henry, *This Fascinating Railroad Business*, pp. 46–47.

3. NCRR, *Report of the Chief Engineer on the Survey, 1851*, p. 17; "H" in *Greensboro Patriot*, 3, 10 July 1862; Raleigh *Daily Sentinel*, 5 July 1867. See also NCRR, *Annual Report*, 1867, p. 45.

4. George Rogers Taylor and Neu, *American Railroad Network*, pp. 12–14; Stover, *Iron Road*, pp. 22, 49, 187–89.

5. Salisbury *Carolina Watchman*, 19 May 1857. See also Charlotte *Western Democrat*, 28 Aug. 1855; *Lexington and Yadkin Flag*, 16 May 1856.

6. Printed contract, 30 June 1851, with John Reich, Gorrell Papers, SHC.

7. Jervis, *Railway Property*, pp. 71–77, 118–21.

8. NCRR, *Report of the Chief Engineer on the Survey, 1851*, pp. 17–18; Reich contract, 30 June 1851, Gorrell Papers, SHC.

9. Greensboro *Times*, 17 Jan. 1856.

10. NCRR, *Annual Report*, 1857, p. 11; 1859, p. 10; 1860, pp. 6, 20; 1861, p. 6.

11. See annual reports of the Petersburg Railroad, 1859, pp. 17–18; C&SCRR, 1859, p. 27; WNCRR, 1860, p. 22; and R&GRR, 1861, p. 8.

12. Jervis, *Railway Property*, pp. 73–77.

13. NCRR, *Report of the Chief Engineer on the Survey, 1851*, p. 17; Reich contract, 30 June 1851, Gorrell Papers, SHC.

14. NCRR, *Annual Report*, 1857, p. 11; 1859, p. 10.

15. Charlotte *North Carolina Whig*, 29 May 1860; NCRR, *Annual Report*, 1860, pp. 6–7; 1861, p. 6; C. F. Fisher to P. C. Cameron, 29 Jan. 1861, Cameron Family Papers, SHC.

16. Jervis, *Railway Property*, pp. 88–91; "H" in *Greensboro Patriot*, 3, 10 July 1862.

17. Jervis, *Railway Property*, pp. 92–98.

18. NCRR, *Report of the Chief Engineer on the Survey, 1851*, p. 18; Reich contract, 30 June 1851, Gorrell Papers, SHC.

19. NCRR, *Circular to the Resident Engineers*, p. 7 (my pagination). The *Greensboro Patriot* (7 May, 11 June 1853) contains detailed descriptions of two substantial stone culverts then under construction across Bull Run near Jamestown and across Rock Creek near Gibsonville, both in Guilford County. The latter is still in use, seemingly unchanged (see fig. 12). The Bull Run culvert has received at least a resurfacing of concrete.

20. XV. Property Inventory, v. 95, NCRR Records, Archives.

21. Charlotte *North Carolina Whig*, 13 June 1854; NCRR, *Annual Report*, 1860, pp. 6, 20; 1861, p. 5.

22. Raleigh *North Carolina Standard*, 6 Sept. 1856; McRae, *Defence of John C. McRae*, pp. 13–15; NCRR, *Annual Report*, 1857, p. 7; 1860, pp. 6, 20; 1861, p. 5; 1862, pp. 26–27.

23. Jervis, *Railway Property*, pp. 122–24; Black, *Railroads of the Confederacy*, p. 13; Olson, *Depletion Myth*, pp. 12–13, 22–23, 63–64. For the life of sills in the South, see Doster, "Were Southern Railroads Destroyed?" p. 313.

24. Jervis, *Railway Property*, pp. 125–26. George L. Vose, writing at about the same time, makes virtually the same recommendations as to size and spacing (*Handbook of Railroad Construction*, pp. 72–73, 273). Colburn and Holley indicate that actual practice in New York State in the 1850s adhered closely to Jervis's recommendations (*Permanent Way*, p. 61).

25. *Greensboro Patriot*, 14 Feb. 1852; Raleigh *North Carolina Standard*, 10 Nov. 1852.

26. NCRR, *Annual Report*, 1860, pp. 7, 20. In 1867 specifications for white or post oak required a length of eight feet, with a thickness of seven inches and a width of at least eight inches, to be sawed square at the ends, hewn smooth on two sides and the other two sides to be barked. Pine sills were to measure ten by seven inches. See book of contracts, 1867–69, in V. Contracts, v. 16; and printed form in XXII. Contracts, v. 19, NCRR Records, Archives.

27. Statement of Superintendent Edmund Wilkes in undated railroad investigation papers, Robins Papers, SHC; NCRR, *Annual Report*, 1868, p. 28.

28. NCRR, *Annual Reports*, 1859–63, 1866–71; "H" in *Greensboro Patriot*, 3, 10 July 1862.

29. Jervis, *Railway Property*, pp. 128–29, 134–42; Colburn and Holley, *Permanent Way*, pp. 80–81, 110; Stover, *Iron Road*, pp. 190–93; Kirkland, *Men, Cities, and Transportation*, 1:287–88. For an explanation of how rails were manufactured, wore out, and were re-rolled, see Temin, *Iron and Steel*, pp. 48–49.

30. See annual reports of the R&DRR, 1856, p. 11; 1861, p. 157; C&SCRR, 1859, p. 10; CC&ARR, 1871, p. 14; and Black, *Railroads of the Confederacy*, p. 13.

31. NCRR, *Report of the Chief Engineer on the Survey, 1851*, p. 18; NCRR, *Annual Report*, 1852, p. 8; 1857, p. 7; 1859, p. 10; 1860, pp. 8, 20–21; 1861, p. 6.

32. Condit, *American Building: Materials and Techniques*, pp. 71–72.

33. Kirkland, *Men, Cities, and Transportation*, 1:291–92; Tyrrell, *History of Bridge Engineering*, p. 121; Jervis, *Railway Property*, pp. 99–112.

34. Plowden, *Bridges*, p. 37.

35. Condit, *American Building Art*, pp. 90–92, 297; Allen, *Covered Bridges of the South*, pp. 3–7; Plowden, *Bridges*, pp. 37–38.

36. Condit, *American Building Art*, pp. 92–99; Plowden, *Bridges*, pp. 38–40.

37. Quoted in Ringwalt, *Development of Transportation Systems*, p. 202.

38. NCRR, *Report of the Chief Engineer on the Survey, 1851*, p. 18. Much information about the bridges was presented in President Fisher's (NCRR) *Report of the President, January 20, 1859*, p. 28. A good deal more data was compiled for an inventory made in September 1871 at the time of the road's lease. See XV. Property Inventory, v. 93–95, NCRR Records, Archives. The remainder of the information is gleaned from bits of information in the annual reports, newspaper articles, and other sources.

39. NCRR, *Annual Report*, 1861, p. 6; 1869, p. 15. Cf. President Fisher's statement in 1857 that "there is no trestle frame on the line" (ibid., 1857, p. 7).

40. Goldsboro *Republican and Patriot*, 17 May 1853.

41. See NCRR, *Annual Report*, 1858, p. 10; 1860, p. 8; 1861, p. 6. The four multiple-span bridges were constructed as follows:

Yadkin River: 658 feet overall; four spans of 150 feet each on three stone piers; a deck-type Howe truss covered with sheet iron in 1871. For a description of the design and construction of this bridge, see Salisbury *Carolina Watchman*, 29 Mar. 1855.

Neuse River: 264 feet overall in 1859, 360 feet in 1871 after replacement; two spans of 100 feet each in both years; a through Howe truss bridge, with double arches in 1871.

Haw River: 260 feet overall; two spans of 100 feet each; a deck-type lattice bridge without arches, repaired in 1868 with a sheet iron cover.

Abbott's Creek: 223 feet overall; two spans of 100 feet each; a through bridge in 1859 rebuilt as a through Howe truss in 1867 with double arch spans and a shingle roof.

42. NCRR, *Report of Col. Walter Gwynn, Jan. 10, 1856*, p. 6; NCRR, *Annual Report*, 1856, pp. 18–19, 22; 1857, p. 7; 1860, p. 8.

43. *Hillsborough Recorder*, 19 Mar. 1856; Charlotte *Western Democrat*, 18 Mar. 1856. See also P. C. Cameron to T. Ruffin, 15 Mar. 1856, in Ruffin, *Papers*, 2:509.

44. NCRR, *Annual Report*, 1860, pp. 8–9. Three bridge watchmen were listed as on the road in January 1859 (NCRR, *Report of the President, January 20, 1859*, p. 29).

45. Timber for a third street bridge in Raleigh was contracted for in 1856, but it does not appear in an 1859 list (NCRR, *Report of Col. Walter Gwynn, Jan. 10, 1856*, p. 6; *Report of the President, January 20, 1859*, p. 28).

46. Charlotte *Western Democrat*, 10, 17 Mar. 1854; Charlotte *North Carolina Whig*, 21 Mar., 16 May, 1 Sept. 1854; Salisbury *Carolina Watchman*, 7 Sept. 1854.

47. *John Coon v. NCRR*, 65 *N.C. Reports* 507.

48. Salisbury *Carolina Watchman*, 23 Nov. 1854.

49. NCRR, *Annual Report*, 1854, pp. 6–7.

50. Charlotte *North Carolina Whig*, 24 Mar. 1852.

51. NCRR, *Annual Report*, 1857, p. 7; Charlotte *Western Democrat*, 2 Dec. 1856, 16 June 1860.

52. NCRR, *Annual Report*, 1854, p. 5; 1857, p. 7.

53. Bob Johnson and Norwood, *History of Wayne County*, pp. 99–100, 104, 111.

54. Raleigh *North Carolina Standard*, 15 July 1854; *Raleigh Register*, 29 Mar. 1856; R&GRR, *Annual Report*, 1857, p. 9; 1858, p. 6; NCRR, *Annual Report*, 1860, pp. 9, 19; 1861, p. 8.

55. Salisbury *Carolina Watchman*, 19 Apr. 1855; Agreement with the WNCRR, 27 May 1857, in XXII. Contracts, v. 19, NCRR Records, Archives; NCRR, *Annual Report*, 1858, p. 10.

56. WNCRR, *Annual Report*, 1859, p. 26; 1860, p. 22; Salisbury *Carolina Watchman*, 24 July 1859.

57. NCRR, *Annual Report*, 1860, pp. 9, 19.

58. Ibid., 1857, p. 7; NCRR, *Report of the President, January 20, 1859*, p. 29. In 1871 the road listed only three turntables, at Charlotte, Company Shops, and Raleigh. The one at Goldsboro had been replaced by a triangular wye permitting locomotives to reverse direction. XI. Maps, v. 67–68; XV. Property Inventory, v. 93, v. 95, p. 91 and plan at end of volume, NCRR Records, Archives.

59. NCRR, *Annual Report*, 1860, pp. 9, 19; 1861, pp. 7–8.

60. Ibid., 1857, pp. 7–8; NCRR, *Report of the President, January 20, 1859*, p. 29.

61. NCRR, *Annual Report*, 1856, p. 11; Licht, *Working for the Railroad*, pp. 231–32.

62. See Stokes, *Company Shops*, esp. pp. 30–35.

63. NCRR, *Report of the President, January 20, 1859*, pp. 11–12.

64. Stokes, *Company Shops*, pp. 13–16, 21–29, 71; NCRR, *Annual Report*, 1856, pp. 12–13; 1857, pp. 8–9; Memorial [of NCRR] to the General Assembly, December 1856, N.C. *Public Documents*, 1856–57, #21, pp. 2–3; NCRR, *Report of the President, January 20, 1859*, pp. 12–15; Whitaker, *Centennial History of Alamance*, pp. 109–11; Report of Joint Select Committee, N.C. *Public Documents*, 1858–59, #71, p. 17; NCRR, *Communincation* [sic] *from the President*, 14 Feb. 1859, pp. 19–21.

65. Emma to Nephew, 25 Feb. 1859, Grimes-Bryan Papers, ECU.

66. NCRR, *Annual Report*, 1858, p. 7.

67. From Senate debate, 3 Jan. 1859, in Raleigh *North Carolina Standard*, 4 Jan. 1859. See also *Lexington and Yadkin Flag*, 20 June 1856. For the Report of the Joint Select Committee, see N.C. *Public Documents*, 1858–59, #71, pp. 17–19.

68. NCRR, *Annual Report*, 1857, pp. 9–10; 1858, pp. 7, 11; 1860, pp. 9–10; 1861, p. 8.

69. Stover, *Iron Road*, pp. 90–91. It may be impossible to reconstruct the NCRR's locomotive roster with complete accuracy, as some engines were rebuilt and returned to service under different names without precise records being kept of their former identities. But table 8 provides a close approximation.

70. White, *American Locomotives*, pp. 33–59; Black, *Railroads of the Confederacy*, pp. 15–16; Jervis, *Railway Property*, pp. 174–76.

71. John H. White's *American Locomotives* is far and away the leading authority on early locomotive manufacture. See especially pp. 14–19, including an account of the Norris Works, and even more particularly White's article, "Once the Greatest of Builders," concentrating on Norris. William D. Edson's companion article, "The Norris Construction Record," lists all but one of the NCRR engines I attribute to Norris. See also White's *Short History of American Locomotive Builders*.

72. NCRR, *Report of Col. Walter Gwynn, Jan. 10, 1856*, p. 14; White, *American Locomotives*, pp. 21–22.

73. NCRR, *Annual Report*, 1854, p. 11.

74. White, *American Locomotives*, pp. 19–20. For a newspaper notice of the new locomotive, see Raleigh *North Carolina Standard*, 27 Aug. 1859.

75. Hunter, *History of Industrial Power*, 2:403.

76. See White, *American Locomotives*, pp. 83–89, 223, 231; Stover, *Iron Road*, pp. 200–203.

77. Compiled from the annual reports for those years. The disparity between the two periods is hard to account for. The lower figure corresponds with data from other railroads. See *American Railway Review*, 7 Nov. 1861, p. 135; *American Railway Times*, 5 Nov. 1864, p. 358; 29 July 1865, p. 239; 12 Aug. 1865, p. 255.

78. F. A. Stagg to W. A. Caldwell, 29 Jan. 1870, XXIII. Correspondence, v. 52; V. Contracts, v. 16 (book of contracts, 1867–69); XXII. Contracts, v. 19 (printed forms), all in NCRR Records, Archives.

79. White, *American Locomotives*, pp. 218–21.

80. Raleigh *North Carolina Standard*, 12, 13 Feb. 1869; Raleigh *Daily Sentinel*, 20 Feb. 1869.

81. See, for example, NCRR, *Annual Report*, 1867, pp. 72–76; 1869, pp. 48–50; 1870, pp. 31–32.

82. Black, *Railroads of the Confederacy*, pp. 18–19; Stover, *Iron Road*, pp. 204–5.

83. Jervis, *Railway Property*, pp. 179–80; White, *American Railroad Passenger Car*,

1:20–29, 35; White, "Splendor and Gloom," pp. 40–42 (including the quotations); Mencken, *Railroad Passenger Car*, pp. 17–18; Stover, *Iron Road*, pp. 204–5.

84. NCRR, *Annual Report*, 1860, p. 37; Stover, *Iron Road*, p. 91.

85. Raleigh *North Carolina Standard*, 15 Feb. 1854; Raleigh *North Carolina Star*, 22 Feb., 14 Sept. 1854.

86. NCRR, *Annual Report*, 1859, p. 11; 1860, p. 10.

87. Ibid., 1854, p. 11.

88. Ibid., 1859, pp. 9–11; 1860, pp. 10, 22.

89. Ibid., 1855, p. 11; 1860, p. 37.

90. See White, *American Railroad Passenger Car*, 2:462–63, 473–75; Klein, *History of the Louisville & Nashville*, p. 56.

91. NCRR, *Annual Report*, 1860, p. 37. For a reference to a conductor's car, see *Hillsborough Recorder*, 23 Jan. 1861.

92. Stover, *Iron Road*, p. 203; list by E. Burns [September 1869], in XXIII. Correspondence, v. 23, NCRR Records, Archives.

Chapter 4

1. See Kirkman, *Railway Revenue*, pp. 18–27.

2. Jervis, *Railway Property*, pp. 251–53, 259–60; Kirkman, *Railway Revenue*, pp. 59–77.

3. NCRR, *Annual Report*, 1857, p. 16; 1861, p. 15; 1862, p. 18.

4. Ibid., 1856, pp. 11–12; board of directors' minutes, 16 Aug. 1867, NCRR Office.

5. Ibid., 1856, p. 20; 1860, pp. 24–25; Responses of Edmund Wilkes, undated Railroad Investigation papers [1867], Robins Papers, SHC.

6. NCRR, *Regulations and Instructions*, 1854, pp. 40–44; 1857, pp. 22–24.

7. Kirkman, *Railway Revenue*, pp. 100–108, 113–18.

8. NCRR, *Annual Report*, 1860, p. 25; 1861, p. 15; board of directors' minutes, 14 Jan. 1860, 18 July 1862, NCRR Office.

9. NCRR, *Regulations and Instructions*, 1854, pp. 29–33.

10. NCRR, *Annual Report*, 1860, pp. 38–39.

11. *Greensboro Patriot*, 7 May 1858; NCRR, *Annual Report*, 1859, p. 5; 1860, p. 38. Greensboro's J. P. Balsley was the only agent on the road earning $600 in 1860, the nearest year for which salaries were published.

12. See Henson, "Industrial Workers," pp. 39–40.

13. See Stover, *Iron Road*, p. 213.

14. Henson, "Industrial Workers," p. 77.

15. NCRR, *Report of the President, January 20, 1859*, pp. 18–19; *Greensboro Patriot*, 3 Apr. 1857.

16. Richard C. Wade, *Slavery in the Cities: The South, 1820–1860* (New York: Oxford University Press, 1964), p. 37; Stover, *Iron Road*, p. 92.

17. Dozier, "Trade and Transportation," p. 239; Black, *Railroads of the Confederacy*, p. 30.

18. NCRR, *Report of the President, January 20, 1859*, pp. 18–19; Salisbury *Carolina Watchman*, 10 Jan. 1860.

19. Ulrich B. Phillips, *American Negro Slavery* (1918. Reprint. Baton Rouge: Louisi-

ana State University Press, 1966), pp. 370, 377; Dew, *Ironmaker to the Confederacy*, p. 31; Henson, "Industrial Workers," pp. 110–14; Randall M. Miller, "The Fabric of Control: Slavery in Antebellum Southern Textile Mills," *Business History Review* 55 (Winter 1981): 477–78.

20. Dozier, "Trade and Transportation," p. 239.

21. NCRR, *Annual Report*, 1856, pp. 5–6, 16–18. Two successive presidents of the R&GRR made similar recommendations in 1857 and 1860, using much the same arguments (R&GRR, *Annual Report*, 1857, p. 11; 1860, p. 9). In 1861, after the war had begun, the R&G stockholders appropriated $125,000 for slave purchases (Black, *Railroads of the Confederacy*, p. 29).

22. NCRR, *Report of the President, January 20, 1859*, pp. 18–19; NCRR, *Annual Report*, 1860, p. 27.

23. Bill of sale, 11 May 1857, in Bills of Sale for Slaves, 1864 [*sic*], XXIII. Correspondence, v. 22, NCRR Records, Archives; NCRR, *Annual Report*, 1858, pp. 13, 25; 1859, pp. 19, 23.

24. NCRR, *Annual Report*, 1856, p. 17; NCRR, *Regulations and Instructions*, 1854, pp. 44–45; 1857, p. 25.

25. Statement by C. F. Fisher, May 1858, in Bills Receivable, 1854–65, XXIII. Correspondence, v. 22, NCRR Records, Archives. For Dave, see ibid., receipts in 1857 folder.

26. *Greensboro Patriot*, 3 Apr. 1857.

27. Licht, *Working for the Railroad*, pp. 181–96; White, "Short History of Railway Brakes," p. 6; Lightner, *Labor on the Illinois Central*, pp. 118–19; Henson, "Industrial Workers," pp. 111–12; Usselman, "Air Brakes," pp. 30–31.

28. See Berlin, *Slaves Without Masters*, pp. 227–28.

29. The 1860 census in North Carolina listed only thirty-seven free black railway employees; only six of these lived in counties adjoining the NCRR. See Franklin, *Free Negro in North Carolina*, pp. 134–35.

30. Lightner, *Labor on the Illinois Central*, p. 89. See also Kirkman, *Railway Expenditures*, 1:149–50.

31. Henson, "Industrial Workers," pp. 114–25; Licht, *Working for the Railroad*, pp. 147–49, 214–24.

32. Henson, "Industrial Workers," pp. 41–43.

33. Licht, *Working for the Railroad*, pp. 38–41, 161–63; Lightner, *Labor on the Illinois Central*, p. 171; Henson, "Industrial Workers," pp. 75–78.

34. Jervis, *Railway Property*, pp. 219–20; Henson, "Industrial Workers," pp. 91–101.

35. Charlotte *North Carolina Whig*, 28 July 1857. See Henson, "Industrial Workers," p. 95; Licht, *Working for the Railroad*, pp. 95–97; Kirkman, *Railway Revenue*, pp. 176–84; *American Railroad Journal*, 15 Sept. 1860, pp. 817–18; *American Railway Review*, 12 Sept. 1861, p. 72.

36. Licht, *Working for the Railroad*, pp. 80–88; NCRR, *Regulations and Instructions*, 1854, esp. pp. 3–5; 1857, esp. pp. 3–5.

37. Licht, *Working for the Railroad*, pp. 188–89; Kirkman, *Railway Expenditures*, 1:143–62; Cochran, *Railroad Leaders*, pp. 178–79; Henson, "Industrial Workers," pp. 118–24.

38. Licht, *Working for the Railroad*, pp. 127–30.

39. Ibid., pp. 130–31.

40. Ibid., pp. 132–33; Richardson, *Locomotive Engineer*, pp. 113, 144–45.

41. Licht, *Working for the Railroad*, p. 137.

42. For NCRR figures, see *Annual Report*, 1856, p. 36; 1860, pp. 38–39; entries for June and July 1859, in Journal, 1852–60, in VIII. Expenditures, v. 39, NCRR Records, Archives. For the national averages, see Licht, *Working for the Railroad*, p. 126, which gives daily figures. I have converted these into annual amounts by multiplying them by twenty-six days, then by twelve months. Average wages for Massachusetts conductors and engineers appear in U.S. Department of Labor, *History of Wages*, pp. 432, 437.

43. NCRR, *Annual Report*, 1860, p. 10; Charlotte *North Carolina Whig*, 29 Mar. 1859.

44. Licht, *Working for the Railroad*, pp. 175–77. The seventy-hour week for trainmen is confirmed for Massachusetts in U.S. Department of Labor, *History of Wages*, pp. 430–41.

45. Licht, *Working for the Railroad*, pp. 88, 197–207; Lightner, *Labor on the Illinois Central*, pp. 122–25.

46. NCRR, *Regulations and Instructions*, 1854, pp. 5, 46; 1857, pp. 4, 20.

47. Licht, *Working for the Railroad*, pp. 212–13.

48. Ibid., pp. 240–48; Cochran, *Railroad Leaders*, pp. 179–80; Richardson, *Locomotive Engineer*, pp. 107–9.

49. *Lexington and Yadkin Flag*, 4 July 1856.

50. Three were natives of Rhode Island, one of Mississippi, two of Maryland, two of Pennsylvania, three of Massachusetts, one of Delaware, one of Kentucky, three of Virginia, three of Alabama, one of the District of Columbia, five of Ireland, and two of Scotland (Stokes, *Company Shops*, pp. 23–25).

51. T. E. Roberts to Isaac Richardson, 1 Apr. 1856, Richardson Paper, Duke.

52. NCRR, *Annual Report*, 1860, p. 25; *Hillsborough Recorder*, 26 Jan. 1870.

53. Licht, *Working for the Railroad*, pp. 65–67; Henson, "Industrial Workers," p. 26.

54. NCRR, *Annual Report*, 1860, pp. 9–10. The president of the Raleigh and Gaston announced a similar policy dating from before 1853 (R&GRR, *Annual Report*, 1853, pp. 8–9).

55. Several Georgia roads had northern managers, including J. Edgar Thomson of the Georgia Railroad and later of the Pennsylvania (Henson, "Industrial Workers," p. 22).

56. *Lexington and Yadkin Flag*, 4 July 1856; NCRR, *Annual Report*, 1860, p. 25.

Chapter 5

1. NCRR, *Annual Report*, 1860, p. 23.

2. *American Railway Review*, 7 Nov. 1861, p. 135; Weber, *Northern Railroads in the Civil War*, p. 12; Angus James Johnston, *Virginia Railroads in the Civil War*, pp. 13–14.

3. Greensboro *Times*, 7 Feb., 21 Aug. 1856.

4. Salisbury *Carolina Watchman*, 23 Sept. 1856.

5. Raleigh *North Carolina Standard*, 23 July 1856; Charlotte *Western Democrat*, 30 Dec. 1856.

6. White, *American Railroad Passenger Car*, 2:462; Greensboro *Times*, 27 Mar. 1856; board of directors' minutes, 17 Aug. 1855, NCRR Office.

7. NCRR, *Regulations and Instructions*, 1854, p. 35; 1857, p. 32; statement of W. B. Dusenberry, 24 Oct. 1857, Cameron Family Papers, SHC.

8. Weber, *Northern Railroads in the Civil War*, p. 12; Angus James Johnston, *Virginia Railroads in the Civil War*, p. 14; NCRR, *Annual Report*, 1862, p. 30.

9. Charlotte *Western Democrat*, 28 Aug. 1855.

10. Jervis, *Railway Property*, pp. 154–56, 278–80, 287–88; Daniel C. McCallum in *Railroads: Pioneers in Modern Management*, ed. Chandler, pp. 41–44; Colburn and Holley, *Permanent Way*, p. 15; Whiton, *Railroads and Their Management*, pp. 41–42; White, *American Locomotives*, pp. 71–74; Angus James Johnston, *Virginia Railroads in the Civil War*, p. 14; Weber, *Northern Railroads in the Civil War*, p. 12; Stover, *Iron Road*, p. 19.

11. NCRR, *Report of Col. Walter Gwynn, Jan. 10, 1856*, pp. 13–14; *Greensboro Patriot*, 28 Mar. 1856.

12. Raleigh *North Carolina Standard*, 4 Mar. 1857; NCRR, *Report of the President, January 20, 1859*, pp. 17–18; Report of the Joint Select Committee, N.C. *Public Documents*, 1858–59, #71, pp. 12–15.

13. Black, *Railroads of the Confederacy*, p. 31.

14. Raleigh *North Carolina Standard*, 22 Mar. 1856; Greensboro *Times*, 17 Apr. 1856.

15. NCRR, *Regulations and Instructions*, 1854, p. 11; 1857, p. 9.

16. Greensboro *Times*, 17 Apr. 1856; *Lloyd's Southern Railroad Guide*, May 1863, p. 38.

17. Thompson, *Wiring a Continent*, p. 205; NCRR, *Regulations and Instructions*, 1854, pp. 7–10; 1857, pp. 6–8.

18. Thompson, *Wiring a Continent*, pp. 203–12; Daniel C. McCallum in *Railroads: Pioneers in Modern Management*, ed. Chandler, pp. 44–52.

19. Thompson, *Wiring a Continent*, maps on p. 140 and facing p. 240.

20. Charlotte *Western Democrat*, 11 Aug., 13 Oct. 1854; Salisbury *Carolina Watchman*, 15 Feb. 1855.

21. Contract, 24 July 1858, with Magnetic Telegraph Co., in 1869 folder, XXII. Contracts, v. 19, NCRR Records, Archives; Charlotte *Western Democrat*, 3 Mar. 1857, 24 Aug. 1858.

22. NCRR, *Annual Report*, 1859, pp. 5, 11; 1861, p. 8.

23. Shaw, *History of Railroad Accidents*, pp. 40–43.

24. *American Railroad Journal*, 4 Mar. 1865, p. 201.

25. *Raleigh Register*, 21 Oct. 1854; *Greensboro Patriot*, 19 Oct. 1855; Charlotte *Daily Bulletin*, 4 Jan. 1861; Greensboro *Times*, 5 Jan. 1861; NCRR, *Annual Report*, 1861, p. 15.

26. NCRR, *Regulations and Instructions*, 1854, p. 35; 1857, p. 32; NCRR, *Annual Report*, 1861, p. 15.

27. Raleigh *North Carolina Star*, 15 Nov. 1854; Salisbury *Carolina Watchman*, 1 Apr. 1856; Raleigh *North Carolina Standard*, 6 Sept. 1856.

28. Greensboro *Times*, 9 Oct. 1856; Charlotte *Western Democrat*, 24 May 1859; *Hillsborough Recorder*, 23 Jan. 1861; *Greensboro Patriot*, 31 Jan. 1861.

29. Stover, *Iron Road*, p. 210; NCRR, *Annual Reports*, 1856–61, esp. 1860, pp. 18–19; 1861, p. 15.

30. Charlotte *Western Democrat*, 14 Sept. 1858; Charlotte *North Carolina Whig*, 4 July 1859.

31. Charlotte *Western Democrat*, 2 June 1857; Schenck, *Digest of Decisions*, pp. 60–61; *Poole v. NCRR*, 53 *N.C. Reports* 340.

32. *Greensboro Patriot*, 3 July 1857; Charlotte *Western Democrat*, 7 July, 22 Sept. 1857.

33. Charlotte *North Carolina Whig*, 21 Apr. 1857, 26 Jan. 1858; Greensboro *Times*, 23 Apr. 1857.

34. One of the clearest expositions of this doctrine was presented by Justice William Battle of the North Carolina Supreme Court, in *Laws v. NCRR*, in 1860 (52 *N.C. Reports* 468). See also *Jones v. Witherspoon*, ibid., 557.

35. Raleigh *North Carolina Standard*, 14 Jan. 1857; Salisbury *Carolina Watchman*, 4 Dec. 1855.

36. White, *American Locomotives*, pp. 211–12.

37. N.C. *Public Laws*, 1856–57, chap. 7, p. 6; *Aycock v. W&WRR* (1858), 51 *N.C. Reports* 232; *Laws v. NCRR* (1860), 52 ibid. 468.

38. NCRR, *Regulations and Instructions*, 1857, p. 34; Raleigh *North Carolina Standard*, 14 Jan. 1857; C. F. Fisher to J. H. Bryan, 6 Sept. 1859, Bryan Collection, Archives.

39. See Davidson County Railroad Records, Dec. 1857, Archives.

40. *American Railway Times*, 29 Oct. 1864, p. 350; J. Crawford King, "Closing of the Southern Range," p. 62.

41. For accounts of the storm and its impact on the railroad, see Greensboro *Times*, 22 Jan. 1857; *Greensboro Patriot*, 23 Jan. 1857; Salisbury *Carolina Watchman*, 27 Jan. 1857 (including quotation); Charlotte *Western Democrat*, 27 Jan. 1857; Charlotte *North Carolina Whig*, 27 Jan., 24 Feb. 1857; Raleigh *North Carolina Standard*, 28 Jan. 1857; Concord *Weekly Gazette*, 31 Jan. 1857.

42. *American Railroad Journal*, 23 Dec. 1854, p. 801; 7 June 1856, p. 356; *Hillsborough Recorder*, 17 May 1854; Licht, *Working for the Railroad*, pp. 179–80; Stover, *Iron Road*, pp. 211–12; Stover, *History of the Illinois Central*, p. 69.

43. *Hillsborough Recorder*, 17 May 1854; NCRR, *Annual Report*, 1855, pp. 5, 17.

44. Charlotte *North Carolina Whig*, 24 Apr. 1855; Greensboro *Times*, 5 June 1856; *Lexington and Yadkin Flag*, 20 June 1856; Concord *Weekly Gazette*, 12 July 1856.

45. Salisbury *Carolina Watchman*, 8 Apr. 1856.

46. *Greensboro Patriot*, 10 Oct. 1856. See also *Hillsborough Recorder*, 23 July 1856.

47. Greensboro *Times*, 4 June 1857. The postmaster general had already announced in July 1856 that such roads as desired could discontinue one Sunday mail if the other was carried regularly (*American Railroad Journal*, 9 Aug. 1856, p. 505).

48. *Hillsborough Recorder*, 15 July, 30 Sept. 1857, 31 Aug. 1859; Greensboro *Times*, 17 Sept. 1857; Charlotte *Western Democrat*, 23 Aug. 1859.

49. Charlotte *Western Democrat*, 26 Mar. 1861.

50. Fuller, *American Mail*, pp. 164–70; Harlow, *Old Postbags*, pp. 313–17.

51. Fuller, *American Mail*, pp. 164–65. The *American Railway Times* in January 1865 heralded the arrival of the new post office cars on several northern and western roads (*Times*, 28 Jan. 1865, p. 26).

52. *Greensboro Patriot*, 23 Dec. 1854.

53. NCRR, *Annual Report*, 1855, pp. 9–10. The lesser receipts of $19,892 for 1855–56 were no doubt occasioned by the road's lack of completion before late January 1856.

54. Charlotte *Western Democrat*, 3, 31 Mar., 12 May 1857; Charlotte *North Carolina*

Whig, 12 May 1857; Raleigh *North Carolina Standard*, 20 May 1857; *American Railroad Journal*, 29 May 1858, p. 345.

55. Raleigh *North Carolina Standard*, 9 May 1860; Charlotte *North Carolina Whig*, 24 Apr., 8 May 1860; Charlotte *Western Democrat*, 1, 8, 15 May 1860.

56. Harlow, *Old Waybills*, pp. 65–69; Stimson, *History of the Express Business*, pp. 159–63; Chandler, *Visible Hand*, pp. 126–27.

57. Offer of 10 June 1856, in XXII. Contracts, v. 19, NCRR Records, Archives.

58. Memorandum of agreement, 26 Jan. 1859; C. F. Fisher to W. H. Trego, 28 Jan. 1859; memorandum of C. F. Fisher, 10 July 1860, all in 1869 folder in XXII. Contracts, v. 19, NCRR Records, Archives; NCRR, *Annual Report*, 1859, p. 25. See Adams Express Co. advertisements in *Greensboro Patriot*, 4 Mar. 1859; Charlotte *North Carolina Whig*, 29 Mar. 1859.

Chapter 6

1. NCRR, *Annual Report*, 1855, p. 8; Concord *Weekly Gazette*, quoted in *Hillsborough Recorder*, 27 Sept. 1854; Raleigh *North Carolina Standard*, 9 Dec. 1854.

2. Raleigh *North Carolina Standard*, 3 Jan. 1855; NCRR, *Annual Report*, 1855, p. 9. See NCRR contracts with James M. Bland, 19 June and 8 Sept. 1855, and with E. T. and J. W. Clemmons, 8 Sept. 1855, in XXII. Contracts, v. 19, NCRR Records, Archives.

3. *Hillsborough Recorder*, 3 Jan. 1855; Raleigh *North Carolina Standard*, 2 Jan. 1856. See also the travel account by "Puffenbarker," in *Raleigh Register*, 5 May 1855.

4. NCRR, *Annual Report*, 1867, pp. 18–19.

5. *American Railroad Journal*, 17 June 1854, p. 376. See also ibid., 30 Aug. 1856, p. 553.

6. White, *American Railroad Passenger Car*, 1:26–30.

7. *American Railway Times*, 11 Feb. 1865, p. 46; *Greensboro Patriot*, 17 Oct. 1856.

8. NCRR, *Annual Report*, 1860, p. 37; report of W. B. Dusenberry, 12 May 1858, J. H. Bryan Papers, ECU. For general discussion, see White, *American Railroad Passenger Car*, 2:462–63; Kirkland, *Men, Cities, and Transportation*, 1:300; Black, *Railroads of the Confederacy*, p. 19; Klein, *History of the Louisville and Nashville*, p. 56.

9. Mencken, *Railroad Passenger Car*, pp. 14–15; Salisbury *Daily Union Banner*, 11 Dec. 1865.

10. The NCRR *Regulations and Instructions* of 1854 (p. 49) forbade passengers to smoke in the cars or station houses, but that ban was omitted from the 1857 revision.

11. Klein, *History of the Louisville and Nashville*, p. 56; Stover, *Iron Road*, p. 186; White, *American Railroad Passenger Car*, 2:429; NCRR, *Regulations and Instructions*, 1857, p. 11.

12. See Stover, *Iron Road*, pp. 186, 205–7; White, *American Railroad Passenger Car*, 1:208–11; Mencken, *Railroad Passenger Car*, pp. 59–60, 75.

13. See White, *American Railroad Passenger Car*, 1:311–20; Mencken, *Railroad Passenger Car*, pp. 27–28.

14. NCRR, *Regulations and Instructions*, 1857, pp. 10–11.

15. Ibid., 1854, p. 36.

16. For the donation of NCRR land to Trollinger, see protest by Paul C. Cameron (written in December 1855 but dated 10 Jan. 1856), in Cameron Family Papers,

SHC. For glowing (and perhaps subsidized) accounts of the Haw River House, see Raleigh *North Carolina Standard*, 16 Apr., 23 July 1856; Raleigh *Advocate*, quoted in Greensboro *Times*, 29 May 1856; Charlotte *Western Democrat*, 30 Dec. 1856, 27 Jan. 1857.

17. For highly divergent accounts of these proceedings, see *Lexington and Yadkin Flag*, 12 Sept. 1856; *Hillsborough Recorder*, 10 Sept. 1856; Greensboro *Times*, 11 Sept. 1856.

18. Salisbury *Carolina Watchman*, 20 Jan. 1857; Charlotte *Western Democrat*, 27 Jan., 17 Mar. 1857; Raleigh *North Carolina Standard*, 28 July, 4 Aug. 1858.

19. Pierpont, "Development of the Textile Industry in Alamance," pp. 48–49; Hughes, *Development of the Textile Industry in Alamance*, pp. 5, 12.

20. *Milton Chronicle*, quoted in Raleigh *North Carolina Standard*, 28 July 1858.

21. See Stokes, *Company Shops*, pp. 26–30; Whitaker, *Centennial History of Alamance*, pp. 110–11. For public and private endorsements of "Miss Nancy" and her hotel, see Raleigh *North Carolina Standard*, 6 Oct. 1860, and Emma to her Nephew, 25 Feb. 1859, Grimes-Bryan Papers, ECU.

22. Elizabeth Doris King, "First-Class Hotel," p. 186.

23. Charlotte *Western Democrat*, 26 Aug., 30 Dec. 1856.

24. Ibid., 17 Mar. 1857; Raleigh *North Carolina Standard*, 6 Oct. 1860.

25. *Greensboro Patriot*, 17 Aug. 1855.

26. Raleigh *North Carolina Standard*, 2 Jan. 1856.

27. Cochran, *Railroad Leaders*, p. 172.

28. This brief account is greatly indebted to the perceptive discussions of early railroad leaders and their strategies in Chandler, *Visible Hand*, pp. 134–37; Cochran, *Railroad Leaders*, pp. 167–72; and Klein, *Great Richmond Terminal*, pp. 10–20. Klein may well exaggerate the persistence of insular "territorial" attitudes and policies among railroad leaders in the 1850s, when the desire for through traffic had already become a driving force.

29. Letter of E. G. Palmer in Raleigh *North Carolina Star*, 13 Aug. 1851.

30. See, for instance, the message of Governor Charles Manly in November 1850 (Governors' Letterbooks, #39, Archives).

31. NCRR, *Annual Report*, 1857, p. 12.

32. The *Greensboro Patriot*, which for a time opposed the NCRR management on every conceivable occasion, argued in 1856 that local travelers were apt to be the mainstay of the road and that daytime trains should be adhered to even at the cost of losing the mails and many through passengers (*Patriot*, 28 Mar. 1856).

33. L. O'B. Branch to D. S. Reid, 28 Dec. 1854, Reid Papers, Archives.

34. See R&GRR advertisement in *Greensboro Patriot*, 5 May 1855; *Patriot*, 17 Aug. 1855; Salisbury *Carolina Watchman*, 23 Sept. 1856.

35. *Raleigh Register*, 13 Feb. 1856; letters of C. F. Fisher and Wm. Johnston in Salisbury *Carolina Watchman*, 1, 15 July 1856.

36. Salisbury *Carolina Watchman*, 23 Sept. 1856; R&GRR, *Annual Report*, 1856, p. 7 (also in Raleigh *North Carolina Standard*, 8 Nov. 1856).

37. *Raleigh Register*, 3 Jan. 1855.

38. Salisbury *Carolina Watchman*, 18 Jan., 1 Feb., 19 Apr. 1855; letter of C. F. Fisher in *Watchman*, 1 July 1856.

39. Charlotte *North Carolina Whig*, 12 Feb. 1856; *Greensboro Patriot*, 25 Apr. 1856; Salisbury *Carolina Watchman*, 27 May 1856; letters of C. F. Fisher and Wm. Johnston

in *Watchman*, 1, 15, 29 July 1856.

40. See letters of Fisher and Johnston, Salisbury *Carolina Watchman*, 1, 15, 29 July 1856. See also editorial support for Johnston's position in Charlotte *Western Democrat*, 17 June 1856.

41. *Hillsborough Recorder*, 20 May, 22 July 1857. For preceding vacillation, see *Greensboro Patriot*, 20 Feb. 1857 (including legislative remarks of Senator Ralph Gorrell), 20 Mar. 1857.

42. Quoted in Greensboro *Times*, 29 Aug. 1857.

43. For the shift in policy in 1857, see NCRR, *Annual Report*, 1857, pp. 13–14; R&GRR, *Annual Report*, 1857, pp. 9–10, reprinted in Raleigh *North Carolina Standard*, 4 Nov. 1857; NCRR, *Communincation* [sic] *from the President*, 14 Feb. 1859, pp. 16–18.

44. NCRR, *Communincation* [sic] *from the President*, 14 Feb. 1859, pp. 16–18; C&SCRR, *Annual Report*, 1859, p. 25.

45. Charlotte *Daily Bulletin*, 5 Mar. 1861. The R&G discontinued one of its two trains in 1859, citing the wear and tear on its locomotives (R&GRR, *Annual Report*, 1859, pp. 10–11).

46. NCRR, *Annual Report*, 1859, p. 11; Charlotte *Western Democrat*, 26 Apr. 1859.

47. Letters of S. L. Fremont to Wilmington *Herald*, quoted in *Greensboro Patriot*, 19 Aug. 1859, and of "Morganton," in Salisbury *Carolina Watchman*, 6 Sept. 1859.

48. *American Railroad Journal*, 29 May 1858, p. 345; N.C. *Public Documents*, 1858–59, #48, p. 8; *Greensboro Patriot*, 28 May, 4 June 1858; W&WRR, *Annual Report*, 1867, p. 10; W&MRR, *Annual Report*, 1858, p. 1.

49. *Greensboro Patriot*, 28 May 1858; Charlotte *Western Democrat*, 22 June 1858; and tables showing numbers of through passengers by month, 1857–61, in NCRR, *Annual Reports*, 1858–61, esp. 1861, p. 22.

50. R&GRR, *Annual Report*, 1858, p. 8; C&SCRR, *Annual Report*, 1859, quoted in *American Railroad Journal*, 24 Mar. 1860, p. 244. The C&SC did better than the NCRR in through passenger receipts during calendar 1859 compared with 1858, gaining $14,100 to the NCRR's $4,300, despite the fact that the C&SC was only about half as long a road. That increase should be kept in perspective, however. The two Wilmington roads each reported total through passenger receipts of nearly $140,000 during the year ending in September 1858; equivalent revenues of the NCRR (a longer road) were only $41,000 in that period (W&MRR, *Annual Report*, 1858, p. 1; W&WRR, *Annual Report*, 1858, p. 10; NCRR, *Annual Report*, 1858, p. 20; 1859, p. 25).

51. Cecil K. Brown, *State Movement*, pp. 106–25. See *Raleigh Register*, 13 Aug. 1853, for Morehead's explanation of his simultaneous conflicting interests as the developer of Morehead City and director of the survey to determine the route of the A&NCRR.

52. Cecil K. Brown, *State Movement*, pp. 126–47; NCRR, *Annual Report*, 1858, pp. 11–12.

53. Dawson, *Reminiscences*, p. 30. For early efforts to promote Beaufort Harbor, see Raleigh *North Carolina Star*, 20 Feb. 1850; Raleigh *North Carolina Standard*, 21 May 1851.

54. Charlotte *Western Democrat*, 10 July, 4 Sept. 1860; Raleigh *North Carolina Standard*, 6 Oct. 1860.

55. The dip in 1858–59 appears even after June 1859 is added to it; fiscal 1858–

59 was only eleven months long due to a shift in the fiscal year from July–June to June–May.

56. I have included here the amounts collected by conductors as part of the local passenger revenues. That is surely a proper allocation, and in any case the conductor revenues are not large enough to affect the generalizations materially.

57. See tables in NCRR, *Annual Reports*, 1858, pp. 19–20; 1859, pp. 24–25; 1860, p. 29b; 1861, pp. 22–27 (my pagination in a few cases, as some pages are not numbered).

58. See tables in ibid., 1860, p. 29a; 1861, p. 24.

59. Stover, *Iron Road*, p. 19; George Rogers Taylor, *Transportation Revolution*, p. 144; Joubert, *Southern Freight Rates*, p. 8; Angus James Johnston, *Virginia Railroads in the Civil War*, p. 15.

60. NCRR, *Report of the President, January 20, 1859*, p. 16; *Greensboro Patriot*, 30 Sept. 1854.

61. *Hillsborough Recorder*, 4 Oct. 1854, 19 Sept. 1855. The board authorized an even lower drop, to 3 cents, but Fisher induced them to leave it at 3½ (Fisher to P. C. Cameron, 25 Aug. 1855, Cameron Family Papers, SHC).

62. *Greensboro Patriot*, 28 Mar. 1856.

63. See *Greensboro Patriot*, 19 Nov. 1858; NCRR, *Report of the President, January 20, 1859*, p. 16.

64. This was a national phenomenon. See Allan Pred, *Urban Growth and City-Systems in the United States, 1840–1860* (Cambridge, Mass.: Harvard University Press, 1980), pp. 150, 270n.

65. *Hillsborough Recorder*, 16 May 1855; Salisbury *Carolina Watchman*, 20 July 1858.

66. Thomas Ruffin to P. C. Cameron, 1 May 1856, Cameron Family Papers, SHC; Raleigh *North Carolina Standard*, 14 May 1856, 14 Oct. 1857.

67. *American Railroad Journal*, 29 Jan. 1859, p. 72. Marshall M. Kirkman, another leading railway authority, agreed with this argument, at least as regards employees (*Railway Expenditures*, 1:116–17).

68. Charlotte *North Carolina Whig*, 7 Feb. 1854; Raleigh *North Carolina Standard*, 30 Dec. 1854.

69. NCRR, *Regulations and Instructions*, 1854, pp. 37–38; 1857, p. 34.

70. Note by C. F. Fisher, 23 Oct. 1856, Cameron Family Papers, SHC; Greensboro *Times*, 4 June 1857.

71. Thomas Ruffin to D. L. Swain, and Swain to Ruffin, 31 May, 7 June 1858, Ruffin, *Papers*, 2:596–98.

72. *Greensboro Patriot*, 22 July 1859; NCRR, *Annual Report*, 1859, pp. 4–5.

Chapter 7

1. See discussion of freight train frequency and service in Jervis, *Railway Property*, pp. 286–90.

2. Greensboro *Times*, 7 Aug., 18 Sept. 1856.

3. Contract with H. Pennington, 21 Sept. 1856, in XXII. Contracts, v. 19, NCRR Records, Archives.

4. Charlotte *Western Democrat*, 8 Sept. 1857.

5. See *Lexington and Yadkin Flag*, 22 Feb. 1856; Salisbury *Carolina Watchman*, 10

Jan., 27 Mar. 1860; *Greensboro Patriot*, 23 Mar. 1860.

6. Stover, *Iron Road*, pp. 17, 68–69; Charles W. Turner, "Railroad Service to Virginia Farmers," p. 243.

7. C&SCRR, *Annual Report*, 1854, p. 15; 1860, p. 18; R&GRR, *Annual Report*, 1859, p. 18.

8. See NCRR, *Annual Report*, 1856, p. 15; 1858, pp. 11–12; 1859, p. 12. For President William Johnston's comments on economic conditions and their effects on the region's railways, see C&SCRR, *Annual Report*, 1857, p. 12 (reprinted in Charlotte *North Carolina Whig*, 16 Feb. 1858).

9. For general discussions of freight rate making, see Cochran, *Railroad Leaders*, pp. 153–56, 159, 167–72; Joubert, *Southern Freight Rates*, pp. 5–16; McPherson, *Railway Freight Rates*, pp. 148–66; Chandler, *Visible Hand*, pp. 125–27.

10. Stover, *Iron Road*, pp. 19–20, 215.

11. NCRR, *Annual Report*, 1857, p. 16; NCRR, *Report of the President, January 20, 1859*, p. 16; *Greensboro Patriot*, 30 Sept., 14 Oct. 1854; C. F. Fisher to P. C. Cameron, 25 Aug. 1855, Cameron Family Papers, SHC.

12. Salisbury *Carolina Watchman*, 15, 22 Mar. 1855; *Hillsborough Recorder*, 2 May 1855; *Lexington and Yadkin Flag*, 14 Dec. 1855. See in particular the letters of Caleb Phifer and Archibald Henderson in *Watchman*, 1 July 1856.

13. Concord *Weekly Gazette*, 10 Jan. 1857.

14. Ibid., 12 July 1856; NCRR, *Annual Report*, 1856, p. 4; 1857, p. 12.

15. NCRR, *Annual Report*, 1857, p. 12; Raleigh *North Carolina Standard*, 23 July 1856; *Hillsborough Recorder*, 30 July 1856.

16. NCRR, *Annual Report*, 1857, p. 12; Salisbury *Carolina Watchman*, 4 Aug. 1857.

17. See letters of "Justice" in Charlotte *Western Democrat*, 19 May 1857; of "Pilot Mountain" in *Greensboro Patriot*, 19 Nov. 1858; and Minority Report of J. M. Morehead et al. in N.C. *Public Documents*, 1858–59, #48, pp. 6–7.

18. NCRR, *Annual Report*, 1860, p. 50.

19. NCRR, *Report of the President, January 20, 1859*, p. 16; agreement with Francis Fries, 8 July 1857, in XXII. Contracts, v. 19, NCRR Records, Archives.

20. NCRR, *Annual Report*, 1859, pp. 22, 25, 28–34; 1860, pp. 29b, 51.

21. Based on ibid., 1858–61.

22. The annual report for 1860 (p. 51) contains itemized tables listing specific categories and quantities of freight sent from each station in either direction. Unfortunately it omits Goldsboro and Raleigh, the two stations receiving all of the westbound freight coming from other roads. The report for 1859 (p. 22) indicates tonnage figures by station but does not itemize the kinds of freight sent by each station.

23. Ibid., 1859, pp. 28–33.

24. Drawn from ibid., 1856, 1857, 1860, 1862–70. The information does not appear in other years.

25. Ibid., 1859, p. 22.

26. C&SCRR, *Annual Report*, 1858, pp. 25–26.

27. W&WRR, *Annual Report*, 1861, p. 23.

28. For general discussion, see Lindstrom, "Southern Dependence," pp. 110–13. For statements of wheat destinations on the NCRR, see *Greensboro Patriot*, 8 Feb. 1856; speech of Ralph Gorrell in state senate, in *Patriot*, 20 Feb. 1857; and Minority Report of J. M. Morehead et al. in N.C. *Public Documents*, 1858–59, #48, pp. 6–7.

29. The Salisbury *Carolina Watchman* (12 Feb. 1856) provided a list of freight

charges on various commodities from Salisbury to Wilmington and Charleston, respectively. Wilmington was slightly lower in almost every category at that point.

30. Soule, "Vegetables, Fruit and Nursery Products," pp. 237, 239.

31. For the beginnings of the nursery business in Greensboro, see Arnett, *Greensboro*, pp. 204–5; B. M. Jones, *Rail Roads Considered*, p. 39.

32. *Hillsborough Recorder*, 7 May 1856; *Lexington and Yadkin Flag*, 7 Dec. 1855; *Raleigh Register*, 22 Mar. 1856; Raleigh *North Carolina Standard*, 16 Feb. 1856.

33. *Hillsborough Recorder*, 12 June 1867; *Greensboro Patriot*, 21 June 1867; Raleigh *Daily Sentinel*, 8 Oct. 1867 (for a description of a kiln).

34. Raleigh *North Carolina Standard*, 30 July 1859.

35. Ibid., 2 Apr., 1, 12 Oct. 1859, 7 Nov. 1860; B. M. Jones, *Rail Roads Considered*, pp. 38–39.

36. Gray, *Agriculture in the Southern United States*, 2:759, 769, 773; Robert, *Tobacco Kingdom*, pp. 53–55, 62–67, 72–73, 161–65, 170–81, 187–88, 219, 222–24; Robert, "Tobacco Industry," pp. 120–29. Although Robert (*Tobacco Kingdom*, p. 224) says that the tobacco boxes averaged 100 pounds, sources familiar with NCRR shipments placed them at 125 pounds. See N.C. *Public Documents*, 1858–59, #48, p. 2; *Lexington and Yadkin Flag*, 7 Dec. 1855.

37. *Lexington and Yadkin Flag*, 7 Dec. 1855.

38. For information concerning origins and destinations of the tobacco, see the Minority Report of J. M. Morehead et al. advocating a railroad from Danville to Greensboro, in N.C. *Public Documents*, 1858–59, #48, pp. 1–3; Raleigh *North Carolina Standard*, 4 Aug. 1858.

39. Hammond, *Cotton Industry*, pp. 288, 290n; Fishlow, *American Railroads*, pp. 270–71.

40. See Chandler, *Railroads: The Nation's First Big Business*, p. 22.

41. NCRR, *Annual Report*, 1867, pp. 18–19.

42. Standard and Griffin, "Cotton Textile Industry," pp. 22–23, 138–39, 145–46.

43. Fries, "One Hundred Years," p. 18.

44. Raleigh *North Carolina Standard*, 11 Apr. 1860.

45. NCRR, *Annual Report*, 1857, p. 12; 1859, p. 31; 1860, p. 18. For general information about guano and its use and importation, see Gray, *Agriculture in the Southern United States*, 2:805–6; Rosser H. Taylor, "Fertilizers and Farming," pp. 307–19.

46. Chandler, *Visible Hand*, pp. 122–25; Fishlow, *American Railroads*, pp. 269–70.

47. Raleigh *North Carolina Standard*, 24 Feb. 1855; *Hillsborough Recorder*, 28 Feb., 14 Mar. 1855; W&WRR, *Annual Report*, 1856, p. 13; 1866, p. 7; agreement of 26 Mar. 1856, in XXII. Contracts, v. 19, NCRR Records, Archives.

48. S. M. Wilson to C. F. Fisher, 24 Apr. 1856, in Fisher Family Papers, SHC; agreement of 29 May 1856 with R&G and Petersburg Railroads, agreement of 1 June 1856 with W&WRR, and contract of 13 Dec. 1856 with W&WRR and S&RRR, in XXII. Contracts, v. 19, NCRR Records, Archives; R&GRR, *Annual Report*, 1856, p. 7; W&WRR, *Annual Report*, 1856, p. 14; NCRR, *Annual Report*, 1857, p. 11. See NCRR advertisement of the through service to Wilmington, in *Greensboro Patriot*, 22 Aug. 1856.

49. Salisbury *Carolina Watchman*, 17, 31 Mar., 7 Apr. 1857.

50. See *Greensboro Patriot*, 22, 29 Apr., 1 July 1859.

51. Raleigh *North Carolina Standard*, 30 Apr. 1859.

52. Agreement of 17 May 1859, in XXII. Contracts, v. 19, NCRR Records, Ar-

chives. This was printed with a covering letter from Fisher to Ellis, in Raleigh *North Carolina Standard*, 21 May 1859. For evidence of an earlier through freight agreement with the WNCRR, see its advertisement, dated 22 Feb. 1859, in Salisbury *Carolina Watchman*, 3 Jan. 1860.

53. Report of Superintendent S. L. Fremont, pp. 6–7 (paginated separately), in W&WRR, *Annual Report*, 1859; advertisements of W&WRR and of H. B. Cromwell & Co., in Charlotte *Western Democrat*, 22, 29 May 1860, 26 Mar. 1861.

54. Charlotte *Western Democrat*, 10 July 1860; NCRR, *Annual Report*, 1860, pp. 4–5, 11; Raleigh *North Carolina Standard*, 6 Oct. 1860; A&NCRR, *Annual Report*, 1861, cited in Black, *Railroads of the Confederacy*, p. 37.

55. Charlotte *Western Democrat*, 9 Oct. 1860.

Chapter 8

1. Alfred M. Chandler, Jr., has made this point in masterful fashion. See particularly his *Visible Hand* and *Railroads: The Nation's First Big Business*. Another important contribution to railroad and management history is Thomas C. Cochran's *Railroad Leaders*.

2. See Stephen Salsbury's excellent study, *The State, the Investor, and the Railroad: The Boston & Albany, 1825–1867* (Cambridge, Mass.: Harvard University Press, 1967).

3. In addition to the previously cited works, see Ward, *J. Edgar Thomson*, esp. pp. 107–8.

4. Chandler, *Visible Hand*, pp. 145–48.

5. "Railroad Management," in *American Railroad Journal*, 29 Aug. 1857, p. 554. See the similar views of Jervis, in *Railway Property*, pp. 67–70; but cf. Cochran, *Railroad Leaders*, p. 67, who says that nineteenth-century railroad directors commonly were powerful initiators and vetoers of policy who sometimes acted without the approval or even knowledge of the president.

6. *American Railroad Journal*, 11 June 1859, p. 369. A prototype of the strong, experienced president was J. Edgar Thomson of the Pennsylvania Railroad. See the portrait drawn by James A. Ward in his *J. Edgar Thomson*.

7. See the rather indifferent biography of Morehead by Burton A. Konkle.

8. NCRR Charter, sec. 36, in *Annual Report*, 1850, p. 15; NCRR, *Report of the President and Directors*, 1852, pp. 283–84; resolution of 17 Dec. 1852, in N.C. *Public Laws*, 1852, p. 637.

9. The final installment of the $2 million was authorized by the legislature in January 1855. See NCRR, *Communication of the President*, 1854, p. 5; resolution of 9 Jan. 1855, in N.C. *Public Laws*, 1854–55, p. 133.

10. These were 6 percent, 30-year bonds. NCRR Charter, sec. 38, in *Annual Report*, 1850, p. 16; Cecil K. Brown, *State Movement*, pp. 265–67.

11. Raleigh *North Carolina Standard*, 8 Oct. 1853; *Hillsborough Recorder*, 8 Mar. 1854; Cecil K. Brown, *State Movement*, p. 265. For accounts of the marketing of American railroad securities, and state securities issued in support of railroads before the Civil War, see Redlich, *Molding of American Banking*, 2:348–54; Chandler, *Visible Hand*, pp. 91–92; Chandler, "Patterns of American Railroad Finance," pp. 262–63; Adler, *British Investments*, pp. 12–13.

12. NCRR, *Annual Report*, 1854, pp. 9–10, 27; NCRR, *Communication of the President*, 1854.

13. N.C. *Public Laws*, 1854–55, chap. 32, secs. 1–2.

14. N.C. *Public Documents*, 1854–55, #12, 2:111–12; ibid., #21, pp. 223–26. The 1854–55 legislature, marking the prewar "highwater mark" in railroad building, also chartered and provided state aid for the Wilmington, Charlotte, and Rutherford Railroad. See Connor, *North Carolina*, 2:52.

15. NCRR, *Communication of the President*, 1854, p. 11; N.C. *Public Laws*, 1854–55, chap. 32, sec. 5.

16. NCRR, *Annual Report*, 1855, p. 5.

17. NCRR, *Communication of the President*, 1854, pp. 7–8; J. M. Morehead to W. A. Graham, 27 Mar., 10 May 1855, in Graham, *Papers*, 4:595–97; NCRR, *Annual Report*, 1855, p. 7. During 1855 state bonds sold at a discount instead of the premium enjoyed earlier. The NCRR seems to have suffered less from this condition than did the A&NCRR and the WNCRR (Cecil K. Brown, *State Movement*, pp. 266–67). President Fisher sold some in New York in August at par (C. F. Fisher to P. C. Cameron, 25 Aug. 1855, Cameron Family Papers, SHC).

18. Goodrich, "American Development Policy," p. 457.

19. NCRR Charter, sec. 43, in *Annual Report*, 1850, p. 17.

20. See Governor Reid's special message to the legislature on this subject, 9 Dec. 1852, Governors' Letterbooks #40, Archives.

21. N.C. *Public Laws*, 1852, chap. 139.

22. NCRR, *Annual Report*, 1853, pp. 10–13; Raleigh *North Carolina Standard*, 23 July 1853; Raleigh *North Carolina Star*, 27 July 1853; *Hillsborough Recorder*, 3 Aug. 1853; letter of Rufus Barringer in Raleigh *Daily Sentinel*, 9 Feb. 1867.

23. NCRR, *Annual Report*, 1854, pp. 25–27; *Hillsborough Recorder*, 19 July 1854.

24. D. S. Reid to J. W. Ellis, 22 June 1853, Governors' Letterbooks #41, Archives; NCRR, *Annual Report*, 1853, pp. 6, 11.

25. N.C. *Public Laws*, 1854–55, chap. 32; NCRR, *Annual Report*, 1855, p. 5; Raleigh *North Carolina Standard*, 14 Mar. 1855.

26. *Raleigh Register*, 18 July 1855; NCRR, *Annual Report*, 1856, p. 4; remarks of James T. Leach and B. M. Edney in Senate debate, in Raleigh *North Carolina Standard*, 4 Jan. 1859.

27. T. Bragg to T. Ruffin, 6 July 1857, in Ruffin, *Papers*, 2:559. Subsequently a critic accused Ruffin of using a parliamentary stratagem to defeat an important measure rather than voting against it openly (*Greensboro Patriot*, 31 July 1857). I have found no confirmation of this incident, which is not mentioned in the 1857 annual report.

28. NCRR, *Annual Report*, 1858, p. 7; NCRR, *Report of the President, January 20, 1859*, p. 31.

29. NCRR, *Report of the President, January 20, 1859*, p. 16; NCRR, *Annual Report*, 1857, p. 17; C. F. Fisher to J. G. Ramsay, 28 Dec. 1859 [1858], in Raleigh *North Carolina Standard*, 6 Jan. 1859.

30. Report of the Joint Select Committee, N.C. *Public Documents*, 1866–67, Supplement, pp. 19–20.

31. Stockholders were publicly listed (without locations) for the first time in NCRR, *Report of the President, January 20, 1859*, pp. 36–46, and subsequently in the annual reports of 1860, 1863–70, and 1872. The geographical distribution of stockholdings

was published in the Raleigh *North Carolina Star*, 3 Apr. 1850, the *Greensboro Patriot*, 6 Apr. 1850, and in the 1854 annual report, but not thereafter.

32. See Stock Transfers #9–18, Transfer of Stock Index, in XVIII. Stock, v. 84, NCRR Records, Archives.

33. The following information is derived from NCRR, *Report of the President, January 20, 1859*, pp. 36–46.

34. For the Whig preponderance, see *Lexington and Yadkin Flag*, 2 May 1856; *Fayetteville Observer*, quoted in *Hillsborough Recorder*, 27 July 1859.

35. See NCRR, *Annual Report*, 1865, pp. 44–52; 1870, pp. 40–46.

36. Ibid., 1859, p. 8.

37. NCRR By-Laws, 1851, in ibid., 1855, p. 21; ibid., 1858, p. 6.

38. See C. F. Fisher to T. Ruffin, 27 June 1857, in Ruffin, *Papers*, 2:558; *Greensboro Patriot*, 22 July 1859. See also two undated slips of paper in the Gorrell Family Papers (6.2: Non-Gorrell Items), Greensboro Historical Museum, listing the names of Fisher, Fries, Saunders, and Alexander McRae. These men were elected in 1855 and 1856.

39. *Greensboro Patriot*, 2 June 1855.

40. For a discussion of the duties of these two officials as they generally operated in the 1860s, see Kirkman, *Railway Revenue*, pp. 32–48.

41. NCRR, *Report of the President, January 20, 1859*, p. 3. Andrew Mickle of Chapel Hill was appointed Mendenhall's successor as treasurer in 1859, and he posted bond; but he resigned after two weeks, and Ruffin was chosen in his place. See *Raleigh Register*, 2 Apr. 1859; bonds of Lindsay, Mendenhall, Mickle, and Ruffin, in XXI. Bonds, Box 1, NCRR Records, Archives; board of directors' minutes, 25 Mar., 8 Apr. 1859, NCRR Office.

42. See NCRR, *Annual Reports*, 1850–61.

43. Salisbury *Carolina Watchman*, 11 Sept. 1855. See letters of C. F. Fisher to P. C. Cameron, 1857–59, in Cameron Family Papers, SHC; board of directors' minutes, 9 July 1858, NCRR Office.

44. C. F. Fisher to P. C. Cameron, 9, 17 Mar. 1859, Cameron Family Papers, SHC. The salary was $1,250 in 1856 and $1,500 in 1860.

45. NCRR, *Annual Report*, 1857, p. 16. James S. Morrison, one of the construction engineers, was appointed superintendent in December 1856, but he seems not to have served (*Greensboro Patriot*, quoted in Greensboro *Times*, 11 Dec. 1856). In July 1858 the directors voted to hire a superintendent to relieve Fisher, whose health was said to be suffering due to overwork, but no appointment was made. See Raleigh *North Carolina Standard*, 14 July 1858.

46. NCRR, *Annual Report*, 1855, pp. 11–12; 1856, pp. 20, 35; 1857, p. 16.

47. For the best account of these managerial reforms, see Chandler, *Visible Hand*, pp. 95–107.

48. *Hillsborough Recorder*, 25 Jan. 1860.

49. See Chandler, *Railroads: Pioneers in Modern Management*, p. 38.

50. NCRR, *Annual Report*, 1859, pp. 10–11; 1860, pp. 24–25, 38.

51. Ibid., 1860, p. 23.

52. Stover, *Iron Road*, p. 213.

53. NCRR, *Annual Report*, 1856, p. 35.

54. Ibid., 1855, p. 17. "One of the Hundred" (stock subscribers) wrote to the same effect in 1856. See his letter in *Lexington and Yadkin Flag*, 23 May 1856, reprinted in *Greensboro Patriot*, 11 Mar. 1859.

55. Reid so promised during his campaign. See his letter of 28 June 1850 and his inaugural address, in Raleigh *North Carolina Standard*, 21 June 1851.

56. *Greensboro Patriot*, 5, 12 Mar. 1853, 24 June, 1 July 1854; *Hillsborough Recorder*, 16 Mar. 1853; *Raleigh Register*, 5 July 1854. The Democratic rejoinder is in Raleigh *North Carolina Standard*, 28 June 1854.

57. Raleigh *North Carolina Standard*, 20 July, 3 Aug., 23 Oct. 1861.

58. The first Whig proxy was John W. Thomas, the longtime NCRR backer in Davidson County. For the controversy that followed his appointment, see *Greensboro Patriot*, 22 July, 5 Aug. 1859.

59. See the breakdown of stockholders' votes in NCRR, *Annual Report*, 1853, p. 11; 1854, pp. 26–27. For allegations of political motivation in this vote, see *Greensboro Patriot*, 30 July 1853.

60. Raleigh *North Carolina Standard*, 31 Aug., 7, 24 Sept. 1853, 28 June 1854; *Fayetteville Observer*, quoted in *Greensboro Patriot*, 15 Oct. 1853; T. Burr to D. F. Caldwell, 29 Oct. 1853, Caldwell Papers, SHC; remarks of William T. Dortch in House debate, in *Standard*, 15 Jan. 1859; letters of Jonathan Worth in *Patriot*, 7 Oct. 1859 (as "Plebs"), and 10 Feb. 1860.

61. NCRR, *Annual Report*, 1853, p. 12; W. A. Graham to S. W. Graham, 6 July 1853, and W. A. Graham to J. W. Bryan, 4 Aug. 1853, in Graham, *Papers*, 4:499, 501; Raleigh *North Carolina Standard*, 23 July, 3 Aug. 1853; *Greensboro Patriot*, 23, 30 July 1853, 7 Oct. ("Plebs" letter), 28 Oct. 1859.

62. Raleigh *North Carolina Standard*, 24 Sept. 1853; "Plebs," in *Greensboro Patriot*, 7 Oct. 1859.

63. See NCRR, *Annual Report*, 1854, p. 28; *Raleigh Register*, 19 July 1854; Raleigh *North Carolina Standard*, 19, 29 July 1854; Raleigh *North Carolina Star*, 26 July 1854; Salisbury *Carolina Watchman*, 27 July 1854; Jonathan Worth, in *Greensboro Patriot*, 10 Feb. 1860.

64. J. M. Morehead to W. A. Graham, 27 Mar., 10 May 1855, in Graham, *Papers*, 4:595–97; NCRR, *Annual Report*, 1855, pp. 16–17.

65. Konkle, *John Motley Morehead*, p. 321.

66. NCRR, *Annual Report*, 1855, p. 16; *Greensboro Patriot*, 2 June, 13 July 1855, 28 Oct., 9 Dec. 1859; *Raleigh Register*, 18 July 1855, 19 Jan. 1859.

Chapter 9

1. The *Lexington and Yadkin Flag*, a Whig paper, was the exception (2 May 1856), charging Democrats with appointing certain station agents for political reasons. For other political attacks that year (or references to them), see *Flag*, 23 May 1856; *Greensboro Patriot*, 27 June 1856; Raleigh *North Carolina Standard*, 21 May, 21 June, 16 July 1856; Charlotte *Western Democrat*, 29 July 1856.

2. *Greensboro Patriot*, 7 Aug. 1857.

3. See letter of "Dividend" and accompanying editorial in *Greensboro Patriot*, 31 July 1857.

4. Jonathan Worth, in *Greensboro Patriot*, 7 Oct. 1859 (as "Plebs") and 10 Feb. 1860.

5. *Greensboro Patriot*, 9 Dec. 1859. The *Patriot* further accused Fisher of neglecting NCRR freight shipments in order to carry rails to the WNCRR. See Raleigh *North Carolina Standard*, 28 Mar. 1860.

6. See Fisher's letter in *Greensboro Patriot*, 9 Dec. 1859.

7. Ibid., 28 Aug. 1857, 17 Dec. 1858.

8. NCRR, *Report of the President, January 20, 1859*, p. 7.

9. C. F. Fisher to P. C. Cameron, 11 Apr. 1857, Cameron Family Papers, SHC.

10. *Greensboro Patriot*, 17 Aug. 1855; Charlotte *Western Democrat*, 19 May 1857.

11. Raleigh *North Carolina Standard*, 15 July 1857.

12. Poor pointed out that rails, ties, machinery, bridges, and many other structures had to be replaced every ten years or so; he urged roads, therefore, to set aside annually 10 percent of the cost of these items as a depreciation fund (*American Railroad Journal*, 17 Sept. 1859, p. 600). See also Jervis, *Railway Property*, p. 233. Although railroads contributed greatly to the theory and practice of depreciation, the concept was not far advanced until the last quarter of the century. See Littleton, *Accounting Evolution*, pp. 227–38; Chatfield, *History of Accounting Thought*, pp. 94–97. Professional accountancy developed out of the need to differentiate capital and income. See Newman, "Historical Development of Early Accounting," pp. 178, 180; Brief, "Nineteenth Century Accounting Error," pp. 25–29; Boockholdt, "Influence of Nineteenth and Early Twentieth Century Railroad Accounting," pp. 187–89, 195.

13. Ward, *J. Edgar Thomson*, p. 100; Angus James Johnston, *Virginia Railroads in the Civil War*, p. 16.

14. This rate is obtained by dividing the excess of receipts over operating expenses for that year ($234,167) by Fisher's 1859 estimate of the total construction cost ($4,912,653) (NCRR, *Report of the President, January 20, 1859*, p. 7). Angus Johnston says that the Richmond and Danville, with an operating ratio of 53.5 percent, gave a rate of return of 5.6 percent (*Virginia Railroads in the Civil War*, p. 16).

15. See Jervis, *Railway Property*, pp. 300–303.

16. For a helpful discussion of the question of stocks versus bonds and why each was resorted to, see Ripley, *Railroads: Finance and Organization*, pp. 10–13, 105–6.

17. NCRR, *Annual Report*, 1856, pp. 4–6, 13–14.

18. Memorial [of NCRR] to the General Assembly, December 1856, N.C. *Public Documents*, 1856–57, #21, pp. 3–8.

19. The author of the aid bill and probably the road's chief legislative representative this session was Senator Paul C. Cameron of Orange County, a leading stockholder, state director, and later Fisher's successor as president. For the measure's hairbreadth escape from defeat, see Raleigh *North Carolina Standard*, 24 Dec. 1856, 10, 14, 21 Jan., 4 Feb. 1857, and letters from Fisher to Cameron, 20 Dec. 1856, 31 Jan., 2 Feb. 1857, Cameron Family Papers, SHC.

20. N.C. *Public Laws*, 1856–57, chap. 32, p. 27.

21. NCRR, *Annual Report*, 1857, pp. 22–23.

22. Ibid., 1857, pp. 15, 19; 1858, pp. 5–6; 1867, p. 20. For accounts of the bond issue and its causes, see NCRR, *Report of the President, January 20, 1859*, pp. 7, 19–21; NCRR, *Communination* [sic] *from the President*, 14 Feb. 1859, pp. 18–19; Cecil K. Brown, *State Movement*, pp. 83–84, 94; *Greensboro Patriot*, 28 Aug. 1857, 17 Dec. 1858. Thomas Ruffin, the state proxy, was responsible for the resolution creating the sinking fund. He was also one of the bondholders. See Carlson, "Iron Horse in Court," pp. 170–71.

23. NCRR, *Annual Report*, 1859, pp. 8, 12.

24. Chandler, *Visible Hand*, pp. 103–5, 109–10.

25. Whiton, *Railroads and Their Management*, p. 66.

26. *American Railway Times*, 17 Jan. 1863, p. 22.

27. *American Railroad Journal*, 3 July 1858, p. 424. See also ibid., 19 Sept. 1857, p. 593; 26 June 1858, pp. 401–2; 17 Sept. 1859, p. 600.

28. Ibid., 8 Oct. 1853, pp. 641–42; 17 Sept. 1859, p. 600.

29. Jervis, *Railway Property*, pp. 271–75.

30. This discussion is based on the annual reports of 1856 and following years.

31. Ibid., 1853, p. 20. Fisher claimed that the practice had ended by January 1859. NCRR, *Report of the President, January 20, 1859*, p. 6.

32. See NCRR, *Annual Report*, 1857, pp. 14–15; 1868, p. 38; letter of C. F. Fisher in Raleigh *North Carolina Standard*, 2 Mar. 1859; Report of the Joint Select Committee, 1867, N.C. *Public Documents*, 1866–67, pp. 3–7.

33. NCRR, *Annual Report*, 1858, pp. 21–23; *Greensboro Patriot*, 16 July 1858.

34. Letter of C. F. Fisher in Raleigh *North Carolina Standard*, 2 Mar. 1859.

35. Ibid.; C. P. Mendenhall card in *Greensboro Patriot*, 25 Feb. 1859.

36. Quoted in *Greensboro Patriot*, 5 Nov. 1858.

37. Fisher-Mendenhall correspondence, 21–25 Feb. 1859, in *Greensboro Patriot*, copied in *Raleigh Register*, 19 Mar. 1859.

38. NCRR, *Annual Report*, 1859, pp, 8, 16–17.

39. *Greensboro Patriot*, 7 Jan. 1854; *Hillsborough Recorder*, 25 Jan. 1854; Raleigh *North Carolina Standard*, 1, 4 Feb. 1854.

40. *Greensboro Patriot*, 4 Feb. 1854; *Raleigh Register*, 15 Feb. 1854; Raleigh *North Carolina Standard*, 15 Feb. 1854; Raleigh *North Carolina Star*, 15, 22 Feb. 1854.

41. Charlotte *North Carolina Whig*, 29 Jan. 1856.

42. *Greensboro Patriot*, 31 July 1857, 26 Nov., 3 Dec. 1858; NCRR, *Annual Report*, 1860, p. 29.

43. See Charlotte *Western Democrat*, 14 Apr. 1857, copied in Raleigh *North Carolina Standard*, 22 Apr. 1857; *Greensboro Patriot*, 31 July, 14 Aug., 6 Nov. 1857, 16 July, 5, 26 Nov., 10, 17 Dec. 1858.

44. NCRR, *Annual Report*, 1858, p. 7; NCRR, *Report of the President, January 20, 1859*, p. 31; T. Bragg to T. Ruffin, 24 June, 6 July 1857, in Ruffin, *Papers*, 2:558, 559.

45. Salisbury *Banner*, quoted in Charlotte *Western Democrat*, 12 May 1857; Raleigh *North Carolina Standard*, 13 June 1857.

46. C. F. Fisher to P. C. Cameron, 23 July 1858, Cameron Family Papers, SHC; *Greensboro Patriot*, 16 July 1858.

47. *Greensboro Patriot*, 17 Feb. 1860.

48. The bill would similarly have affected the A&NCRR and WNCRR. Democrats voted predominantly to defeat the measure, Whigs to save it. See N.C. *Senate Journal*, 1858–59, pp. 152–53; Raleigh *North Carolina Standard*, 21 Dec. 1858, 4, 6 Jan. 1859. Turner quotation in *Standard*, 6 Jan. 1859.

49. Resume of Senate debate and letter of C. F. Fisher to J. G. Ramsay, in Raleigh *North Carolina Standard*, 6 Jan. 1859.

50. Mauney, Memorial, in N.C. *Public Documents*, 1858–59, #57; legislative debate in Raleigh *North Carolina Standard*, 6 Jan. 1859. For background information on Mauney and his offer, see Glass, "King Midas and Old Rip," pp. 62, 97–98, 161–62, 182–84, 191, 258.

51. Raleigh *North Carolina Standard*, 30 Nov. 1858.

52. See, for example, *Greensboro Patriot*, 10, 17 Dec. 1858, 14 Jan. 1859, and speech by J. G. Ramsay in *Raleigh Register*, 12 Jan. 1859. (A notable exception was the

Whig *Carolina Watchman* of Salisbury, Fisher's hometown, which praised his management and advised restraint [*Watchman*, 18 Jan., 8 Feb. 1859].)

53. Reprinted in Raleigh *North Carolina Standard*, 10 Oct. 1860.

54. See C. F. Fisher to P. C. Cameron, 2 Dec. 1858, Cameron Family Papers, SHC. The Democratic press so regarded it also. See the views of the *Wilmington Journal* and Raleigh *North Carolina Standard*, in *Standard*, 9 Mar. 1859.

55. Report of the Joint Select Committee, 1859, in N.C. *Public Documents*, 1858–59, #71, pp. 32–33.

56. NCRR, *Report of the President, January 20, 1859*.

57. C. F. Fisher to R. W. Mills, 22 Jan. 1859, Mills Collection, ECU.

58. See Worth's and Fisher's accounts of the proceedings and their comments about each other, respectively, in Report of the Joint Select Committee, 1859, N.C. *Public Documents*, 1858–59, #71, esp. pp. 1–3, 23–26; Worth, in *Greensboro Patriot*, 10 Feb. 1860; NCRR, *Communincation* [sic] *from the President*, 14 Feb. 1859, esp. pp. 1–12. See also the account by Richard L. Zuber, rather more favorable to Worth than mine, in his *Jonathan Worth*, pp. 94–95.

59. J. Worth to Messrs. Long and Sherwood, 2 Mar. 1859, in Worth, *Correspondence*, 1:63; Worth to E. J. Hale, 15 Feb. 1859, Hale Papers, Archives.

60. The majority report is the Report of the Joint Select Committee, 1859, N.C. *Public Documents*, 1858–59, #71. Commoner William F. Green's minority report is ibid., #74.

61. NCRR, *Communincation* [sic] *from the President*, 14 Feb. 1859, p. 19. This document was reprinted in Raleigh *North Carolina Standard*, 2 Mar. 1859, and *Greensboro Patriot*, 4 Mar. 1859.

62. See the account of the legislative uproar, featuring the equally excitable Josiah Turner, in Raleigh *North Carolina Standard*, 23 Feb. 1859.

63. Appendix of 18 Feb. 1859, in NCRR, *Communication from the President of the N.C. Railroad*, 1859, reprinted in Raleigh *North Carolina Standard*, 2 Mar. 1859; Worth, in *Raleigh Register*, 16 Mar. 1859. See also Worth's reply in *Register*, 12 Mar. 1859, partly missing but reprinted in *Greensboro Patriot*, 25 Mar. 1859; correspondence between Worth ("Plebs") and Fisher in *Patriot*, 7 Oct., 9 Dec. 1859, 10 Feb. 1860; and Worth's letters of this period as contained in Worth, *Correspondence*, vol. 1. Worth's later charges (even more prone to accusations of fraud) centered around Fisher's role as a contractor on the WNCRR. For modern accounts of the controversy, see Zuber, *Jonathan Worth*, pp. 94–105; Cecil K. Brown, *State Movement*, pp. 85–90; Stokes, *Company Shops*, pp. 32–35.

64. I borrow freely here from Cecil K. Brown's lucid account of the controversy, reordering and adding to his list of five categories. See his *State Movement*, pp. 85–90.

65. See the Report of the Joint Select Committee, N.C. *Public Documents*, 1858–59, #71, pp. 3–9; Worth's later emendations in *Greensboro Patriot*, 7 Oct. 1859 (as "Plebs") and 10 Feb. 1860; and Fisher's two replies, in NCRR, *Communincation* [sic] *from the President*, 14 Feb. 1859, pp. 13–14; and in Salisbury *Banner*, 18 Nov. 1859, as reprinted in *Patriot*, 9 Dec. 1859. See also McRae's replies, in *Defence of John C. McRae*, and *Patriot*, 28 Oct. 1859.

66. Report of the Joint Select Committee, N.C. *Public Documents*, 1858–59, #71, pp. 17–19; Worth, in *Greensboro Patriot*, 10 Feb. 1860; NCRR, *Communincation* [sic] *from the President*, 14 Feb. 1859, pp. 19–23; Stokes, *Company Shops*, pp. 32–34.

67. Report of the Joint Select Committee, N.C. *Public Documents*, 1858–59, #71, pp. 15–16; NCRR, *Communincation* [sic] *from the President*, 14 Feb. 1859, p. 18.

68. Report of the Joint Select Committee, N.C. *Public Documents*, 1858–59, #71, pp. 9–10, 36–37; Worth, in *Greensboro Patriot*, 10 Feb. 1860; NCRR, *Communincation* [sic] *from the President*, 14 Feb. 1859, pp. 14–15, and edition with appendix of 18 Feb. 1859, pp. 7–8; *Raleigh Register*, 16 Mar. 1859.

69. Report of the Joint Select Committee, N.C. *Public Documents*, 1858–59, #71, pp. 11–12; Worth, in *Greensboro Patriot*, 10 Feb. 1860; NCRR, *Communincation* [sic] *from the President*, 14 Feb. 1859, p. 16.

70. Report of the Joint Select Committee, N.C. *Public Documents*, 1858–59, #71, pp. 12–15; Worth, in *Greensboro Patriot*, 10 Feb. 1860; NCRR, *Communincation* [sic] *from the President*, 14 Feb. 1859, pp. 16–18. See my discussion of this matter in Chapter 6.

71. Report of the Joint Select Committee, N.C. *Public Documents*, 1858–59, #71, pp. 19–30; Worth, in *Greensboro Patriot*, 7 Oct. 1859 (as "Plebs"), 10 Feb. 1860; NCRR, *Communincation* [sic] *from the President*, 14 Feb. 1859, pp. 24–27; C. F. Fisher to C. P. Mendenhall, 21 Feb. 1859, in *Raleigh Register*, 19 Mar. 1859.

72. See accounts of the voting in NCRR, *Annual Report*, 1859, pp. 4–6; Raleigh *North Carolina Standard*, 20 July 1859; and *Greensboro Patriot*, 22 July 1859.

73. J. Worth to D. F. Caldwell, 20 July 1859, to C. P. Mendenhall, 26 Oct. 1859, and to C. B. Mallett and Tod R. Caldwell, 4 Nov. 1859, in Worth, *Correspondence*, 1:75–81.

74. See Jervis, *Railway Property*, pp. 300–308.

75. Stover, *Iron Road*, pp. 62, 215–16. See also the discussion in Shaw, "Profitability of Early American Railroads," pp. 56–67.

76. Shaw, "Profitability of Early American Railroads," p. 67.

77. Jervis, *Railway Property*, pp. 304–5.

78. NCRR, *Annual Report*, 1858, p. 7; NCRR, *Report of the President, January 20, 1859*, pp. 31–32.

79. NCRR, *Annual Report*, 1859, pp. 7–8, 12.

80. See W. Edwards to T. Ruffin, 8 Apr. 1859, in Ruffin, *Papers*, 3:30.

81. NCRR, *Annual Report*, 1860, p. 16; 1861, p. 19; report of state comptroller, 1860, in N.C. *Public Documents*, 1860–61, #8, p. 157.

82. NCRR, *Annual Report*, 1861, pp. 13, 18–19.

83. Ibid., 1860, p. 23.

84. Raleigh *North Carolina Standard*, 21 July 1860; *Greensboro Patriot*, 27 July 1860; C. F. Fisher to T. Ruffin, 18 Sept. 1860, in Ruffin, *Papers*, 3:92–93.

85. Raleigh *North Carolina Standard*, 2 June, 8 Aug. 1860.

86. NCRR, *Annual Report*, 1861, p. 9.

87. For an account of Fisher's role in raising and leading the Sixth North Carolina Regiment until his untimely death, see Iobst and Manarin, *The Bloody Sixth*, pp. 3–25.

Chapter 10

1. Raleigh *North Carolina Standard*, 20 July, 3 Aug., 23 Oct. 1861.

2. See Kruman, *Parties and Politics*, chaps. 9–10.

3. For Johnson's background, see Raleigh *North Carolina Standard*, 23 Oct. 1850, 16 Feb. 1856, 5, 26 July 1864. For Hutchings, see Raleigh *Daily Confederate*, 5 July 1864. For the political controversy engendered by these replacements, see *Standard*, 26 June 1863, 5 July 1864; *Confederate*, 5 July 1864.

4. *Hillsborough Recorder*, quoted in Raleigh *North Carolina Standard*, 20 July 1861.

5. NCRR, *Annual Report*, 1863, p. 4.

6. Kenzer, *Kinship and Neighborhood*, p. 44.

7. Letter of P. C. Cameron in Raleigh *North Carolina Standard*, 9 July 1856. For examples of the outcry against him, see Salisbury *Carolina Watchman*, 20, 27 Jan. 1862.

8. The first reference I have to Wilkes as superintendent documents his attendance at Fisher's funeral late in July 1861. See Raleigh *State Journal*, 31 July 1861.

9. Salisbury *Carolina Watchman*, 20 Jan. 1862. See also issue of 25 Nov. 1861.

10. Ibid., 27 Jan. 1862.

11. Charlotte *Western Democrat*, 28 Jan. 1862; Raleigh *North Carolina Standard*, 29 Jan. 1862.

12. Raleigh *North Carolina Standard*, 8 Feb. 1862. Italics in original.

13. NCRR, *Annual Report*, 1862, pp. 25, 30–31.

14. Wm. Johnston to P. C. Cameron, 1 Feb. 1862, Cameron Family Papers, SHC.

15. NCRR, *Annual Report*, 1862, p. 19.

16. Ibid.; *Hillsborough Recorder*, 19 Mar. 1856.

17. In the 1860 manuscript census, Webb is listed with $2,575 in real and $15,000 in personal estate (Orange County, Part 1, p. 160, Archives). For other scraps of information about his background, see *Hillsborough Recorder*, 24 July 1850, 25 Aug. 1852 (when he was secretary of a Whig party meeting), 19 Sept. 1855, 20 Feb. 1861; Daniel L. Grant, ed., *Alumni History of the University of North Carolina*, 2d ed. (Durham: Christian & King Prtg. Co., 1924), p. 653; William James Webb, *Our Webb Kin*, pp. 12, 21, 70, 74, 97.

18. Raleigh *North Carolina Standard*, 28 June 1862. For similar brief evaluations, see ibid., 12 Feb., 9 July 1862.

19. NCRR, *Annual Report*, 1862, p. 5; board of directors' minutes, 11, 18 July 1862, NCRR Office. My evidence of the effort to make Sumner president consists of a bare mention in the Raleigh *North Carolina Standard*, 9 Aug. 1862, plus the otherwise strange effort to elect someone in his position (superintendent of another road) to the board at all.

20. NCRR, *Annual Report*, 1862, p. 6; board of directors' minutes, 18 July, 29 Aug. 1862, NCRR Office.

21. Ibid., p. 18.

22. See Raleigh *North Carolina Standard*, 9 Aug. 1862; affidavit of E. Wilkes, 21 Sept. 1865, in Piedmont Railroad, *Annual Report*, 1866, p. 20.

23. *Raleigh Register*, 4 July 1863; NCRR, *Annual Report*, 1863, pp. 5–6; board of directors' minutes, 9 July 1863, NCRR Office.

24. Raleigh *North Carolina Standard*, 8, 12 Feb., 28 June 1862.

25. Holden chose not to comment directly on Johnson's fate, instead copying a caustic editorial by his ally, editor J. L. Pennington of the Raleigh *Daily Progress*, 5 July 1864.

26. Raleigh *North Carolina Standard*, 2 Mar. 1859.

27. Board of directors' minutes, 12 July, 15 Aug., 9 Sept., 6 Oct. 1861, NCRR

Office; NCRR, *Annual Report*, 1862, pp. 13–14, 19. In applying for the job Bryan offered as qualification his experience as a bank teller (J. H. Bryan to R. Gorrell, 4 Oct. 1861, Gorrell Family Papers, Greensboro Historical Museum).

28. Concord *Carolina Flag*, quoted in Salisbury *Carolina Watchman*, 20 Jan. 1862; Raleigh *North Carolina Standard*, 8 Feb. 1862.

29. NCRR, *Annual Report*, 1863, p. 5; 1864, p. 5.

30. Ibid., 1862, pp. 4, 15, 40–41; 1863, pp. 4–5, 12–13, 26; board of directors' minutes, 31 July 1863, NCRR Office.

31. Board of directors' minutes, 23 Oct. 1863, NCRR Office; Raleigh *North Carolina Standard*, 27 Oct. 1863.

32. Board of directors' minutes, 5 Nov. 1863, NCRR Office; NCRR, *Annual Report*, 1864, pp. 14–15, 23–24; Stokes, *Company Shops*, pp. 36–37, 71–72.

33. NCRR, *Annual Report*, 1864, p. 5. For other examples of the "Vance" heading, see Raleigh *Daily Confederate*, 19 Mar., 23 May 1864.

34. NCRR, *Annual Report*, 1863, p. 5.

35. See W. A. Dunn testimony, railroad investigation papers, in Robins Papers, SHC.

36. See Black, *Railroads of the Confederacy*, pp. 134–35, 219–20. Charles L. Price makes the same points in his valuable overviews of North Carolina roads during this period. For their comparative finances, see his published "North Carolina Railroads during the Civil War," pp. 298–300, and unpublished "Railroads of North Carolina during the Civil War," pp. 126–30.

37. C&SCRR, *Annual Report*, 1864, pp. 7–8.

38. NCRR, *Annual Report*, 1863, p. 15.

39. Other North Carolina roads had about the same experience. See Price, "Railroads of North Carolina," pp. 126–27.

40. I have used a chronological currency/gold conversion table subsequently adopted by the North Carolina legislature in 1866. See copy in *Greensboro Patriot*, 12 May 1870. All such formulas for measuring the real value of paper currency are estimates. My figure for the 1865 dividend is based on a currency-to-gold ratio of 50 to 1, according to the table just cited. Price gives a figure of $22,222 in gold for that dividend, using a ratio of 45 to 1 obtained from Todd, *Confederate Finance*, p. 114 (Price, "North Carolina Railroads," p. 300).

41. NCRR, *Annual Report*, 1865, p. 10; J. Worth to T. Ruffin, 21 July, 31 Aug. 1864, in Ruffin, *Papers*, 3:407, 421–22.

42. Charlotte *Daily Bulletin*, 13 Nov. 1863; Charlotte *Western Democrat*, 27 Jan. 1863, citing Raleigh *Daily Progress*; Salisbury *Carolina Watchman*, 16 Mar. 1863.

43. See the discussion by Price of the debt policies of the North Carolina roads, in "Railroads of North Carolina," pp. 132–42.

44. N.C. *Public Laws*, 1856–57, chap. 32, p. 27.

45. NCRR, *Annual Report*, 1859, pp. 7–8; 1860, pp. 15–16; 1861, p. 19.

46. Ibid., 1862, pp. 20–22; 1863, pp. 17–18; board of directors' minutes, 2 July 1862, NCRR Office.

47. Memorandum by P. B. Ruffin, 31 May 1862, in Reports of Finance Committee folder, XXVII. Miscellaneous, Box 90; Treasurer's ledger, in X. Ledgers, v. 57, p. 142, NCRR Records, Archives.

48. NCRR, *Annual Report*, 1862, pp. 3, 7, 20–22; 1863, pp. 17–18.

49. Ibid., 1863, pp. 19–21.

50. Copy of board of directors' minutes, 9 July 1863, Robins Papers, SHC.

51. NCRR, *Annual Report*, 1864, pp. 18–19; 1867, p. 20; board of directors' minutes, 12 Jan. 1865, NCRR Office; Report of Joint Select Committee, 1867, N.C. *Public Documents*, 1866–67, pp. 16, 40.

52. NCRR, *Annual Report*, 1864, pp. 18–19.

53. Ibid., 1865, p. 17; 1867, p. 21. For evidence of the committee's effort to acquire these bonds, see notice in Raleigh *Daily Confederate*, 11 Mar. 1864. In November 1864, $50,000 in NCRR bonds (of $500 denomination) sold at auction in Raleigh for $300 and $305 (*Confederate*, 29 Nov. 1864). By that time the sinking fund committee probably lacked the means to buy them.

54. Report of Joint Select Committee, 1867, N.C. *Public Documents*, 1866–67, pp. 16–19, 38–41; *NCRR v. G. W. Swepson et al.*, 71 *N.C. Reports* 350; answer of Swepson, 10 Oct. 1868, in Wake County Railroad Records, 1837–73, Archives; NCRR, *Annual Report*, 1867, p. 20.

55. See testimony of W. A. Dunn in railroad investigation papers, 1867, in Robins Papers, SHC.

56. NCRR, *Annual Report*, 1865, pp. 17–18, 33; 1867, p. 21.

57. Ibid., 1868, p. 19. See records of the case in Wake County Railroad Records, 1837–73, 1876–77, Archives; 71 *N.C. Reports* 350; 73 ibid. 316.

58. See director John Berry's indignant reaction when the Robins committee of the legislature revealed Mendenhall's action in 1867 (Berry to Jonathan Worth, 7 Mar. 1867, Worth Papers, Archives).

59. NCRR, *Annual Report*, 1866, p. 22; 1867, p. 27; 1868, p. 41; 1869, pp. 27, 33.

60. Agreement with Chatham Railroad, 25 Nov. 1862, in XXII. Contracts, v. 19, NCRR Records, Archives; Battle, *Memories*, pp. 175–76; Spencer, *Last Ninety Days*, p. 240; NCRR, *Annual Report*, 1864, p. 5; 1865, p. 33; Price, "Railroads of North Carolina," pp. 43–47, 50.

61. Raleigh *North Carolina Standard*, 16 Nov. 1861; Todd, *Confederate Finance*, pp. 130–36.

62. Todd, *Confederate Finance*, pp. 140–41.

63. T. Webb to W. J. Hawkins, 31 Dec. 1863, Hawkins Family Papers, SHC; Price, "Railroads of North Carolina," pp. 144–45.

64. Todd, *Confederate Finance*, pp. 150–53.

65. NCRR, *Annual Report*, 1864, p. 11; J. Worth and D. L. Swain to T. Ruffin, 4, 13 June 1864, W. Edwards to J. Worth, 15 June 1864, in Ruffin, *Papers*, 3:389–90, 395–97. State Treasurer Jonathan Worth, Fisher's old foe, was unsure whether the state could legally accept Confederate bonds, but he ended up taking them. See correspondence in ibid., 3:399–400, 403, 405, 407, 420–22; Price, "Railroads of North Carolina," pp. 145–47.

66. NCRR, *Annual Report*, 1864, pp. 10, 27; 1865, pp. 8, 31. These payments went to the Confederate government; the NCRR had been exempt from state and local taxes all along.

67. See Angus James Johnston, *Virginia Railroads in the Civil War*, p. 227.

68. NCRR, *Annual Report*, 1862, pp. 8, 10–11; Price, "Railroads of North Carolina," p. 131.

69. NCRR, *Annual Report*, 1864, pp. 11–12.

70. T. Webb to J. Worth, 31 Aug. 1864, in Ruffin, *Papers*, 3:421–22.

71. NCRR, *Annual Report*, 1865, pp. 8–10. For cotton and other goods at Greensboro and Gibsonville at the end of the war, see T. J. Sumner to S. R. Chisman, 11

Apr. 1865; S. P. Carter to T. Cox, 27 May 1865; J. A. Campbell to S. P. Carter, 30 May 1865, in Goods Turned Over to NCRR by U.S. Government, 1865 folder in XXIII. Correspondence, v. 22, NCRR Records, Archives.

72. NCRR, *Annual Report*, 1863, p. 5; 1864, p. 12; 1865, p. 28; 1866, pp. 4, 13; 1867, pp. 40–41, 51–56; 1868, p. 19; response of President Webb, undated railroad investigation papers, 1867, Robins Papers, SHC. The C&SCRR purchased 1,000 bales as early as 1862, "as a medium of exchange and basis of credit abroad after the blockade of our ports is relieved," according to President William Johnston. See his annual report for 1862 in Charlotte *Western Democrat*, 24 Feb. 1863. For the actions of other roads in North Carolina, see Price, "Railroads of North Carolina," pp. 142–44, 205–6. For the wartime trade in cotton generally, see Woodman, *King Cotton*, pp. 226–27, 236–38; Schwab, *Confederate States*, pp. 230–31, 236, 274.

73. Raleigh *Daily Confederate*, 7 Feb. 1865. These accusations had surfaced much earlier. See Raleigh *North Carolina Standard*, 26 June 1863. For further examples of outrage over railroad speculators' exploitation of the public and the military effort, see John Beauchamp Jones, *Rebel War Clerk's Diary*, 2:60–61, 82, 282, 337–38.

74. See responses of Webb, J. G. Moore, and E. Wilkes in undated railroad investigation papers, 1867, Robins Papers, SHC.

75. Affidavits or testimony in 1867 of E. W. Bull, W. A. Dunn, H. K. Winslow, A. H. March, and B. Y. Hunt, and copy of entries from NCRR private freight book at Charlotte, 1864–65, in Robins Papers, SHC.

76. Testimony of W. A. Dunn in railroad investigation papers, 1867, Robins Papers, SHC.

77. Order of J. C. Breckinridge, 23 Apr. 1865; statement by T. J. Sumner, 15 Feb. 1867; and copy of statement by A. H. Ragland, 23 June 1865, all in Robins Papers, SHC.

78. See deposition by G. W. Swepson, 22 Apr. 1870, in case of *NCRR* v. *Swepson and Mendenhall*, Wake County Railroad Records, 1837–73, Archives.

79. Testimony of T. J. Sumner, E. Wilkes, and NCRR employees J. G. Moore and W. A. Dunn. Dunn (a former passenger train conductor) was the purchasing agent whose testimony was most incriminating against Sumner. See also copy of Sumner to S. R. Chisman, 11 Apr. 1865, with Chisman's endorsement of 12 Apr., and copy of Sumner to T. Webb, 12 Apr. 1865. These documents are all in Robins Papers, SHC, some of them in a special category of railroad investigation papers. Senator Marmaduke Robins of Randolph was chairman of the legislative investigating committee of 1867.

80. Capt. J. W. Berry, Inventory of goods turned over to T. J. Sumner, 16 June 1865, in Goods Turned Over to NCRR by U.S. Government, 1865 folder in XXIII. Correspondence, v. 22, NCRR Records, Archives. A copy is in the Robins Papers, SHC.

Chapter 11

1. NCRR, *Annual Report*, 1861, p. 14.

2. Ibid., 1862, pp. 12, 26–27, 36–37. See also the comments on the roadbed's original construction and present shortcomings by "H" in *Greensboro Patriot*, 3, 10 July 1862.

3. NCRR, *Annual Report*, 1862, pp. 26–27.

4. Charlotte *Western Democrat*, 25 Nov. 1862.

5. *Greensboro Patriot*, 22 Jan. 1863; *Official Records*, Series 4, 3:598–601.

6. NCRR, *Annual Report*, 1863, pp. 11, 23–24.

7. Ibid., 1864, pp. 14, 21; *Official Records*, Series 4, 3:598.

8. Dew, *Ironmaker to the Confederacy*, pp. 272–74.

9. NCRR, *Annual Report*, 1863, p. 11; Black, *Railroads of the Confederacy*, pp. 85–88, 124–25; Price, "North Carolina Railroads," p. 301.

10. Price, "North Carolina Railroads," p. 301; Black, *Railroads of the Confederacy*, pp. 204–5.

11. R&GRR, *Annual Report*, 1866, p. 11; U.S. Congress, *House Reports*, 39 Cong., 2 sess., #34, p. 119.

12. A. M. Powell to Z. Vance, 14 Feb. 1865, and Vance's endorsement, Vance Papers, Archives.

13. NCRR, *Annual Report*, 1862, pp. 27–28, 34–36; 1863, pp. 22–23; 1864, pp. 20–21; 1865, pp. 13, 20–22.

14. Ibid., 1862, pp. 12, 16–17, 29–30.

15. T. Webb to Z. Vance, 28 Feb. 1863, Governors' Letterbooks, Archives; NCRR, *Annual Report*, 1862, p. 30; 1863, p. 11.

16. *Official Records*, Series 4, 2:484.

17. T. J. Sumner to J. D. Whitford, 31 Jan. 1864, Whitford Papers, Archives; NCRR, *Annual Report*, 1864, p. 13.

18. NCRR, *Annual Report*, 1862, p. 40; T. Webb to Z. Vance, 28 Feb. 1863, Governors' Letterbooks, Archives.

19. NCRR, *Annual Report*, 1864, p. 13; 1865, pp. 12, 23; Salisbury *Carolina Watchman*, 11 July 1864, quoting Raleigh *State Journal*.

20. Black, *Railroads of the Confederacy*, pp. 103, 116.

21. I find no record of their arrival. See contract with Chamberlain & Co., 23 Oct. 1862, in XXII. Contracts, v. 19, NCRR Records, Archives.

22. NCRR, *Annual Report*, 1863, pp. 10, 26. If the improved maintenance reflected an increase in shop personnel, it does not appear in the payroll records, the only evidence at hand. Shop payroll costs rose 143 percent between October 1862 and August 1863, but that was far less than the inflation rate in that period. See monthly payroll entries, in Journal, 1860–64, pp. 498, 622, VIII. Expenditures, v. 40, NCRR Records, Archives.

23. NCRR, *Annual Report*, 1864, pp. 13, 23; 1865, pp. 11, 23. See the firsthand evidence of decrepitude from wartime riders, especially prisoners of war, in Chapter 12.

24. NCRR, *Annual Report*, 1860, p. 37; 1862, pp. 29–30, 49; *Official Records*, Series 4, 2:484.

25. NCRR, *Annual Report*, 1863, pp. 11, 26; 1864, pp. 13–14.

26. W. Y. Raoul to J. H. Cooper, 28 Mar. 1865; T. Webb to T. J. Sumner, 30 Mar. 1865, Boyd Papers, Duke.

27. NCRR, *Annual Report*, 1862, pp. 18, 32; 1864, p. 23; 1865, p. 12.

28. Ibid., 1862, pp. 29–30, 40; 1863, pp. 10, 26; 1864, pp. 13, 23; 1865, p. 23.

29. Raleigh *North Carolina Standard*, 2, 12 Dec. 1862.

30. T. J. Sumner to J. D. Whitford, 29 Sept. 1863; ? to W. W. Pierce, 2 Oct. 1863; Pierce to Whitford, 16, 19 Oct. 1863; Whitford to F. W. Sims, 23 Oct. 1863; Whitford to T. Webb, 3 Nov. 1863, all in Whitford Papers, Archives.

31. Regarding conscripts, see J. M. Robinson to J. M. Otey, 20 Mar. 1865, Otey Papers, Duke. For the NCRR's wood problem, see *Annual Report*, 1862, pp. 15–16, 29; 1863, pp. 13–14, 25; 1864, pp. 15, 23; 1865, p. 13; Price, "Railroads of North Carolina," pp. 102–3.

32. NCRR, *Annual Report*, 1862, pp. 15–16, 28–29, 38; 1863, pp. 13–14, 25; 1864, pp. 15–16, 23; 1865, p. 23; Price, "Railroads of North Carolina," pp. 101–2.

33. *Raleigh Register*, 12 Feb. 1862.

34. NCRR, *Annual Report*, 1862, pp. 28, 37; 1863, pp. 4, 25; 1864, pp. 15, 22–23. See also Raleigh *North Carolina Standard*, 7 Nov. 1862, 14 July 1863.

35. NCRR, *Annual Report*, 1862, pp. 28, 38; 1863, p. 25; 1864, pp. 22–23; Charlotte *North Carolina Whig*, 24 June 1862.

36. NCRR, *Annual Report*, 1862, pp. 28, 37; 1863, p. 24; 1864, pp. 21–22.

37. Goldsboro *Tribune*, quoted in Charlotte *Western Democrat*, 16 July 1861; *Greensboro Patriot*, 4 June 1863.

38. Salisbury *Carolina Watchman*, 1 Aug. 1861; Salisbury *Banner*, quoted in Charlotte *Western Democrat*, 6 Aug. 1861.

39. *Greensboro Patriot*, 7 May 1863.

40. Ibid., 21 May 1863; Charlotte *Western Democrat*, 26 May 1863; Raleigh *North Carolina Standard*, 26 May 1863; Raleigh *Daily Progress*, 1 June 1863.

41. NCRR, *Annual Report*, 1865, p. 13; Salisbury *Carolina Watchman*, 18 July 1864; *Greensboro Patriot*, 21 July 1864; Raleigh *Daily Progress*, 23 July 1864; Charlotte *Western Democrat*, 26 July 1864.

42. NCRR, *Annual Report*, 1862, p. 12; 1863, pp. 26–27; 1864, pp. 15, 23–24; Stokes, *Company Shops*, pp. 36–37.

43. *Official Records*, Series 4, 1:1081, 2:161.

44. Moore, *Conscription and Conflict*, pp. 53, 67, 83–84, 90–91; Price, "Railroads of North Carolina," pp. 104–6; Black, *Railroads of the Confederacy*, pp. 129–30, 215–16. For an example of impressing laborers to cut wood for the NCRR, see J. M. Robinson to J. M. Otey, 20 Mar. 1865, and telegram from B. T. Johnson to Otey, same date, Otey Papers, Duke.

45. Secretary of War Seddon called for an investigation of the NCRR's plight before detailing men to it. The records do not reveal the result of the study, but Webb's protests did not continue. See *Official Records*, Series 4, 3:598–601; Price, "Railroads of North Carolina," pp. 106–7; Stokes, *Company Shops*, pp. 38–41.

46. Price, "Railroads of North Carolina," p. 108; Henson, *Industrial Workers*, pp. 159–60, 165.

47. In May 1865 they were listed at $45 per month, but that figure persisted in 1866 and represents wages earned in postwar United States currency (NCRR, *Annual Report*, 1862, p. 40; 1865, p. 42; 1866, p. 67).

48. See NCRR, *Annual Report*, 1862, pp. 15, 24, 43; 1865, pp. 8, 31; record of slaves used by NCRR, 1862–64, in XVII. Slaves, v. 81; printed slave hire form, in 1862–63 and Hire of Slaves, 1864–65 folder, in XXIII. Correspondence, v. 22, NCRR Records, Archives.

49. NCRR, *Annual Report*, 1865, pp. 8, 31; Hire of Slaves, 1864–65 folder, XXIII. Correspondence, v. 22, NCRR Records, Archives; Raleigh *North Carolina Standard*, 3 Jan. 1865; Raleigh *Daily Confederate*, 5 Jan. 1865.

50. Nelson, "Some Aspects of Negro Life," pp. 162–64.

51. NCRR, *Annual Report*, 1862, p. 15; 1863, pp. 4, 13.

52. The total cost varies a bit from one document to another. The road listed its loss of slave property at the end of the war at $139,237, which seems to include $138,087 for the persons acquired in 1864–65 and the $1,150 paid for the man purchased in 1857, but not $400 for the person (Cherry) bought in 1858. My total of the 1864–65 bills of sale comes to $138,681. See NCRR, *Annual Report*, 1865, pp. 28, 33; 1866, pp. 50, 51; bills of sale, December 1864 to January 1865, in Bills of Sale folder, XXIII. Correspondence, v. 22, NCRR Records, Archives.

Chapter 12

1. Price, "Riding the Rails," pp. 13–14 (including quotation); Price, "Railroads of North Carolina," p. 115.

2. NCRR, *Annual Report*, 1862, pp. 30–31.

3. Ibid., pp. 38–39.

4. See Charlotte *Daily Bulletin*, 21 Sept. 1861; Charlotte *Western Democrat*, 5 Nov. 1861; *Raleigh Register*, 2 Nov. 1861; Raleigh *North Carolina Standard*, 6 Nov. 1861; Raleigh *Daily Progress*, 17 Mar. 1863.

5. See Raleigh *Daily Progress*, 10, 14 Jan. 1863; Raleigh *North Carolina Standard*, 13, 16 Jan. 1863; Charlotte *Daily Bulletin*, 30 Mar. 1864; Charlotte *Western Democrat*, 28 June 1864.

6. *Greensboro Patriot*, 22 Jan. 1863; Raleigh *North Carolina Standard*, 20 Feb. 1863.

7. Shaffner, *Diary*, p. 3.

8. Raleigh *Daily Progress*, 11, 13 Apr., 24 Dec. 1864; Charlotte *Western Democrat*, 12 Apr. 1864; Raleigh *Daily Confederate*, 9, 17 Mar. 1865.

9. Conner, *Letters*, p. 32; NCRR, *Annual Report*, 1862, p. 40.

10. Salisbury *Carolina Watchman*, 11 Jan. 1864; Raleigh *Daily Progress*, 5 Apr. 1864.

11. Charlotte *Daily Bulletin*, 31 July 1861.

12. Charlotte *Western Democrat*, 28 Oct. 1862; *Greensboro Patriot*, 6 Nov. 1862; Raleigh *Daily Progress*, quoted in Raleigh *North Carolina Standard*, 16 Jan. 1863.

13. See *Hillsborough Recorder*, 18 Mar. 1863.

14. Raleigh *Daily Progress*, 28 Oct. 1863; response of T. Webb in undated railroad investigation papers, 1867, Robins Papers, SHC.

15. Salisbury *Carolina Watchman*, 11 Jan. 1864.

16. Raleigh *Daily Confederate*, 7 Feb. 1865.

17. Thompson, *Wiring a Continent*, pp. 211–12.

18. Ibid., pp. 333, 373–74.

19. Copy of contract with Southern Express Co., 8 Jan. 1862, in Robins Papers, SHC, and in NCRR Records, VPI; NCRR, *Annual Report*, 1861, p. 8; 1862, pp. 14, 31–32, 39.

20. NCRR, *Annual Report*, 1863, pp. 25–26.

21. Ibid., 1865, p. 26.

22. Ibid., 1862, pp. 17–18, 39. For the Selma accident, see ibid., pp. 26–27; Raleigh *North Carolina Standard*, 31 May 1862; and the slightly misdated account of a Union prisoner of war traveling on the train: [Bixley], *Incidents in Dixie*, pp. 81–87.

23. Raleigh *State Journal*, 16 Nov. 1861; Raleigh *North Carolina Standard*, 26 Apr. 1862.

24. NCRR, *Annual Report*, 1862, pp. 30–31; *Raleigh Register*, 15 Feb. 1862; Salis-

bury *Carolina Watchman*, 17 Feb. 1862; Charlotte *Western Democrat*, 18 Feb. 1862.

25. Raleigh *State Journal*, 5 Apr. 1862.

26. Salisbury *Carolina Watchman*, 9 June 1862.

27. Concord *Carolina Flag*, 20 May 1862, quoted in Salisbury *Carolina Watchman*, 26 May 1862. For the navy yard and its location, see Violet G. Alexander, "Confederate States Navy Yard," pp. 29–34; Simmons and Lindsay, *Charlotte and Mecklenburg*, p. 11.

28. *Raleigh Register*, 11 June, 2 July, 29 Oct. 1862.

29. NCRR, *Annual Report*, 1863, pp. 25–26. For examples, see Raleigh *Daily Progress*, 21 Dec. 1863, 8 Apr. 1865; Salisbury *Carolina Watchman*, 2 May 1864.

30. See the account by a prisoner of war traveling on a train that derailed: Abbott, *Prison Life*, p. 184.

31. Joseph E. Johnston, *Narrative of Military Operations*, pp. 400–401.

32. Raleigh *Daily Progress*, 10 July 1863.

33. Raleigh *Daily Confederate*, 19 July 1864; Raleigh *North Carolina Standard*, 27 July 1864; Greensboro *Daily Southern Citizen*, 12 Aug. 1864.

34. Raleigh *Daily Confederate*, 15, 23 Sept. 1864.

35. Charlotte *Daily Bulletin*, 27 Jan. 1865, quoted in Raleigh *Daily Confederate*, 30 Jan. 1865.

36. Louis Alexander Brown, *Salisbury Prison*, pp. 20–22, 59–61, 144, 147, 167–68, 171; Andrews, *South since the War*, pp. 102–4. Andrews provides a good description of the place but says incorrectly that it was not used as a prison until 1863 and as a prisoner of war facility until 1864. As early as May 1862, the Salisbury *Carolina Watchman* noted the departure of several trainloads of Yankee prisoners, headed homeward after a stay in the prison there. Others arrived in June (*Watchman*, 26 May, 9, 16 June 1862).

37. *Official Records*, Series 2, 8:263–64, 269, 287–88, 294, 297–98, 300, 449–50, 454.

38. Abbott, *Prison Life*, pp. 46–51; Isham, *Prisoners of War*, p. 37. For accounts of similar trips at about the same time, see Abbott, *Prison Life*, p. 185; Sprague, *Lights and Shadows*, p. 77; Stearns, *Narrative*, pp. 20–23.

39. Small, *Road to Richmond*, p. 164; Sprague, *Lights and Shadows*, p. 50. Colonel Sprague was on the same train. Two weeks later he was taken back to Danville, about 350 men being crowded into five freight cars (*Lights and Shadows*, p. 77). Benjamin F. Booth told of a similar trip in November 1864, when the men, having been fed salted codfish in Virginia, were driven almost insane by thirst until permitted access to water at Greensboro the next morning. Thirteen prisoners died on the train during the day's trip (Booth, *Dark Days*, pp. 109–12).

40. Booth, *Dark Days*, pp. 284, 304–6, 313.

41. Black, *Railroads of the Confederacy*, pp. 52–54, 227.

42. Contract Office, U.S. Post Office, to C. F. Fisher, 28 May 1861, in XXIII. Correspondence, v. 22, NCRR Records, Archives.

43. Charlotte *Daily Bulletin*, 21 Sept. 1861. The competing Charlotte *Western Democrat*, however, went out of its way soon afterward to thank President Cameron for bringing the mail to Charlotte fifteen hours earlier than before (*Democrat*, 24 Sept. 1861).

44. *Greensboro Patriot*, 22 Jan. 1863; Raleigh *North Carolina Standard*, 20 Feb. 1863.

45. Raleigh *Daily Progress*, 19 Feb. 1863.

46. Charlotte *Western Democrat*, 9 Feb. 1864; *Hillsborough Recorder*, 1 Mar. 1865.

47. Raleigh *Daily Progress*, 11 Apr. 1864; Charlotte *Western Democrat*, 12, 19 Apr. 1864; Raleigh *Daily Confederate*, 13 Apr. 1864, 9, 17 Mar. 1865.

48. Harlow, *Old Waybills*, pp. 288–89; Stimson, *History of the Express Business*, pp. 159–60.

49. See copies of R. B. Bullock to W. Johnston, 6 Nov. 1861; agreements with Southern Express Co. by Presidents Johnston, Hawkins, and Cameron, November 1861; and P. C. Cameron to Bullock, 8 Jan. 1862, all in 1869 folder, XXII. Contracts, v. 19, NCRR Records, Archives.

50. NCRR, *Annual Report*, 1862, p. 25.

51. See account book, 1863–71, in XXVII. Freight, v. 90, NCRR Records, Archives.

52. See John Beauchamp Jones, *Rebel War Clerk's Diary*, 2:60–61, 82; Angus James Johnston, *Virginia Railroads in the Civil War*, p. 176; Salisbury *Carolina Watchman*, 29 Aug., 12, 19 Sept., 3 Oct. 1864; Charlotte *Western Democrat*, 27 Sept. 1864.

53. *Greensboro Patriot*, 10 Dec. 1863; Raleigh *Daily Progress*, 7 Dec. 1863. See also *Progress*, 23 Aug., 16, 21 Sept. 1864; Charlotte *Daily Bulletin*, 7 Mar. 1864; Raleigh *North Carolina Standard*, 2 Sept. 1864; *Patriot*, 22 Sept. 1864.

54. NCRR, *Annual Report*, 1862, p. 25.

55. Ibid., 1864, p. 4; Salisbury *Carolina Watchman*, 12, 19 Sept. 1864; Charlotte *Western Democrat*, 20 Sept. 1864.

56. See J. D. Whitford to T. Webb, 17 Aug. 1864, Whitford Papers, Archives; WNCRR, *Annual Report*, 1864, pp. 2–3; Price, "Railroads of North Carolina," p. 124.

57. See Charlotte *Western Democrat*, 8 Mar. 1864; Raleigh *Daily Progress*, 4, 25 Oct., 28 Nov., 3 Dec. 1864, 3 Mar. 1865.

58. NCRR, *Annual Report*, 1862, pp. 18, 32; 1863, p. 14; 1864, p. 16.

59. Ibid., 1863, p. 14; 1864, p. 16; Raleigh *Daily Progress*, 20 Jan. 1863. For later incidents, see Charlotte *Western Democrat*, 25 Aug. 1863; Salisbury *Carolina Watchman*, 18 July 1864.

60. Response of T. Webb, in railroad investigation papers, 1867, Robins Papers, SHC.

61. Charlotte *Daily Bulletin*, 4 Mar. 1864; Charlotte *Western Democrat*, 8 Mar., 4 Oct. 1864; NCRR, *Annual Report*, 1864, p. 22.

62. Charlotte *Daily Bulletin*, 8 Jan. 1865, copied in Raleigh *Daily Progress*, 10 Jan. 1865; Charlotte *Western Democrat*, 10 Jan. 1865. See Chapter 13.

63. Charlotte *Daily Bulletin*, 9 Jan. 1862.

64. *Proceedings at a Called Convention, Petersburg, 12th of March, 1862*; Price, "Railroads of North Carolina," p. 151.

65. *Raleigh Register*, 1 Oct. 1862; Raleigh *North Carolina Standard*, 5 Feb. 1864; Raleigh *Daily Confederate*, 19 Mar. 1864.

66. See Lerner, "Money, Prices, and Wages," pp. 29–31.

67. See editorials in Charlotte *Western Democrat*, 26 Nov. 1861; *Raleigh Register*, 2 May 1863.

68. D. K. McRae, in Raleigh *Daily Confederate*, 7 Feb. 1865; Price, "Railroads of North Carolina," pp. 153–54; *Official Records*, Series 4, 3:616–17.

69. Board of Internal Improvements Minutes, 19 June 1863, Archives.

70. NCRR, *Annual Report*, 1863, p. 4.

71. Ibid., 1860, p. 34; 1861, p. 27; 1862, p. 46; Price, "Railroads and Reconstruction," pp. 43–46.

72. NCRR, *Annual Report*, 1862, p. 11.
73. Price, "Railroads of North Carolina," pp. 123–24.

Chapter 13

1. Emory M. Thomas, *The Confederacy as a Revolutionary Experience* (Englewood Cliffs, N.J.: Prentice-Hall, 1971), and *The Confederate Nation, 1861–1865* (New York: Harper & Row, 1979).
2. Price, "Railroads of North Carolina," pp. 158–61; Black, *Railroads of the Confederacy*, esp. pp. 104, 114–15.
3. Black, *Railroads of the Confederacy*, pp. 72–73.
4. For discussion and examples of government regulation of railroads, see ibid., esp. p. 63ff; Ramsdell, "Confederate Government and the Railroads;" Goff, *Confederate Supply*, pp. 17, 199–202, 215–16, 224–26, 247–51; Price, "Railroads of North Carolina," pp. 154–67.
5. *Official Records*, Series 4, 3:616–17; Angus James Johnston, *Virginia Railroads in the Civil War*, pp. 226–27.
6. Black, *Railroads of the Confederacy*, pp. 52–56.
7. Ibid., pp. 81–82.
8. *Proceedings of a Convention, Augusta, Ga., December 15, 1862*; Price, "Railroads of North Carolina," pp. 147–54; Ramsdell, "Confederate Government and the Railroads," p. 796; Lerner, "Money, Prices, and Wages," p. 15.
9. Price, "Railroads of North Carolina," pp. 151–53.
10. *Official Records*, Series 4, 3:616–17; Angus James Johnston, *Virginia Railroads in the Civil War*, pp. 226–27.
11. See Catton, *Reflections on the Civil War*, pp. 139–40.
12. Raleigh *State Journal*, 20 Apr., 1 May 1861; Charlotte *Daily Bulletin*, 22 Apr. 1861.
13. Greensboro *Times*, 4 May, 8 June 1861; *Greensboro Patriot*, 3, 28 May 1861; NCRR, *Annual Report*, 1862, p. 30.
14. NCRR, *Annual Report*, 1862, pp. 11–12, 17, 24–25, 29.
15. Auman, "Neighbor against Neighbor," pp. 60–66; Auman and Scarboro, "Heroes of America," p. 332.
16. Letters of H. T. Clark to R. C. Pearson and P. C. Cameron, 22 Nov. 1861, Governors' Letterbooks; A. M. Powell to Clark, 25 Nov. 1861, Governors' Papers, Box 156, Archives.
17. See WNCRR, *Annual Report*, 1862, p. 9; J. W. Wilson to President and Directors of R&GRR, 22 Feb. 1864, Hawkins Family Papers, SHC.
18. Salisbury *Carolina Watchman*, 27 Jan., 3 Feb. 1862; Charlotte *Western Democrat*, 28 Jan. 1862; *Wilmington Journal*, quoted in Raleigh *North Carolina Standard*, 8 Jan. 1862.
19. Raleigh *North Carolina Standard*, 11 Jan. 1862.
20. *Proceedings of a Convention, Goldsboro, April 1, 1862*; Price, "Railroads and Reconstruction," pp. 47–48.
21. *Official Records*, Series 4, 3:600.
22. *Proceedings of a Convention, Goldsboro, April 1, 1862*, pp. 3–7; Black, *Railroads of the Confederacy*, p. 147; *Wilmington Journal*, quoted in Charlotte *Daily Bulletin*, 7 Apr. 1862.

23. Raleigh *North Carolina Standard*, 5 Apr. 1862.

24. Goff, *Confederate Supply*, pp. 105–6.

25. Ibid., pp. 107–8; *Official Records*, Series 1, 18:874; 25, pt. 2: 610–11, 688; Angus James Johnston, *Virginia Railroads in the Civil War*, pp. 133–35.

26. Angus James Johnston, *Virginia Railroads in the Civil War*, p. 127; Raleigh *Daily Progress*, 31 Mar. 1863.

27. Z. Vance to President and Directors of NCRR, 26 Feb. 1863; T. Webb to Vance, 28 Feb. 1863, Governors' Letterbooks; J. D. Whitford to T. J. Sumner, ? Oct. 1863, Whitford Papers, Archives.

28. *Official Records*, Series 4, 2:483–86; Black, *Railroads of the Confederacy*, p. 119.

29. NCRR, *Annual Report*, 1863, pp. 11, 23–24; F. W. Sims to Q. M. General Lawton, 16 Aug. 1864, in *Official Records*, Series 4, 3:598; Raleigh *North Carolina Standard*, 2 June 1863.

30. Goff, *Confederate Supply*, p. 197.

31. Ibid., pp. 108–11; Black, *Railroads of the Confederacy*, pp. 119–22.

32. *Official Records*, Series 1, 51, pt. 2: 808; Goff, *Confederate Supply*, pp. 196, 208; Ramsdell, "General Lee's Horse Supply," pp. 766, 769, 773–77.

33. Goff, *Confederate Supply*, pp. 198–99; Charlotte *Western Democrat*, 22 Mar. 1864; Raleigh *Daily Progress*, 11 Apr. 1864.

34. Goff, *Confederate Supply*, pp. 199–202.

35. Raleigh *Daily Progress*, 2 May, 24 Dec. 1864; Charlotte *Daily Bulletin*, 16 Nov. 1864.

36. For the history of this controversial issue, see Cecil K. Brown, "History of the Piedmont Railroad."

37. Ibid., pp. 202–11; Black, *Railroads of the Confederacy*, pp. 148–53, 227. For the first train, see *Greensboro Patriot*, 26 May 1864.

38. Black, *Railroads of the Confederacy*, pp. 224, 227–28.

39. See letters of J. M. Morehead (now a member of the Confederate Senate) to T. Ruffin, November 1861 to February 1862, in Ruffin, *Papers*, 3:194–95, 200–202, 213–14.

40. P. C. Cameron to [D. M. Barringer], 29 Nov. [1861], Barringer Papers, SHC.

41. NCRR, *Annual Report*, 1864, pp. 16–17; R&GRR, *Annual Report*, 1864, pp. 6–7; Price, "Railroads of North Carolina," pp. 72–73.

42. *Official Records*, Series 1, 46, pt. 2: 1026–27; Black, *Railroads of the Confederacy*, p. 228. See Raleigh *North Carolina Standard*, 8 June 1865, for a description of the Piedmont road a year after it opened.

43. Telegrams of O. P. Mears and T. J. Sumner to Z. Vance, 24, 25 Dec. 1864, Governors' Papers, Archives.

44. Ramsdell, "Confederate Government and the Railroads," p. 810; Goff, *Confederate Supply*, pp. 215–16, 224–25.

45. Charlotte *Daily Bulletin*, 1 Jan. 1865, quoted in Raleigh *Daily Progress*, 3 Jan. 1865.

46. Ramsdell, "Confederate Government and the Railroads," pp. 809–10.

47. NCRR, *Annual Report*, 1864, p. 17.

48. *Official Records*, Series 1, 42, pt. 3: 1334–35.

49. Ibid., Series 1, 42, pt. 3: 1348–49; 46, pt. 2: 1026–27; Price, "Railroads of North Carolina," pp. 74–75.

50. Copy of telegram, A. R. Lawton to J. R. Chisman, 3 Jan. 1865, Governors' Papers, Archives.

51. Black, *Railroads of the Confederacy*, p. 229.

52. Charlotte *Daily Bulletin*, 8 Jan. 1865, quoted in Raleigh *Daily Progress*, 10 Jan. 1865; Charlotte *Western Democrat*, 10 Jan. 1865.

53. Dew, *Ironmaker to the Confederacy*, p. 172.

54. Raleigh *North Carolina Standard*, 13, 17 Jan. 1865; Raleigh *Daily Confederate*, 20 Jan. 1865.

55. Goff, *Confederate Supply*, pp. 225–27, 233–34; Angus James Johnston, *Virginia Railroads in the Civil War*, pp. 230–31.

56. Goff, *Confederate Supply*, p. 218; Angus James Johnston, *Virginia Railroads in the Civil War*, pp. 230–31.

57. Cecil K. Brown, "History of the Piedmont Railroad," pp. 214–16; Angus James Johnston, *Virginia Railroads in the Civil War*, pp. 228–29, 304n; Price, "Railroads of North Carolina," pp. 189–90; *Official Records*, Series 1, 46, pt. 3: 1391–92.

58. J. Worth to J. J. Jackson, 4 Mar. 1865, in Worth, *Correspondence*, 1:362; F. W. Sims to J. M. Otey, 26, 27 Feb. 1865, Otey Papers, Duke; *Official Records*, Series 1, 47, pt. 2: 1312; pt. 3: 724.

59. Letters of P. Adams and D. F. Caldwell to Z. Vance, 27 Feb. 1865, with Vance's endorsements, Vance Papers, Archives.

60. *Official Records*, Series 1, 47, pt. 2: 1311–12, 1425, 1440; Black, *Railroads of the Confederacy*, p. 274; Price, "Railroads of North Carolina," pp. 187–88.

61. *Official Records*, Series 1, 47, pt. 2: 1319, 1321, 1323, 1324, 1328, 1331, 1339–40, 1346–47, 1353, 1355, 1360–61, 1366, 1371–74, 1376–78, 1380, 1395, 1398–99, 1406–7 (including General Johnston's complaint), 1426, 1442, 1445, 1448; pt. 3: 712; Series 2, 8:263–64, 294; Black, *Railroads of the Confederacy*, p. 277.

62. Barrett, *Civil War in North Carolina*, pp. 350–54; Van Noppen, "Significance of Stoneman's Last Raid," pp. 28–39, 149–63.

63. Robertson, *Michigan in the War*, pp. 723–24; R. S. Patterson to Father, 14 Mar. [Apr.] 1865, Jones and Patterson Papers, SHC; *Official Records*, Series 1, 49, pt. 1: 324, 332; Kirk, *History of the Fifteenth Pennsylvania*, pp. 501–3, 546–48, 553–55, 698–99; R. A. Jenkins reminiscences, Jenkins Papers, Duke; R. L. Beall account, August 1866, pp. 3–4, Spencer Papers, Addition, SHC; Barrett, *Civil War in North Carolina*, p. 355; Van Noppen, "Significance of Stoneman's Last Raid," pp. 167–71; Fries, "One Hundred Years," pp. 18–19.

64. *Official Records*, Series 1, 49, pt. 2: 446. For the raid on Salisbury, see ibid., Series 1, 47, pt. 1: 29; 49, pt. 1: 324, 334; R. L. Beall account, August 1866, pp. 3–7, Spencer Papers, Addition, SHC; WNCRR, *Annual Report*, 1865, p. 23; NCRR, *Annual Report*, 1865, p. 20; Barrett, *Civil War in North Carolina*, pp. 356–62; Van Noppen, "Significance of Stoneman's Last Raid," pp. 341–61, 500–502; Spencer, *Last Ninety Days*, pp. 199–208.

65. This was the view of Spencer, *Last Ninety Days*, pp. 207–8.

66. *Official Records*, Series 1, 49, pt. 2: 457–58, 465.

67. Ibid., Series 1, 47, pt. 3: 762, 765–66.

68. Ibid., Series 3, 5:32, 965–66; Price, "United States Military Railroads," p. 255.

69. NCRR, *Annual Report*, 1865, p. 13.

70. Price, "United States Military Railroads," pp. 254–57.

71. *Official Records*, Series 1, 47, pt. 3: 788–89, 802.

72. Ibid., p. 798.

73. Raleigh *North Carolina Standard*, 17 Apr. 1865. See also Raleigh *Daily Progress*, 15 Apr. 1865.

74. J. Worth to A. Worth, 22 Apr. 1865, Worth Papers, SHC.

75. J. Worth to J. J. Jackson, 21 Apr. 1865, and to J. A. Worth, 22 Apr. 1865, in Worth, *Correspondence*, 1:380–81; 2:1288, 1291–92.

76. Sherman, *Memoirs*, 2:345; Barrett, *Civil War in North Carolina*, pp. 373–75.

77. J. E. Johnston to Z. Vance, 19 Apr. 1865, Vance Papers, Archives; Stokes, *Company Shops*, pp. 42–44.

78. Stokes, *Company Shops*, pp. 46–48.

79. Hanna, *Flight into Oblivion*, pp. 5, 31–35, 38–45, 90–92, 100–101. For Davis and the leaky railroad car, see *Greensboro Patriot*, 23 Mar. 1866.

80. Sherman, *Memoirs*, 2:346–63; Sherman, *General Sherman's Official Account*, pp. 116–22; *Official Records*, Series 1, 47, pt. 3: 841.

Chapter 14

1. NCRR, *Annual Report*, 1865, pp. 19–22; telegram, T. J. Sumner to J. F. Boyd, 8 May 1865, Boyd Papers, Duke.

2. NCRR, *Annual Report*, 1865, pp. 12–14, 21, 26; statement of E. Wilkes, 18 Jan. 1867, Robins Papers, SHC; Andrews, *South since the War*, p. 109.

3. Doster, "Were Southern Railroads Destroyed?"

4. Price, "Railroads and Reconstruction," pp. 202–13.

5. *Official Records*, Series 3, 5:32–33, 298–99, 589–90, 963–66; report of E. C. Smeed, 15 May 1865, Boyd Papers, Duke; Sherman, *General Sherman's Official Account*, pp. 116–17; U.S. Congress, *Senate Executive Documents*, 45 Cong., 2 sess., #99, pp. 2–3; U.S. Congress, *House Reports*, 39 Cong., 2 sess., #34, pp. 118–19, 138–39, 440–41; Price, "United States Military Railroads," pp. 243–55.

6. Price, "United States Military Railroads," pp. 257–63.

7. NCRR, *Annual Report*, 1866, pp. 23–24.

8. U.S. Congress, *House Reports*, 39 Cong., 2 sess., #34, pp. 118–19; Price, "United States Military Railroads," pp. 255–57; R&GRR, *Annual Report*, 1866, p. 11.

9. NCRR, *Annual Report*, 1866, pp. 21, 23–24.

10. Ibid., 1865, pp. 12, 20.

11. Ibid., 1865, p. 12; 1867, pp. 15, 32; statement of E. Wilkes, 18 Jan. 1867, Robins Papers, SHC.

12. NCRR, *Annual Report*, 1868, p. 24; 1871, p. 5. See also ibid., 1869, pp. 15, 30; 1870, p. 11; Raleigh *North Carolina Standard*, 2 Aug. 1869.

13. Report of W. P. Raiford, 11 May 1870, in XXIII. Correspondence, v. 24, NCRR Records, Archives.

14. XV. Property Inventory, v. 96, pp. 71–78, NCRR Records, Archives.

15. Response of E. Wilkes, in undated railroad investigation papers, 1867, Robins Papers, SHC.

16. NCRR, *Annual Report*, 1865, pp. 12, 26.

17. Bills of sale, September 1865, in XXIII. Correspondence, v. 22, NCRR Records, Archives; responses of N. Boyden and W. A. Caldwell, railroad investigation papers, 1867, Robins Papers, SHC; NCRR, *Annual Report*, 1867, p. 32.

18. Statement of E. Wilkes, 18 Jan. 1867, Robins Papers, SHC; NCRR, *Annual Report*, 1867, pp. 15, 32.

19. NCRR, *Annual Report*, 1867, pp. 15–16; Price, "Railroads and Reconstruction," pp. 187–89.

20. NCRR, *Annual Report*, 1868, pp. 22, 24, 28; 1869, p. 15; 1870, p. 11; 1871, p. 8. For the only example I have seen of fifty-pound rail ordered after 1865, see order to W. B. Richards & Co., 28 Oct. 1870, in XXIII. Correspondence, v. 53, NCRR Records, Archives.

21. See relevant contracts, receipts, shipment statements, and correspondence of 1867–70, in V. Contracts, v. 16; XXII. Contracts, v. 19; Iron 1868–69, and January–June 1869 folders in XXIII. Correspondence, v. 23; F. A. Stagg to Tredegar, 10 May 1870, in XXIII. Correspondence, v. 53, all in NCRR Records, Archives. For Tredegar's business activity, see Dew, *Ironmaker to the Confederacy*, esp. p. 316.

22. Atack and Brueckner, "Steel Rails," pp. 339–57.

23. NCRR, *Annual Report*, 1867, pp. 32–33.

24. N.C. *Private Laws*, Special session, 1868, chap. 35.

25. NCRR, *Annual Report*, 1869, p. 5; R&GRR, *Annual Report*, 1869, p. 35.

26. XV. Property Inventory, v. 94, pp. 112–16, v. 96, pp. 71–78, NCRR Records, Archives.

27. Ibid., v. 93. See also v. 94, pp. 99–100, v. 95, pp. 88–89.

28. Ibid., v. 93, 95, p. 91. See 1850s city plans of Goldsboro, Raleigh, and Charlotte, in XI. Maps, v. 67, 68, and 71, respectively; 1871 plans at end of XV. Property Inventory, v. 95; and plan of Company Shops in the 1880s in XI. Map NCRR 3-A, all in NCRR Records, Archives.

29. For temporary repairs by the Union army in the east, see *Official Records*, Series 3, 5:32–33, 966; report of E. C. Smeed, 15 May 1865, Boyd Papers, Duke.

30. Raleigh *North Carolina Standard*, 9 Nov., 28 Dec. 1865, 10 Jan. 1866; Raleigh *Daily Sentinel*, 29 Dec. 1865, 12 Jan, 21 Feb., 1 Mar. 1866.

31. For information on the condition and repair of the bridges, 1865–71, see NCRR, *Annual Report*, 1865, pp. 19–20; 1866, pp. 16–17, 25–26; 1867, pp. 16, 31; 1868, pp. 24–25; 1869, pp. 15, 30; 1870, p. 11; 1871, p. 8; statement of E. Wilkes, 18 Jan. 1867, Robins Papers, SHC. See lists of bridges in table 7 of this book, and in XV. Property Inventory, v. 93–95, NCRR Records, Archives.

32. See NCRR, *Annual Report*, 1866, pp. 15, 24; 1867, esp. pp. 30–31; 1869, p. 30; 1870, p. 11; 1871, p. 8; and XV. Property Inventory, v. 93, p. 206, NCRR Records, Archives.

33. Report of the Joint Select Committee, 1867, N.C. *Public Documents*, 1866–67, p. 20.

34. Raleigh *North Carolina Standard*, 7 Nov. 1870; Report of Superintendent of Public Works, 1870, N.C. *Public Documents*, 1870–71, #14, pp. 2–3.

35. Price, "Railroads and Reconstruction," pp. 165–73; Price, "Railroads of North Carolina," p. 198.

36. T. J. Sumner to J. F. Boyd, 19 May 1865; telegram, E. Wilkes to Boyd, 16 Aug. 1865, Boyd Papers, Duke.

37. Andrews, *South since the War*, p. 201.

38. NCRR, *Annual Report*, 1865, pp. 11–12, 23; 1866, pp. 60–61.

39. Ibid., 1866, p. 48; Fisher, "United States Military Railroads," pp. 63–66; U.S. Congress, *House Reports*, 39 Cong., 2 sess., #34, pp. 121–22; bills of sale, 11 Dec. 1865, in Bills of Sale for U.S. Property, 1865–71, in XXIII. Correspondence, v. 22, NCRR Records, Archives; statement, 3 Jan. 1866, of NCRR purchases, in December 1865 folder, Boyd Papers, Duke.

40. NCRR, *Annual Report*, 1866, p. 19; responses of N. Boyden, railroad investigation papers, 1867, Robins Papers, SHC.

41. NCRR, *Annual Report*, 1866, pp. 18–19, 28; 1867, pp. 17, 33–34; 1868, pp. 25, 54–55; 1869, p. 30; 1870, p. 11; statement of E. Wilkes, 18 Jan. 1867, Robins Papers, SHC. According to property inventories submitted by the road annually to the state, the number of locomotives fell to twenty-two in May 1870 and twenty-three in June 1871. But the number was twenty-seven (including one out of order) at the time of the lease in September 1871. Cf. NCRR Property Inventories, 29 May 1869, 31 May 1870, 15 June 1871, in Internal Improvements, Boxes 19–20, Treasurers' and Comptrollers' Papers, Archives; and R&DRR, *Annual Report*, 1872, pp. 100–102; NCRR, *Annual Report*, 1878, p. 9.

42. Raleigh *North Carolina Standard*, 12, 13 Feb. 1869; Raleigh *Daily Sentinel*, 20 Feb. 1869; NCRR, *Annual Report*, 1871, p. 5.

43. Andrews, *South since the War*, p. 109. See similar comments as to the comfort of coaches, in Raleigh *North Carolina Standard*, 30 Oct. 1865.

44. NCRR, *Annual Report*, 1865, pp. 11–13, 20, 23, 26; 1866, pp. 9–10, 18–19, 27–30; 1871, p. 5; statement of E. Wilkes, 18 Jan. 1867, Robins Papers, SHC; *Greensboro Patriot*, 8 June 1866; Price, "Railroads of North Carolina," p. 199.

45. XV. Property Inventory, v. 93, NCRR Records, Archives; White, *American Railroad Passenger Car*, 1:35.

46. NCRR, *Annual Report*, 1869, p. 16.

47. Ibid., 1867, pp. 13–14.

48. Ibid., 1867, p. 70.

49. Report of Supt. Albert Johnson for Oct. 1869–Jan. 1870, with board of directors' minutes, 12 Apr. 1870, in XXVI. Minutes, v. 63, NCRR Records, Archives.

50. NCRR, *Annual Report*, 1867, p. 70.

51. Ibid., 1865, pp. 13, 22–23.

52. Ibid., 1866, p. 26; 1867, pp. 28–29.

53. Ibid., 1865, p. 22.

54. Ibid., 1867, p. 29; R&GRR, *Annual Report*, 1866, p. 9; Raleigh *Daily Sentinel*, 12 Feb. 1867; and XV. Property Inventory, v. 93, 95 (including map), NCRR Records, Archives.

55. Raleigh *North Carolina Standard*, 16 Jan. 1865, 2 Feb. 1866.

56. Raleigh *Daily Sentinel*, 19 Oct. 1866; Raleigh *North Carolina Standard*, 26 Feb. 1869, 28 Feb. 1870.

57. R&GRR, *Annual Report*, 1868, p. 25; Raleigh *North Carolina Standard*, 18 Feb. 1869; *Greensboro Patriot*, 14 Oct. 1869; Charlotte *Western Democrat*, 19 Sept. 1871.

58. NCRR, *Annual Report*, 1867, pp. 29–30; R&DRR, *Annual Report*, 1866, p. 78; 1867, pp. 178, 203.

59. *Greensboro Patriot*, 10 Mar. 1870.

60. XV. Property Inventory, v. 93, NCRR Records, Archives.

61. NCRR, *Annual Report*, 1866, pp. 26–27; 1870, p. 11; WNCRR, *Annual Report*, 1865, pp. 23, 30; 1868, p. 33.

62. NCRR, *Annual Report*, 1866, p. 17.

63. XV. Property Inventory, v. 93, NCRR Records, Archives.

64. Charlotte *Western Democrat*, 21 Sept. 1869, 1 Aug. 1871; NCRR, *Annual Report*, 1866, pp. 26–27; 1867, p. 30; 1870, p. 11.

65. Raleigh *Daily Sentinel*, 4 Apr., 19 Sept. 1867, 22 July 1868.

66. Minutes of directors' meeting, 16 Apr. 1869, in XXVI. Minutes, v. 63, NCRR Records, Archives.

67. Ibid., meeting of 15 Oct. 1869; C. M. Crump to agent at Holtsburg or Linwood, 31 May 1870, in XXIII. Correspondence, v. 53, NCRR Records, Archives; NCRR, *Annual Report*, 1871, p. 8.

68. Raleigh *North Carolina Standard*, 18 June 1870.

69. NCRR, *Annual Report*, 1869, p. 29; and XV. Property Inventory, v. 93–94, NCRR Records, Archives.

70. NCRR, *Annual Report*, 1865, pp. 13, 23; 1866, p. 26; 1867, pp. 17, 33; 1869, p. 15.

71. XV. Property Inventory, v. 93–94, NCRR Records, Archives.

72. NCRR, *Annual Report*, 1869, pp. 28–30. About 500 acres of the land were in Cabarrus or Rowan County and 400 more in Johnston County. See Thomas Webb, *Thomas Webb vs. NCRR*, p. 3.

73. Undated report of J. R. Harrison, in XV. Property Inventory, v. 95; minutes of directors, September 1871, in XXVI. Minutes, v. 63, NCRR Records, Archives.

74. NCRR, *Annual Report*, 1868, pp. 25–26; 1869, p. 16. Superintendent Wilkes reported in 1867 a far larger locomotive consumption of 1,700 to 1,900 cords per month, or over 20,000 per year. Statement of E. Wilkes, undated railroad investigation papers, 1867, Robins Papers, SHC.

75. NCRR, *Annual Report*, 1865, pp. 13, 23; 1866, p. 27.

76. Statements of E. Wilkes, undated railroad investigation papers, 1867, Robins Papers, SHC; NCRR, *Annual Report*, 1867, p. 33; 1868, pp. 25–26; 1869, pp. 16, 21, 23; 1870, p. 15; 1871, p. 13.

77. NCRR, *Annual Report*, 1866, p. 17; and XV. Property Inventory, v. 93, NCRR Records, Archives.

78. NCRR, *Annual Report*, 1868, pp. 30, 39.

79. Minutes of directors, 15 Oct. 1869, in XXVI. Minutes, v. 63, NCRR Records, Archives; Stokes, *Company Shops*, p. 72.

80. Stokes, *Company Shops*, pp. 71–72, 76–80; Raleigh *North Carolina Standard*, 13 Feb. 1869.

81. X. Ledgers, v. 57, p. 155; XIV. Payrolls, v. 81, NCRR Records, Archives; responses of T. Webb, in railroad investigation papers, 1867, Robins Papers, SHC; NCRR, *Annual Report*, 1867, p. 37; Stokes, *Company Shops*, pp. 87–89.

82. N.C. *Private Laws*, 1866, chap. 19, pp. 91–92.

83. Stokes, *Company Shops*, pp. 72–75, 144; Whitaker, *Centennial History of Alamance*, p. 134.

84. "Itinerant," in Raleigh *Daily Sentinel*, 29 July 1867.

85. NCRR, *Annual Report*, 1868, pp. 11–12; 1869, p. 39; Raleigh *Daily Sentinel*, 14 July 1868; Raleigh *North Carolina Standard*, 13 Feb. 1869; Stokes, *Company Shops*, pp. 99–104, 108–9.

86. Stokes, *Company Shops*, pp. 62–69, 93–99; Trelease, *White Terror*, esp. chaps. 12–13.

87. NCRR, *Annual Report*, 1866, pp. 17, 30; 1869, pp. 29, 31; Raleigh *Daily Sentinel*, 29 July 1867; *Hillsborough Recorder*, 16 Mar. 1870; Stokes, *Company Shops*, p. 58.

Chapter 15

1. Employees are enumerated in the annual reports from 1865 through 1871 by department, occupation, and (in 1865 and 1866) by race, with the wages paid to those in each occupation.

2. *Greensboro Patriot*, 22 Nov. 1867; NCRR, *Annual Report*, 1867, pp. 37, 41–43. See the table on p. 43, showing the number of workers employed at intervals between October 1865 and April 1867. For Turner's boast of having "dismissed all supernumeraries" in the interest of "retrenchment and reform," see *Annual Report*, 1868, p. 18.

3. NCRR, *Annual Report*, 1871, p. 28. The agents and their salaries are listed with the company officers in each annual report.

4. Ibid., 1866, p. 67; 1869, p. 53; responses of E. Wilkes, railroad investigation papers, 1867, Robins Papers, SHC.

5. See NCRR, *Annual Report*, 1867, p. 42.

6. Ibid., 1865, pp. 26–27; see also p. 13.

7. Ibid., 1866, pp. 31, 67.

8. For the temporary abolition of the ration system, but without any indication of the reason, see ibid., 1867, p. 37.

9. Ibid., 1868, p. 20. See Trelease, *White Terror*, esp. chaps. 12–13.

10. See T. Webb to M. S. Robins, 14 Feb. 1867, Robins Papers, SHC; payroll for February 1871, in XXVIII. Payrolls, v. 92, NCRR Records, Archives.

11. Fels, *Wages, Earnings and Employment*, pp. 21, 44–45, 51–52. In Massachusetts from 1840 into the 1870s or later, the seventy-hour workweek was standard on railroads. The sixty-hour week prevailed on Ohio railroads in 1870–71. Other states reporting wages in those years did not report hours (U.S. Department of Labor, *History of Wages*, pp. 430–31).

12. The national averages are based on tables in Licht, *Working for the Railroad*, pp. 64, 126, which vary slightly according to somewhat different chronological and data bases. Roughly comparable averages appear in U.S. Department of Labor, *History of Wages*, pp. 430–31.

13. See February 1871 payroll, in XXVIII. Payrolls, v. 92, NCRR Records, Archives. For a discussion of the trip system of determining engineers' pay, see Richardson, *Locomotive Engineer*, pp. 144–51.

14. Engineers on the Nashville, Chattanooga, and St. Louis Railroad received $104 per month in this period, conductors $69 to $78, based on a twenty-six-day month (Fels, *Wages, Earnings and Employment*, pp. 44–45, 51–52).

15. See E. G. Rike to A. J. Rike, 19 June, 4 Oct. 1867, and J. W. Willis to A. J. Rike, 14 Sept. 1867, in Rike Papers, SHC.

16. NCRR, *Annual Report*, 1868, p. 39.

17. Responses of T. Webb, in undated railroad investigation papers, 1867, Robins Papers, SHC.

18. NCRR, *Annual Report*, 1867, pp. 21–22.

19. For postwar NCRR labor costs (prewar figures were not published), see *Annual Reports*, 1866–1871. Nationally, labor costs averaged 60 percent of total *operating* costs. The latter were not carefully delineated by NCRR bookkeepers, however, making that comparison difficult (Licht, *Working for the Railroad*, p. 25n).

20. *Greensboro Patriot*, 12 May 1870.

21. NCRR, *Annual Report*, 1868, p. 21.

22. For a general discussion of railway recruitment and promotion practices, see Licht, *Working for the Railroad*, pp. 36–59, 147–49.

23. *Greensboro Patriot*, 22 Nov. 1867.

24. *William B. Lewis* v. *NCRR*, Davidson Superior Court, Spring term, 1868, in Davidson County Railroad Records, 1847–89, Archives. Lewis went to court and eventually won a settlement. See below.

25. NCRR, *Annual Report*, 1871, p. 30.

26. *Hillsborough Recorder*, 29 June 1870; minutes of directors, 18 Aug. 1871, in XXVI. Minutes, v. 63, NCRR Records, Archives; NCRR, *Annual Report*, 1878, p. 4. For general practice, see Licht, *Working for the Railroad*, pp. 197–207.

27. See Charlotte *Western Democrat*, 3 Sept. 1867.

28. Raleigh *North Carolina Standard*, 22 Feb. 1870.

29. See copies of reports of secretaries and auditors, 1869–72, in XII. Minutes, v. 80, NCRR Records, Archives.

30. See the criticism by the stockholders' inspection committee, in NCRR, *Annual Report*, 1868, p. 31. For correspondence on car exchanges in 1869–70, see XXIII. Correspondence, v. 23, 53, NCRR Records, Archives. For a complaint about the selective use of cars in dull seasons, see report of R&GRR Supt. A. B. Andrews in R&GRR, *Annual Report*, 1871, p. 20.

31. There is a multitude of evidence on the size and composition of NCRR trains arising from President William A. Smith's requirement in 1869 and 1870 that station agents inform him by telegraph of the numbers of cars carried on passing freight trains, together with the numbers of cars dropped off and picked up at their stations. See telegrams in XXIII. Correspondence, v. 23–25, and XXVII. Miscellaneous, v. 62, NCRR Records, Archives.

32. Cf. Andrews, *South since the War*, p. 109; *American Railroad Journal*, 23 Sept. 1865, p. 915; report for 1866 (dated 31 Aug. 1867) made to Bureau of Statistics, Treasury Department, in Statistics Furnished Washington, D.C., 1866 folder, XXIII. Correspondence, v. 22, NCRR Records, Archives.

33. Evidence concerning trains and schedules is derived primarily from the frequent newspaper notices. The NCRR reported to the Bureau of Statistics in Washington that in 1866 its express trains attained an average speed of twenty-five miles per hour, its slower passenger trains fifteen, and its freight trains twelve, all including stops (report for 1866 [dated 31 Aug. 1867] made to Bureau of Statistics, Treasury Department, in Statistics Furnished Washington, D.C., 1866 folder, XXIII. Correspondence, v. 22, NCRR Records, Archives). This does not correspond with the train schedules published in the newspapers, which do not mention express trains. Four separate schedules were published between January and November 1866, each of them for mail (or passenger) trains and for freight or accommodation trains. After calculating the times and distances, the mail trains show average speeds of 13.6 to 19.7 miles per hour from Raleigh to Charlotte and the freight/accommodation trains 10.5 to 11.5 miles per hour, all including stops. See Raleigh *Daily Sentinel*, 17 Jan., 11 June, 25 Sept. 1866; Raleigh *North Carolina Standard*, 10 Nov. 1866. The distance from Raleigh to Charlotte was 174 miles.

34. The evidence here is scanty, but an engineer reported picking up his train at Company Shops and taking it to Charlotte in 1869 or 1870. Also, an engineer and conductor were both recorded as taking a train from the shops to Charlotte and

back on a single run involving two successive days. See undated telegram of Agent Newlin at High Point to W. A. Smith, [1869 or 1870], in XXVII. Miscellaneous, v. 62; and manuscript table of running times, Charlotte to Company Shops, 24–25 Aug. 1871, in XXIII. Correspondence, v. 25, NCRR Records, Archives.

35. See NCRR, *Annual Report*, 1867, p. 38 (for an attack on Sunday trains on moral grounds); Raleigh *North Carolina Standard*, 21 Nov. 1868, 4 Feb. 1869; Raleigh *Daily Sentinel*, 19 Jan. 1869. The board of directors authorized the president and superintendent in December 1869 to run trains on Sunday or not, as they thought the road's interest dictated. But there is no evidence that Sunday service was again curtailed (directors' minutes, 3 Dec. 1869, in XXVI. Minutes, v. 63, NCRR Records, Archives).

36. See correspondence of June and July 1871 between President W. A. Smith and officers of S&A Telegraph Co., in XXII. Contracts, v. 19, and in XXIII. Correspondence, v. 53, NCRR Records, Archives.

37. Raleigh *Daily Progress*, 31 May 1865. See also affidavit of accident on 12 May 1865 near High Point, in Boyd Papers, Duke.

38. NCRR, *Annual Report*, 1867, p. 19.

39. Charlotte *Western Democrat*, 22 June 1869; S. F. Phillips to W. A. Smith, 2 Oct. 1869, with directors' minutes of October 1869, in XXVI. Minutes, v. 63, NCRR Records, Archives.

40. Raleigh *Daily Progress*, 28 Oct., 20 Dec. 1865; Raleigh *North Carolina Standard*, 30 Oct., 9 Nov., 20 Dec. 1865; Raleigh *Daily Sentinel*, 23 Dec. 1865; Charlotte *Western Democrat*, 26 Dec. 1865; NCRR, *Annual Report*, 1866, pp. 20, 29.

41. Raleigh *North Carolina Standard*, 9 Nov., 28, 30 Dec. 1865, 4, 5, 10 Jan., 22 Feb. 1866; Raleigh *Daily Sentinel*, 29 Dec. 1865, 12 Jan., 21, 22, 27 Feb., 1 Mar. 1866.

42. NCRR, *Annual Report*, 1867, p. 19.

43. Raleigh *Daily Sentinel*, 12, 13 Sept. 1866; *W. B. Lewis* v. *NCRR*, Davidson Superior Court, Spring term, 1868, in Davidson County Railroad Records, 1847–89, Archives; *W. B. Lewis* v. *NCRR*, N.C. Supreme Court Records, case #9535, Archives; and X. Ledgers, v. 60, p. 372, NCRR Records, Archives.

44. Charlotte *Western Democrat*, 20 Oct. 1868.

45. *Greensboro Register*, 8 Sept. 1869; Raleigh *Daily Sentinel*, 31 Dec. 1870; Charlotte *Western Democrat*, 3 Jan. 1871; *Greensboro Patriot*, 17 Feb. 1870.

46. *Greensboro Patriot*, 4 Nov. 1869, 5 Jan. 1871; Raleigh *Daily Sentinel*, 21 Jan. 1870; Raleigh *North Carolina Standard*, 21 Jan., 22, 23 Feb., 4 Mar. 1870.

47. *Raleigh Daily Telegram*, 18 Mar. 1871.

48. *Hillsborough Recorder*, 29 Sept. 1869.

49. Affidavit of accident of 17 May 1865, and telegrams from C. W. Leffingwell to J. F. Boyd, 11, 13 Aug. 1865, Boyd Papers, Duke.

50. Raleigh *North Carolina Standard*, 25 Sept. 1865.

51. Ibid., 5 Oct. 1865; Raleigh *Daily Progress*, 5 Oct. 1865; Raleigh *Daily Sentinel*, 5 Oct. 1865.

52. NCRR, *Annual Report*, 1866, p. 20; Salisbury *Carolina Watchman*, 10 Dec. 1866; *Smith & Melton* v. *NCRR*, 64 *N.C. Reports* 235; 68 ibid. 107.

53. NCRR, *Annual Report*, 1868, p. 24; 1870, p. 13. Cf. treasurer's report, ibid., 1868, p. 33, listing disbursements during the year of $10,759 for freight damages; perhaps most of this was carried over from previous years.

54. Ibid., 1866, p. 20.

55. Telegram, 27 Aug., and letter, 29 Aug. 1865, E. Wilkes to J. F. Boyd; affidavit of Boyd, 16 Feb. 1869, in Abstract and Letterbook, 1861–69, Boyd Papers, Duke.

56. Raleigh *North Carolina Standard,* 17 Oct. 1865.

57. Charlotte *Western Democrat,* 11 May 1869; *Greensboro Register,* 18 Aug. 1869.

58. Charlotte *Western Democrat,* 21 Aug. 1866; Raleigh *North Carolina Standard,* 18 May 1870 (about the ejectee); *Raleigh Daily Telegram,* 12 May 1871.

59. W. P. Raiford to W. D. Holt, 4 Feb. 1869, Arthur Collection, ECU.

60. See NCRR, *Annual Report,* 1868, pp. 37–38.

61. Ibid., 1867, p. 12.

62. Order of board, 15 Feb. 1867; board resolution, 15 Mar. 1867; printed copy of preceding, dated 30 Dec. 1868, with board minutes of 16 Apr. 1869, all in XXVI. Minutes, v. 63, NCRR Records, Archives.

63. NCRR, *Annual Report,* 1868, pp. 20, 37–38; 1870, p. 17.

64. Raleigh *Daily Progress,* 21 Aug. 1865; contract with Post Office Department, 5 Nov. 1867, stipulating $16,725 per year (or $75 per mile) from October 1867 to June 1871, in XXII. Contracts, v. 19, NCRR Records, Archives. For the Post Office Department formula, see P. M. General J. A. J. Creswell, 25 Jan. 1870, in U.S. Congress, *House Executive Documents,* 41 Cong., 2 sess., #90, pp. 1–2.

65. Charlotte *Western Democrat,* 13 June, 25 July 1865; Raleigh *North Carolina Standard,* 12, 28 Aug. 1865; Raleigh *Daily Progress,* 21 Aug. 1865; *Hillsborough Recorder,* 1 Nov. 1865, 2 Feb. 1870; Raleigh *Daily Sentinel,* 11 Jan. 1866. NCRR conductors were required to report occasions when they failed to make their normal mail connections. These notices were then forwarded by the road to the second assistant postmaster general in Washington. See XXIII. Correspondence, v. 53, NCRR Records, Archives.

66. Harlow, *Old Waybills,* pp. 288–89, 300, 304.

67. For the references to Adams Express, see Raleigh *Daily Progress,* 24 Apr., 24 July 1865; Raleigh *Daily Sentinel,* 19, 21, 24 Jan. 1867; NCRR, *Annual Report,* 1869, p. 43; 1870, p. 27. For National Express, see *Annual Report,* 1866, p. 15.

68. Charlotte *Western Democrat,* 8, 29 Aug. 1865; NCRR, *Annual Report,* 1866, p. 15; Southern Express account book, 1863–71, in XXVII. Freight, v. 90; contract with Southern Express, 4 Feb. 1869, and attached documents, in XXII. Contracts, v. 19, NCRR Records, Archives.

Chapter 16

1. Runyan, *Eight Days with the Confederates,* pp. 9–35.

2. She said seventy miles (Smiley, "Jottings of a Journey to North Carolina in the Fifth Month of 1865," pp. 75–76, Friends Historical Collection, Guilford College). Daniel M. Barringer, a leading prewar political figure, felt it too dangerous to travel at all at this time. See Barringer to Wife, 9 May 1865, Barringer Papers, SHC.

3. T. J. Sumner to J. F. Boyd, 16 May 1865, Boyd Papers, Duke.

4. Salisbury *Daily Union Banner,* 22 June 1865. Cf. the great improvement noted in ibid., 13 Oct. 1865.

5. Andrews, *South since the War,* p. 109.

6. NCRR, *Annual Report,* 1866, p. 14; 1867, p. 13.

7. Raleigh *Daily Sentinel,* 12 June 1867.

8. Rae, *Westward by Rail*, pp. 31, 34.

9. For generalized praise of NCRR service, see Raleigh *Daily Sentinel*, 4 June 1868; Raleigh *North Carolina Standard*, 2 Jan. 1869, 23 Mar. 1870.

10. Raleigh *North Carolina Standard*, 27 Jan. 1869; Raleigh *Daily Sentinel*, 20 Sept., 26 Oct. 1870; G. Z. French to W. A. Smith, 26 Jan. 1870, XXIII. Correspondence, v. 24, NCRR Records, Archives.

11. See Stover, "Ruined Railroads of the Confederacy," pp. 379, 385. For evidence of segregation on the Richmond, Fredericksburg and Potomac in 1867 and the Richmond and Danville in 1869, see *Hillsborough Recorder*, 2 Oct. 1867, 8 Sept. 1869.

12. See the general orders as well as an account of Johnson's trip, in Raleigh *Daily Sentinel*, 13 June 1867. An order of the NCRR board of directors in January 1867 seemingly relegated blacks to the second-class coaches (board of directors' minutes, 9 Jan. 1867, NCRR Office).

13. Ibid., 22 Aug. 1871.

14. J. W. Hoover to W. A. Smith, 17 Jan. 1870; telegram, J. C. Phillips to Smith, 19 Mar. 1870, in XXIII. Correspondence, v. 24, NCRR Records, Archives.

15. Raleigh *Daily Sentinel*, 11 July 1871.

16. See Trelease, *White Terror*, chaps. 12–13.

17. This is the total of receipts listed for "Government Transportation" that year (NCRR, *Annual Report*, 1871, p. 12). There is a voluminous file of militia transportation accounts in XXIII. Correspondence, v. 24, NCRR Records, Archives.

18. White, *American Railroad Passenger Car*, 1:208–21, 249–53.

19. Ibid., pp. 35, 210–11, 250; Mencken, *Railroad Passenger Car*, pp. 59–69. For an appreciative account of the Pullman cars by an English traveler of 1869, see Rae, *Westward by Rail*, pp. 50–55.

20. Raleigh *North Carolina Standard*, 1 Feb. 1866; Charlotte *Western Democrat*, 29 May 1866.

21. Raleigh *Daily Sentinel*, 8 June, 19 July 1866; Raleigh *North Carolina Standard*, 24 July 1866; NCRR, *Annual Report*, 1866, p. 14; contract with Van Rensselaer & Van Nortwick, 22 June 1866, in XXII. Contracts, v. 19, NCRR Records, Archives.

22. Contract with Southern Transportation Co., 12 Mar. 1869, in XXII. Contracts, v. 19, NCRR Records, Archives.

23. See Raleigh *North Carolina Standard*, 12 Apr., 15, 20 Dec. 1869; Raleigh *Daily Sentinel*, 16, 22 Dec. 1869.

24. *Greensboro Patriot*, 13 Jan. 1870.

25. A. S. Buford to W. A. Smith, 12 Apr. 1870; E. N. Kimball to Smith, 9 May 1870, in XXIII. Correspondence, v. 24, NCRR Records, Archives.

26. *Greensboro Patriot*, 30 Mar., 6 Apr. 1871; Charlotte *Western Democrat*, 28 Mar. 1871.

27. Leigh, *Ten Years on a Georgia Plantation*, pp. 6–8.

28. Raleigh *Daily Sentinel*, 21 Dec. 1866.

29. Charlotte *Western Democrat*, 26 Nov. 1867; Raleigh *Daily Sentinel*, 21 Dec. 1866.

30. Raleigh *Daily Sentinel*, 2, 14, 18 Sept., 8 Oct. 1867.

31. *Raleigh Daily Telegram*, 22 June 1871. See adverse advice concerning this choice from an NCRR official in undated [1870?] telegram of W. W. Davis to W. A. Smith, filed with 1870 items in 1872 folder in XXIII. Correspondence, v. 25, NCRR Records, Archives.

32. *American Railroad Journal*, 2 Sept. 1865, pp. 825–26, 843.

33. Petersburg Railroad, *Annual Report*, 1866, p. 9; *Wilmington Journal*, quoted in Charlotte *Western Democrat*, 14 June 1864.

34. NCRR, *Annual Report*, 1868, pp. 6, 9, 20; agreement, 30 July 1868, in XXII. Contracts, v. 19, NCRR Records, Archives.

35. Richmond and Petersburg Railroad, *Annual Report*, 1867, in *American Railroad Journal*, 10 Oct. 1868, p. 974; Petersburg Railroad, *Annual Report*, 1866, pp. 10, 25; 1867, pp. 8, 15.

36. Raleigh *Daily Progress*, 3 Aug. 1865.

37. Raleigh *Daily Sentinel*, 7 Apr. 1866; Charlotte *Western Democrat*, 12 June 1866.

38. R&DRR, *Annual Report*, 1866, pp. 84–85; Piedmont Railroad, *Annual Report*, 1866, p. 10; Cecil K. Brown, "History of the Piedmont Railroad," pp. 214–16.

39. See *Danville Times*, quoted in *Greensboro Patriot*, 17 Mar. 1870.

40. Alexander Crosby Brown, *Old Bay Line*, pp. 69–74, 85–89.

41. S&RRR, *Annual Report*, 1867, pp. 16–17; 1869, pp. 7–8; 1870, p. 7.

42. Raleigh *North Carolina Standard*, 22 Aug. 1865; Piedmont Railroad, *Annual Report*, 1866, p. 12.

43. *Hillsborough Recorder*, 30 May 1866.

44. *Greensboro Patriot*, 15 June 1866; Piedmont Railroad, *Annual Report*, 1866, pp. 11–12; 1867, pp. 42–46.

45. NCRR, *Annual Report*, 1866, p. 21; Charlotte *Western Democrat*, 12 June 1866.

46. Raleigh *North Carolina Standard*, 12 Jan. 1867; R&DRR, *Annual Report*, 1867, quoted in *American Railroad Journal*, 28 Mar. 1868, p. 297; NCRR, *Annual Report*, 1867, pp. 15, 33.

47. NCRR, *Annual Report*, 1866, p. 21; S&RRR, *Annual Report*, 1867, pp. 18–19.

48. Turner explained his actions in the *Hillsborough Recorder*, 11 Dec. 1867. The story was copied in the Raleigh *Daily Sentinel*, 23 Dec. 1867.

49. See Raleigh *Daily Sentinel*, 9, 17, 18 Oct. 1867; Raleigh *North Carolina Standard*, 10 Oct. 1867; *Raleigh Register*, 18 Oct. 1867.

50. J. M. Robinson to W. J. Hawkins, 20 Jan. 1868, Hawkins Family Papers, SHC.

51. See Raleigh *Daily Sentinel*, 4 Apr., 4 June 1868.

52. Unsigned draft of letter, W. A. Smith to P. V. Daniel, 20 Feb. 1871, in XXIII. Correspondence, v. 25, NCRR Records, Archives.

53. Raleigh *North Carolina Standard*, 29 Aug. 1868; letter of W. A. Smith in Charlotte *Observer*, copied in *Standard*, 1 June 1870. The NCRR also agreed with the R&GRR and other connecting roads in July 1869 not to discriminate against each other in passenger and freight rates (R&GRR, *Annual Report*, 1869, pp. 7–8).

54. R&GRR, *Annual Report*, 1869, pp. 11–12.

55. See R&DRR, *Annual Report*, 1868, p. 299; R&GRR, *Annual Report*, 1869, pp. 11–12; telegram, W. Johnston to W. A. Smith, undated but included with 1870 items in 1872 folder in XXIII. Correspondence, v. 25, NCRR Records, Archives; Johnston to A. B. Andrews, ? Aug. 1871, Andrews Papers, SHC.

56. Board of directors' resolution, 3 Dec. 1869, with minutes of that date, in XXVI. Minutes, v. 63, NCRR Records, Archives.

57. Raleigh *Daily Sentinel*, 16 Dec. 1869; Raleigh *North Carolina Standard*, 20, 21, 28 Dec. 1869.

58. *Danville Times*, quoted in *Greensboro Patriot*, 17 Mar. 1870.

59. A. S. Buford to W. A. Smith, 12 Apr. 1870; E. N. Kimball to Smith, 9 May 1870, in XXIII. Correspondence, v. 24, NCRR Records, Archives; letter of W. A.

Smith in Charlotte *Observer*, copied in Raleigh *North Carolina Standard*, 1 June 1870.

60. Smith wrote later that he had favored the Raleigh connection over the Greensboro one from the fall of 1868 until about August 1870 (draft of letter, W. A. Smith to P. V. Daniel, 20 Feb. 1871, in XXIII. Correspondence, v. 25, NCRR Records, Archives). For the change in connections and its effect, see R&GRR, *Annual Report*, 1871, pp. 10, 17–18.

61. R&DRR, *Annual Report*, 1870, p. 488; *Greensboro Patriot*, 20 July 1871.

62. NCRR, *Annual Report*, 1870, pp. 4–5; Charlotte *Western Democrat*, 15 Nov. 1870; R&DRR, *Annual Report*, 1870, pp. 468–69 (including quotation), 488.

63. NCRR, *Annual Report*, 1866, p. 59. A number of NCRR accounts for military transportation appear in the Boyd Papers, Duke.

64. For a clear statement of the postwar southern rate structure (if that is the word), see Klein, *History of the Louisville & Nashville*, pp. 65–67.

65. For details of this agreement, see Fitch, *Through Rates and Proportions*, p. 4ff.

66. *Hillsborough Recorder*, 11 Dec. 1867.

67. Information on rates was more apt to appear in the newspapers than in the annual reports. For information on rate changes between 1865 and 1871, see responses of W. A. Caldwell in railroad investigation papers, 1867, Robins Papers, SHC; Charlotte *Western Democrat*, 10 Oct. 1865; *Greensboro Patriot*, 8 Feb. 1867; Raleigh *Daily Sentinel*, 8, 11, 15 Aug. 1868, 2 Feb. 1869; Raleigh *North Carolina Standard*, 18 Jan. 1869 (including an offhand and perhaps incorrect reference to an 8-cent fare); NCRR, *Annual Report*, 1869, p. 5.

68. Board of directors' minutes, 30 June 1871, in XXVI. Minutes, v. 63, NCRR Records, Archives.

69. For local press efforts to lower rates on the NCRR and its neighbors, see Raleigh *North Carolina Standard*, 31 Jan. 1866, 23 Feb., 13 Apr., 28 Oct. 1869; Raleigh *Daily Sentinel*, 2, 5 July 1867 (the latter including a reply by President Webb); *Raleigh Register*, 29 Oct. 1867; *Greensboro Patriot*, 18 Feb. 1869; Goldsboro *Daily Messenger*, 29, 30 June 1869.

70. For the rate changes in these two years, see citations in note 69. For the figures on passenger volume and receipts, see NCRR, *Annual Report*, 1867, p. 66; 1868, pp. 52–53; 1869, p. 42. In the case of local passenger numbers as well as receipts, I have included the tickets sold by conductors on the trains.

71. Raleigh *Daily Sentinel*, 11 July 1871; *Greensboro Patriot*, 21 Sept. 1871. My passenger volume figures represent my best estimate, given the incomplete reporting in the NCRR *Annual Report*, 1871, p. 8. I have tried to flesh them out (particularly with regard to conductors' fares) with figures from 1869–70, to which the next year's report makes reference. R&DRR figures are from its *Annual Report*, 1872, pp. 36, 98.

72. Charlotte *Western Democrat*, 27 Oct. 1868; Raleigh *North Carolina Standard*, 7 Jan. 1869.

73. *Greensboro Patriot*, 7 July 1870.

74. Raleigh *North Carolina Standard*, 20 July, 18 Oct. 1870.

75. *Proceedings of a Convention of the Officers, Columbia, July 15, 1869*, p. 7; Raleigh *North Carolina Standard*, 21 July 1869.

76. Stokes, *Company Shops*, pp. 59–61.

77. NCRR, *Annual Report*, 1868, p. 21.

78. *Greensboro Patriot*, 16 Nov., 14 Dec. 1866, 25 Jan., 8, 15 Feb. 1867; Raleigh *North Carolina Standard*, 15 Nov. 1866.

79. Raleigh *North Carolina Standard*, 15 Nov. 1866; *Greensboro Patriot*, 4 Mar., 1 Apr. 1869, 23 Mar. 1871; Greensboro *Republican*, 9 Apr. 1870.

80. *Hillsborough Recorder*, 16 Mar. 1870.

81. Responses of T. Webb in undated railroad investigation papers, 1867; Webb to M. S. Robins, 14 Feb. 1867, both in Robins Papers, SHC. The tabulation appears in Report of the Joint Select Committee, 1867, N.C. *Public Documents*, 1866–67, pp. 32–33.

82. NCRR, *Annual Report*, 1867, p. 46.

83. Ibid., 1868, p. 39. See also p. 30.

84. Ibid., 1868, p. 9.

85. See XXIII. Correspondence, v. 23–24, NCRR Records, Archives.

86. Raleigh *Daily Sentinel*, 24 May 1871; *Raleigh Daily Telegram*, 25 May 1871.

87. *Raleigh Daily Telegram*, 12, 15 July 1871.

88. Raleigh *Daily Sentinel*, 18 Nov. 1868.

89. *Turner v. R&DRR*, 70 N.C. 1 (1874), in Schenck, *Digest of Decisions*, p. 69.

90. See *Greensboro Patriot*, esp. 2 Sept. 1869, 13 Jan. 1870.

91. C. M. Crump to Editor, Raleigh *Daily Sentinel*, 12 Aug. 1871, in XXIII. Correspondence, v. 53, NCRR Records, Archives.

Chapter 17

1. Statement of E. Wilkes, 18 Jan. 1867, Robins Papers, SHC; Raleigh *Daily Progress*, 5 Aug. 1865.

2. Raleigh *North Carolina Standard*, 28 July 1865.

3. NCRR, *Annual Report*, 1866, pp. 14, 28–29; Raleigh *North Carolina Standard*, 18, 19, 26 Jan., 6 Mar. 1869.

4. See letter from "Eno" in Raleigh *Daily Sentinel*, 22 Sept. 1869.

5. NCRR, *Annual Report*, 1867, pp. 14–15.

6. Based on NCRR annual reports, 1867–71, and (for the first year after the lease) R&DRR, *Annual Report*, 1872, p. 96. Besides the lack of local/through freight receipts comparable to those for passengers, no comparable tonnage figures were reported before 1867.

7. The only exceptions to this rule were in the highly eccentric years 1864–65 and 1865–66. See table 15. In 1865–66 this phenomenon seems to have resulted from the war-deferred shipment of large quantities of southern produce, especially cotton, to the North and an inability to buy many northern goods in return. Unfortunately the NCRR made no record of the kinds of freight carried this year.

8. W. A. Smith to W. A. Graham, 2 Nov. 1869, Graham Papers, SHC. There is no postwar breakdown between east- and westbound receipts by month.

9. R&DRR, *Annual Report*, 1872, pp. 96, 99.

10. See Chandler, *Visible Hand*, pp. 125–26; Klein, *History of the Louisville & Nashville*, pp. 65–67; Joubert, *Southern Freight Rates*, pp. 16–30.

11. NCRR, *Annual Report*, 1866, pp. 10–11, 14.

12. Raleigh *Daily Sentinel*, 13 Mar. 1867.

13. *Raleigh Register*, 6, 22, 26 Nov. 1867; *Greensboro Patriot*, 22 Nov. 1867.

14. Raleigh *Daily Sentinel*, 4 Dec. 1867; 13 May 1868; letter of Turner in *Hillsborough Recorder*, 11 Dec. 1867, copied in *Sentinel*, 23 Dec. 1867; NCRR, *Annual Report*, 1868, pp. 18–19.

15. *Raleigh Register,* 17, 20 Dec. 1867; Raleigh *Daily Sentinel,* 14, 16 Dec. 1867.

16. See W. J. Hawkins to T. Ruffin, 15 Aug. 1868, in Ruffin, *Papers,* 4:205.

17. Raleigh *North Carolina Standard,* 20 Jan. 1869.

18. Telegrams, W. W. Davies, 18 [?] 1869, and J. T. Ecton, 20 [?] 1869, to W. A. Smith, in Freight, 1869–75, in XXVII. Miscellaneous, v. 62; contract, 30 Sept. 1870, between W. A. Smith and firms of Smith & Melton and Hardin & Co., in XXII. Contracts, v. 19, NCRR Records, Archives.

19. Agreements with D. G. Fowle, 10 Jan. 1871; Wilson & Shober, 28 Mar. 1871; and J. R. Harrison, 30 June 1871, in XXII. Contracts, v. 19, NCRR Records, Archives.

20. T. L. McCready and J. M. Robinson to W. A. Smith, 8 May 1869; W. J. Hawkins to Smith, 18 May 1869; and McCready to Smith, 17 July 1869, in XXIII. Correspondence, v. 23, NCRR Records, Archives.

21. Letter of W. A. Smith in Raleigh *North Carolina Standard,* 27 May 1870; board of directors' minutes, 8 Nov. 1870, 21 Apr. 1871, in XXVI. Minutes, v. 63, NCRR Records, Archives.

22. Letter of W. A. Welker, [Sept. 1869], in XXIII. Correspondence, v. 23, NCRR Records, Archives; Raleigh *Daily Sentinel,* 8 Nov. 1869.

23. See Raleigh *Daily Sentinel,* 14 June, 16 July 1869, 18 Jan. 1870; Raleigh *North Carolina Standard,* 17 June, 5 July 1869. For an argument in support of the idea, see paper of Dr. Thomas D. Hogg delivered at the 1869 state fair, in *Sentinel,* 24 Dec. 1869. For information on the use and shipment of guano and other fertilizers in this period, see Rosser H. Taylor, "Fertilizers and Farming in the Southeast," pp. 310–28.

24. See Woodman, *King Cotton,* pp. 96–97, 272–73; Hammond, *Cotton Industry,* pp. 290n, 294–95, 299–300; Wright, *Old South, New South,* pp. 34–38; Cary W. Jones, *Guide to Norfolk,* pp. 98–99; Wertenbaker, *Norfolk,* pp. 271–86.

25. For the local destination, see NCRR, *Annual Report,* 1867, p. 18.

26. Ibid., 1860, p. 50a; 1868, p. 23; 1870, p. 11; 1871, p. 8. The predominant destination of Norfolk (rather than Petersburg and points farther north) is suggested by a number of sources. In addition to the preceding, see T. L. McCready to W. A. Smith, 25 Sept. 1869, in XXIII. Correspondence, v. 23; telegrams, J. T. Ecton to Smith, 13 Oct. 1869, in ibid.; and 22, 23 [Oct.?] 1869, in Freight, 1869–75, XXVII. Miscellaneous, v. 62, NCRR Records, Archives.

27. J. T. Ecton to W. A. Smith, 27 Dec. 1869, in XXIII. Correspondence, v. 23; J. W. McCarrick to Smith, 8 Aug. 1871, in ibid., v. 25, NCRR Records, Archives. A loaded boxcar held about twenty-five bales.

28. For such instructions, see the circular of a Philadelphia commission merchant printed in *Greensboro Patriot,* 12 July 1867 and Raleigh *North Carolina Standard,* 16 July 1867.

29. See Raleigh *Daily Sentinel,* 6 Sept., 27 Oct. 1866, 8 Oct. 1867, 18 May 1868; *Hillsborough Recorder,* 12 June 1867, 27 Sept. 1871; *Greensboro Patriot,* 21 June 1867, 22 May 1868; Charlotte *Western Democrat,* 27 Oct., 3 Nov. 1868.

30. Albright, *Greensboro, 1808–1904,* p. 16. There is a good deal of correspondence regarding dried fruit shipments in the files of President W. A. Smith in 1868 and later. See Correspondence, v. 23, NCRR Records, Archives.

31. Raleigh *Daily Sentinel,* 6 Sept. 1866; Charlotte *Western Democrat,* 27 Oct. 1868; *Greensboro Patriot,* 19 Aug. 1869.

32. S&RRR, *Annual Report,* 1869, p. 7; Raleigh *North Carolina Standard,* 20 Oct. 1870.

33. Tilley, *Bright-Tobacco Industry*, pp. 206–7, 222.

34. See J. Crane to W. A. Smith, 17 Aug. 1869, XXIII. Correspondence, v. 23, NCRR Records, Archives. Greensboro was also a shipping point for whiskey headed south, in substantial but unrecorded quantities. See telegrams in Freight, 1869–75, in XXVII. Miscellaneous, v. 62, ibid.

35. Charlotte *Western Democrat*, 18 Dec. 1866; Raleigh *Daily Sentinel*, 26 Oct. 1867; *Greensboro Patriot*, 13 Mar. 1868; references from 1869 in board of directors' minutes, XXVI. Minutes, v. 63, NCRR Records, Archives.

36. NCRR, *Annual Report*, 1869, p. 14.

37. Most of these references are in correspondence and telegrams, 1869–71, in XXIII. Correspondence, v. 23, 53, and in Freight, 1869–75, in XXVII. Miscellaneous, v. 62, NCRR Records, Archives.

38. The *Hillsborough Recorder*, 1 May 1867, reported that people there had been importing flour from the North recently and that Hillsboro had just sent off its first postwar shipment of flour. The R&DRR reported a very bad wheat crop in southside Virginia in 1867, but in 1868 the road shipped large quantities northward from southwestern Virginia and Tennessee. See R&DRR, *Annual Report*, 1867, 1868, as quoted in *American Railroad Journal*, 28 Mar. 1868, p. 297; 12 Dec. 1868, p. 1227.

39. S&RRR, *Annual Report*, 1867, p. 15. Nearly all of that road's fiscal year 1866–67 fell in calendar 1866.

40. CC&ARR, *Annual Report*, 1870, p. 4.

41. S&RRR, *Annual Report*, 1867, p. 8.

42. Charlotte *Western Democrat*, 6 Mar. 1866; letter of Josiah Turner in Raleigh *Daily Sentinel*, 4 Feb. 1868.

43. Report of Superintendent S. L. Fremont, in W&WRR, *Annual Report*, 1866, p. 7 (his report paginated separately); Raleigh *North Carolina Standard*, 13 Feb. 1866.

44. Speech of James Sinclair in House debate, Raleigh *North Carolina Standard*, 20 Jan. 1869. For continuing efforts of the A&NCRR to generate through traffic, including steamship and railroad agreements and ultimately a complete merger with the NCRR, see A&NCRR, *Annual Report*, 1866, p. 4; 1867, p. 13; 1868, pp. 9–13; *Raleigh Register*, 23 Aug. 1867; advertisement in Raleigh *Daily Sentinel*, 31 Aug. 1867; correspondence between Presidents J. D. Whitford and Josiah Turner in *Sentinel*, 24, 25 Jan., 4 Feb. 1868. The consolidation or merger efforts will be discussed in more detail in Chapter 20.

45. See Cecil K. Brown, "History of the Piedmont Railroad," p. 218.

46. Notice from R&GRR in Raleigh *North Carolina Standard*, 10 Apr. 1866; NCRR, *Annual Report*, 1866, pp. 14, 29; S&RRR, *Annual Report*, 1867, pp. 14–15.

47. Raleigh *North Carolina Standard*, 11, 18, 25 Aug. 1866.

48. NCRR, *Annual Report*, 1867, p. 14; S&RRR, *Annual Report*, 1868, pp. 5–6.

49. See reports of Superintendent S. L. Fremont in W&WRR, *Annual Report*, 1866, pp. 7–8; 1867, pp. 14, 16–17, 20, 25–26.

50. J. Worth to J. Turner, 25 Feb. 1868, in Worth, *Correspondence*, 2:1164; NCRR, *Annual Report*, 1867, pp. 4–5.

51. Letter of Josiah Turner in Raleigh *Daily Sentinel*, 4 Feb. 1868; report of Superintendent S. L. Fremont in W&WRR, *Annual Report*, 1867, p. 17; *Wilmington Journal*, copied in Raleigh *North Carolina Standard*, 3 Sept. 1867.

52. Raleigh *Daily Sentinel*, 20 July, 9 Oct., 23 Dec. 1867; NCRR, *Annual Report*, 1868, p. 20. See adjoining advertisements for the new through freight line and its competition, in *Sentinel*, 22 Aug. 1867.

53. R&GRR, *Annual Report*, 1868, pp. 6–7.

54. NCRR, *Annual Report*, 1868, p. 23; 1869, p. 14.

55. See *Wilmington Journal*, copied in Raleigh *Daily Sentinel*, 20 Sept. 1867; correspondence addressed to R&GRR President W. J. Hawkins and Superintendent A. B. Andrews, 5–29 Oct. 1867, in Andrews Papers, SHC.

56. Advertisements in Raleigh *Daily Sentinel*, 31 Aug., 30 Sept. 1867.

57. Letter of J. D. Whitford in Raleigh *Daily Sentinel*, 25 Jan. 1868; ibid., 29 Feb. 1868; NCRR, *Annual Report*, 1868, p. 20.

58. R&GRR, *Annual Report*, 1869, p. 11; Raleigh *Daily Sentinel*, 21 Jan. 1870.

59. J. Worth to J. Turner, 25 Feb. 1868, in Worth, *Correspondence*, 2:1164–65; NCRR, *Annual Report*, 1868, p. 11.

60. This was the view of the pre-Turner Raleigh *Daily Sentinel*, 9 Oct. 1867.

61. Agreement, 30 July 1868, between NCRR, Columbia & Augusta Railroad, R&GRR, and C&SCRR, with supplementary statement by R&GRR, 11 Sept. 1868, in XXII. Contracts, v. 19, NCRR Records, Archives; letter of W. A. Smith in Raleigh *North Carolina Standard*, 16 Jan. 1869.

62. T. S. Morton to W. J. Hawkins, 4 Sept. 1868, Hawkins Family Papers, SHC; W&WRR, *Annual Report*, 1868, pp. 17, 20; 1869, p. 9; 1870, p. 4; Raleigh *Daily Sentinel*, 14 Nov., 22 Dec. 1868.

63. Goldsboro *Carolina Messenger*, 15 Feb. 1870.

64. See Raleigh *Daily Sentinel*, 25 Jan. 1869, and Raleigh *North Carolina Standard*, 27 Jan. 1869, for a bitter exchange between Smith and the *Wilmington Journal*, speaking for the W&WRR.

65. See E. G. Ghio to W. J. Hawkins, 13 Sept. 1870, Hawkins Family Papers, SHC.

66. See W. Johnston to A. B. Andrews, 18 Feb. 1871, Andrews Papers, SHC.

67. Charlotte *Western Democrat*, 22 Feb. 1870; letter of W. A. Smith in Charlotte *Observer*, copied in Raleigh *North Carolina Standard*, 1 June 1870.

68. Copy of letter from committee of WNCRR board to W. A. Smith, 15 Oct. 1869, in letterbook, Tate Papers, SHC. See the similarly bitter letter from Tate to Smith, 31 Dec. 1869, in XXIII. Correspondence, v. 23, NCRR Records, Archives.

69. Agreement, 5 Feb. 1870, in XXII. Contracts, v. 19, and XXIII. Correspondence, v. 53, NCRR Records, Archives.

70. Ibid.

Chapter 18

1. See Raleigh *North Carolina Standard*, 23 Oct. 1865.

2. See J. D. Whitford to J. Worth, 5 Apr. 1866, Worth Papers, SHC; Raleigh *Daily Sentinel*, 7, 11 July 1866.

3. Raleigh *North Carolina Standard*, 17 July 1858, 19 July 1866. For a similar view of Holden's railroad patronage policies and appointments, see Price, "Railroads and Reconstruction," pp. 248–50.

4. See Raleigh *Daily Sentinel*, 12 Aug. 1865, 14 July 1866.

5. T. Ruffin to J. Worth, 15 May 1866, Worth Papers, SHC.

6. Board of directors' minutes, 13 July 1865, NCRR Office; *Greensboro Patriot*, 22 July 1865; responses of T. Webb, undated railroad investigation papers, 1867, Robins Papers, SHC.

7. *Greensboro Patriot*, 22 July 1865; NCRR, *Annual Report*, 1865, p. 5.

8. Salisbury *Carolina Watchman*, 11 July 1864; Charlotte *Western Democrat*, 26 July, 2 Aug. 1864; Chamberlain, *This Was Home*, pp. 130–31; Louis Alexander Brown, *Salisbury Prison*, pp. 154–55. According to Boyden family tradition, Abraham Lincoln (whose one congressional term coincided with Boyden's) was going to appoint Boyden provisional governor of North Carolina before his assassination (Max Williams, "Nathaniel Boyden," in *Dictionary of North Carolina Biography*, ed. William S. Powell, 3 vols. to date [Chapel Hill, University of North Carolina Press, 1979–], 1:204).

9. NCRR, *Annual Report*, 1866, p. 11; Report of the Joint Select Committee, 1867, N.C. *Public Documents*, 1866–67, p. 16; Raleigh *Daily Sentinel*, 14 July 1866.

10. See Andrews, *South since the War*, pp. 138–51; Dennett, *South As It Is*, pp. 158–60.

11. Charles L. Price provides a good discussion of Worth's railroad appointment policies and practice. See his "Railroads and Reconstruction," pp. 250–61.

12. Raleigh *North Carolina Standard*, 9 Nov. 1869. Josiah Turner, Sr., had been one of the road's construction contractors. As such he owned forty shares of NCRR stock from 1850 to 1866, when the number decreased to thirty-five and his son first appeared as a stockholder, with five shares.

13. Worth kept a much fuller record than other governors of the process by which he arrived at his appointments. See (for the NCRR) Worth, *Correspondence*, 1:559–62, 568–69, 630–31, 646–47, 649–56 (quotation from p. 653); 2:669, 711–15, 720–24, 732–33, 1272–73; J. F. Foard to Z. Vance, 26 Apr. 1866, and K. P. Battle to Vance, 3 May 1866, in Vance Papers, Archives; letters to Worth from T. Ruffin, 15 May 1866, L. Hanes, 17 May 1866, and A. G. Foster, 20 May 1866, Worth Papers, SHC. For Worth's pardon campaign in Turner's behalf, see Worth, *Correspondence*, 2:660–62, 676–78, 925–27, 981–82, 984.

14. The stockholders departed from custom in staging a spirited vote between two slates of candidates for the finance committee. For years they had routinely chosen three men, John U. Kirkland, Edwin M. Holt, and Jeduthun H. Lindsay. These were replaced in 1865 by vote of Holden's state proxy. But when some of the old guard in 1866 thought to restore Kirkland, Holt, and Lindsay, a rival slate was offered, consisting of Rufus S. Tucker, Rufus Barringer, and William A. Caldwell. (Caldwell had been one of those chosen in 1865 and then served as chairman.) For reasons never made public, the rival slate was elected by a vote of more than two to one, Governor Worth's proxy not voting. Caldwell continued as chairman (NCRR, *Annual Report*, 1866, pp. 6–7). Then, in 1867, Worth's new proxy, John Berry, cast his 30,000 votes to elect Caldwell, Barringer, and B. B. Roberts, a recent director who had worked with the committee. No explanation survives. Caldwell became treasurer of the road that year and left the committee (Ibid., 1867, p. 7).

15. Board of directors' minutes, 13 July 1866, NCRR Office; J. Worth to L. Hanes, 5 July 1866, and to Englehard & Price, 27 Jan. 1869, in Worth, *Correspondence*, 2:669, 1272–73; J. Turner to J. Worth, 7 July 1866, Worth Papers, SHC. The vote was seven for Webb and three for Turner. My figure of four assumes that both Webb and Turner abstained. For a more generic account of the political dealings prior to selecting a president, which must have referred in part to this occasion, see letter of Rufus Barringer in Raleigh *Daily Sentinel*, 13 Feb. 1867.

16. J. Worth to J. Turner, 25 June 1867; Turner to Worth, 1 July 1867; Worth to N. Boyden, 3 July 1867; Worth to R. Strange, 3 July 1867; Worth to J. M. Coffin, 8

July 1867; Worth to Englehard & Price, 27 Jan. 1869, all in Worth, *Correspondence*, 2:986, 990–91, 998, 1273–74; J. Turner to J. Worth, 7 July [1867], Worth Papers, Archives. Turner even enlisted George W. Swepson to help line up support (Swepson testimony, in *State v. Josiah Turner*, 1876, pp. 25–28, 37–38, 46–50).

17. Board of directors' minutes, 12 July 1867, NCRR Office; Raleigh *North Carolina Standard*, 9 Nov. 1869; "Veritas," in *Greensboro Patriot*, 19 July 1867.

18. Raleigh *North Carolina Standard*, 28 July 1866.

19. See, for example, Charlotte *Western Democrat*, 31 Dec. 1867; letter of "H. Bossa," in Raleigh *Daily Sentinel*, 8 Jan. 1868. For biographical sketches, see S. A. Ashe, *Biographical History of North Carolina*, 3:415–26; J. G. de Roulhac Hamilton, in *Dictionary of American Biography*, ed. Allen Johnson and Dumas Malone, 22 vols. (New York: Scribners, 1928–44), 19:68–69; Ezra J. Warner and W. Buck Yearns, *Biographical Register of the Confederate Congress* (Baton Rouge: Louisiana State University Press, 1975), pp. 241–42.

20. For two possible exceptions, see D. L. Swain to W. A. Graham, 12 July 1866, in Graham, *Papers*, 7:154; Raleigh *Daily Sentinel*, 3 May 1867; Raleigh *North Carolina Standard*, 11 May, 15 June 1867.

21. NCRR, *Annual Report*, 1867, pp. 46, 91, 93, 95.

22. See J. Turner to wife, 29 Oct., 4 Nov. 1867, 22 May 1868, Turner Papers, SHC.

23. Charlotte *Western Democrat*, 23 Dec. 1871.

24. Board of directors' minutes, 13 July 1865, 15 Feb. 1867, NCRR Office; NCRR, *Annual Report*, 1867, p. 25; Raleigh *Daily Sentinel*, 29 Mar. 1867.

25. Fortunately the annual reports from 1865 onward list all of the company officers with their salaries. The ensuing discussion is based on that information.

26. Raleigh *North Carolina Standard*, 13 Feb. 1869; Raleigh *Daily Sentinel*, 17 Dec. 1869; *Hillsborough Recorder*, 16 Mar. 1870; investigating committee report, 18 Jan. 1870, in XXIII. Correspondence, v. 52, NCRR Records, Archives.

27. NCRR, *Annual Report*, 1868, p. 21.

28. Board of directors' minutes, 18 Aug. 1871, in XXVI. Minutes, v. 63, NCRR Records, Archives; NCRR, *Annual Report*, 1870, pp. 17, 21; 1871, pp. 10, 17; 1878, p. 4.

29. NCRR, *Annual Report*, 1867, p. 98; statement by E. Wilkes, undated railroad investigation papers, 1867, Robins Papers, SHC.

30. NCRR, *Annual Report*, 1868, p. 21.

31. Ibid., 1867, pp. 91, 95, 97–98, 101; 1868, pp. 30, 36, 38; 1870, p. 37; 1871, p. 28; E. S. Parker to W. A. Graham, 11 Aug. 1871, Graham Papers, SHC.

32. NCRR, *Annual Report*, 1865, p. 4; 1866, pp. 64–65; 1867, pp. 77–78; 1868, pp. 60–61; 1869, pp. 6–7, 51–52; 1870, pp. 5, 37–38; 1871, pp. 28–29.

33. The following discussion of the road's postwar financial situation sometimes follows and always benefits from the careful research of Price, "Railroads and Reconstruction," esp. p. 220ff, as well as Cecil K. Brown, *State Movement*, p. 149ff.

34. NCRR, *Annual Report*, 1866, p. 11; responses of T. Webb in undated railroad investigation papers, 1867, Robins Papers, SHC.

35. NCRR, *Annual Report*, 1865, pp. 9–10.

36. Ibid., 1868, p. 19; Chapter 10, above.

37. See statement of amount of tobacco; J. V. Moore to P. B. Ruffin, 25 Dec. 1866; responses of T. Webb and E. Wilkes in undated railroad investigation papers, 1867, all in Robins Papers, SHC. Also accounts and correspondence of Moore and others

in Tobacco, 1866–67 folder, in XXIII. Correspondence, v. 22, NCRR Records, Archives; J. Turner to J. Worth, 28 July 1867, Waddell Papers, Archives; and (for the apparent bottom line so far as proceeds from sales are concerned) NCRR, *Annual Report*, 1867, p. 58; 1868, p. 50.

38. Responses by T. Webb in undated railroad investigation papers, 1867, Robins Papers, SHC.

39. NCRR, *Annual Report*, 1867, pp. 12, 24.

40. Ibid., 1866, pp. 10–11; Report of the Joint Select Committee, 1867, N.C. *Public Documents*, 1866–67, p. 16; answer of G. W. Mordecai to questions of 9 Jan. 1867, undated statement of F. A. Stagg, and copy of statement by N. Boyden, 27 Sept. 1865, in Robins Papers, SHC.

41. See Charlotte *Western Democrat*, 16 Jan. 1866; Raleigh *North Carolina Standard* (quoting other papers and a correspondent), 28 June, 3 July 1866; Raleigh *Daily Sentinel*, 2 July 1866; Salisbury *Old North State*, quoted in *Greensboro Patriot*, 13 July 1866.

42. Report of the Joint Select Committee, 1867, N.C. *Public Documents*, 1866–67, pp. 8–12, 14–16, 26–30, 34–38; responses by W. A. Caldwell in undated railroad investigation papers, 1867, and copy of board minutes, 12 Dec. 1866, in Robins Papers, SHC.

43. Responses of E. Wilkes and W. A. Caldwell in undated railroad investigation papers, 1867, Robins Papers, SHC.

44. See, for example, Rufus Barringer in Raleigh *Daily Sentinel*, 13 Feb. 1867.

45. Webb claimed to have laid off over 200 hands (NCRR, *Annual Report*, 1867, p. 23) and probably did, at least temporarily, but the numbers of employees listed in the annual reports of 1866 and 1867 indicate a decrease of only 107.

46. Raleigh *Daily Sentinel*, 18 Jan. 1867; NCRR, *Annual Report*, 1867, pp. 21–23. For a listing of the lenders, see response of T. Webb in undated railroad investigation papers [1867], Robins Papers, SHC.

47. F. A. Stagg to T. Ruffin, 9 Jan. 1867, in Ruffin, *Papers*, 4:142–43.

48. NCRR, *Annual Report*, 1867, pp. 8–9, 24; 1868, p. 15.

49. Ibid., 1868, pp. 18, 30–32. See Turner's solicitation of bondholders to make the exchange, in *Raleigh Register*, 22 Nov. 1867.

50. See G. W. Mordecai to P. C. Cameron, 29 Oct., 28 Dec. 1867, 2 Jan., 6, 19 Apr. 1868, Cameron Family Papers, SHC.

51. NCRR, *Annual Report*, 1868, pp. 13, 27–29, 31. Despite his opposition to the dividend, Turner himself invited it by exaggerating the year's surplus as $316,000. The dispassionate Secretary Stagg recorded the year's proceeds at $585,411, the expenses at $508,526. Cf. *Annual Report*, 1868, pp. 15, 46–47.

52. Report of State Treasurer, 14 Nov. 1868, N.C. *Public Documents*, 1868–69, #5, p. 6; Report of the Commission to Investigate Fraud, ibid., 1871–72, #11, pp. 199–201, 343–44, 538, 555–56.

53. Raleigh *Daily Sentinel*, 4 Jan. 1869, 21 July 1870.

54. See bond quotations in the Raleigh press, the *North Carolina Standard* in particular.

55. F. A. Stagg to H. W. Fries, 22 Mar. 1870, in XXIII. Correspondence, v. 52, NCRR Records, Archives. For the references to Morehead and Swepson, see NCRR, *Messages to the People*, p. 7; *Raleigh Daily Telegram*, 10 July 1871.

56. For NCRR stock quotations see Charlotte *Western Democrat*, 9 Jan. 1866 (quot-

ing *Salisbury Gazette*), 9, 30 June 1868; *Greensboro Patriot*, 31 May, 19 July (letter by "Veritas"), 9 Aug. 1867, 24 Apr. 1868; Raleigh *North Carolina Standard*, 3 Sept. 1868.

57. NCRR, *Annual Report*, 1858, pp. 21–23.

58. Ibid., 1866, pp. 33–38. George W. Mordecai gave a similar diagnosis of the system. See questions put to him by the legislative investigating committee, 9 Jan. 1867, and his answers, in Robins Papers, SHC. See also President Webb's explanation of how this laxity had occurred, in his responses in undated railroad investigation papers, 1867, Robins Papers, SHC.

59. NCRR, *Annual Report*, 1867, pp. 36–44; copy of directors' minutes, 12 Dec. 1866, Robins Papers, SHC; board of directors' minutes, 13 July 1866, 15 Feb., 19 Apr. 1867, NCRR Office; Report of the Joint Select Committee, 1867, N.C. *Public Documents*, 1866–67, p. 8.

60. N.C., *Memorial [of NCRR] to the Honorable General Assembly*, [1866]; resolution creating committee, in N.C. *Public Laws*, 1866–67, pp. 232–33; Report of the Joint Select Committee, 1867, N.C. *Public Documents*, 1866–67, pp. 1–2.

61. Report of the Joint Select Committee, 1867, N.C. *Public Documents*, 1866–67, pp. 2–3. These materials—the interrogatories, responses, testimony, and other documents—now reside in the Robins Papers, SHC. They are a mine of information about the road's management and operations up to this time, but particularly after the war.

62. Ibid., pp. 3–21.

63. J. Berry to J. Worth, 7 Mar. 1867, Worth Papers, Archives; Worth to Berry, 8 Mar. 1867, in Worth, *Correspondence*, 2:915. Turner rehearsed many of the charges taken up by the committee, in a speech to a special stockholders' meeting in December 1866. See Raleigh *Daily Sentinel*, 18 Dec. 1866.

64. NCRR, *Annual Report*, 1867, pp. 39–44.

65. Ibid., 1867, pp. 40–43.

66. By-laws, and report of the committee on by-laws, in ibid., 1867, pp. 91–103.

67. Raleigh *North Carolina Standard*, 7 Feb. 1868.

68. NCRR, *Annual Report*, 1868, pp. 28–30, 36–37; 1869, p. 25; 1871, p. 11.

69. Responses of N. Boyden and T. Webb in undated railroad investigation papers, 1867, and answers of G. W. Mordecai to questions of 9 Jan. 1867, all in Robins Papers, SHC.

70. Board of directors' minutes, 13 July 1866, 12 July 1867. For Wilkes, see remarks of Josiah Turner in special stockholders' meeting, in Raleigh *Daily Sentinel*, 18 Dec. 1866.

71. J. Worth to Englehard & Price, 27 Jan. 1869, in Worth, *Correspondence*, 2:1272–73. This notion of NCRR subservience to the R&GRR was by no means confined to Worth. See editorial by David F. Caldwell (brother of NCRR Treasurer William A. Caldwell) in *Greensboro Patriot*, 18 Oct. 1867.

72. J. Worth to J. Turner, 25 Feb. 1868, in Worth, *Correspondence*, 2:1164–65; NCRR, *Annual Report*, 1867, pp. 4–5.

73. NCRR, *Annual Report*, 1868, p. 11.

Chapter 19

1. J. D. Whitford to S. McD. Tate, 15 May 1868, Tate Papers, SHC.
2. General Orders, No. 125, 2 July 1868, N.C. *Public Documents*, 1868–69, #4; Zuber, *Jonathan Worth*, p. 287. Worth's nominees for the NCRR board were Josiah Turner, O. G. Parsley, James M. Leach, R. Y. McAden, William C. Means, R. B. Haywood, Peter Adams, and J. M. Coffin, some of them being reappointments. His choice as state proxy was the same as in 1867: John Berry.
3. Charlotte *Western Democrat*, 24 Aug., 14 Sept., 6 Oct. 1869, 21 June 1870.
4. Raleigh *North Carolina Standard*, 6 Apr. 1853, 15 Feb. 1854; Charlotte *North Carolina Whig*, 8 Nov. 1859.
5. Charlotte *Western Democrat*, 2 Apr. 1867.
6. Resolution and Report in Regard to the Lease, N.C. *Public Documents*, 1871–72, #27, pp. 7, 65; Raleigh *Daily Sentinel*, 15 July 1871.
7. NCRR, *Annual Report*, 1868, pp. 3–5, 9, 19–20; Raleigh *Daily Sentinel*, 11 July 1868.
8. NCRR, *Annual Report*, 1868, pp. 4, 6–8.
9. Board of directors' minutes, 10 July 1868, NCRR Office; Raleigh *North Carolina Standard*, 11 July 1868; Raleigh *Daily Sentinel*, 13 July 1868.
10. *Raleigh Daily Telegram*, 9 June 1871.
11. Raleigh *Daily Progress*, 19 Oct. 1863, copied in Raleigh *North Carolina Standard*, 20 Oct. 1863; letter of W. A. Smith in Raleigh *Daily Sentinel*, 29 May 1869.
12. Raleigh *North Carolina Standard*, 7 Aug. 1863, 11 July 1865.
13. Hamilton, *Reconstruction in North Carolina*, p. 538.
14. For biographical sketches, see John Gilchrist McCormick, "Personnel of the Convention of 1861," *James Sprunt Historical Monographs*, No. 1 (Chapel Hill: University of North Carolina Press, 1900), pp. 76–77; Wheeler, *Reminiscences*, p. 226; obituary in Stephen B. Weeks Scrapbook, III, #134, North Carolina Collection, University of North Carolina, Chapel Hill.
15. See newspaper clipping in Stephen B. Weeks Scrapbook, VIII, #176, North Carolina Collection, University of North Carolina, Chapel Hill; Raleigh *North Carolina Standard*, 26 July 1864, 20 Apr. 1865; A. Johnson to J. F. Boyd, 1 Sept. 1865, Boyd Papers, Duke; Boyd to M. C. Meigs, 6 Jan. 1866, in U.S. Congress, *House Reports*, 39 Cong., 2 sess., #34, p. 120.
16. See *Greensboro Patriot*, 16 July 1868; Raleigh *Daily Sentinel*, 20 July, 12 Aug. 1868; Raleigh *North Carolina Standard*, 21 July 1868; and editorials from *Milton Chronicle* and Salisbury *Old North State* a year later, in *Greensboro Register*, 7 July 1869; C. J. Cowles to W. A. Smith, 17 July 1869, in XXIII. Correspondence, v. 23, NCRR Records, Archives.
17. Raleigh *North Carolina Standard*, 4 June 1869; W. Johnston to A. B. Andrews, 20 Nov. 1870, Andrews Papers, SHC.
18. Board of directors' minutes, 8 July 1869, NCRR Office; Raleigh *Daily Sentinel*, 13 July 1869. The state directors in 1869 were the same as in 1868. The private stockholders reelected Davis but replaced Thomas Webb, John L. Morehead (two previous favorites), and William A. Caldwell with Thomas M. Holt (son of Edwin), John I. Shaver, and Dr. Richard B. Haywood.
19. See W. A. Smith to W. A. Graham, 30 Aug., 2 Nov. 1869, Graham Papers, SHC; Smith to D. F. Caldwell, 28 Aug. 1869, Caldwell Papers, SHC; Smith to P. C. Cameron, 26 Dec. 1870, Cameron Family Papers, SHC.

20. In Caldwell Papers, SHC.

21. G. W. Mordecai to M. C. Cameron, 7 Sept. 1870, Cameron Family Papers, SHC.

22. W. A. Smith to W. A. Graham, 2 Nov. 1869, Graham Papers, SHC.

23. Price, "Railroads and Reconstruction," pp. 266–71.

24. At least one white shopworker thought he was fired to make room for a black, however (E. J. Rike to A. J. Rike, 28 Apr. 1869, Rike Papers, SHC).

25. Board of directors' minutes, 21 July, 4 Sept. 1868, NCRR Office; Charlotte *Western Democrat*, 1 Dec. 1868.

26. NCRR, *Annual Report*, 1869, p. 24. See Smith's later explanations and defense of his hiring policies, in Raleigh *North Carolina Standard*, 25 Aug. 1869; *Raleigh Daily Telegram*, 27 Apr. 1871.

27. Raleigh *Daily Sentinel*, 22 Jan., 3 Apr. 1869, 21 June 1871.

28. Records of Lawsuits, pp. 9–19, in VI. Deeds, v. 48, NCRR Records, Archives.

29. W. A. Smith to directors, 17 Dec. 1869, with directors' minutes, December 1869; order of directors, 18 Jan. 1870, with attached committee report; directors' minutes, 16 Feb. 1870, in XXVI. Minutes, v. 63, NCRR Records, Archives.

30. Board of directors' minutes, 4 Sept. 1868, NCRR Office; Raleigh *Daily Sentinel*, 7, 26 Aug., 10, 11 Sept. 1868, 10 Aug. 1871; Raleigh *North Carolina Standard*, 2 Sept. 1868.

31. *Milton Chronicle*, quoted in Raleigh *Daily Sentinel*, 22 Feb. 1869; Raleigh *North Carolina Standard*, 5 Apr. 1869.

32. Raleigh *Daily Sentinel*, 17 Dec. 1870; Jonathan Daniels, *Prince of Carpetbaggers*, pp. 225–26; Stokes, *Company Shops*, p. 70.

33. Raleigh *Daily Sentinel*, 9 July, 6, 9, 10, 16, 17 Dec. 1869.

34. *Wilmington Journal*, 2 Jan. 1869; Raleigh *Daily Sentinel*, 7, 11, 17 Nov. 1868.

35. See Raleigh *Daily Sentinel*, 20, 28 Apr. 1871; and Smith's reply in *Raleigh Daily Telegram*, 27 Apr. 1871.

36. *Greensboro Patriot*, 28 July, 4 Aug. 1870; Raleigh *Daily Sentinel*, 19 Dec. 1870, 9, 14 June 1871. Cf. denial by W. A. Strayhorn, gravel engineer, in Raleigh *North Carolina Standard*, 19 Dec. 1870.

37. Raleigh *Daily Sentinel*, 17 Dec. 1870, 5 Jan. 1871.

38. NCRR, *Messages to the People*, pp. 3–4.

39. See Price, "Railroads and Reconstruction," pp. 276–79.

40. See Miller, *Railroads and the Granger Laws*, p. 32ff; Licht, *Working for the Railroad*, pp. 120–21.

41. Report of Governor Worth to the General Assembly, 8 Dec. 1866, in Board of Internal Improvements minutes, Archives; Raleigh *North Carolina Standard*, 27 Jan. 1866.

42. Constitution of North Carolina, in *Public Laws*, 1868–69, pp. 15, 18.

43. Ibid., 1868–69, chap. 270, secs. 97–100; chap. 271.

44. N.C. *Senate Journal*, 1868–69, p. 263; letter from "Stockholder," in *Hillsborough Recorder*, 2 Mar. 1870.

45. Horace Raper, in his biography of Holden, says that Holden had persuaded Harris in February 1868 to run for superintendent of public works instead of trying for the NCRR presidency, which had previously been promised him. Raper provides no source for this statement (Raper, *William W. Holden*, p. 290n).

46. Report of Superintendent of Public Works, 9 Dec. 1869, N.C. *Public Documents*, 1869–70, #5, p. 5; *New-Berne Daily Times*, 3, 21, 26 Aug. 1869.

47. W. A. Smith to W. W. Holden, 4 June 1869; L. P. Olds to Holden, 21 June 1869, in Governors' Papers, Archives.

48. Report of Superintendent of Public Works, 9 Dec. 1869, N.C. *Public Documents*, 1869–70, #5, pp. 5–6; Raleigh *Daily Sentinel*, 8, 9, 12 July, 2 Aug., 18 Nov. 1869; Raleigh *North Carolina Standard*, 7, 10, 30 July, 2, 3, 4 Aug. 1869; NCRR, *Annual Report*, 1869, pp. 4–5.

49. Report of Superintendent of Public Works, 9 Dec. 1869, N.C. *Public Documents*, 1869–70, #5, pp. 6–8, 11–12.

50. Remarks of Mr. Ingram in House debate, in Raleigh *North Carolina Standard*, 3 Mar. 1870; Raleigh *Daily Sentinel*, 9 June 1871.

51. N.C. *Public Laws*, 1869–70, chap. 112.

52. Price, "Railroads and Reconstruction," p. 584.

53. See S. F. Phillips to W. A. Smith, 25 May 1871, in XXIII. Correspondence, v. 25, NCRR Records, Archives; Raleigh *Daily Sentinel*, 9 June 1871.

54. Report of President and Speaker, N.C. *Public Documents*, 1871–72, #19, pp. 2–3.

55. *Greensboro Patriot*, 14 Sept. 1871. Caldwell's appointees included William A. Smith and Rufus Barringer; three were reappointments from 1870, five were new. See *Raleigh Daily Telegram*, 14 July 1871.

56. Board of directors' minutes, 30 June 1871, in XXVI. Minutes, v. 63, NCRR Records, Archives.

57. Stafford, *Joseph B. Stafford vs. Ed. J. Warren*; Resolution and Report in Regard to the Lease, N.C. *Public Documents*, 1871–72, #27, pp. 13, 69–70; *Raleigh Daily Telegram*, 9 July 1871; Raleigh *Daily Sentinel*, 10 July, 21 Sept. 1871.

58. Raleigh *Daily Sentinel*, 10, 17 July 1871; *Greensboro Patriot*, 13 July 1871.

59. Minutes of Greensboro stockholders' meeting, 13 July 1871, in XXVI. Minutes, v. 68, NCRR Records, Archives.

60. Ibid.; J. A. Hedrick to B. S. Hedrick, 17 July 1871, Hedrick Papers, Duke; Thomas Webb, *Thomas Webb vs. NCRR*, p. 4; Resolution and Report in Regard to the Lease, N.C. *Public Documents*, 1871–72, #27, pp. 70, 73; *Raleigh Daily Telegram*, 12, 15 July 1871; Raleigh *Daily Sentinel*, 15, 17 July 1871; *Greensboro Patriot*, 13 July 1871; *Wilmington Journal*, 14 July 1871.

61. *Greensboro Patriot*, 21 Sept. 1871.

62. *Clark* v. *Stanly*, 66 N.C. *Reports* 60; Cecil K. Brown, *State Movement*, pp. 177–78.

63. See Raleigh *Daily Sentinel*, 22 July 1870.

64. This is calculated by dividing the excess of receipts over expenditures in 1870–71 ($361,063) by the cost of constructing the road as given by President Fisher in 1859 ($4,912,653).

65. NCRR, *Annual Report*, 1871, p. 5. See the glowing commendation of Smith's management by the stockholders' finance committee in 1870 (Ibid., 1870, p. 16).

66. Ibid., 1870, p. 13.

67. Ibid., 1868, pp. 7–9.

68. Ibid., 1871, p. 11.

69. Ibid., 1871, pp. 4, 11. In 1872, nearly a year after the lease, Smith and Lea reported that $790,000 of the 1867 bonds had been issued, that the bonded debt (old and new) was $550,000, and the total debt (bonded and floating) was $598,000 (Ibid., 1872, pp. 8–9, 17). By that time the NCRR managers had little more to do than collect rent from the R&DRR and decide on its allocation. The annual rental amounted to $260,000. Of that amount about $120,000 was required to pay the

interest on the debt and build up the sinking fund on schedule. The remaining $140,000 could be devoted to retiring the debt early or paying dividends or both. See ibid., 1872, pp. 4–5, 8; W. A. Smith to C. H. Brogden, 13 Jan. 1875, in N.C. *Public Documents*, 1874–75, #18, p. 4.

70. See Stover, "Southern Railroad Receivership," pp. 44–45.

71. Raleigh *Daily Sentinel*, 4, 9 Jan., 10 Apr., 9 Aug. 1869; NCRR, *Annual Report*, 1870, p. 8.

72. Raleigh *Daily Sentinel*, 8 Feb., 4 Mar., 10 Apr., 9 Aug. 1869, 1 Feb. 1870; Raleigh *North Carolina Standard*, 12 Feb. 1869; F. A. Stagg to H. W. Fries, 22 Mar. 1870, in XXIII. Correspondence, v. 52, NCRR Records, Archives.

73. Raleigh *Daily Sentinel*, 9, 23 Jan., 8 Feb., 4 Mar., 10 Apr., 9 Aug. 1869; Raleigh *North Carolina Standard*, 18 Oct. 1869; NCRR, *To the Stockholders, October 20th, 1869*, p. 1.

74. Raleigh *Daily Sentinel*, 1 Feb., 17 Sept. 1870, 4, 31 Oct. 1871; NCRR, report to superintendent of public works, 31 May 1870, in Treasurer and Comptroller's Papers, Box 19, Archives; C. M. Crump to J. C. Justice, 27 Aug. 1870, in XXIII. Correspondence, v. 53, NCRR Records, Archives.

75. Quoted in Raleigh *Daily Sentinel*, 29 Oct. 1869.

76. NCRR, *Annual Report*, 1869, pp. 6, 26; Raleigh *North Carolina Standard*, 18 Dec. 1869.

77. Resolution of board, 18 Jan. 1870, in XXVI. Minutes, v. 63, NCRR Records, Archives.

78. N.C. *Public Laws*, 1869–70, chap. 47.

79. Directors' minutes, 16 Feb. 1870, in XXVI. Minutes, v. 63, NCRR Records, Archives; Report of State Treasurer, 1870, N.C. *Public Documents*, 1870–71, #4, p. 4.

80. See Charlotte *Western Democrat*, 22 Feb. 1870; *Greensboro Patriot*, 24 Feb. 1870.

81. Letter of W. W. Holden in Raleigh *News and Observer*, 1 Dec. 1881.

82. N.C. *Public Laws*, 1870–71, chap. 39; Cecil K. Brown, *State Movement*, p. 264.

83. Directors' minutes, 16 Dec. 1870, in XXVI. Minutes, v. 63, NCRR Records, Archives.

84. See Raleigh *Daily Sentinel*, 19 Jan. 1871.

85. Cecil K. Brown, *State Movement*, pp. 269–73; *NCRR vs. Anthony H. Swasey*, pp. 14, 17.

Chapter 20

1. Goodrich, *Government Promotion of American Canals and Railroads*, pp. 289–92. See also Goodrich, "Revulsion against Internal Improvements," pp. 161–64, 168–69; Hartz, "Laissez-Faire Thought in Pennsylvania," pp. 74–77; Heath, "Public Railroad Construction," pp. 49–51; Reed, *New Orleans and the Railroads*, pp. 84–86.

2. See, regarding the Western and Atlantic Railroad in Georgia, Goodrich, *Government Promotion of American Canals and Railroads*, pp. 118–19, 211; and regarding the Chesapeake and Ohio Canal in Maryland, Sanderlin, *Great National Project*, pp. 208–9, 220, 225–26, 229, 248, 286–87.

3. See also Trelease, "The Passive Voice."

4. N.C., *Ordinances and Resolutions, 1866*, chap. 21, pp. 47–49.

5. Raleigh *Daily Sentinel*, 23 May, 24 July, 22 Aug. 1866.

6. NCRR Charter, sec. 41, in *Annual Report*, 1850, p. 17; Raleigh *Daily Sentinel*, 22 Aug. 1866.

7. Raleigh *Daily Sentinel*, 2 Nov. 1866; N.C. *Public Laws*, 1866–67, chap. 106, pp. 177–78.

8. Raleigh *North Carolina Standard*, 13 Aug. 1868. These obstacles did not keep the House of Commons from voting in February 1867 to transfer $500,000 of its NCRR stock to another projected railroad (Charlotte *Western Democrat*, 26 Feb. 1867). The Senate did not concur.

9. Raleigh *Daily Sentinel*, 22 Aug. 1866.

10. NCRR, *Annual Report*, 1866, pp. 3–4.

11. N.C., *Memorial [of NCRR] to the Honorable General Assembly*, [1866].

12. Ibid.; NCRR, minutes of called stockholders' meeting, 12 Dec. 1866, Microfilm S.79.2 N&P, Archives; Raleigh *Daily Sentinel*, 12, 18 Dec. 1866.

13. Report of the governor, 8 Dec. 1866, with editorial endorsement, in Raleigh *Daily Sentinel*, 18 Jan. 1867. The *Sentinel* held this opinion until Josiah Turner took over the paper in December 1868. See issues of 20 July 1867 and 5 Aug. 1868.

14. Raleigh *North Carolina Standard*, 27 Jan. 1866.

15. From record of Senate debate in ibid., 6 Jan. 1859.

16. Raleigh *Daily Sentinel*, 18 Dec. 1866; Raleigh *North Carolina Standard*, 22 Dec. 1866.

17. Raleigh *Daily Sentinel*, 9 Feb. 1867.

18. Ibid., 13, 16 Feb. 1867.

19. Raleigh *Daily Sentinel*, 19 Feb. 1867.

20. "Veritas," in *Greensboro Patriot*, 19 July 1867.

21. Summers, *Railroads, Reconstruction, and the Gospel of Prosperity*, pp. 261–63.

22. N.C. *House Journal*, 1868–69, p. 576; *Sentinel—Extra. What we know*; Price, "Railroads and Reconstruction," pp. 420–27; Price, "Railroad Schemes of George W. Swepson," pp. 35–40.

23. See Charlotte *Western Democrat*, 21 July 1868; Raleigh *North Carolina Standard*, 21 July 1868; Raleigh *Daily Sentinel*, 5 Aug. 1868; *Greensboro Patriot*, 21 Jan. 1869.

24. Raleigh *North Carolina Standard*, 4 June 1869.

25. Letter of W. A. Caldwell in *Greensboro Patriot*, 11 Nov. 1869; W. A. Smith to W. A. Graham, 25 Nov. 1869, Graham Papers, SHC.

26. E. Belo to D. F. Caldwell, 11 Dec. 1869, Caldwell Papers, SHC; W. A. Smith to W. A. Graham, 2 Dec. 186[9?], in 1866 folder, Graham Papers, SHC.

27. *Raleigh Daily Telegram*, 15, 17, 25 Mar. 1871. See also Raleigh *Carolina Era*, 31 Aug. 1871.

28. See Raleigh *Daily Sentinel*, 14 Dec. 1869, 29, 31 Jan., 1, 2 (including quotation), 9, 19, 21 Feb., 29 Dec. 1870. See also opposition by the Charlotte *Western Democrat*, 4 Apr. 1871.

29. Governor's message, 16 Nov. 1869, N.C. *Public Documents*, 1869–70, #1, p. 8; governor's message, 22 Nov. 1870, ibid., 1870–71, #1, pp. 6–7.

30. See Cecil K. Brown, *State Movement*, pp. 269–76; state auditor's report for 1881–82, N.C. *Public Documents*, 1883, #4.

31. N.C. *House Journal*, 1858–59, p. 124; N.C. *Senate Journal*, 1865–66, p. 176; Raleigh *Daily Sentinel*, 3 Mar. 1866. For continuing efforts in 1866, see report of the A&NCRR president and board, June 1866, in [Stanly et al.], *To the Stockholders of the NCRR and the A&NCRR*, p. 8.

32. NCRR, *Annual Report*, 1866, pp. 42–47.

33. *Wilmington Journal*, as reported in Raleigh *Daily Sentinel*, 23 Nov. 1866; Charlotte *Western Democrat*, 6 Mar., 8 May, 17, 24 July 1866.

34. Raleigh *Daily Sentinel*, 24 Nov. 1866; Charlotte *Western Democrat*, 24 July 1866.

35. Letter of "A Stockholder in Both Roads," in Raleigh *North Carolina Standard*, 3 June 1869. Cecil Brown's superb study of North Carolina's nineteenth-century effort to create a statewide railway system is openly sympathetic to that objective and laments its defeat. Yet Brown regretfully concludes that the two ports at New Bern and Beaufort/Morehead City were fatally flawed and the state network should have led to Norfolk. See *State Movement*, esp. pp. 280–82.

36. NCRR, *Annual Report*, 1866, pp. 4–5.

37. For eloquent reports on the A&NCRR's problems and its efforts to combat them, see its *Annual Report*, 1866, p. 4; 1868, pp. 9–13.

38. See "A Member of the Legislature," in Raleigh *Daily Sentinel*, 22 June 1869.

39. Raleigh *North Carolina Standard*, 14 Dec. 1868, 26 Jan. 1869; N.C. *Public Laws*, 1868–69, chap. 27.

40. NCRR, *Annual Report*, 1869, p. 12. See also W. A. Smith to W. A. Graham, 29 May 1869, Graham Papers, SHC.

41. Raleigh *Daily Sentinel*, 7 Jan. 1869; Raleigh *North Carolina Standard*, 21 May 1869; *Greensboro Patriot*, 7 Jan., 20, 27 May 1869.

Letters to the editors were much more committed. For affirmative arguments in newspapers and elsewhere, see the letter of "NCRR Stockholder" in *Standard*, 8 Dec. 1868; another under the same designation in *Sentinel*, 28 May 1869; letter of "A Friend of Internal Improvement," in *Standard*, 11 Jan. 1869; speech of A. S. Seymour in House debate, ibid., 21 Jan. 1869; "Iota," in *Sentinel*, 23 June 1869; *Consolidation of the A&NCRR and the NCRR*; Stanly, *To the Stockholders of the NCRR*; [Stanly et al.], *To the Stockholders of the NCRR and the A&NCRR*.

For opposing views, see printed communication from W. A. Smith to the NCRR stockholders, 29 Dec. 1868, in Swepson Papers, Archives; Smith, *Is it to the Interest of the NCRR to Consolidate?* (reprinted in *Standard*, 4 Jan. 1869); letter of "A Radical Railroad Man," in ibid., 7 Jan. 1869; speech of J. Sinclair in House debate, ibid., 20 Jan. 1869; letter of "A Stockholder in Both Roads," ibid., 3 June 1869 (reprinted in *Sentinel*, 7 June 1869); NCRR, *To the Stockholders, May 18, 1869* (reprinted in *Standard*, 24 June 1869).

42. Printed invitation from E. R. Stanly addressed to W. A. Graham, May 1869, Graham Papers, SHC; Stanly to W. W. Holden, 1 May 1869, Governors' Papers, Archives.

43. See Charlotte *Daily Carolina Times*, 5, 7, 8 June 1869; Charlotte *Western Democrat*, 1, 8 June 1869; Raleigh *North Carolina Standard*, 9 June 1869.

44. Raleigh *Daily Sentinel*, 10 June 1869; W. A. Smith's letter of invitation to W. A. Graham, 6 June 1869, Graham Papers, SHC.

45. Raleigh *Daily Sentinel*, 18 June 1869; *Greensboro Patriot*, 24 June 1869. See also Charlotte *Daily Carolina Times*, 12, 16, 19 June 1869.

46. Raleigh *North Carolina Standard*, 28 June, 10 July, 6 Aug. 1869.

47. *New-Berne Daily Times*, 11 July, 3, 21, 26 Aug. 1869.

48. NCRR, *Annual Report*, 1869, pp. 5–6; Raleigh *Daily Sentinel*, 9 July 1869. Turner printed the text of Smith's speech in *Sentinel*, 19 July 1869.

49. Raleigh *North Carolina Standard*, 10, 11, 12, 18 Feb. 1870; E. R. Stanly to D. F. Caldwell, 16 Feb. 1870, Caldwell Papers, SHC.

50. Board of directors' resolution, 16 Feb. 1870, in XXVI. Minutes, v. 63, NCRR Records, Archives.

51. Letter of W. A. Smith in Raleigh *North Carolina Standard*, 22 Feb. 1870.

52. Raleigh *Daily Sentinel*, 3, 21 Mar. 1871; *Raleigh Daily Telegram*, 28 Mar. 1871; Charlotte *Western Democrat*, 4 Apr. 1871; N.C. *Public Laws*, 1870–71, chap. 270.

53. NCRR, *Annual Report*, 1871, p. 6.

54. Cecil K. Brown, *State Movement*, pp. 163–64.

55. R&GRR President W. J. Hawkins, in R&GRR, *Annual Report*, 1871, pp. 8–9.

56. J. Turner to W. J. Hawkins, 1 Aug. 1867, Andrews Papers, SHC; board of directors' minutes, 16 Aug. 1867, NCRR Office; W. A. Smith to D. F. Caldwell, 1 Nov. 1869, Caldwell Papers, SHC. For thoughts about a lease in 1867, see E. G. Ghio of the S&RRR to A. B. Andrews, 28 Aug. 1867, and H. E. Orr to Andrews, 6 Oct. 1867, Andrews Papers, SHC; *Greensboro Patriot*, 18 Oct. 1867.

57. These figures were reported by Josiah Turner, and I have not seen them contradicted (Raleigh *Daily Sentinel*, 21 Jan. 1870).

58. W. J. Hawkins to President and Directors of NCRR, 14 Oct. 1869, orders of board to negotiate and to call a stockholders' meeting, all with board minutes for October 1869, in XXVI. Minutes, v. 63, NCRR Records, Archives.

59. NCRR, *To the Stockholders, October 29, 1869*.

60. Raleigh *North Carolina Standard*, 18 Oct. 1869; NCRR, *To the Stockholders, October 20th, 1869*, p. 1.

61. For information on the Chatham Railroad, see Price, "Railroads and Reconstruction," pp. 327–30; Cecil K. Brown, *State Movement*, pp. 168–70.

62. For Smith's defense of the R&G lease offer, see NCRR, *To the Stockholders, October 20th, 1869*, p. 1; ibid., *October 29, 1869*; Smith to W. A. Graham, 2 Nov. 1869, Graham Papers, SHC.

63. For Turner's opposition, see Raleigh *Daily Sentinel*, 20, 21, 23 (including the bribery charge), 25, 26, 27, 29, 30 Oct., 4, 5, 6, 8, 10, 11 Nov. 1869, 29, 31 Jan. 1870. For other papers, see Raleigh *North Carolina Standard*, 18, 23, 26, 27 Oct., 4, 10, 11 Nov. 1869; *Greensboro Patriot*, 21 Oct. 1869; Charlotte *Western Democrat*, 26 Oct. 1869; Charlotte *Daily Carolina Times*, 10 Nov. 1869; *Rutherford Star*, in *Sentinel*, 28 Oct. 1869. The *New-Berne Daily Times* saw a lease as the nemesis of consolidation with the A&NCRR, and opposed it bitterly (*Times*, 21, 24 Oct. 1869). Smith eventually wrote to the *Sentinel* refuting some of the charges launched against him and the lease (*Sentinel*, 8 Nov. 1869).

64. NCRR, *Proceedings of a Called Meeting, November 11th, 1869*; Raleigh *Daily Sentinel*, 12, 13, 15 Nov. 1869; Raleigh *North Carolina Standard*, 17 Nov. 1869; Charlotte *Western Democrat*, 16 Nov. 1869. The private stockholders also voted, as in 1866, to memorialize the legislature in favor of private stockholder control of the road. Even less came of the request than previously.

65. Governor's message, 16 Nov. 1869, N.C. *Public Documents*, 1869–70, #1, p. 8.

66. *Greensboro Patriot*, 13 Mar., 1 May 1868.

67. NCRR, *Annual Report*, 1870, pp. 23–24; contract with NWNCRR, 22 July 1869, in XXII. Contracts, v. 19, NCRR Records, Archives; Price, "Railroads and Reconstruction," pp. 499–508.

68. NCRR, *Annual Report*, 1870, pp. 4–5; W. A. Smith to W. A. Graham, 3 Oct. 1870, Graham Papers, SHC.

69. Smith to Graham, 3 Oct. 1870, Graham Papers, SHC.

70. Smith to Graham, 2 Nov. 1869, ibid.

71. *Greensboro Patriot*, 1, 8 Dec. 1870, 26 Jan. (including card from W. A. Smith), 9 Feb., 9 Mar. 1871; Raleigh *Daily Sentinel*, 21, 24, 25, 26, 28 Jan., 3, 18 Feb., 3, 4 Mar. 1871.

72. N.C. *Public Laws*, 1870–71, chap. 177, pp. 265–66.

73. NCRR, *Annual Report*, 1871, p. 6; board of directors' minutes, 16, 30 June 1871; resolution approving contract, with minutes for August 1871; minutes and accompanying resolutions of September 1871, all in XXVI. Minutes, v. 63, NCRR Records, Archives; *Winston Sentinel*, in Charlotte *Western Democrat*, 29 Aug. 1871; *Greensboro Patriot*, 21 Sept. 1871; Price, "Railroads and Reconstruction," p. 507.

Chapter 21

1. For a comprehensive account of these developments, see Klein, *Great Richmond Terminal*, pp. 18–22, or the similar discussion in his *History of the Louisville & Nashville Railroad*, pp. 60–69. See further Klein's "Southern Railroad Leaders."

2. See Trelease, "The Passive Voice."

3. See report of R&DRR committee on examination, in R&DRR, *Annual Report*, 1868, p. 299.

4. NCRR, *Annual Report*, 1872, pp. 12–13; Klein, *Great Richmond Terminal*, pp. 55–60.

5. Stover, "Pennsylvania Railroad's Southern Rail Empire," p. 28.

6. See ibid., pp. 28–31; Klein, *Great Richmond Terminal*, pp. 61–62; Harrison, *History of the Southern Railway*, pp. 93–94.

7. For accounts of the Pennsylvania's southward expansion, see Stover, "Pennsylvania Railroad's Southern Rail Empire," pp. 31–36; Grodinsky, *Transcontinental Railway Strategy*, pp. 15–19; Chandler, *Visible Hand*, pp. 153–54; Klein, *Great Richmond Terminal*, pp. 11, 61–62; Ward, *J. Edgar Thomson*, pp. 150–51.

8. R&DRR directors' minute book, 1869–83, p. 13, R&DRR Records, VPI; *Hillsborough Recorder*, 13 July 1870.

9. NCRR, *Annual Report*, 1870, pp. 4–5, 9; 1872, pp. 10–11.

10. R&DRR directors' minute book, 1869–83, p. 13, R&DRR Records, VPI; W. A. Smith to W. A. Graham, 3 Oct. 1870, Graham Papers, SHC.

11. Letter of W. A. Smith in Raleigh *Daily Sentinel*, 2 Nov. 1870; NCRR, *Annual Report*, 1872, p. 12; W. A. Smith to W. A. Graham, 3, 8 Oct. 1870, Graham Papers, SHC.

12. Board of directors' minutes, 8 Nov. 1870, in XXVI. Minutes, v. 63, NCRR Records, Archives; Raleigh *Daily Sentinel*, 10, 12 Nov. 1870.

13. W. Johnston to A. B. Andrews, 20, 21 Nov. 1870, Andrews Papers, SHC.

14. Draft of letter, A. B. Andrews to W. Johnston, 23 Nov. 1870, Andrews Papers, SHC.

15. Governor's message, 22 Nov. 1870, N.C. *Public Documents*, 1870–71, #1, pp. 6–7. It was a measure of Josiah Turner's paranoia where Holden was concerned that he continued to charge the governor with scheming to alienate the road. See Raleigh *Daily Sentinel*, 29 Dec. 1870.

16. Raleigh *Daily Sentinel*, 24 Jan. 1871; NCRR, *Annual Report*, 1872, p. 12.

17. W. J. Hawkins to P. C. Cameron, 23, 27 June 1871, Cameron Family Papers, SHC; W. Johnston to A. B. Andrews, 25 June 1871, Andrews Papers, SHC; P. C. Cameron to W. S. Battle, 29 June 1871, Battle Family Papers, SHC.

18. W. Johnston to A. B. Andrews, 21 July, 4, 7 Aug. 1871, Andrews Papers, SHC.

19. R&DRR directors' minute book, 1869–83, p. 43, R&DRR Records, VPI; printed circulars, 26 June 1871, from R&GRR board of directors and from B. F. Moore et al., W. J. Hawkins to P. C. Cameron, 27 June 1871, Cameron Family Papers, SHC; W. Johnston to A. B. Andrews, 25 June, 4, 7 Aug. 1871, Andrews Papers, SHC; Raleigh *Daily Sentinel*, 29 June, 3, 6, 8 July 1871.

20. NCRR, *Annual Report*, 1871, pp. 5–6.

21. Raleigh *Daily Sentinel*, 11, 31 Oct. 1870, 10, 17 July 1871.

22. See ibid., 17 July 1871; Thomas Webb, *Thomas Webb vs. NCRR*, p. 5.

23. Raleigh *Daily Sentinel*, 19 July 1871.

24. P. C. Cameron to sister, 17 July 1871, Cameron Family Papers, SHC; *Raleigh Daily Telegram*, 21 July 1871.

25. Resolution and Report in Regard to the Lease, N.C. *Public Documents*, 1871–72, #27, pp. 67, 68, 71; NCRR, *Annual Report*, 1872, p. 13.

26. *Greensboro Patriot*, 13 July 1871.

27. R&DRR directors' minute book, 1869–83, pp. 42, 45, R&DRR Records, VPI; A. S. Buford to W. A. Graham, 26 July, 23 Aug. 1871, Graham Papers, SHC; legal opinion of Ralph Gorrell, 21 Aug. 1871, in XXIII. Correspondence, v. 25, NCRR Records, Archives.

28. R&DRR directors' minute book, 1869–83, p. 44, R&DRR Records, VPI; W. R. Albright, in Resolution and Report in Regard to the Lease, N.C. *Public Documents*, 1871–72, #27, p. 72. Cf. J. R. Harrison testimony, saying that no comparable offer had ever been made from the R&D before September (Ibid., p. 66). None is mentioned in the surviving board minutes of June, July, or August 1871.

29. A. S. Buford to W. A. Smith, 6 Sept. 1871, and handwritten copy of lease, in XXII. Contracts, v. 19, NCRR Records, Archives; Resolution and Report in Regard to the Lease, N.C. *Public Documents*, 1871–72, #27, pp. 2–4, 58–75.

30. The lease appears in NCRR, *Annual Report*, 1872, pp. 37–47, and in Resolution and Report in Regard to the Lease, N.C. *Public Documents*, 1871–72, #27, pp. 47–57. For the property inventory, see XV. Property Inventory, v. 93–96, NCRR Records, Archives.

31. Resolution and Report in Regard to the Lease, N.C. *Public Documents*, 1871–72, #27, pp. 45–47. Smith's letter also appears in *Greensboro Patriot*, 14 Sept. 1871, and Raleigh *Carolina Era*, 16 Sept. 1871.

32. R&DRR, *Annual Report*, 1871, pp. 581–82.

33. W. A. Graham to R. Gorrell, 19 Sept. 1871, Gorrell Papers, SHC. See also Raleigh *Daily Sentinel*, 20 Sept., 2, 3 Oct. 1871. For favorable newspaper comment, see Charlotte *Western Democrat*, 19 Sept. 1871; *Hillsborough Recorder*, 13 Dec. 1871.

34. NCRR Charter, sec. 19, in *Annual Report*, 1850, p. 10; Resolution and Report in Regard to the Lease, N.C. *Public Documents*, 1871–72, #27, p. 75; board of directors' minutes, 27 Oct. 1871, in XXVI. Minutes, v. 63, NCRR Records, Archives.

35. *Clark v. Stanly*, 66 *N.C. Reports* 60.

36. Resolution and Report in Regard to the Lease, N.C. *Public Documents*, 1871–72, #27, pp. 1–18.

37. Ibid., pp. 16–18, 71, 74; NCRR, *Messages to the People*, p. 6.

38. NCRR, *Annual Report*, 1872, pp. 4, 10–14.

39. *State v. R&DRR et al.*, 72 *N.C. Reports* 634, 73 ibid. 527; N.C. *Public Laws*, 1874–75, chap. 159, pp. 185–86; R&DRR, *Annual Report*, 1875, pp. 325–26; Cecil K. Brown, *State Movement*, pp. 179–81.

40. Stokes, *Company Shops*, pp. 121–25, 137.

41. Ibid., pp. 124–38.

42. Adams, "North Carolina's Railroads," p. 8.

43. Ibid.; NCRR, *Annual Report*, 1891, pp. 9–10; 1893, pp. 13–14; 1894, p. 1.

44. Stover, *Railroads of the South*, pp. 233–53. The most detailed account of these events, and a superb generic study of railway consolidation, is Klein, *Great Richmond Terminal*.

45. See Jeffrey J. Crow and Robert F. Durden, *Maverick Republican in the Old North State: A Political Biography of Daniel L. Russell* (Baton Rouge: Louisiana State University Press, 1977), pp. 79–116; and Allen W. Trelease, "The Fusion Legislatures of 1895 and 1897: A Roll-Call Analysis of the North Carolina House of Representatives," *North Carolina Historical Review*, 57 (July 1980): 301–5.

46. See Cecil K. Brown, *State Movement*, pp. 265–76.

47. For Robert J. Brown, see *Greensboro News and Record*, 29 Oct. 1985.

48. N.C. Department of Transportation, *Report on the NCRR and A&NCRR*, pp. 2, 7; N.C. Legislative Research Commission, *Railroad Operations*, p. A-5. This total includes several years' worth of state dividends in the 1870s and early 1880s that were actually paid out to state bondholders under the Swasey decision.

49. Klein and Yamamura, "Growth Strategies of Southern Railroads," pp. 365–70.

50. NCRR, *Annual Report*, 1895, p. 5.

51. Adams, "North Carolina's Railroads," p. 13.

52. Ibid., pp. 12–13.

53. For a discussion of the state's current interests in both the NCRR and the A&NCRR, and its options for the newly merged roads in 1994, see ibid., pp. 2–16.

54. *Greensboro News and Record*, 19 June, 21 Aug. 1987, 15 Aug. 1989. For a sketch of the A&NC's history, see N.C. Department of Transportation, *Report on the NCRR and A&NCRR*, pp. 4–5.

55. Ibid., p. 14; *Greensboro News and Record*, 24 Apr., 12 July 1986.

Chapter 22

1. Jenks, "Railroads as an Economic Force," pp. 4–11; Lebergott, *The Americans*, pp. 93, 98–199; Fishlow, *American Railroads*, pp. 14–16, 23.

2. For a discussion of this process in two northern Virginia counties, see Schlotterbeck, "The 'Social Economy' of an Upper South Community," pp. 19–22.

3. For an argument in behalf of the last theory, see Weiss, "Southern Business Never Had It So Good!" pp. 28–33.

4. *Raleigh Daily Telegram*, 18 Apr. 1871. See also Raleigh *Daily Sentinel*, 13 May 1868.

5. *Greensboro Patriot*, 27 Dec. 1899; Wright, *Old South, New South*, pp. 34–38, 107–11.

6. See Goldfield, *Cotton Fields and Skyscrapers*, pp. 65–66; Raymond L. Cohn, "Local Manufacturing," pp. 80–83, 88.

7. Coatsworth, "Indispensable Railroads," pp. 953–58.

8. Goldfield, *Cotton Fields and Skyscrapers*, pp. 67–68.

9. Ibid., pp. 32, 34, 65; Goldfield, *Urban Growth in the Age of Sectionalism*, pp. 236–37.

10. Goldfield, *Cotton Fields and Skyscrapers*, pp. 89–90.

11. See Jenks, "Railroads as an Economic Force," pp. 6–11; Chandler, *Railroads: The Nation's First Big Business*; Chandler, *Visible Hand*.

12. Report of the Committee on Internal Improvements, N.C. *Public Documents*, 1854–55, #21, p. 304.

13. *Lexington and Yadkin Flag*, 7 Dec. 1855; NCRR, *Annual Report*, 1859, p. 12.

14. O'Brien, *Legal Fraternity*, pp. 146–47.

15. *Hillsborough Recorder*, 14 Apr. 1852; Connor, *North Carolina*, 2:56.

16. Chamberlain, *History of Wake County*, pp. 211–13; Chamberlain, *This Was Home*, pp. 80–81; John B. Alexander, *History of Mecklenburg County*, p. 379.

17. Charlotte *Western Democrat*, 28 Aug. 1855. For NCRR policies, see Chapters 7 and 17, above.

18. For the predictions of Walter Gwynn in 1851, see NCRR, *Report of the Chief Engineer on the Survey, 1851*, p. 21. There were ten counties until 1881, when Durham County was created from Orange and Wake.

19. Pressly and Scofield, *Farm Real Estate Values*, pp. 13–14. This book begins with the 1850 census.

20. The state comptroller reportedly said that the landed property along the NCRR was valued at $11,166,687 in 1853 and at $20,821,976 in 1860, an increase of almost 90 percent (speech of Mr. Love in state convention, reported in Raleigh *Daily Sentinel*, 23 June 1866).

21. *Greensboro Patriot*, 25 June 1858.

22. Escott, "Yeoman Independence and the Market," pp. 290–96; B. M. Jones, *Rail Roads Considered*, p. 27; *Lexington and Yadkin Flag*, 25 July 1856.

23. *Winston Sentinel*, quoted in Raleigh *North Carolina Standard*, 30 June 1858.

24. Hilgard, "Report on Cotton Production," pp. 21–22, 56.

25. For national cotton production, see U.S. Bureau of the Census, *Historical Statistics of the United States, Colonial Times to 1957* (Washington: Government Printing Office, 1960), pp. 301–2.

26. Ibid., pp. 297, 302.

27. O'Brien, *Legal Fraternity*, pp. 16, 61.

28. Wright, *Old South, New South*, pp. 43–44.

29. William Kenneth Boyd, *Story of Durham*, pp. 57–77; Durden, *Dukes of Durham*, p. 15.

30. U.S. Census, 1860, 3:430; 1880, 2:318.

31. Unfortunately the 1850, 1890, and 1900 censuses did not break down individual industries by county.

32. Griffin, "North Carolina: The Origin and Rise of the Cotton Textile Industry," p. 103.

33. Pierpont, "Development of the Textile Industry in Alamance," p. 55. Pierpont, in contrast with the census, mentions only six active mills in the county in 1880.

34. Raleigh *North Carolina Standard*, 13 Feb. 1869.

35. Pierpont, "Development of the Textile Industry in Alamance," pp. 53–54; Hall, Korstad, and Leloudis, "Cotton Mill People," pp. 247–48.

36. Phillips, "North Carolina's Rich Crescent," p. 186; Goldfield, *Cotton Fields and Skyscrapers*, p. 124.

37. Blicksilver, *Cotton Manufacturing*, p. 17.

38. U.S. Census, 1860, 3:420–34, 437; 1880, 2:160, 317–19. Again, the census does not give county data on individual industries after 1880.

39. The table includes the NCRR counties with and without Wake County, which

seems to have been erroneously reported in 1870. See also Tryon, *Household Manufactures*, pp. 370–74.

40. *Greensboro Patriot*, 14 Sept. 1850.

41. Wright, *Old South, New South*, p. 42.

42. Goldsboro *Republican and Patriot*, 28 Feb., 20 June, 22 Nov. 1854.

43. Goldsboro *Daily Messenger*, 15 Feb. 1870; Frank A. Daniels, *History of Wayne County*, chap. 10 (not paginated).

44. *Raleigh Daily Telegram*, 19 Apr. 1871.

45. Byrd, *Around and About Cary*, pp. 1–6, 25.

46. Raleigh *Daily Sentinel*, 30 Aug. 1867; Raleigh *North Carolina Standard*, 13 Feb. 1869; Kenzer, *Kinship and Neighborhood*, p. 116.

47. William Kenneth Boyd, *Story of Durham*, pp. 97–98. For accounts of Durham's early development, see ibid., p. 26ff; Durden, *Dukes of Durham*, p. 11ff; Kenzer, *Kinship and Neighborhood*, pp. 114–26.

48. Raleigh *North Carolina Star*, 10 Sept. 1851; *Raleigh Register*, 5 May 1855; *Fayetteville Observer*, quoted in *Hillsborough Recorder*, 14 Nov. 1855; *Recorder*, 18 Apr. 1860.

49. Kenzer, *Kinship and Neighborhood*, pp. 114–17; *Hillsborough Recorder*, 26 Jan. 1859, 14 June 1871.

50. Kenzer, *Kinship and Neighborhood*, pp. 32–33.

51. Whitaker, *Centennial History of Alamance*, pp. 138–40; Pierpont, "Development of the Textile Industry in Alamance," pp. 85–86.

52. Pierpont, "Development of the Textile Industry in Alamance," pp. 59–60, 74–75, 84–85.

53. See accounts of Greensboro in the *Raleigh Register*, 5 May 1855; *Greensboro Patriot*, 25 Apr. 1856.

54. Albright, *Greensboro*, pp. 101, 110; Arnett, *Greensboro*, pp. 167–68; Greensboro *The Topic*, 21 May 1869; Raleigh *Daily Sentinel*, 24 May 1869; Raleigh *North Carolina Standard*, 5 June 1869.

55. The first plant seems to have been new when described by the *Greensboro Patriot*, 5 June 1868. See also issues of 28 Jan., 11 Feb. 1869, 22 Dec. 1870, 16 Feb., 6 Apr. 1871; Raleigh *North Carolina Standard*, 13 Feb., 5 June 1869; Arnett, *Greensboro*, p. 167; Otto H. Olsen, *Carpetbagger's Crusade: The Life of Albion Winegar Tourgee* (Baltimore: Johns Hopkins University Press, 1965), pp. 176–78.

56. *Greensboro Patriot*, quoted in Raleigh *North Carolina Standard*, 1 Feb. 1869; *Greensboro Register*, 13 Oct. 1869; *Patriot*, 19 May 1870. See also *Standard*, 5 June 1869. For the number of businesses, see Iota, in Raleigh *Daily Sentinel*, 24 May 1869. Iota surely exaggerated in claiming that the town had gained a thousand people since the war, for a total of over 4,000. The 1870 census, the first to list Greensboro separately, just as surely undercounted it at 497.

57. Kipp, "Urban Growth," esp. pp. 24–27, 53–55, 70–117, 153–54, 172–83. For Cone Mills, see Arnett, *Greensboro*, pp. 171–74.

58. *Greensboro Patriot*, 29 Oct. 1853, 20 Jan. 1855, 22 July 1859; Ebert, "Furniture Making in High Point," pp. 333–39.

59. Griffin, "North Carolina: The Origin and Rise of the Cotton Textile Industry," pp. 181–83; Fries, "One Hundred Years," pp. 17–19.

60. Matthews and Sink, *Wheels of Faith and Courage*, pp. 11–21; Sink and Matthews, *Pathfinders*, pp. 230–31; Sink, *Davidson County*, p. 13; Leonard, *Centennial History of Davidson*, pp. 344, 347, 351, 355–57, 362. For contemporary accounts of Thomas-

ville's early days, see *Greensboro Patriot*, 24 Aug. 1855, 26 June 1857, 4 May 1860, 26 Aug. 1869; Greensboro *Times*, 23 Oct. 1856; Raleigh *Daily Sentinel*, 6 July 1867.

61. *Greensboro Patriot*, 26 June 1857; Sink and Matthews, *Pathfinders*, pp. 83–84.

62. Charlotte *Western Democrat*, 28 Aug. 1855; Greensboro *Times*, 30 Oct. 1856.

63. Salisbury *Carolina Watchman*, 29 Jan. 1856; *Lexington and Yadkin Flag*, 1 Feb. 1856; Salisbury *Banner*, quoted in Charlotte *Western Democrat*, 10 Mar. 1857.

64. Salisbury *Carolina Watchman*, 28 Apr. 1857; *Greensboro Patriot*, 26 June 1857; Raleigh *North Carolina Standard*, 29 Aug. 1857, 13 Oct. 1858. For the history of the Boyden factory, see Louis Alexander Brown, *Salisbury Prison*, pp. 22–26.

65. Salisbury *Carolina Watchman*, 8 Sept. 1857; Raleigh *North Carolina Standard*, 13 Oct. 1858; Salisbury *Daily Union Banner*, 28, 29 Sept. 1865.

66. Brawley, *Rowan Story*, pp. 168, 215–24, 265–66; Beck, "Building the New South," pp. 447–70.

67. Brawley, *Rowan Story*, pp. 293–94; Triplette, "One-Industry Towns," pp. 133–34. For John McDonald, see Griffin, "Reconstruction of the North Carolina Textile Industry," p. 45.

68. Raleigh *North Carolina Star*, 15 Oct. 1851; Charlotte *North Carolina Whig*, 4 Feb., 22 Sept. 1852, 13 June 1854; Raleigh *North Carolina Standard*, 6 Oct. 1860.

69. Charlotte *Western Democrat*, 21 Sept., 28 Dec. 1858, 3 May 1859. In September 1862 Wilkes put the two enterprises up for sale, so as to join his brother in building the Piedmont Railroad between Greensboro and Danville (*Democrat*, 9, 16 Sept. 1862). For the navy yard, see Simmons and Lindsay, *Charlotte and Mecklenburg*, p. 11.

70. Blythe and Brockmann, *Hornets' Nest*, pp. 272–73; Tompkins, *History of Mecklenburg County*, pp. 151–52. For contemporary accounts of the city's early postwar growth, see Charlotte *Western Democrat*, 29 Aug. 1865, 6 Nov., 18 Dec. 1866, 4 June 1867, 27 July 1869, 18 Oct. 1870; Raleigh *North Carolina Standard*, 2 Nov. 1868, 30 Jan. 1869. For the Rock Island mill, see *Democrat*, 3 Dec. 1867.

71. See Scott, *Railroad Development Programs*, pp. 4–14.

72. Earley, "Quail Paradise," pp. 18–23.

73. Phifer, *Burke*, pp. 238–39, 244.

74. Browning and Parker, "Urbanization," pp. 54–57.

75. Cates, "Piedmont Crescent and the NCRR," pp. 1–9.

76. Phillips, "North Carolina's Rich Crescent," pp. 183–86.

77. Ibid., pp. 182, 185–86.

78. Birdsall and Florin, *Regional Landscapes*, p. 170.

BIBLIOGRAPHY

Primary Sources

Manuscript Collections

Duke University Manuscript Collection, Perkins Library, Durham, N.C.
  Joseph Fulton Boyd Papers
  William Alexander Graham Papers
  Benjamin Sherwood Hedrick Papers
  Gertrude Jenkins Papers
  John Marshall Otey Papers
  Isaac Richardson Paper
East Carolina University Manuscript Collection, University Library, Greenville, N.C.
  Sara Holt Arthur Collection
  John Herritage Bryan Papers
  Grimes-Bryan Papers
  Hugh Harrison Mills Collection
Friends Historical Collection, Guilford College, Greensboro, N.C.
  Nereus Mendenhall Collection
  Sarah F. Smiley Manuscript
Greensboro Historical Museum, Greensboro, N.C.
  Gorrell Family Papers
North Carolina Archives, Division of Archives and History, Raleigh, N.C.
  County Railroad Records: Davidson, Johnston, and Wake counties
  North Carolina Railroad Company Records
  North Carolina State Records
    Board of Internal Improvements Minutes, 1851–1912
    Governors' Letterbooks and Papers, 1850–71
    Supreme Court Records
    Treasurers' and Comptrollers' Papers:
      Internal Improvements
  Private Collections
    John H. Bryan Collection
    Edward Jones Hale Papers
    G. W. Pearson Collection
    David S. Reid Papers
    George W. Swepson Papers
    Zebulon Baird Vance Papers
    James I. Waddell Papers
    John D. Whitford Papers
    Jonathan Worth Papers
  United States Census, 1860. Manuscript Return, Orange County

North Carolina Railroad Company Office, Raleigh, N.C.
  Minutes of the Proceedings of the Board of Directors, 1850–84. 2 vols.
Southern Historical Collection, Wilson Library, University of North Carolina,
  Chapel Hill, N.C.
  Alexander Boyd Andrews I Papers
  Daniel Moreau Barringer Papers
  Battle Family Papers, Series A
  David Franklin Caldwell Papers
  Cameron Family Papers
  Edmund J. Cleveland Diary
  Davis and Walker Family Papers, Series A
  Fisher Family Papers
  Ralph Gorrell Papers
  William A. Graham Papers
  Hawkins Family Papers
  Hobbs-Mendenhall Papers
  Edwin M. Holt Diary
  Jones and Patterson Papers
  Thomas David Smith McDowell Papers
  George W. Mordecai Papers
  Andrew Jackson Rike Papers
  Marmaduke Swaim Robins Papers
  Cornelia Phillips Spencer Papers
  Springs Family Papers
  David L. Swain Papers
  Samuel McDowell Tate Papers
  Josiah Turner, Jr. Papers
  Zebulon Baird Vance Papers
  Thomas Webb Papers
  Mrs. J. S. Welborn Papers
  Calvin Henderson Wiley Papers
  Edmonia Cabell Wilkins Papers
  Jonathan Worth Papers
Virginia Polytechnic Institute and State University Library, Special Collections Department, Blacksburg, Va.
  North Carolina Railroad Company Records
  Northwestern North Carolina Railroad Company Records
  Richmond and Danville Railroad Company Records

North Carolina Official Publications

An Act to Consolidate the Atlantic and North Carolina Railroad Co. and the North Carolina Railroad Co. [Raleigh: 1869?] 4pp. North Carolina Collection, University of North Carolina, Chapel Hill.
Bill for the Completion of the North Carolina Railroad. *Public Documents*, 1854–55, #12.
Bill to Make the Killing of Stock by Railroads Prima Facie Evidence of Negligence. *Public Documents*, 1854–55, #22.
Department of Transportation. *Report on the North Carolina Railroad Company and At-*

lantic and North Carolina Railroad Company. [Raleigh]: 1976.

General Orders, No. 125, 2 July 1868. Relating to the Organization of the State Government. *Public Documents*, 1868–69, #4.

Legislative Research Commission. *Railroad Operations. Report to the General Assembly, 1981*. Raleigh: 1982.

Mauney, Ephraim. Memorial. *Public Documents*, 1858–59, #57. Also published separately.

Memorial [of NCRR] to the General Assembly, December 1856. *Public Documents*, 1856–57, #21.

Memorial [of NCRR] to the Honorable the General Assembly, with *House Bill No. 169, Sess. 1866–67. A Bill to Amend an Act to Incorporate the North Carolina Rail Road Company*. N.p. [1866].

Minority Report on the Bill to Incorporate the Greensboro and Danville Railroad Company. *Public Documents*, 1858–59, #48.

North Carolina Reports. State supreme court decisions.

Ordinances and Resolutions Passed by the North-Carolina State Convention, Second Session, 1866. Raleigh: W. W. Holden & Son, 1866.

Private Laws of the State of North Carolina, 1868.

Public Laws of the State of North Carolina, 1852–72.

Report of President of Senate and Speaker of House in Reference to their Action in Appointing Railroad Proxies and Directors. *Public Documents*, 1871–72, #19.

Report of the Commission to Investigate Fraud and Corruption Under Act of Assembly, Session 1871–72. *Public Documents*, 1871–72, #11.

Report of the Committee on Internal Improvements on the Bill for Completion of the North Carolina Railroad. *Public Documents*, 1854–55, Senate Document #21.

Report of the Joint Select Committee on the North Carolina Railroad. *Public Documents*, 1858–59, #71.

Report of the Joint Select Committee on the North Carolina Railroad. *Public Documents*, 1866–67.

Report of the State Treasurer, 1868, 1870. *Public Documents*, 1868–69, #5; 1870–71, #4.

Reports of the Superintendent of Public Works, 1869–72. *Public Documents*, 1869–70, #5; 1870–71, #14, 15; 1871–72, #30.

Report Upon the North Carolina Railroad. *Public Documents*, 1858–59, #74.

Resolution and Report in Regard to the Lease of the North Carolina Railroad. *Public Documents*, 1871–72, #27.

North Carolina Railroad Publications

Located in North Carolina Collection, University of North Carolina, Chapel Hill, unless otherwise noted.

Annual Reports, 1850–78, 1891–95. Title varies.

By-Laws and Regulations of the North Carolina Railroad Co. Raleigh: 1867.

Charter and By-Laws of the North Carolina Railroad, With the Proceedings of the First Meeting of Stockholders. Salisbury: 1850.

Circular to the Resident Engineers of the North Carolina Railroad. N.p. [1852].

Communication of the President of the N.C. Railroad Co. to the General Assembly. Raleigh: 1854.

Communincation [sic] *from the President of the N. Carolina Railroad, in Reply to the Report of the Chairman of the Joint Committee on the North-Carolina Railroad*. N.p. [1859]. Reprinted in Raleigh *North Carolina Standard*, 3 Mar. 1859.

_____. A variant edition of preceding, with same title but using name *N. C. Railroad* and containing an appendix of 14 Feb. 1859.

Disbursements by C. P. Mendenhall, Treasurer, of the N.C. Rail-Road Company, for the Fiscal Year . . . 1857 . . . 1858. Greensboro: 1859.

Messages to the People, by Maj. W. A. Smith, President N.C.R.R. Co. [Princeton, N.C.: 1874].

Proceedings of a Called Meeting of the North Carolina Rail Road Company. Held in Raleigh on November 11th, 1869. [Raleigh?: 1869]. In David F. Caldwell Papers, Southern Historical Collection.

Regulations and Instructions for the Government of the Transportation Department and the Running of Trains. Raleigh: Seaton Gales, 1854. Rev. ed. Salisbury: J. J. Bruner, 1857.

Report of Col. Walter Gwynn, Chief Engineer North Carolina R.R. Co., to the Board of Directors at Meeting in Salisbury, Jan. 10, 1856. Salisbury: J. J. Bruner, 1856.

Report of the Chief Engineer on the Survey of the N.C. Railroad, May, 1851. Greensborough: 1851.

Report of the President and Directors of the North Carolina Railroad Company to the Legislature. Raleigh: 1852.

Report of the President of the North Carolina Railroad to the Governor of the State, January 20, 1859. Salisbury: 1859.

Time Table . . . Express Train. Salisbury: 1858. Broadside.

To the Stockholders of the N.C.R.R. Co. May 18, 1869. Company Shops, N.C.: NCRR, 1869. 1p. In David F. Caldwell Papers and William A. Graham Papers, Southern Historical Collection.

To the Stockholders of the North Carolina Railroad Company . . . October 20th, 1869. N.p. [1869]. 4pp. In William A. Graham Papers, Southern Historical Collection.

_____. Nearly identical title and date. 7pp.

To the Stockholders of the North Carolina Rail Road Company . . . October 29, 1869. N.p. [1869]. 1p.

Railroad Annual Reports (other than NCRR)

Atlantic and North Carolina Railroad, 1856–60, 1865–72.

Charlotte and South Carolina Railroad, 1855–69.

Charlotte, Columbia, and Augusta Railroad, 1870–71.

Petersburg Railroad, 1859–67.

Piedmont Railroad, 1865–67.

Raleigh and Gaston Railroad, 1852–71.

Richmond and Danville Railroad, 1856–76.

Seaboard and Roanoke Railroad, 1867–72.

Western North Carolina Railroad, 1859–71.

Wilmington and Manchester Railroad, 1856–61.

Wilmington and Weldon Railroad, 1856–70.

Newspapers and Serial Publications

American Railroad Journal, 1849–71.
American Railway Review, 1860–62.
American Railway Times, 1863–67.
Charlotte *Daily Bulletin,* 1859–69.
Charlotte *Daily Carolina Times,* 1864–69.
Charlotte *North Carolina Whig,* 1852–63.
Charlotte *Western Democrat,* 1852–71.
Concord *Weekly Gazette,* 1855–57.
Goldsboro *Carolina Messenger,* 1869–70.
Goldsboro *Daily Messenger,* 1869.
Goldsboro *Ku Klux Kaleidoscope,* 1869.
Goldsboro News, 1867, 1869.
Goldsboro *Republican and Patriot,* 1851–54.
Goldsboro Telegraph, 1850–55.
Greensboro Daily News, 1956.
Greensboro *Daily Southern Citizen,* 1864.
Greensboro News and Record, 1985–88.
Greensboro Patriot, 1849–72.
Greensboro Register, 1869.
Greensboro *Republican,* 1869.
Greensboro *Times,* 1856–68.
Greensboro *The Topic,* 1869.
Hillsborough Recorder, 1849–71.
Lexington and Yadkin Flag, 1855–57.
New-Berne Daily Times, 1869.
Raleigh *Carolina Era,* triweekly ed., 1871.
Raleigh *Daily Confederate,* 1864–65.
Raleigh *Daily Conservative,* 1864.
Raleigh *Daily Progress,* 1862–67.
Raleigh *Daily Sentinel,* 1865–71.
Raleigh Daily Telegram, 1871.
Raleigh *North Carolina Standard,* daily ed., 1865–70; semiweekly and triweekly ed., 1850–68; weekly ed., 1849–50, 1864–65.
Raleigh *North Carolina Star,* 1849–56.
Raleigh *North Carolinian,* 1868.
Raleigh Register, daily and semiweekly eds., 1849–68.
Raleigh *State Journal,* daily, triweekly, and semiweekly eds., 1860–64.
Salisbury *Carolina Watchman,* 1849–66.
Salisbury *Daily Union Banner,* 1865–66.

Other Published Sources

Abbott, Allen O. *Prison Life in the South.* New York: Harper & Bros., 1865.
Andrews, Sidney. *The South since the War.* Boston: Ticknor & Fields, 1866. Reprint. Boston: Houghton Mifflin, 1971.
Averill, J. H. "Richmond, Virginia. The Evacuation of the City and the Days Preceding It." *Southern Historical Society Papers* 25 (1897): 267–73.

Battle, Kemp Plummer, *Memories of an Old-Time Tar Heel.* Edited by William James
    Battle. Chapel Hill: University of North Carolina Press, 1945.
[Bixley, O. H.] *Incidents in Dixie.* Baltimore: James Young, 1864.
Booth, Benjamin F. *Dark Days of the Rebellion.* Indianola, Iowa: 1897.
Bradley, George S. *The Star Corps.* Milwaukee: Jermain & Brightman, 1865.
Brewster, Frederick Carroll. *Argument of Hon. F. Carroll Brewster in the Case of Swasey
    vs. North Carolina Railroad Co.* Philadelphia: J. B. Chandler, 1874.
Brogden, Curtis H. "Communication from the Governor." N.C. Public Documents,
    1874–75, #18. Also published separately.
Chandler, Alfred D., ed. *The Railroads: Pioneers in Modern Management.* New York:
    Arno Press, 1979.
Colburn, Zerah, and Holley, Alexander L. *The Permanent Way.* New York: Holley &
    Colburn, 1858.
Conner, James. *Letters of General James Conner, C.S.A.* [Columbia, S.C.: The State,
    1933.]
Consolidation of the Atlantic & N.C.R.R. Co. and the N.C.R.R. Co. N.p. [1869]. 3pp.
    Duke University.
Cooper, Alonzo. *In and Out of Rebel Prisons.* Oswego, N.Y.: R. J. Oliphant, 1888.
Dawson, Francis W. *Reminiscences of Confederate Service, 1861–1865.* 1882. Reprint.
    Baton Rouge: Louisiana State University Press, 1980.
Dennett, John Richard. *The South As It Is, 1865–1866.* Edited by Henry M. Christ-
    man. New York: Viking Press, 1965.
Edson, William D., comp. "The Norris Construction Record." *Railroad History,* no.
    150 (Spring 1984): 57–86. List of Norris-built locomotives, their dates, specifica-
    tions, and purchasers.
Ellis, John Willis. *The Papers of John Willis Ellis.* Edited by Noble J. Tolbert. 2 vols.
    Raleigh: Archives & History, 1964.
Emmons, Ebenezer. *Geological Report of the Midland Counties of North Carolina.* New
    York: G. P. Putnam; Raleigh: Henry D. Turner, 1856.
Fitch, Charles L. *Through Rates and Proportions Between New Orleans . . . and the North-
    ern and Eastern Cities . . . June, 1866.* New York: Sanford, Harroun, 1866.
George, Charles B. *Forty Years on the Rail.* 2d ed. Chicago: Donnelley, 1887. Reminis-
    cences of a railroad conductor.
Graham, William A. *Message, Transmitting a Plan . . . to Establish a Continuous Line of
    Railroad from Gaston to Charlotte.* N.C. Public Documents, 1848–49, #4.
————. *The Papers of William Alexander Graham.* Edited by J. G. de Roulhac Hamilton
    and Max R. Williams. 7 vols. to date. Raleigh: Archives & History, 1957–.
Guilford Land Agency. *Facts for Capitalists and Parties Desirous to Settle in North Caro-
    lina.* Lynchburg, Va.: Johnson & Schaffter, 1867.
Hitchcock, Henry. *Marching with Sherman.* Edited by M. A. de Wolfe Howe. New
    Haven: Yale University Press, 1927.
Holden, William W. *Address Delivered Before the Cumberland County Agricultural Society
    . . . 1859.* Fayetteville: 1859. Railroads and fruit production.
————. *Message from the Governor.* N.C. Public Documents, 1869–70, #1.
Iota [pseud.]. *Facts and Figures in Regard to the Relative Merits of the North Carolina &
    Atlantic & North Carolina Railroads: Why the Railroads Should be Consolidated!* Ra-
    leigh: Raleigh Sentinel, [1869]. Broadside. North Carolina Collection, University
    of North Carolina, Chapel Hill.

Isham, Asa Brainard, et al. *Prisoners of War and Military Prisons*. Cincinnati: Lyman & Cushing, 1890.

Jervis, John B. *Railway Property. A Treatise on the Construction and Management of Railways*. New York: Phinney, Blakeman & Mason, 1861.

Johnston, Joseph E. *Narrative of Military Operations*. New York: D. Appleton, 1874.

Jones, B. M. *Rail Roads Considered in Regard to Their Effects*. Richmond: Ritchie, Dunnavant, 1860.

Jones, John Beauchamp. *A Rebel War Clerk's Diary at the Confederate States Capital*. 2 vols. Philadelphia: J. B. Lippincott, 1866.

Keasbey, Anthony Quinton. *From the Hudson to the St. Johns*. Newark, N.J.: Daily Advertiser, [1874].

Kirk, Charles H., ed. *History of the Fifteenth Pennsylvania Volunteer Cavalry*. Philadelphia: 1906. Part of Stoneman's command.

Kirkman, Marshall M. *Railway Expenditures*. 2 vols. Chicago: Railway Age, 1880.

———. *Railway Revenue*. 2d ed. New York: Railroad Gazette, 1879.

Lardner, Dionysius. *Railway Economy: A Treatise on the New Art of Transport*. New York: Harper & Bros., 1850.

Leigh, Frances Butler. *Ten Years on a Georgia Plantation Since the War*. London: R. Bentley & Son, 1883. Rode on the NCRR in 1866.

Lillington, John A., et al. *To our Constituents*. N.p. [1849]. Broadside. Duke University.

Lloyd's Southern Railroad Guide, 1863.

Lyell, Sir Charles. *Lyell's Travels in North America in the Years 1841–2*. Edited by John P. Cushing. New York: C. E. Merrill, 1909.

McRae, John C. *A Defence of John C. McRae & Co. From the Imputations Cast Upon Them as Contractors on the North Carolina Railroad*. N.p., n.d.

North Carolina Railroad Company vs. Anthony H. Swasey et al. Raleigh: [1874].

Olmsted, Frederick Law. *The Cotton Kingdom*. 1861. Reprint, edited by Arthur M. Schlesinger. New York: Knopf, 1953.

———. *A Journey in the Seaboard Slave States*. New York: Dix & Edwards, 1856.

———. *The Papers of Frederick Law Olmsted*. Edited by Charles E. Beveridge and Charles Capen McLaughlin. 4 vols. to date. Vol. 2, *Slavery and the South, 1852–1857*. Baltimore: Johns Hopkins University Press, 1981.

Pressly, Thomas J., and Scofield, William H., eds. *Farm Real Estate Values in the United States by Counties, 1850–1959*. Seattle: University of Washington Press, 1965.

Proceedings at a Called Convention of the Representatives of the Railroad Companies between Richmond and . . . Savannah, Held at . . . Petersburg on the 12th of March, 1862. [Petersburg?: 1862]. In John D. Whitford Papers, North Carolina Archives.

Proceedings of a Convention of Presidents and Superintendents of Railroads in the Confederate States Held in Augusta, Ga., December 15, 1862. N.p. [1862?].

Proceedings of a Convention of Rail Roads, Connecting with the Wilmington & Weldon Rail Road, Held at Goldsboro, April 1, 1862. Raleigh: 1862. In John D. Whitford Papers, North Carolina Archives.

Proceedings of a Convention of the Officers of the Railroads Composing the Atlantic Coast and Inland Lines and Their Connections Between Washington City and New Orleans, Held at Columbia, July 15, 1869. Columbia: Presbyterian Pub. House, 1869. North Carolina Collection, University of North Carolina, Chapel Hill, bound with Charlotte, Columbia, and Augusta Railroad Annual Report, 1870.

Proceedings of a Convention of the Presidents, Superintendents and Other Officials of Southern Railways, for the Promotion of Immigration to the South, Held in . . . Atlanta, Jan. 4th, 1869. Atlanta: Atlanta Intelligencer, 1869. North Carolina Collection, University of North Carolina, Chapel Hill, bound with Charlotte, Columbia, and Augusta Railroad Annual Report, 1870.

Proceedings of a Railroad Convention, Held at Richmond, Va., April 3rd and 4th, 1867. Richmond: 1867. In North Carolina Collection, University of North Carolina, Chapel Hill.

Rae, W[illiam] F[raser]. *Westward by Rail: The New Route to the East.* 1871. Reprint. New York: Arno Press, 1973.

Richmond and Danville Railroad. *Through Rates and Proportions for Through Tickets by the Great Central Route . . . August 1866.* Richmond: Gary & Clemmitt, 1866.

Robertson, John, comp. *Michigan in the War.* Rev. ed. Lansing, Mich.: W. S. George, 1882.

Ruffin, Thomas. *The Papers of Thomas Ruffin.* Edited by J. G. de Roulhac Hamilton. 4 vols. Raleigh: Edwards & Broughton, 1918–20.

Runyan, Morris C. *Eight Days with the Confederates and Capture of their Archives, Flags, &c.* Princeton, N.J.: W. C. C. Zapf, 1896.

Schenck, David. *Digest of Decisions by the Supreme Court of North Carolina Pertaining to Railroads, from 1837 to 1883.* Richmond: Wm. Ellis Jones, 1883.

Sentinel—Extra. What we know about the bill . . . entitled an act to amend the charter of the North Carolina Railroad Company. [Raleigh: 1875?]. Broadside. Duke University.

Shaffner, J. F. *Diary of Dr. J. F. Shaffner, Sr., Sept. 13, 1863–Feb. 5, 1865.* N.p., n.d. In North Carolina State Library, Raleigh.

Sherman, William Tecumseh. *General Sherman's Official Account of His Great March Through Georgia and the Carolinas.* New York: Bunce & Huntington, 1865.

———. *Memoirs of Gen. W. T. Sherman, Written by Himself.* 2d ed. 2 vols. New York: D. Appleton, 1904.

Small, Abner Ralph. *The Road to Richmond. The Civil War Memoirs of Major Abner R. Small.* Edited by Harold Adams Small. Berkeley: University of California Press, 1939.

Smith, W[illiam] A. *A Card.* N.p. [1871]. 1p. In David F. Caldwell Papers, Southern Historical Collection.

———. Interview, *New York Tribune,* 9 August 1870, p. 5.

———. *Is it to the Interest of the North Carolina Rail Road Company to Consolidate their Company with the Atlantic & North Carolina Rail Road?* N.p. 1868. 4pp. In David F. Caldwell Papers, Southern Historical Collection.

Sprague, Homer Baxter. *Lights and Shadows in Confederate Prisons; A Personal Experience, 1864–5.* New York: G. P. Putnam's Sons, 1915.

Stafford, Joseph B. *Joseph B. Stafford vs. Ed. J. Warren . . . et als.* N.p. [1871?]. 7pp. In North Carolina Collection, University of North Carolina, Chapel Hill.

Stanly, E[dward] R. *To the Stockholders of the North Carolina Railroad Company.* N.p. [1869]. 2pp. In Cameron Family and William A. Graham Papers, Southern Historical Collection.

[———, et al.] *To the Stockholders of the North Carolina Rail Road Company, and the Atlantic & North Carolina Rail Road Company.* N.p. [1869]. 9pp. In North Carolina Collection, University of North Carolina, Chapel Hill.

State v. Josiah Turner. *Indictment for Libel: Evidence of George W. Swepson, Raleigh,*

N.C., 1876. N.p. [1876?]. 90pp. In North Carolina Collection.

Stearns, Amos E. *Narrative of Amos E. Stearns . . . a Prisoner at Andersonville*. Worcester, Mass.: Franklin P. Rice, 1887.

U.S. Census, 1840–1910. Abstracts and volumes on population, agriculture, manufactures.

U.S. Congress. House. *House Executive Documents*. 39 Cong., 1 sess., #155 (Serial 1267). Railroad Property in the Possession of the United States Government, 1 May 1865.

――――. *House Executive Documents*. 41 Cong., 2 sess., #90. Letter of Postmaster General J. A. J. Creswell.

――――. *House Reports*. 39 Cong., 2 sess., #34 (Serial 1306). Affairs of Southern Railroads. 4 vols.

U.S. Congress. Senate. *Senate Executive Documents*. 45 Cong., 2 sess., #99 (Serial 1781). Report of Secretary of War.

――――. *Senate Miscellaneous Documents*. 32 Cong., 2 sess., #32 (Serial 670). Resolution of North Carolina Legislature.

――――. *Senate Reports*. 41 Cong., 3 sess., #321. Report of Senator Joseph C. Abbott.

U.S. Department of Labor. *History of Wages in the United States, Colonial Times to 1928*. Bulletin 604, 1934. Reprint. Detroit: Gales Research, 1966.

Vance, Zebulon Baird. *Papers*. Edited by Frontis W. Johnston. 1 vol. to date. Raleigh: Archives & History, 1963.

Vose, George L. *Handbook of Railroad Construction: For the Use of American Engineers*. Boston and Cambridge: James Munroe, 1857.

The War of the Rebellion: The Official Records of the Union and Confederate Armies. 128 vols. Washington, D.C.: Government Printing Office, 1880–1901.

Webb, Thomas. *Thomas Webb vs. North Carolina Railroad Co. and the Richmond and Danville Railroad Co.* N.p. [1873]. 15pp. In North Carolina Collection.

Wheeler, John H. *Reminiscences and Memoirs of North Carolina, and Eminent North Carolinians*. 1884. Reprint. Baltimore: Genealogical Publishing, 1966.

Whiton, James M. *Railroads and Their Management*. Concord, Mass.: McFarland & Jenks, 1856.

Willson, H. Bowlby. *North Carolina, Its Debt and Financial Resources, 1st September 1869*. New York: John Medole, 1869.

Woodlock, Thomas F. *Anatomy of a Railroad Report*. New York: U.S. Book Co., 1895.

Worth, Jonathan. *The Correspondence of Jonathan Worth*. Edited by J. G. de Roulhac Hamilton. 2 vols. Raleigh: Edwards & Broughton, 1909.

Secondary Sources

Works on Railroading, Transportation, Engineering, and Accounting

Adams, Steve. "North Carolina's Railroads: What Track for the Future?" *North Carolina Insight* 6 (June 1983): 2–16.

Adler, Dorothy R. *British Investments in American Railways, 1834–1898*. Charlottesville: University Press of Virginia, 1970.

Allen, Richard Sanders. *Covered Bridges of the South*. Brattleboro, Vt.: S. Greene Press, 1970.

Atack, Jeremy, and Brueckner, Jan K. "Steel Rails and American Railroads, 1867–

1880." *Explorations in Economic History* 19 (October 1982): 339–59.

Barringer, Rufus. *History of the North Carolina Railroad.* Raleigh, N.C.: [1894]. 21pp.

Black, Robert C., III. *Railroads of the Confederacy.* Chapel Hill: University of North Carolina Press, 1952.

Boockholdt, James L. "Influence of Nineteenth and Early Twentieth Century Railroad Accounting on Development of Modern Accounting Theory." In *The Academy of Accounting Historians, Working Paper Series,* edited by Edward N. Coffman, 2:184–205. N.p. 1979.

Boyd, J. Hayden, and Walton, Gary M. "Social Savings from Nineteenth Century Rail Passenger Services." *Explorations in Economic History* 9 (Spring 1972): 233–54.

Brief, Richard P. "Nineteenth Century Accounting Error." *Journal of Accounting Research* 3 (Spring 1965): 12–31.

Brown, Alexander Crosby. *The Old Bay Line.* Richmond, Va.: Dietz Press, 1940.

Brown, Cecil K. "A History of the Piedmont Railroad Company." *North Carolina Historical Review* 3 (April 1926): 198–222.

———. *The State Highway System of North Carolina: Its Evolution and Present Status.* Chapel Hill: University of North Carolina Press, 1931.

———. *A State Movement in Railroad Development: The Story of North Carolina's First Effort to Establish an East and West Trunk Line Railroad.* Chapel Hill: University of North Carolina Press, 1928.

Calhoun, Daniel H. *The American Civil Engineer.* Cambridge, Mass.: Harvard University Press, 1960.

Carlson, James A. "The Iron Horse in Court: Thomas Ruffin and the Development of North Carolina Railroad Law." M.A. thesis, University of North Carolina, Chapel Hill, 1972.

Chandler, Alfred D., Jr. "Patterns of American Railroad Finance, 1830–1850." *Business History Review* 28 (September 1954): 248–63.

———. *The Visible Hand: The Managerial Revolution in American Business.* Cambridge, Mass.: Harvard University Press, 1977.

———, ed. *The Railroads: The Nation's First Big Business.* New York: Harcourt, Brace, World, 1965.

Chatfield, Michael. *A History of Accounting Thought.* Rev. ed. Huntington, N.Y.: Robert E. Krieger, 1977.

Clark, Malcolm Cameron. *First Quarter Century of the Richmond & Danville, 1847–1871.* Washington, D.C.: Privately printed, 1959.

Cleveland, Frederick A., and Powell, Fred W. *Railroad Promotion and Capitalization in the United States.* 1909. Reprint. New York: Johnson Reprint Co., 1966.

Coatsworth, John H. "Indispensable Railroads in a Backward Economy: The Case of Mexico." *Journal of Economic History* 39 (December 1979): 939–60.

Cochran, Thomas C. "The Executive Mind: The Role of Railroad Leaders, 1845–1890." *Business History Society Bulletin* 25 (December 1951): 230–41.

———. *Railroad Leaders, 1845–1890: The Business Mind in Action.* 1953. Reissued. New York: Russell & Russell, 1966.

———. "The Social Impact of the Railroad." In *The Railroad and the Space Program: An Exploration in Historical Analogy,* edited by Bruce Mazlish, pp. 163–81. Cambridge, Mass.: MIT Press, 1965.

Condit, Carl W. *American Building Art: The Nineteenth Century.* New York: Oxford University Press, 1960.

———. *American Building: Materials and Techniques from the First Colonial Settlements to the Present.* Chicago: University of Chicago Press, 1968.

Cooper, Theodore. "American Railroad Bridges." *Transactions of the American Society of Civil Engineers* 21 (July 1889): 1–58.

Cotterill, R. S. "Southern Railroads, 1850–1860." *Mississippi Valley Historical Review* 10 (March 1924): 396–405.

Doster, James F. "Were Southern Railroads Destroyed by the Civil War?" *Civil War History* 7 (September 1961): 310–20.

Dozier, Howard Douglas. "Trade and Transportation along the South Atlantic Seaboard before the Civil War." *South Atlantic Quarterly* 18 (July 1919): 231–45.

Dunaway, Wayland Fuller. *History of the James River and Kanawha Canal Company.* New York: Columbia University Press, 1922.

Fels, Rendigs. *Wages, Earnings and Employment—Nashville, Chattanooga & St. Louis Railway, 1866–1896.* Nashville, Tenn.: Vanderbilt University Press, 1953.

Fisher, Charles E. "The United States Military Railroads." *Railway and Locomotive Historical Society Bulletin* 108 (April 1963): 49–79.

Fishlow, Albert. *American Railroads and the Transformation of the Antebellum Economy.* Cambridge, Mass.: Harvard University Press, 1965.

Flint, Henry M. *Railroads of the United States, Their History and Statistics.* 1868. Reprint. New York: Arno Press, 1976.

Fogel, Robert William. "Notes on the Social Saving Controversy." *Journal of Economic History* 39 (March 1979): 1–54.

Fuller, Wayne E. *The American Mail: Enlarger of the Common Life.* Chicago: University of Chicago Press, 1972.

Gilbert, John F., comp. *The Tree of Life: A History of the North Carolina Railroad.* Text by Grady B. Jefferys. Raleigh, N.C.: NCRR, 1972.

Goodrich, Carter. "American Development Policy: The Case of Internal Improvements." *Journal of Economic History* 16 (December 1956): 449–60.

———. *Government Promotion of American Canals and Railroads, 1800–1870.* New York: Columbia University Press, 1960.

———. "Public Aid to Railroads in the Reconstruction South." *Political Science Quarterly* 71 (September 1956): 407–42.

———. "The Revulsion against Internal Improvements." *Journal of Economic History* 10 (November 1950): 145–69.

Grodinsky, Julius. *Transcontinental Railway Strategy, 1869–1893: A Study of Businessmen.* Philadelphia: University of Pennsylvania Press, 1962.

Harlow, Alvin F. *Old Postbags: The Story of the Mail Service.* New York: D. Appleton, 1928.

———. *Old Waybills: The Romance of the Express Companies.* New York: Appleton-Century, 1934.

Harrison, Fairfax. *A History of the Legal Development of the Railroad System of the Southern Railway Company.* Washington, D.C.: 1901.

Heath, Milton S. *Constructive Liberalism: The Role of the State in Economic Development in Georgia to 1860.* Cambridge, Mass.: Harvard University Press, 1954.

———. "Public Railroad Construction and the Development of Private Enterprise in the South before 1861." *Journal of Economic History* Supplement 10 (1950): 40–53.

Henry, Robert Selph. *This Fascinating Railroad Business.* Indianapolis, Ind.: Bobbs Merrill, 1942.

Henson, Stephen Ray. "Industrial Workers in the Mid-Nineteenth Century South:

Atlanta Railwaymen, 1840–1870." Ph.D. dissertation, Emory University, 1982.

Hill, Forest G. *Roads, Rails, and Waterways: The Army Engineers and Early Transportation.* Norman: University of Oklahoma Press, 1957.

Holmes, Oliver W., and Rohrbach, Peter T. *Stagecoach East: Stagecoach Days in the East from the Colonial Period to the Civil War.* Washington, D.C.: Smithsonian Institution Press, 1983.

Hunt, Robert S. *Law and Locomotives: The Impact of the Railroad on Wisconsin Law in the Nineteenth Century.* Madison: State Historical Society of Wisconsin, 1958.

Jenks, Leland H. "Railroads as an Economic Force in American Development." *Journal of Economic History* 4 (May 1944): 1–20.

Johnston, Angus James, II. *Virginia Railroads in the Civil War.* Chapel Hill: University of North Carolina Press, 1961.

Joubert, William Harry. *Southern Freight Rates in Transition.* Gainesville: University of Florida Press, 1949.

Kirkland, Edward C. *Men, Cities, and Transportation: A Study in New England History.* 2 vols. Cambridge, Mass.: Harvard University Press, 1948.

Klein, Maury. *The Great Richmond Terminal.* Charlottesville: University Press of Virginia, 1970.

———. *History of the Louisville & Nashville Railroad.* New York: Macmillan, 1972.

———. "Southern Railroad Leaders, 1865–1893: Identities and Ideologies." *Business History Review* 42 (Autumn 1968): 288–310.

———. "The Strategy of Southern Railroads." *American Historical Review* 73 (April 1968): 1052–68.

Klein, Maury, and Yamamura, Kozo. "The Growth Strategies of Southern Railroads, 1865–1893." *Business History Review* 41 (Winter 1967): 358–77.

Lash, Jeffrey N. "Major George Whitfield and Confederate Railway Policy (1863–1865)." *Journal of Mississippi History* 42 (August 1980): 172–93.

Licht, Walter. *Working for the Railroad: The Organization of Work in the Nineteenth Century.* Princeton, N.J.: Princeton University Press, 1983.

Lightner, David L. *Labor on the Illinois Central Railroad, 1852–1900: The Evolution of an Industrial Environment.* New York: Arno Press, 1977.

Littleton, A[nanias] C. *Accounting Evolution to 1900.* New York: American Institute Publishing Co., 1933.

McGuire, Peter S. "The Railroads of Georgia, 1860–1880." *Georgia Historical Quarterly* 16 (September 1932): 179–213.

McPherson, Logan G. *Railway Freight Rates in Relation to the Industry and Commerce of the United States.* New York: Henry Holt, 1909.

Mencken, August. *The Railroad Passenger Car.* Baltimore: Johns Hopkins University Press, 1957.

Meyer, Balthasar Henry, ed. *History of Transportation in the United States before 1860.* 1917. Reprint. New York: P. Smith, 1948.

Miller, George Hall. *Railroads and the Granger Laws.* Madison: University of Wisconsin Press, 1971.

Newman, Maurice S. "Historical Development of Early Accounting Concepts and Their Relation to Certain Economic Concepts." In *The Academy of Accounting Historians, Working Paper Series*, edited by Edward N. Coffman, 1:157–86. N.p. 1979.

Olds, Fred A. "The Development of North Carolina Railroads." *North Carolina Historical and Genealogical Record* 1 (April 1932): 47–52.

Olson, Sherry H. *The Depletion Myth: A History of Railroad Use of Timber*. Cambridge, Mass.: Harvard University Press, 1971.

Plowden, David. *Bridges: The Spans of North America*. New York: Viking Press, 1974.

Potter, David M. "Historical Development of Eastern-Southern Freight Rate Relationships." *Law and Contemporary Problems* 12 (Summer 1947): 416–48.

Price, Charles L. "North Carolina Railroads during the Civil War." *Civil War History* 7 (September 1961): 298–309.

———. "Railroads and Reconstruction in North Carolina, 1865–1871." Ph.D. dissertation, University of North Carolina, 1959.

———. "The Railroad Schemes of George W. Swepson." In *East Carolina Publications in History*. Vol. 1: *Essays in American History*, pp. 32–76. Greenville, N.C.: East Carolina University, 1964.

———. "The Railroads of North Carolina during the Civil War." M.A. thesis, University of North Carolina, 1951.

———. "Riding the Rails in Civil War Days." *The New East* 3 (May–June 1975): 12–15.

———. "The United States Military Railroads in North Carolina, 1862–1865." *North Carolina Historical Review* 53 (July 1976): 243–64.

Ramsdell, Charles W. "Confederate Government and the Railroads." *American Historical Review* 22 (July 1917): 794–810.

Reed, Merl E. *New Orleans and the Railroads: The Struggle for Commercial Empire, 1830–1860*. Baton Rouge: Louisiana State University Press, 1966.

Richardson, Reed C. *The Locomotive Engineer, 1863–1963: A Century of Railway Labor Relations and Work Rules*. Ann Arbor: Bureau of Industrial Relations, University of Michigan, 1963.

Ringwalt, John L. *Development of Transportation Systems in the United States*. 1888. Reprint. New York: Johnson Reprint Co., 1966.

Ripley, William Z. *Railroads: Finance and Organization*. New York: Longmans, 1923.

Sanderlin, Walter S. *The Great National Project: A History of the Chesapeake and Ohio Canal*. Baltimore: Johns Hopkins University Press, 1946.

Scanlon, Ann M. "The Building of the New York Central: A Study in the Development of the International Iron Trade." In *An Emerging Independent American Economy, 1815–1875*, edited by Joseph R. Frese and Jacob Judd, pp. 99–126. Tarrytown, N.Y.: Sleepy Hollow Press, 1980.

Scott, Roy V. *Railroad Development Programs in the Twentieth Century*. Ames: Iowa State University Press, 1985.

Shaw, Robert B. *A History of Railroad Accidents, Safety Precautions and Operating Practices*. 2d ed. Potsdam, N.Y.: Northern Press, 1978.

———. "The Profitability of Early American Railroads." *Railroad History* 132 (Spring 1975): 56–69.

Starling, Robert B. "The Plank Road Movement in North Carolina." *North Carolina Historical Review* 16 (January, April 1939): 1–22, 147–73.

Stimson, Alexander Lovett. *History of the Express Business*. New York: Baker & Godwin, 1881.

Stover, John F. *History of the Illinois Central Railroad*. New York: Macmillan, 1975.

———. *Iron Road to the West: American Railroads in the 1850s*. New York: Columbia University Press, 1978.

———. "The Pennsylvania Railroad's Southern Rail Empire." *Pennsylvania Magazine of History and Biography* 81 (January 1957): 28–38.

————. *The Railroads of the South, 1865–1900: A Case Study in Finance and Control.* Chapel Hill: University of North Carolina Press, 1955.

————. "The Ruined Railroads of the Confederacy." *Georgia Historical Quarterly* 42 (December 1958): 376–88.

————. "Southern Railroad Receivership in the 1870s." *Virginia Magazine of History and Biography* 62 (January 1955): 40–52.

Summers, Mark W. *Railroads, Reconstruction, and the Gospel of Prosperity: Aid under the Radical Republicans, 1865–1877.* Princeton, N.J.: Princeton University Press, 1984.

Taylor, George Rogers. *The Transportation Revolution, 1815–1860.* New York: Rinehart, 1951.

Taylor, George Rogers, and Neu, Irene D. *The American Railroad Network, 1861–1890.* Cambridge, Mass.: Harvard University Press, 1956.

Thompson, Robert L. *Wiring a Continent.* Princeton, N.J.: Princeton University Press, 1947.

Trelease, Allen W. "The Passive Voice: The State and the North Carolina Railroad, 1849–1871." *North Carolina Historical Review* 61 (April 1984): 174–204.

Tunnell, George Gerard. *Railway Mail Service: A Comparative Study of Railway Rates and Service.* Chicago: Lakeside Press, 1901.

Turner, Charles W. "Early Virginia Railroad Entrepreneurs and Personnel." *Virginia Magazine of History and Biography* 58 (July 1950): 325–34.

————. "Railroad Service to Virginia Farmers, 1828–1860." *Agricultural History* 22 (October 1948): 239–48.

Turner, George E. *Victory Rode the Rails: The Strategic Place of Railroads in the Civil War.* Indianapolis, Ind.: Bobbs Merrill, 1953.

Tyrrell, Henry Grattan. *History of Bridge Engineering.* Chicago: Author, 1911.

Usselman, Steven W. "Air Brakes for Freight Trains: Technological Innovation in the American Railroad Industry, 1869–1900." *Business History Review* 58 (Spring 1984): 30–50.

Ward, James A. *J. Edgar Thomson: Master of the Pennsylvania.* Westport, Conn.: Greenwood Press, 1980.

————. "A New Look at Antebellum Southern Railroad Development." *Journal of Southern History* 39 (August 1973): 409–20.

Weber, Thomas. *The Northern Railroads in the Civil War, 1861–1865.* 1952. Reprint. Westport, Conn.: Greenwood Press, 1970.

White, John H., Jr. *American Locomotives: An Engineering History, 1830–1880.* Baltimore: Johns Hopkins University Press, 1968.

————. *The American Railroad Passenger Car.* 2 vols. Baltimore: Johns Hopkins University Press, 1978.

————. "Once the Greatest of Builders: The Norris Locomotive Works." *Railroad History* 150 (Spring 1984): 17–56.

————. *A Short History of American Locomotive Builders in the Steam Era.* Washington, D.C.: Bass, Inc., 1982.

————. "A Short History of Railway Brakes." *National Railway Historical Society Bulletin* 40, no. 5 (1975): 6–17.

————. "Splendor and Gloom: The Decoration of Victorian Railroad Cars." *Nineteenth Century* 3 (Spring 1977): 38–47.

Wicker, E. R. "Railroad Investment before the Civil War." In Conference on Research in Income and Wealth, *Trends in the American Economy in the Nineteenth Century*, pp. 503–45. Princeton, N.J.: Princeton University Press, 1960.

State and Local Works

Albright, James W. *Greensboro, 1808–1904*. Greensboro, N.C.: Jos. J. Stone, 1904.

Alexander, John B. *The History of Mecklenburg County from 1740 to 1900*. Charlotte, N.C.: Observer Printing House, 1902.

Alexander, Violet G. "The Confederate States Navy Yard at Charlotte, North Carolina, 1862–1865." *North Carolina Booklet* 22 (1926): 28–37.

Amis, Moses N. *Historical Raleigh with Sketches of Wake County . . . and Its Important Towns*. Raleigh, N.C.: Commercial Printing, 1913.

Anderson, Jean Bradley. *Piedmont Plantation: The Bennehan-Cameron Family and Lands in North Carolina*. Durham, N.C.: Historic Preservation Society of Durham, 1986.

Arnett, Ethel Stephens. *Greensboro, North Carolina, the County Seat of Guilford*. Chapel Hill: University of North Carolina Press, 1955.

Ashe, Samuel A., et al. *Biographical History of North Carolina*. 8 vols. Greensboro, N.C.: C. L. Van Noppen, 1905–17.

Auman, William T. "Neighbor against Neighbor: The Inner Civil War in the Randolph County Area of Confederate North Carolina." *North Carolina Historical Review* 61 (January 1984): 59–92.

Auman, William T., and Scarboro, David D. "The Heroes of America in Civil War North Carolina." *North Carolina Historical Review* 58 (Autumn 1981): 327–63.

Barrett, John G. *The Civil War in North Carolina*. Chapel Hill: University of North Carolina Press, 1963.

Beck, John J. "Building the New South: A Revolution from Above in a Piedmont County." *Journal of Southern History* 53 (August 1987): 441–70.

Bishir, Catherine W. "Black Builders in Antebellum North Carolina." *North Carolina Historical Review* 61 (October 1984): 423–61.

Blackwelder, Ruth. *The Age of Orange: Political and Intellectual Leadership in North Carolina, 1752–1861*. Charlotte, N.C.: W. Loftin, 1961.

Blythe, LeGette, and Brockmann, Charles Raven. *Hornets' Nest: The Story of Charlotte and Mecklenburg County*. Charlotte, N.C.: Charlotte Public Library, 1961.

Boyd, William Kenneth. *The Story of Durham, City of the New South*. Durham, N.C.: Duke University Press, 1925.

Brawley, James S. *The Rowan Story, 1753 to 1953: A Narrative History of Rowan County, North Carolina*. Salisbury, N.C.: Rowan Printing, 1953.

Brown, Louis Alexander. *The Salisbury Prison: A Case Study of Confederate Military Prisons, 1861–1865*. Wendell, N.C.: Avera Press, 1980.

Browning, Clyde E., and Parker, Francis H. "Urbanization." In *North Carolina Atlas: Portrait of a Changing Southern State*, edited by James W. Clay et al., pp. 53–69. Chapel Hill: University of North Carolina Press, 1975.

Byrd, Thomas. *Around and About Cary*. Raleigh, N.C.: N. C. Daniel, 1970.

Cappon, Lester J. "Iron-Making—A Forgotten Industry of North Carolina." *North Carolina Historical Review* 9 (October 1932): 331–48.

Cates, D. Brooks. "The Piedmont Crescent and the North Carolina Railroad." Unpublished manuscript in possession of author.

Cathey, Cornelius Oliver. *Agricultural Developments in North Carolina, 1783–1860*.

Chapel Hill: University of North Carolina Press, 1956.

Chamberlain, Hope Summerell. *History of Wake County, North Carolina*. Raleigh, N.C.: Edwards & Broughton, 1922.

———. *This Was Home*. Chapel Hill: University of North Carolina Press, 1938.

Connor, Robert Diggs Wimberly. *North Carolina: Rebuilding an Ancient Commonwealth, 1584–1925*. 4 vols. Chicago and New York: American Historical Society, 1929.

Daniels, Frank A. *History of Wayne County*. 1914. Reprint. Goldsboro, N.C.: n.p., 1956.

Daniels, Jonathan. *Prince of Carpetbaggers*. Philadelphia and New York: J. B. Lippincott, 1958.

Durden, Robert F. *The Dukes of Durham, 1865–1929*. Durham, N.C.: Duke University Press, 1975.

Earley, Lawrence S. "Quail Paradise in the Piedmont." *Wildlife in North Carolina* 50 (December 1986): 18–23.

Ebert, Charles H. V. "Furniture Making in High Point." *North Carolina Historical Review* 36 (July 1959): 330–39.

Escott, Paul D. "Yeoman Independence and the Market: Social Status and Economic Development in Antebellum North Carolina." *North Carolina Historical Review* 66 (July 1989): 275–300.

Franklin, John Hope. *The Free Negro in North Carolina*. 1943. Reprint. New York: Russell & Russell, 1969.

Fries, Adelaide L. "One Hundred Years of Textiles in Salem." *North Carolina Historical Review* 27 (January 1950): 1–19.

Glass, Brent D. "King Midas and Old Rip: The Gold Hill Mining District of North Carolina." Ph.D. dissertation, University of North Carolina, 1980.

———. "'Poor Men with Rude Machinery': The Formative Years of the Gold Hill Mining District, 1842–1853." *North Carolina Historical Review* 61 (January 1984): 1–35.

Goldfield, David R. *Urban Growth in the Age of Sectionalism: Virginia, 1847–1861*. Baton Rouge: Louisiana State University Press, 1977.

Griffin, Richard W., "North Carolina: The Origin and Rise of the Cotton Textile Industry, 1830–1880." Ph.D. dissertation, Ohio State University, 1954.

———. "Reconstruction of the North Carolina Textile Industry, 1865–1885." *North Carolina Historical Review* 41 (Winter 1964): 34–53.

———, ed. "List of North Carolina Cotton Manufacturers to 1880." *Textile History Review* 3 (October 1962): 222–31.

Hamilton, Joseph Gregoire de Roulhac. *Party Politics in North Carolina, 1835–1860*. Durham, N.C.: Seeman Printery, 1916.

———. *Reconstruction in North Carolina*. New York: Columbia University Press, 1914.

Harden, John W. *Alamance County: Economic and Social*. Chapel Hill: University of North Carolina Press, 1928.

Harris, William C. *William Woods Holden: Firebrand of North Carolina Politics*. Baton Rouge: Louisiana State University Press, 1987.

High Point Chamber of Commerce. *The Building and the Builders of a City—High Point, North Carolina*. High Point, N.C.: Hall Printing Co., 1947.

Hughes, Julian W. *Development of the Textile Industry in Alamance County*. Burlington, N.C.: Burlington Letter Shop, 1965.

Iobst, Richard W., and Manarin, Louis H. *The Bloody Sixth*. Raleigh, N.C.: Confederate Centennial Commission, 1965.

Jeffrey, Thomas E. "Internal Improvements and Political Parties in Antebellum North Carolina, 1836–1860." *North Carolina Historical Review* 55 (Spring 1978): 111–56.

———. "The Progressive Paradigm of Antebellum North Carolina Politics." *Carolina Comments* 30 (May 1982): 66–75.

Johnson, Bob, and Norwood, Charles S. *History of Wayne County, North Carolina.* Goldsboro, N.C.: Wayne County Historical Association, 1979.

Johnson, Guion Griffis. *Ante-Bellum North Carolina: A Social History.* Chapel Hill: University of North Carolina Press, 1937.

Jones, Cary W. *Guide to Norfolk as a Business Centre.* 4th ed. Norfolk, Va.: Hume & Parker, 1884.

Kenzer, Robert C. *Kinship and Neighborhood in a Southern Community: Orange County, North Carolina, 1849–1881.* Knoxville: University of Tennessee Press, 1987.

Kipp, Samuel Millard, III. "Urban Growth and Social Change in the South, 1870–1920: Greensboro, North Carolina, as a Case Study." Ph.D. dissertation, Princeton University, 1974.

Konkle, Burton Alva. *John Motley Morehead and the Development of North Carolina, 1796–1866.* Philadelphia: William J. Campbell, 1922.

Kruman, Marc W. *Parties and Politics in North Carolina, 1836–1865.* Baton Rouge: Louisiana State University Press, 1983.

Lefler, Hugh, and Wager, Paul, eds. *Orange County—1752–1952.* Chapel Hill, N.C.: Orange Printshop, 1953.

Leonard, Jacob Calvin. *Centennial History of Davidson County, North Carolina.* Raleigh, N.C.: Edwards & Broughton, 1927.

Lounsbury, Carl. "The Building Process in Antebellum North Carolina." *North Carolina Historical Review* 60 (October 1983): 431–56.

Matthews, Mary G., and Sink, M. Jewell. *Wheels of Faith and Courage: A History of Thomasville, North Carolina.* High Point, N.C.: Hall Printing Co., 1952.

Mitchell, Memory F. *Legal Aspects of Conscription and Exemption in North Carolina, 1861–1865.* Chapel Hill: University of North Carolina Press, 1965.

Nelson, B. H. "Some Aspects of Negro Life in North Carolina during the Civil War." *North Carolina Historical Review* 25 (April 1948): 143–66.

Norton, Clarence Clifford. *The Democratic Party in Ante-Bellum North Carolina, 1835–1861.* Chapel Hill: University of North Carolina Press, 1930.

O'Brien, [Roberta] Gail Williams. *The Legal Fraternity and the Making of a New South Community, 1848–1882.* Athens: University of Georgia Press, 1986. Relates to Greensboro and Guilford County.

———. "Power and Influence in Mecklenburg County, 1850–1880." *North Carolina Historical Review* 54 (April 1977): 120–44.

Paul, Hiram V. *History of the Town of Durham, N.C.* Raleigh, N.C.: Edwards & Broughton, 1884.

Phifer, Edward William, Jr. *Burke: The History of a North Carolina County, 1777–1920.* Morganton, N.C.: Author, 1977.

Phillips, Coy T. "North Carolina's Rich Crescent." *Journal of Geography* 54 (April 1955): 182–87.

Pierpont, Andrew W. "Development of the Textile Industry in Alamance County, North Carolina." Ph.D. dissertation, University of North Carolina, 1953.

Ramsdell, Charles W. "General Robert E. Lee's Horse Supply, 1862–1865." *American Historical Review* 35 (July 1930): 758–77.

Raper, Horace W. *William W. Holden: North Carolina's Political Enigma.* Chapel Hill: University of North Carolina Press, 1985.

Robert, Joseph Clarke. "The Tobacco Industry in Ante-Bellum North Carolina." *North Carolina Historical Review* 15 (April 1938): 119–30.

———. *The Tobacco Kingdom: Plantation, Market, and Factory in Virginia and North Carolina, 1800–1860.* Durham, N.C.: Duke University Press, 1938.

Sanders, Charles Richard. *The Cameron Plantation in Central North Carolina (1776–1973) and Its Founder Richard Bennehan.* Durham, N.C.: Author, 1974.

Sanders, William Marsh, Jr. *Johnston County: Economic and Social.* Smithfield, N.C.: Smithfield Observer, 1922.

Schlotterbeck, John T. "The 'Social Economy' of an Upper South Community: Orange and Greene Counties, Virginia, 1815–1860." In *Class, Conflict, and Consensus: Antebellum Southern Community Studies*, edited by Orville Vernon Burton and Robert C. McMath, Jr., pp. 3–28. Westport, Conn.: Greenwood Press, 1982.

Simmons, William T., and Lindsay, L. Brooks. *Charlotte and Mecklenburg County: A Pictorial History.* Norfolk, Va.: Donning, 1977.

Sink, Margaret Jewell. *Davidson County, Economic and Social.* Chapel Hill: Department of Rural Social Economics, University of North Carolina, 1925.

Sink, Margaret Jewell, and Matthews, Mary Green. *Pathfinders Past and Present: A History of Davidson County, North Carolina.* High Point, N.C.: Hall Printing Co., 1972.

Smith, A. Davis, comp. *Western North Carolina, Historical and Biographical.* Charlotte, N.C.: Smith, 1890.

Spencer, Cornelia Phillips. *The Last Ninety Days of the War in North Carolina.* New York: Watchman Publishing Co., 1866.

Standard, Diffee W., and Griffin, Richard Worden. "The Cotton Textile Industry in Ante-Bellum North Carolina." *North Carolina Historical Review* 34 (January, April 1957): 15–35, 131–64.

Stokes, Durward T. *Company Shops: The Town Built by a Railroad.* Winston-Salem, N.C.: John F. Blair, 1981.

Tilley, Nannie May. *The Bright-Tobacco Industry, 1860–1929.* Chapel Hill: University of North Carolina Press, 1948.

Tompkins, Daniel Augustus. *History of Mecklenburg County and the City of Charlotte, from 1740 to 1903.* 2 vols. Charlotte, N.C.: Observer Printing House, 1903.

Triplette, Ralph R., Jr. "One-Industry Towns: Their Location, Development, and Economic Character." Ph.D. dissertation, University of North Carolina, 1974.

Van Noppen, Ina W. "The Significance of Stoneman's Last Raid." *North Carolina Historical Review* 38 (January–October 1961): 19–44, 149–72, 341–61, 500–526.

Weatherly, Andrew Earl. *The First Hundred Years of Historic Guilford, 1771–1871.* Greensboro, N.C.: Greensboro Printing Co., 1972.

Webb, William James. *Our Webb Kin of Dixie.* Oxford, N.C.: Author, 1940.

Wertenbaker, Thomas Jefferson. *Norfolk: Historic Southern Port.* 2d ed. Durham, N.C.: Duke University Press, 1962.

Whitaker, Walter. *Centennial History of Alamance County, 1849–1949.* Burlington, N.C.: Burlington Chamber of Commerce, 1949.

Williams, James W. "Emigration from North Carolina, 1789–1860." M.A. thesis, University of North Carolina, 1939.

Zuber, Richard L. *Jonathan Worth: A Biography of a Southern Unionist.* Chapel Hill: University of North Carolina Press, 1965.

Other Works

Aldrich, Mark. "Flexible Exchange Rates, Northern Expansion and the Market for Southern Cotton, 1866–1879." *Journal of Economic History* 33 (June 1973): 399–416.

Bateman, Fred, and Weiss, Thomas. *A Deplorable Scarcity: The Failure of Industrialization in the Slave Economy.* Chapel Hill: University of North Carolina Press, 1981.

Berlin, Ira. *Slaves without Masters: The Free Negro in the Antebellum South.* 1974. Reprint. New York: Vintage Books, 1976.

Birdsall, Stephen S., and Florin, John W. *Regional Landscapes of the United States and Canada.* New York: Wiley, 1978.

Blicksilver, Jack. *Cotton Manufacturing in the Southeast: An Historical Analysis.* Atlanta: Georgia State College of Business Administration, 1959.

Bradlee, Francis Boardman Crowninshield. *Blockade Running during the Civil War.* Salem, Mass.: Essex Institute, 1925.

Catton, Bruce. *Reflections on the Civil War.* 1981. Reprint. New York: Berkley Books, 1982.

Coelho, Philip R. P., and Shepherd, James F. "Differences in Real Wages: The United States, 1851–1880." *Explorations in Economic History* 13 (April 1976): 203–30.

Cohn, David L. *The Life and Times of King Cotton.* 1956. Reprint. Westport, Conn.: Greenwood Press, 1973.

Cohn, Raymond L. "Local Manufacturing in the Antebellum South and Midwest." *Business History Review* 54 (Spring 1980), 80–91.

Cullum, George W. *Biographical Register of the Officers and Graduates of the U.S. Military Academy . . . 1802–1890.* 6 vols. Boston and New York: Houghton Mifflin, 1891–1920.

Dew, Charles B. *Ironmaker to the Confederacy: Joseph R. Anderson and the Tredegar Iron Works.* New Haven, Conn.: Yale University Press, 1966.

Earle, Carville, and Hoffman, Ronald. "The Foundation of the Modern Economy: Agriculture and the Costs of Labor in the United States and England, 1800–60." *American Historical Review* 85 (December 1980): 1055–94.

Goff, Richard D. *Confederate Supply.* Durham, N.C.: Duke University Press, 1969.

Goldfarb, Stephen J. "A Note on Limits to the Growth of the Cotton-Textile Industry in the Old South." *Journal of Southern History* 48 (November 1982): 545–58.

Goldfield, David R. *Cotton Fields and Skyscrapers: Southern City and Region, 1607–1980.* Baton Rouge: Louisiana State University Press, 1982.

Gray, Lewis C. *History of Agriculture in the Southern United States to 1860.* 2 vols. Washington, D.C.: Carnegie Institute of Washington, 1933.

Hall, Jacquelyn Dowd; Korstad, Robert; and Leloudis, James. "Cotton Mill People: Work, Community, and Protest in the Textile South, 1880–1940." *American Historical Review* 91 (April 1986): 245–86.

Hammond, Matthew. *The Cotton Industry: An Essay in American Economic History.* Part 1: *The Cotton Culture and the Cotton Trade.* New York: Macmillan, 1897.

Hanna, Alfred Jackson. *Flight into Oblivion.* Richmond, Va.: Johnson Publishing Co., 1938.

Hartz, Louis. "Laissez-Faire Thought in Pennsylvania, 1776–1860." *Journal of Economic History* 3 (Supplement, December 1943): 66–77.

Hilgard, Eugene W. "Report on Cotton Production in the United States." Part 2. In

Tenth Census of the United States, vol. 6. Washington, D.C.: Government Printing Office, 1884.

Hunter, Louis C. *A History of Industrial Power in the United States, 1780–1930*. Vol. 2: *Steam Power*. Charlottesville: University Press of Virginia, 1985.

King, Elizabeth Doris. "The First-Class Hotel and the Age of the Common Man." *Journal of Southern History* 23 (May 1957): 173–88.

King, J. Crawford, Jr. "The Closing of the Southern Range: An Exploratory Study." *Journal of Southern History* 48 (February 1982): 53–70.

Lebergott, Stanley. *The Americans: An Economic Record*. New York: Norton, 1984.

Lerner, Eugene M. "Money, Prices, and Wages in the Confederacy, 1861–65." *Journal of Political Economy* 63 (February 1955): 20–40. Also in *The Economic Impact of the American Civil War*, edited by Ralph Andreano, pp. 11–40. Cambridge, Mass.: Schenkman, 1962.

Lindstrom, Diane. "Southern Dependence upon Interregional Grain Supplies: A Review of the Trade Flows, 1840–1860." In *Structure of the Cotton Economy of the Antebellum South*, edited by William N. Parker, pp. 101–13. Washington, D.C.: Agricultural History Society, 1970.

Lively, Robert A. "The American System: A Review Article." *Business History Review* 29 (March 1955): 81–96.

Lossing, Benson John. *The Pictorial Field Book of the Revolution*. 2 vols. New York: Harper & Bros., 1851–52.

McDonald, Forrest, and McWhiney, Grady. "The South from Self-Sufficiency to Peonage: An Interpretation." *American Historical Review* 85 (December 1980): 1095–1118.

Moore, Albert Burton. *Conscription and Conflict in the Confederacy*. New York: Macmillan, 1924.

Redlich, Fritz. *The Molding of American Banking: Men and Ideas*. 2 vols. 1947–51. Reprint. New York and London: Johnson Reprint Co., 1968.

Schwab, John Christopher. *The Confederate States of America, 1861–1865: A Financial and Industrial History of the South during the Civil War*. 1901. Reprint. New York: Burt Franklin, 1968.

Soule, Andrew M. "Vegetables, Fruit and Nursery Products, and Truck Farming in the South." In *The South in the Building of the Nation*. Vol. 5: *Economic History, 1607–1865*, pp. 236–42. Richmond, Va.: Southern Historical Publication Society, 1909.

Starobin, Robert S. *Industrial Slavery in the Old South*. New York: Oxford University Press, 1970.

Swank, James M. *History of the Manufacture of Iron in All Ages, and Particularly in the United States*. 2d ed. Philadelphia: American Iron & Steel Institute, 1892.

Switzler, William F. *Report on the Internal Commerce of the United States*. Washington, D.C.: Government Printing Office, 1886. House Executive Documents, 49 Cong., 2 sess., #7, part 2 (serial 2476).

Taylor, Rosser H. "Fertilizers and Farming in the Southeast, 1840–1950. Part I: 1840–1900." *North Carolina Historical Review* 30 (July 1953): 305–28.

Temin, Peter. *Iron and Steel in Nineteenth-Century America: An Economic Inquiry*. Cambridge, Mass.: MIT Press, 1964.

Todd, Richard C. *Confederate Finance*. Athens: University of Georgia Press, 1954.

Trelease, Allen W. *White Terror: The Ku Klux Klan Conspiracy and Southern Reconstruction*. New York: Harper & Row, 1971.

Tryon, Rolla Milton. *Household Manufactures in the United States, 1640–1860.* Chicago: University of Chicago Press, 1917.

Vandiver, Frank E. *Ploughshares into Swords: Josiah Gorgas and Confederate Ordnance.* Austin: University of Texas Press, 1952.

Weiss, Thomas. "Southern Business Never Had It So Good!: A Look at Antebellum Industrialization." In *Business in the New South: A Historical Perspective*, edited by Fred Bateman, pp. 27–34. Sewanee, Tenn.: University of the South Press, 1981.

Wiley, Bell I. *Southern Negroes, 1861–1865.* New Haven, Conn.: Yale University Press, 1938.

Woodman, Harold D. *King Cotton and His Retainers: Financing & Marketing the Cotton Crop of the South, 1800–1925.* Lexington: University of Kentucky Press, 1968.

Wright, Gavin. *Old South, New South: Revolutions in the Southern Economy since the Civil War.* New York: Basic Books, 1986.

INDEX